WHILE MESSIAH TARRIED

WHILE MESSIAH TARRIED

Jewish Socialist Movements, 1871–1917

NORA LEVIN

SCHOCKEN BOOKS · NEW YORK

First published by SCHOCKEN BOOKS 1977

Copyright © 1977 by Schocken Books Inc.

Library of Congress Cataloging in Publication Data

Levin, Nora.
  While messiah tarried.

  Includes bibliographical references and index.
  1. Labor and laboring classes—Jews. 2. Socialists,
Jewish. 3. Jews in the United States—Politics and
government. 4. Ogólny Zydowski Związek Robotniczy
"Bund" na Litwie, w Polsce i w Rosji. 5. Jews in
Russia—Politics and government. 6. Labor Zionism.

I. Title.
HD6305.J3L46   331.6   75-7769

Manufactured in the United States of America

Contents

Contents

IV: SOCIALIST ZIONISM

A section of illustrations follows page 280.

Foreword

Although Jews have been conditioned for centuries to adapt to situations and accommodate to the pressures and demands of the prevailing culture, some have also been on the frontiers of radical political thought and activity. From the Jewish Saint-Simonists to Karl Marx, Ferdinand Lassalle, Rosa Luxemburg, Leon Trotsky and other Bolsheviks, to the New Left of recent years, there has developed a tradition of radicalism among some Jews. Whether or not rooted in the Jewish prophetic vision or messianism, this strain of radicalism very consciously and deliberately broke completely with all aspects of Jewish tradition and life. Having abandoned their own origins and identity, yet not finding, or sharing, or being fully admitted to any other living tradition, such Jews found their ideological home in revolutionary universalism. They dreamt of a classless and stateless society, supported by a faith and doctrine that transcended the particularities of Jewish existence, and often economic and political realities as well.

Less familiar than these non-Jewish Jews—most of them of middle-class origin and a cast of mind pitched toward the abstract and theoretical— have been *Jewish* socialists, who have had a no less fervent vision of an ultimately universalist order, but who have also wrestled with the immediate realities of Jewish life and tried to solve the idiosyncratic, often intractable, problems facing Jewish workers within a Jewish and socialist framework. This consciousness of uniquely Jewish needs and dilemmas came slowly. At first, like other socialists, the Jewish socialists in Russia and the United States accepted prevailing doctrine, namely, that *all* workers were involved in a common struggle against exploitation, and that cultural differences would be resolved by assimilation. But, gradually, it became clear that general socialist formulations blurred or evaded the evidence of anti-Jewish persecution, the pull of a past culture which could not be totally denied or repressed, and the need of Jewish workers to find a Jewish, as well as socialist, identity.

There were Jewish labor and socialist movements prior to World War I in many countries: England, Austria, Rumania, France, Canada, Greece, Argentina, as well as Russia, Palestine, and the United States. Each was propelled by persecution and economic misery, but became infused with a fiery hope in the future—the search for redemption that is so strong in Jewish history. Each of these movements not only struggled to achieve economic gains for Jewish and non-Jewish workers but also developed an interesting, value-rich subculture of schools, newspapers, cooperatives, mutual aid societies, political parties, and trade unions, which shaped a secularized group identity for those Jews who could no longer accept old religious traditions. These movements, moreover, were linked with an immigration process, which gave them a character different from other socialist movements.

The three movements I have described—in Russia, the United States, and Palestine—were on the cutting edge of history, sharpening the sense of social struggle, taking pioneering steps that others followed, and facing existing political forces in historically important interactions. All had their origins in tsarist Russia. In the United States, the movement that arose had given up all hope of achieving any social or political change in Russia. In adapting to a free society, it moderated its early radical dogma and left a heritage of liberal and reformist tendencies to later generations. It also created a remarkably vibrant culture in Yiddish. The movement in Russia, however, led by the Jewish Labor Bund, remained in Russia and struggled there. Although defeated in the end, first by political reaction and then by the Bolshevik Revolution, the Bund left a legacy of genuine achievements and created a theoretical model that combined socialism with cultural autonomy for Jews and other minorities in Russia—still a live idea whose time may yet come in the Soviet Union. Moreover, the Bund's influence on the early socialist-democratic movement in Russia was considerable but has seldom been acknowledged. In Palestine, a third synthesis was hammered out—the most radical of the Jewish socialist responses: the abandonment of the Diaspora as hopelessly saturated with anti-Semitism and crippling to Jews, and the shift of socialist efforts to Palestine. Socialist Zionists there have struggled to create a "new Jew" as well as a new kind of society in the ancient homeland. This revolution has been arrested by Arab hostility, war, and complications that could scarcely have been imagined by the pre-World War I generation. But their vision is not dead.

All three movements had their share of dogmatism and intellectual stubbornness, but I have been struck by their willingness to bend to reality when ideological rigor failed, to give up dogmas and shibboleths when they were clearly irrevelant to the special problems and needs of Jewish workers.

These movements throb with life. Their experiences and insights were of and for a past time, but they cannot help inspire us with their energy, self-starting boldness, and courage in propelling oppressed Jewish workers into the modern world. They also remind us of a time when intellectuals found ways of reaching the poor and uneducated, yearning for a better life, tapping their strength, and working together for shared goals. Moreover, in the three formulations of Jewish ways of looking at society and possible Jewish roles as social catalyst, we may find past sources for renewed social idealism and action.

Two of the Jewish socialist movements I have examined—the one in Russia and the other in America—have, in a sense, played out their historic roles. Yet, even so, influences, echoes, and ideas reverberate. One can even hope that some day Jews in the Soviet Union will be able to learn about the struggles of their fathers and grandfathers in the Bund, without the perversities and distortions of Soviet historiography.

In writing this work, I have been very conscious of today's young Jews groping for ways to reconcile their own social radicalism with Jewishness. Their search will have to be their own, but perhaps they will be heartened in their quest by the knowledge that there have been several generations of other young Jews who have made a similar struggle. The landscape now may seem bleak but hardly bleaker than the Russia of the 1870's where the remarkable saga started. I have also been conscious of the absence of material on Jewish socialist movements in general histories of socialism, and hope that this study will help re-assess their contribution.

I am indebted to a number of people who have helped my research, most particularly Mr. Hillel Kempinski, archivist of the Bund Archives in New York, who gave unstintingly of his time and erudition. I am also grateful to my old friend and former librarian of Gratz College, Mr. Joseph Yenish, and to Mr. Elkan Bukhhalter, librarian of Gratz College, for their help in obtaining materials in Yiddish; to Miss Dina Abramowicz and Mr. Mark Webb of the YIVO Institute for Jewish Research; and to the American Jewish Periodical Center for the loan of Yiddish newspapers on microfilm. I also wish to thank Miss Francine Cohen and Miss Becky Ney, who patiently typed a sometimes indecipherable manuscript. I am especially indebted to the students at Gratz College who took a course with me several years ago on The Jew as Radical. Their interest turned from alienated Jews such as Marx and Lassalle to unalienated Jewish radicals, and their turning suggested the possibility of a book on Jewish socialists. I hope they are still interested in such models.

Nora Levin
Philadelphia, 1976

Guard the portal-song
Of tomorrow's hope
Which is forever etched
Into your believing bones

JACOB GLATSTEIN

I

THE BEGINNINGS IN RUSSIA

THE JEWISH PALE OF SETTLEMENT AT THE END OF THE NINETEENTH CENTURY

BALTIC SEA

• Riga

• Moscow

KOVNO
Kovno

VITEBSK
Vitebsk

Vilna

GERMANY

VILNA

• Minsk

Mogilev
MOGILEV

Bialystock
GRODNO

Warsaw •

POLAND

MINSK

Gomel

CHERNIGOV

VOLYNIA
Zhitomir •

POLTAVA

GALICIA

Poltava •

AUSTRIA-HUNGARY

PODOLIA

KIEV

Ekaterinoslav •
EKATERINOSLAV

Kishinev •

KHERSON
Odessa

TAURIDA

Northwest provinces
(main area of Bund
activity to 1917)

BESSARABIA

RUMANIA

Polish provinces

Southwest provinces

BLACK SEA

Southern provinces   BULGARIA

1. The Long Jewish Night in the Pale

Three important Jewish socialist movements developed in the late nineteenth century—in Russia, in the United States, and in Palestine. They profoundly changed Jewish life in those countries and affected the non-Jewish world as well. Although each movement developed its own version of socialist thought and institutions, each influenced the other and each had to confront Jewish as well as general social and economic realities. This meant dealing with anti-Semitism, Jewish national consciousness, and dilemmas of identity. Each movement took a different course in meeting these problems and the problems besetting Jewish and non-Jewish workers. Yet each involved a curious, perhaps exceptional, relationship between workers and intellectuals, without which none of them could have developed as effective, even transforming forces in modern Jewish life. All three movements, moreover, arose in the huge Russian ghetto called the Pale of Settlement and were shaped by conditions of life in the Pale and by the crosscurrents of thought that battered the ghetto under oppressive Russian tsars. None of the Jewish socialists in these movements forgot the Pale and how it had deformed the Jew.

The oppression of the Jew in Russian history can be traced to the beginnings of the Jewish experience under Russian rule and, with few and brief episodes of surcease, has persisted until our own time. This history is the history of the Jews of Poland under the regime of the Russian tsars—and, more recently, of Soviet Russia. But, unlike the generosity and benign tolerance of the early Polish kings, the fundamental anti-Jewish policy of Russia coincided with the expansion of the Principality of Muscovy, which was the nucleus of the emerging Russian state in the sixteenth and seventeenth centuries. Recollecting the conversion of the Khazars to Judaism [1] in the seventh century and the so-called Judaizing heresy [2] of the fifteenth, the Muscovite kings beginning with Ivan IV (Ivan the Terrible) held to a strong anti-Jewish line.[3] In 1550, for example, he refused the demand of the Polish king that, under existing commercial treaties, Lithuanian Jews be admitted into Russia for business purposes. "It is not convenient to allow Jews to come with their goods to Russia," Ivan IV replied, "since many evils result from them. For they import poisonous herbs [medicines] into our realm, and lead astray the Russians from Christianity." Some years later, when he occupied the Polish border city of Polotzk, he ordered all local Jews to be converted or drowned in the Dvina River.

In the seventeenth century, Peter the Great, who imported thousands of foreigners to help modernize his semi-barbaric kingdom, refused to admit any Jews. In the next century, this anti-Jewish policy was clinched by the Empress Elizabeth who in 1741 ordered the immediate expulsion of all Jews "from our entire empire, both from the Great Russian and Little Russian cities, villages and hamlets."[4] No Jews were to be admitted unless they converted to Russian Orthodoxy, in which case they could live in Russia, but not leave it. Even the enlightened Catherine II, admirer of the French *philosophes,* and herself a religious skeptic, added the oft-repeated Russian formula *kromye zhydov* ("except the Jews") to her invitation to foreigners to settle in Russia (1762). A few years later, during the political and economic anarchy that engulfed Poland, the Russians encouraged the Ukrainian Haidamacks to perpetrate unspeakable butcheries upon Jews—a fateful omen of what was to come. Thus, before Polish Jewry fell under Russian rule, as one historian has put it, Russia managed to have a Jewish problem without having any Jews.[5]

The three partitions of Poland in 1772, 1793, and 1795 gave Russia large chunks of a disintegrating Poland, which she grasped eagerly, and also almost one million Jews, whom she took grudgingly and, finally, with undisguised hatred. In 1772, taking an enlightened posture, Catherine II promised her new Jewish subjects all of the rights they had enjoyed in Poland. However, by the second (1793) and third partitions (1795), when hundreds of thousands of additional Jews came into the Russian Empire, Catherine abandoned her liberal pretensions. In 1794, she issued a ukase that was to have fateful consequences for Russian Jews until 1917, and even later. This ukase created the Pale of Settlement (see map, p. 2), a huge ghetto roughly conforming to the boundaries of the former Polish kingdom. Confined to this area, Jews began their life under Russian tsarism—an experience of physical constraint, oppressive taxation, Russian Orthodox anti-Semitism, and a long night of tormenting disabilities punctuated by very occasional gleams of humanity or the suggestion of relief.

Not until March 20, 1917, three weeks after the fall of tsarism, were all of the restrictions on Jews revoked—a total of some 140 statutes covering 120 years. At the time, the new government also found reports of countless commissions that had been created periodically to examine legislation dealing with Jews. The commissions invariably concluded that the existing restrictions did not achieve their purpose and should be revoked, yet their recommendations were never applied. From Catherine II on, no guiding objective informed government policies; rather, justification for the restrictions spanned the whole gamut of religious, economic, and political reasons. The Jew was infidel, murderer of Christ, and should convert to Christianity; he was also accused of exploiting the rural population and having "useless occupations"; toward the end of the nineteenth century, he was charged with being politically subversive. Each of these charges involved elaborate administrative schemes for keeping the non-Jewish population "uncontaminated," while at the same time officials spoke of the need for "fusion," "russification," and "assimilation." Tsarist Russia never resolved these mutually exclusive aims.

Nevertheless, however much bureaucratic thinking weaved and drifted, Jews were invariably victims of an onslaught against their religious, cultural, and economic patterns of life. Motives and control mechanisms might vary, but for the masses of Jews penned up in the Pale, life was wretched, cramped, and precarious. Yet they would not fuse or disappear. At the same time, the government refused to allow them to be citizens. This impasse led to ever-intensifying persecutions and culminated in the officially inspired pogroms of 1881–82 that outraged world opinion and reached a new pitch of savagery in modern anti-Semitism prior to the Holocaust.

The boundaries of the Pale were first explicitly defined in the "Statute Concerning the Jews," issued in 1835. Roughly, the Pale included the regions of "New Russia"—the Ukraine, Belorussia-Lithuania, Polish territories added to the Empire after the Napoleonic wars, and certain areas in the Baltic provinces. Occasionally, restricted categories of Jews were permitted to leave for brief visits to St. Petersburg, Moscow, the seaports and the big fairs. Others could leave to become "russified"—that is, to give up their Jewishness. Some, in "useful" categories, were later permitted to reside for uncertain terms in Russia proper. But the Jewish masses remained in the Pale. Yet, despite the strong physical constraint placed upon them—virtual isolation from general Russian society—the Russian government was implacably opposed to "Jewish separateness," which meant any cultural or religious distinctiveness.

Hundreds of decrees were churned out, aimed at robbing the Jew of his traditional identity by banning his language and dress; crippling his highly developed educational system; slashing the functions of the *kahals*, the autonomous Jewish communities; wrenching Jewish youth from their homes at the age of twelve for a lifetime of brutal military conscription and forced conversion. Further poisoning the atmosphere in which Russian Jews lived were the tormenting ritual murder trials and recurring attacks on the Talmud. Regarded as stubbornly alien, harmful, and intrusive, Jews were peculiarly and persistently vulnerable. Yet when they tried to reach outside the imposed restrictions and aspire to a fuller life, they were blocked by the regime.

Jews were also stigmatized by other minority people in the empire. As the internal life of the Russian Empire swelled with the complications and tensions of numerous national minorities, Jews were not only separated from Russians but also from non-Russians, particularly from their closest neighbors: Belorussians, Lithuanians, Poles, and Ukrainians. These groups marked the stigma the regime placed on the Jewish population through special taxes, periodic expulsions from rural areas in the Pale, and denial of certain occupations. In the struggle that these groups waged for ethnic emancipation, Jews had no leverage—no land to redeem, no armed forces, no economic power or political influence, and no allies. Moreover, their own traditional cohesiveness and spiritual armor were weakening under the impact of new forces.

By the time Polish Jews were absorbed into the Russian Empire, rabbinic Judaism, which had enwrapped the *shtetl* in an all-encompassing religious culture for several centuries, was already in decline. The annihilation of almost 700 Jewish communities in Poland during the Khmielnitzki massacres of 1648 traumatized Jewish life in a way that was never overcome, except perhaps in Lithuania. The earlier vigor of Polish Jewry, with its diversified economic and social life, halakhic creativity, and highly developed communal organization had been shattered by the massacres. Most of the Jews who survived were dispersed throughout the countryside, without the possibility of educating themselves or living a full communal and religious life. On this bleak landscape, there blazed, from time to time, Messianic expectations; and prophets of redemption appeared and vanished, gripping the masses with ecstatic visions. This was the era of the imposters Sabbatai Tzevi and Jacob Frank, of Frankist attacks on the Talmud, of the contracting scholasticism of rabbinic Judaism.

Talmudic study, divorced from the realities of daily life, became the province of an elite and took on a cold, formalistic cast. There was deep contempt for the artisan or laborer who had no skill in Talmudic dialetics. Gloom and superstition engulfed Jewish towns and villages. Into this darkness and stagnation moved the radiant Israel of Miedzybodz, the Baal Shem Tov, who infused Jewish life with a new warmth, simple piety, and joyful intimacy with God. Never comfortable with the intricacies of Talmudic study, he settled with his second wife in the heart of the Carpathians. In the midst of magnificent natural beauty, he learned the healing properties of herbs and plants, ministered to the peasants of the region, prayed, and expounded his teachings to humble Jews and adoring disciples.

The Baal Shem Tov launched a movement of religious renewal known as Hasidism, which subordinated learning to faith, and which transformed worldly pleasures into service to God. Masses flocked to his call, challenging the religious and administrative leaders of the declining and defensive *kahals*. Several years after his death, the first partition of Poland took place, but neither old nor new borders could stem the surge of the new movement that quickly filled the Yiddish-speaking world. It continued to spread during subsequent partitions, giving spiritual comfort and emotional warmth to the Jews of Europe, and buffering the frightening political changes taking place. Jewish life, with its daily misery and oppressions, became not only endurable but occasionally joyous.

Eventually, Hasidism made its peace with rabbinic Judaism—and very possibly saved it from petrifaction. However, certain harmful abuses and extravagances also developed: the cult of the miracle-working rebbes, entrenchment of *tzaddik* dynasties, the downgrading of learning—it became axiomatic in many Hasidic circles that "where there is much learning, there is little piety"—the advent of charlatans who lived off the credulity of ignorant masses, and excessive sensuality. A balance between the extremes of both Hasidism and Talmudic Judaism was essential to give Russian Jewry the necessary strength to survive the struggle against the fanaticism of the Greek Orthodox clergy and the pressures of an essentially anti-Semitic government.

By the 1840's, the schism in Eastern European Jewry had narrowed, enabling the two factions to make common defense against the threat that was directed against all forms of Judaism. The healing of the schism occurred in time for Russian Jewry to resist the relentless efforts of Nicholas I (1825–55)—one of the most despotic and anti-Semitic of the Russian tsars—to destroy Judaism in Russia. In this mobilization for survival, Hasidism contributed not only vehement resistance, but a new expression of that resistance. Hasidic communities and courts became cells of opposition to the Russian government—the first such force in Russian Jewry which balked at the role into which the government had maneuvered the *kahal*, and through it, all Russian Jews. This role derived from the medieval notion of Jews as a religious-social corporation within general society. While the *kahal* leaders maintained inner discipline within the Jewish community, the government used them as agents for tax purposes and tight administrative control. Jews perforce were "cooperative" subjects. They relied on the government to legitimatize their corporate existence; the government expected and received their loyalty. The spirit of independence and dissent in a political-secular sense was still a generation away, but the spread of Hasidism did much to embolden religious Jews to disobey the *kahals*, and, by extension, the government. When Nicholas I withdrew the legal recognition of the *kahals* in 1844, he was moved by the growing rebellious spirit of the Jews. By this act, the government hoped to crush the seeming internal unity of the Jews.

Before the liquidation of the *kahals*, Nicholas I subjected Jewish boys of twelve to a six-year preliminary "cantonment" in addition to twenty-five years of military service, a brutal measure aimed at achieving conversion. The tsar also tried sudden expulsions, book burnings, severe censorship of Jewish religious literature, harsh taxes and, finally, the lure of crown schools to drive the "perversity" out of the Jews. But nothing availed. The Jews remained a generally cohesive mass. The more they were abused, the more stubbornly separate and threatening to Nicholas' dream of amalgamation they became. Even the destruction of the *kahals*, which left them in a political and legal limbo, merely caused a shift in communal discipline. Voluntary self-help associations, called *hevras*, took the place of the *kahals*, answering a variety of communal needs and regulating the major areas of Jewish community life. There were *hevras* that provided schooling for poor children, those that arranged funerals, maintained orphanages and homes for the aged, and regulated crafts in Jewish life. In the same sense in which the guilds of Western Europe were the forerunners of European trade unions, the *hevras* of the Pale were the forerunners of Jewish trade unions.

In the West, the destruction of Jewish corporate life ushered in, if not full citizenship for Jews, at least the breakdown of ghetto walls and disabilities. In Russia, the destruction of corporativism not only failed to extend citizenship, but ensured the cohesion Nicholas aimed to destroy. Yet Jewish resistance, the reflex of a desperate will to survive, exacted a great price. The determination to preserve Jewish tradition at all costs protected both obsolete parts of the culture as well as its foundations. The old patriarchal scheme of family life, for example, remained rigidly conservative. Parents arranged marriages between young teenage children. Boys of school age often became husbands and fathers, while continuing to attend the *heder* or *yeshivah*, weighed down by the triple tutelage of father, father-in-law, and teacher. Jewish youths knew nothing of the sweetness or rebelliousness of youth, but withered under the weight of family responsibilities, hallowed customs, and old habits of thought. A short jacket or trimmed beard was condemned as a dangerous sign of freethinking. The reading of books in foreign languages, or secular works in Hebrew brought severe punishment, even excommunication.

The traditional *heder* was also a cramping experience. The historian Simon Dubnow, who at the age of twelve composed a diatribe in Hebrew against religious fanaticism and whose *bar mitzvah* discourse was an exercise on the subject of how a left-handed person should wear his *tefillin* (phylacteries), recalled the *heder* with revulsion, as did so many others:

> The entire pale is filled with thousands of children's prisons. These children are criminally tortured both in spirit and in body. Emaciated youngsters leave these institutions. They know nothing of childhood, fields, meadows or blue skies. They pass away their finest years of childhood within four walls, in sticky air, in spiritual tension that is far too much for their meager energies, under the rod of ignoramuses. An enormous storehouse of Babylonian wisdom is forcibly injected into the brains of these youngsters. They are told nothing about the

real world, about nature and life, but only about the next world and about death.[6]

Minds sharpened by the *pilpul* (the subtle method of argumentation and dialectics of the Talmudic academies) could not wrestle with the "extraneous sciences" nor could they make direct contact with tides of thought swirling outside Russia. Thus, the isolation imposed by the regime drove the Jews deeper into their own self-protective but ossifying shell. Unquestionably, they were also frightened by the price emancipated Jews in the West—especially Germany—were paying, resulting in a diluted Judaism, filed down to Western niceties and practices, or—much more shocking—the frequent recourse to baptism.

With the increase of trade and the awakening of secular intellectual interests—part of the general response in Russia to Western ideas—some shock waves were felt in the Pale in the early nineteenth century. Even earlier, the great Vilna Gaon (Rabbi Elijah ben Saloman Zalman) had labored to end the tyranny of *pilpul,* to reform the schools and broaden the scope of studies to include mathematics, astronomy, grammar, and other secular studies. Although his influence was greatest in Lithuania, it was felt also by the early *maskilim* (humanists) in Russia. A far greater influence, however, was exerted by Moses Mendelssohn, who opened German culture to Jews through his translation of the Bible, and subsequently by the German Jews themselves who rushed into Western culture, political emancipation, and, often, conversion. Berlin became a mecca for Galician and Russian Jews who impotently raged against the cramping life of the Pale. Galicia became the crossroad between "enlightened" Germany and "backward" Russia, and Lemberg, Brody, and Tarnopol, in Galicia, and Odessa, in Russia, became new centers for restless Jewish intellectuals and enterprising merchants.

This new breed of *maamike behokhmah*—"delvers in knowledge"— tramped, begged and peddled their way to Berlin under scarcely believable hardships. The tenacity of these pathbreakers is awesome. Solomon Maimon,[7] the brilliant, erratic, insatiable searcher, was only the most dramatic and extreme of a great number of Jewish autodidacts of the time who set out on lonely pilgrimages, abandoning family, *shtetl,* and the old culture. Secretly they taught themselves German, Latin, and Greek, contrived armillary spheres out of twisted rods in order to get a visual picture of the universe, smuggled forbidden books in and out of hiding places, collected slugs of Russian type, and learned to read Russian.

Many other early *maskilim* found the light of their new world not quite so blinding; they were more selective. In Galicia, Russia, and Congress Poland, old and new forces interacted, creating a Haskalah (Enlightenment) in Eastern Europe, very different from the process in Germany, where the attack against traditional Judaism was more sweeping. In Eastern Europe, there developed many tones of Haskalah, early and late phases, and gradations of sympathy or hostility toward Hasidism, German culture, *shtetl* folkways, Yiddish, the Talmud, Jewish schools, government authority, Russian culture, and secular studies.

Pain and dislocation accompanied the conflicts and accommodations unleashed by the *maskilim*. Critics of the Haskalah still deplore the blows it delivered against the traditional religious culture of the Pale. Yet, during the first quarter of the nineteenth century, that culture was already being undermined by inner stresses. Change was inevitable. The Haskalah in Eastern Europe accelerated the change and generated forces in Jewish life that developed a new tradition or, at least, patterns for new kinds of Jewish life based on the struggle of the *maskilim* to absorb the modern world without surrendering all of the old religious culture.

Some of the early *maskilim* became uncritical *Berlinchiks* who lived off the reflected glory of the Mendelssohn enlightenment.[8] But, in time, Mendelssohn's defense (largely for Christian critics) of Orthodox Judaism in terms of "revealed legislation" became as unpalatable as his disciples' immersion in German culture. The Russian *maskilim* admired German dress, German manners, the German emphasis on science and academic research, but did not want to Germanize themselves. In strong contrast with those Jews who followed Mendelssohn in Germany, the Russian *maskilim* typically sought not the de-Judaized Jew, but the modern Jew. Men like Joseph Perl, Solomon Rapoport, and Nachman Krochmal were devoutly religious, devoted to Jewish tradition, and eager to perpetuate it—without, however, the superstitions that had crusted around it and obscured the meaningful values of the past.

It was this reverence for Judaism that explains, in large measure, the choice of Hebrew, rather than German or Russian, as the medium of expression of the Russian Haskalah. Moreover, although some Eastern European Jews of this period thought they could assimilate into general society in the manner of the German Jews, the early *maskilim* could not excite young Russian Jews with the promise of a rich Russian culture once they had breached the four ells of the *halahkah*, as the followers of Mendelssohn could do. In the early nineteenth century, Russia was a cultural wasteland; whatever was interesting in Russia at the time was imported. The language itself was still in a primitive state in the early 1800's, and Russian literature was sparse, unoriginal, and uninspiring. There were no profound philosophical systems, no Rousseau, Goethe, or Kant to seize hold of restless minds. The whole royal library of Alexander I (1801–25), founded, curiously enough, by a Jew, the court physician Sanchez, contained only eight Russian books; not many more were added by his successor.[9] The nation's best energies seemed turned to the military, and most young men of intelligence at the time were drawn to the army— or to agonizing self-scrutiny.

Alexander Herzen has given us a vivid picture of the young intellectuals during the regime of Nicholas I, in some ways a self-portrait:

A terrible crime must be laid at the door of the regime of Nicholas—moral abortion and the killing of the souls of the young. . . . The whole system of public education was reduced to the preaching of a religion of blind obedience, leading to official position as the natural reward. The naturally expansive feelings of youth were roughly driven inwards, and were replaced by ambition and by jealous, spiteful rivalry. Those who did not perish emerged sick in mind and soul. Rampant vanity was combined with a sort of hopelessness, a consciousness of impotence, a weary disinclination for work. Young people became hypochondriacal, suspicious, worn-out before they reached the age of twenty. They were all infected with the passion for self-observation, self-examination, self-accusation; they carefully studied their own psychological symptoms, and loved endless discussions and stories about their own nervous case-history. . . . No happiness could exist for them; they did not know how to retain it. On the slightest pretext they reacted inhumanly and dealt brutally with their neighbor. . . .[10]

Not only was Russia undeveloped intellectually in the early nineteenth century; its political and social institutions were also far behind those of Western Europe. Fifty million Russian serfs were fastened to the land or owned by the state. Little wonder, then, that some of the early Russian *maskilim* found nothing in their own society to stimulate them, and sought Germany, like moths seeking a flame. Coming at another time in Russian history, the vehement Jewish reaction against Emancipation probably would not have erupted; in large part it was a reaction to the harsh policies of the last years of the reign of Alexander I and the whole reign of Nicholas I, a period of political reaction in Europe (1815–48), which assumed particularly repressive forms in Russia.

The early Russian *maskilim* tapped feebly at the doors of this Jewry under seige and were roared down. But, in strong contrast with the German disavowal of Hebrew and Yiddish, these *maskilim* did not reject the linguistic core of Jewish experience. Instead, they laid the foundations for a national literary renaissance,[11] which later became an important social and ideological force. The work of many lonely figures made the first cracks in traditional Jewish society in the Russian Pale.

These cracks were widened by the emergence of a new Jewish merchant-scholar group and the development of centers of new cultural interests: Odessa and Vilna within the Pale, Brody and Lemberg in Galicia, and Courland in Prussia. Having for long filled the role of middlemen in the towns and cities of Poland and the unenviable role as economic link between landlord and peasant in the villages, Jews were locked in the same pattern in Russia. A class of Jews who became wealthy tax farmers (collecting liquor excises) and their employees in mills, storehouses, and offices, and Jews in wholesale commerce began to find traditional Judaism a liability blocking their upward mobility. Increasingly they saw practical benefits in a secular education and, like some of the early *maskilim*, urged basic reforms in Jewish schools and synagogues.

Jewish school reform ran a tumultuous course in Russia. In one phase, in 1842, it culminated in the establishment of crown schools for Jewish children and two rabbinical seminaries, whose graduates could become crown rabbis. These schools aroused intense opposition from most Jews, for the government's aim was soon made all too clear: to destroy Jewish "separatism" and lead students to conversion. From this development, moreover, a new small class of Jews appeared, further splitting the solid edifice of *heder* and *yeshivah* schooling. This was a Jewish intelligentsia, supported precariously by the government, who taught Jewish subjects in the crown schools, censored Jewish books on behalf of the government, and wrote government-financed textbooks and manuals for the general public. Dependent as they were on government employment and favor, they were severed from the Jewish masses and generally disliked by them. The graduates of the state-supported seminaries were also estranged from *shtetl* life. Often they entered the universities and became skeptics, socialists, and disaffected Jews. Only occasionally did these university graduates return to Jewish life—until after the pogroms of 1881.

Possibly the most profound forces creating a new dynamic in Jewish life in the Pale were the reforms of the early years of Alexander II's regime and the immense expectations aroused by them. Alexander II came to the throne in 1855, following the disastrous Crimean War, and quickly began to introduce social and economic reforms that profoundly affected Russia, though they stopped short of genuine political freedom and civic equality and eventually created disillusionment, frustration, and explosive revolutionary movements. Jews at first hailed the benevolent and liberal tsar with great rejoicing. In 1856, he abolished the seizure of juvenile cantonists and equalized military service for Jews. The sealed Pale was finally breached, and Jewish merchants of the First Guild,[12] persons with "learned degrees,"[13] artisans, mechanics, and distillers could reside in all parts of the empire. State schools were opened to all children, and Jewish children were especially encouraged to attend. By 1873, the Jewish crown schools were closed, and officials viewed the general Russian schools as the most effective agencies of civil and cultural fusion. A Hebrew press flourished under official encouragement. Nicholas I's efforts to "diminish the Jews" by religious assimilation were eschewed.

Although these radical changes did not directly or immediately affect the masses of Jews still languishing in the Pale, a thin layer made a rapid cultural, economic, and social advance. Some Jewish youths were admitted into the *gymnasia* and universities and thrilled to new ideas of freedom and brotherhood, the new discipline of science, and the lure of contemporary European literature and philosophy. The bright banner of socialism was already making young hearts beat faster. Certain journals in both Hebrew and Russian appeared, exploring the pleasures and challenges of modernism, secularism, and even patriotism. Some dealt harshly with Talmudic law and ritualistic quibbles, uncovering new levels of Jewish consciousness, even helping to bring the new Russian-Jewish intelligentsia into closer contact with the Jewish people, their problems and needs. The journals had fitful, irregular life spans. Some ceased publication for several years and then resumed; others lasted only a year or two. The Hebrew weekly *Ha-Melitz* (*The Advocate*) and its Yiddish supplement *Kol Mevasser* (*The Messenger*) published virtually every important Hebrew writer at the time. The powerful monthly *Ha-Shahar* (*The Dawn*), edited by Peretz Smolenskin in Vienna, but widely read by East European *maskilim*, lasted longer than the others and influenced an entire generation.

Ha-Melitz bore down harshly on Hasidism and the obscurantism of rabbinical Judaism, while Smolenskin slashed equally at the fanaticism of the Orthodox and the pale Jewishness of the Berlin-influenced *maskilim*. He inveighed against Mendelssohn and his followers for draining the national substance out of Jewish life. For Smolenskin, Jews had never ceased to be a nation, but had become weak and defenseless because they did not possess a land of their own. A forerunner of Pinsker and Herzl, Smolenskin developed national, nonreligious elements in the outlook of modernist Russian Jews. A glimpse of the effect of *Ha-Shahar* on religious youth can be found in the following reminiscence by Samuel Citron, a Yiddish and Hebrew writer:

> For the Orthodox youth educated in the yeshivas and prayer houses, *Ha-Shahar* was practically a revolutionary upheaval. Every copy in the hands of these young people was like a match put to a powder keg. *Ha-Shahar* revolutionized their minds, undermined old ideas infested with traditional moldiness, stimulated them to new ideas. . . . Woe to the yeshiva student caught with *Ha-Shahar!* He took a drubbing, he suffered various indignities (his "eating" days were withdrawn). Sometimes he was even expelled from the yeshiva. Yet, despite their vigorous efforts, the officials of the yeshiva failed to bar *Ha-Shahar*. When they chased it from one door, it came in through seven others. . . . The young people devised cunning ways to deceive their guardians. They read *Ha-Shahar* on the Gemara and under the Gemara and sat up nights with it. . . .[14]

Even more influential than the journals were the early Hebrew novels, especially those of Abraham Mapu, who carried ghetto youths away from painful reality with romanticized splendors of ancient Israel and tore the mask from hypocritical figures he saw in the declining Pale. These novels were read surreptitiously and made the problem of fathers and sons a burning question long before Turgenev wrote his famous novel, setting off inner spiritual struggles that were as disruptive as the external conflicts. There are countless memoirs of the torments experienced by *yeshivah* students as their minds and spirits were tossed by new intellectual excitements and pulled by old loyalties. The crisis in values was especially keen for the many Jewish youths who by age thirteen or fourteen became dialectical wizards panting for new challenges. It was these youths who devoured the fine spinnings of philosophy, the precise exercises of mathematics and science, and the enchantments of French, German, and Russian literature.

Moreover, by the 1860's, Russian literature had its own towering figures—Tolstoy, Dostoevsky, and Turgenev—who stimulated a rage to learn Russian. Mastery of Russian also drew Jews into diverse russification movements, some frankly conversionist, some linked with general emancipation efforts, some aimed at cultural fusion. The Russian language also gave Jews access to the progressive and radical political circles of the time. These groups gathered momentum during the last half of Alexander II's reign, when early reforms stopped short of realization and signalled an unexpectedly bitter turn of events.

Most critical were the failures of the emancipation edict of 1861 which freed the serfs. As the edict was being put into effect, peasant rioting in hundreds of places poisoned the widespread rejoicing the edict aroused. The serf was indeed free; he could no longer be bought and sold; but for this, he soon realized that he would pay a heavy price. The land he had used still belonged to the landowner.[15] Thus, if the serf was to be released with land, he must pay for it. Moreover, how much land and what kind of land he received was arbitrarily decided by the landlord. The effect was shocking: peasants actually received less land than they had been free to use in the pre-emancipation period, and for these lesser amounts they paid more than the land would normally sell for. Four million peasants received no land at all, and had no choice but to drift to towns and the bitter competitive struggle to survive. The peasant population as a whole became impoverished. Burdened by debts and taxation, land-hungry, undernourished, yet forced to sell the grain they and their families needed, the peasants of Russia were worse off after emancipation than before.[16] Their suffering was to have profound effects on the Pale.

There was another fundamental deficiency in Alexander II's reforms: his refusal to cap early reforms with a constitution and genuine political liberty. This refusal widened the breach between the government and all progressive elements in Russia, whose hopes were riveted on this goal. The struggle for complete emancipation, driven underground by the dreaded Third Section of the police, assumed the character of a revolutionary movement among Russian youth. As if suddenly unfettered, some young Jews rushed headlong into this movement.

Emancipation of the serfs generated yet other problems fraught with danger as well as opportunity for the Jews. As serfs poured into the cities, the way was opened for the development of capitalism in Russia, which brought about the disintegration of the traditional Jewish economic structure. In pre-industrial Russian society, Jews filled important functions in the distribution and exchange of agricultural and consumer goods. According to an occupational estimate made in 1825,[17] about 30 percent of Russian Jews were engaged in trade; 30 percent were innkeepers, farm tenants, and leaseholders; 18 percent were artisans (selling as well as producing goods); and about 18 percent—the *luftmenschen*—were in "undetermined occupations," generally, uncertain work from day to day, that gave a Jew a very precarious living. Only 1 percent were farmers. A few years later, in 1832, we find Jews owning 149 factories (out of 528) in eight provinces in the northeastern and southwestern territories.[18] Moreover, in the 1840's, Jews began to operate as well as finance sugar refineries and textile factories. These changes reflected certain changes in the general Russian economy: the development of light industry, the increase in serf and hired factory labor, and the importation of foreign machinery. In turn, these transitions reflected the growing rebelliousness of the serfs and the pressuring effect of the industrial achievements in Western Europe.

A small proportion of Jews were drawn into this change. In the early 1800's, especially after the War of 1812, the government had tried to enlist Jews to supply the Russian army. This role enabled some Jews to accumulate capital, which was later invested in factories, mining, transportation, and banking. Some Jews had also amassed capital through liquor production and distribution, or as commission merchants, in the 1860's. At the same time, many thousands of petty liquor agents and innkeepers lost their livelihood.

Meanwhile, the masses of Jews in the *shtetlach* became more impoverished than ever. As ex-serfs poured into cities and began to wear manufactured boots and ready-made clothes, factory production displaced the labor of the Jewish bootmaker, weaver, and tailor. The building of railroad networks (often financed by wealthy foreign Jews) also hurt local Jewish shopkeepers, draymen, and letter carriers. As the population increased, the Pale of Settlement became an even more crowded prison for the masses. Between 1847 and 1897, the Jewish population tripled, and crowding and competition became more acute. The overcrowding was particularly felt in the northwestern provinces (Vilna, Grodno, Minsk, Vitebsk, Kovno, and Mogilev), which were, together with Poland, the areas of densest Jewish population. By 1897, when the Jewish Labor Bund was founded, the Jews represented 58 percent of the urban population in Russia.

In the 1880's, Christians, too, began to stream into the cities, looking for work in the factories. Many Jewish workers remained in their traditional crafts—tailoring, shoemaking, and baking. But some now moved into factories manufacturing cigarettes, leather, brushes, and cloth, where they confronted Christian workers for the first time, in a setting of cultural isolation and economic discrimination and insecurity. Such economic and social dislocations in the Pale created an unwholesome number of Jews who became what Mendele Mocher Seforim called "lick and smell" or "walking-stick" businessmen who barely subsisted. Between 1870 and 1880—before the year of pogroms—41,057 Jews left Russia to go to the United States. A sharpened class consciousness was felt by the Jewish proletariat that remained. In 1888, the Pahlen Commission, which was set up to examine legislation governing Jewish life, found that about 90 percent of the Jewish population were "a mass of people that are entirely unprovided for . . . a mass that lives from hand to mouth, amidst poverty, and most oppressive sanitary and general conditions. This very proletariat is occasionally the target of tumultuous popular uprisings. . . ." [19]

Nevertheless, the growing affluence of a small fraction of the Jewish population aroused envy, suspicion, and hostility among non-Jews, feelings that were inflamed by the activities of a Jewish apostate, Jacob Brafman, in the late sixties. Brafman had become embittered by *kahal* agents who had been forced to fill quotas of military conscripts among Jews in the last years of Nicholas I. Appointed a Hebrew teacher in the seminary for Russian preachers in Minsk, he was charged by the Holy Synod with promoting Christianity among Jews. He produced a *Book on the Kahal*, in which he alleged that the *kahal* worked in secret, together with similar organizations all over the world, that it wielded despotic power over the Jewish communities, incited the Jewish masses against the state, and fostered a dangerous separatism. The charges were soon enough disproved, but the tsar and crown prince were strongly impressed by Brafman's disclosures and his work was printed at public expense and distributed to all government offices. In this mood of heightened suspicion, the Council of State set up a special commission to consider ways of "weakening as far as possible the communal cohesion among the Jews." In the midst of its deliberations, a pogrom erupted in Odessa.

The background to the pogrom lay in the antagonism between Jews and Greeks, rooted in competition in the corn trade and grocery business. Traditionally during Easter, the Greeks would discharge their pistols in front of their church in the Jewish district.[20] In 1871, the mob was aroused by a rumor that Jews had stolen a cross from the church fence. Then on Palm Sunday (March 28), and for three straight days, Greeks and Russians beat Jews, burned and robbed Jewish property, and desecrated synagogues. The police stood by until the fourth day, when order was restored. As for the central government, the only thing it wanted to know was whether the pogrom had any connection with secret revolutionary propaganda that might set the mob against the Russian nobility and bourgeoisie.[21] For the victims, the pogrom excesses were put aside as "a crude protest of the masses against the failure to solve the Jewish question," but for the Christian population, they were deemed a manifestation of resentment against Jewish economic "exploitation" in the Pale. Official reports followed showing that Jews were becoming a "great economic power" in the southwestern provinces, that they possessed a "World Kahal" (the Alliance Israélite Universelle) and constituted a "religio-political caste" that must be dissolved.

Throughout the 1870's, the gravity of the "Jewish peril" filled journals and government reports. A new trumped-up charge of ritual murder further inflamed the anti-Jewish atmosphere. Anti-Semitic literature, already rampant in Germany, was enthusiastically imported. At the Congress of Berlin in 1878, the Russian minister Gorchakov was the only important statesman who opposed legal equality for the Jews of Eastern Europe. Meanwhile, the movement for social reform and political liberty at home was being brutally silenced. Alexander II, the symbol of this bitter failure, increasingly became the target of terrorist assassins, and on March 3, 1881, he was killed by an exploding bomb—ironically, just after he had approved a moderate constitutional project.

The opposing forces now polarized sharply, putting Jews in great jeopardy. The rationale for repressive absolutism was proclaimed by Konstantin Pobiedonostzev, Procurator of the Holy Synod and confidant and advisor of the new tsar, Alexander III, who had once been his pupil. Pobiedonostzev's ideal of autocracy was a pan-Slav, pure Russian Orthodox conformism. All minorities suffered wretchedly during his ministry, but none more than the Jews, who were blamed for the tsar's assassination. A Jewish girl, Hessia Helfmann, was the one Jewish member of the group that organized the murder of Alexander II. Her role was actually a secondary one—she kept a secret residence for the others—but her connection with the terrorists was the pretext for a wave of government-inspired pogroms that brought death and terror to 160 Jewish towns and cities in southern Russia throughout the spring and summer of 1881.[22]

The pogrom agitation was started before the assassination of the tsar by agent-provocateurs. These attacks on Jews were not instigated by the national government but were tolerated by it and, even more, involved the active participation or tacit consent of the authorities. Circumstances point to a secret group of high officials called the Sacred League, formed in 1881, and made up of arch-reactionaries and rabid anti-Semites. They planned and guided the pogroms, which became a recurring feature of Russian life from 1881 to the fall of tsarism in 1917.[23] The usual pattern was to spread a rumor that an imperial ukase had been issued, calling upon Russians to attack Jews during the Greek Orthodox Easter. Christians on the streets and in stores told each other that "the Zhyds are about to be beaten." The first outbreaks took place in Elizabethgrad on April 16, 1881, and spread through the provinces of Kiev, Chernigov, Poltava, Kherson, and Ekaterinoslav. Western public opinion expressed outrage at the ferocity of these events. The Russian government mulled over what line to take.

At first, the government developed the rationale that the anti-Jewish actions were caused by revolutionary agitators seeking to channel the resentment of the masses against the Jews. Later, it was said, they would incite the masses against the Russian upper classes. Publicly, the tsar maintained that the disorders were the work of "anarchists." However, the government later abandoned this view and spoke of Jewish "exploitation" as the inciting factor. Not only did the government fail to aid the victims but, rather, began expulsions of the "privileged" Jews outside the Pale, signalling fresh encouragement to the pogrom-raisers. A new wave of pogroms began early in July in Pereyaslav, Poltava, infecting nearby villages and spreading fires in the areas of Lithuania and White Russia.

Before the year ended, a three-day pogrom assaulted the Jews of Warsaw. Some Polish intellectuals and clergymen tried to establish a civil guard and restore order, but the governor-general was not interested in stopping the street mobs too quickly. Finally, the army had to be called in to crush the riots—"a sad thing in all these Jewish disorders," the tsar commented. News of these "disorders" reached the government while the Central Committee on Jewish Affairs under the Minister of the Interior, Nicholas Ignatiev, an active member of the Sacred League, was preparing new legal and administrative restrictions against Jews. In the spring of 1882, the so-called Temporary Rules, or May Laws, were announced and remained in effect until the collapse of tsarist Russia in 1917.

The "rules" created a pale within the Pale and constituted a permanent and administrative legal pogrom. Dubnow estimates that Jews were now dislodged from nine-tenths of the territory previously available.[24] They were forbidden to leave the towns and hamlets they lived in to settle elsewhere in the Pale. They could not own mortgages, leases, or merchandise outside these towns. Except for the few Jews already in agricultural colonies, they were cut off from all connection with the land. Sojourn permits were suddenly cancelled, residence registers "disappeared," and local *kulaks* (literally "fists" or "bosses") convened peasant assemblies that expelled Jews. Driven by the terrible congestion within the Pale, Jews fled to the forbidden cities of St. Petersburg, Moscow, Kiev, and Kharkov, but were soon hounded and expelled. Forbidden to carry on business on Sundays or Christian holidays, poor Jews became still poorer. The right of residence of "trained artisans" in the interior was continually undermined by sudden reclassifications: if a watchmaker sold watch chains that he had not made himself, or if a pastry cook served coffee with his pastry, they became "merchants" and forfeited their right as artisans. Bribes served mainly to incite officials to new tricks, new demands, and new blows.

The Jews of Russia were now faced with a crisis of unprecedented magnitude. The pogroms of 1881–82 constituted a turning point in Jewish history. The convulsions that rocked Russian Jewry soon involved hundreds of thousands in a massive migration to the United States, there establishing a new center of Jewish life after a generation of struggle. There also developed an intensely introspective search for other answers to the dilemmas of Jewish survival and identity. Radical critiques of diaspora life led to Zionist formulations and the organization of the first *aliyot* to Palestine. For other Jews with a radical bent, neither America nor Palestine was satisfying. They did not want to leave Russia—despite everything they had endured—and slowly worked their way toward a unique ideological formulation compounded of Yiddish, Jewish cultural autonomy, and socialism. Each of these directional pulls was wrenched out of the common *shtetl* experience in Russia and changes agitating the *shtetl* and the larger society. The Haskalah, new economic and political forces, and the trauma of pogroms dislocated traditional Jewish life in the Pale and set new forces in motion. These collisions created remarkable new configurations in Jewish life that have profoundly affected Jews during the past century. The Russian Jewish generation of renewal and transformation produced three strands of Jewish socialism: the Yiddish-oriented Jewish labor movement in the United States, the Bund movement in Russia (and later Poland), and the socialist Zionist movement which laid the foundations for modern Israel. The extraordinary vigor of these movements, coming as they did out of a long-oppressed people, lay in the creative vision and energies of Russian Jewry—the tap root of modern Jewish life.

2. *The Jewish* Narodniki

As has often happened in history, the era of rising expectations in Russia—roughly the decade from 1856 to 1866—produced its antithesis: frustration, alienation and rebellion, spearheaded by a generation of iconoclastic students. Rejecting all past traditions at odds with their present, they developed a movement called *narodnichestvo*, or populism, an amalgam of disparate, even self-contradictory, ideas, which eventually turned into a strong affirmation of the power of the radicalized intelligentsia to lead the people to revolutionary changes in the teeth of government reaction and oppression in the 1870's.

Russian populism [1] was not a single party or a coherent body of doctrine, but a widespread radical movement in Russia in the middle of the nineteenth century, growing in influence during the sixties and seventies, and reaching its culmination with the assassination of Alexander II in 1881, after which it swiftly declined. Its leaders were men of dissimilar origins, outlooks, and capacities, and their followers consisted of small independent groups of conspirators and sympathizers who sometimes united for common action. These groups differed about ends and means but had sufficient moral and political solidarity to render them a movement. The essence of their belief was that "government and the social structure in Russia" were a "moral and political monstrosity" [2] and must be destroyed. The Russian universities provided populism with its first leaders. For at least three decades, the revolutionary movement as a whole was to be a youth movement, manned chiefly by undergraduates, some of whom were Jews.

At the end of the fifties and the beginning of the sixties, the thought of the young generation was dominated by Alexander Herzen and the influential journal he published in London, *The Bell*. But Herzen lost some of his influence when his support for the tsar was undermined by the terms of the Emancipation Edict and the crushing of the Polish uprising of 1863. His hope for "reform from above" and faith in Western liberalism disenchanted the new student generation, made up of children of minor officials, professional men, and minority groups now permitted to attend the universities as a result of Alexander II's liberalizing of school admissions. These "new men of the sixties" also included students from the provinces who experienced the frustrations and sectarian religious ideas of the less developed regions of Russia. Among them were an unusually large number of former seminarians, who "brought with them a certain passion for absolute answers ... which hypnotized and seduced many of their uprooted fellow-students." [3] The most important were the "two St. Nicholases," Chernyshevsky and Dobroliubov, who dominated the editorial staff of the journal *The Contemporary* with a philosophy compounded of nihilism, materialism, practical rationalism, utilitarianism, and concern for suffering humanity.

Chernyshevsky, particularly, radiated an influence that survived twenty years of Siberian exile. In 1855, he published his *Aesthetic Relations of Art to Reality,* urging meticulously rendered realism in literature and the social responsibility of the artist. In 1862 he was arrested, and while in prison, wrote his vastly popular didactic novel *What Is To Be Done?* Borrowing from the ideas of Robert Owen, Charles Fourier, and John Stuart Mill, Chernyshevsky synthesized a new Russian hero, the aristocrat Rakhmetov, who became the idol of a generation of self-sacrificing youth. Rakhmetov renounces everything for the people: he sleeps on a bed of nails, eats only what the poorest peasant eats, and gives up all pleasures. The characters Vera Pavlovna, the new emancipated woman, and Kirsanov, the rationalist physician, also served as models for radical youth of the time.

But the seminarians were only one force in the student upheaval. The peasant disorders following the Emancipation Edict were matched by turbulence in the Russian universities, which erupted as a result of the confused, fumbling policies of the regime and a growing awareness of peasant unrest. At first, fitfully trying to overcome long years of repression of academic life and a near-military regimen, Alexander II opened admission to large numbers of poor, sometimes destitute, students, who gradually gained control over their own affairs and developed a strong esprit de corps. They also developed the habit of publicly voicing approval or disapproval of lecturers. Writers who wished to be influential began to take notice of student opinion. The student body came into increasing contact with intellectual circles and all manner of political thought. Students were particularly responsive to the work of Herzen and to the men spreading populist ideas, such as Peter Lavrov and Chernyshevsky, the more so as they began to lose respect for liberal teachers, who at first had gained concessions from the government for the students, but then hesitated as repressions were re-introduced.[4] By 1861, the universities had become a political battlefield.

A crisis developed in the spring of 1861 when the turmoil in the universities was so great that the tsar threatened to close some of them. Instead, in May, he called for a drastic cut in the number of government scholarships and the abolition of the student meetings. In July, an inflammatory leaflet appeared, calling on the students in St. Petersburg to take "energetic measures" and a stormy meeting was held protesting against the new rules.[5] A student march across the city to the home of the rector followed, with students boycotting classes, and bystanders along the Nevsky Prospect waving their hands and shouting, "Revolution! Revolution!" In the end, several hundred youths, some of whom had been roughly handled by police and soldiers, were arrested and imprisoned for several months; others were deported to the provinces. The university was closed late in 1861 for two years, giving Herzen the occasion for creating the expression that would thereafter be the populist slogan: "Whither should you go, youth, from whom science has been taken away? Into the people, to the people ... there is your destination, banished men of science. ..."[6]

Herzen's plea had already been answered to a large degree by the extraordinary Sunday school movement which provided part-time instruction to the poor. This movement flourished in Russia between 1859–62 and may properly be described as the "first of the large-scale penitent efforts of the urban intellectuals to take the fruits of learning to the ordinary people."[7] All aspects of rural life—peasant revolts, tavern life, traditions of popular religious dissent, and communal patterns in the *obshchina* (peasant commune)—now began to seize the interest of the students. Peasant virtues were idealized and, in the peaceful transformation of society that was heralded, the peasant would be the carrier and the communes the peculiar institution that would save Russia from a landless proletariat and the oppression of a centralizing authority. Herzen, too, believed that the foundation for a new, just and equal society was the peasant social structure, based on the *obshchina*, and that the communal life of the peasant imbued him with the consciousness necessary to transform the wretchedness and oppression of Russian society into a socialist order. If the peasant lacked this awareness, the *narodnik* could arouse it, and a new order would soon take shape.

Of all European radical figures of the time, the French socialist-anarchist Pierre-Joseph Proudhon influenced populism the most. A French provincial who hated all authority and élites, Proudhon developed a kind of mystical belief in "the people" as a mighty force capable of rejuvenating Europe. Proudhon was also deeply interested in Christ as a social reformer—a view that also appealed to some of the early populists who viewed socialism as an outgrowth of suppressed traditions within heretical Christianity.[8] In fact, they pinned their hopes for the coming revolution on Proudhon and France until Germany's defeat of France in 1871. Thereafter, their hopes were transferred to Russia.

There was also a growing belief that progress was an inevitable historical law. In the late sixties, Auguste Comte's vision of progress in his "religion of humanity" and Peter Lavrov's *Historical Letters* helped overcome the alienation of the intellectuals by enabling them to feel united in the service of suffering humanity. The iconoclasts became what Lavrov called "critically thinking personalities" who would become agents of society's transformation. Lavrov's *Historical Letters* gave a historical rationale for repentance: since the educated minority had acquired their education at the expense of the downtrodden masses, they must now repay their debt by awakening the people to an awareness of their misery and showing the way toward a new social order.

A strain of revolutionary violence also formed a thin rivulet in the populist stream. For a time, early in 1861, some radicals like Chernyshevsky believed that the liberation of the serfs had precipitated a situation of revolutionary potentiality. Inflammatory appeals and leaflets derided the emancipation as a bone thrown to an angry dog and called on the people to rise up against a dying despotism. But a revolutionary situation did not develop; the leaflets and appeals merely intensified government repression. Yet belief in a mass revolt persisted, and in May 1862, people in Moscow and St. Petersburg found on their doorsteps a piece of underground literature called "Young Russia." [9] This was a bloodthirsty revolutionary manifesto that originated in a circle of Moscow students who had previously reprinted and distributed forbidden books and set up "Sunday schools" in which adults were taught to read and learn the message of revolt. "Russia," it ran, "is entering the revolutionary period of its existence"; the plundering of the people can only be stopped by a "bloody, implacable revolution." Though the masses are to be relied upon, initiative is to be taken by the army and "our youth." The manifesto ends with a call to destroy the tsar. If the "Imperial party" comes to his aid, "we will shout with one voice: 'Get your axes!' " [10]

A few days after the appearance of "Young Russia," a succession of fires broke out in St. Petersburg and several provinces. Herzen speculated that the fires may have been started by the police in order to intimidate the tsar and weak souls, but it was rumored that the fires were the work of the students and Poles. The government's crushing reaction was predictable. All of the "Sunday schools" were closed, as were the reading rooms and chess club in St. Petersburg. In July, there were more arrests, among them Chernyshevsky himself. Few students—Jew or Gentile—could fail to be electrified by these events.

Such secret extremist groups launched a tradition of active revolutionary terrorism which attempted the assassination of the tsar in 1866 and led to Sergius Nechayev's vision of a professional revolutionary cadre linked with a vast conspiratorial organization—a religion of revolutionary terrorism which gave Dostoevsky the theme of *The Possessed*. For a time, the road to terrorism and violence was deflected by the failure of the followers of Nechayev (and Bakunin) to win student support. The dominant populist note was still optimistic and evolutionary in the early seventies; most members of the movement still cultivated the "religion of humanity," studied the works of Proudhon, Marx, Lavrov, and Blanc, engaged in peaceful propaganda, and developed lofty ideas about the full development of the human personality through the *obshchina* form.

The government, meanwhile, did nothing to regain student confidence. Expulsions from universities multiplied; careers were destroyed; despair about one's future gave way to ever more extremist ideas about changing society. The poor judgment of the government in 1874–75 further alienated the youthful radicals. In the "mad summer" of 1874, stung by guilt over a famine the previous winter, several thousand *narodniki* "went to the people" in a great surge of compassion.

> Suddenly, without any central leadership or direction, more than two thousand students and a number of older people and aristocrats were swept away by a spirit of self-renunciation. In almost every province in European Russia, young intellectuals dressed as peasants and set out from the cities to live among them, join in their daily life, and bring them the good news that a new age was dawning. Rich landowners gave away their possessions or agreed to let students use their estates for social propaganda and experiment; agnostic Jews had themselves baptized as Orthodox in order to be more at one with the peasantry; women joined in the exodus in order to share equally in the hopes and suffering.[11]

The regime was perplexed and frightened by this movement of the people. It responded with mass trials. Over 700 participants were arrested; many more were molested in the government's effort to crush the movement. But the "mad summer" of 1874 was repeated the following summer. Again the government cut the movement down ruthlessly. No concessions of any kind were made or suggested. Such harsh repression of a largely nonviolent movement served to push populism into more violent and extremist paths. Moreover, the inertness of the peasants was very disturbing. They were bewildered by their would-be saviors, dazed and suspicious, and resumed their stubborn unenlightened ways. Vera Zasulich, a populist heroine, said of them: "They listen to our people as they do to a priest—respectfully, without understanding, without any effect on their actions." Nekrasov's words were apt:

> There is noise in the capitals.
> The prophets thunder.
> A furious war of words is waged,
> But in the depths, in the heart of Russia,
> There all is still . . .

Nowhere had the populists been able to arouse a revolt or upheaval, but the spread of the movement began to assume proportions that seriously worried the government.

For their part, the young populists grieved and sometimes despaired, but they did not give up. In 1876, they stepped up their demands: Zemlya i Volya (Land and Liberty) was founded, largely inspired by Mark Natanson, a Jewish organizer of a student study circle, demanding land for the peasants and the "destruction of the state." Natanson brought scattered groups together into a secret society on a national scale for the first time.

Unfortunately, the movement was caught by a wave of Pan-Slavism, which the regime was using to counter the idealism of populism.[12] This form of Russian nationalism had already been used to discredit the populists and other Polish sympathizers during the Polish uprising of 1863 and was further exploited in the war against Turkey in 1877–78, a war of imperialist expansion which made a moderate populism very difficult indeed. The two forces now churned toward a polarization. Pan-Slavism became Alexander II's alternative to populism; populism now moved toward the spirit of "Young Russia" of 1862—revolutionary Jacobinism.

What the program of Land and Liberty lacked in clarity, it made up in organization. Here was a closely knit, highly disciplined and dedicated underground of no more than 200 members,[13] who refused to own any property. Zemlya i Volya had its own printing press and network of sympathizers, and was organized in regional groups, with special units to protect members from the police and plan escapes. It acted in the name of the people and encouraged all signs of popular discontent but had given up all hope of popular support. In one of its first actions, a mass demonstration in front of the Kazan Cathedral in St. Petersburg, the governor of the city was shot for ordering the flogging of a revolutionary who had been arrested. The young woman who shot him was acquitted by a civil jury, but thereafter all such trials were conducted by military courts. As administrative repression increased, terrorist attempts grew bolder and more frequent, until the issue of terrorism split Land and Liberty in 1879.

The populists were now forced to consider the long-neglected question of a political alternative to autocracy. The absence of any parliamentary or legal opposition with which to work and the enduring suspicion of liberal reformers propelled them into the whirlpool of revolution. The terrorist wing of Land and Liberty, called Narodnaya Volya (The Will of the People) formed in the summer of 1879 with the conscious political objective of overthrowing tsarism. It took the path of regicide and was responsible for the assassination of Alexander II in 1881. Its original peasant-orientation was later picked up by the non-Marxist Social Revolutionary party. The second faction formed a more purely populist fragment called Chorny Peredel (Black Redistribution), led by George Plekhanov, the man who later introduced Marxism into Russia. This was a tiny splinter group that favored redistributing the land to the dispossessed and strongly opposed terrorism. The failure of terrorism and the absence of peasant response soon led Plekhanov to focus on the growing industrial proletariat as the prime force that could achieve socialism.

The first Jewish plunge into radicalism in Russia was taken by a few Jews in the 1860's. The most important of them was a converted Jew, Nicholas Utin, one of the first Russian Marxists. First attracting attention in 1861 for his active role during the anti-government student demonstrations,[14] he later collaborated with the leaders of the Polish rebellion of 1863 and was obliged to flee abroad. Utin finally settled in Geneva, where he met a number of other Russian political emigrés, including Bakunin, Marx's arch rival in the struggle in 1868 at the so-called First International.[15] Utin became one of Marx's ardent followers as well as one of the first of the Russian Marxists, in a pre-Marxist stage of radical activity, throwing himself wholeheartedly into the struggle against Bakunin. In 1870, he organized the Russian Section of the International, trying to adapt what he knew of Marxism to the situation in Russia.[16]

Utin was not a fully developed Marxist, but it is of some interest that he rejected Bakunist-terroristic extremism in favor of a Western social-democratic orientation. Some writers [17] have suggested that Utin's Jewishness was responsible for his revulsion against the "deep irrationality" of Bakuninist terrorism and the criminality of Nechayev, the arch-terrorist. His Jewishness was certainly unimportant to him on a conscious level, but as so often has happened in the radical movement, it gave his enemies— Bakunin most particularly—a prime argument against Utin's position. Utin had embraced Russian Orthodoxy, but Bakunin persisted in calling him a Jew, and thus "hostile to Russia and particularly to the Slavs." Other aspects of Utin's life illuminate the psychological and ideological storms of similar non-Jewish Jews. Besides having to deal with the repressed Jewishness of his make-up, he found himself caught in the conflict between his universalist and nationalist fervors. Utin was an ardent supporter of the Polish war for independence in 1863 and the Italian and Irish national liberation movements of the time. These loyalties posed no particular problems, but during the Russian-Turkish War of 1877–78, Utin was so stirred by Russian patriotic fervor that he petitioned the tsar, repenting his revolutionary sins, and asking for permission to return to Russia.[18] He was granted an amnesty, eventually forsook revolutionary activity, and became involved in building a strategic railway line to facilitate the movement of Russian troops against Turkey— a strange ideological passage.

Another important early figure—also an estranged Jew—was Mark Natanson. In addition to his student activist role, he also formed the first of the revolutionary-educational units called the Chaikovsky cells,[19] which were amalgamated in 1876 into "The Northern-Revolutionary Narodny Group," which, in turn, later emerged as the revolutionary party Zemlya i Volya. Their members came mostly from the intelligentsia of the upper and middle classes, with a sprinkling of army officers. The primary purpose of these circles was self-education through the study of the works of Marx, Proudhon, Lassalle, and other revolutionary thinkers, and extensive help to urban and peasant masses, who would then be drawn into future political action.

The Chaikovsky cells were organized in Moscow, Odessa, Kharkov, and Vilna, as well as St. Petersburg. Their members were the first to plant the seeds of a genuine working-class organization—a significant development in the 1860's before there was a genuine movement of factory workers. In this early phase of random protests, disorders, and isolated strikes, which broke out spontaneously, the Chaikovskists provided the impulse for a working-class movement, which despite its early limitations and the violence of the persecutions it had to endure, grew in scope and influence as revolutionary populism developed during the seventies.[20]

The spirit of rebellion spread to the non-Russian minorities of the empire, but at first affected Jews as a group scarcely at all. Of all the minorities, Jews were most loyal [21] to the government of Alexander II and were deeply grieved by his death, despite the reversal of his earlier "liberal" course. No doubt, their isolation, centuries of oppression, and lack of political power contributed to their submissiveness. But children of middle-class and educated Jews as well as *yeshivah* students became susceptible to radical ideas in the seventies.

The story of the involvement of Jews in the revolutionary movement in Russia begins in this decade, when the Russian revolutionary movement as a whole began to take shape. Just as there could be no general revolutionary movement without an intelligentsia, there could be no Jewish involvement or, for that matter, any specific Jewish socialist movement without such an intelligentsia. The emergence of this élite was a direct result of the liberal reforms of the early years of Alexander II's regime, especially the opening up of schools and universities to Jewish youths without conversion pressure. The number of Jewish boys in secondary schools increased from 1.25 percent of the total number in 1853, to 13.2 percent in 1873.[22] Universities also opened their doors to Jewish youths in the exhilarating liberal atmosphere of the early sixties, and their numbers rose from 160 in 1865 to 1,684 in seven universities in 1886. Jewish supervisors and teachers in the new crown schools meanwhile zealously promoted secular studies in Russian and general "modernization." Interest in general culture even penetrated the *yeshivot*, and the two government rabbinical seminaries in Vilna and Zhitomir, which had been shunned under Nicholas I, now attracted young Jews. The institute in Vilna was to become an important center of Jewish radical activity.

The emergence of some Jews from a long and introspective isolation had profound social and psychological effects. Accustomed to a life of humiliation and the need to find solace in devotion to religious faith and tradition, the Jewish intelligentsia now became painfully sensitive to gentile opinion. They began to be preoccupied with the question of full civil rights and hoped for deliverance from the imprisonment of the Pale. However, these high hopes did not materialize—either for Jews or non-Jews in Russia. The liberalism of the "Liberator-Tsar" was greatly exaggerated, it seems; the views of some of his ministers were much more enlightened than his, and the anticipated changes never came.

As young Russian radicals were being swept into the struggle for emancipation of the Russian people, a growing Jewish student group came into closer contact with the Russian intelligentsia and new political ideas. It is not surprising that some Jewish intellectuals should have been attracted to radical ideologies. A Russian Jew with a gymnasium certificate, or even a university degree, could scarcely hope for a career in Russian academic or bureaucratic circles.[23] Nor was it easy to enter other professions. Exposure to modern thought meant exposure to radical social ideas. In the 1870's and early 1880's—before Marxism had yet made an impact on Russian radicals—the social awakening of Russian and Jewish student youth developed along populist lines.

The movement that drew them with such compelling power held out the vision of a society built on social justice and social equality, the essence of which presumably already existed in Russia in the peasant commune— the *obshchina*. Furthermore, it was believed that Russia could bypass capitalism and avoid the brutalization of factory workers attending industrialization, which was afflicting Western Europe.

Jewish youths attracted to this movement felt culturally and spiritually estranged from the contemporary culture of Russian Jewry—whether it was religious orthodoxy,[24] the Jewish bourgeois affluence of those who had successfully entered the middle class, or even the secularized outlook of the *maskilim*. The *maskilim* might be "modern," but they were too busy with the struggle against religious and cultural obscurantism to deal with gnawing social and economic problems of Russia. These young Jews who became *narodniki* found no outlet for their burning social idealism in the Pale. The Jewish masses were inert—there were no forces protesting or even challenging existing conditions. There was only unquestioned obedience to established authority. Blocked on every side, yet yearning to enter the great stream of humanity and help carry it forward, these Jews succumbed to the vision of total redemption through revolution. In the process, all of the complex, idiosyncratic Jewish problems were swept into the surging tide of revolution, and were thus ignored or dismissed. Because the peasant and peasant culture were at the heart of Russian populism, there was no way, given the role that Jews played in the general economy, of integrating them into populist ideology. Quite the reverse—the Jewish revolutionary was alienated from his people. A historian of this movement has described this alienation:

> . . . the Jewish revolutionary intelligentsia did not find appropriate terrain in his own surroundings from which to practically direct his ideology. The decision to "go to the people," that is, the peasant, primarily, entailed leaving the Jewish

people. Without much concern, the Jewish revolutionary brushed off the dust of the ghetto together with its downheartedness, grieving, need and naiveté. The Jewish worker of the small artisan workshop was then not as widely separated from his employer economically or consciously. The classes were mixed, hence not evoking the interest of the socialist.[25]

The Jewish *narodniki* plunged into radicalism not as Jews but as Russians and, as they put it, "natural brothers" of the muzhiks. Toward the Jewish masses, many of whom were impoverished artisans, they had only contempt. Lev Deutsch, one of the best known of the early socialists, admitted:

> For us there were essentially no Jewish workers. We looked upon them through the eyes of the Russifiers. The Jew had to dissolve among the native population as had happened in Western Europe. . . . We looked upon artisans almost as exploiters. Because the majority of the Jewish workers were artisans and had to occupy themselves with small trade, we were ready to call them businessmen. To conduct any propaganda for socialism among them—and yet in jargon [Yiddish]—appeared to us, if not harmful, at least a waste of time and energy.[26]

"The idea," he continued, "of waging propaganda for socialism among the backward Jewish people . . . was received by us with surprise if not with sarcasm."

Another well-known Jewish activist, Vladimir Jochelson, came from a respectable middle-class family in Vilna, where he received his education in the traditional Jewish *heder*. At the age of eighteen, he entered the Vilna Rabbinical School, where much underground radical literature had already found its way, and became a revolutionary zealot. In his memoirs he admitted that:

> We were negatively disposed to the Jewish religion as to every religion in general. We considered the jargon [Yiddish] a synthetic language and Hebrew a dead language. . . . National aspirations, traditions and language were generally considered worthless, from a universal point of view. We were convinced assimilationists and found salvation for the Jew in the Russian enlightenment. . . . As to the laboring masses of Jews, we believed that the liberation of the Russian people from despotism and the oppression of the ruling classes would liberate all other people in Russia, including Jews. . . .[27]

Jochelson also admitted that "the Russian literature which has imbued us with affection for the Russian peasant, created in our minds a picture of the Jews not as a people, but as a class of parasites. Such opinions were often uttered by radical Russian writers, and that was the reason which prompted us to desert the Jewish people."[28]

These ideas were generally accepted by the Jewish *narodniki* of the time—even by Aaron Zundelevich, whom the historian Tscherikover calls "the most Jewish of the Jewish revolutionaries." At about the same time that Natanson was carrying on his activities as a student rebel in St. Petersburg, Zundelevich organized a clandestine circle of students at the

Vilna Rabbinical Seminary. This circle was a loose association of acquaintances who met on various occasions at the homes of its members to read the covertly circulated literature and discuss means of propagandizing socialism among those nearest them—namely, the Jewish workers—but, more importantly, the peasants. Among the more prominent Jewish members whom Zundelevich enrolled were Aaron Lieberman [29] (the first Jewish socialist who tried persistently to organize a movement of Jewish workers), Vladimir Jochelson, Lev Davidovich, and Anna Epstein (who had belonged to the Chaikovskists and had brought illegal literature from St. Petersburg). Anna was the first Jewish woman in a Russian university. She is often referred to in revolutionary literature as "chief nurse and smuggler of the revolution."

Through Zundelevich's efforts, the group established Vilna as a central point in the Russian underground network. Smuggling of illegal literature had always been risky and haphazard until Zundelevich organized operations on the Russian-Prussian border.[30] Vilna's proximity to the border made it ideal as a base of operations; it was far enough from the frontier to escape rigid surveillance and large enough to enable underground groups to camouflage their activities. By 1876, when Zundelevich helped Natanson found Zemyla i Volya, his own field of work primarily involved illegal transport. Besides the transport of literature, he personally escorted fugitives back and forth across the border. He also established important contacts outside of Russia, and was often referred to as "Minister of Foreign Affairs" for the revolution.

Zundelevich was also responsible for the establishment of the first successful clandestine printing press in 1877. In his book *Underground Russia*, S. M. Kravchinsky, the Russian populist, dramatically recounts this achievement:

> After the innumerable attempts which had been made and had failed, the establishment of a secret press was universally recognized not as being merely difficult, but impossible; it was only an idle dream, a waste of money, and a useless sacrifice of men. . . .
>
> There was, however, a "dreamer" who . . . maintained, in the teeth of everyone, that a secret printing office could be established in St. Petersburg itself, and that he would establish it, if supplied with the necessary means. This dreamer was Aaron Zundelevich. . . . About 400 zloty was allotted to him; he went abroad, brought everything necessary to St. Petersburg, and having mastered the compositor's art, he taught it to four other persons, and established with them in 1877 the free printing office in St. Petersburg, the first deserving that name, as it kept going regularly, and printed works of some size.
>
> The plan upon which he established his undertaking was so well conceived and arranged, that for four consecutive years the police, notwithstanding the most obstinate search, discovered nothing until treachery and mere accident came to their aid.[31]

In 1878, Zundelevich set up the so-called "Free Russian Press" which, upon the dissolution of the Zemlya i Volya, was transferred to the Narodnaya Volya. In late 1879, Zundelevich, together with Jochelson, set up a press for the Narodnaya Volya with Layzer Tsukerman as a typesetter.[32]

Some of the Jewish intellectuals—the first generation of Russian Jews exposed to a secular education—were doubtless attracted to the counter-culture of the time, the so-called nihilism of Dmitri Pisarev whose verve and truculence thrilled rebellious youths of the time. The term "nihilism" was popularized by Turgenev's *Fathers and Sons*, but hardly defined the views of Pisarev. His nihilists made a great point of defying conventions and authority and sneering at delicate feelings, the arts, and all restraints, but they actually worshiped a crude determinism and empiricism under the name of science. Nihilism was an aspect of the revolt of a generation with no deep roots in any cultural tradition against the values of an exhausted past. All of the *narodniki* were nihilists of a sort; they all disowned the past. Their appeal to "reason" was also compelling and had a special attraction for Jewish youth. "It would not be an exaggeration," commented Deutsch, "were I to say that nihilism exerted a greater influence among Jewish students than among Christians." The nihilist axiom to live in accordance with reason attracted Jews even from the remotest provinces. Deutsch continued: "It is quite understandable that nihilism should find so much success among Jewish youths. The appeal to logic, reason . . . and need to find a purpose in everything . . . would satisfy the spiritual needs which drove able and talented youths to the study of Torah and in which they found no gratification for their thirst . . . for knowledge." [33]

Deutsch may have exaggerated when he wrote that the rationalist mystique of nihilism swept the *yeshivot*, but a number of such students were surely affected and turned their backs on tradition. Yet others seem to have inherited from a previous generation of *maskilim* the inner struggle between "man" and "Jew," expressed in Judah Leib Gordon's formula: "Be a Jew at home and a man outside." Unable to create the necessary synthesis between the two, they abandoned the "Jew" as well as home, left the university and, occasionally, promising careers, and plunged into the exalted new life with the fervor and intensity possible only to those who live by abstract ideas and transcendent visions.

In the sudden ideological and emotional shifts that occurred, there are many curious paradoxes. From the densely textured Jewish world of the self-protective *shtetl*, Jewish youths took up the dangerous life of underground revolutionary activity. Some, fresh from *yeshivot*, became deeply imbued with the teachings of the New Testament and the spirit of Jesus. Despite the atheistic and nihilist underpinnings of Russian populism, a number of the Jewish radicals could be found praying and weeping over the Gospels in preparation for their revolutionary mission.[34] On yet another level, the ascent to the Russian cultural Olympus was such a heady experience for *shtetl*-bound Jewish youths, they lost their spiritual balance. The Talmud was no match for Herzen, Bakunin, Lavrov, Tolstoy, and Dostoevsky. The Jewish problem, moreover, shrank into insignificance in the face of the vast suffering in Russia and the coming revolution which would liberate the poorest and most downtrodden. Whenever the particular suffering of Jews was mentioned, the Jewish *narodniki* dismissed it by saying that the emancipation of Jews depended on the general emancipation of the Russian people. Later, during the pogroms of 1881 and subsequent persecutions, some of them realized that a severe crisis in Jewish life had developed, raising fundamental questions about Jewish survival. But for many of the Jewish *narodniki*, this crisis was evaded or displaced. The Jewish question remained insignificant or insoluble or was buried.

The first generation of alienated Russian Jewish youth worked underground under assumed names, sometimes as teachers, vagabond preachers, advisers and propagandists, farm hands and factory workers. They struggled to "go to the people," to share their wretchedness, teach them simple skills, and arouse them to rebellion. In this new life, they had to crush out or repress all vestiges of the old life. To signify their break from Judaism and strengthen their identification with the Russian people, many Jewish *narodniki* converted to Russian Orthodoxy. Often this was done to expedite marriage to a non-Jew, or to make it easier to "go to the people." Quite a large number were women. Indeed, the revolutionary movement created an internal upheaval among Jewish women,[35] possibly more profound than among the men. Some Jewish women evoked exceptional praise from their comrades. Betty Kaminskaya, for example, was the first woman to work as a factory hand in order to explain the harmful rules under which workers were forced to work and to talk to them about the struggle of workers in the West against exploitation.[36] The workers were amazed by her stories, and her spirit of sacrifice bore some fruit. But despair finally overtook her and she committed suicide. Hessia Helfmann, the young woman sentenced to death after the assassination of Alexander II, drew a beautiful tribute from Kravchinsky: "There are unknown heroines, obscure toilers, who offer up everything upon the altar of their cause without asking anything for themselves. . . . Without their labor, the party could not exist; every struggle would become impossible." [37]

Although Jewish youths made extreme efforts to melt into the *narodniki*, they were fated to remain outsiders in every sense, for the movement was altogether Russian. Its idealization of peasant culture, Mother Russia, and the adored Russian literary heritage had deep roots in Russian history—a compound that the Jewish revolutionary might earnestly try to possess but could not. Moreover, although the Russian *narodniki* were moved by a sense of guilt for the generations of peasant suffering, the Jewish *narodniki*, most of whom had never seen a Russian peasant, could not authentically feel this same moral debt. They had nothing to atone for, yet somehow had to try to feel guilt—an impossibility—as admitted in many of the memoirs. Osip Aptekman, for example, one of the most devoted of the converted wrote: "I had no trace of feelings of contrition. And whence should such a bad conscience have come to me? Rather should I, a son of an oppressed people, have presented a bill, than feel obligated to pay some imaginary debt!" [38] As a town dweller, he had no contacts with the countryside, and was aware of having "foreign blood." He kept asking himself how Russian peasants would respond to him—a Jew. Then a religious exaltation seized him. By fusing his socialist world view with the Christian evangelical vision, he apparently resolved his conflict and became "newborn." Before going to the people, he was baptized into the Russian Orthodox faith and tried to rid himself of his "foreignness." [39] But the gap could not be bridged.

Lev Deutsch, dressed in a peasant's garb, in one of his missions to the people, was asked, "Aren't you a *Zhid?*" Many Jews never grasped the nuances of the muzhik's language and could not control a Yiddish accent. Besides, the desired physical strength, a knowledge of peasant folksongs, even of dancing, were hardly skills developed in the ghettos.

Russian traditions thus had to be grasped intellectually—a very contrived way to live. Moreover, the break with Jewish tradition also involved a difficult passage; the Jewish *narodnik* became an outsider in this realm, too—pitied, mocked, and condemned by Jews. Among others, Pavel Akselrod, who together with Plekhanov and Deutsch organized the Group for the Liberation of Labor in 1883—the first genuine Russian Marxist unit—has also recounted his desertion of Judaism and the ideological cycle that he and others experienced.[40] Born in 1850 of a very poor family in the village of Tchernigov, Akselrod wrote: "The poverty in our family was simply horrifying. My parents were terrified when the landowner called on them for the rent for the inn which they had leased." In Shklov, where the family moved, the Jewish community sent him to a Russian school where he distinguished himself as a brilliant and industrious student. Then, in the gymnasium in Mogilev he fell under the spell of the radical Russian intelligentsia and the works of Turgenev and Belinsky.

At first he tried rallying fellow Jews to a spiritual and social renewal:

> When I was still in the fourth class I consciously tried to disseminate culture among the Jewish youth. I wanted these young Jews to liberate themselves from their religious and national superstitions and I thought to accomplish this quite simply: I intended to disseminate among them the ideas, the concepts, and the aspirations which developed in my head under the influence of these Russian writers and also under the influence of Borne and Dobroliubov.[41]

But Akselrod soon became ashamed of his interest in a "handful of Jews" after reading Lassalle's "Program for Labor," which spread before him a vision of revolutionary change that would liberate all working masses:

What significance can the interest of a handful of Jews have, I thought, compared with the interests and the "Idea of a working class," with which socialism was imbued? For there is really no Jewish problem, but only the general question of liberating the working classes of all nations, including the Jewish masses as well. With the victory of socialism, this so-called Jewish question will be solved. How foolish, then, and indeed how criminal to devote oneself to the Jews who are only a small part of the vast Russian Empire.[42]

"The idea of the Fourth Estate," as Lassalle called it, thereafter claimed Akselrod. In 1872, he began his revolutionary activity in Kiev, almost immediately devoting himself to propaganda among peasant and factory workers there. He soon realized the populist error of staking everything on the peasantry, blindly accepting the *obshchina* as the only instrument of revolution, and the movement's naive belief that revolution was imminent. He did not, however, stop his agitation for an agrarian revolution as a first step toward the reconstruction of society on socialist foundations. But after the populist movement was crushed, following the assassination of the tsar, Akselrod fell under the influence of Western socialism—that is, Marxism, which had been thought inapplicable to Russia.

In the autumn of 1883, a few expatriates living in Switzerland, including Akselrod and Plekhanov, formed the Group for the Liberation of Labor. Its aims were to spread "scientific socialism" among the intelligentsia and to create the nucleus of a Russian labor party modeled on that of Germany. By the end of the decade, the group counted fewer than a dozen, calling forth Plekhanov's famous joke when he and several comrades went boating on Lake Geneva: "Be careful; if we drown, Russian socialism will perish." But the group proved to be the first cell of the future Russian Social-Democratic Labor party. The historian Tscherikover credits Akselrod and Zundelevich with being the first to recognize the importance of Western European workers' movements and the only ones who served as intermediaries between European and Russian socialism: "In the Russian-emigré literature, Akselrod, from the first, informed his Russian comrades about the German (and also Swiss) workers' movement although he was critical of it, and wrote lucidly on these matters in Russian emigré papers in Geneva." [43]

Akselrod turned his back on the Jews of the Pale until 1881. The pogroms of that year stirred his guilt and compassion, and almost drew from him an exposé of the position of the populists, who justified the pogroms as expressions of true revolutionary fervor. But he gave up the idea as imprudent. Lev Deutsch, in a letter to Akselrod analyzing the dilemma faced by the Jewish revolutionary, also admitted that he had "no practical answer to the Jewish question."[44]   Such strains and conflicts were not lost on the non-Jewish *narodniki* and account, at least in part, for the absence of Jews among the ideological leaders of the Russian populist movement. Besides, their Russian patriotism was frequently questioned and they were not usually assigned to take the lead in actions or demonstrations. Nevertheless, Jews played important roles in the populist movement: they smuggled illegal literature and persons to and from Russia, organized propaganda, planned escapes, operated the vitally important printing presses, and "went to the people." Later, of course, their role in the Russian social-democratic movement was greater and more significant—a shift that evolved out of populist failures.

It has been suggested that some Jews [45] were also responsible for a shift from the characteristic apolitical stand of the populists toward a more political orientation. This occurred within Zemyla i Volya in the late 1870's, when the self-destroying cycle of assassination and death of the revolutionaries led to a re-examination of the use of terror. Terror, it was argued, was costly and wasteful. The emphasis on terror was also a populist heresy: the real business of the revolutionaries was to arouse the masses to active protest in the name of their economic interests, not the killing of government officials. And yet, the attempt to arouse the masses was failing. If the greater revolution could not be carried out, could not a constitutional regime prove a worthwhile intermediate goal?

These questions were sharpened by the end of the Russian-Turkish War, which involved the granting of a constitution to newly created Bulgaria, and which laid bare incompetence and corruption in the Russian bureaucracy. The Treaty of Berlin, signed in 1878, was a humiliating conclusion to an inglorious and costly war. Wasn't this a good time to overthrow the regime? Many of the young revolutionaries, indeed, thought that the revolution was only a matter of days, perhaps of hours. Some Russian liberals wanted to negotiate a common front with the revolution-aries; others believed it was still possible to wring a constitution from the tsar. The lull of terrorist acts in the winter of 1878–79 was probably a manifestation of these developments.

Zundelevich was possibly the first *narodnik* to speak out against terror, believing that it could not lead to political freedom in Russia.[46] He also was among the first to realize that because Russia lacked bourgeois-constitutional organs and a parliament, the revolution would have to go over to a political struggle—through terror—if other means were lacking.[47] Zundelevich felt much more sympathy with the German social-democratic movement—which the *narodniki* hated—than with the Russian brand of revolutionary activity. While observing labor movements in Germany and Switzerland in 1879–80, he concluded that revolution could be achieved only through an industrial proletariat. He thus developed an essentially Marxist view and argued heatedly with his comrades over the futility of *narodnichestvo.*

The shift to a political orientation was strongest in the south, in the Ukraine, where radicals of Jewish birth were most active. Aptekman, for example, led a group in Kharkov that represented the less violent wing of the revolutionary forces in southern Russia. During this period, we also have a *cri de coeur* from the less well-known Abram Magat of Vilna, in the form of a letter to his sister in November 1879:

> Jews realize that they lack freedom, rights. "How has this come about?" they ask: we are the oldest, the most intelligent, best educated and most energetic people and we are deprived of all the rights possessed by the other subjects of Russia. . . . We are not even free to run our own affairs. . . . No! We have to fight for our rights and our equality, no matter what the cost. . . . I see before me two and a half million people in bondage and say: one has to take the side of the oppressed and defenseless, to fight for their liberation.

Some leading Jews, he added, have decided to resort to the written word. But for him, not words, but only deeds—a revolution—could wrest a constitution from the rulers of Russia, a constitution "which would grant also the Jews equal rights." [48]

There were a few Jewish terrorists in the early revolutionary move-ment—for example, Solomon Wittenberg, Aaron Gobet, and Grigori Goldenberg—but, in general, Jews were not well-suited for terroristic roles. As Deutsch expressed it: "Neither by our nature nor by our training were we qualified to shed human blood." Nor did the *narodnik* leadership particularly want to entrust assassinations and bombings to people who would put a Jewish cast on the revolution and create hostility instead of sympathy.

One of the most important expressions of a new political direction lay in the activity of the Northern Union of Russian Workers, organized by metal workers in the winter of 1876–77. It had an exclusively working-class character, and adhered closely to the functions of the social-democratic parties of the West, calling for the destruction of the unjust political and economic structure of the state. Much of its platform, published in 1879, had familiar populist planks, but the most original feature was its unequivocal statement on the need for political freedom and guaranteed civil liberties. There were also small working-class groups in several Russian cities, who opposed terrorism and found it impossible to support the peasants against the government and landlords without minimal legal guarantees and political freedom.[49]

But the state did not bend. The hounding and killing of the young revolutionaries intensified, spreading despair and escalating terror. Mean-time, with immense problems besetting the country, it was expedient for the government to divert attention from them by recourse to anti-Semitic persecution. The involvement of Jews in revolutionary activity served perfectly to justify waves of pogroms that began in 1881.

For the handful of Jewish youths who joined the radical movement, the experience was doubly revealing and arduous. For the first time, they were exposed to social theory, political activism, organizational tech-niques, an examination of the phenomenon of power, propaganda, and political agitation. They began to think of social forces such as the peasantry and, later, the factory proletariat; of the oppressive power of the state; of individual autonomy; of the role of civil liberties and political freedom; of the relationship between a leadership élite and a dormant mass; of the development of Western social thought and socialist change, especially in Germany. Autonomous activity in the small *narodnik* groups or cells—a fundamental element in the political and personal searching—was another valuable experience toward an autonomous life, which the Russian schools, for example, did not encourage.

The Jewish *narodniki* failed to apply their new perceptions and activity to Jewish misery. Populism proved to be no answer at all to the great predicament facing Jews in Russia, but the revolutionary activity of the *narodniki* swept towns and villages in the Pale, shaking many Jews into their first awareness of the great economic and social forces convulsing the empire. The social revolutionaries who organized the Bund were, at first, populists. Moreover, there is evidence that a number of Orthodox Jews gave refuge to *narodniki* fleeing the police. Possibly the least evaluated gain for Jews was the fact that even in the very condemnation of them, they realized that the *narodniki* agitated the prevailing stagnation and challenged the existing order. Could not, then, even lowly Jews organize for change? The narodniki also provided an early prototype of a revolutionary chimera, to which certain Jews have been peculiarly addicted, in which the all-comprehending, all-enveloping vision turns out to be an eclipse blotting out intractable problems and contradictions.

The Jewish *narodnik* is usually treated unsympathetically. Yet, it should be remembered that populism was the only political movement in the 1870's in Russia—small and fragmented as it was—available to anyone, Jew or non-Jew, who could no longer endure the economic and social misery that gripped Russia. There were no alternatives, and terrorism, deplored by many of the *narodniki* themselves, became a strategy of desperation only after it became obvious that there would be no spontaneous revolt by the peasants or change on the part of the regime.

The Jew who rebelled against traditional authority in the *shtetl* and needed an ideological channel for his outrage against the widespread human oppression in all of Russia could find it only in *narodnichestvo*. Virtually every shade of Jewish radicalism later on, and every subsequent radical movement in Russia were affected by populism. Many young Bundists and socialist-Zionists were deeply influenced by it. The movement failed; it did not create a new order in Russia, but it was an indispensable consciousness-raising and politically maturing experience for a generation of idealistic youths who left a legacy of ideas and personal commitment to revolutionary action that made subsequent changes possible. The Jewish condition was not changed by the *narodniki*—indeed, it grew worse—but their ideas deeply affected certain Jews who eventually revolutionized Jewish life in ways that would have startled the *narodniki*.

3. Aaron Lieberman Perceives the Jewish Worker

During this period, industrialization was already changing Russian life, and even affecting the Pale of Settlement in ways that the *narodniki* could scarcely imagine. Marx himself seems to have been largely ignorant of these changes. A phenomenal increase in the production of iron and coal was creating the conditions for the emergence of a proletarian class and a socialist movement among Russian Jews. Following the emancipation edict of 1861, the influx of landless peasants into factories and the Russian-Turkish War of 1877–78 created a demand for consumer goods and assured a market for cheap, standardized garments. Industrial production gradually displaced the labor of the Jewish artisan and doomed the traditional *shtetl* economic structure. By 1886, the number of Jewish industrial workers had swelled to 300,000, according to the report of the Pahlen Commission,[1] thus changing Jewish economic existence. Graduates of Talmudic academies, artisans, and the sons of petty traders were increasingly compelled to enter industry. From the 1870's on, groups of Jewish workers appear in the northwestern provinces of Russia and in Congress Poland, in Warsaw, Bialystok, Vilna, and Minsk.[2] In the tanneries in Belorussia, for example, Jewish workers occupied the skilled trades connected with the finishing of tanned leather and bristle-making, which developed in the small towns in the provinces of Vitebsk, Grodno, Mogilev, and Suvalki and was virtually monopolized by Jews.[3] They were destined to play a crucial role in the Jewish socialist movement.

In the 1870's, Jewish capital was already being invested in beet-sugar refineries, textile industries, flour mills, tobacco factories, and beer breweries, and some Jewish workers were employed by them. But the only factories of any size that used large numbers of Jewish workers were those which manufactured cigarettes and matches. Located in almost every major city in Belorussia-Lithuania, these factories were mostly owned by Jews and involved Jewish labor almost entirely. Shereshevsky's cigarette factory, for example, in Grodno, which was founded in 1862, was the second largest in the empire, employing 100 workers in 1881, 885 in 1885.[4] Women and children made up perhaps 70 percent of the working force in these factories and they were considered fair game for the most shocking exploitation.

The first traces of a recurring economic struggle involving Jewish workers appeared in the 1870's, although there is a record[5] of an association of women clothing workers organized in Mogilev in 1864. The association offered financial aid and sick and death benefits to its members and even conducted strikes. But the association had a strongly religious character and was groping without organized planning or class consciousness. In the main, the women were dealt with harshly by employers and the police. The earliest strike of Jewish workers about which there is fairly reliable information occurred in November 1871, in a Vilna tobacco factory.[6] The striking workers were recent arrivals from southern Russia, where apparently similar strikes had taken place even earlier. Another strike at the same factory occurred four years later and is described by Aaron Lieberman in the December 15, 1875, issue of *V'period (Forward)*.[7] Still other spontaneous strikes of Jewish workers are mentioned in correspondence in a journal of the same period, unsigned, but attributed to Zundelevich. The first documented strike fund was set up by the hosiery workers in Vilna in 1882. In the 1880's, hundreds of Jewish women were drawn into hosiery manufacture, concentrated mainly in the Vilna province, and centered mostly in homes under the control of middlemen. There was also a strike in a Bialystok tobacco factory, where the women workers demanded that they be separated from the male workers by a special partition. Bialystok, in fact, was the chief center of agitation during the prehistory (before 1897) of the Jewish labor movement. By the end of the nineteenth century, 2,000 to 3,000 Jews worked as weavers and brushmakers in small shops and factories in Bialystok. The Polish socialist Feliks Kon, who visited the city in the early 1880's, was amazed to find Jewish factory workers there. "In Poland at that time," he remarked, "there were Jewish artisans—journeymen—but Jewish proletarians were not heard of. . . . Here in Bialystok there were hundreds of them in the textile factories. . . ."[8]

This observation, however, must be set against the fact that the average Jewish weaver did not profit from the industrial revolution which had made Bialystok a boom town. The great majority of Jewish weavers worked for middlemen known as *loynketniks,* who received looms and raw materials from the factory owners and put the weavers to work in small shops where conditions were deplorable, where the working day averaged between sixteen and eighteen hours, and where wages were far lower than in the conventional factories.[9] Moreover, Jewish as well as Christian factory owners seemed to prefer Christian to Jewish workers, because Jewish workers lacked training in technical factory skills. Christian workers also resisted competition from the admittedly hard-working Jewish workers. There was, besides, the problem of the "Sabbath rest"—Jews would not work on Saturday. But, chiefly, there was fear of the Jewish workers' revolutionary potential, which led owners to prefer the relative stability of the non-Jewish labor force.[10] Even at this point, a dawning proletarian consciousness among Jewish workers could be discerned.

In 1877–78, the years of the Russian-Turkish War, which caused a boom in the textile industry, Bialystok, the most industrialized city in Belorussia-Lithuania, had a labor force of thousands of Germans, Poles, and Jews. During the war, a huge strike was called, lasting three days. Fifteen hundred Jewish workers were involved, and the strikers won their wage demands.[11] "In those quiet, still times," a socialist journal later boasted, "when Jewish workers throughout Russia were sound asleep, dreaming of the Messiah and the world to come, we Bialystok workers were already waging economic battles, beating up the industrialists, breaking looms, striking, struggling." [12] As early as 1882, Jewish weavers staged a strike that was exceptionally well organized for that period, in which the workers achieved their objectives. According to one expert, this was the first strike in Russia that "demonstrated the existence of a trade union organization among the workers." [13] Several years later, Bialystok witnessed the first struggle between the weavers and their arch-enemies, the *loynketniks*.

It is doubtful that socialist intellectuals played any role in the early years of the Bialystok movement. The protest actions seem to have broken out spontaneously and sporadically, uninfluenced by outside agitation, and generally unperceived by the Jewish radicals of the time as possible raw material for their theories. This early movement failed to develop permanent organizational features or long-term goals, but it indicates worker militancy which was later channeled. The organized Jewish labor movement developed only after the Jewish socialists from the intelligentsia made contact with the Jewish workers. That development was still some years ahead, awaiting the transformation of radical intellectuals who happened to be Jews into Jewish socialists.

A few young Jews, however, as early as the 1870's, had become interested in the social problems affecting Jews as a whole and in conditions of the Jewish working class. The earliest such figure is Aaron Lieberman.[14] To him, "going to the people" meant going to the Jewish people. Lieberman grew up in a family influenced by the Haskalah and steeped in Hebrew culture. He was already a father when he entered the Rabbinical Seminary in Vilna (actually a government teachers' seminary), and after graduating, he taught, studied painting and etching in St. Petersburg, and returned to Vilna in 1871, when he made his first contacts with revolutionary circles.

Vilna at this time was not only a Haskalah center, but a point of contact between early Russian revolutionaries and their counterparts in Western Europe. Revolutionary literature from Germany destined for

Russia passed through here, as did political prisoners from the western provinces on their way to Siberia. It was therefore natural that the first Jewish socialists should emerge in Vilna amid the intellectual ferment of the teachers' seminary. In the early 1870's, Aaron Zundelevich, one of the organizers of Zemlya i Volya, founded the first radical circle, consisting almost entirely of the students at the seminary, Lieberman among them.[15] They read illegal socialist literature and "prepared themselves" for revolutionary activity, carrying on their discussions in Russian, but Lieberman would, from time to time, raise the questions of Jewish national consciousness and the cultural uniqueness of the Jewish people. He also stressed the need to publish socialist books in a Jewish language, deciding in favor of Hebrew, with which to prepare propagandists from the ranks of Jewish students. Lieberman had already rejected the Jewish religion, but passionately loved the Hebrew language, to which he remained a lifetime devotee.

Both Lieberman and Zundelevich tried to win the Jewish masses over to socialism. This was unique: all other radicals negated the economic role of Jews and condemned their work as nonproductive. Raised among the Jewish proletariat, both men knew that countless Jews lived by their own toil and were exploited, oppressed workers.

In the summer of 1875, the seminary administration and police discovered evidence of underground activity at the school, and both Lieberman and Zundelevich fled Russia. Zundelevich meanwhile had moved into populist circles, soon becoming a member of the executive committee of Narodnaya Volya, but Lieberman persisted in his focus on an identifiable Jewish socialism. He was stimulated in this interest by the Russian socialist exile Peter Lavrov, the spiritual father of the populist movement and one of the leading figures of the early Russian revolutionary and socialist movement. In the 1870's and 1880's, Lavrov was the only socialist leader who showed an active interest in the Jewish problem.[16] Unlike the others, he did not evade the issue. In the middle 1870's, when this problem was nonexistent even for Jewish revolutionaries, Lavrov was the first to deal with this question in *V'period*, the journal which he edited in London and which was smuggled into Russia. Lavrov encouraged Lieberman and published Lieberman's reports on social conditions among the Jews of Lithuania and White Russia.[17] In one of these articles, Lieberman formulated the idea of Jewish socialism in the following terms: "To us Jews, socialism is not a strange phenomenon. . . . It is we Jews who proclaimed the principle that the land cannot be alienated forever, it is we who proclaimed such a social institution as the seventh and the Jubilee year, and bequeathed to humanity the ideals of equality and brotherhood." Though not a Marxist, Lieberman believed that Marx himself and Lassalle were "brought up in the spirit of our people." [18]

In 1875, Lieberman fled briefly to Berlin, where he tried unsuccessfully to establish a "Jewish Socialist Section of the International," and then went to London. During this time, London served both as inspiration and training ground for Jewish radicals and trade unionists, many of whom later went to America.[19] The first Jewish union, workers' club, radical brochures and newspapers, and the first socialist and anarchist theoretical formulations appeared in London.[20] The beginnings of socialist propaganda and organization among Jews centered around Lieberman. In January 1876, he wrote the statutes for the proposed Social Revolutionary Union Among Jews in London, and on May 20 of that year, at his initiative, ten immigrant workers formed the Agudat Hasotzialistim Haverim (Hebrew Socialist Union). If we except the ephemeral Jewish Socialist Circle in Vilna, formed by him and Zundelevich, this was the first Jewish socialist group in the world. Lieberman composed the group's manifesto, written in a scholarly Hebrew as well as in a Yiddish version. He was also elected secretary of the Union and kept meticulous minutes. The program states, in part:

> We are convinced that the present order, which holds sway everywhere, is ruthless and unjust. The capitalists, rulers, and clergy have taken upon themselves all human rights and property and have enslaved the working masses through the power of their money. . . .
>
> The liberation of humanity can be achieved only through a basic change in the political, economic, and social relations—by uprooting the existing order and constructing in its place a new society based on socialism which will abolish the injustice and domination of capital. . . .
>
> We Jews are an integral part of humanity and cannot be liberated except through the liberation of all humanity. The liberation of humanity . . . can be achieved by the workers only if they unite in a struggle . . . destroying the existing order and replacing it with a reign of labor, justice, freedom, and the fraternity of mankind.
>
> The workers of Europe and America have united in various societies to achieve their aim and are preparing for a revolution. . . . Therefore we, the children of Israel have decided to affiliate ourselves with this noble Alliance of Labor.[21]

The program was adopted unanimously.

In the seven months of its existence, the union attracted thirty-seven members—intellectuals and would-be-intellectuals from the ranks of the Russian-Jewish political refugees who had to adapt to all sorts of manual labor. The aim of the union was to "spread socialist ideas among the Jews, as well as among other nations, and to organize the workers in their struggle against their oppressors." This little group started its agitation among the Jewish workers in the East End with a well-attended meeting of several hundred workers in a hall close to the hovels of Spitalfields on August 26, 1876. The first speakers were enthusiastically received when they described the lot of the Jewish workers and urged their audience to organize and demand a ten-hour day. However, when Lieberman expanded on the view that without the triumph of socialism, equal treatment of Jews was impossible, misgivings arose, and the meeting eventually broke up in an uproar.[22]

Because of the union's anti-religious views, the conservative *Jewish Chronicle* attacked the group in an article entitled "Another Conversionist Trick." [23] The agitation of the union was very likely incomprehensible to the Jewish community except as a "missionary trick" to lure the Jewish poor away from Judaism. Meanwhile, most of the workers identified the anti-religious socialists with the missionaries and rejected their efforts to enlist them into the union. On the other side, doubts were expressed about the wisdom of involving a revolutionary group in such prosaic matters as trade unionism and workers' sick funds. At the second meeting, the organization of a Jewish tailors' union was announced but, together with the parent group, it expired at the end of the year. Altogether, the union met twenty-nine times. Nevertheless, the union was sufficiently aware of its historic significance to have left a careful record of its proceedings.[24]

The meetings and lectures of this pioneer group in the Whitechapel slums also disclosed two opposing pressures which did not split the union, because of its short life, but which foreshadowed the dilemmas and divisions of subsequent socialist movements among Jews. These strains were revealed in the union's reactions to Lieberman's proposal that it refrain from meeting on the Ninth of Av—the date commemorating the destruction of the Temple, when religious Jews fast. The opposition ridiculed the idea. They were socialists, they said, who happened to be Jews, and desired to educate Jews separately but only until their struggle could be merged with the common struggle of the workers. But the meeting date was changed. Lieberman was indeed socialist and internationalist and, although he never succeeded in creating a strong philosophical or political synthesis of his socialism and Jewishness, he recognized the distinctive character and particularity of the Jewish people. The opposition viewpoint did not and, in the early years of the Jewish socialist movement, theirs was the dominant view.

In July 1876, before he left London, Lieberman published his famous manifesto, *El shlome bahure yisrael* ("To the Intelligent Young Men of Israel"), a flaming socialist appeal addressed to Jewish youth. Originally distributed in Hebrew and Yiddish among the *yeshivah* students in Russia and Russian Jewish students in Europe, it was translated into Russian and appeared in Lavrov's *V'period*, as did an article by Lieberman on the Hebrew Socialist Union in London. Opening with, "We, the friends of the Jewish people and of all the suffering masses," Lieberman addressed himself chiefly to enlightened *yeshivah* students. He wrote:

> These students of the Talmudic academies possess rare qualities. They represent the pillars of Jewry. They comprise the elite of our Jewish youth. They are men of an acute mind, they love truth and justice with their very heart. They are the only ones among our youth without a sense of egotism.

They are the only ones who remained faithful to their people.... They
continue to dwell among the Jewish masses whilst the so-called 'educated'
youth deserted the bond of Israel and under the excuse of enlightenment
sought honors, money, and power.[25]

He appealed to the youth to devote their energy to the cause of
general humanity, particularly the struggle for the emancipation of the
working masses of all peoples. Without any support, Lieberman was
painfully searching for a way to implant socialism in Jewish life by
mobilizing a radical intelligentsia among *yeshivah* students, which he
hoped would be the counterpart of the Russian student intelligentsia.[26]
But his appeal to the *yeshivah* students failed, as had his appeal to the
Jewish workers in London.

In December 1876, the Hebrew Socialist Union of London disbanded,
and Lieberman went to Vienna where he met Peretz Smolenskin. In their
discussions, Lieberman negated the Jewish national past and Jewish
nationality. In one of their talks, Lieberman passionately inveighed against
the *yeshivot*, accusing them of consuming "the best we have. The young
people are buried alive in these deserts . . . without dew or sunlight. . . .
We need institutions to educate proud people with uplifted heads who
will have the spirit and the courage to oppose the despotic government
and the feudal order."[27] Smolenskin accused Lieberman of attempting to
wreck the existing order, and spoke excitedly "of the Torah which
obstructs your passage, the Torah of creation, not demolition." Lieberman
retorted, "We do not demolish, we build," and then strangely cited the
Bible and the Talmud to prove that the fundamentals of socialism had
their origins in Torah.

For a short time, Lieberman contributed to Smolenskin's periodical
Ha-Shahar, but he soon went his own way and in May 1876, founded *Ha-
Emet (The Truth),* the first Jewish socialist magazine. Although he
cloaked his ideas in safe phrases to escape the tsar's censors, and published
under the assumed name of Arthur Freeman, *Ha-Emet* survived only three
issues. The Vienna authorities shut it down and arrested its editor.
Lieberman served time in an Austrian prison and later was extradited to
Germany where he was tried and convicted for illegal revolutionary
activity in what was known as "the trial of the Russian Nihilists" in 1879.[28]

Undoubtedly prison life affected Lieberman's mental balance and
prevented or hampered a thorough working out of his ideas which reveal
many contradictions. After his last release, he returned briefly to London
in 1880 and organized a Jewish Workingmen's Benefit and Educational
Society—a more realistic project than the Hebrew Socialist Union. He was
now willing to deal with concrete matters and to address the workers "in
their own tongue." But this, too, failed to take hold, and Lieberman left
London later that year for the United States under dramatic circumstances. Broken and depressed by his political failures, he clung to a fragile
hope of personal happiness.

Lieberman had met a young woman who ran an East End restaurant, Rachel Sarasohn. She was a young *agunah*—a deserted wife whose husband could not be declared dead and who was thus not eligible to remarry. Lieberman was then thirty-six; an earlier marriage had been dissolved. A romance developed, but in the fall of 1880, a letter arrived from Rachel's missing husband, requesting that she join him in Syracuse, New York. A steamship ticket was enclosed with the letter. She left England and Lieberman went with her to Syracuse. Once there, apparently finding his suit futile, he killed himself on November 18, 1880.

In his essay on Lieberman, Ber Borochov, the socialist Zionist ideologist, refers to him as the "father of Jewish socialism," whose theoretical work not only does not create a *weltanschauung*, but reveals deep conflict.[29] His cosmopolitanism came from the prevailing belief of all socialists that they were on the eve of a great social revolution, yet he could not harmonize his socialism with his intense Jewish consciousness. He denied that Jews had a culture or a nationality of their own, yet insisted on using an ancient language which for centuries had served as a cultural tie for scattered Jews. He rightly felt that a Jewish socialist movement could not be framed in the Russian language, which was foreign to the Jewish masses, but deprecated Yiddish as a jargon and, like a typical *maskil*, insisted on using Hebrew. In his memoirs, Morris Winchevsky portrays Lieberman as stormy and paradoxical, unable to desecrate or renounce Tishah be-Av, but denying the existence of a Jewish people, as is evident in his article in the first issue of *Ha-Emet*: "We Jews do not possess a culture of our own which differentiates and isolates us from the nations among whom we live. . . . Any bond which may ever have existed between us has long been torn asunder." [30] He believed that Jews should move closer toward the people in whose midst they lived, but did not believe that assimilation would solve the Jewish problem.

In part, Lieberman failed because of the absence of a coherent, systematically worked out philosophy and program. In part, he failed because, personally, he tended to be overbearing and wilful, without commanding the respect and confidence needed for the leadership of a social movement. But, mainly, he failed because he was ahead of his time— the other Jewish revolutionaries had no positive orientation to the Jewish masses—and because his ideas were a fuzzy composite of Russian populism, Jewish messianism, Western European non-Marxian socialism, and anarchism. "The Russian *muzhik* is our brother," he said; "no national or racial differences exist for socialists. All of us who live in Russia are Russians." On November 23, 1876, he had written to Valerian Smirnov, Lavrov's assistant on *V'period*:

You know very well that I hate Judaism, as I do all that is nationalist or religious . . . I am an internationalist. I am not, however, ashamed of my Jewish origin, and to the degree that I love all who suffer, I love that part of mankind which ... has been isolated as Jews. However, I do not love all of them, but only the suffering masses and those who are capable of uniting with us.[31]

With Lieberman's death, no serious attempt was made to continue his work and, although he was the first to pioneer the idea of a mass Jewish socialist movement, the awakening of the Jewish workers and the spread of socialist ideas in Vilna and Minsk in the late 1880's probably took no account of Lieberman at all. Others who have left no record may have been affected by Lieberman's original approach to the Jewish masses, but we do know that Morris Winchevsky was one of Lieberman's devoted disciples, who aroused the Jewish workers in London—and later America—and even affected radical circles in Russia through the power of his writing. Winchevsky greatly admired Lieberman from the days of the Teachers' Institute in Vilna, where he was also a student, and emulated *Ha-Emet* in his *Asefat Hakhamin* (Assembly of the Wise), which appeared soon after Lieberman's publication ceased. However tenuous his direct influence was, Lieberman was the first Jew in the Pale not only to see and feel the pain of Jewish economic misery as a manifestation of exploitative capitalism but also to perceive that Jews could take their destiny into their own hands by joining other workers in a struggle to destroy the existing order. The awakening of Jewish workers to this reality was still to come.

4. Jewish Radicals and the Pogroms of 1881-82

In the midst of the ideological disarray and eventual disintegration of Narodnaya Volya and Chorny Peredel in the decade following the pogroms of 1881, a small movement of confused Jewish radicals and a mass movement of nonpoliticized Jews came to America. At the time, there was little mass interest in Palestine, then part of the Ottoman Empire, but a small trickle of young idealistic Jews and romantic Zionists went up to the land, oblivious of the harsh practical problems they would have to cope with. This first *aliyah* of 1882, made up of Hovevei Zion (Lovers of Zion), did not establish a vigorous new agricultural society but it did constitute the nucleus of the bridgehead for later settlements. Of the 7,000 or so who left for Palestine in 1882, several hundred survived as farmers who founded a line of settlements at Rosh Pina, Zichron Ya'akov, and Petah Tikvah. More realistic than the fervent Biluim,[1] who could not withstand the exhausting physical ordeals and lack of support, Hovevei Zion secured the first modern Jewish settlements in Palestine on nationalist grounds.[2]

However, America remained the goal of most Jews who yearned for physical safety and economic security in a free land, uncomplicated by ideological twists. A very intensive debate ensued, particularly in the pages of *Ha-Melitz* and *Ha-Yom* (*The Day*, founded in 1886)[3] as to which land—Palestine or America—should be the object of emigration. But for the masses of Jews who were concerned primarily with the day to day struggle for existence, America with its wealth and potential opportunities was the more alluring. By 1887, it became evident that the trend to America was the predominant one. Yet, even this wave, so largely moved by urgent primary needs, became for some youths and intellectuals a burning ideological issue. Simple flight without a meaningful philosophical underpinning was unthinkable.

A movement called Am Olam (The Eternal People) was started in 1881. The founders at first were undecided whether their objective should be Palestine or the United States, but they soon chose the latter. The emblem of the movement was a plow and the Ten Commandments, symbolizing their goal of physical and spiritual rejuvenation of the Jewish people. America, they believed, was a land of freedom where Jews could establish a home based on certain progressive social and economic principles; some members even planned to establish an autonomous Jewish state or "canton" in the United States. The important thing was to "productivize" Jewish life in order to make it more normative, to eliminate "unproductive" fields such as business and functions of the middleman. Arguments against Jewish "parasitism" would thus be refuted and anti-Jewish feeling would then abate. Some members, who had come from revolutionary ranks, inveighed against the evils of private property and planned to establish collective settlements patterned after the Russian *obshchina*.[4] Interestingly, there was a sympathetic response to such ideas even among artisans and tradesmen, who were attracted by the idealism of the movement. The young Abraham Cahan, who became a well-known Jewish labor leader and editor of the *Jewish Daily Forward*, joined one of the Am Olam groups for a time. He commented that:

> Quite ordinary people, as well, were attracted by the idealistic side of the movement. They, no less than the intelligentsia, showed real enthusiasm. Simple artisans and tradesmen, who did fairly well in Russia, sold all their belongings and joined the groups leaving for America, to begin a new life. They did this in a spirit of religious devotion and self-sacrifice.[5]

The founders of the movement, Moshe Herder and Monye Bokal, came from unpretentious origins. Herder was a private tutor in a small town who felt the need to systematically organize Jewish emigration after the pogroms. When he settled in Odessa, he met Bokal, the son of a scholar and *hasid*, who had been greatly influenced by Haskalah currents and Isaac Ber Levinson's views on the importance of learning a trade. He himself came to Odessa and learned goldsmithing. In 1881, he and Herder[6] launched Am Olam in Odessa, envisioning cooperative colonies in the spirit of Owen, Fourier, and Tolstoy. Bokal contributed all of his possessions to the "common fund" and bore the brunt of speaking, traveling to organize branches, writing and bucking up the disheartened. Neither he nor Herder was a profound social theoretician or socialist, but merchants, tavernkeepers, half-baked intellectuals, and many students rallied around the two teachers. Bokal especially inspired great trust by virtue of his gentle and ascetic life. In the shop in Odessa where he worked as a goldsmith, drifting souls found comfort and guidance.

In November 1881, soon after the pogroms, Am Olam sent its first group of seventy young people, led by a student Paul Kaplan, to America to establish a collective agricultural settlement; several months later, a second group left. Numerous groups subsequently organized in Odessa and other Russian cities. In the first group, two factions began to clash with each other: petty tradesmen, artisans, and workers, on one hand, and students on the other. Bokal had admitted the intellectuals reluctantly, believing that they would not only feel superior but would think of ordinary workers in terms of bookish theories. Sharp conflicts also resulted from ideological differences. The tradesmen and workers were imbued with a strong Jewish national consciousness, while the students were essentially Russianized and stressed the socialist aspect of their commitment. Gradually, leadership passed into the hands of the russified students who were considered more presentable to the non-Jewish world and generally had better contacts both in Russia and abroad.[7] The groups from Odessa, Kremenchug, and Vilna had pronounced socialist leanings, while the group from Kiev, next largest after Odessa, was not particularly interested in socialism, but in the rehabilitation of the Jewish people through productive work. Its constitution provided for the needs of Orthodox as well as secular members. When this group arrived in Brody, the collection center, an Orthodox member described most of the members as students from the universities and institutes of technology, true idealists who renounced careers to become farmers, while the older members included former wealthy merchants.[8]

The Kiev group of seventy was joined in February 1882 by twenty students from Vilna, who dreamed of establishing an autonomous "Jewish canton" in America, basing their ideas on the federal nature of the American Constitution, which reserves certain rights to the states. These notions as well as those of other Am Olam groups and the Biluim were held with the ardor befitting youthful idealists, but they had neither a grasp of the enormous practical tasks involved nor a firm anchorage in Jewish tradition and culture. They thought they had heeded Smolenskin's plea to work in behalf of their people, but being Russianized intellectuals, they had been largely alienated from Jewish life and could not acquire a new culture by mere feeling—strong as it might be—or by participating with emotion in a communal fast following the pogroms. Nevertheless, before their departure, they were warmly and sympathetically accepted by Jews in the Russian cities and given aid and comfort by Jewish organizations as they passed through communities in central and Western Europe. They were also given financial aid by the Alliance Israélite Universelle and other philanthropic organizations, as well as individual sympathizers, including the famous German scholar Theodor Mommsen, and plied with gifts ranging from Marx's *Capital* to Torah scrolls. But this enthusiasm and their own zeal were not enough to sustain the long pull of actual experience in America, which was grim, both in terms of the attitude of American Jews and life on the land.

Although it was not the first agricultural colony of Russian Jews in America,[9] the first Am Olam group from Odessa established itself in the summer of 1882 near Portland, Oregon. It had already had a difficult break-in adjustment of a year, including arrival on Ward's Island in New York in the midst of an uprising of other Jewish immigrants against American agents who wanted them to scab for striking longshoremen. After the incident on the island, the members of the Odessa group drew up a report,[10] which was translated and published in the *New Yorker Volkzeitung,* a socialist daily. Through the paper's co-editor, Alexander Jonas, a leading figure in the Socialist party, they were introduced to Michael Heilprin.

Heilprin was a well-educated Polish Jew whose family had moved to Hungary where he joined the press division of the revolutionary government in 1848. After the revolution failed, Heilprin lived in France, England, and finally America, where his articles appeared in the *Nation.* When he met the Am Olam group, he was editor of the prestigious *Appelton New American Cyclopaedia* and worked day and night for the cause of the new immigrants. He was also a colonization enthusiast and gave the youths from Odessa unstinting moral support and considerable financial aid. On Heilprin's advice, they sent three members to choose a suitable farm in Oregon, where both the soil and climate were reputed to be good for colonization. A farm of 910 acres was purchased for $4800, of which $1800 was paid immediately. A letter, written by a member of the group, dated November 1, 1882, conveys the quality of the first months in preparation:

> Our organization, Brethren of New Odessa, consists of some 70 young people of Odessa, from 20 to 30 years old. Last summer we spent on a farm near Hartford, Connecticut, and we succeeded in gaining some experience in practical American farming. Being green, we received for our work no more than from 12 to 15 dollars a month. But I can truly say that we have earned the reputation of industrious and capable workers. Frequently, the owner would request us to slow our pace so that he could keep up with us. Our organization, which numbers several people with university degrees, has succeeded in interesting several wealthy and prominent Jews of New York [Jacob Schiff, Dr. Felix Adler, and Julius Goldman] in the plan to establish an agricultural colony.... We have selected a place in the State of Oregon on the Pacific coast, which is known for its moderate climate and fertile soil. On July 30 [1882] the first group in our organization, consisting of 21 men and 5 women left by boat for Oregon, which they reached after a journey of one month.... Our capital amounted to $4000 ... one-fifth of which was spent for travelling expense.... The group arriving in Oregon found suitable employment there. The other members have taken jobs in New York, Boston and St. Louis, whence I write. In the spring we, too, shall leave for Oregon.[11]

One serious problem emerged immediately. Although the farm was large, not more than 150 to 200 acres were suitable for cultivation—clearly not enough for the first fifty settlers. The remainder was dense forest. Transportation, the cost of several cows, oxen, and farm implements used up all of the group's money and put them into debt. Besides, the colonists did not realize that cattle-raising, not corn, which they intended to grow, was the principal profit-making activity of Oregon farmers. Their corn crop was good, but they made little profit on it because the grain market was being monopolized by railroad owners. What saved them from total disaster was a contract to deliver 2,000 cords of lumber at $2.50 per cord to a railway;[12] all of the energy of the colony was mobilized toward this end. Even so, life was very hard. Food consisted of bread, potatoes, peas, beans and a little milk; shelters were very primitive and cold; there seemed no way out of debt. Cosmopolitan socialist tendencies had rather quickly dominated the group, and the original leaders, Bokal and Herder, broke off and joined a New Jersey colony called Alliance. The colonists' difficulties were dramatized by the arrival of William Frey and his family.

The arrival of the Frey family in July 1883 was, in one sense, a milestone for the colony, yet in another, the beginning of its disintegration. William Frey was a Russian nobleman of German extraction, whose real name was Vladimir Heins. An ardent disciple of Auguste Comte, he had tried to establish religious communist colonies in Kansas in the 1870's. When these failed, Frey came to New York, where his "religion of humanity," asceticism, and striking personality made a deep impression on all radical immigrants, especially the Am Olam idealists. They invited him to join their colony in Oregon and, for a time, he became the ideological leader of the group, introducing religious-positivist services, the cult of nonresistance, baking of bread, vegetarianism, and ennobling acts of self-discipline. He converted everything he did into religious acts and won many zealous converts—but he had no grasp of the daily problems facing the colony. His opposition to all struggle and the use of force led him to oppose the battle then being waged by factory workers for decent working conditions and a living wage. Some of the members seethed quietly. For a while, the commune lacked the heart to deny Frey his eccentricities, but his ideas became more and more burdensome and unrealistic. Open differences arose between Frey and Paul Kaplan, the secretary of the colony. The economy of the farm—and therefore the work load—involved cutting timber. As the aura of spiritual elevation surrounding physical labor began to diminish, the girl members, who at first insisted on equal rights, did not have the physical strength to take their turns in the forest and had to return to kitchen chores. The group discipline and orderliness that some visitors had admired struck Cahan as a facade concealing an oppressive, unhappy mood.

> While one saws or chops wood, another stands around and pretends to mix gruel, meanwhile gossiping with the women. . . . The forty young communards were all quite intelligent. So there were no loud out-bursts, no quarrels. But, quietly the dissatisfaction grew and spread, turning into misunderstandings, intrigues, bitter jokes. Life in the commune became dull and monotonous for the former city-dwellers. Then there were jealousies that resulted from sex relations. The commune included a small number of married couples and

several single girls. But the majority consisted of single young men for whom there were too few girls. Amorous intrigues and some free love existed. The young men were moody, jealous, isolated. Nor was there enough privacy in the commune. . . . Some insisted that communism required literal togetherness: eating from the same bowl, sleeping in the same bedrooms.[13]

Frey and fifteen of his most devout followers finally left New Odessa, and after a five-year struggle, the colony finally dissolved in 1887, the last of the Am Olam groups to maintain itself. A few persistent members tried to continue New Odessa, first in San Francisco, then in New York, where they settled in a tenement house on Henry Street and opened a cooperative laundry also called New Odessa. But this, too, collapsed in a few years. The other units of Am Olam had tried to establish colonies in Louisiana, Kansas, and South Dakota, each effort accompanied by soaring hopes, great publicity in the Jewish press, and appeals for financial support. But there were too many elements that foredoomed their efforts—lack of farm experience, tension within the group, and loss of spirit, as well as economic factors precluded the success of almost all Jewish agrarian projects of the time.

Under the immense pressure of large-scale immigration, there could be no comprehensive well-organized planning for land settlement. The American Jewish philanthropic agencies were themselves somewhat caught up in the enthusiasm for getting the Jew back to the land. But the basic problem was to meet the dire needs of the large masses in the Eastern cities. Even so, it was the wrong time to believe in the future of the American farm. By 1870, American agriculture was in steady decline, prices were falling, and farm tenancy was increasing. Very possibly, some of the zeal to return the Jew to the land to become "productive," was defensive, even apologetic,[14] in reaction to charges that Jews were exploitative middlemen. Settlement schemes were also diffuse, uncoordinated, and erratic. In their ambivalence, some of the Jewish agencies were anxious to scatter the compact mass of immigrants in order to relieve the congestion in the large cities and blunt the antagonism of many Americans to the influx of foreign poor—a reflex that showed how much their own hard-won status was threatened. Of all the colonies established throughout the country, only those in New Jersey endured, and these were established by private enterprise.

Orthodox socialists took a jaundiced view of the colonizing furor, labeling it a capitalist conspiracy to disperse the masses. Soon after Cahan founded *The Jewish Daily Forward* in 1897, it, too, was sharply critical.[15] The *Forward*'s idea of sound agrarianism was based on farmer-labor cooperatives and misty evocations of the Brook Farm experiments.

As a youthful idealist himself, Cahan had come to America in the Balta group of Am Olam. Soon after his arrival, he realized that he was too much a city man ever to adapt to the life of a farmer. He also had strong reservations about New Odessa's philosophy and had late-in-the-night discussions with Paul Kaplan, the secretary, who shared with him the attic floor of the house at 213 Clinton Street when Kaplan was in New York promoting the interests of the group. Cahan was at the time moving toward Marxist socialism and believed that fundamental change in capitalism could never be achieved by samples of a grand idea, or by small, isolated groups of communes, no matter how committed their members were. In analyzing the cause of the failure of New Odessa, Cahan argued:

> You were not true communists but rather simple proletarians when you chopped and sawed wood for the capitalist railroad companies. And as farmers, you were being robbed by the capitalist system as all farmers are robbed by it. Every dollar you earned was the target of all sorts of idlers: the shareholders of the railroads that took your products to market, brokers and bankers, agents, and so on. Because of them, your members had to work hard. Without them, you could have worked fewer hours and even the hard, physical work would not have been so burdensome. There would have been no evasions, no jealousies. Life would have been easier, more comradely.[16]

The groping of Cahan mirrored the ideological confusion of many Jewish radicals in the aftermath of the pogroms of 1881, but comparatively few of them emigrated from Russia. Those who stayed behind were at a critical ideological crossroads. Though the fire had gone out of the *narodnik* movement after the assassination of Alexander II, the model of Russian populism still had theoretical appeal for certain radical Jewish intellectuals. Some began to ponder the specific problems of the Jewish masses and the struggle for Jewish rights, without predicating their thinking on or even imagining a specifically Jewish national renascence. Opposition to emigration was central to this orientation. The Jewish intelligentsia must move toward the Jewish people, help return them to the land and a more productive life, and thus hasten their civil and political emancipation. In this view, however, Jews were still potential Russian citizens. Other Jewish (and non-Jewish) revolutionaries in the *narodnik* movement strained their theories to see something good in the anti-Semitic massacres: the pogroms were an instinctive outpouring of anger of the Russian masses against all of their oppressors. After the Jewish "bloodsuckers," they would attack the rest of the oppressive structure and topple it.

At the same time, there is no doubt that many of the youthful Jewish revolutionaries anguished not only over the sufferings of the Jews during and after the pogroms, but were also deeply chagrined and bewildered by the indifference of Russian liberals to the torments of Jews. The progressive forces, the great Russian writers—with whom the Jewish intelligentsia had so ardently identified—were either silent in the face of the pogroms or perfunctory in their sympathy, in contrast with the emotional indignation expressed in Western Europe. Russian literature of this period is full of remorseful and repentant self-revelations of disillusioned Jewish intellectuals.[17] Typical were such expressions as:

When I remember what has been done to us, how we have been taught to love Russia and Russian speech, how we have been induced and compelled to introduce the Russian language and everything Russian into our families so that our children know no other language but Russian, and how we are now repulsed and persecuted, then our hearts are filled with sickening despair from which there seems to be no escape. This terrible insult gnaws at my vitals.[18]

A correspondent writing in *Russky Evrei (The Russian Jew)* expressed his deep hurt:

The "enlightened" Jews had repudiated their history, forgotten their traditions, and come to despise everything that made them conscious of belonging to an eternal race. Without an intelligent understanding of Jewish ideals, and burdened by Judaism even as an escaped convict is hampered by heavy chains, what could compensate for their belonging to a tribe of "Christ-killers" and "exploiters"? How pathetic is the position of those who advocated fusion with the Russian people through national self-abnegation. Life and logic of events demand that the Jew define his position, for it has become impossible to occupy a seat between two chairs. Either one openly declares himself a renegade or one decides to share the sufferings of his people.[19]

There were a few expressions of sympathy for Jews by revolutionaries: on June 15, 1881, Zemlya i Volya and the South Russian Workingman's Union denounced the pogroms.[20] But these were exceptions to the main response of the revolutionary movement. Most shocking to the young idealists was the stand taken by Narodnaya Volya. In the barbarous attacks of the peasants upon the Jews, the prevalent attitude was one of sympathy for the perpetrators, not the victims; indignation was directed at the police for arresting the rioters. The pogroms, it was argued, were an authentic mass protest—a prelude to a broader movement, indeed a harbinger of the revolution. On August 30, 1881, in the midst of the pogroms, a faction of the party called The People's Freedom issued a call to the Ukrainian people: "The Ukrainian people suffer above all from the Zhid. . . . The Zhid is sucking its blood. . . . The Czar has sided with the Zhid. . . . Arise, laborers, avenge yourselves on the landlords, plunder the Jews and slay the officials. . . ."[21] On October 23, 1881, the Actions Committee of this wing of the party confirmed the Ukrainian proclamation as the official position:

The people's discontent has begun to express itself in a mass revolutionary movement, which, due to local conditions, has assumed an anti-Jewish character. . . . All the attention of the resisting masses is concentrated on merchants, innkeepers, usurers, in a word, on Jews, this local bourgeoisie which hurriedly and passionately is fleecing the toiling masses. . . . We have no right whatsoever to react negatively, nor even to remain indifferent to this true people's movement.[22]

It has been established that the author of the proclamation was the journalist G. G. Romanenko,[23] the author of numerous subsequent anti-

Semitic articles in the paper *Narodnaya Volya* and subsequently a member of the editorial staff of the yellow *Bessarabets*, which incited the pogrom in Kishinev in 1903. The affairs of the Narodnaya Volya at the time of the 1881 pogroms were no longer in the hands of the responsible leaders of the party, many of whom were languishing in prison or had been executed. Moreover, a few of the older members had joined the ranks of the monarchists, as Romanenko eventually did. By 1884, the editors of *Narodnaya Volya* had second thoughts about the pogroms and acknowledged that morally and tactically it had been a mistake to welcome them.[24]

A well-known theoretician of the Russian Social-Revolutionary party, M. B. Ratner, later wrote of the "utter indifference of the *narodovoltsy* [member of the Narodnaya Volya] to the sufferings of the Jewish people. . . . That section of the Jewish intelligentsia within its ranks shared the joy at this 'revolt against the bourgeoisie,' their ears stone-deaf to the weeping of hungry Jewish children from the bloody and ravaged homes." [25] Ratner also found a definite anti-Semitic current in the ranks of all early Russian socialists, a feeling he ascribes to lack of understanding of the Jewish situation and political immaturity. All of the major revolutionary papers but one (*Zerne*, published by Chorny Peredel and intended primarily for urban workers) carried articles hailing the pogroms as the first sign of a mass stirring.[26]

How much the Jewish *narodniki* themselves were infected by this attitude or helped to strengthen it is difficult to evaluate. But alienated as they were from Jews and ignorant of the historical background of Jewish economic life, assimilated radical Jewish youth were contemptuous of petty Jewish traders whom they regarded as swindlers and exploiters. They, too, believed the pogroms would trigger the revolution by spreading to attacks upon the Russian power structure. The pogromists, however, showed no interest in carrying forward the revolution. Having ruined the poorest quarters of the Jewish population, the mobs showed no similar zeal to destroy the property of the Russian rich. This fact in itself undermined the faith of a number of Jews in revolutionary activity and wrought much anguish and confusion. In addition, there was the open anti-Semitism of many of their Russian comrades, who made no distinction between Jewish traders and Jewish socialists. Stripped now of their most vital beliefs, many Jewish youths underwent a severe spiritual and ideological crisis.

These intense inner conflicts are revealed in a brochure that Pavel Akselrod, a leading Jewish revolutionary living in Zurich, wrote in 1882, but was deterred from publishing by his radical friends, including some who were Jews. These emigré radicals were less compromising and more politically mature on the Jewish question than those still in Russia, but their misgivings proved too weak for an effective counterblast against the *narodniki*.

Among the Jewish students in Switzerland disillusioned by the turn of events in Russia was Gregory Gurevich, who had been a close friend of Akselrod in Mogilev and was now living with the Akselrods in Zurich. Gurevich was an active member of a circle studying the Jewish question in Russia who, unlike Akselrod, had never severed his ties with Jews. Indeed, he was among the first to advocate agitation in Yiddish among Jewish workers. At a social gathering one evening, Gurevich reproached Akselrod, then the most prominent Jewish revolutionary, for not speaking out against the pogroms. Akselrod pleaded the lack of sufficient information, but Gurevich would not be put off. "I objected to this," he wrote, "by saying that for a declaration of one's attitude towards the outrageous pogroms it was not necessary to engage in scholarly research or to be acquainted with the literature on the question." [27] All that was necessary, as far as Gurevich was concerned, was for Akselrod to register a protest.

But for Akselrod, the matter was not quite so simple. He had already given thought to the pogroms and his assessment was not so different from that of other revolutionaries. In an article published in *Volnoe Slovo* (*The Free Word*) on December 13, 1881,[28] Akselrod argued that had the organized socialist groups expended sufficient effort, the anti-Jewish disorders could have constituted

> the beginning of a socialist *class* movement in the name of "land and freedom" for the laboring masses. It was only necessary, in Kiev, for example, to direct the crowd to the quarter of the Jewish capitalists, to the banks, where the capital of the upper classes of all nationalities is concentrated. Of course, if the "disorder" had received this sort of direction the further course of the movement would inevitably have been such as to lead the rebellious masses into direct clashes with the wealthy elements in general and with their natural ally, the government.

But, to the shame of the socialists, Akselrod continued, they had permitted the disorders to develop into a general campaign against an entire nation, during which tens of thousands of proletarians and small shopkeepers had been ruined. In Akselrod's view, then, the pogroms had degenerated into senseless rioting only because the socialists had botched up a fine opportunity to bring about the long-awaited social upheaval.

But the continued pressure of the Jewish colony in Zurich, coupled with wringing letters from Jewish intelligentsia in Russia expressing their disillusionment with the revolutionary movement, had their impact on Akselrod. In February 1882, he discussed with Plekhanov, Lavrov, Deutsch, and Stepniak—all political comrades—the advisability of publishing a brochure protesting the pogroms and the stand of the revolutionary press. They all agreed that such a brochure would be desirable, and that a non-Jew should write it. At first Plekhanov was too busy with other work; Lavrov and Stepniak said they were not equipped to write on the subject. Finally, vexed by his comrades' inaction, Akselrod decided to write the pamphlet himself. It was to have been approved by his comrades and signed a "Group of Socialist Revolutionaries." Their inhibitions are significant.

From London, Lavrov, virtually the only Russian socialist leader of the time who interested himself in the Jewish question, wrote back guardedly that it was difficult for Russian socialists to take a stand in the matter because they had to have the masses on their side. "Such a brochure could be published," he wrote,

> but ... I must admit to you that I consider this question to be a very complex one. Moreover, for a party that is trying to establish closer contacts with the [Russian] people and to arouse them against the government, it is most difficult to deal with this problem in practical terms. In theory and on paper, the solution is easy, but with the prevailing popular passion [i.e., anti-Semitic feeling] and with the need of the Russian Socialists to get the people on their side as far as possible, the problem is quite different.[29]

Akselrod also urged the executive committee of Narodnaya Volya to publish a pamphlet for Jewish readers, reassessing events and their own position, but apparently the committee was not interested. Meanwhile, Akselrod himself began his article dealing with the need for a systematic campaign against anti-Semitism by all revolutionary factions. He called it "On the Tasks of the Jewish Socialist Intelligentsia," addressing himself primarily to Jewish radicals in an effort to clarify their future political tasks. In his draft,[30] Akselrod expressed sympathy with their despair at discovering that their attempts to assimilate into Russian culture and politics had been rebuffed by the "truly disgraceful spectacle" of anti-Semitism. He understood how disheartened they felt as they realized that many Russians still regarded them as members of an alien national group. Nevertheless, he was convinced that the pogroms were not merely the manifestation of deep-seated national and religious prejudice, but also of the position of the Jews in the economic structure of the country.

Because of their long history of persecution and exclusion from "productive" work—especially from agriculture—an inordinately large number of Jews served as traders, shopkeepers, and money lenders. Most of them were far from wealthy, as he could well enough recall from his own childhood. Many were actually proletarians, but the peasants looked upon all Jews as exploiters, as people who did not earn their living by the sweat of their brows. On the other hand, the gentile petty bourgeoisie and capitalists despised Jews because they saw them as competitors. Russian professionals also were threatened by the university-educated Jews. "In Russia, therefore," Akselrod concluded, "the Jews are an economic force that in the struggle for existence and wealth comes into conflict with the most varied strata of the population." Thus, the gentile capitalists and the government were prepared to exploit this hostility in order to provide an outlet for the widespread popular unrest.

Akselrod also recalled that the Jewish socialists deserted the Jewish masses because they felt ashamed of their interest in Russian Jews who, after all, were only a small part of the Russian Empire. There is no separate Jewish problem, they believed, only the problem of liberating the masses of all nations. When socialism triumphs, the so-called Jewish question will be solved. Thus, severed from the Jewish masses, totally committed to the Russian revolution, the Jewish radicals

> eliminated the last bit of our interest in the fate of our people, which needed the help of its own intellectuals as much as the other poor classes in Russia. . . . We forgot, also, that a large part of Russian Jewry was proletarian in the literal sense of the word, and that even the petit bourgeois elements among Jews, though parasitic exploiters of the peasants, were, in the great majority, themselves terribly poor, grossly exploited by the military, the upper middle classes, and the government. . . . The cosmopolitan aspect of socialism did not require that we be indifferent to the conditions of life among the Jewish masses. . . . We should have approached the Jewish masses . . . with propaganda about class conflict and the solidarity of the oppressed working masses regardless of nationality or religion. Jewish socialists might surely have been associated with Russian revolutionary groups in the larger Jewish centers like Odessa, Kharkov, and Kiev. This would have brought them closer to Christian workers' groups. Such Jewish groups would undoubtedly be of great help in the general social revolutionary struggle in Russia. (Many revolutionaries found that observant Jews were wholehearted in their help when they had to flee Russia as political criminals.)[31]

Lamenting the lost possibilities of Jewish-Russian socialist collaboration which could have blunted the "unworthy one-sided national aspect" of the pogroms, Akselrod then quotes excerpts of letters from certain students and Jewish socialist youths—all horrified and shocked by the savage attitude of *all* classes in Russia to Jews. "The Jewish student youth suffered their greatest disappointment," Akselrod comments, "when they realized that the socialist-minded students sympathized with the crusade against the Jewish masses and, worse yet, demonstrated their anti-Semitic feelings toward their Jewish fellow-revolutionaries." This lesson and the realization that the bulk of the Russian masses had not yet reached that stage of class consciousness where they could understand that their interests were the same as those of other masses—including Jews—led Akselrod to conclude that the Jewish situation was unique. He was forced to admit that conditions of life for Jews *were* different from those of the rest of the population and that their special forms of oppression might not be touched by the revolutionary programs then being advocated. This aspect of the problem he deals with very sketchily, very possibly reflecting the conflicting pressures and inner uncertainties under which he labored.[32]

By this time, Akselrod conceded that it was legitimate for Jewish socialists to concern themselves primarily with the oppression of the Jewish lower classes, but not for the purpose of achieving a "national renaissance of Judaism" or the establishment of a Jewish state. Rather, this interest must go no further than concern for the well-being of poor Jews.

As soon as persecution of Jews ended, "Jewish socialists must be entirely indifferent to the fate of their own capitalists." For the Jewish masses, he projected a two-fold development: conversion into a genuine proletariat engaged in physical labor, and their "fusion" with the native population, apparently meaning cultural assimilation. But these ideas are not elaborated; Akselrod conceded that it would be difficult to realize them. Already under the growing influence of the Marxist notion that Russia had to undergo a bourgeois revolution as a first stage toward socialism, Akselrod also urged replacement of the existing autocracy and political reforms.

While working on his essay, Akselrod considered another possibility then being discussed by Gurevich and his friends: that Russian Jews be encouraged to emigrate to Palestine and take up farming—not to establish a Jewish state but simply to escape from persecution. On this proposition, Akselrod consulted the geographer and Bakunist K. E. Reclus, who found the idea impracticable. Deutsch also urged Akselrod to give up the Palestine project because of the danger that it would recognize Jews as a separate national group. As to Akselrod's persistence in wanting to publish his article, Deutsch said that Chorny Peredel, now very close to an open advocacy of Marxism, were operating under extremely difficult circumstances and should be "firmly united and act in complete solidarity." On May 26, 1882, he wrote: "We are very sorry that you persist in your decision with respect to the Jewish brochure," but left the final decision up to Akselrod.[33] Personally, a rather timid man, Akselrod was not willing to act on his own and withdrew from the issue, at least publicly. His manuscript was never finished, and the draft that has survived—sketchy and somewhat disjointed—was not published until 1924.[34] Persuasive pressure from his comrades in Chorny Peredel and his own inability to work out coherent alternatives to the familiar socialist solutions to the Jewish question very probably blocked him. There is evidence to suggest that he later came to have misgivings about his silence in 1882.[35]

Akselrod's true center of gravity did not shift. He remained in the revolutionary movement, a spiritual and ideological father of Russian Marxist socialism, a founder of the Russian social-democratic movement in 1883, and one of the editors of its paper, *Iskra (The Spark)*. Yet his uneasiness over Jewish persecution was never completely buried, surfacing again during the Dreyfus trial, when he was shocked by the "atrophy of the elemental sense of justice and of wild, tribal, shameful chauvinism" of the whole nation, and by the indifference of the French labor movement to the trial of Émile Zola.[36] He agonized and, again, suggested that the Russian colonies in Zurich and Geneva act together in protest. But they did not, and Akselrod was not prepared to act on his own. Once more, in 1913, during the trial of Menahem Beilis, who was falsely charged with ritual murder, Akselrod's will to act failed, though he undoubtedly suffered deeply.

The Russian *narodnik* writer Stepniak described the mood of the Jewish revolutionaries during the pogroms in his novel, *The Career of a Nihilist*. In talking to a Russian comrade, the hero, modeled after Aaron Zundelevich, expresses the conflict of the Jewish *narodniki*:

> We Jews, we love our race, which is all we have on earth. I love it deeply and warmly. Why should I love your peasants, who hate and ill-treat my people with blind barbarity? . . . No there is nothing in your Russia worth caring for, But I knew the Nihilists, and I loved them even more than my own race. I joined and fraternized with them, and that is the only tie which binds me to your country.[37]

The Jewish comrades of Akselrod in Chorny Peredel and others may have stiffened their revolutionary resolve in the face of the pogroms and evaded or repressed a natural response to Jewish suffering, but other youthful Jewish radicals were remorseful. Plekhanov's wife recalled, "Deep down in the soul of each of us, revolutionaries of Jewish birth, there was a sense of hurt pride, and infinite pity for our own, and many of us were strongly tempted to devote ourselves to serving our injured, humiliated, and persecuted people." [38]

Jewish students began to participate in the organization of Jewish self-defense units (which most Russian Jews opposed strenuously); in Odessa they helped to blunt the ravages of the pogrom of May 3–5, 1881.[39] They joined about one hundred and fifty people armed with sticks, pipes, and a few revolvers and fought off the attackers in several Jewish quarters. The police arrested about sixty of the resisters, beat them up, and jailed them without food for several days.

In his reminiscences about the first pogrom in Odessa in 1881, M. Ben Ami (Rabinovich) describes the change that came over Jewish students after the outbreaks. When, in 1880, he had approached them for contributions toward the establishment of a trade school, he found no interest. But after the pogrom, they were among the first to organize the self-defense unit.[40] This was the first widely noticed instance of young Jewish intellectuals spontaneously identifying with and responding, *as Jews*, to other Jews in a time of crisis.[41] The response of older Jews to this involvement was overflowing. In Odessa, on the eve of the ominous pogrom, some students had gone to the synagogue and appealed to the congregation to resist. Ben Ami describes the moving reception of the young men as they spoke:

> Those who spoke to the people in Yiddish, particularly when quoting passages from Biblical and rabbinic literature, evoked a strong response. Many burst into tears at the sight of this rapprochement. . . . [The students] felt as children who have returned after many years in an alien world, to their mother.[42]

At the same time, those who spoke in Russian and urged self-defense were suspected of being provocateurs or "nihilists," both of whom were known to be supporters and even instigators of the pogroms.[43]

Students also participated in the public fasts that took place in all Jewish communities in Russia on January 18, 1882. A well-known Hebrew writer recalled that "Jews wherever they happened to be in the vastness of Russia . . . responded enthusiastically to the idea of a fast day. The stores and shops were shut and the synagogues were crowded from the early hours of the day. . . . Everyone observed the fast, including the entire intelligentsia—even more strictly than the common people. . . . The demonstration seemed to be completely spontaneous." [44]

In Kiev, there were stormy debates among the students and, finally, a unanimous decision to go to the synagogue, not to remain silent while prayers were being said, but to console the people in their misery.[45] Their speeches were also in Russian and "jargon." In Kiev the Am Olam group responded with great feeling to the fast. Cahan wrote that a student addressed the congregation in Russian: "We are brothers. We are Jews just like you. We repent over our feelings that we were Russians—not Jews. The events of the last few years have shown us that we were sadly mistaken. Yes, we are Jews." [46]

Yet these tragic events did not lead to a total rejection of assimilation and a wholehearted return to Jewish concerns. Lev Deutsch, for example, wanted an even more intensified effort at assimilation into the revolutionary movement.[47] He, too, was shaken by the pogroms, and agreed with Akselrod that the revolutionary movement should analyze the pogroms and accusations against the Jews from the viewpoint that Jews, too, were an oppressed group. He also wanted such a brochure to be written by an eminent gentile socialist, preferably Plekhanov or Lavrov, but neither considered himself "suitable." Consequently, as he later wrote, "a printed defense of the oppressed nationality by a Russian socialist, extremely necessary at that time, never appeared." [48] He reverted to his revolutionary posture, regretting Akselrod's movement toward the "ranks of the Judeophilic *Razsvet* regarding emigration to Palestine." While opposing the effort to move Jews into "productive" occupations (this paid too much special attention to the problems of Jews *qua* Jews), and their emigration to Palestine or America, Deutsch was unable or unwilling to pursue the dilemma that he had scarcely opened. In a letter to Akselrod, dated April 4, 1882, he wrote:

> In practice, a revolutionary cannot resolve the Jewish question; *nu*, just what are we to do now, for example, in Balta, where Jews are being beaten? Going to their defense would, as Reclus has put it, "arouse the hatred of the peasants against the revolutionaries, who have not only murdered the Czar, but also defend the *Zhidy*." Thus we are faced with an insoluble dilemma. . . . Please do not think this is of no concern to me, that I am not depressed by this. Nevertheless, I will always remain a member of the Russian revolutionary party and I will not leave it even for a day.[49]

Nor did he. The same could be said for other Jewish radicals—despite the pogroms, conflicts, intermittent guilt, and repressed feelings about

While Messiah Tarried

Jewishness. Indeed, there was an *increase* in the involvement of Jews in the revolutionary movement *after* the pogroms. A secret police survey for the years 1884–90 reports 579 Jews out of 4,307 arrested for political activity[50]—almost 14 percent, as against 6.5 percent for the years 1873–77.[51] For every one arrested, moreover, there were undoubtedly other activists and sympathizers who escaped the police. This increased involvement of Jews was certainly in part a reaction to the pogroms (although, paradoxically, it helped fan them), but was also a reaction to the mounting oppressiveness of the regime and the frustrations that found no outlet other than rage and terror.

By the mid-eighties, however, the revolutionary movement underwent important ideological changes. Marxism, which rejected terrorism, began to take hold. The Jewish elements dispersed over a broader radical spectrum. Shaken by the pogroms, a few radicals emerged affirmatively Jewish. A Jewish working-class movement was also beginning to dawn.

II

THE AMERICAN JEWISH LABOR MOVEMENT

5. The Uprooting: Jewish Radicals Come to America, 1881-83

Although the populist movement had been unable to rouse the Russian peasantry, on whom it had pinned its hopes for a social revolution in Russia, it had sent shock waves into the stagnant Russian air, and had even penetrated the Pale of Settlement where young *yeshivah* students bursting to taste the literature, science, and philosophy of the "other" world, and restless sons and daughters of middle-class Jews, enrolled in government schools and institutes and felt their first whiffs of revolutionary ideas. It was this student generation that confronted the horror of the pogroms, struggled with the immense dilemmas and practical hardships created by them, and eventually found ways to energize the stricken masses with alternatives to the cold-blooded prophecy dooming Russia's Jews, made by Constantin Pobiedonostzev, the procurator of the Holy Synod and intimate of the new tsar: "One-third will die out, one-third will leave the country, and one-third will be completely dissolved in the surrounding population."

The year 1881 left the Jews of Russia terrified, dazed, and unguided. The traditional leadership remained characteristically submissive; it could propose no initiatives. A conference of Jewish notables had met in April 1882, soon after the bloody pogrom of Balta, to consider the question of emigration. For Jews, the conference was a mixture of pathos, tragedy, and timidity; for the Russians it was a field for cynicism, sophistry, and sport. Russian law forbade emigration and, because the conference was unwilling to confront the law, delegates were mocked and scorned. A travesty of emigration—deportations to Central Asia—was dangled by the government as a resettlement scheme. The delegates, completely out of touch with the real forces now in motion, petitioned the government to abolish discriminatory treatment of the Jews and to compensate those who had suffered during the pogroms. A pathetic disclaimer of an alleged secret Jewish *kahal* ended their deliberations.

Intense debates raged in the Hebrew journals, some declaring that

America was the only solution for Russian Jewry; others pressed the case for Palestine. Yet other Jews staked their future on a more progressive Russia, and a few radicalized intellectuals believed that Jews should become more "productive" and settle in agricultural colonies within Russia. All of these activities were agitated, often insubstantial, and edged with despair, because of the recurring pogroms and anti-Jewish policies of the government, which provided no time for adequate preparation. At the same time, the years 1881–82, in retrospect, were to become the fulcrum against which many ideological levers pushed and clashed, eventually turning Russian Jews from helpless victims into a self-directing force capable of at least partially controlling its destiny.

After the first days and weeks of shock and grief following the pogroms, an unorganized flight of the Jews of southern Russia began. Each day, several hundred set out only to find themselves stranded in Brody, Hamburg, or Berlin. Some had to return to Russia, victims of desperate, unplanned emigration. Yet, rumors of help from "committees" of West European Jews and fantasies of warm welcome in America swelled the emigration fever.[1] "America was in everybody's mouth," Mary Antin recalled,

> Businessmen talked of it over their accounts; the market women made up their quarrels that they might discuss it from stall to stall; people who had relatives in the famous land went around reading letters for the enlightenment of less fortunate folks; the one letter-carrier informed the public how many letters arrived from America, and who were the recipients; children played at emigrating—all talked of it, but scarcely anybody knew one true fact about the magic land.[2]

Sudden emigration decisions were fused to idealized visions of America and, despite the crushing poverty of most Jews in the Pale, the flight broke through all restraints. Until 1892, Jewish emigration from Russia remained legally forbidden. But Count Nikolai Ignatiev, the interior minister, had made a suggestive reference to the western frontier: "The Western border is open to them," he had declared sardonically to Dr. Isaac Orshanky, a well-known Jewish scholar and publicist, giving quasilegality to flight. To emigrate was no longer an act of rebellion. Yet Jews had to pay for this privilege. Special permission had to be secured in provincial capitals—often arranged with bribes. Many documents were required, frequently costing up to twenty-five rubles [3] (about seventeen dollars, which many Jews could not afford). Consequently, much of the emigration in the 1880's was illegal, and "stealing the border" became a dangerous but common way out.

By the time the refugees reached the frontier, they had been packed into third-class railway cars for anywhere from twenty to sixty hours, and they disembarked exhausted and stupefied. At the border towns they encountered strange sights: tall buildings, storage depots, warning flares, menacing soldiers and policemen, and passengers milling about in great confusion. The refugees then had to present passports and exit permits, without which they could not enter neighboring Austria or Germany. Always eager for military conscripts, Russian bureaucrats gave few of these documents to Jews and when they were issued, border officials often found technical discrepancies. These requirements so frightened Jews that many chose illegal crossings, disguising themselves as *muzhiks* and bribing guards to take them on foot or by boat across forest swamps and rivers.

Western Jewish leaders, meanwhile, were completely unprepared psychologically and organizationally for what was to become a mass exodus. Throughout 1881, hundreds of immigrants—penniless, Yiddish-speaking, strange-looking *Ostjuden*—streamed into Brody, the Austrian frontier station, placing Austrian and German Jews in a quandary. Sympathy for the pogrom victims was certainly genuine, but Western European Jews, who were fairly comfortable and decades removed from ghettos, were desperately anxious to maintain their still precarious status. Culturally far removed from the *shtetl* Jew, they could not easily identify with him. Nor could they envision the need for long-term large-scale emigration and commensurate organization and planning. The prospect of an exodus of hundreds of thousands was not academic: in 1881-82, over 20,000 Jews emigrated to the United States alone, more than half of whom had to have financial aid.[4]

Table 1. Estimates of Jewish Immigration into U.S. from Russia, 1881-1914 *

Year	Number	Year	Number
1881	3,125	1898	14,949
1882	10,489	1899	24,275
1883	6,144	1900	37,011
1884	7,867	1901	37,660
1885	10,648	1902	37,846
1886	14,092	1903	47,689
1887	23,103	1904	77,544
1888	21,216	1905	92,388
1889	18,338	1906	125,234
1890	20,981	1907	114,932
1891	43,457	1908	71,978
1892	64,253	1909	39,150
1893	25,161	1910	59,824
1894	20,747	1911	65,472
1895	16,727	1912	58,389
1896	20,168	1913	74,033
1897	13,063	1914	102,638

* For the period 1881-98, statistics are available only for the number of Jews admitted at the ports of New York, Philadelphia, and Baltimore.

Based on Samuel Joseph, *Jewish Immigration to the United States* (New York, 1914), p. 93.

The initial task of providing food and shelter for the Jews decamped in

Brody was assumed by the world's largest and most prestigous philanthropic agency, the Alliance Israélite Universelle. The early refugees found
the Alliance representatives kind and generous, bringing hope and
compassion to the distraught Jews in Brody. The Jewish writer Ahad Ha-
Am, then a youth of twenty-six, passed through Brody on his way to
Vienna during this time. In his reminiscences he comments that

> Charles Netter [one of the founders of the Alliance] and his assistants were . . .
> sending off parties of refugees to America. One of these parties traveled by the
> train on which I went to Vienna, and so I had the good fortune to see that
> remarkable man at the railway station, distributing money to the refugees. The
> expression on his face reflected his kindness of heart and deep sympathy. The
> refugees themselves were cheerful, and their looks betrayed his hope.[5]

But this initial generosity was short-lived. Toward the end of November
1881, Netter was instructed first to stop and then to slow down the influx.

The Alliance assumed the leading role in the movement by virtue of its
authority, international affiliations, and financial resources—recently enlarged by a gift of one million francs from Baron de Hirsch for a special
emigration fund. Almost half of this was made available to Russian Jews,
and America was at first seen as an ideal solution to the mounting problem
of Russian Jewish refugees. But Jewish leaders in New York were becoming
alarmed not only by the numbers of Russian Jews coming in, but by their
luftmensch and petty-bourgeois character. Many from small towns had
been small shopkeepers with sparse stock, rabbis living on a pittance, part-
time *melamdim*, sextons, cantors, and "tradesmen" barely eking out a
living. In November 1881, the New York leaders remonstrated with the
Alliance in Paris:

> You were to send us the strong and able bodies, willing to work and possessing a
> knowledge of some handicraft. . . . Fully one-third of those who have arrived
> thus far possess none of the requisite qualifications . . . not over one-third are
> really desirable emigrants. . . . Very few are farmers. . . . Most that we have seen
> are clerks or tradesmen; they know no handicraft and wish to peddle. . . .
> [Many] are too old to learn any trade and not a few of them are burdened with
> large families. . . . Our charities [are considering] a proposition to refuse relief to
> persons who have not been at least two years in this country. . . . It has also been
> proposed by many, to take means to return to Europe all those who are paupers
> or likely to become such.[6]

It became clear to the leaders of the Alliance in Europe that their
earlier plans to direct the stream of immigrants to America had to be
abandoned. Toward the end of 1881, American Jewish leaders, frightened
by the prospect of waves of "unfit" immigrants flooding American cities,
demanded the immediate stoppage of all further transports. However, a
compromise was agreed upon, permitting those Jews still in Brody to be
sent on, with the guarantee that "no other people" be accepted.

The European leaders thereupon decided to liquidate the center in

Brody.[7] Of the 1,258 Jews there early in 1882, 458 were given 75 francs apiece to settle somewhere in Western Europe, while the rest—mostly artisans—were given 20 francs each on condition that they return to Russia. Most of them, however, did not return to Russia but made their way to Paris and London, awaiting a chance to go to America.

In the spring of 1882, a new flow of emigrants descended upon Brody in such numbers that a conference of the German, Austrian, and British committees was called. The delegates issued warnings and dire threats of stern measures should the emigration continue, but the flow was not checked. On May 11, 1882, 1,300 new refugees arrived in Brody, 400 on foot. Shocking accounts of their condition began to fill the Jewish press, but the New York committee insisted on stopping all emigration. By August 1882, new pogroms swelled the number in Brody to 12,000. Polish workers in Lwow began to protest against the arrival of the refugees. Finally, the Austrian government—previously very benevolent—ordered the border closed to all but holders of steamship tickets, or the cash equivalent. By the end of the year, Brody was closed to Russian Jews, but the refugee exodus did not stop. Other routes were devised from northern Russia into old Poland by way of Dünaburg and Vilna into East Prussia. From the central part of the Pale, Jews went to Brest-Litovsk through Warsaw, crossing the frontier on the Vistula at Thorn. From the southern Pale, large numbers crossed the Austrian frontier at Podvolochesk. Almost all then made their way to Hamburg and Bremen.

In May 1882, Baron de Hirsch had tried to prevail on the New York committee to change its position, but it remained adamant, and the European groups had to yield. Edward Lauterbach, the representative of the New York committee in Europe, reported to his home office in August 1882 that "there would be no more immigrants."

The return to Russia of many of the 12,000 refugees languishing in Brody became a thorny and painful matter. Complete figures are not available, but it is known that the Berlin committee returned 3,904 people, and the Alliance 3,850.[8] According to its final report, the London committee returned 8,000 emigrants during the whole period of its activity, many of whom included Jews who left the United States in 1882, and some of whom were returned to Russia from England.[9] By January 1883, there were no refugees left in Brody.

Many who came in the first wave (1881–82), after suffering the ordeal of the ocean crossing in steerage and the frightening physical examination on arrival in the United States, languished for days and weeks at Castle Garden, New York. First contacts were often with German Jews in the Hebrew Emigrant Aid Society, who were condescending toward the *Ostjuden* and totally unprepared to help them. The hostility was mutual. Letters to Russia were soon filled with bitter complaints against the HEAS agents. HEAS had set up two immigrant hostels on Ward Island and in Greenpoint, where many of the immigrants spent weeks and even months.

These contacts were the first with Americanized German Jews, and they were distressing. The main office of the HEAS was on State Street, New York, directly opposite Castle Garden. Abraham Cahan, who had arrived in June 1882, recalled:

> When I arrived there, I was interviewed by an American Jew who talked with me in German, which neither of us spoke very well. Unable to communicate effectively, we were uneasy with each other. I left with a strong impression that he was a heartless bourgeois. And he probably suspected that I was a wild Russian. This is what they called us immigrants at that time, sometimes even to our faces.[10]

The arrival place, he said, "looked like a big stable, and the atmosphere smacked of charity and the barracks. . . . I felt we were being treated like recruits at a Russian summons to military duty."

Tension among the immigrants was high and quarrels broke out frequently, sometimes involving the police. Of one riot on October 14, 1882, Emma Lazarus wrote, "the riot is the inevitable consequence of a prolonged encouragement of idleness and pauperism, uncontrolled by the necessary forces of intelligent authority. . . . Not a drop of running water is to be found in dormitories . . . not a single step has been taken to provide [education] . . . the wretched idleness of the emigrants is by no means a voluntary one. . . ." [11]

German Jews tried strenuously to take the Russian Jews out of their primitive situation and "elevate" them—spiritually as well as economically—and to disperse the immigrant population away from the dense cities by colonization schemes. But this sort of directive planning failed. In the end, the masses of immigrants, with their own social and cultural needs and aspirations, went their own way.[12]

During the long and bitter ordeal of life in the squalid tenements and sweatshops, a life often filled with despair and the danger of individual disintegration, the gap between Americanized Jews of German descent and Russian Jews grew. Except for the Employment Bureau of the United Hebrew Charities, the great network of philanthropic and social agencies that German Jews had created was used by surprisingly few immigrants.[13] Russian Jews very quickly created their own mutual-aid institutions and their own distinctive synagogues, *landsmandshaftn* (associations of Jews from the same towns), and political parties. Later admonitions of German Jews to ignore the blandishments of both major political parties were also largely ignored; the Russian Jews wanted to be part of American political life on their terms.

This negative attitude of the German Jews in America and the subsequent experience of the immigrants with many of them as their first employers shaped later relations in the shops and in the Jewish community at large. As official leaders of the American Jewish community, German Jews opposed the radical ideas of the intelligentsia, the "unenlightened" beliefs of the Orthodox masses, the attempts to form non-religious Jewish organizations. German Jews also no longer considered themselves part of a Jewish nation but defined themselves as a religious community and, as such, the truest bearers of the Jewish tradition. Under the leadership of Rabbi Isaac Mayer Wise, this concept became a key element in the rationale for Reform Judaism. As in Germany, the Reform position insisted that Judaism was an evolutionary faith, thus dissociating itself quite completely from the traditional Judaism of Eastern Europe.

The cultural gap between German and Russian Jews widened as the Russian Jews quickly developed their own synagogues and *landsmanshaftn* and later, their distinctive schools, Yiddish press, and labor unions. But in the area of radical ideology and labor unionism, there was much borrowing from the adaptation of German socialism to America. Fresh from a radical break with their own past, the young Russian radical intellectuals groped their way to a socialist orientation with the help of the German socialists and took the mass of Jewish workers with them. Despite their own traditional attachments, the workers came along because there were no other leaders whom they could follow. The established Jewish community, the English-language Jewish press, and much of the Yiddish press openly opposed these dissidents, fearful of shaking the status quo and discrediting American Jewry with radical un-American labels. In large measure, class conflict and polarization split the community and alienated the Jewish labor movement from the rest of the community until World War I, when new forces turned it from socialism.

However, it took several years before the radicalized intellectual met the new Jewish working mass on common ground. Nothing in their respective experiences in Russia had prepared them for such an encounter; at the same time, no Jewish labor movement would have been possible without it. Shocked by the pogroms, some of the Jewish radicals transplanted their idealism and organized groups for emigration to America, where they planned to establish agricultural communes; this idea motivated the creation of the Am Olam movement. Others left Russia together with the masses and shared their experiences in the sweatshops. But the romanticized aura of the revolutionaries who yearned to "go to the people" and be witness to a new social order fell away slowly. For years, these doubly uprooted Jewish youths lived in the overwrought, conspiratorial fantasy world of the revolution-to-come, a world hammered flat by the freedom of America, with its opportunities and embitterments, its utilitarian spirit and materialism, as well as the bread-and-butter needs of Jewish workers. Yet wistful echoes of the grandiose dream continued to reverberate after material security was assured. This sense of unappeased spiritual hunger which Abraham Cahan evoked in his novel *The Rise of David Levinsky* hovered over the American Jewish labor movement, even after it had become "successful" as, indeed, it has hovered naggingly over American Jewish life as a whole.

What Cahan and other young intellectuals brought to America was too rich, too complex, and too self-contradictory to synthesize or reduce to life-size, and the land they came to gave little ground to dreams. That they were able to invest as much social idealism as they did into their lives, that they could transcend the despair and the bone- and soul-aching labor of each day's struggle to survive, and that they could eventually create a movement that gave dignity and meaning to Jewish workers, individually and collectively, is a kind of miracle. That they did not do even more probably stems from the very complexity of their background, their uprootedness, their youthfulness, which denied them time to digest the exciting ideas they were experimenting with and put them into a coherent philosophy. Markedly absent was a sense of what their Jewishness meant to them and how they would manifest it. This was the least of their many preoccupations. Nor could they have worked this out in the context of the *shtetl* culture, when the Jewishness around them was so unacceptable.

This meaning and expression of Jewishness, then, unformed in Russia, was to remain unformed in the Jewish labor movement in America. A quick review of the early experiences of Cahan in Russia [14]—quite typical of other intellectual radicals who helped shape the movement—shows the quantum leaps from *shtetl* traditions, the struggle with parents and subsequent guilt and sharp separations, the unholy intensity of learning, the new knowledge, the intoxication with the new possibilities of life.

Cahan was born in 1860 in Podberezhie, a little hamlet near Vilna, where almost half the population was Jewish. A courtyard away was Cathedral Square, with its theater and riding academy and the home of the Governor-General with its magical water fountain. More of the Russian world lay a bit farther away: an army barracks filled with the sounds of marching feet, drumbeats, and trumpets. Mesmerized by the colors of the banners and uniforms, Cahan soon learned the names of the officers and the insignia of rank. The sounds of Russian words fascinated him and he began collecting slugs of Russian typeface in the courtyard of his *heder*, near a Russian print shop. He soon taught himself to read and by the age of thirteen was so proficient that he was able to translate a government decree making all twenty-one-year-olds subject to conscription.

He attended a *yeshivah* for a while, but his family decided that he needed a trade and apprenticed him to a turner who required him to memorize seventy-seven tools. A week was all that Cahan could stand. The government, meanwhile, had set up schools aimed at assimilating Jews. Cahan applied and was admitted to the second grade, where he delighted in Russian, arithmetic, geometry, and the use of a compass. He also began to envy the smart uniforms and buttons of Jewish boys in the *gymnasium* and felt ashamed of his long *kapote* (long coat), especially after a painful experience in the Vilna public library. Cahan was fifteen before he realized that there was a public library in Vilna where he could read all the Russian books he wanted, without any charge. The library stood opposite the Governor-General's home, and he had often passed the gilt sign "Public Library," but he had not thought of himself as one of the "public." It took him a full year to gird himself to enter. Timidly he asked for a book by Turgenev. The librarian brought it, but said he would have to remove his overcoat before he could use the reading room. Cahan explained that he was not wearing an overcoat but a *kapote*, with nothing underneath except his underwear, and walked out humiliated. At home, he insisted on getting a short jacket, much to his parents' chagrin.

As he began to perfect his Russian, he lost all interest in Yiddish and Hebrew and his religious faith and began giving Russian lessons to a fur dyer. The money he earned enabled him to buy maps and geography books. At this time, he also entered his first "modern" home, where the floor was covered with carpets instead of sand and where all the books were Russian. A friend who had a talent for drawing encouraged him to join his art class, a project he pursued so rigorously that he became cross-eyed from eye strain. The drawing class also brought him into contact with gentiles and a more relaxed, even gayer, atmosphere than he had yet known. By now he and his friends were earning enough to have their own apartment where they studied for admission to the Teachers' Institute. On Saturdays, while other Jews prayed, these young men learned ballroom dancing.

When he was admitted to the institute, where he lived six days a week, life there opened up still more novelties: sheets on beds, parquet floors, cases of minerals and anatomical models, his own uniforms, meat every day, and other amenities and blandishments the government was offering to "humanize" the Jews of Russia. A few Jewish instructors were on the staff, including an outstanding Hebraist and creative teacher, but the Jewish boys not only had no interest in him or his courses or anything that smacked of Judaism; they felt ashamed of these associations. The novelties soon wore off, however, and Cahan's insatiable curiosity was scarcely nourished by the rote memorization required by most teachers. Once, reacting sharply to a recitation he failed, he was sentenced to three days' solitary confinement and bread and water in the bathroom of the infirmary. There, for the entire time, he luxuriated reading *War and Peace*.

Inside the institute, moreover, companionship was not very stimulating; the prospect of a dreary eight years of teaching in some village in a grade school depressed him. Outside, however, other influences were at work. He began to talk with "modern" Jewish girls from westernized homes who attended the *gymnasium*, had elegant manners, and discussed rarefied intellectual topics. In the summer of 1880, he learned about revolutionary activity for the first time. On a visit to a classmate at a nearby resort, he noticed that a number of students often gathered near the railroad tracks. When his friend gave him some illegal literature, he realized that this group was an underground circle. This first perception of a movement of self-sacrifice and social idealism struggling against a crushing despotism acted like a thunderbolt; he was thrilled by the very touch of the first illegal brochure given to him:

> A forbidden object, its publishers are those . . . who live together like brothers and are ready to go to the gallows for freedom and justice. This knowledge had an indescribable influence on me, and the danger connected with reading this brochure heightened its power. I touched the little book as one touches a holy thing.

Cahan's life thereafter was completely changed. He avidly read all of the socialist material he could get and learned at first hand the selflessness, intimacy, and complete sharing in a revolutionary circle where Jew and gentile lived as comrades. The revolution soon became a holy cause with him and, inevitably, estranged him from his father—they quarreled and stopped talking to each other—and the old life. He did not declare his new allegiance, but his mother suspected him of being in a radical circle when she saw him riding in a droshky with a non-Jewish student.

The institute did not tell the students that the tsar was assassinated on March 1, 1881, but merely that he had died. Cahan learned the truth soon enough and, like his revolutionary friends, anticipated that a revolution would soon follow. This expectation he offered as a partial explanation for the notorious anti-Semitic proclamations issued by the People's Will party in the Ukraine on August 30, 1881. The emigration panic among Jews after the pogroms did not touch Cahan at all, but events soon ended his brief revolutionary rapture.

After completing his course at the institute, he was sent to teach in a little hasidic village called Velisz. At first he concealed his revolutionary inclinations by attending synagogue, but he soon found kindred spirits and tried to lead a double life. After a few months, his mother, in covert language, wrote that the rooms of his old circle in Vilna had been raided and that his name was known to the police. In Velisz, they searched his place three times. All suspect literature had been removed except a copy of Marx's *Das Kapital*. When the police asked what kind of book it was, Cahan casually replied, "Oh, a book about business." Knowing he would be hounded, he left Velisz disguised as a *yeshivah* student, going by rowboat down the Dvina to Vitebsk and by steamer to Mogilev. He spent Passover at an inn, passing as an army deserter who could count on every Jew's sympathy, and managed to secure a forged passport, which enabled him to get to the Austrian border by way of Kiev.

In the course of these journeys, Cahan met Samuel Belkin, who was traveling secretly from city to city signing up young men for agricultural settlements in Palestine. But Cahan did not respond—he wanted a more universal cause. In their long talk, Belkin mentioned a movement of young socialists gathering in Brody, waiting to go to America to form communes and "begin a new chapter in the life of the Jewish people." *This* idea did arouse his enthusiasm:

> I saw a fantastic picture of agricultural communes in far-away America, a life which does not know of mine and thine, where all are brothers and all are happy. Previously, I had thought that this could be realized only in the future. Now it was going to be realized in the present, and I would be a participant.

Cahan arrived in Brody in the spring of 1882 and relished the company of a number of young idealists in the Am Olam group from Odessa, but he realized, after his arrival in America, that he was too much of an individualist to join any of the communes—even the urban groups organized by his friends from Vilna.

In complaining about the dry and lifeless approach to subjects at school, Cahan had once said, but "if a subject interests me, it takes complete possession of me." The first such subject in a lifetime of many enthusiasms was English. During the week in Hull, England, waiting for the ship to America, Cahan bought a used copy of Appleton's grammar and studied English diligently. He continued his study during the two weeks' voyage and, later, sat among twelve and thirteen-year-olds in a New York East Side public school in order to learn the language efficiently.

But neither Cahan nor any of the other young radicals could avoid the sweatshops and manual labor. Unused to physical labor, and coming from a culture that frowned on it, they had no choice but to endure it, then master it and, finally, invest it with dignity. The starry-eyed visions of those who beheld a new utopia in America and who were nourished by the soaring ideas of socialism and anarchism bent or broke under the day-to-day struggle with fiendishly exhausting labor, squalor, and the traumas of culture shock.

The relatives and *landslayt* (acquaintances from one's town of origin) of the immigrant played an important role in absorbing Jewish workers, and in both blunting and sharpening the conflicts between worker and boss. A common device of the Jewish contractor in the clothing industry, for example, which became the prime field of Jewish labor, was to seek out his *landslayt* and, in the role of a benefactor, take them into his shop, where they worked at a low rate. At first, it was natural and helpful for the workers to gravitate to those they had known back home. Here were kinsmen who had gone to the same *heder* as the new immigrant. How could a *landsman* take advantage of a greenhorn, someone from his own town? However, the employer expected special consideration from "his own" people and was bitterly disappointed when his demands boomeranged and caused hostility among the greenhorns who eventually refused to endure their appalling conditions of work and went on strike.[15]

Landslayt connections were the dominant factor in determining the personnel of the various trades. A machine operator took on a new immigrant as learner; he in turn, did the same favor for another *landsman* who arrived several months later. Soon many people from a particular town "produced" mostly cloak operators, kneepants operators, or dress pressers, and from single towns this occupational specialization spread to chains of neighboring towns. For some time, moreover, old regional prejudices were carried over into the shops. The Litvaks (from Lithuania and the northern Pale) affected a superior air toward the Russians, while the Ukrainians considered the Litvaks *shnorrers* (beggars). All three looked down on the Galitzianer (from Galicia and southern Poland).

Jewish immigrants worked at anything available: peddling bread, fish, pins and needles; selling cheap goods from pushcarts; working machines in tenements; sewing and pressing coats, jackets, and pants in dark workrooms; making pillows, ribbons, chairs; digging ditches; stripping tobacco. On Saturdays, many would rush to the Hester Street Pig Market in New York, and similar improvised labor exchanges in other cities, where contractors would come to hire workers for the coming week. There was little bargaining about terms. The boss or his agent stipulated the wage he would pay and the workers took whatever was offered.

The Jews who came to America in the early 1880's were the poorest, least skilled, and the least educated of all who came. But they had the courage to leave home and a familiar culture and plunge into a strange and menacing life. It was this first wave, moreover, that assisted the later mass migration from 1885 to 1890, by saving money and sending it to relatives still in Russia. The sweatshop experience in the Lower East Side of New York became the crucible of suffering and testing, which ultimately forged them into new men. All of the organizers of the first Jewish unions and socialist movement underwent the experience of the sweatshops, wandering from job to job, paying five or ten dollars a week "tuition" out of future earnings to learn an operation, and toiling for twelve and fourteen hours a day. Many of the intellectuals took jobs in shirt factories, where the work was relatively tolerable. Morris Hillquit, the future Socialist party leader, has recorded this experience:

> I was frail and untrained for any trade and almost inevitably gravitated into a shirt shop. For some fortuitous reason, shirt making had become the favorite occupation of the circle of young Russian intellectuals in which I moved. It was a trade easy to learn principally because of the minute division of labor. . . . Nobody made a complete shirt. The task of each worker was confined to one small and uniform operation, such as making the front or the sleeve, the collar or the cuff. . . . The operators in the stuffy little workshop spent at least as much time in discussing social and literary topics as in turning out shirts, and the whir of the sewing machines was often accompanied by the loud and hearty sound of revolutionary songs. . . . The "boss," i.e., the contractor, who ran the shop, took no business chances. He practically paid no rent, since the work was done in one of the rooms of his living quarters. He had no outlay on machinery because every worker hired his own sewing machine at a rental of two dollars per month.

Wages were low and were paid "by the piece." Work was seasonal and irregular. The machine rent was the only constant element in the peculiar industrial scheme, so that a worker of my skill and productivity sometimes wound up the month with a deficit in earnings.[16]

Cahan at first worked in a cellar on South Fifth Avenue in New York stripping tobacco. He, too, was unaccustomed to physical work and relieved the boredom and strain by daydreaming and talking to a fellow radical, Bernard Weinstein, who later became a leader in the Jewish labor movement. Cahan raged against the lives being broken by the uprooting and was ambivalent about America—he reveled in the freedom, but kept thinking, "All of this is a capitalist prison." He longed to distribute revolutionary leaflets, a task that once had a special aura of danger and consecration. But how could there be socialism without conspiracy? How could a permitted activity be worthy of the revolution? If all is permissible and there is no danger, socialism loses its glow and revolutionary heroism becomes impossible. On his second job, feeding tin plate into a machine while standing all day, he was fired for his daydreaming. His monotonous job was an example of the way capitalism subdivides every task, diminishing the need for skilled workers. Like the rest, he was being reduced to a dead tool, Cahan believed.

However, the idea of going to the workers, of organizing them to press for more humane working conditions and better wages did not, as yet, occur to him or other young radicals. They were just as devoid of a proletarian tradition and just as ignorant of union practices as the masses of Jewish workers. Moreover, their own liberation from the bonds of the *shtetl* culture meant a revolt against established religious tradition. There seemed little they had in common. Besides, the radicals had been nurtured on the notion of an aroused peasantry, not an aroused industrial proletariat. Thus, for a time, the radicals continued to debate in a void. They argued about nuances of socialist thought and the specific events of the revolutionary struggle in Russia, in whose milieu, in fact, they still lived imaginatively. As they tried to repress the sordidness of their actual lives, waves of nostalgic longing for the landscape of Russia and the intellectual life they had given up often engulfed them.

But, inevitably, American realities forced their way into consciousness, and the plight and ignorance of the Jewish worker into insistent challenges. This process took several years as the young radicals struggled with their own economic problems and painfully groped for intellectual clarity amid the turmoil of their new lives. A faint beginning of contact between Jewish worker and intellectual was made in the early months of the mass inflow in the summer of 1882.

One afternoon in June 1882,[17] shortly after Cahan's arrival in America, a barge pulled up alongside the harbor outside Castle Garden. A young man stepped out and approached a group of immigrants sitting on the grass. Addressing them in German, he told them that he had jobs for about five hundred men unloading steamships; the pay would be two dollars a day plus meals. The men were overjoyed and the following morning boarded a boat which took them to the dock. For three days they worked loading and unloading heavy cases. On the fourth day, during the lunch break, one of the men was suddenly rushed by two burly Irishmen and beaten up. His cries for help brought police and several of his fellow workers. Two of them, members of Am Olam, who understood a little English, quickly learned that the dock workers were on strike, and that the Jewish workers had "scabbed." No one understood what the word meant, but they didn't dare continue working. That night a large crowd gathered on the grass at Battery Park to listen to the longshoremen, several of whose union leaders were exiled social democrats from Germany. An immigrant Jewish radical from St. Petersburg named Mirovitsch addressed the crowd in Russian and called upon them to demonstrate their solidarity with the American longshoremen. They voted overwhelmingly not to work any longer and to demand their pay the following day. A few days later, a street parade of the strikers and their families was held. More than five hundred Jewish immigrants joined the several thousand dock workers in a two-mile march from Battery Park along Broadway to Union Square, where a rally was held.

The workers themselves soon scattered to the sweatshops on the East Side, peddler's packs, and pushcarts, but the intellectuals began to organize after this episode. The German social democrats told Mirovitsch that they would help him form a socialist discussion group which, they hoped, would attract some of the immigrants. A handbill [18]—probably the first printed Yiddish socialist handbill in America—was distributed, calling people to a meeting on Friday night, July 7, 1882, at Eisel's Golden Rule Hall at 125-27 Rivington Street. The handbill struck familiar notes: it was sent out in the name of the Propaganda Verein, a name modeled after German socialist associations, and urged all Jews to attend to hear about the persecution of Jews in Russia, Hungary, and Germany. Speeches in Yiddish, Russian, English, and German were scheduled. The title of the handbill, "When will the persecution of the Jews cease?" was intended to veil the more radical theme intended, namely, the evils of strike-breaking and the need for labor solidarity.

The German socialists connected with the influential labor daily, the *Volkszeitung,* had arranged to have one of its editors, Sergius Schevitsch, as the opening speaker. Schevitsch's name inspired great excitement among the young radicals of the time. He was married to Helene von Racowitza (von Dönniges), for whose love Ferdinand Lassalle had died in a duel. Every Russian-Jewish radical had adored Lassalle. Schevitsch started his speech with a reference to the pogroms:

The pogroms that have forced you Russian Jews to seek a new home were the work of ignorant peasants who did not understand what they were doing. When the day of understanding comes to them, they will attack, not Jewish homes, not the Jewish inhabitants of Elizabethgrad, Balta, or Kiev, but the Tsar's palace in St. Petersburg. There they will indeed make a pogrom. Then they will do away with despotism and organize a government founded upon freedom, equality, and brotherhood.[19]

He soon passed on to the longshoremen's strike and warned the immigrants against scabbing.

In his memoirs, Cahan describes his impressions of Schevitsch: "He was a tall, handsome, dark-haired man . . . with an aristocratic manner. . . . He was a brilliant speaker. The fact that his wife was the heroine of Lassalle's romance and fatal duel lent his personality a particular magnetism. His pronunciation of the Russian language made an indescribable impression on me. . . . We hung on every word." [20]

The other speakers were German anarchists and an Irish socialist. When they finished, Mirovitsch asked if anyone in the audience wanted to speak. Overcoming his anxiety, Cahan responded in a strong, angry Russian:

> We are now in a land that is relatively free. We are seeking a new home here. But we must not forget the great struggle for freedom that we left behind in our old home. While we worry about our own problems, our comrades, our heroes and martyrs are carrying on the struggle, suffering in Russian prisons and in Siberia. . . . There is not much that we can do from such a distance, but we can raise money for the sacred cause. And we must keep the memory of the revolutionary struggle deep in our hearts.[21]

A storm of applause broke out, and Cahan, no longer shy, listened with astonishment and delight. After the meeting, a group gathered around him, eager to find out who he was. Twenty new members joined the Verein that night. Later that night, Cahan and Mirovitsch discussed the group's future. Cahan felt that speakers would have to use Yiddish to reach Jewish workers, but Mirovitsch, a thoroughgoing Russian radical, shared the contempt for Yiddish common among intellectuals. "Why don't you deliver a speech in Yiddish," he taunted Cahan. Cahan agreed, and the Verein rented a hall—more in jest than in earnest—for what was to be the first socialist lecture in America in Yiddish.

Yiddish handbills were printed and distributed in the Jewish neighborhoods. The meeting took place on August 18, in a small hall, called Internationale Arbeiter Halle, the meeting place of the German anarchists, in the rear of a German beer saloon in lower Manhattan. The subject of Cahan's lecture was nothing less than the theory of scientific socialism: Marx's theory of surplus value, the theory of the class struggle, and the inevitable evolution from capitalism to socialism—heavy going for most of his audience. Cahan spoke for two hours, but he used the simplest Yiddish and vivid, homely examples to make his subject intelligible. When he finished, he was greeted by tumultuous applause

On September 1, he delivered another lecture before an even larger audience. At one point he shouted for the workers to march on Fifth Avenue with their tools and axes, and to seize the wealth which their labor had produced. He cursed the millionaires with expressive and elaborate Vilna curses. Later, Cahan said it was a foolish speech, but acknowledged that others—wiser and more sophisticated—were uttering similar revolutionary platitudes.[22] The speech was in the style of Johann Most, the fiery, hypnotic anarchist who preached "propaganda through deeds." Most had come to America in December 1882 and soon became the leader of the American anarchists and one of the idols of the Jewish radicals.

Until the Haymarket Affair in May 1886, anarchism did not exist as an organized movement among Jews, but some, including Cahan, considered themselves anarchists or social revolutionaries even earlier. Dissatisfied with social-democratic tactics and slogans, they demanded a "revolutionary" program in "revolutionary" language—that is, violence and terror. But Marxism was often intermixed in their ideological brew, as well as the positivism of William Frey and the ethical culturalism of Felix Adler. Still gripped by the romanticized danger surrounding illegal activities, they were skeptical of a socialist movement that did not have to go underground. Nevertheless, despite the excitement of so many compelling ideas, Cahan, for one, soon began to have misgivings about his lack of a clear political orientation. "It's a joke," he wrote in a letter to a friend. "I debate, I argue, I get excited, I shriek, and in the middle of all this, I remind myself that I am an empty vessel, an empty man without a shred of knowledge, and I begin to blush. I am ashamed of myself." [23] He envies others who seem sure of their ideas, but he has nothing to lean on. He must study more, he concludes.

However, as with many of the Jewish radicals, for the first four or five years of life in America, Cahan lived in a foggy web of numerous ideological strands and colors. A great deal of the perplexity stemmed from the divided life of many of the radicals: on one level, they still lived the daring exalted life of Russian revolutionaries; on another, they faced menial work every day, the ugliness of the tenements, and an American scene that rejected visionaries. Cahan sensed this dilemma soon after he met Mirovitsch. The incident in the dock strike had shown the necessity of a practical program to organize Jewish workers. Mirovitsch had called meetings of the new immigrants to stress the shamefulness of scabbing. Then why didn't he take the next step, Cahan asked himself, and organize Jewish tailors? "The answer," Cahan wrote,

> is that such a program would have lacked revolutionary fire; it would have been too mundane, and in this respect, I shared his feelings. Mirovitsch looked at the young American labor movement through the rosy glasses of the Russian struggle. He had named his firstborn Andrei Zheliabov, in honor of the leader

of the group that had assassinated the tsar—a hero of the *Narodnaya Volya*. What interest could we have in naive, legal American trade unions? There was no danger involved in working with them—and no socialism. . . . How could a revolutionary talk about such lowly matters? [24]

The Verein, which attracted some Am Olam members, lasted only about a year. Instead of continuing the plan to educate the Jewish people politically, it confined itself to lectures and discussions among a narrow circle. At the end of 1882, some of the Am Olam members left for their experimental colonies; others drifted away into training at night school for careers. Meanwhile, fresh boatloads of bewildered immigrants poured into the country. Radical youths as yet had no coherent philosophy or course of action. Nostalgia for the Russian revolutionary movement still seemed to dominate their lives. They celebrated New Year for the first time in America on January 1, 1883, with a decided Russian flavor, and on the first anniversary of the assassination of Alexander II, staged a solemn public ceremony commemorating the martyrs of Narodnaya Volya. Through the Popov family, with whom the Russian revolutionaries in Geneva, Paris, and London conducted a continuous correspondence, a flow of memoirs, articles, and pamphlets dealing with the terrorist heroes streamed into Cahan's hands, and through him, to the Russian radical intelligentsia in New York. Every scrap of information about the lives of the *narodniki* was read with fascination; the current trials of the executive committee were followed with intense interest. In the summer of 1883, a book of exceptional interest appeared—an account of the Russian revolutionary movement written by an exile in Italy, Sergei Kravchinsky (under the pseudonym Stepniak). The book appeared in English under the title *Underground Russia* and provided spiritual nourishment for the ardent, still floundering radicals. Revolutionary fetishes were also cherished. Someone brought to New York a black silk scarf that had belonged to Sophia Perovskaya, one of the young *narodnik* martyrs. Cahan confessed, "I cradled the sacred thing in my hands."

With the collapse of several of the Am Olam colonies in 1883–84, the perplexities of the intellectuals deepened. After another period of soul-searching, a new group was formed at the iniative of Nicholas Aleinikoff, a somewhat older, much admired intellectual and former leader of the Kiev Am Olam, who taught English with Cahan at an evening school for immigrants. This group attracted the drifting, dispirited Am Olam members groping for ideological clarification. It called itself the Russian Workers' Union and aimed to educate Russian workers in the United States—but no workers joined. Russian problems and Russian culture still claimed first priority, and the library, consisting largely of Russian works, which had been left by the Propaganda Verein, was a major attraction of the group.

Personal clashes and the group's limited goals caused dissatisfactions and a split among the members. Cahan and Louis Bandes (better known as

Miller), who later became a leading socialist leader, rented a hall at 165 East Broadway, where they had already had their first garment "union" meeting, and announced the formation of a new organization: the Russian Labor Lyceum. This group, too, attracted mainly intellectuals and also was short-lived, but it has a certain historic importance because it came to grips with the difference between socialism and anarchism. This was achieved by a Dr. M. Merkin, a former Latvian *yeshivah* scholar and an active member of the Social-Democratic party during Bismarck's anti-socialist regime. Merkin was a fountainhead of knowledge for the Lyceum members, a mature thinker, a political activist, a strong speaker—and a confirmed Marxist.[25] His vehement opposition to anarchism clarified the thinking of some, but this group, too, was conducting hair-splitting discussions in an ideological hothouse. Real workers were still missing. Only after radicals had created a framework called the United Hebrew Trades in 1888 were workers drawn in. The UHT was a mere shell within which the radicals hoped to develop a solid kernel of worker-members. Astonishingly enough, the scheme worked, and small groups of workers joined the "shell."

6. Socialist Intellectuals Encounter Jewish Workers, 1881-87

The history of the early Jewish unions in cigar factories, bakeries, and the garment industry, to a large degree parallels the early experience of American unions in general. The cycle became almost predictable: from intolerable conditions to unionization, strikes, an inability to maintain worker interest in the union, apathy and, finally, disorganization. If their demands were met, the workers generally lost interest in their union, and within a short time, it disappeared from sight. If the strike failed, it was felt there was no need to have a union.

The needle trades, in their various branches, were the major area of proletarian experience for masses of Jewish immigrants. By the 1870's, there were a considerable number of Jewish workers from Germany, Hungary, and Galicia in the garment industry—skilled cutters who worked on expensive garments—who helped organize several local assemblies of the Knights of Labor. Later, Polish and Russian Jews, who worked on cheaper garments, joined these locals, but such early unions were short-lived. The Austro-Hungarian socialists were influenced by German socialism but were more concerned with the immediate problems of the workers than were the soul-searching Russian-Jewish radicals of the time. In July 1883, the former called a large strike of about 750 inside shopworkers in the Dress and Cloak Makers' Union, which they had recently organized. Half the work force were German and Austro-Hungarian Jewish men; the rest were non-Jewish girls. The union demanded a wage of $2.50 per workday, from 8 A.M. to 6 P.M., and in shops on piecework rates, they insisted on a rate high enough to enable a worker to earn $15 per week. A strike conducted by Jewish workers was a newsworthy event—one New York paper called it "the first emigrants' strike"—and described it as follows:

> The members of the new Cloak and Dress-Makers' Association [Union] have never before been on strike, and had never before taken part in labor

movements. Nevertheless the men and women who compose the union have realized all the hopes of the leaders in standing by the association and holding out against the bosses. There were fears that the great poverty of many of them and the wealth of the bosses, who at first stoutly declared that they would make no concession whatever, might induce these poor people to return to their daily toil for the pittance they were receiving, but the weak ones were encouraged and now they all seem determined to stand out until their wages are raised.[1]

This strike revealed the complex relations of manufacturers, contractors, and inside shopworkers. The contractors had offered to strike with the cloakworkers if the latter would refuse to work for certain contractors who were taking out work from the manufacturers at rates lower than the rest.[2] No agreement, however, was reached between the strikers and the contractors. (In the course of the strike, a cloak manufacturers' association was formed, directed against both contractors and workers.) Despite many handicaps, the strike was eventually won by the workers, and virtually all of the union's demands were met. The union achieved status as an assembly of the Knights of Labor and sent representatives to the Central Labor Union. Yet, soon after the strike, it went out of existence.

In January 1884, the Gotham Knife Cutters' Association of New York and Vicinity, which included several different crafts in the ladies' garment industry, was also chartered by the Knights of Labor. Here, too, no sooner had the workers concluded an agreement with their employers than interest in the union faded.

A loose reorganization of the Gotham Knife Cutters' Association took place in the summer of 1885, and on August 15, about 1,500 cloakmakers, mostly Jewish, in thirty inside shops responded to a strike call. Finishers, pressers, and operators were in this union, which cut across craft lines. Many of the operators had been recruited from among former university and *yeshivah* students, who urged the workers to protest against intolerable conditions. The terms of the final agreement included not only a wage increase but worker representation in the fixing of prices for new styles and arbitration in case of any misunderstanding regarding the quality of work or the rate of payment [3]—possibly the first in the industry. Yet, in a few weeks, union meetings were unattended.

In the course of this development, yet another local was accepted into the Knights of Labor. One of the members, Abraham Rosenberg, who was to become president of the International Ladies' Garment Workers Union (ILGWU) from 1908 to 1914, has drawn a touching picture of the terrors of initiation for religiously orthodox Jewish workers who had recently come from the Russian Pale.

> I still retain in my memory a vivid picture of the scene which took place when the District Master Workman and his deputies, all Irish, came to perform the ceremony of installing us. We were all new in America and we did not understand a word of what was said. We could only see how one of them took a piece of chalk and drew a large circle on the floor and told us to stand around

the circle. Then another deputy placed a small sword on the table, and a globe was hung on the side of the door of the meeting-hall.

. . . .

Many of us on seeing the sword were not sure whether we were all going to be slaughtered or drafted into the army. Many of us had already made their peace with themselves. . . . Only later did some of those who understood a little of the ceremony explain to the rest the meaning of it all, namely, that if any one of us broke his oath and became untrue to the interests of Labor, he would be pursued by the sword and be unable to escape because the Knights were strong the world over.[4]

The Knights adopted the principle of secrecy and elaborate, Masonic-like rituals—appropriate perhaps in an era of labor spies and blacklisting—but such notions eventually handicapped the growth and influence of the organization.

The rise and fall of the early Jewish unions reflected the escalating and de-escalating fortunes of the parent union, the Knights of Labor, to which the early Jewish locals belonged, and which held center stage in the early drama of the American labor struggle. Organized in 1869 by a Philadelphia tailor, Uriah Stephens, and largely native-American in membership, the Knights of Labor attempted to unite the workers of America into one big union under centralized control. Membership was open to all workers—men, women, white, black, skilled, unskilled, farmers, and even merchants and capitalists—but excluded liquor dealers, gamblers, lawyers, and bankers.

The Knights had lofty goals, including "the complete emancipation of the wealth producers from the thraldom and loss of wage slavery, the entire redemption of the world's toilers from the political tyranny of unjust laws, and the annihilation of the great anti-Christ of civilization manifest in the idolatry of wealth." [5] They hoped to achieve these goals through vaguely sketched producers' cooperatives, arbitration, an eight-hour day, the abolition of child labor, and other social and economic reforms, many of which were eventually adopted in America.

The growth of the Knights of Labor was nothing short of phenomenal. When Terence Powderly, a Pennsylvania machinist, became Grand Master in 1878, the membership was under fifty thousand. Powderly was an idealist who disliked the tactics of belligerent unionism; nevertheless, the new organization became powerful by winning a railroad strike in the Southwest in 1884. Capital met labor on more or less equal terms for the first time when the New York financier Jay Gould conferred with the Knights' executive board and conceded their demands. The prestige of this victory was so great that the membership reached 700,000 the following year.

But parallel with the rise of the Knights of Labor, other labor groups sprouted and multiplied, seriously competing with the Knights and contributing to its decline. The Haymarket bomb explosion in 1886 in the midst of a mass meeting of striking union workers demonstrating against the McCormick Harvester Company also hurt the Knights. Seven persons were killed and over sixty injured as police broke up the demonstration. The Knights were in no way responsible, but popular revulsion against "radicalism" began to taint the movement. Indiscriminate strikes, Powderly's mismanagement, and the difficulties of holding together both skilled and unskilled labor within one organization also weakened its ranks. By 1887, it was supplanted by a new and more vigorous organization, the American Federation of Labor.

Meanwhile, palpable changes in the American economic and social landscape pressed in upon the consciousness of the young Jewish radicals. The large Jewish immigration of the mid-eighties was bringing a clearly definable Jewish proletariat into being. The typical immigrant was now more likely to remain a worker for some time, condemned to the filthy sweatshops for long hours. The increasing militancy of American labor and the challenge of political campaigns also prodded thoughtful radicals to re-evaluate their theoretical positions. Nor could they any longer remain isolated from the Jewish masses or from the slashing forces in American society.

The Jewish Workers' Association,[6] organized in April 1885, fused several parallel streams that had preserved this isolation and brought Jewish intellectuals into meaningful contact with Jewish workers. It also was the first of the early groups to use the word "Jewish" in its name in order to attract new immigrant workers. Most of its lectures and discussions were conducted in Yiddish and took a definitely social-democratic, rather than anarchist, direction, thus aiming at a specific place in the general American radical movement. The antecedent of this group was the Russian Workers' Party, which first met in January 1885, but soon changed its name to the Russian-Jewish Workers' Association (RJWA), under the impetus of the Gretch brothers, Mitia and Niuma, who had engaged in illegal activity in Odessa. Once in America, they came under the influence of the German socialist paper, the New York *Volkszeitung*, and believed that Jewish workers must be led away from the perils of anarchism. Many of the intellectuals at the time held back. For example, Abraham Cahan could not join the RJWA because he still considered himself an anarchist.[7] However, the Gretch brothers were not effective speakers, and Cahan was often invited to lecture for them, but only after the text of every speech he prepared was first carefully read.

The first meeting of the RJWA in April 1885 drew only twenty intellectuals or so, and like earlier such groups soon exhausted itself. But it had latched on to a genuine workers' force which gave it new life. This was the Jewish Workingmen's Newspaper Association, which had been started a bit earlier by central European Jewish immigrant tailors—fairly well educated socialists who had already made contact with the German radical movement in America.[8]

The Jewish Workingmen's Newspaper Association was organized to create a fund for a Yiddish labor newspaper—a proposal which aroused some fear of Jewish separatism but which gained the support of the *Volkszeitung*. Far removed from workers, the members of the RJWA had not even heard of the central European group. One of their members wrote:

> One day there was an announcement in the German *Volkszeitung* of a meeting to be held in some hall on Cannon Street to discuss the publication of a Yiddish labor paper. The members of the "Russian Jewish Verein" could not figure out what benevolent heaven had sent such a god-send. At the meeting, the Russian comrades met an association of Hungarian-Jewish socialists. After some brief discussion between the members of both groups, it was agreed to combine them into one.[9]

This fusion, which created the JWA, took place April 8, 1885, and proved to be an important milestone in the early history of Jewish labor.[10] The new Verein could not raise enough money for a Yiddish labor paper, but it became the focal point for the small, slowly coalescing radical intellectual–Jewish worker force and a center of leadership and guidance for immigrant Jewish labor. Within six months, boasting 107 members, it discussed concrete economic, political, and social questions confronting the workers, helped organize unions and deal with problems posed by strikes. Jacob Schoen, for example, an early union organizer, analyzed the role of spies, scabs, courts, and police, and wrote a pamphlet in Yiddish on the issue, which the association published. Niuma Gretch spoke on the eight-hour day as a solution to the problem of unemployment. Moreover, with the help of the association, the first Jewish printers' union was formed; Jewish theater choristers, bakers, and capmakers were also organized with its help. Events in 1886 further drew the association into the turbulence of contemporary American society.

The year 1886 was a momentous one for the struggling American labor movement. It was the year of the Haymarket Affair, of widespread labor-capital warfare, and the Henry George mayoralty campaign in New York City. The Jewish Workers' Association (JWA) was affected by all of these issues and directly involved in some. Injunctions were hailing down on unions, blocking the right to organize and strike, forcing labor to shift to political action and electoral campaigns. Central labor bodies in the large cities moved to an important position in American politics. The Henry George campaign in New York particularly aroused great excitement and hope through the creation of an independent, progressive movement of trade unionists, liberals, reformers, and radicals of all sorts.

A journalist and one-time printer's devil in Philadelphia, George perfected his single-tax theory in the midst of a prolonged struggle with the West Coast monopolies. Land monopoly, he concluded, was the cause of poverty. By taxing away the unearned increment in land values, great speculative holdings in the West would be broken up while abolition of all other taxes would destroy monopolies dependent on the protective tariff. Thus, a single decisive use of taxing power would restore both liberty and equality of opportunity to American economic life. After leading a fruitless land-reform movement on the West Coast during the depressed seventies, George moved to New York City where he published his *Progress and Poverty* in 1880. The appeal to natural rights, the indictment of the existing business system, and the utopian and moral overtones of the book profoundly influenced public opinion here and in Great Britain and had enormous impact on the American labor movement.[11]

George exposed the grave economic and social problems of urban America and gave discontented workers and intellectuals an alternative to Marxian socialism. The central body of organized workers in New York City, the Central Labor Union,[12] the AFL unions,[13] and elements of the Knights of Labor enthusiastically joined the broad coalition that campaigned for George. At first, the Socialist Labor party withheld its support but eventually warmed to the campaign. They disparaged George's theory, but realized that the campaign riveted attention on the class struggle in the largest city in America and that George would later "be driven to demand the abolition of the wage system." Anarchists opposed any concessions to "the system," but some, like Cahan, campaigned.

Jewish socialists soon found themselves in the thick of the campaign and began to feel involved for the first time in a general American issue. Expressive of this new feeling was a drive for citizenship, spearheaded by the *Nu Yorker Yidishe Folkstsaytung,* a paper for Jewish workers started in June 1886, whose editors were active in the JWA. Through the *Yidishe Folkstsaytung,* the JWA came forward with the slogan, "Jewish immigrants, become citizens!" The paper exhorted Jewish workers to "lend your ears to the sound of liberty, merge yourselves with the representatives of the labor movement, and join the fighters for general human rights."

Although George was defeated, the campaign was an important experience in American politicking for the Jewish socialists. During October, the JWA held daily meetings on the East Side, and the unions they helped to organize created Henry George clubs and Americanization programs. The campaign took on the mood of a religious revival, climaxing in a mass meeting on October 28, when George himself compared current events to those of the Jewish exodus out of Egypt.[14]

Because Tammany Hall bought votes and controlled the tallies, the exact number cast for George was never known. The Tammany election inspectors reported 60,000 for Theodore Roosevelt, the Republican candidate, 90,000 for Abram Hewitt, the winning Democrat, and 62,000 for George, of which an estimated 15,000 were Jewish votes.[15] Despite the defeat, there was initial elation over the large vote for George. Raw political recruits, it was said, had struck a blow against the political machines and monopoly capital. But the groups that comprised the

United Labor party lacked basic cohesion. The common front between the socialists and the single taxers could not hold and the political bonds that had been forged under waves of emotion now weakened. Each group soon began to think of its particular programs and goals, and the old bitterness erupted. The socialist leader Sergius Schevitsch challenged George to a debate shortly after the election, and George failed lamentably. To Schevitsch's question: "Let George tell us how a worker with a piece of land, and nothing more, can single-handedly compete with the capitalist who owns the tools and the machinery?" George replied: "If the worker has no tools and cannot produce factory-made products—let him go fishing. He can live from that." Many of the workers and radicals in the audience—including Cahan—shouted derisively in the pandemonium ending the meeting: "Go fishing! Workers, go fishing!" [16]

The socialists in the JWA now saw their role in the campaign as a sorry compromise; simultaneously, George's defeat also fanned the sparks of anarchism. Anarchists had frequently ridiculed the socialists for their collaboration in a capitalist institution—a political election. But, above all, the death sentence hanging over the seven men condemned in the Haymarket Affair and the hanging of four on November 11, 1887, made new anarchist converts and sharpened the ideological lines that had been hitherto blurred. Anarchism also gradually infiltrated the Jewish Workers' Association, creating an open split in July 1887, and the end of the group as such.

The thought of the leading anarchist of the time, Johann Most, was a mixture of Marx, Bakunin, and Proudhon. He had not created a consistent or reasoned philosophy, but his speeches electrified his listeners. Even his inability to speak Yiddish (he lectured in German) apparently did not diminish the hypnotic effect he exerted on many of the immigrant workers. His pamphlets, which were translated into Yiddish, also intoxicated his followers, especially the young Jewish radicals still under the spell of the *narodniki,* and were an important weapon in the antireligious attacks of the time. In October, his Jewish followers had organized an independent group called Pioneers of Liberty, formed to raise bail for the convicted Chicago Haymarket anarchists. The group soon came into conflict with social-democratic elements in the JWA and developed as an independent anarchist movement. This struggle polarized radicals and foreshadowed the coming turbulent battles between Jewish anarchists and socialists.

The social-democratic faction of the defunct JWA decided to reconstitute itself as an official component of the Socialist Labor party in New York. At the time, although most of the members were German, the party constitution permitted the formation of sections along linguistic or nationality lines. Seven such units already existed. Section Eight, the first Jewish section in the country, followed the pattern of the JWA and cut across lines of national origin, ostensibly uniting Yiddish-speaking "comrades," even though it was a heavily Germanized Yiddish, and sometimes Russian. Compared to its rather impotent parent body, which suffered from serious internal conflicts, Section Eight was a lively and confident unit.

Bernard Weinstein, in his reminiscences of this period,[17] had to admit that the anarchist Pioneers of Liberty had more members than Section Eight in 1888, and attracted more people to their Friday night meetings. Section Eight also suffered financial stringencies. The twenty-cent monthly dues paid by members went to the central party; no funds were left to hire halls. There were also political failures. The party ran Alexander Jonas as its mayoralty candidate but obtained a pathetically poor vote. Weinstein tried to comfort himself by remembering that few of the Jewish socialists were as yet citizens.[18] The anarchists, as usual, denounced the election. The socialists faced quite a different opposition from the Anglo-Jewish and Orthodox press. Garment manufacturers urged their workers to vote Republican to ensure a continuation of the high tariff, without which, they said, they would have to reduce wages.[19]

Section Eight also had to withstand the challenge of a small group of Russian radicals who had organized themselves into the Russian Progressive Association and clung together as Russians in spite of philosophical differences. Occasionally the Jewish problem came up for discussion. On January 9, 1887, for example, Nicholas Aleinikoff, who believed there was a Jewish as well as an economic problem, proposed the formation of a special Russian Jewish society to protect the interests of the Jewish immigrants, but opposed separate Jewish workers' organizations as undesirable.[20] The anarchist wing of the association opposed the union movement as the greatest obstacle to revolutionary salvation. Reverence for the revolutionary martyrs in Russia seems to have been the main force that held the group together, but it finally split in May 1888. The socialists within it, under the leadership of Louis Miller (who had been in the radical circle with Cahan), now decided to form a Russian-speaking section of the SLP, and much against the wishes of Section Eight, Section Seventeen came into being.

The leading members of Section Seventeen were Louis Miller (formerly Bandes), his brother Leo, Morris Hilkowitz (later Hillquit), his brother Jacob and, for a time, Joseph Barondess. Both sections were Jewish, Russian, radical, and cosmopolitan, but the meetings of Section Seventeen were conducted on a somewhat higher intellectual level. Some bitterness continued, but gradually both groups were drawn into election campaigns and union activity until the anarchist elements here, too, sheared off. Within a short time a Russian group called Samorassvetie (Self-education) was formed, including a number of the same people, and Section Seventeen disappeared, but not before it gave support to a federation effort.[21]

Section Eight, meanwhile, continued to prosper and Jewish branches were formed in Philadelphia, Chicago, Baltimore, and Boston, along the lines of the New York group. Yiddish materials were issued. Most important, it took the initiative in organizing a central Jewish labor body, Faraynikte Yidishe Geverkshaftn (United Hebrew Trades) in October 1888. Its formation was the most important single event in the early history of the American Jewish labor movement. The young visionaries realized that it would take decades to build a Jewish labor movement from the bottom up, educating individual workers, organizing them, and finally uniting them into one body. So, in the words of Hillquit, they were "forced to reverse the logical process and to attempt to build from the top down." [22]

Many factors contributed to this reverse process. Most serious was the virtual disintegration of all of the Jewish unions that had been formed. There had been unions of shirt makers, cloak operators, and bakery workers, but they had collapsed. Strikes had been quelled and, thanks to the constant flow of immigration, the mass of unorganized workers grew steadily. Jewish workers had not had any experience with collective bargaining and seemed unorganizable. Besides, few of the radical leaders spoke Yiddish well enough to embark on a broad program of propaganda, while the hostility of the radicals toward traditional religious beliefs and practices alienated most Jewish workers. Yet, some of the radical intellectuals yearned to make contact with the workers. They looked to the central federation of German workers—the United German Trades (Vereinigte Deutsche Gewerkschaften)—as their model. The UGT consisted of labor unions which were strong in several important industries in New York. Originally, it was formed primarily to support the German labor press, but gradually it broadened its work and became a vital factor in strengthening the union movement and spreading socialist views.

In September 1888, nineteen-year-old Jacob Magidow from Odessa, a member of Section Eight, proposed that the two Jewish sections—Eight and Seventeen—organize a federation among the Jewish workers. The basic idea of his proposal, he later wrote, "was simple: if the Jewish unions could be made to realize that other unions were ready to support them, that all of those other unions were organized for mutual aid, they would then feel more faith in themselves." [23] Magidow was also anxious to reverse the downward trend in labor standards in the Jewish trades and worried about the reputation that Jewish workers had acquired for working long hours.[24] The two sections agreed to cooperate in trying to create a Jewish trade union movement. Joining Magidow from Section Eight was Bernard Weinstein, a modest, shy, but utterly devoted member, also from Odessa, who worked alongside Samuel Gompers in a cigar factory. The "Russian" section was represented by Leo Bandes, a former *narodnik* who had served time in Russian prisons, and nineteen-year-old Morris Hillquit, recently arrived from Riga.

Before the first joint meeting, Hillquit and Weinstein had made a painstaking search of all remnants of Jewish unions in New York and found only two: typesetters and choral singers, with a combined membership of forty.[25] It was reported that these unions wanted to affiliate with the proposed central union. The typesetters' union, made up of workers of the struggling newspaper and job printing shops on the lower West Side, was only a few months old. The chorus singers worked hard during the day for low wages—the men mostly as shirtmakers, the women as garment finishers—and suffered from harsh treatment by theater managers. Undaunted by this slim foundation, lack of funds, and inexperience, on October 9, the youthful representatives formally organized the United Hebrew Trades.[26] Besides Magidow and Weinstein from Section Eight, and Hillquit and Bandes from Section Seventeen, there were two fraternal delegates from the United German Trades, one delegate from the typesetters, two from the choristers, and one from an actors' union who had answered the following call:

> It is time that the Jewish proletarian should know the protection of a central union to which he can apply for help in his many wage struggles, as well as for advice as to how to attach himself to the ranks of organized labor. It is time that such a central body should be called into being and the Jewish workman should have the opportunity more quickly to free himself from the "Pig Market" [labor exchange], to throw off the yoke of different kinds of contract systems ... and other living examples of the vile, capitalistic system of wage slavery.[27]

The declared triple aim of the new organization was: mutual aid and cooperation among the Jewish trade unions, the organization of new unions, and socialist propaganda among the Jewish workers. The delegates agreed to keep minutes in "Yiddish jargon." A committee was appointed to work out a constitution and platform. The United German Trades contributed ten dollars to the as yet empty treasury.

Just before adjournment, the delegate from the actors' union gave the new body its first taste of practical trade union politics.[28] In his request for affiliation and help from the new federation, the delegate attached certain conditions. Actors are artists, he explained, and cannot be expected to receive instruction in coarse and common Yiddish. The federation speaker would have to address them in German, the language of poets and thinkers. All eyes turned to Hillquit, who knew German perfectly—and Yiddish scarcely at all. Somewhat uncertainly, he nodded assent. But the delegate had yet another condition. "To have the attention and respect of the audience," he said quite calmly, "the speaker will have to appear in proper attire, that is, dressed in frock coat and silk hat." Hillquit heard this with consternation and suppressed humor. He could not guarantee *this* request and the actors' union met without benefit of a UHT representative. For years afterward, a favorite subject of debate was whether actors were wage workers with a legitimate place in the labor movement. It was finally decided that they were.

The UHT soon began working in earnest among the simon-pure proletariat. Its first effort was to revive the defunct shirtmakers' union. Prior to the mass Jewish immigration, the workers employed in the shirt industry had been almost exclusively American girls, earning between five and six dollars a week. By 1885, immigration forced wages down to three and four dollars. It will be recalled that shirt manufacturers were mostly German Jews who had found it both profitable and charitable to use the cheap immigrant labor; but instead of taking the workers into the factories, they gave work to outside contractors, and they, in turn, rented a two-room or three-room apartment and took in boarders, each with his own rented sewing machine. Many of the Russian-Jewish intellectuals—Hillquit, Louis Miller, Michael Zametkin—entered the ranks of the proletariat as shirtmakers. But the income was very meager. Work was seasonal and irregular and wages were paid "by the piece." Frequently workers wound up a month's work with an earnings deficit.

The first shirtmakers' union had been organized in 1884. It included both workers and contractors, but it did not last very long. In March 1886, another effort was made to organize the shirtmakers, but this time the union decided to fight against the contracting system by organizing a producers' cooperative that would work directly for the large manufacturers. By the end of 1886, practically all of the shirtmaker shops were organized; in December of that year, the union was strong enough to boycott two firms that refused to recognize it. Then, suddenly, the union collapsed, and there was apparently no further activity until May 1888,[29] when the Rahway, New Jersey, shirtmakers conducted a successful strike. This stimulated the New York workers to reorganize their union—but this fresh effort lasted only a few months. Then, on the iniative of the UHT, a union of shirtmakers was once again organized, and this time, it experienced steady growth. By March 1890, it boasted one thousand members, and in the same month, it successfully concluded a sixteen-day strike, which greatly strengthened its structure and prestige.

Union organizing was infinitely more difficult in the other branches of the needle trades, but gradually a technique of organization was developed, more unions were started, and representation in the UHT increased steadily. By March 1889, there were 1,200 UHT members and at the first congress of the Second (Socialist) International,[30] in July 1889, UHT delegate Louis Miller reported the following ten constituent unions: typographers, shirtmakers, actors, choristers, tailors (men's garments), dressmakers, knee-pants workers, mattress-makers, silk ribbon weavers, and musicians. By the beginning of 1890, there were 22 unions with 6,000 members.[31]

UHT's success with the knee-pants workers shows how the neophytes began to acquire practical techniques.[32] In 1890, there were about one thousand knee-pants makers in New York, all "green," and most of them illiterate. A sweatshop industry par excellence, knee-pants making was done entirely on the contracting system. Typically, a contractor employed about ten workers and operated his shop in his living quarters. His sole function was to procure bundles of cut garments from the manufacturer and have them made up by the workers. He did not furnish sewing machines, needles, or thread; the operators brought these. The work day—from dawn to dusk—brought the most experienced operators only six or seven dollars a week. Often the contractor would abscond with a week's pay; more often the worker would be discharged because he was not fast enough to suit the contractor, or would quit because of mistreatment or intolerable working conditions. Every time a knee-pants operator changed contractors, he was compelled to put his sewing machine on his back and carry it through the streets to his new place of employment. The patience of the workers finally gave out, and in the early part of 1890 they struck. The strike was spontaneous, without program, leadership, or organization. "It was," as Hillquit said, "a blind outbreak of revolt, and was destined to collapse if left to itself, sharing the fate of many similar outbursts in the past." But the UHT stepped in during the very first hours of the strike and took complete charge of the situation. Hillquit recalled:

> Our first step was to hire a meeting hall large enough to accommodate all of the strikers. There were about nine hundred, and we gathered them in from all shops and street corners. In the hall we held them in practically continuous session, day and night, allowing them only the necessary time to go home to sleep. We feared to let them go, lest they be tempted to return to work, and we entertained them all the time with speeches and such ... instruction and amusement as we could devise. While the continuous performance was going on in the main hall, we tried to bring order and system into the strike and to organize the strikers into a solid and permanent union.
>
> In consultation with the most intelligent men and women from the ranks of the strikers, we worked out a list of demands centering upon the employer's obligation to furnish sewing machines and other work tools at his own expense. Then we chose pickets, relief committees, and settlement committees, all operating under our direct supervision and guidance.... Our discourses on the principles of trade unionism and the philosophy of socialism were interspersed with elementary lessons in parliamentary procedure and practical methods of organization. We tried to pick out the most promising among them and train them for leadership of their fellows. The strike was a course of intensive training and education, but it was of short duration. After one week without a break in the ranks of the workers, the contractors weakened; one Saturday night they became panicky and stormed the meeting hall of the strikers in a body, demanding an immediate and collective settlement on the workers' terms.[33]

The UHT thus scored a great victory and was encouraged to new efforts in other fields. One of the most significant was the breakthrough in the organization of Jewish bakery workers.

In the early days of Jewish immigration, bakeshops had sprung up on the East Side, specializing in Jewish rye bread. The bakeries were in dark, moldy subcellers, without ventilation, and infested with rats. All of the work was done by hand. The few hundred Jewish workers were from Galicia, Hungary, and Poland, more "stolid, unemotional, irresponsive" than the bulk of Russian workers:[34]

They worked seventeen to eighteen hours a day, except on Thursday, when their "work day" began early in the morning and lasted until noon on Friday. They worked at the ovens naked from the waist up and slept in the bakery cellars. When they did not receive board and lodging, their wages averaged six to seven dollars a week. Their only leisure time was between making the dough and its rising, and these hours they spent in their favorite saloons, drinking beer and playing cards. The beer saloons, particularly one on the corner of Ludlow and Hester Streets, provided the only romance in their drab lives. Here were their social clubs and also their labor bureaus. Here they would exchange information about jobs and here also employers would come in quest of "hands." Pale-faced, hollow-chested, listless and brutified, they seemed to be hopeless material for organization and struggle. In 1887, the newly organized Bakery and Confectioner Workers' International Union of America had succeeded in enlisting a number of them into a Jewish local union, but the organization collapsed within a year, for a reason very characteristic of the workers' mentality. The United Hebrew Trades launched a new campaign to organize the bakers in 1889. After some preparatory propaganda, a strike was called. The principal demand of the strikers was for the six-day week, with one day of rest, on Saturdays, a radical demand in those days.[35]

The strike call met with a good general response and within a few days, the proprietors yielded. As in the case of the knee-pants makers, the workers were given an intensive course in the principles and methods of trade unionism, and within a few months, the union numbered four hundred members—practically all of the Jewish bakery workers. The union became their religion for a time.

A tragic incident [36] which occurred soon after the organization of the Jewish bakers' union called public attention to the revolting conditions in the bakeries of New York's East Side and led to important consequences in the field of labor legislation. Early one morning, the secretary of a newly organized union reported to Bernard Weinstein at the UHT office that a baker had collapsed while working at night and was still in the bake shop, critically ill. When Weinstein reached the bakery he found appalling conditions. Three emaciated and exhausted bakers were working at the side of their stricken comrade. Weinstein arranged to have the sick man taken to a hospital and reported the case to the Labor Department. An investigation of the bakeshops on the East Side followed, resulting in a sensational report condemning the inhuman labor conditions found in the shops, and branding them as a standing menace to public health.

In spite of its promising beginning, the bakers' union founded by the UHT, like so many early unions, had a short life. With the immediate objects of their strike attained, members lost interest and within a short time, the union disbanded. A new cycle then started: decline in labor standards, a new revolt, another strike, and a revival of the union. This process was repeated every two or three years for the next fifteen to twenty years until workers understood that unions could be much more than instruments of strikes. The bakers' union subsequently became one of the strongest, most progressive, and disciplined among the Jewish unions in America. An essential factor that contributed to eventual union stability was the consolidation of numerous branches of the needle-trade crafts into large unions embracing all parts of a related industry, such as the International Ladies' Garment Workers Union, extending over all branches of the manufacture of women's apparel, and the Amalgamated Clothing Workers Union, composed of all workers in the men's tailoring industry. This development, however, was still two decades away.

7. The Jewish Question and the Socialist International

American Jewish socialists of this early period did not consider it necessary to formulate their attitude toward specifically Jewish problems. However, the fact that they had helped to form separate Jewish unions and the UHT had provoked much discussion of the issue of separateness. The American Jewish socialist press and literature were being developed simultaneously with the Jewish trade union movement and were having a strong impact on Jewish life, but were not at all intended to create new Jewish traditions. They were mainly concerned with giving the Jewish worker a sense of his own worth and capacity to change the conditions of his life and a sense of his involvement in a large proletarian struggle. The formation of separate Jewish unions was an expedient. Nor was there any organizational framework uniting Jewish workers throughout the country (the UHT covered only Jewish workers in New York). By the end of the 1880's, many American cities had organized groups of Jewish workers, socialists, and anarchists, each with its periphery of unorganized workers and sympathizers, but there was no coordination among them. On August 18, 1890, members of the Jewish section of the Socialist Labor party proposed that the UHT convene a national congress of all organized Jewish workers in the United States. On October 4–6, the first such congress was held in New York, to which eighty-seven delegates from thirty-six organizations came, nine of them from outside New York City.

The walls of Clarendon Hall were bedecked with slogans reading, "The world is our fatherland, socialism our religion," and the resolutions, besides demanding the end of the sweating system, support of the eight-hour day and creation of a strike fund, urged all Jewish workers to join the Socialist Labor party.[1] A Hebrew Federation of Labor was formed to link together the fragmented movement. Cahan, who was chosen organizer, traveled as far west as Chicago to organize new unions. Enthusiasm ran high. Soon after the congress, the executive committee of the federation issued a statement of aims and purposes. The condition of the Jewish worker, it said, is infinitely worse than that of the American "wage slave." Thus, the major task of the federation was to

> equalize the Jewish worker with his American brother and to help him understand the labor question—the question of the enslaved class, to which he belongs. . . . There is no Jewish question in America. The only Jewish question which we recognize is the question, how to prevent the development of such "Jewish questions." Only because we alone, Yiddish-speaking citizens, can have an influence among the Jewish immigrants; only because we speak their language and are familiar with their lives—only because of this, are we organizing this special Jewish body. The Yiddish language is our tool; one of our goals is to erase all divisions between Jew and non-Jew in the world of the workers.[2]

This refusal of the Jewish socialists in America to think in terms of an ideologically Jewish base had an enormously important influence not only on the development of the Jewish labor movement, but also on the process of the absorption of Jewish workers into American life. The pull to become part of the "melting pot" was stronger than the pull to remain Jewish. The lack of a specifically Jewish ideology doomed the embryonic Hebrew Federation of Labor. Despite its early promise, there was no strong philosophical reason for a national movement of Jewish workers. Jewish workers were engulfed in anarchist-socialist strife and the struggle to establish and maintain unions. Within a year, the Hebrew Federation of Labor collapsed.

However, the issue of the "Jewish Question" was raised soon again— but this time in the context of the international socialist movement. Jewish affairs were not discussed at all at the first congress of the Second International, held in Paris in 1889. But Louis Miller, one of the two UHT delegates [3] gave a somewhat exaggerated picture of the labor situation in America, claiming that a "deep class-consciousness is rooted among Jewish workers as can be seen from the fact that the Jewish capitalist papers find it necessary, in order to exist, to hide behind socialist trappings." [4] He also tried to reassure the other socialists on the matter of Yiddish, explaining that Jewish socialists had to use it because it was the only language they knew, but they had no intention of secluding themselves and, in fact, participated fully in the socialist movement in England, the United States, and Russia.

The Second International was organized in 1889 and signaled the swift rise of Marxist socialism in Europe. Created as a federation of national sections, representatives of socialist parties and labor unions dealt with problems of common interest at periodic congresses, and formulated programs and goals which, it was hoped, would achieve the eventual triumph of socialism. Representation in the International was the aim of all socialist parties and was particularly important for Jewish socialists in the early stages of their development, for it meant prestige, recognition, and the right to enter the European socialist movement.[5] It also meant socialist sanction to exist, for many socialist organizations questioned that right because of the lack of a Jewish territorial base and the age-old difficulties of defining Jews in national terms. Nevertheless, the United Hebrew Trades and a few Jewish socialist branches had representatives at the congresses in 1889, 1891, and 1893.

The Jewish issue was raised following the publication of a statement "To All the Jewish Unions and Labor Organizations in America," in the New York *Arbayter Tsaytung*, June 26, 1891, after the UHT had decided to send a delegate to the Socialist International in Brussels:

> At a time when the Jew is everywhere regarded and treated as a savage beast, hounded and persecuted at every step, when the anti-Semites are shouting in unison that all Jews are only bloodsuckers, thieves, robbers, and swindlers, that none of them earns an honest living—at such a time, it is more important than ever to show the world that the Jews have not only workers, but also a labor movement, and a progressive and strong one at that. The United Hebrew Trades of New York has thoroughly understood the need and usefulness of sending a representative to the Jewish labor movement to the Congress of the International in Brussels, in order to show the world what Jewish workers can accomplish in a country where they have the same rights as everyone else.

Abraham Cahan was the delegate to this congress from both the UHT and the Jewish section of the Socialist Labor party. By this time, he had come a long way from a sometime *narodnik* and anarchist, having had nine years' experience in the thick of Jewish socialist activity. Interestingly, he asked and received permission from the UHT to place the "Jewish Question" on the agenda of the congress: What shall be the attitude of the organized working classes of all countries toward the Jewish question? This marked the first time the world-wide socialist movement was to consider the "Jewish Question."

At first, Cahan received a cordial reception in Brussels.[6] Socialists were gratified to hear about the emergence of a Jewish proletariat in the United States. Then, in order to clarify the question he had placed on the agenda, Cahan circulated information on the Jewish labor movement in America and on the persecution of Jews in various countries. He also urged the delegates to condemn anti-Semitism.

In raising this question, Cahan identified himself, not as a Jew, but as a worker. Like Miller, he discounted the use of "the German-Jewish dialect" (Yiddish) by members of the UHT, adding that "our organization has nothing to do with either religion or nationality, and received its name only because of the language spoken by our members." [7] Cahan reported a membership of about 30,000 Jewish workers in the UHT and also referred to uncounted Jewish workers in American unions. "Our aim is to bring the Jewish worker to the same economic level as that enjoyed by the American worker." Cahan added, "We are very pleased that our workers stand together with all other workers and do not separate themselves. . . . The quicker we merge with our American brothers, the quicker we can make disappear the national grouping. . . . Capitalism . . . is our worst enemy and Christian and Jewish workers must march together against it."

But despite his reassurances, the atmosphere soon chilled. Murmurs of disapproval vibrated around him. To his astonishment, Cahan found that strong opposition was coming from certain Jews at the congress.

The issue was a delicate and potentially explosive one for the International—especially for certain of its Jewish delegates who feared that Cahan's resolution asking for a declaration of sympathy for Jewish workers would raise embarrassing questions and play into the hands of the enemies of socialism. These enemies, they reasoned, would say that socialism itself was a Jewish product. If the congress were to adopt Cahan's resolution, they would say the congress, too, had become a Jewish affair.[8] Victor Adler, an Austrian social democrat, and Paul Singer, a German social-democratic leader, both from well-to-do assimilated Jewish families, urged him to withdraw his resolution. Rabbi Dreyfus of Brussels likewise pressed him. But Cahan was adamant: socialists should not be frightened by lies and libels, he insisted. Point 4 on the "Jewish Question" remained on the agenda, and Cahan opened the discussion of the issue by requesting a firm stand against discrimination:

> Socialists must adopt an attitude toward the attempt to stir up a war between Jews and Christians. They must express their sympathy for Jewish workers who found themselves in a state of permanent war against the sweatshop system in the United States. . . . All the Russian newspapers attack the Jews and claim that the socialist workers detest them. . . . It is asked that you deny this, to say that you are the enemies of all exploiters, whether Christians or Jews—and that you have as much sympathy for Jewish workers as for Christian workers.[9]

After this appeal, the Belgian socialist Jean Volders, probably inspired by Adler and Singer, took the floor and said that such a proposition was superfluous at a socialist congress, since socialists are everywhere in favor of the oppressed and exploited and against the oppressors and exploiters.[10] Discussion of the Jewish question has only one purpose: to serve as a counter-irritant to the social question by exciting one group against another, who have the same interests regardless of whether they are Jews or Christians. The anti-Semitic campaign, he added, is the invention of big capitalism; therefore, a debate on the Jewish question is not necessary.[11]

To the argument that such a resolution was superfluous among socialists, Cahan reminded delegates that a discussion of militarism among socialists was also superfluous, yet it was an issue that the congress dealt with. He continued, "I urge that you repudiate anti-Semitism, that you declare for the whole world that you condemn every form of Jewish persecution." His speech was interrupted several times by applause, which encouraged Cahan to believe that his resolution would pass. But he was mistaken. The discussion took a strange course. A French delegate, Paul

Argyriades, who carried considerable weight, declared that there existed not only anti-Semitism, but "philo-Semitism," and insisted that the congress disapprove "the provocations of certain Semites," as well as those of anti-Semites. He also made malicious remarks about Jewish bankers.

Cahan, stunned by this notion, once more took the floor to ask Argyriades where he dug up the word "philo-Semitism." Where did he see Christians persecuted in the interests of Jews? Where did he ever hear about Jews organizing pogroms against gentiles? Or about privileges granted exclusively to Jews? "And why should Jewish bankers be singled out? A banker is a banker, whether he be Jewish or gentile. And what has the origin of bankers to do with the Jewish question?" "Very much indeed," retorted Argyriades.[12] Cahan appealed to the congress to ignore the "unsocialist ideas" of Argyriades, and to vote his own motion. When he left the rostrum, a heated debate still continued, but no record of it has been preserved. The resolution which terminated the debate dismayed and disillusioned him.

Argyriades proposed that both anti-Semitic and "philo-Semitic excitations" be condemned. In the final text, the resolution [13] affirmed that Jewish workers could achieve emancipation only by uniting with socialists of their respective countries in the class struggle. It also condemned "anti-Semitic and philo-Semitic outbursts as one of the means by which the capitalist class and reactionary governments seek to divert the socialist movement and divide the workers." The question posed by Cahan "has no place here and passes to the order of the day." Commenting on the resolution, the London *Times* (August 20, 1891) stated that Argyriades' amendment, "insofar as it had any definite bearing on the Jewish question, was deprived of any point it ever possessed." The *New York Times* of the same date called it a "diffuse resolution."

Cahan was shattered by the frank unwillingness of world socialism to express solidarity with the specifically Jewish socialist movement. Yet, for the next thirty-five years, he remained absolutely silent about his experience. In his letters to the *Arbayter Tsaytung*, not a word of it appeared. Only in his memoirs did he finally reveal this silence, explaining that he preferred not to share publicly the details of the debate.[14] Obviously, the details were too unpleasant to share with the rank and file of a struggling movement and would give the anti-socialist press more ammunition in their attacks on radical movements. However, the British organ of the social democrats, *Justice*, reported quite openly its disappointment while the congress was still sitting: "There appears to be a strong feeling against the Jews in the congress. This is a pity. Even on the grounds of tactics, apart from general humanity, we need the poor Jews to beat the rich Jews." [15] The Yiddish papers in the United States "washed over" the whole episode.[16]

Interestingly enough, the resolution was severely criticized by Plekhanov for putting anti-Semitism on the same plane as philo-Semitism and for the failure of the International to make a strong attack on anti-Semitism.[17] The ambivalence of the International on the Jewish question is perhaps best revealed by the fact that its official resolution was never formally revoked but, rather, was supplanted by events—particularly the aftermath of World War I. Moreover, the Brussels resolution is probably unique in the annals of international socialism, in that special sympathy for an oppressed people is condemned by the same body that often expressed solidarity with other oppressed peoples.

After the congress, Plekhanov and the Liberation of Labor Group in Geneva wrote a strong condemnation of the resolution [18] and expressed the hope that the next congress would revise it. Plekhanov attended the Third Congress of the International in Zurich in 1893, but the resolution was not revised. The question was laid open at the Fourth Congress in 1896 in London in the form of a report from a Rumanian Jewish social-democratic group called Lumina, in which the whole matter of Jewish disabilities and denial of equality was propounded.[19] The group did not attend the congress but said that "the International must become interested in and respond to the Jewish question. It must open a discussion of the issue." This was as much a thrust against the anti-Semitic tendencies in the Rumanian Social-Democratic party as a challenge to the International. The great French socialist Jean Juarès, who came as a delegate to the International for the first time at this Congress, made a speech dealing with oppressed peoples, acknowledging the justice of Lumina's analysis.[20] But nothing tangible was done in behalf of Jews. Nor was there any coverage of this matter in the English or German translation of the deliberations.[21]

Thus, although Cahan had exposed a raw nerve in the socialist perception of the Jewish condition, neither he nor most other Jewish socialists at the time saw any fundamental flaws in the Marxist answer to the Jewish predicament. Or, perhaps, a flaw was perceived but repressed, because of the insecurity of the Jewish socialists present at the congress. It was painfully obvious that few socialists were willing to deal with the phenomenon of anti-Semitism, except as a footnote in the large Marxist canon.

The whole question of the attitude of socialists toward the Jewish question is one of wracking complexity and suspicious ambiguity. A case can be made—and has been—showing evidence of a strong anti-Semitic tradition in socialist thought and behavior.[22] In large part, this was, as the penetrating analyst of socialism George Lichtheim has put it, "in its origins, the poisoned root of a tree planted—alongside the more familiar tree of liberty—in the decades following the French Revolution." [23] The Enlightenment following the Revolution, to which Jews owed their liberty, also brought about an economic upheaval, in which some Jews rose to prominence as financiers and industrialists. The unleashing of individualism from the outworn constraints of the old order seemed to confer disproportionately great benefits upon Jews, already a widely hated group. This formed the basis of the anti-Semitism of Charles Fourier, one of the founders of socialism. The emancipation of Jews, he said, was among "the most shameful" of all "the recent vices" of contemporary society.

This tradition in French socialism, which, of course, antedated Marx, was part of the overflow of hatred heaped upon Jews by the casualties of the French Revolution. They saw Jews as main beneficiaries, profiting from the misfortunes of the losers and disrupting stable forms, ranks, and relationships. International finance, commodity exchanges, mass production, free trade, international news agencies, banking—all of which were part of a process that dissolved the old stable order and venerable symbols—were seen as "Jewish phenomena." [24]

The Industrial Revolution in England was no more made by Jews than was the French Revolution, but there were the Rothschilds, spread across Europe, the Pereiras in France and Austria, and somewhat later, the Hirschs in Turkey, and the Poliakovs in Russia—conspicuous, restless, and risk-taking men. The very fact that Jews had not yet gained equal rights, but could be audacious and prominent in industry and finance only intensified the resentment and hatred toward the Jew-upstart on the part of those who were left behind.

It was a favorite argument with the early socialists that capitalism had indeed abolished feudalism, only to re-establish a neo-feudalism, which was bound to perpetuate the distinction between the haves and have-nots and plunge the poor into untold penury. In this formulation, Jews were destined to become the feudal lords of the modern world—Alphonse Toussenel's "industrial-financial feudalism." In their horror of a world tossed by unnerving change and the anonymity of industrial society, the pre-Marxist socialists—Toussenel, Pierre Leroux, and Proudhon—fused their sense of menace onto the Jew and heaped on him the stigma that had previously been the province of the Christian churches. They offered familiar-sounding phrases such as: "The Jew is, so to speak, a traitor by definition": Jews carefully shun agriculture in order to devote themselves exclusively to "mercantile depravities"; "Europe is entailed to the domination of Israel"; "The Jew is by temperament an anti-producer. . . . He is an intermediary, always fraudulent and parasitic, who operates in trades as in philosophy, by means of falsification, counterfeiting, horse-trading." Marx then built up yet another structure of anti-Jewish images and concepts which have become embedded in socialist thought.

The young Karl Marx began writing in the 1840's when the ideas of the French socialists were well-known and influential. This was also the period in which certain Jewish bankers were prominent in the Orléanist regime (1830–48), when it was frequently said that the Rothschilds and their associates controlled the government.[25] During that period, Marx's fundamental ideas on the Jewish question were expressed in his famous essay, "Zur Judenfrage," written in 1844 in response to two essays ("Die Judenfrage") by the German philosopher Bruno Bauer. Bauer took the position that Jews were not ready for emancipation and, in fact, did not deserve it. Only by giving up their "exclusive religion, morality, and customs," only by surrendering "their constricting oriental faith," could they qualify for emancipation, according to Bauer.[26]

Marx,[27] on the other hand, says that Jews *are* entitled to political equality, since political—in contradistinction to "human"—emancipation, does not require the renouncing of religion. Religion, of course, is a defect, but this defect is no reason to deny emancipation to Jews. But, for Marx, political emancipation was no emancipation at all. It is not a thoroughgoing emancipation from religion, but the only form of emancipation available within the existing order. Marx then goes into the heart of his attack: the Jew has already attained a remarkable degree of emancipation, appropriating to himself financial power to such a degree that the "practical Jewish spirit has become the practical spirit of Christian nations." His language becomes scorching: the secular morality of the Jews is egoism, their secular religion is huckstering, their secular god is money. The real God of the Jews is the bill of exchange. "Money is the jealous God of Israel, before whom no other god may exist." For Marx, Judaism is an expression of a self-alienated society, not yet emancipated humanly: "It was only then [when Christianity had made the alienation of man from himself and from nature theoretically possible] that Judaism could attain universal domination and could turn alienated man and alienated nature into *alienable*, saleable objects in thrall to egoistic need and huckstering."

The Jew thus represents that which has destroyed the cohesion of society, replacing the proper relation of the human personality to other people and to things by the factor of money and the market, which atomize society. Marx's solution is a return to social cohesion. This involves the elimination of "Judaism," which, in Marx's view, has become the embodiment of *Schacherei*—huckstering. The Jewish problem can thus be solved only by doing away with the present social system, or what Marx calls "the Jewish limitations of society." Moreover, as soon as "society succeeds in abolishing the *empirical* essence of Judaism, the huckster and its basis, the Jew, will become *impossible*, because the subjective of Judaism, namely practical needs, will have been humanized. . . . The *social* emancipation of the Jew is the *emancipation of society from Judaism*." Ultimately, Jews, whom Marx defines as a "caste," will disappear with the disappearance of capitalism.

Marx was then only twenty-five, not yet a fully developed socialist or communist, and quite anxious, as were many Jewish intellectuals of the time, to divest himself of all Jewish ties, associations, and the fact of his Jewish birth. (He was baptized in 1824, but his Jewish origins exposed him to anti-Jewish taunts throughout his life.) His essay is so shockingly full of the standard anti-Jewish stereotypes that it has often been interpreted as an expression of the self-hatred of a Jew who cannot be a non-Jew. Anti-Semitism was particularly virulent in post-Napoleonic Germany and bred self-contempt among many of those who were its targets. More generous critics have described Marx's essay as part of his immature and un-developed work. But, that aside, the influence of his essay on subsequent socialist thinking about Jews has been immense. The same contempt for Jews has been pronounced in the work of later socialists, while Marx's own essay has been read by "hundreds of thousands, if not millions, of his adepts." [28] Thus, one scholar concludes, Marx "contributed powerfully to provoke or to strengthen anti-Jewish prejudice among his Christian followers, and to estrange from their own people a good number of his Jewish admirers." [29]

Franz Mehring, an influential German socialist who wrote a massive biography of Marx, referred to Marx's essay as having "greater value than the huge pile of literature on the Jewish problem which appeared since that time." Karl Kautsky a well-known German socialist theoretician who influenced Lenin, used Marx's language in referring to the Jews in Galicia and Russia as a "caste." Lenin used the same word and said repeatedly that the solution of the Jewish problem in Russia should take the same course that it followed in Western Europe—namely, "their assimilation with the surrounding population."

Marx's analysis gave socialist thinkers an easy way out—to ignore or minimize the Jewish problem. It also gave Jewish-born socialists justifica-tion for assimilating and for ignoring the needs of Jewish masses in Western Europe, as well as in Russia. Those who were more sensitive—for example, Moses Hess, a contemporary of Marx, and later, the Bundists, who struggled against Lenin over the issue of Jewish national autonomy—were treated contemptuously by fellow socialists.

In the Bund struggle with Lenin, no one quoted from Marx's essay "for fear that its outspoken and quite vulgar anti-Semitism must prove out of place in a social-democratic audience." [30] The Bund later advanced the opinion that the views expressed in "Zur Judenfrage" were out of date, but Marx did not modify his ideas about Jews or Judaism. After 1845, in various articles, some written anonymously, he concentrated his fire on Jewish finance. In at least three anonymous articles in the New York *Tribune* (November 9 and 22, 1855; January 4, 1856), he analyzed the alleged power of Jewish financiers and the network of Jewish banks in Europe. From 1848 on, Marx saw the Jews chiefly as a financial and reactionary group. He showed an extraordinary interest in Jewish bankers, describing them as latter-day moneychangers backing every tyranny in the world. But he assiduously avoided differentiating Jews: in abusive lan-guage, *all* were identified with the exploiting Jewish bourgeoisie. Par-ticularly insulting slurs on Jews are also found in Marx's correspondence with Engels. Moreover, he never made any attempt to study or investigate the condition of the Jewish working masses.[31]

During the last ten years of his life, Marx could hardly have avoided knowing that there was a large Jewish proletariat in Russia and a smaller but significant one in England. During those years, he was keenly interested in Russia and studied the Russian language and Russian social and economic institutions. He must have known something of the life of the Jews in the Pale. Moreover, he was living in London during this period and it is scarcely possible that he knew nothing of the struggle of the Jewish workers in the East End. Articles on the Jewish proletariat were appearing in the socialist press during this time, and a voracious reader like Marx could hardly have missed all of them. The distinguished scholar Edmund Silberner has unraveled some very interesting evidence bearing on this.[32]

It is known that Marx was a reader of *V'period*, which was edited in London in 1875 and 1876 by his friend, the famous Russian philosopher and social revolutionary, Peter Lavrov. Lavrov, it will be remembered, was one of the few socialists interested in the Jewish socialist movement, and *V'period* published material on developments in this movement. An almost complete file of *V'period* was found in Marx's private library and Silberner points to two issues particularly—Numbers 37 and 38—to which Marx had drawn Engels' attention. These issues contain articles on the possible unification of the two rival internationals, a matter in which Marx was keenly interested. In those issues there also appeared an article called "The Foundations of a Social-Revolutionary Association of the Jewish Workers in London" and Aaron Lieberman's famous appeal, "To the Intelligent Young Men of Israel." Silberner also mentions a German socialist review, the *Jahrbuch für Sozialwissenschaft und Sozialpolitik*, which also dealt with the revolutionary movement among Jews. Marx also knew this *Jahrbuch*. Thus, his absolute refusal to confront the issue of Jewish working people cannot have been caused by his lack of awareness. Moreover, although he often expressed sympathy for oppressed peoples, he never did so in behalf of oppressed Jews, not even during the terrible pogroms of 1881.[33]

Cahan was apparently not aware either of Marx's judeophobia or of the substantial anti-Semitic strain in socialist notions about Jews. He said he had come with a "heart full of international love" and was shocked by what he heard and saw in Brussels. Moreover, at the time that Cahan was in Europe, political anti-Semitism was sweeping Germany, France, and Austria and carried a number of socialists in its wash, for anti-Semitic political leaders were arousing the masses against Jewish capitalists (just as was happening in Russia), and socialists were not eager to quarrel with popular hatred of the Rothschilds or to discriminate between anti-capitalism and anti-Semitism. The very belated reaction of socialists to the Dreyfus affair reveals this reluctance. Not until 1898 did socialists acknowledge that the royalist-military-Catholic attack on the republic was using anti-Semitism to undermine a form of government this bloc despised. Even then, some were afraid to have the Socialist party come to the defense of a wealthy Jew. In addition, such leading socialist periodicals as *La Revue Socialiste, Le Socialiste,* and *La Petite République* lent their support to anti-Semitic literature, while many leading socialists were sympathetic to the work of Edouard Drumont, the chief architect of modern anti-Semitism, who called anti-Semitic socialist appeals to win over the masses "the social function of anti-Semitism." For many socialists, anti-Semitism was coiled around the same growths as popular prejudices. Moreover, as in Russia, some of the most vehement attacks on Jews came from other Jews, alienated intelligentsia, children in revolt against bourgeois families, who were struggling to find a new home in the trans-national proletariat. Like Marx, they supported certain struggles of national liberation but strongly rejected the possibility of *Jewish* national liberation, believing that the only road to genuine Jewish emancipation lay in complete assimilation. Moreover, not until 1905, with the end of the Dreyfus affair and the creation of a single socialist party in France, did the French socialists renounce anti-Semitism.

In the German socialist movement,[34] there were frequent manifestations of anti-Semitism in the 1870's and 1880's, although the movement as a whole was opposed to political anti-Semitism. Among the more important German socialists who showed a definite anti-Jewish bias were Johann von Schweitzer, Wilhelm Hasselmann, Rudolf Calwer, and Franz Mehring. As early as 1862, Moses Hess complained bitterly about anti-Jewish feeling in the ranks of German socialists. Generally speaking, the attacks follow Marx in showing that the Jew and capitalist exploiter are synonymous, with the party press reprinting the well-known anti-Jewish passages from Marx's essay.

The manifestations of open anti-Jewish feeling diminished in the 1880's and 1890's, and German socialists opposed anti-Semitic parties, but they believed that, in the last analysis, anti-Semitism served to advance the cause of socialism—very much like the *narodniki* in Russia who welcomed the pogroms. Red-baiting which was said to be encouraged by Bismarck in the 1880's was justified: "In this respect, too, the Imperial Chancellor is proving to be a revolutionary despite himself. On the path that he incited the masses to follow, the Jews are being killed *today*, and tomorrow it will logically be the turn of the court chaplains, imperial chancellors, kings, emperors, and all the rest of the 'unproductive' gang." [35]

The historian Mehring warned particularly against the "dangers" and "brutalities" that "philo-Semitism" commits against everyone who opposes capitalism. He also felt certain that anti-Semitism would pull hundreds of thousands into the social movement, which they would enter as anti-Semites and come out as social democrats. In 1893, a year after the movement officially condemned anti-Semitism and the same year in which Auguste Bebel made a long analysis of anti-Semitism at the Social

Democratic party congress, Wilhelm Liebknecht said: "Yes, the anti-Semites plow and sow, and we Social Democrats will reap. Their successes are therefore not at all unwelcome to us." In the same year, after the spectacular electoral victory of the anti-Semites, *Vorwärts*, the central organ of the party, observed:

> Anti-Semitism . . . is the last phase of the dying capitalist society. . . . Barbarous as it [anti-Semitism] is, it is against its will a bearer of culture—cultural *manure*, in the truest sense of the word, for social democracy. Let us therefore rejoice over the successes of anti-Semitism, which are a heavy blow for all other capitalist parties, almost as much as we do over our own. These enemies are our best friends; the more fiercely they attack us, the greater service do they do us, and the more quickly do they dig their own grave.

Bebel's resolution, passed unanimously by the party congress at Cologne in the same year, conveyed the same meaning, though perhaps in less toxic language:

> Social Democracy opposes anti-Semitism as a *movement which is directed against the natural development of society*, but *despite* its reactionary character and *against* its will, it exerts an ultimately *revolutionary* effect, because the petty-bourgeois and small-farmer strata of society, who are aroused against the Jewish capitalists by the anti-Semitic movement, must finally realize *that their enemy is not merely the Jewish capitalist but the capitalist class as a whole, and that only the attainment of Socialism can free them from their misery.*[36]

Why such groups *must* recognize that socialism is preferable to anti-Semitism is not explained. After the Russian pogroms of 1904–05, Bebel seems to have realized, for the first time, the counterrevolutionary potentialities of anti-Semitism, but believed that such a force "in Germany will never have a chance to exert a decisive influence on the life of state or society."

The Internationals, too, condemned anti-Semitism after the outbreak of World War I, under persistent prodding by Jewish socialist movements, and as a result of splits within the International, which made even socialist Zionists desirable as members to fill depleted ranks.

The positions taken by the International regarding the national question and the Jewish question were to have an important effect on the position it eventually took regarding Jewish representation. The efforts to gain recognition—and the attendant frustrations—are enmeshed in the nationality issue and the complex forces behind the resistance toward condemning anti-Semitism. All of these matters constitute an important chapter in the history of Jewish socialism.

In 1868, the First International through its official organ *Vorbote* had endorsed the idea of national self-determination. The International was seen as a society of equal nations, a federation of equally free collectives. The smallest nation, in this view, must be given full guarantees of free and independent existence, while each nationality, being an organic part of the large human family, must contribute its share to the common culture. The International was thus actively sympathetic to all the national movements of liberation of the period: Polish, Irish, Italian. Moreover, nationality came to mean more than political entities. Politically dependent nations, such as Finland, Australia, and South Africa enjoyed full national status within this definition.[37]

The delegates at Brussels in 1891, however much or little they were motivated by anti-Jewish feelings, accepted the conventional socialist position on the necessity of Jewish assimilation. They were convinced that the Jewish question had nothing to do with nationality, that it was not relevant to the interests of the International, and that the problem would solve itself.[38]

In 1893, Cahan again represented the UHT at the International in Zurich; he was joined by nine delegates of Jewish trade unions in England. Also present at this congress was Jacob Stechenberg, the delegate of the Jewish Social-Democratic Workers of Lemberg and Cracow, the first representative of a Jewish social-democratic group. Jewish social-democratic circles from the Russian Pale were first represented at the London International in 1896 but not as *Jewish* socialists. Unable to send their own delegates, Jewish socialists in Warsaw, Minsk, Vilna, and Smorgon arranged for members of Plekhanov's Liberation of Labor group (in exile) to represent them in London.[39] This congress also received the first report sent by the Russian Jewish labor movement even before its own component parts were officially unified in the Bund, a report which made a very favorable impression on the Russian delegates.[40]

References to contacts between Jewish workers and the International are made in letters from Pavel Akselrod, Plekhanov's colleague in the Liberation of Labor and a leading Russian socialist. In one such letter to an Israel Peskin in 1893, Akselrod complains that Russian workers have no contacts with the International, that they have failed to express their solidarity with other workers and socialists. "It is time," he writes, "that Russian social democrats, like Jewish socialists, show European comrades that we are no longer Asiatics and are ready to stand with the international proletarian army." [41] The Jewish workers, even before the formal organization of the Bund (1897), were considerably ahead of the Russian movement. The organization of Jewish *kassy* (self-help funds or unions) was already well advanced by 1893, and in that year, when Engels died, over one thousand workers, representing twenty-seven *kassy*, held a memorial meeting in Vilna and sent a message to the International.[42]

From the time of its founding, the Bund tried to send the largest possible delegations, and by 1900, had already achieved strong representation at the International. In that year, twelve of the twenty-nine mandates held by the entire Russian delegation were held by the Bund.[43] In anticipation of the Paris congress, the "Foreign Committee of the Bund" issued a statement which reveals the importance it attached to representation in the International:

> We have become a power which plays no minor role in the Russian revolutionary movement. We have therefore the right to be represented by a large delegation which would express our relative strength, our activities, our real significance. Let us see to it that it be recognized. We must not lag behind the others; let us make use of our right and fulfill our duty.[44]

The Bund was the largest single bloc in the Russian delegation at this congress, but in 1903, it severed its connection with the Russian Social-Democratic Labor party because of the latter's refusal to accept the Bund's nonterritorial stand on Jewish cultural autonomy, a position which had crystallized in 1901. At the 1904 congress in Amsterdam, the question of the Bund's status as an unaffiliated Jewish movement arose for the first time. The Russian national section had two votes—one for the Marxist Social Democrats, the other for the non-Marxist Social Revolutionaries. Since the Bund was no longer affiliated with the former and could not join the latter because of ideological differences, the Bund had no place to go. At the same time, it refused to leave the Russian national section. Eventually, a compromise was worked out, with the Bund and Social Democrats splitting the vote. The Bund rejoined the Social Democrats in 1906, but a year later, when it tried to achieve independence at the International, it failed.

In 1906, the International had accepted the "national" as against the "state" principle of representation. It regarded as nationalities "the agglomerations of peoples whose aspirations toward autonomy and moral unity, the result of a long historical tradition, have persisted despite their dependence upon one or more governments." Thus, the Polish, Finnish, Australian, and South African delegations enjoyed full national status. However, the International never recognized the possibility of representation on an extra-territorial basis and so foreclosed the possibility of accepting a Jewish national representation prior to the establishment of the State of Israel.

In 1907, Poale Zion (the Labor Zionist party) challenged this formulation, asserting that the decision of 1906 to recognize nationalities and not limit delegations to states should serve as the basis for Jewish representation.[45] The Jewish worker, they said, was in every respect equal to the workers of other nationalities. They were supported on this issue by the territorialist branch of the Jewish labor movement—the Jewish Socialist Workers' party (called SERP from the Russian initials of its name)—and by the Zionist Socialist Workers party (SS), and all three parties became enmeshed in a bitter controversy with the Bund over it. The three parties believed in the national character of the world Jewish proletariat, while the Bund was hostile to this notion as well as to the search for a *territorial* solution to the problems of Jewish insecurity. The Bund was anchored in Russia and favored a Diaspora solution to the

Jewish question. For its part, the International, unwilling or unable to sift out these important differences, referred the applications of the three parties to the Russian section, on the assumption that they were *Russian* Jewish organizations. Ber Borochov the prominent Poale Zion leader, vehemently attacked this decision, which, in effect, delivered the Jewish parties to the mercies of the Bund and Russian Social Democrats. Inevitably, the Russians condemned the territorialist trends within the Jewish parties and refused to admit them to the Russian section.[46] The SS then appealed to the International Socialist Bureau for reconsideration of the issue and a temporary compromise was agreed upon: the SS was granted a "consultative" voice. This was a significant victory, but it was short lived, for the Russian branches utterly rejected the idea, and the SS was cast out of the International.

The Zionist and territorialist parties then launched a campaign to establish a Jewish section within the International, with independent representation of all Jewish proletariat. Again, there was intra-Jewish conflict. The Bund argued that such a section was impossible as well as undesirable. The International was a political not a cultural organization and could not admit extra-territorial peoples. Moreover, the Bund claimed that the Jewish parties would use the International as a forum for their views, which the Bund found "reactionary." For their part, the Zionist and territorialist parties claimed the right of representation and accused the International of being discriminatory. Borochov asked the embittered question: "Are we, the Jewish workers, to blame, if due to certain historical reasons it has become our fate to shed our blood for socialist freedom not in one country, but in all countries?" [47]

The struggle, led by Poale Zion, lasted until 1911, but the International did not yield. The Bund's opposition and the International's refusal to accept extra-territorial nations fitted nicely into the prevailing socialist attitude toward the Jewish question and, in fact, fortified it. Assimilation of Jews was the accepted solution; recognition of a specifically Jewish socialist movement was out of the question.

Emigration and immigration of workers, which were first discussed at the Amsterdam congress, also agitated Jewish delegates. The Bund, particularly, played a vital role in this struggle. At Amsterdam, a large bloc voted against immigration restrictions, but American, Dutch, and Australian delegates favored restriction of the immigration of "backward nationalities." The Bund advanced its own proposals at the Stuttgart congress in 1907, issuing a special brochure containing a detailed analysis of the issue and introducing its own resolution. Faced with the mass emigration of Russian Jews to America, the Bund was obliged to protect the immigrants from discriminatory legislation, as well as underscore a principle. Stressing persecution as a major cause of mass emigration, the Bund's resolution proclaimed the right of all workers, regardless of race or nationality, to escape from starvation, persecution, and pogroms and to seek refuge in more hospitable lands. Restrictive legislation "clouds the conscience of the working class, diverts the proletariat from the class struggle, and creates a favorable climate for the development of racial and national conflict." [48] The final resolution adopted at Stuttgart was essentially a compromise, not very well received by the Bund. It distinguished between individual immigrants and the mass importation of unorganized labor, favoring the curtailment of the latter because of its injurious effect on the worker's standard of living and the free immigration of the former.

On the question of anti-Semitism, the Bund had submitted a petition to the steering committee of the Paris congress in 1900, urging a message of sympathy for the persecuted Jews of Russia, but the congress took no action, although this same congress did not hesitate to adopt a resolution, moved by Rosa Luxemburg, expressing its "close and ardent solidarity" with the oppressed Armenian people.[49] In 1901, the International Socialist Bureau protested the restrictions on Jewish admissions to Russian universities. Belatedly, in 1903, after the Kishinev pogrom, the Bureau addressed an appeal to the workers of all countries to protest the massacres and denounce the Russian government. Yet even this appeal avoided the word anti-Semitism, and did not specifically urge non-Russian workers to fight anti-Semitism in their own countries.[50] At the next International in Amsterdam in 1904, several delegates submitted a resolution "against discriminatory legislation and persecution of the Jews of Russia," [51] but the official record does not contain its text—an indication that it was not considered very important. The 1891 Brussels resolution "condemning anti-Semitic and philo-Semitic outbursts" was never formally abrogated by subsequent congresses.

It is difficult to avoid Silberner's conclusion, namely, "that prior to World War I, the International was rather hostile to the Jewish cause." [52] As late as 1915, a Labor Zionist memorandum complained that "in the labor movement in Western Europe, the attempts to secure the active sympathy of the proletariat for the Jewish cause are occasionally met by the uneasy feeling that it is desired to convert social democracy into a bodyguard of the Jews." After World War I, of course, the Jewish problem took on dimensions that could not be ignored or buffered by formulas "condemning anti-Semitic and philo-Semitic outbursts." Furthermore, the International was weakened by the split with the communists and welcomed Jewish workers and Labor Zionists to its reduced ranks. During and after the war, various socialist conferences even endorsed the right of the Jewish people to create a national home in Palestine. More recently, however, a new cycle of overlapping anti-Jewish, anti-Israel and anti-Zionist thought has emerged out of certain left-wing movements. This "new" anti-Semitism has its roots in the clash of Jewish national aspirations with the global dynamics of Russian communism wearing varied masks, and the immense economic power of the Arab world combined with its hostility toward Israel and Zionism. In leftist circles, communist states, and Third World movements, the old Marxist clichés dealing with Jews have had an ugly resurgence.

8. The Early Labor Press and Yiddish Poets

The struggle for dignity, acceptance, and recognition by the Second International was only one aspect of the complex battle waged by Jewish workers in America. They struggled also to overcome the stigma of Jews as crafty traders and Jews as the most sweated labor of all. Physically and spiritually uprooted from their old culture, they had to build new lives in a cultural wilderness. Thrust out of the compact *shtetl* into an impersonal, industrializing, un-Jewish life, the immigrants had immense adjustments to make. Many fatalistically accepted their hard lot, living out their lives embittered by the collapse of their dreams, spending days upon days bent over machines, crushed by squalid tenements, lonely for familiar sights and sounds, and sapped of energy by grinding toil, insufficient food, and despair.

In time, when the struggle for sheer material survival was overcome, the old values were often discarded as being irrelevant, and financial success—which paved the way to social recognition—became the total good, synonymous with Americanization.[1] A host of "allrightnicks" crowded the Jewish scene. A new breed of Jew, they scrambled for status, boasted that they knew how to handle a fork and knife, vulgarized Yiddish with Americanisms, and presented a coarse facade of Jewish adjustment to America. This scene, too, became the occasion for another kind of struggle on the part of Jewish workers. The East Side socialists fought vigorously against the insidious materialism and success ethic that characterized so much of American urban life; they gave a new faith to large masses of Jewish workers who otherwise would have slid into shame and despair. Much more than a program for a political party or utopia for the future, socialism gave the workers dignity, self-respect, and a philosophy meaningful enough to overcome hopelessness, poverty, and the blandishments of a materialistic culture. In part, the bold initiative and self-confidence Cahan displayed at the Second International was not only an expression of a proud, combative man, but the reflection of a movement defending its newly won sense of worth. This movement was also winning for Jewish workers the respect of the non-Jewish labor movement and was a living demurrer to the nay-sayers and prophets who believed "the nature of the Jew" and his "non-working class instincts" unfitted him for the discipline of a sustained labor organization.[2]

It is true, of course, that many workers considered their status as workers temporary. The tangible examples of social mobility in America were tantalizing. Freed from the strait-jacketed economy of the Pale, many sought to improve their condition by going into "business," attending night school, and struggling with professional training. But continuing immigration created a permanent Jewish working class, even if there was an inner shifting of its composition. At any moment after 1880, a substantial proportion of Jews were workers (see Table 2), and by 1890, there was a substantial core who had been employed, for example, in the garment industry for five, ten, or even fifteen years.[3] Moreover, a truly mass emigration to America took place in the 1890's. By that time, the dislocation and displacement of large numbers of Jews from the existing economic structure in Russia—mostly workers, this time, rather than petty

Table 2. Occupations of East Side Jews, 1890

Occupation	Number
Tailors	9,595
Peddlers	2,440
Cloakmakers	2,084
Clerks	1,382
Laundry workers	1,043
Cigar workers	976
Hat makers	715
Painters	458
Carpenters	443
Tinsmiths	417
Butchers	413
Food suppliers	370
Goldsmiths	287
Bakers	270
Cigar merchants	270
Hebrew teachers	251
Saloon keepers	248
Machinists	149
Glaziers	148
Printers	145
Old clothes dealers	86
Shoemakers	83
Musicians	67
Milk dealers	62

Based on table in E. Tscherikover, ed., *Geshikhte fun di yidishe arbeter-bavegung in di feraynikte shtatn* (New York, 1943–45), vol. I, pp. 258–59.

bourgeois elements—had become pronounced, and mass emigration became imperative.[4] The entire process was more orderly, the preparations were better organized than in the previous decade, and the immigrants themselves were more realistic. There were fewer rosy illusions. Many already had family in America; they were more self-confident and more independent than the earlier immigrants. "Modern" ideas, new experiences and contacts had already somewhat broken the isolation of the *shtetl,* and relentless government-inspired hostility and persecution in the last decade of the century caused further disintegration of traditional Jewish life in the Pale and the stark realization that for hundreds of thousands, Russia as home was clearly untenable.

The young Jewish socialist movement had to find approaches to this diffused, nonideological mass. The grip of religious traditionalism was one of the most difficult obstacles. The religious Jew clung to any job that permitted him to rest and pray on the Sabbath, while the Jewish socialist had already emancipated himself from such needs and preached a strong anti-religious line. This not only alienated religiously observant workers, but created a philosophy alienated from Judaism. The Jewish socialists had no Jewish substitute for religious tradition, but their intense commitment to socialism became their religion, and they threw themselves into the ideological debates and quarrels of the radical movement with great fervor. Moreover, Jewish socialists—unlike non-Jewish socialists, who had little permanent influence on labor unions—were the very leaders who organized the Jewish unions. Thus, the Jewish labor movement became one of the major sources of strength for the general socialist movement in America.

Jewish intellectuals played a vital role in raising the immigrant worker out of his physical and spiritual wretchedness and giving him a new awareness of his capacities for individual and group change. The intellectuals themselves had to undergo complicated and difficult experiences for which their background had not prepared them. Many had felt the menace of the Okhrana, the tsarist secret police, and were possessed of a burning sense of social injustice which kept their socialist dogmas aflame. However, nothing in their experience prepared them to be union organizers. Often from middle-class homes, and coming from a land where there was, as yet, no labor movement, they could not draw on their own past for guidance. Nor could they feel any inspiration from the Jewish proletariat in the United States in the 1880's and 1890's. Yet the labor union came to mean not only the catalyst for improving material conditions but became the symbol and sometimes the surrogate of the coming socialist society.

Jewish intellectuals spoke Yiddish, rather than Russian or German, to the workers, strengthening the bond between them. They also had to make a living in exactly the same way as did other workers, tasting the same daily misery, and thus destroying whatever class lines had been created in the Pale. Another unanticipated change came almost imperceptibly: the union became a school of politics and a practical laboratory in Americanization. Election campaigns, political rallies, union meetings and organization involved knowledge of democratic processes and consciousness of the larger American scene. Gradually, the intellectual himself gave up many of his socialist shibboleths and saw America as a different kind of land. He, too, seized new opportunities and gained new perspectives, finally deciding not to make the Revolution a permanent career.

The complex dilemmas, challenges, and problems of Jewish socialist action, as well as philosophy, might easily have led to aimless drift, disorientation, or collapse of the movement. Instead, even when the movement was enmeshed in bitter factional conflict, it tried to maintain itself as an instrument of education and moral uplift for the working mass. The solidarity of the working class was passionately felt and taught. This role was achieved through union meetings, lectures, educational societies and clubs, dramatic groups, and the labor press. Many contemporary observers were astonished by the burning idealism of Jewish workers who endured great suffering during strikes for the sake of exposing and abolishing social evils. When there were no strikes, union meetings became the main forum for the discussion of socialism and principles of labor solidarity—often to the neglect of strictly union business. However, the main underpinning for the movement was developed by the labor press and a body of literature that eventually elevated Yiddish to the level of a literary instrument.

Several Yiddish newspapers had appeared in the United States in the 1870's, but only one weekly, *Di Yidishe Gazeten* (*The Jewish Gazette*), which had been founded in 1874, survived the 1880's. For two months in 1881—during the height of the pogroms in Russia—it actually became the first Yiddish daily in the world, and by 1885, it was successful enough to begin publishing the *Tageblatt* (*The Daily Gazette*), which appeared about four times a week. The publisher, Kasriel Sarasohn, initially had such difficulty in finding a typesetter who could handle Yiddish that, at last, having found one, he was compelled to take him into partnership. Moreover, the two kinds of relatively learned immigrants—the religiously observant and the religiously emancipated—had little time for or interest in Yiddish publications. The former believed that all spare time should be spent in sacred studies, while the latter was ashamed of the rudimentary Yiddish being published. Besides, early journalistic efforts in Yiddish were held in contempt by the English-language press and by English and German-speaking Jews; and the Yiddish-speaking masses, too, had still to acquire the habit of reading a newspaper or book.[5] In 1882, there were about 30,000 or 40,000 Jewish workers in the United States, but many of them could not read Yiddish. Within a few years, however, the situation changed greatly. Mass immigration brought not only many competent workers and job printing shops but also an almost insatiable demand for printed matter in Yiddish.[6] By 1885, the circulation of *Tageblatt* stood at eight thousand.

Sarasohn's papers were essentially pietistic and politically conservative, and Sarasohn himself was often embroiled in anti-union efforts involving his own shop and the general Jewish labor struggle of the time. He tried to identify union organization with anarchism and condemned separate Jewish unions as a violation of the "fundamental law of democracy." [7] The Jewish radicals naturally detested him and were alarmed over his near-monopoly of the Yiddish press. Spurred by the Haymarket trial and the Henry George mayoralty campaign and by the success of his popular Yiddish lectures, Abraham Cahan took up the challenge in the summer of 1886. Together with Chaim Rayevsky, a former member of Am Olam and an exponent of Yiddish in the Jewish Workers' Association, Cahan found a printer who gave them credit and a desk in his shop. Rayevsky, who worked in a soap factory at the time, contributed all of his savings—ten dollars—for the project and time after work. Cahan, who by this time was earning a living by giving English lessons to immigrants at night, went from store to store soliciting ads during his free time. For their first issue, which appeared during the festival of Shavuot, Cahan had persuaded a fellow immigrant from Lithuania, Alexander Harkavy, also a former member of Am Olam, to write an article linking the theme of Shavuot to the lot of the worker and socialism. Harkavy was already embarked on his life's work—to redeem the Yiddish language and proclaim it part of the family of languages. He wrote a semi-popular essay called "The Worker in Our Teacher Moses' Times," and Cahan reinforced the lesson with an editorial showing that socialism was the Torah of the modern worker—a formulation that earned him the jibes of fellow socialists. But such incipient conflicts were academic—their newspaper, the *Naye Tsayt*, lasted for only four issues.

For the next few years, Cahan, who was later to become a powerful influence as editor of the Yiddish socialist daily, the *Forverts* (*Forward*), dropped out of Yiddish writing and speaking except for an occasional lecture. He strengthened his social-democratic convictions through his association with the German socialists Alexander Jonas and Sergius Schevitsch, and in the winter of 1887–88, met Wilhelm Liebnecht and Eleanor Marx and her husband, Dr. Eveling. He also joined the Socialist Labor party but affiliated with the English-speaking, not Yiddish, branch on Eighth Street near Broadway. He soon began contributing regularly to the SLP's weekly, the *Workmen's Advocate* and continued his diligent study of English and English literature. He also discovered the general press and had some short articles on the East Side placed in the *Sun, Star, and Press*. Occasionally, he submitted articles to Russian journals. Already dreaming of a literary career as an American writer, he felt no particular pull toward Jewish affairs, but a chance invitation by his friend Louis Miller to a meeting set him on an unexpected path. Miller, by then, was teaching English in an evening school for immigrants, but was known among East Side radicals chiefly as co-editor of a Russian-language socialist weekly called *Znamya (The Banner)* and as a fiery orator, whose gifts had already recommended him as delegate to the congress of the International the previous summer. The meeting involved forty-seven delegates representing some thirty Jewish radical and labor organizations concerned with founding a radical Jewish newspaper. Cahan came as an observer.

Plans for the publication of a Yiddish weekly labor paper had often been discussed among the early leaders of the movement, and from 1886 to 1889 the *Nu Yorker Yidishe Folkstsaytung*, edited by Aba Braslavsky and Moshe Mintz, attempted to fill the need. It also attempted to deal with specific Jewish dilemmas. Mintz was unusual then in that he was a Jewish nationalist and an advocate of settlement in Palestine without ceasing to be a revolutionary. It may be assumed that he was the author [8] of the "Program of the *Nu Yorker Yidishe Folkstsaytung*," published in its first issue, June 25, 1886, which asserted that the Jewish socialist should feel united with Jewish workers as well as with workers of the world. The aim of the paper, "socialist and Jewish," in the words of Mintz, was to shed light on the labor problem, the situation of the Jewish worker in the world—particularly in America—the general development of culture, and movements in Jewish history. However, by 1889, it came under fire from the socialists for its failure to make a complete commitment to the Socialist party. In the last few months of its existence, it did not print a single report of the UHT.[9]

The anarchists similarly felt the need to publish a paper, and in 1889 their *Varhayt (Truth)* appeared briefly. Toward the end of the year, the anarchists proposed a joint, bi-partisan weekly, with two editors, one from each party. They said that they wanted Jewish workers to be acquainted with many streams of thought. The socialists accepted their call for a conference, but without much enthusiasm, believing that a labor paper must have a clear stand on issues and that labor unions be represented in policy making. A conference was called on December 25, 1889, but after six days of bitter argument, the two groups parted for good. The conference, Cahan wrote, "closed amid scenes of mutual accusations and extreme language." [10] Personal as well as political relations were poisoned by these acrimonious sessions, in the midst of which some of the socialists met in caucus to discuss the possibility of their own paper.

Cahan's interest was fired. The socialists left the hall in the Essex Street Market and immediately opened their own conference on the publication of a newspaper. Weeks of continuous preparatory work followed. Funds had to be raised, the paper planned, and its management organized. Among the most active promoters were Cahan, Louis Miller, and Hillquit. For several months, almost every night, they solicited contributions for the projected paper among Jewish trade unions and friendly German labor organizations. They finally succeeded in raising eight thousand dollars, and on March 7, 1890, the first issue of their *Arbayter Tsaytung (Worker's Newspaper)* appeared. It was an event of first magnitude in the Jewish socialist and labor movements and an occasion for boundless rejoicing. Hillquit has recalled those early days:

> For hours a throng of eager sympathizers stood in front of the printer's shop waiting for the first copies to come off the press. As fast as they did, they were handed out to the waiting crowds and snatched up by them with reverence and wonder. Here it was "in the flesh," a four-page paper neatly printed in the familiar Hebrew characters, all written for them and about them. Their hopes and dreams of many months were finally realized.
>
> The paper was an instantaneous success. For weeks and weeks we had carefully planned every detail of its contents. It was our idea to conduct the paper along broad educational lines rather than to confine it to dry economic theories and Socialist propaganda. The Jewish masses were totally uncultured. They stood in need of elementary information about the important things in life outside the direct concerns of the Socialist and labor movement. Without a certain minimum of general culture, they could not be expected to develop an intelligent understanding of their own problems and interest in their own struggles.[11]

Alongside a weekly chronicle of socialist and labor-movement activity, the *Arbayter Tsaytung* printed simple expositions of their philosophies, articles on popular science, travel, good fiction, and even poetry. Hillquit contributed editorials, historical sketches, and articles on socialist theory and doubled as business manager, bookkeeper, and social poet. Cahan supplied "human interest" features. The editor-in-chief was Jacob Rombro, using the pseudonym Philip Krantz, who had edited the *Arbayter Fraynd (Worker's Friend)*, a small radical Jewish weekly in London, and was lured to New York by the promise of a larger and more fruitful field of activity and the princely salary of seven dollars a week.

Selling for three cents a copy, the paper soon reached a circulation of eight thousand and increased its size to eight pages. Hillquit kept the income of the paper in a desk drawer and "petty cash" in his pockets. His weekly poems, he felt, were a "liability" rather than an asset to the paper, but he thought better of his prose. However, Cahan was severely critical of it. "It is not Yiddish," he would say, "it is German written in Hebrew characters." [12] But there were no recognized authorities on written Yiddish at the time. The literary style of the language was in the making. Cahan advocated a faithful reproduction of the spoken Yiddish with all its crudities, while Hillquit argued that Yiddish was nothing but a corrupted, ungrammatical German, that the task of the Yiddish writer was to purify it and ultimately convert it into modern German.[13]

The evolution of a literary Yiddish was still to come. The powerful influence of the *Arbayter Tsaytung* on Jewish laboring masses also lay ahead. But a portent of its influence could be discerned in the joyous discovery of an early issue of the paper by a Jewish worker:

One Friday, going home from work and considering what paper to buy, I noticed a new Yiddish paper with the name *Arbayter Tsaytung*. I bought it and began to read it, and remarkable, this was the thing I wanted. It was the first Yiddish socialist newspaper. Although till then I never heard about socialism and its doctrine, still I understood it without any interpretation. I liked it because its ideas were hidden in my heart and in my soul long ago; only I could not express them clearly. . . . That paper preached, "Happiness for everyone"; this has always been my ardent desire; it preached "peaceful development",— excellent. I always liked peace. It said that "new changes for the betterment of the people could be reached by free and decent speech, and free and decent press." This I could sign with both my hands. What person with common sense could deny them? [14]

By May 1890, a few months after its founding, the *Arbayter Tsaytung* was enthusiastically caught up in the May Day demonstration, involving almost ten thousand Jewish workers, called by the United Hebrew Trades and the Socialist Labor party. Cahan reported fulsomely:

This imposing demonstration is the beginning of the great revolution which will overthrow the capitalist system and create a new society on the foundations of genuine liberty, equality and fraternity. Standing here, between the palaces of the millionaires on Fifth Avenue, the rich stores of Broadway on one side and the dark miserable tenement section on the other side, let us swear, comrades, that we will lay down our lives to abolish the present inequality. [15]

The great era of the Jewish socialist press had begun.

The *Arbayter Tsaytung* also marked the beginning of Cahan's career as a Yiddish publicist. Cahan soon enough found his stride. Energetic, proud, and self-confident, he sensed that he, not the sedate Krantz, was the right man to edit the *Arbayter Tsaytung*. He knew Yiddish better than any of the others, had already had some experience in American journalism, and believed he could apply its popularizing techniques to Yiddish. He also felt more thoroughly "American" than the others. Besides, he was a born *melammed* and loved lecturing to the ordinary folk-Jew and worker, a gift he could easily transfer to a Yiddish newspaper.

Anxious to confirm what he already suspected, Cahan read through a whole bound volume of the *Arbayter Fraynd*, which Krantz had edited in London, and found it impossibly dry and full of the *deitshmerish* style cultivated by writers who aimed to raise Yiddish to the level of German—a style which Cahan disliked intensely. He had fully expected to find Krantz similarly stiff and formal; instead, when they met, he found him exuberant, charming, and fluent in Russian. But though he had no official job on the newspaper and liked Krantz personally, Cahan soon found himself criticizing the editorial policy and style of the *Arbayter Tsaytung*. Krantz and his comrades wanted the paper to be a vehicle for the theoretical and political clarification of socialism. Cahan, for his part, sure of his grasp of the Jewish immigrant mind, wanted to write for the largest possible number of readers and to attract them with dramatic captions.

Believing that popular science articles should be a regular feature, Cahan submitted an article on cannibals in Africa, to be used in the first issue. Krantz at first refused it, having already accepted two of Cahan's articles for the first issue, but he finally accepted it under deadline pressure. Tension developed between the men. Krantz himself wrote the lead article, a rather heavy, serious statement of "Our Program." [16] It began: "Our general goal is the building of a social order on the principles of genuine freedom, equality, and brotherhood, in place of the present capitalist order, which is based on oppression, mass poverty, and civil strife." Across from this was an unsigned piece entitled "Two Worlds in the World," written in colloquial Yiddish and containing rather crudely sketched scenes of poverty contrasted with scenes of wealth. This, of course, was written by Cahan who may have wanted as much to mock Krantz's ponderous tone as to cater to low-brow tastes. In the same issue, Cahan also experimented with an idea he had tried out briefly in *Naye Tsayt* some years earlier, when he used the theme of Shavuot to illustrate socialist principles. He was convinced that there was a connection between Judaism and socialism and that religious associations familiar to all Jews— even those like himself who were skeptics or secularists—could be drawn on to spark socialist lessons. He took on the mantle of a *maggid*, the traveling preacher of his childhood, and wove a weekly socialist sermon around the *sidra*, the portion of the Torah that is read each week in the traditional synagogue service. The *sidra* for the first issue dealt with God's specifications to Moses for the building of a sanctuary and necessary taxation. From this scaffolding, Cahan discussed the exploitativeness of capitalism, the current unfair tax system, and new alternatives opening up to workers in Germany in the form of a Social-Democratic party. Interspersed throughout the sermon were Biblical quotations, homilies and personal comments aimed at appealing to the most humble reader. Cahan's *sidra* was signed *Der Proletarishker Maggid*.

His column became one of the most popular features of the *Arbayter Tsaytung* and signaled the course of the future editor of the *Forverts*. Under Cahan's peculiar genius, Jewish readers cultivated an intense interest—even zest—for the special amalgam that he created in the *Arbayter Tsaytung*. The newspaper became a kind of popular university, offering its readers understandable socialism, translations from European and American literary classics, popular science, simplified essays on political economy and American history, poetry, and exhortatory essays. Cahan frequently used several pseudonyms to conceal his multiple authorship. Most important, perhaps, he was creating an instrument of popular Jewish socialist culture in America.

The labor press combined the functions of educator, organizer, cultivator of "manners," and instrument of Americanization. Far superior to the commercialized press, the radical *Arbayter Tsaytung*, and later the *Fraye Arbayter Shtimme*, the *Abendblatt*, and *Forverts* worked heroically in a barren field. They were bearers not only of a new social faith but of a vastly diversified universe. They widened the horizons of their readers by making accessible great works of literature—the novels of Tolstoy, Zola, and Hugo were daily fare—popularizations of material from the natural and social sciences, American history and politics, and homely advice for bewildering personal problems. The gamut of material was very wide and revealed to the immigrants, who were getting used to reading a newspaper regularly, the immense complexities of the modern world. But it was the Jewish labor poets who gave voice to the anguished cries of the sweated workers, who had the most compelling influence. A verse that evoked the misery of the sweatshops, the exhaustion of the pale, emaciated women and children, and the hatefulness of exploiters, combined with a call for solidarity and struggle, had a more immediate effect than preachy articles and editorials. The poems were sung at work across the machines and work tables, creating a living bond among the oppressed and a pulsing hope for a better world the poets promised.

The labor poets—Morris Rosenfeld, David Edelstadt, Yossef Bovshover, and Morris Winchevsky—are generally regarded as the founders of Yiddish poetry, the pioneers of Yiddish literature. Of the four, only Winchevsky came to feel a deep unqualified love for the Yiddish language. The others, in common with most of the Jewish political writers and socialist spokesmen of the time, looked upon Yiddish as an impure and transitory jargon.[17] By the 1880's some of the periodicals had begun to free themselves of Germanized Yiddish, and a few of the leaders, like Cahan, were no longer ashamed of "simple Yiddish." In his *Naye Tsayt*, for example, he had tried to use an idiomatic, unalloyed Yiddish. In 1886, when the *Nu Yorker Yidishe Folkstsaytung* appeared, it, too, tried to keep close to spoken Yiddish. It was in number 26 of the *Folkstsaytung* (December 31, 1886) that Rosenfeld published his first poem, a lament for the passing year and a call to the Jewish people to arise and be ready for the world struggle that would end the gap between poor and rich.

The son of a poor Polish fisherman, Rosenfeld [18] worked as a youth in a sweatshop in Whitechapel, London, and emigrated to New York in 1886. While still a boy, he loved the work of Eliakum Zunser, Abraham Goldfadden, and Michael Gordin, and learned many of their poems and songs by heart. By the time he was fifteen, he yearned to be a poet; in London, he circulated his verses among fellow workers and several songs became popular. Having heard that tailors in New York had won a strike and worked only ten hours a day (not true), he came to New York in 1886, intending to save enough money to bring over his wife and children. Like so many other immigrants, he worked inhumanly long hours in a filthy shop, bent over a sewing machine or pushing a hot iron as the precious hours vanished forever. The humiliating work filled him with despair; the shop became a living hell. In poetry [19] of great anguish and pathos,

Rosenfeld wailed over the human waste, self-pity, and grinding monotony of the interminable days.

Hutchins Hapgood, a non-Jewish writer and sensitive observer of nineteenth-century social and esthetic movements, who knew all of the East Side writers personally, described Rosenfeld as "small, dark, and fragile in body with fine eyes and drooping eyelashes, and a plainative, child-like voice . . . weary, sick—a simple poet, a sensitive child, a bearer of burdens . . ." who sang "to the maimed spirit of the Jewish slums." [20] The note of revolt was less audible than the note of lamentation, but hope did occasionally break through in Rosenfeld's songs of Zion, which recalled ancient glories and times when Jews were not a people of mourners. Typical was the mood of "Mayn rueh platz" ("My Place of Rest"):

> Don't look for me where myrtle grows,
> You won't find me there, my love.
> At the machines, where lives wither,
> There you'll find my place of rest.
>
> Don't look for me where birds are singing,
> You won't find me there, my love.
> I am a slave where chains are ringing;
> There you'll find my place of rest.[21]

Despite the remorseless poverty he suffered, Rosenfeld succeeded in having his first volume of poetry, *The Bell*,[22] published in 1888; two other collections appeared within a few years. Then, in 1897, Leo Wiener, an instructor in Slavic literature at Harvard who had published an early history of Yiddish literature, reviewed Rosenfeld's *Das Lieder Buch (Book of Songs)* in the *Nation* and proclaimed it the work of a great poet, whose intensity "approached the vivid realism of Dante's *Inferno*." Later critics have been much less fulsome. Yet Rosenfeld's historic significance is undeniable. He wrote when there was no Yiddish poetry except the ballads of the popular bards. Later Yiddish poets scorned him but, as one of them admitted, "Rosenfeld is in the blood of everyone of us."

In the United States, he was for a time the leading poet produced by Jewish immigrant culture. The piercing misery of the Jewish worker has rarely been rendered more soulfully; but at times his overwrought feelings spill over into sentimentality. The few radical publications of the time gladly printed his poems—he was a regular contributor to *Arbayter Tsaytung*—and Jewish workers read and quoted him ardently. Many of his poems were set to music and sung by workers and socialists in the 1930's and 1940's and even today, by children in secular Yiddish schools and choruses. Especially popular were "In the Sweat-Shop," "My Little Boy," "The Teardrop Millionaire," and "The Hanukkah Candles" (often the part dealing with the wandering Jew dreaming of Eretz Israel was omitted).

Although Rosenfeld identified closely with the Jewish working masses, he did not have the typical socialist outlook. He was strongly conscious of himself as a Jew, and some of his poems, "Songs of Nation and People," have a nationalist tone. Indeed, in 1900, he was a delegate to the Fourth World Zionist Congress in London.

Professor Wiener's discovery of Rosenfeld developed for him a broad reading public; his *Songs from the Ghetto* (so titled by Wiener) was translated into many languages, and Rosenfeld was invited to speak at several American universities. William Dean Howells, the noted novelist and literary critic, also wrote favorably of his work. But Rosenfeld's sudden fame and health were shattered by the death of his fifteen-year-old son. A poem of vehement power called "Earth" was written later:

> O earth, you angry, filthy, gluttonous
> Ripped throat swallowing everything
> And leaving pain alive
> Torn to pieces in your great belly—
>
> Only the tombstones say what you have devoured
> My rage and pain curse you, bitch—
> But how can I curse you now
> That my child sleeps in your black bosom?
> Swallowed, O you have swallowed the sweet light
> Of that clear-eyed look, my happiness!
> It is not here now, and what it was is earth.[23]

Subsequently, Rosenfeld's health improved somewhat, and for several years he wrote for the *Forward*, though he considered this a period of "pen slavery." Poor health dogged him, and his irascible nature and growing nationalist orientation made his stay on the paper untenable. After a quarrel, Cahan dismissed him. Even as his poems were recited and sung by Jewish workers, Rosenfeld died penniless and unattended. Although his later poetry was marked by polemical outbursts, his early lyrics were written in a simple, idiomatic Yiddish that helped create a literary standard which made possible an authentic Yiddish literature in America.

David Edelstadt [24] telescoped his career as a poet into a few short years. Born far from the Jewish Pale in the Russian city of Kaluga, Edelstadt knew little about Jewish life. He developed a great love for the Russian language and its literature and began writing poetry at the age of twelve. In Kiev, where he went to prepare for university, he lived through an experience that jolted him back to his Jewish origins. During the pogroms, in the spring of 1881, he was attacked by hoodlums and barely escaped with his life. Unable to remain in Russia, he joined an Am Olam group and set out at sixteen for America, landing in Cincinnati where he found work as a button-hole maker. The execution of the Haymarket anarchists agonized him, and he determined to devote his life to the emancipation of workers. He learned Yiddish from fellow workers and began to write polemical verse in the Russian anarchist literary tradition, condemning government and capitalist exploiters. He also wrote in memory of the executed Russian revolutionaries and the Haymarket martyrs. One poem, "In Kampf," became a favorite with prisoners in tsarist jails, as well as with Jewish workers in America.

Edelstadt came to New York and became one of the editors and founders of the anarchist *Fraye Arbayter Shtimme (Free Worker's Voice)*, plunging into the sharp rivalry between anarchists and socialists, and labeling the socialists "parlor revolutionaries." His poems, he explained, "were not born in a flower garden, [but] in the dark world of slavery." The struggle for bread is his muse; the factory hell, his boss:

> The sick heart under the worker's blouse
> Is the sweet nectar of our street.

Much more than Rosenfeld, Edelstadt wanted his poetry to transform the amorphous Jewish masses into a militant working class. He did not deny the peculiar problems faced by the Jewish worker, but wrote passionately out of his rage against every worker's misery and his struggle for freedom. The following lines, which were inscribed on his tombstone, place him within the revolutionary romantic tradition:

> O, good friend! When I die,
> Carry our flag to my grave—
> The free flag colored red
> Splattered with the blood of workers!

Edelstadt's poems won great popularity among Jewish workers, but his promising career was cut down swiftly. At twenty-six he died of tuberculosis in Denver.

Yossef Bovshover [25] arrived in America a few months after Edelstadt had gone to a hospital in Denver. The two never met, but Bovshover was inspired by Edelstadt's poetry, and on the day of his death, wrote an elegy that was hailed in radical circles as a masterpiece. Unlike Rosenfeld, Bovshover does not cry out with the pain of workers lashed to a machine but, like Edelstadt, he tries to rouse workingmen out of their apathy. An occasional bitter vein of contempt of the worker's life also appears in Bovshover:

> Your senseless chat is wearisome to me;
> Your shallow joy is not the joy I like . . .
>
> You live, and know not what existence is:
> You die, and know not what the grave entombs;
> You trust, and know not what your faith implies;
> You hope and know not what it is to hope.

Yet, at times, he sang of the worker's pride and is capable of a genuine intimacy, as in the poem, "Tsu Mayne Brider" ("To My Brothers"):

I am the violin, you are the strings;
You alone can awaken the music in me.

Indeed, Bovshover was the most lyrical of the labor poets. His best-known poem "A Gezang Tsum Folk" ("A Song to the People") is a noble apostrophe to the people, calling on them to open their eyes to behold the fruits of their labor—from which they are alienated—and by enjoying what they have created, to learn the joy of creating.[26] In Bovshover's vision, the wealth that the workers create embraces locomotives and factories as well as socks and shirts—of which they are deprived. The lyricism as well as sense of alienation in this poem are reminiscent of Shelley's "To the Men of England." Other poems call on the workers to break their chains and liberate themselves and all of mankind. Influenced by Heine and Shelley, Bovshover also wrote love poetry and poems dealing with nature. He mastered English sufficiently to translate some of his own poetry, which appeared in *Liberty,* an anarchist magazine. The publisher thought he had discovered a new and great poet, another Whitman, but others did not share his enthusiasm, and Bovshover's emotional balance, never very steady, slipped. Suffering from neglect and emotional conflicts, his behavior grew more and more bizarre, and at twenty-six he was admitted to a hospital for the mentally ill. Only after this tragic breakdown did his poetry reach the masses and receive the acknowledgment he had craved.

The literary quality of the labor poets is not of first rank, although the radical journals of the day boasted of their greatness. Jewish life in America was still too turbulent, too transitional for the development of a literature of stature.[27] Most of all, there was the absence of roots, of a Yiddish heritage, of unifying generations. Old traditions had to be thrown off before new roots could take hold. Many immigrants of the first exodus yearned to return to Russia; they felt no affection as yet for America. That the labor poets were essentially propagandistic may have detracted from their artistry, but their mission as enlighteners and uplifters created a bond among the workers and a hope that their lives could be bound up with a cause, and that cause, with their own liberation. Moreover, the poems were often sung, and the singing created a special charm and, indeed, outlet, for the singers. The singing also created a poetic mood, even if the poems themselves were of lesser quality. The effect of poetry and song transformed a moral or political message into an esthetic experience—often without a conscious awareness by the reader or singer.[28] Workers became accustomed to poetic enjoyment, or at any rate prepared for it, although the poems themselves were often far from poetic. The workers could read into the lines more than was in them—a significant step in the creation of a cultural climate. "In no other movement," it has been said, "at any period, has poetry been such a potent force." [29]

The most influential of the poets, by far, was Morris Winchevsky, the oldest of four, but the last to settle in the United States. When he arrived in 1894, Winchevsky was already widely known in Yiddish-speaking labor circles not only as a labor editor in London, but for his songs of labor's struggle, probably the first in Yiddish, which were reprinted in America. Winchevsky is also importantly linked with Lieberman during their days together at the Teachers' Institute in Vilna and later, with the Jewish socialist culture that flourished briefly in London. He was also intimately involved in all of the great issues and complications of the young Jewish socialist movement.

Born Lippe Ben-Zion Novakhovitch,[30] Winchevsky was raised in a politically and intellectually enlightened home in Kovno, Lithuania, an old Jewish city known for its rabbinical learning, and a center of the early Haskalah. His father could never make a living for their large family of eleven children, but had strongly independent ideas about education and encouraged Lippe to read widely in German and Russian, as well as Hebrew. From a very early age, Lippe aspired "to do literary work for humanity" [31] in general and for Jews in particular. He came under the compelling spell of the populist and revolutionary writers in Russia, but his earliest writings also reveal the persistent influence of the prophet Isaiah. He lived through the typical youthful rebel's ideological swirl of the period, translated German and Russian poetry into Hebrew, and wrote columns, couplets, and social satire in Hebrew for the Hebrew weekly *Ha-Maggid*.

Toward the end of 1876, he read Lieberman's "To the Intelligent Young Men of Israel" and, deeply moved by it, began a lively correspondence with its author.[32] Lieberman was then about to start publishing his *Ha-Emet*, the first Jewish socialist magazine, and Novakhovitch was invited to contribute. He began to write poems with a definite socialist orientation, but Lieberman was thrown into prison before any of his poems could appear. Though barely twenty-one, he was invited by the young publisher Michael Ratkinson to become editor of a socialist magazine in Hebrew, *Asefat Hakhamim (Assembly of the Wise)*, and his poems, political articles, fantasies, and book reviews practically filled the magazine until it was banned, after eight issues, in October 1878.

At this time, Novakhovitch was working as a bank clerk in Königsberg, Germany. Here he was exposed to German socialist literature and came in touch with a lively socialist movement, but in order to keep his job at the bank and maintain his double life, he had to resort to several pseudonyms—of which Winchevsky became the most lasting and best known. In November 1878, a few weeks after Bismarck's anti-socialist laws went into effect, Winchevsky was arrested. After almost five months in prison, he was expelled from Germany, eventually made his way to London, in 1879, and resumed his contacts with Lieberman.

In London, he also met his idol Johann Most,[33] the well-known anarchist, and members of the famous Communist Workers' Educational Society, founded by Marx and Engels. But both experiences disappointed him—Most by his gluttony, and the communists, by their beer drinking, billiards, and card playing. More important, for the first time, he confronted the Whitechapel sweatshops and the Jewish proletariat and Lieberman, who had returned to London after two years in prison. For a time, he helped Lieberman organize the short-lived Jewish Workers' Benefit and Educational Verein and began to write in Yiddish. By this time, Lieberman himself had accepted the necessity of using Yiddish as a vehicle for spreading socialist ideas among Jewish workers, but the failure of the Verein and Lieberman's sudden departure for America, followed by his suicide, left Winchevsky politically alone, stunned, and unable to challenge the German atmosphere that surrounded radical immigrant activity in London. His own highly Germanized Yiddish also handicapped his efforts to reach Jewish workers.

For the next four years, Winchevsky withdrew from active political life, maintaining himself by again working as a bank clerk. But in 1884, his life changed, and for the next ten years until his emigration to America, Winchevsky became the hub of Jewish socialist activity—not as a political leader but as a writer. In that year, he could no longer resist the pull of the vast exodus of Jews from Russia to London and Manchester and the compelling call to resume socialist agitation among the Jewish workers. He and A. V. Rabinovich, his old comrade from Königsberg who had introduced him to German socialist thought, decided to publish a weekly paper for workers in Yiddish.

The new paper, the first of its kind, was called *Der Poylisher Yidel* (*The Polish Jew*). On July 25, 1884, the first issue appeared, humorously chiding the reader for doubting that it would last longer than other Yiddish papers. In its approach to socialism, it was cautious, proposing to be a teacher of those who knew only Yiddish, a guide for "greenhorns," and a source of news. It renounced interest in "religious matters or in personalities," and kept an appearance of bland neutrality: "We treat the Jew . . . as a man, as a Jew, and as a worker. . . . We wish to speak . . . about everything which concerns labor and the laboring man." But it limited its radical propaganda to descriptions of proletarian life, particularly the exploitation of Jewish immigrant workers by Jewish contractors.[34]

Winchevsky was variously bland, coy, indecisive, and even obtuse in his handling of burning issues of the day, but he aroused the deepest feelings in the Jewish workers and kindled hopes of social change. However, the wealthy Jews in England became uncomfortable; unfavorable publicity in their *Jewish Chronicle* and questions in Parliament drew attention to Jewish East European "agitators." Moreover, the title of the paper, *Der Poylisher Yidel*, which was intended as an expression of defiance and pride, was apparently felt to be insulting by some of its readers.[35] It was dropped after the sixteenth issue and renamed the *Zukunft* (*The Future*).

In 1885, after struggling with many technicalities and exacting Litvak readers, Winchevsky left *Zukunft*[36] and returned to the idea he had developed with Lieberman earlier—that of socialist pamphleteering in

Yiddish. Actually, he had written the first pamphlet,[37] called *Yehi or: eyne unterhaltung iber di farkerte velt (Let There Be Light: A Discourse on the Topsy-Turvy World)*, in 1879 in Königsberg, but had not published it for lack of funds. Money was raised in 1884 and the first printing was soon sold out. The text is in the form of a dialogue between two workers, Morris and Hyman, who discuss the world situation in the conversational Yiddish of immigrant workers. Socialist ideas were cast in simple terms and were popularized both in England and America through the pamphlet. In the introduction, Winchevsky listed "The Thirteen Articles of Socialist Faith," modeled after Maimonides' Thirteen Articles of Faith, thus throwing the gauntlet down to exploiters and capitalists.

These articles removed the sugar coating from socialist ideas and shocked Orthodox Jews but helped materialize the first avowedly socialist Yiddish publication, the *Arbayter Fraynd (Worker's Friend)*. On July 15, 1885, it started publication, first as a monthly and from December 1886, as a weekly. During this time, Winchevsky was asked to serve as its editor, but he demurred, recommending instead the *Zukunft* correspondent, Jacob Rombro, who had recently returned from Russia. The serious Rombro, who changed his name to Philip Krantz, accepted, but Winchevsky unofficially collaborated and wrote voluminously for the paper. In the first few years of its existence, *Arbayter Fraynd* was open to all wings of radical opinion, but anarchists fought pitched polemical battles with socialists, and moderates like Winchevsky were deeply disturbed by the rancor of the quarrels and the terrorist orientation of the anarchists. The paper also made biting attacks against Jewish religious traditions and Zionist aspirations. Winchevsky at this time had a "cosmopolitan" orientation and satirized institutional religion, but he was pained by the total absence of Jewish fellow-feeling in the paper and thought back longingly to the more tender days of *Der Poylisher Yidel*.[38]

The arguments deteriorated into factional strife which became particularly venomous in 1889. In that year, Joseph Jaffe, the anarchist-spokesman, became editor of the *Varhayt* in New York and wrote severe attacks on the social-democratic faction in London, whose position was upheld by Krantz. In the summer of that year, Krantz was a delegate to the First Congress of the Second International in Paris, where anarchism was strongly denounced. Reflecting the violent partisanship engendered by the congress, Krantz became aggressively partisan, labeling nonpartisans like Winchevsky *pareve lokshn* (literally, neutral noodles—neither fish nor fowl), and left for New York to become editor of the new socialist paper *Arbayter Tsaytung*. Soon, the anarchists on *Arbayter Fraynd* became bitterly hostile. The socialists were edged out, and by April 1891, the paper officially adopted an anarchist position. Winchevsky and other intermediate "socialist-revolutionaries" then started a monthly called *Di Fraye Velt (The Free World)*, but it lasted for only ten issues.

It is of some interest that the question of Yiddish was raised at the congress of the International in 1889. In his report on the emigré Russian revolutionary movement, Lavrov referred to the Jewish socialists in London and the *Arbayter Fraynd*, "which is issued in a Hebraic dialect." The Jewish socialists, he said, "assure the congress that, although they are compelled to use the sole language which the Jewish workers understand, they are indeed distant from the notion of national separation and participate in the socialist workers' movements wherever they may be." [39] All radicals of the time justified the use of Yiddish as an unfortunate expedient.

Meanwhile, Winchevsky was also writing Yiddish poetry, some of it influenced by Shelley, Heine, Hugo, and even Yeats, much of it of deep social significance for Jewish workers. Mistreatment of workers, the helplessness of the abused poor and their sorrows became his main themes. He also wrote fighting songs, filled with indignation and protest, which were sung with fervor in garment shops in London and New York and in basements in Warsaw and Vilna. Workers' choruses can still be heard singing "Vikelt fanander di fone di roite" ("Unfurl the Red Flag"), "In die gassen tsu di massen" ("To the Masses in the Streets"), and "Hert kinder, vie es riert zich" ("Listen Children, Something Is Stirring").[40] Winchevsky's translation of Thomas Hood's stirring "Song of the Shirt" also became a favorite of Jewish workers. In contrast with Rosenfeld, who voiced the pain of the individual worker, Winchevsky, like Edelstadt, aroused him to the social struggle.

Bending his literary talents to the Jewish proletariat cause, Winchevsky did not mind being called a socialist propagandist. But he was no starry-eyed visionary. Though deeply compassionate and gentle, even timid, in manner, he had a realistic grasp of the grubby hard work needed in all social movements—socialist and otherwise—and understood the need for mastering organizational matters in the newly formed unions. He was the first to explain the essence of trade unionism in Yiddish—in fictional form, for greater appeal—in *The Alef-Bet of Trade Unionism: An Engagement after a Wedding*, published in 1884 by the first union of Jewish garment workers.[41]

Winchevsky's unique literary talents also inspired a generation of labor leaders and even found an echo in revolutionary circles in Russia.[42] He wrote in Hebrew, Russian, German, and English and drew on all cultures to fashion and polish his Yiddish material. Of all the early labor poets, he was the only one to create an authentic bridge from the Haskalah to socialism. Indeed, from 1884 until his emigration to the United States, socialist propaganda activity among certain Jewish workers in London centered around Winchevsky. But Jewish radical circles in London were far from strong or united, and defections increased as the socialist-anarchist struggle wore on. Anarchist terrorism repelled some; the Zionist movement drew off others; and reaction in Russia threw still others into despair. Rumors that Jews would be expelled from Moscow hung in the air early in 1891, and the expulsion order was published March 28 and 29 (the first two days of Passover) and within a few days the entire Jewish population of Moscow—about 30,000—was uprooted.

Winchevsky chided those Jewish radicals who left the revolutionary barricades and continued to identify himself as a "radical cosmopolitan." Religious orthodoxy and "Palestinophilism" particularly aroused his anger. Nevertheless, he spoke at a mass meeting on November 1, 1890, in London, protesting the anticipated Russian anti-Jewish decrees—probably the only action of its kind taken by London radical circles in those years.[43]

Meanwhile, all attempts by the socialists in London at the time to form a durable organization had failed. The Jewish anarchists seemed more successful for a while. Periodically, they felt infusions of strength from leading European anarchist refugees who came to London. Krantz believed that social democracy was too demanding a theory to be of much attraction to young Jews who had escaped from the police regime of Russia. The state—whether Russian or British—was deemed the cause of all social evil. Winchevsky's closeness to the British socialist movement was apparently rather exceptional among Jewish radical immigrants in London.[44]

Even so, Jewish anarchists in London were not making real contact with Jewish workers. Their wrangling with the socialists was conducted on a rarefied theoretical level in a social vacuum. For example, in the midst of the misery of unemployed Jewish workers during the economic crisis of 1889, *Arbayter Fraynd* was involved in anti-religious issues. The paper taunted a London rabbi about a sermon in behalf of unemployed demonstrators and sponsored the first "Yom Kippur Ball"—a revolt against Orthodox prayer and fasting. In the great strike by Jewish tailors at the end of August 1889, the anarchists played no role whatsoever, and the socialists, still largely withdrawn from bread-and-butter concerns of workers, little more. Both groups of radicals considered trade-union activity of little value in the coming transformation of society. The unions, meanwhile, were being organized for concrete, everyday gains: a ten-hour workday, the elimination of homework, limits on child labor, higher wages. Little attention was paid to the dogmatic, high-flown theories of the radical philosophers. At the same time, the unions that were formed were highly competitive, fragmented, and generally unstable. They burst forth, and quickly died out, ruined by personality clashes, internal strife, chaotic conditions of work, and failures. In the garment industry, for example, there were Jews in an operators' union, others in a pressers' union, and still others in the British Amalgamated Society of Tailors. Even in the late 1880's, when the socialists had begun to modify their antagonism toward unions and made some efforts to unite Jewish workers, they were still torn by ideological struggles.

The outstanding effort of the English radicals in union organization of the early nineties was that of the socialist revolutionaries, who called themselves Proletariat and sponsored *Di Fraye Velt*. On their initiative, a conference of union representatives was called in the summer of 1892, where the formation of a General Council of Jewish Workers' Societies was proposed. On September 17, a mass meeting was organized, chaired by Winchevsky. Eleanor Aveling, Karl Marx's daughter, who had become deeply interested in the Jewish masses,[45] and Abraham Cahan spoke. At the time, anti-immigrationist feeling was growing in the ranks of British labor and many unions refused to accept Jews as members. For some Jewish radicals, these facts obliged them to re-examine their views against Jewish separatism and support of specifically Jewish-worker interests. But the council's work in this direction was denounced by the more traditional cosmopolitan radicals as a betrayal. Nor could the valiant efforts of Karl Lieberman, writing in *Di Fraye Velt* [46] and calling for a Jewish "patriotic revolution," win them over. Lieberman insisted that Jews need not be ashamed of being Jewish. But the prevailing radical attitude toward the Jewish masses was negative, even contemptuous. Jewish workers in London, nevertheless, were miserably exploited and isolated while the most capable men were still gripped by doctrinaire radical formulations. Summarizing this period in later years, Winchevsky wrote: "The tragic social democratic-anarchist civil war worked havoc in the unions, the only field in which we could have achieved anything of significance among Jewish workers." [47]

Only in their opposition to religion did anarchists and socialists agree. The anti-religious position of the anarchists was particularly vehement, forming the main thrust of their struggle against the existing social order. Jewish immigrant workers, meanwhile, struggling for new economic and cultural anchors, had nothing to replace the traditions and customs from which they had been uprooted. Winchevsky shared these anti-religious views and admitted that "disbelief and hatred toward all faiths reached a high pitch of fanaticism. . . . My greatest delight was to prove that Moses did not write the Pentateuch, that Joshua did not cause the heavens to stand still." [48] Yet, curiously, Biblical metaphors and images keep recurring in his writing.

Arrival in America did not diminish the anti-religious views or the intense antagonisms of the hostile parties. Moreover, the movement of many Jewish radicals from England to the United States simply transferred the scene of ideological battles between socialists and anarchists. Until the 1890's, London was the source of inspiration for Jewish radicals and union leaders in America. Many Jews who later became labor leaders in America had their first proletariat experiences in London. Workers' clubs, radical pamphlets and newspapers and radical theorizing had their beginnings in London. But the 1890's saw increasing migration of Russian Jews to America,[49] causing a shift of the center of gravity of the Jewish labor movement from London to New York and characteristically American-Jewish patterns.

In groping for new social and cultural props, Russian Jews had to adapt traditional religious practices to the new life. Many synagogues were established, which filled social, educational, as well as religious functions, but the rigidity of ghetto orthodoxy had to give way. The Sabbath was compromised very early. Work on Friday lengthened, and work on Saturdays was endured guiltily. A new breed of rabbis sprang up—often poorly educated, grasping, looking for a soft job—and chroniclers complain of the indignities to which traditional rabbis were subjected. In the sometimes boorish social climbing and crude materialism of the "all-rightniks," the traditional old-country respect for the pious rabbi and scholar, as well as for the *maskil*, was eroded, leaving the way open for the gradual rise of the Jewish radical intelligentsia to leadership in some segments of Jewish life.

Psychologically, Jewish workers were being forced into religious transgressions by the terms of their work: the Sabbath, *kashrut*, and prayer obligations were violated. Anarchist anti-religious propaganda only aggravated their guilt and left them without any anchorage. The socialists tempered their anti-religious activity somewhat by rejecting the vulgar public assaults of the anarchists and Yom Kippur balls. Instead, they stressed the opposition of science to religious dogmas and the need to educate the masses in the history of religion and evolution.

Interestingly, the *landsmanshaftn*, which were made up overwhelmingly of workers, owed nothing to the Jewish radicals or intellectuals of the time. They arose out of the deep need for community among the Jewish masses and flourished in the United States. Moreover, the radical assault on religion backfired and alienated most Jewish workers. In their extreme vehemence, many Jewish radicals seemed to be shouting down their own doubts and guilt about their own rejection of Jewish observances. The cleverness of their parodies and satirical references to religious texts disclose an intimate knowledge of the religious sources. On an ideological level, it was apparently necessary for the radical to liberate himself from the imprisonment of Judaism, which like all religion in the Marxist view, was as great an evil as the state, the existing social order, and capitalism.

Quite typical was the tone of Edelstadt's poem "To the Defenders of Obscurantism," which appeared in the *Fraye Arbayter Shtimme* a few days before Yom Kippur in 1890:

> Why complain, you orthod-oxen?
> Do you want Jewry to consist only of animals
> Ignorant and stupid
> Do you wish us to bow down
> to your archaic god,
> Lower our heads
> before every pious idiot?
> Each era has its new Torah—

Ours is one of freedom and justice:
For us, the greatest transgression
is to be an obedient slave.
We also have new prophets—
Börne, Lassalle, Karl Marx;
They will deliver us from exile,
But not with fasts and prayers! [50]

Orthodox defenders hurled invectives of their own, and from time to time the public witnessed Jewish antagonists warring against each other, even resorting to boycotts, court injunctions, and arrests. These abusive battles continued for about ten years, to the early 1900's, when the struggle for trade unions became uppermost.

Winchevsky came to the United States in 1894, at thirty-eight (by forty he was already called *zayde*—grandfather). He was not explicitly a Marxist socialist and shunned party labels, but in America he very quickly became identified with the opposition to the existing (De Leon) leadership of the Socialist Labor party. Winchevsky also became a steady contributor to the *Abendblatt,* the first Jewish socialist daily, which started publication two days after his arrival. It was an exciting time for an aspiring Jewish writer to be in America. A cultural revolution was brewing, with Yiddish its instrument and catalyst.

9. Yiddish in the Cultural Growth of Jewish Workers

The history of Yiddish literature in America is in large measure the history of the cultural development of Jewish workers. The Yiddish culture of the 1890's and early 1900's paralleled the rise of the Jewish labor movement and was, in large part, the result of its growth and influence. A Yiddish literature of great scope was created, perhaps the most important non-English literature ever to arise in the United States.[1] Simultaneous with the cultural development of Jewish workers there was a cultural evolution centering around Yiddish. The "jargon," as Yiddish was called, slowly became a literary instrument.

In its early phase, Yiddish literature in America was confined almost exclusively to journalism. About seventy Yiddish writers had their work published in the ephemeral periodicals of the 1880's.[2] Practically no writing of substance appeared in book form. The first Yiddish book in the United States, a volume of verse by Jacob Z. Sobel, appeared in 1877; the few writers of books generally sought publication in Europe, where printing was more accessible and cheaper. In the United States, the first Yiddish literary works were serialized in weeklies, and later, dailies. Gradually, these periodicals began to free themselves of German and Germanized Yiddish, which had dominated the early Yiddish press. *Naye Tsayt* avoided Germanized Yiddish, and the *Nu Yorker Yidishe Folkstsaytung* was freer of Germanisms than earlier papers. "The Yiddish langauge," one of its editorials asserted,

> is composed of words of various origin. It is without rules of grammar. We deem it inadvisable to have in our periodical only one sort of Yiddish. Our readers need not be surprised, therefore, that different articles are written in different sorts of Yiddish. We only believe it important to eliminate all Russian words from our periodical.[3]

Its articles, nevertheless, approximated the spoken language. Of equal significance was the promise of the *Folkstsaytung* to publish "interesting original stories and good translations of the most recent writers," as well as articles on general culture and movements in Jewish history. To keep the promise of publishing original Yiddish stories in the 1880's was at least as difficult as being both socialist and Jewish.[4] Except for Abraham Cahan, none of the Yiddish writers who were to lay the foundation of Yiddish fiction—Leon Kobrin, Zalman Libin, and Jacob Gordin—had yet arrived in the United States. The *Folkstsaytung* did what it could to be a literary organ, but like the *Fraye Arbayter Shtimme* and *Arbayter Tsaytung*, had to content itself mostly with poetry.

However, the range of subjects treated in Yiddish expanded, giving more flexibility and richness to the language. Cahan, Krantz, Benjamin Feigenbaum and others began to write popularizations of natural and social sciences in Yiddish, thus widening the readers' horizons and preparing them for material of a higher quality, literary criticism, and belles-lettres.[5] Attracting intellectuals, previously alienated from Yiddish, was also an important achievement, for which the radical press was largely responsible. Writers and speakers whose language had been Russian, German, or Hebrew, studied Yiddish in order to be read. Every important Jewish writer began his work by writing for the Yiddish press, and many eventually became salaried employees of the newspapers. Increasingly, the press originated and disseminated Yiddish literature in all its forms. There was at first no distinction between journalism and belles-lettres, and little to differentiate one literary genre from another, or even prose from poetry. All writing in the early radical press was propagandistic; literary artistry as such developed later.

The popularization of high culture in Yiddish has often been criticized for being superficial, but long before a sophisticated, critical audience could emerge, the mass of readers had to be educated in secular, contemporary matters and awakened to new interests. The literary critic Shmuel Niger has pungently summarized the importance of this role:

> The Yiddish press in America was the midwife of Yiddish literature. If the Yiddish newspaper was a home (frequently, to be sure, an asylum) to the Yiddish writer, to the reader it was a *heder*, if not a yeshivah. It taught him to read an unvocalized text, it gave him a taste for reading stories and poems in addition to the news, it enlightened him, it told him what was going on in the world, and it gave him a certain degree of sophistication and an interest in social literature.[6]

The self-consciousness of the more serious writers toward the primitive Yiddish abounding in the early years of immigration, often expressed, is reflected in the preface to the first issue of the *Zukunft* in January 1892:

> We announce quite frankly [that we] are undertaking to publish a scientific journal in the jargon—a novelty in the indigent jargon literature—only as an experiment. The Jewish labor movement is growing very rapidly and is developing workmen who want to learn about the social questions of our time

and to become cultured generally; but they cannot do so because until recently only old wives' tales and doggerel were written in the jargon and they are unfamiliar with other languages or know too little.

The *Zukunft* had emerged toward the end of 1891, reflecting the growing tension between Cahan and Krantz, as well as their respective abilities. Cahan had thrust himself forward at the *Arbayter Tsaytung* and soon edged Krantz out as editor. Krantz, in turn, became editor of the new monthly, conceived as a serious socialist journal dealing with literary, scientific, and political questions. The first issue included articles on a variety of topics: the evolution of a proletariat in America, a biography of Karl Marx, a report on the Reichstag elections in Germany, Darwinism and Malthus, and capitalism. Gradually, there appeared more strictly literary pieces and literary criticism. In 1894, *Zukunft* published such articles as Cahan's "Poetry: How It Is Written," and "A Few Words about the Development of Belles-lettres," by K. Paulding.[7]

The struggle against crude Yiddish was taken seriously, especially with the appearance in the early 1890's of a new genre in Yiddish, the cheap novel. B. Gorin, the historian of the Yiddish theater, began his *Yidishe-Amerikanishe Folksbibliotek* in 1897 to wage "open warfare against the yellow journalism that flooded all Jewish homes in America and to clear a new path for a clean decent literature."[8] Yiddish, of course, had already been scrubbed and polished by Mendele Mokher Seforim, Sholem Aleichem, and Yitzchak Leibush Peretz, and their stories began appearing in the *Arbayter Tsaytung* in the 1890's after Cahan became editor. Cahan himself was becoming a local colorist of New York's Jewish quarter and developing a novelistic talent. The first installment of a long moralistic fable called "How Raphael Na'aritzokh Became a Socialist," a work of considerable charm and vividness of characterization, appeared in the July 24, 1894, issue of the *Arbayter Tsaytung*. In the following year, Cahan wrote a short novel, "Yankel the Yankee" in Yiddish, and was encouraged by William Dean Howells to write in English for American magazines.

There was as yet no market for Yiddish books, but writers had outlets for their work in the press and felt sufficiently self-conscious as Yiddish writers to organize an association in 1889—the first "union" of Yiddish writers in America. The union's aim was to improve Yiddish literature both in form and content and organize support of members through weekly dues, public entertainment, and lectures. Hebrew writers, meanwhile, were very agitated. They derogated Yiddish and bewailed the need to "defile" their pens by writing in "the corrupt language of Babylon for the jargon publications." But the lowly jargon was gaining respectability and even the attention of scholars. In 1886, Alexander Harkavy published his little book *Di yidishe-daytshe shprakh* (The Yiddish-German Language), in which he took the position that Yiddish is as good a language as any other. This attracted responses in the press and was prominently featured in the *Folkstsaytung*.[9] Several years later Harkavy started work on his monumental Yiddish Dictionary.

Within a few years of their coming to America, immigrants began to acquire strong cultural appetites. They searched out "literary evenings," poetry readings and story telling, which soon became a major folk institution. And then the newspapers—particularly the radical press—brought the literary evenings into their homes, reprinting the works of European Yiddish writers and translations of European classics. Moreover, during the 1890's, the radical Yiddish press loosened up its intransigently didactic tone occasionally to admit articles on literary criticism and poetry on the strength of their quality. Another slight shift in content can be discerned. The Dreyfus case and the growing influence of Zionism led to greater interest in Jewish social and cultural problems and Jewish national survival. More of this type of writing appeared in the Yiddish conservative press, but some also began to appear in the socialist press.

However, Zionism was slow to make an impact on immigrant as well as established Jews in the United States. At first, only a few were stirred. Emma Lazarus, the Jewish poet, was deeply affected by George Eliot's novel *Daniel Deronda* and wrote fifteen articles for the periodical *American Hebrew* in 1882–83, expressing great sympathy for a restored Palestine. These undoubtedly influenced some Jews to think about Zionism favorably, but their immediate effect was mainly to stimulate a contentious exchange of letters. Hovevei Zion (Lovers of Zion) groups were scant but gradually attracted the attention of the Yiddish press and elements of the Jewish community in the late 1880's, and eventually were considered by the socialist Yiddish press. The first Hovevei Zion branch in New York numbered three hundred at the end of 1886. Soon there was a second branch, with a membership of 116, a woman's branch (Bnot Zion), and a branch in Chicago. This movement, though slight, was first acknowledged in the Yiddish press by the *Yidishe Gazeten*, under the caption "Jewish Colonization in Palestine":

> Under the above caption the *Gazeten* and the *Tageblatt* will feature interesting articles and reports from Palestine every week, particularly reports on the conditions of the colonies, the activities and progress of the organizations Hovevei Zion and the American friends of Jewish colonization in Palestine.[10]

The aims of Hovevei Zion were at first defined largely in traditional philanthropic terms—to aid poor and persecuted Jews. Even the rising nationalist spirit was transposed into a traditional religious key. "Our national pride is not nationalistic but religious," declared the organ of Hovevei Zion. The *Yidishe Gazeten* and other Yiddish publications reported fully on the progress of the colonies, dwelling fondly on every detail: so many thousands of trees planted, so many dunams of land irrigated.[11] Then, in 1885, a quite different note was sounded. A second branch of Hovevei Zion was founded for those who wished to *settle* in Palestine—a situation which created a rift between the two factions. The second group would not accept the prevailing melting-pot conception of America and spoke of the uncertainty of the Jewish future in America. Other groups, too, were disquieted by American press reports on the undesirability of immigrants and talked about Jews as guests and tenants in America who had to be prepared to leave.

The Chicago branch of Hovevei Zion bluntly called on its New York comrades "to unite and leave this alien land." This group, indeed, came to regard farming as the ideal occupation, capable of regenerating an ailing people. They deplored the Jewish "predilection for business" and believed that only settlement in Palestine could transform Jewish social-economic distortions. Another group with similar goals, called Shovei Zion, was created in 1891. The aim of its members was "to settle in Palestine at their own cost within three to five years." Moses Mintz, the former editor and publisher of *Nu Yorker Yidishe Folkstsaytung,* was its moving spirit.

His *Folkstsaytung* had been started in 1886 and offered a bold synthesis of socialism and Zionism. In the first issue, Mintz had declared: "On the battle line, the Jewish worker had many comrades as a worker; as a Jew, he has very few. The Jewish problem is very important and needs careful consideration for a proper solution. He [the Jewish worker] will understand the solution only when he is familiar with Jewish history." [12] Mintz soon became involved in a sharp controversy with Sarasohn, the publisher of the *Tageblatt* and *Yidishe Gazeten,* and other Jewish socialists, and both his paper and colonization effort ended within a few years.

The term "Zionism" began to appear quite frequently in the mid-1890's, but the movement was slow to affect Jewish life in the United States. Herzl's summons to the first Zionist Congress aroused less enthusiasm than criticism. Opposition soon developed into a conflict waged in the press and synagogue. The stand of Reform Judaism and the English-language Jewish press was very hostile. Zionism and its leaders were generally derided, satirized, and discredited. Christian interest was much more generous, if romanticized. Small groups formed and dissolved, and re-formed. Finally, in 1898, a federation of independent Zionist societies was formed, called the American Federation of Zionists. Various organizations and cities were represented, but the Federation was plagued by internal dissension and financial difficulties. American Zionism as a significant force in American Jewish life was not really felt until World War I when Louis Brandeis gave the movement an American and humanitarian stamp. Even then, large segments of American Jewry remained anti-Zionist.

The American labor Zionist movement—Poale Zion—grew out of a few pro-labor branches of the Federation. In 1900–1901, guided by the temperamental Joseph Ziff, these pro-labor groups were closely allied with a small group called Ohavei Zion, which had formed in Philadelphia on June 25, 1897, two months before the first Zionist Congress met.[13] Ohavei Zion, in turn, had been inspired by a Philadelphia Jewish scholar, Dr. Cyrus Adler, who had visited Palestine in 1891. Another very early figure in the Poale Zion movement, Ezekiel Edelstein, organized a group of English-speaking students with a socialist, anti-assimilationist outlook into a pro-labor Zionist group.[14] Later, the Brown brothers, Philadelphia booksellers and publishers, and Dr. Hayim Fineman, a professor of English literature at Temple College, brought the Philadelphia labor Zionist group into formal existence in June 1904.

Meanwhile, the first American Poale Zion branch had been formed in New York in March 1903 and announced its synthesis of socialism and Zionism: "The national struggle and the class struggle, far from being mutually exclusive, are two branches of the same trunk. They strive to accomplish the same ends—to free mankind by various methods and various ways." [15] By 1905, there were four branches in three states, which sent twenty-three delegates to the first American Poale Zion convention, held in Philadelphia, April 29–May 1. The convention promptly split into two groups—one territorialist (believing that any available land could be used for Jewish autonomous settlement, not just Palestine), the other, Palestine-centered. The majority at the time were territorialists, causing the Palestine-oriented wing to secede and reorganize the Poale Zion in Baltimore in December of the same year. That convention actually laid the foundation for what was to become the labor Zionist movement in America. The socialist-territorialists in America, as in Europe, fought the "Palestinians" bitterly, and brought their most fiery advocate, Nachman Syrkin, to edit their weekly *Das Volk* in 1907.[16]

Most of the early members of the Poale Zion were immigrant workers eager to become part of the American socialist movement, but they were rebuffed and indeed subjected to continuous attack. They were also assailed by the Zionist right. Vehemently opposed to the Bund, Labor Zionism in America was nevertheless fated to live with a similar duality—in this case, the difficulty of reconciling the desire for a socialist society in America with a very strong Jewish nationalist position.

After the Kishinev pogroms in 1903, there was a great infusion of Zionist and Bundist literature, and outstanding writers such as Chaim Zhitlovsky and Abraham Liessin challenged socialist shibboleths and reminded the Jewish labor movement of the existence of a Jewish people. But even earlier, there were signs of change. The strongly anti-Zionist *Forward* carried an editorial on October 31, 1902, written by Dr. S. Peskin, which not only admitted the reality of Jewish national feelings, but the possibility of reconciling it with socialism:

> We do not want to see all peoples cooked into one stew. We believe that, even
> as I have a right to wish that there be no poor and rich, so do I have a right to

wish that Jews remain a nation with its own language, its own folkways, culture, and so on. Every other nation may strive toward the same end. In this sense there is no conflict between socialism and nationalism. Everybody can fully be both a nationalist and a socialist.

Some socialists, moreover, began to think about their share of responsibility for continued Jewish existence or, at least, about improving the existing quality of cultural expressions. For most Jewish socialists, however, Jewish culture was not a value in itself but subordinate to cosmopolitan values and the class struggle. Still, demands for a better quality of Yiddish culture—particularly in literature and the theatre—began to be expressed by intellectuals in the 1890's. During this same decade, moreover, a new influx of immigrants, including well-educated and talented Jews, augmented this demand. In literature, fictional sketches began to appear in Yiddish newspapers, ranging from the simplest and most unpretentious to quite subtle and artistically rendered portrayals of life on New York's East Side. The labor press published these sketches frequently, and Jewish workers could now read about themselves, their confusions, fears, and conflicts, as well as hardships. This gave them an interest in "literature." Of special significance were Leon Kobrin and Zalman Libin.

Kobrin,[17] born in Vitebsk, was attracted to Russian culture, though he was the son of poor, Orthodox parents, and began writing sketches in Russian at an early age. When he came to the United States in 1892, he was twenty years old but knew no Yiddish. He had only heard of "Jewish writers who wrote simple tales for servant girls and ignoramuses in the Yiddish jargon." About Mendele and Peretz, he knew only a few translations that he had read in *Voskhod*. He learned Yiddish and began to write in it somewhat apologetically, but came to believe in its literary possibilities after he read stories by Anton Chekhov which Cahan had translated from Russian for the *Arbayter Tsaytung*.

Kobrin could not survive in the sweatshops and failed as a cigar-maker and baker, so he tried writing sketches for the *Arbayter Tsaytung*. Some were satirical, almost burlesque descriptions of ghetto types, but most were in the naturalistic vein that he admired in the French and Russian tradition. They dealt realistically with themes new to the ghettos—the inner life of workers and radical intellectuals, the complexities of sexual passion, the brutalization of workers (as well as bosses), the conflicts and ambivalencies of the emotional struggle to bridge two cultures, and the complications of Americanization. As in David Pinski's plays later, Kobrin dealt with erotic themes, but was less interested in sexuality than in the changing life-styles a freer sexual code involves,[18] often calling into question the assumptions of traditional Jewish morality and conventional American standards.

The stories of American Jewish life were difficult to write, Kobrin admitted:

Writing about Jewish life in Russia, I constantly had before my eyes a defined, developed, complete type, with a definite world outlook, a heritage of generations and generations; but writing about Jewish life in America I constantly had before my eyes confused souls, unsettled characters, a chaotic life. And to create life and people out of chaos—that was easy only for the Almighty himself!

Yet, later, he prided himself on being an *American* Yiddish writer, impatient with authors who devoted their attention to Europe and neglected the American scene. This attitude was not a reflection of any provincialism, for Kobrin, toward the end of his life, was actively involved in the Yidisher Kultur Farband (YKUF), organized in 1937 as an international cultural organization.

Zalman Libin (Israel Hurvitz) wrote many plays for the Yiddish theatre—his theatrical output amounted to over fifty plays—but he is best remembered for his sketches of the sordid conditions of Jewish life in the ghetto. "My muse," he later wrote, "was born in the gloomy sweatshops; it gave its first anguished cry by the side of the Singer [sewing] machine. It was educated in the dark tombs of the tenements." When Hapgood saw him in 1900–1901, he was "a dark, thin, little man, as ragged as a tramp, with plaintive eyes and a deprecatory smile when he speaks. He is uncommonly poor, and at present sells newspapers for a living and writes an occasional sketch, for which he is paid at the rate of $1.50 or $2.00 a column by the Yiddish newspapers." [19] Stealing a few minutes from his long hours as a cap maker, Libin wrote his sketches, which he sent to the *Arbayter Tsaytung* and later to the *Jewish Daily Forward*. Cahan recognized in Libin's misspelled, almost illegible manuscript a certain gift for realism, pathos, and gentle satire and published a number of his sketches. His "Worker's Sigh" was the first Yiddish fictional sketch published. One of the most poignant, called "The New Law," describes an agitated tailor, paid by the piece, who finds that a new law limits the workday in the shop to ten hours and forbids the workers to take any work home. The tailor customarily works nineteen hours a day; his wife and child sew busily at home. How can they live under the new law?

Although the chief vehicle for Kobrin and Libin was the radical Yiddish press, which, at least theoretically, was indifferent to the history and destiny of the Jewish people as a people, the image of the Jew which emerges from their writings is in the main, a sympathetic one.[20] Moreover, these writers retained a genuine warmth for the charm and simple goodness of traditional Jewish life, which was unhinged forever in America.

Despite the attraction of the sketches, however, no newspaper or journal could match the flesh-and-blood immediacy of the Yiddish theatre. The socialist intellectuals knew that they could never displace it, although they found its fare and influence cheap and trashy in the early days. Into the three theatres on the Bowery, in the midst of music halls, dives, cheap lodging houses, saloons, and fake museums, poured the whole ghetto the first four nights of the week, when blocks of seats were bought up by clubs, *landsmanshaften,* and union locals. Generally, before the "new" theatre of Jacob Gordin, the plays catered to primitive, even vulgar tastes. Crude melodrama, vaudeville tricks, and cheap historical spectacles were the usual fare. But the immigrant audience loved it. Many a poor Jew who made no more than ten dollars a week would spend five dollars of it on the theatre, which was his only amusement. But it was not only to see the play; it was to see his friends and especially the actors, who strutted about in the cafés on Canal and Grand streets, fully aware of the adoring crowds, who were often treated with haughty condescension or biting humor.

The sights in the theatres were marvellously picturesque:

> Poor workingmen and women with their babies of all ages fill the theatre. Great enthusiasm is manifested, sincere laughter and tears accompany the sincere acting on the stage. Peddlers of soda water, candy, of fantastic gewgaws of many kinds, mix freely with the audience between acts. Conversation during the play is received with strenuous hisses, but the falling of the curtain is the signal for groups of friends to get together and gossip about the play or affairs of the week. Introductions are not necessary.[21]

The audience came to have a good laugh and a good cry and could switch from the sentimental to the boisterous in a moment. But the more sophisticated Jews were outraged by the typical theatrical fare. In answering a reader's question asking why the *Arbayter Tsaytung* in its first year (1890) was ignoring the Yiddish theatre, Cahan replied: "We cannot devote ourselves to theatre reviews because most Jewish readers, regrettably do not understand what theatre criticism is. Also, it would not help to improve the theatre. Most of the plays on the stage do not deserve serious reviews. The fault lies in the low taste of the Jewish public." [22]

The intellectuals at first despaired of raising the level of the Yiddish theatre from the level of *shund* (vulgarity) and getting the audience to enjoy serious drama until a writer from Russia—Jacob Gordin—came on the scene. Physically, Gordin was a big and impressive figure. "I still see him walking along the streets," Kobrin recalled, "straight as a palm, his princely beard solemnly covering his broad chest, his eyes like two bits of fire, sharp as daggers. In his right hand he carries a cane; in his left, one of his plays. He is going to the theatre to read it to the actors." [23]

Gordin became a figure larger than life, indeed a myth during his lifetime, fiercely independent, possessed of the grand manner, not the least susceptible to bending under the pressures of the socialists, although he deeply identified with the struggle of the poor masses for a better life. Gordin came to America in 1891, intending to establish a Tolstoyan-type agricultural colony. As a youth in Russia,[24] he had worked variously as a farm laborer, longshoreman, journalist, and traveling actor, consciously trying to bypass the customary occupations of Jews in the Pale. His home, a combination of enlightenment and Orthodoxy, had a library that contained Russian as well as Hebrew works and liberal magazines, which Jacob read avidly. He was strongly pulled by Russian literature and received a good Russian education, but he also loved the Bible and tried to create a contemporary movement based on its moral teachings. For a time he wrote sketches of Jewish life in various papers and served as editor of an important Russian paper in Odessa, but he became restless and in 1880, wanting to bring "light, education, and hope" directly to the Jewish masses, he organized a Spiritual Biblical Brotherhood, modeled in part on the peasant sect that influenced Tolstoy.

Gordin's brotherhood acknowledged the Bible only in a Tolstoyan sense and idealized the Jewish peasant type described there. Yet Gordin opposed settlement in Palestine as unacceptably nationalistic. Orthodox Jews looked upon him as an apostate, and after the pogroms of 1881, which he blamed on Jewish love of money and saloon-keeping, he was reviled in the Jewish press. Finally, the Russian government itself closed down the brotherhood and Gordin felt that his life in Russia had become futile. He left for America in 1891.

When he arrived in New York, Gordin was already thirty-eight—much older than the other revolutionary youths—self-educated, unaffiliated with any socialist group, and convinced that the only remedy for Jewish persecution was economic reconstruction. Trade, peddling, and moneylending would have to give way to farming. About sixty of Gordin's followers in the disbanded Biblical Brotherhood had followed him; within a month of his arrival, he addressed a memorandum to the Baron de Hirsch Fund, outlining plans for an agricultural colony.[25] The group contained many skilled individuals, but the fund, already struggling with precarious colonies, turned Gordin down. Gordin made another attempt to establish a farming colony in 1893, in Woodbine, New Jersey, but this, too, was unsuccessful.

Meanwhile, in order to support his large family, Gordin perfected his Yiddish and began to contribute sketches to the *Arbayter Tsaytung*. His first article appeared in the August 21, 1891, issue and dealt with a pogrom in Elisabethgrad, which occurred about a month after he left the city. This time he did not blame the Jews, as he had earlier, but condemned the plundering peasants. The second piece, "Pantole Polge," which possibly inspired Peretz' famous story "Bontshe the Silent," contained superbly written dialogue which was quickly dramaticized and performed at the Union Theatre.[26] The sketch was well received, and Gordin was commissioned by the actor Jacob Adler to write a play. The result was *Siberia*, which Cahan described as "a complete revolution on the Yiddish stage." The play dealt with a Jew who had escaped from exile in Siberia and was caught by the police—a dramatically tense and familiar theme. There was no ad-libbing by the actors—a momentous change—and very little music or dancing. The play was successful and launched Gordin as the pre-eminent Jewish playwright of the period. Intellectuals knew something important was happening to the Yiddish theatre and acclaimed Gordin as the new champion and "apostle of realism."

A rapid succession of plays followed, of greatly varying character, many that leaned heavily on models drawn from world drama, and all reflecting Gordin's conviction that "the greatest educational institution in the world is the theatre." Like so many of the intellectuals in New York's East Side, he wanted to uplift the depressed masses, pointing up moral lessons of one sort or another. In the more than seventy plays Gordin adapted or originated, he consciously used the stage to moralize and instruct. His themes dealt mainly with the grip of tradition, the conflict of generations, the struggle between rich and poor, the scramble for money, family strife, and the struggle of women to emancipate themselves. Some non-Jewish writers compared him to Ibsen. His themes were discussed at home, at work, and in the cafés; he stimulated intellectuals to discuss "realism in the arts." On the Monday following the opening of *Der Yidisher Kenig Lear (The Jewish King Lear)*, a play leaning heavily on Shakespeare but dealing with Jewish children who neglect their parents, lines of young men and women formed in front of the bank on Delancey Street waiting to send money to their parents in Europe.[27]

By modern standards, Gordin's plays are too melodramatic, but at the turn of the century, they infused the Yiddish theatre with fresh ideas and literary style, and gave players dramatic material with which to grow artistically. For young, talented actors like Jacob Adler, David Kessler, Boris Thomashevsky, Bertha Kalish and Keni Liptzen, Gordin was their salvation. He gave them dramatic plays and character types with which they could identify: *Der Yidisher Kenig Lear, Gott, Mensch un Taivel (God, Man and the Devil), Mirele Efros,* and the *Kreutzer Sonata.* The actors became folk heroes. Fabulous stories were told about their exploits and each had his own group of followers and devotees.

Although many characters and locales in his plays are Jewish, Gordin did not draw on the experience of the Jewish people, but aimed at "universalizing" it, actually closing out the immigrant past. Even after the pogroms of 1903, in the great radical debates between the internationalists and those straining to recover their Jewishness, Gordin sided with the former. But his contribution to the Yiddish theatre was considerable. He not only educated the better actors artistically and created respect for the written script, but he exerted a profound cultural influence on the theatre audience.[28] Gradually, both actors and spectators learned to appreciate plays free of the claptrap of cheap operetta and melodrama. Moreover, thanks to him, some of the educated radicals began to take an interest in the Yiddish stage, and in 1896, they established a theatrical association, Di Fraye Yidishe Folksbine [29] (The Free Jewish People's Theatre). Moreover, on Gordin's initiative, an Educational League was established, a sort of people's college where some five hundred young people studied English, social studies, and literature. Gordin himself lectured extensively before many *landsmanshaften* and radical societies and wrote frequently for the socialist press.

The raw life that Gordin dramatized was frowned on by the conventional American theatre of the day, but his insistence on realism and the development of ideas in plays intrigued the avant-garde of the American literary scene. In these non-Jewish circles, he was considered the finest dramatic craftsman in the United States.[30] The better American journals published systematic and critical reviews of the Yiddish theatre in general and of Gordin's plays in particular. Lincoln Steffens, in his autobiography,[31] believed that the best theatre in New York City in his day was the Yiddish theatre.

Under Gordin's influence, other Yiddish writers, particularly Kobrin and Libin, began to write for the theatre. In his plays Kobrin continued his intense interest in the fierce claims of sex upon his characters and in the contrary forces battling within an individual, being much less interested than Gordin in ideas and moral lessons.[32] Probably his most successful play was *Der Dorfsyung (The Swain)* produced in 1908 and based on an earlier story "Yankele Boile," the tragedy of a strong, kind, but dull-witted Jewish youth in a Russian fishing village, embroiled in a complex moral and emotional dilemma that he could resolve only by committing suicide. Libin, also influenced by Gordin, wrote over fifty plays, quite popular in their time, most of them dealing with tense family problems played out in the wretched tenements about which he had written in his sketches.

Later migrations brought other gifted writers: Abraham Reisen, Sholem Asch, David Pinski, Chaim Zhitlovsky, and Abraham Liessin. Together with the vigorous development of the Yiddish theatre, for which a number of the writers wrote plays, they created a rich literary culture which the early Yiddish labor poets and editors would have dismissed as impossible—and even undesirable. Yiddish, they had thought, would dissolve away as the vision of a classless society dawned.

The heightened response to the Yiddish theatre, human interest sketches, literary critism, and poetry contributed enormously to the development of a literate audience and the beginnings of book buying. Although most of the books printed before 1900 were novels of slight literary merit, mostly translations and adaptations, they broadened the immigrant reader's outlook and accustomed him to read books in addition to newspapers.[33]

The interest in Yiddish cultural expression as a value in itself developed more fully in the early 1900's as Bundism, Zionism, and theories of Yiddish as a linguistic base for Jewish culture clashed with the older assumptions, and as a new wave of immigration beat against the old. Yiddish resounded everywhere. The despised jargon was becoming a supple, richly expressive instrument of permanent cultural value.

It is not a little ironic that Yiddish became a central element in the culture of the Jewish socialists, not only as a literary and dramatic tool, but as an important means of adjustment and economic progress. Whereas other ethnic groups became economically productive to the extent that they became anglicized, Jews became productive in and through Yiddish. And Jewish productivity at the end of the nineteenth century meant proletarianization.[34]

Table 3. Number of Jews in Largest Cities in the United States, 1900

City	Population
New York	500,000
Philadelphia	75,000
Chicago	60,000
Boston	40,000
Baltimore	25,000
St. Louis	25,000
Cleveland	20,000
San Francisco	15,000
Newark	15,000
Pittsburgh	10,000
Detroit	10,000
Los Angeles	2,000

Source: Jacob Lestchinsky, "Economic and Social Development of American Jewry," in *Jewish People Past and Present* (New York, 1955), vol. 4, p. 58.

This economic transformation was made possible by the compactness of Jewish life within the ghettos of New York, Chicago, Philadelphia, and Baltimore (see Table 3). Here, Jewish workers worked for Jewish employers and the class conflicts between them were carried on in a Jewish milieu.[35] Everyone spoke Yiddish; frequently, workers and employers came from the same town. Many of the shops were in the homes of the employers, in which workers demanded time off to conduct religious services. The Jewish worker could live in New York for years and not come into contact with the non-Jewish world or have need of the English language. Jewish capital and labor battled on opposite sides of the economic barricades, but they lived within a common culture to a much greater degree than either would have been willing to admit. The socialist founders of Jewish unions may not have had any ideological interest in Jewish culture, yet they were destined to be bearers of that culture in ways they could scarcely have foreseen.

10. Stormy Years, 1890-97

In the years 1890–97, the labor movement in America was torn by bitter ideological conflict and debilitating fragmentation. Socialists battled anarchists for control of the radical press; socialists argued endlessly over the role of trade unions, the possibility of reform within a capitalistic society, and party work in unions. An ultimately ruinous internal struggle within the Socialist Labor party ripped the movement apart. Jewish unions and Jewish socialists were enmeshed in all of these issues.

A maze of internal conflicts in the young and shaky Jewish labor movement of the time twisted around a last-ditch effort by anarchists to oust the socialists from control of the Yiddish labor press—still in its formative stages, but growing rapidly—and an exhausting, unelevating struggle for the Jewish unions themselves. For several years, a pivotal and controversial figure in these struggles was Joseph Barondess,[1] the flamboyant and adored leader of the Cloakmakers' Union. Hardly a party man, Barondess had to take two opponents of the Socialist Labor party into the union's executive board in order to placate anarchist elements in his union. The *Arbayter Tsaytung*, resenting this tolerance, began to attack him abusively and organized socialist groups in the union to oppose him. Deeply hurt by these attacks, Barondess took his union out of the Socialist Labor party labor federation, which the Cloakmakers' Union had joined with the UHT, and brought it into the American Federation of Labor (AFL). Barondess was also an occasional contributor to the *Arbayter Tsaytung*'s anarchist competitor, *Fraye Arbayter Shtimme*, a fact which strengthened the socialist argument that he had anarchist sympathies.

Curiously, the anarchists were no longer condemning all unions out of hand. There were good unions and bad unions, depending on the degree of anarchist influence, and although most members of the Cloakmakers' Union were readers of the *Arbayter Tsaytung*, which backed the SLP, the anarchists were bent on transforming it into a "good" union. The relative power of each see-sawed. The high point in Barondess' influence and popularity came in July 1890, after a very successful strike. Union membership increased rapidly and its prestige soared. But Barondess was soon involved in legal complications over an extortion charge, largely spurred by employers who wanted to undermine the union and crush Barondess. This struggle overlapped a divisive three-cornered battle among the Socialist Labor party, the AFL, and the Knights of Labor, which involved all the Jewish unions, most especially the cloakmakers, the largest prize and, politically, the most excitable. And in the center of this storm was Daniel De Leon.[2]

De Leon was born in the Dutch West Indies of a wealthy Sephardic Jewish family. After studying in Germany, he came to New York in 1872, and studied and taught international law at Columbia University. He first engaged in politics in the Henry George campaign of 1886 and became a Marxist within a few years. When the Socialist Labor party recruited De Leon in 1890, it was the leading revolutionary organization in America,[3] though still somewhat weakened by earlier conflicts over the role of labor unions. Almost immediately, De Leon assumed leadership of the party and brought new vigor to the idea of trying to inoculate the trade unions of the country with socialist revolutionary principles by having socialists bore from within. He vehemently rejected any compromise with the capitalist system and attacked trade-union leaders and socialists who concentrated on immediate demands of workers as enemies of the working class. He grimly admitted that only a determined minority, i.e., the Socialist Labor party, would have the tenacity and spirit to lead the workers to socialism. For a time, De Leon's ideas and methods dominated the party, which consisted mainly of foreigners and intellectuals: mostly Germans and a scattering of Jews, Poles, and Italians. The Jewish socialists on the East Side were won over by De Leon's revolutionary rhetoric and the faint aura of romanticized conspiracy he inspired. His dogmatic solutions to the most complex questions also helped them overcome their recurring fear of being lost in a life without a future.

Under De Leon, the party intensified its efforts to convert local unions and central labor bodies, and through these, the AFL and Knights of Labor, to the principles of socialism. By 1893, sixteen central labor bodies recognized delegates from the Socialist Labor party, and the party controlled seventy-two trade unions united in the powerful Central Labor Federation of New York.[4] In that year, the party polled 25,666 votes in federal elections. It made serious enough inroads in the AFL to influence delegates to the 1894 convention to very nearly adopt a plank calling for collective ownership of all means of production and distribution, and defeat Samuel Gompers for the presidency of the federation.

By the following year, however, Gompers was firmly back in the saddle, intent upon revenge. The socialists were outnumbered three to one, and De Leon concluded that AFL leaders were "labor fakirs . . . doing picket duty for capitalism," and that craft unions as a whole were little more than a "conspiracy of the capitalists and conservative labor leaders against the working class." [5] Under order from De Leon, the Jewish socialists detached their unions from the AFL and affiliated with a new dual New York Central Alliance that De Leon set up. Another sudden switch was soon to come.

Relentlessly, De Leon had also tried to capture the rapidly declining Knights of Labor. Supported by the German, Jewish, and other non-English–speaking socialist-led unions of New York, the SLP won the leadership of the Knights' most powerful body, District Assembly 49, and at the 1893 Knights' convention, it succeeded in ousting Powderly from his fourteen-year sinecure as Grand Master Workman. From this new base, De Leon planned to capture the entire labor movement. But De Leon's influence was very brief. Feuds and personality clashes drove him to withdraw the party's 13,000 members from the Knights in 1895 with his typically vehement blast that "the whole fabric of the organization was rotten to the core and nothing could be gained by capturing what had been reduced to a nest of crooks."

For its part, beginning in 1890, the Knights of Labor had been making a determined effort to regain its lost position, concentrating its drive in the skilled trades. This decision drew it into a fierce struggle with the young AFL. The Knights affiliated with the UHT and, counting on the prestige the UHT enjoyed in the garment trades, they organized a second union in the cloak and suit trade. The cloakmakers also became the target of the SLP, which, having failed to bore from within the AFL, belatedly embarked on a trade-union campaign.

Immediately following his unsuccessful campaigns in the AFL and Knights of Labor, De Leon prepared to implement his Marxian principles by organizing a rival union, the Socialist Trade and Labor Alliance, under strict party control. But the Alliance's union membership raids antagonized many workers, including Jewish socialists and union members. Many of them, under the influence of the *Forward*, refused to follow De Leon and prepared for another split. The leaders of the UHT, however, took their organization into the Alliance, although many of its affiliates remained in the AFL. To counter the shift of the UHT, the socialists of the *Forward* bloc set up the Federated Hebrew Trades, loyal to the AFL.

Adding to the confusion, the anarchists, a small but vociferous group in certain unions, fearing that the new center was squeezing them out of their position, and believing that the socialists were bent on destroying their weekly paper, *Fraye Arbayter Shtimme*, went over to their former archenemies, the AFL. To justify this shocking expediency, the anarchists argued that it was better for the unions to affiliate with the openly conservative AFL, which repudiated political activity, than be dominated by the socialists who engaged in political activity "detrimental to the workers." Gompers, for his part, was eager to win the support of the Jewish workers and accepted the anarchists as allies. Melech Epstein, labor historian, has vividly described the strife-torn scene:

> This reshuffle of allegiances created a curious and catastrophic situation. The fiery adherents of the Social Revolution, the anarchists, did their utmost to keep the unions in the conservative AFL, while the "socialist traitors" of the revolution, of the Socialist Labor party, split unions for a new class-conscious and militant trade union movement.
>
> Intergroup fighting always attains a higher pitch of fervor and vilification than a struggle with an outside enemy. Union meetings became a bedlam. Several of the unions were split down the middle. The weeklies of both the socialists and the anarchists were busily engaged in hurling at each other abuse from the vast arsenal imported from the radical movement in the old country, and spiced with Hebrew and Yiddish invectives. To add to this growing chaos, the socialist-anarchist ideological controversy was becoming more vehement as a result of the organizational struggle. The lines were sharply drawn, and although the mass of workers stood aside from both camps, the active people in the unions and their followers were thrown into the fracas.[6]

These struggles spread to other cities. In Chicago, Baltimore, and Philadelphia, where the anarchists were quite strong, local cloakmakers' unions became part of the AFL. Meanwhile, the two weeklies, ostensibly started for the purpose of teaching and organizing a vast, uneducated Jewish proletariat, were heaping abuse upon each other. So charged was the hostility that the gifted, sensitive young poet David Edelstadt who edited the *Fraye Arbayter Shtimme* for a short time, permitted the rousing demonstration of Jewish workers in New York on May Day 1890 to be ridiculed with sneering phrases.[7] (By the following year, in the zig-zag of allegiances, the anarchists had changed their minds and marched with the very socialists they earlier called clowns, but they did not come together on basic issues.)

Bad feeling was aggravated by a conflict which developed around the typesetters' union and soon implicated the entire Jewish labor movement. In 1891, the typesetters of the *Fraye Arbayter Shtimme* asked for a wage increase. The management said the financial situation of the paper did not warrant an increase. The Knights of Labor, with which the union was affiliated, thereupon approved a strike and the UHT called for a boycott of the anarchist paper. The *Shtimme* charged that the wage demand was a ruse to destroy the paper; after the strike was called, new typesetters were hired, and a rival union was formed affiliated with the AFL. A boycott war between the two papers followed, splitting radical and labor groups and generating a rash of competing unions and abrasive personality clashes.

Very likely, the colorful figure of Joseph Barondess, who figured prominently in the struggle that raged between socialists and anarchists, represented a somewhat threatening, new force in Jewish labor leadership to aggressive and domineering men like Cahan and Louis Miller. As an immigrant youth, Barondess had worked in garment shops, was active in several early spontaneous strikes, and succeeded in forming a small union, which he represented in the new UHT. In 1890, he organized the floundering cloakmakers who were carrying out separate shop strikes and brought them under his tireless and devoted leadership. In describing him as the builder of the union, a trace of envy slips into Cahan's remarks:

> We suddenly saw him as an influential leader of a large organization. . . . Barondess was the commanding figure. His power had grown immensely. He began to pay attention to his clothes and to carry himself with poise. He was unrecognizable. The workers loved him. His devotion in their strike was not the only reason. . . . Barondess possessed a considerable personal magnetism. A soft, good-natured man, it was easy to awaken pity in him, to bring tears to his eyes, and to get a favor from him. . . . His voice alone created respect. . . . I knew many cloakmakers who were literally fascinated by him. They loved him and trembled before him.[8]

Later, Cahan charged that Barondess had become a union leader "by accident." Melech Epstein has speculated that Cahan—and Miller—"were unwilling to see the larger unions slipping away from them. They were not men to permit themselves to be relegated to the position of mere propagandists and advisers. Barondess, a people's tribune, expressed the spirit of independence that was maturing in the new unions." [9]

Eventually, the Cloakmakers' Union was ruined—and with it the career of Barondess as trade union leader—by the ravages of the depression of 1893, and by the refusal of employers to deal with the striking union after it failed to rally support for a general strike. Ironically, Barondess came full circle and joined the socialists he had always been close to. In 1897, he joined Cahan, Miller, and others in their break with the Socialist Labor party and became a co-founder of the *Forward*, which became the fountainhead of opposition to De Leon's inflexible and dogmatic socialism. But he was too independent a spirit to stay within Cahan's orbit for long and ultimately broke with the *Forward* when its attacks on Gompers and the AFL grew particularly venomous. Later, he joined Eugene V. Debs and Victor Berger on a ticket of the newly launched Social-Democratic party, the forerunner of the Socialist party. In 1903 and 1905, he was greatly shaken by the wave of pogroms in Russia, and in contrast with many of his assimilationist friends in the labor movement, he became increasingly conscious of his Jewishness and became active in Zionist affairs.

Yet Barondess maintained contact with the labor movement and as late as 1906 echoed the views of the AFL with regard to separatist Jewish unions, a view that was very critical of union division along national, racial, or religious lines, and thus of the very existence of the UHT. He wrote:

> The Central Labor Union [AFL] has accused us of dishonesty. You preach, "Workers of all lands unite," and in practice you split the strength of organized labor by segregating our German and Jewish co-workers in separate bodies. If we permit this segregation, then the Irish, the English, and workers of other

nationalities will also separate, and the measure of unity that American workers have achieved after so many years will be entirely destroyed.[10]

The struggle over control of the Yiddish labor press also overlapped an inner struggle for editorial independence from a creeping bureaucracy; this, in turn, was enmeshed in the struggle against De Leon's leadership. The *Arbayter Tsaytung* was a weekly published by the *Arbayter Tsaytung* Publishing Association, a body with a small, select membership. The association's executive committee consisted of shop workers who had risen to positions of power. Because of its control of the press (it also published *Das Abendblatt*, a socialist evening paper), it exercised important influence over the UHT, the Jewish unions, and the Socialist Labor party.[11] Its members were unreservedly loyal to De Leon, who wrote for the paper, and the growing number of professional men in the radical movement.[12]

Intellectuals like Cahan and Miller were at first not very much interested in administration. But when control of policy shifted from the relatively broad association to a self-perpetuating management board which imposed its ideas, the independent intellectuals were irked by restrictions on editorial policy, which was shaped to fit De Leon's objectives. Bent on making the trade union movement into a tool of the SLP, De Leon became increasingly arbitrary and relentless. When the UHT and many of its unions affiliated with his Alliance, they had no freedom, but had to follow the SLP political line. The gathering rebelliousness against De Leon was partly instigated and fed by the intellectuals on and around the *Arbayter Tsaytung*. Having developed a strong dislike of De Leon's tyranny, Cahan became particularly active in the opposition. Thus, the struggle for control of the two socialist papers was interlocked with the struggle against De Leon and exacerbated by it.

By 1892, the *Arbayter Tsaytung* had a circulation of about 10,000 and its principal sponsor, the UHT, had grown into a federation comprising forty affiliated unions. The leadership of the two had become interlocked and bureaucratized. In the early stage of the conflict, Cahan demanded that the press be turned over to a delegated body of all labor organizations. "The leaders of the [publishing] association were honest men," Cahan wrote, "but power is sweet and they were not eager to relinquish it." Louis Miller, by now a practicing lawyer, supported him, accusing the management of engaging in "clique business" and closing the door to new members. The growing resistance to the New York bureaucracy found expression in the national convention of Yiddish-speaking branches of the SLP held in January 1894, when Cahan was elected to replace Philip Krantz as editor of the monthly *Zukunft*. Some of these constituent branches had never given up the old notion of "non-partisanship"; some sections also contained anarchist and AFL affiliates. After Cahan's accession as editor, *Zukunft* became a rallying point for the opposition to De Leon.

In 1894, Cahan made his first open move against De Leon's leadership.

At a meeting of socialists in the election districts of the East Side, Cahan introduced a resolution opposing De Leon's policies in the party [13]— particularly dual unionism—but the resolution was defeated. De Leon's prestige was still very high. In that year, the socialist-controlled unions were still in the AFL and defeated Gompers for the presidency. As for Jewish socialists, they were still quite solidly behind De Leon. They were passing through a period of ideological adjustment to American conditions, but the social revolution was still the main theme of their propaganda. The German Social-Democratic party with its growing strength in the Reichstag, its influential trade unions and newspapers, had replaced the Russian revolutionary movement as their model of a socialist movement, and they commonly used German nomenclature. A party branch was a *sektion*, trade unions were *gewerkschaften*, and party members were called *genossen*. But Jewish socialists still clung—at least in principle—to the necessity of a class struggle and drastic changes in the existing system. Many thus accepted De Leon's splitting tactics in the trade unions. Caught in unresolvable but understandable paradoxes, they admired De Leon for his strongly "American" radical experience, as well as his Sephardic origins, while at the same time their own links to American society were still so weak they could accept De Leon's negative policy toward local workers' parties, the widening populist movement, and the essentially pragmatic nature of American trade unionism.

Moreover, with the advent of De Leon, the Jewish labor movement, torn between politically minded socialists and apolitical anarchists, finally accepted political leadership.[14] Politics became infused with a religious intensity and social urgency to which neither major political party could respond. The *Arbayter Tsaytung* hailed Election Day in 1892 as "Judgment Day" and compared the Socialist Labor party to the Abolitionists. The "joy that an honest man gains on fulfilling a sacred duty" was deemed sufficient reward for voting for its candidates.[15] Jewish messianic fervor was beginning to find expression in impassioned political yearning and hope for redemption.

But a storm was brewing within the party, and at the center was Abraham Cahan. At this time, Cahan was far from having crystallized a clear political path for himself. By 1894, he had made several trips to Europe and was overcome by recurring waves of nostalgia for the lost Russian revolutionary still buried within him. He also yearned to become an "American" writer and was sketching out the lines of a novel. Still affiliated with the "American" branch of the SLP in New York, he was convinced that he had a more realistic knowledge of the American scene than any of his fellow intellectuals. In 1894, he wrote a series of articles in the *Arbayter Tsaytung*, in which he urged the formation of a workers' party that would not abandon the class struggle. "We are of the opinion," he said, "that the American workers are already at a stage which makes it possible for them to accept a purely socialist program." The *melamed*, the teacher, in him was also alive: he felt called upon to enlighten the Lower East Side about the dangers of De Leon's leadership.[16] Cahan disliked De Leon's biting sarcasm, dogmatism, and despotic power in the party. Cahan was also convinced that the tactic of dual unionism would lead to the disintegration of the labor movement.

Allied with him were Michael Zametkin, Louis Miller, and Morris Winchevsky. Miller, in 1892, in the second issue of *Zukunft*, had written a fiery article called "What Is To Be Done?" [17] denouncing the factionalism and stagnation of the SLP. Discerning the growing power of the AFL, he also attacked the continuing warfare against the anarchists. Winchevsky, by now a regular contributor to both the *Arbayter Tsaytung* and *Zukunft*, had recently arrived in New York and was soon won over to Cahan's and Miller's side. Toward the end of the year he received an invitation from the Yiddish-speaking socialists in Boston—where anarchists and socialists both belonged to socialist party branches—to come and edit a paper for them. To prevent further disunity among socialists, the paper was to be purely "educational." Winchevsky agreed, and the first issue of *Der Emes* *(The Truth)* appeared on May 3, 1895. It was sub-titled "A Weekly Family Paper for Literature and Enlightenment." However, it did not keep its family character for long. In the August 19 issue, Winchevsky published a provocative editorial titled "Foyl oder Tsugefoylt?" ("Rotten or Rotting?"), in which he accused De Leon and his followers of ruining the socialist movement. "De Leon's tactics," he wrote, "are the worm in the good apple of the SLP." He was soon relieved of his post.

The Boston party section supporting Winchevsky proposed a special convention to consider reforms within the Jewish labor movement. The result was a congress of Yiddish-speaking branches of the SLP. The *Arbayter Tsaytung* Publishing Association did not recognize the assembly because unions were not admitted, but it became the scene of the first confrontation between De Leon's followers and their opposition. Critics of De Leon demanded that the *Arbayter Tsaytung* and *Das Abendblatt* be removed from the existing control of the *Arbayter Tsaytung* Publishing Association, and placed, like *Zukunft*, under the direct authority of the Yiddish-speaking branches of the SLP.[18] They also wanted *Das Abendblatt* to be less sectarian. The battle over De Leon's Trade and Labor Alliance further agitated and confused Jewish workers, but the lines were sharpening. In November 1895, the *Arbayter Tsaytung* editorialized:

> We must say candidly that we are not in the least pleased with Comrade De Leon's "victory" and his whole "struggle," particularly in both national labor organizations. Comrade De Leon goes much too far in his accusations and attacks against the "pure and simple" unionists and the "labor fakirs." He seems to be obsessed with attacking and fighting them on every suitable and unsuitable occasion. . . . These quarrelsome and intolerant tactics are a misfortune to our party and have created enemies among friends of socialism.

An arbitration board worked tirelessly for a compromise and patched up the rift temporarily. But after Cahan resigned as editor of the *Arbayter Tsaytung*, there was persistant talk about forming a separate, independent, socialist newspaper. A secessionist mood spread as it became clear that De Leon's disruptive Socialist Trade and Labor Alliance was splitting the socialist movement.

The final break came in January 1897, when De Leon's opposition was blocked in its efforts to have new members admitted to the *Arbayter Tsaytung* Publishing Association, which Cahan had called a House of Lords. In a highly charged election meeting on January 7, 1897, the tellers of each side brought in a different tabulation of votes. Physical as well as verbal clashes followed. Suddenly Miller shouted, "Comrades, let's go!" and fifty-two dissidents walked out of the meeting. They held their own meeting that night, and as one of them recalled, "It was freezing outside, but we were warm inside." Immediately they began laying plans for the creation of a new Yiddish labor daily.

A convention of all socialist societies, labor unions, and press clubs identified with the opposition to De Leon was called on January 30, at Valhalla Hall on Orchard Street. At that meeting, a new press association was created representing organizations "based on socialism, and of trade unions, based on class struggle, that are in sympathy with our present fight"—that is, free of the influence of De Leon. The paper, it was said, "shall honestly and devotedly serve the movement and not be the property of a clique with income for a dozen business socialists." [19] To assure democratic feedback, independent press clubs were to be formed in various cities. A fund-raising program was mapped out, and the paper's name was borrowed from the influential Social-Democratic newspaper in Berlin, *Vorwärts*. Cahan was unanimously elected editor. He, Zametkin, Miller, Winchevsky and others visited a number of cities and raised money. Remarkable scenes of enthusiasm and sacrifice took place at these meetings. Workers contributed more than they could afford; still others filled collection plates and hats with rings, pocket watches, and watch chains. Some pawned overcoats and Sunday suits. Cahan recalled, "If ever there was a paper supported by a spiritual force, by holy inspiration, it was ours." [20]

On April 22, 1897, the first issue of the *Jewish Daily Forward* appeared—a benchmark in the annals of Jewish labor and the Yiddish press.[21] Starting in a basement with several cases of type and the chases for locking forms, the first *Forward* columns were set by hand and carried to a cheap printer near the Brooklyn Bridge. Later, the editorial and composing rooms were in a rented loft on Duane Street, partitioned off with rough lumber into three rooms. Jacob Gordin joined Cahan in the first editorial sanctum and wrote columns, fictional sketches, and other features. Miller, Zametkin, and Winchevsky contributed regularly; writing from home, Abraham Liessin joined the *Forward* soon after it was launched and wrote editorials and poetry. Cahan himself was the paper's most prolific contributor, writing on all manner of subjects and in varied forms. His special gift lay in creating a magazine-type newspaper of wide appeal, dedicated to essentially sectarian propaganda. His constant injunction to contributors was to make their Yiddish simple, lucid, and understandable to the most elementary level of reader. Most controversial was his introduction of light reading matter, involving human-interest themes from shop and home. Most radically, he put a stop to party polemics, insisting that these bitter quarrels were of no interest to readers and would eventually alienate them.[22]

The new paper began publication in an atmosphere of great excitement, but tensions soon exploded over the question of how to deal with De Leonism, *Das Abendblatt*, and the very nature of the *Forward*. Cahan was virtually alone in wanting to stop what he thought were futile polemics against *Das Abendblatt* and the wasteful cycle of abusive argument. Having already seen the wider possibilities of American journalism, he wanted to move away from ideological generalizations and socialism-in-the-abstract to the more interesting and complex rendering of the actual life of Jewish immigrants, a realism activated by writers with a social consciousness. He believed that the end of literature was social, that Tolstoy and Howells were among the greatest writers because their realistic perception of the world created a literature of social protest, and thus argued for socialism.[23]

The founders of the paper, all devoted socialists, approached their new tasks from different angles. Winchevsky wanted more "fresh air" and a free expression of socialist opinion, which De Leon had made impossible; he also wanted a counteroffensive against *Das Abendblatt*, which was vilifying the dissidents who had founded the *Forward*. The stormy Louis Miller also opposed Cahan's strategy of silence on De Leonism and thought he was too "Jewish." Both wanted the *Forward* to help build a new or reformed party and objected to Cahan's domination of editorial policy. Cahan, for his part, wanted a mass daily, not a dry party organ. His use of sensational headlines and light, even trivial articles agitated his socialist comrades. These personal tensions were aggravated by financial hardships. Each issue of the paper involved urgent appeals for contributions, but times were bad. Thousands of Jews were unemployed and two socialist dailies were too many to support. For several years, the paper was to suffer financial crises, numerous editors, a decline in readers and near-extinction, but it held on, living from hand to mouth, staving off disaster by last-minute appeals to supporters and saved by several lucky political developments.

The leaders of the breakaway movement included some of the most talented men and prominent personalities in Jewish affairs. Their prestige encouraged shifts in allegiance from veterans in the SLP and a favorable response from young immigrants in the 1890's. For a time the men in the "kangaroo exodus" [24] stressed their continued loyalty to the SLP, but the *Forward* faction and the old *Abendblatt* soon plunged into bitter polemics and nasty tirades. Cahan preferred the tactic of silence, but the others disagreed. Harassed and exhausted by the ennervating struggle, he left the paper eight months after it was started, not to return for almost five years. During this interval, he wrote fine essays and stories for English-language newspapers and established a reputation as a literary figure in English.

De Leon, meanwhile, fought back and demanded that the dissidents be ousted from the SLP. A move to excommunicate a member had to be approved by the central body of the party representing various city branches. But the branches balked, whereupon De Leon "reorganized" them and ousted some three hundred members, including the dissidents. Meanwhile, the SLP was itself rushing headlong toward ruin. De Leon's Trade and Labor Alliance was never able to attract more than 20,000 members, while the AFL stood at 300,000.[25] De Leon became more rigid as the opposition increased. The German socialists and their unions, representing highly skilled workers, were deeply disturbed over the rupture with the AFL and De Leon's repudiation of the populist movement and workingmen's parties that mushroomed in the late 1890's. De Leon insisted that these groups demand socialization of all means of production and distribution, while the German socialists were demanding a more conciliatory approach. In Wisconsin, for example, the two movements were drawing together. In Milwaukee, a German socialist center, built up by the energetic Victor Berger, was strong enough to threaten the old Republican machine. But after the Wisconsin State Federation of Labor supported the Populists in July 1894, creating the basis of a Labor-Populist alliance, Berger brought his socialist following into the Milwaukee People's party.[26] Similar fusions developed elsewhere in the Middle West where the desire for immediate social and economic reforms outweighed the dream of social revolution.

These arrangements did not last long, but they added pressure to the already boiling dissension in the SLP. Berger's friend and Illinois labor leader Eugene V. Debs, who had become a socialist while serving a jail sentence during the Pullman strike, followed Berger's example. In 1896, many German socialists had already left the ranks of the SLP; the group around Debs and Berger followed suit, and the following year they launched the Social-Democratic party. The Jewish insurgents of the SLP, who had been thrown out of the party, were among the first to join the new party. Politically homeless, "without a synagogue," as Cahan put it, the group behind the new *Forward* proclaimed their support at a convention in July 1897.[27]

The election campaign in the East Side in the fall of 1898 saw the depressing spectacle of two competing socialist tickets, assuring a victory to their common enemy, Tammany Hall. The rancor continued to seethe over the conflicting interpretations of the Spanish American War and the

Dreyfus case. These issues not only tested the political acuteness of each side, but determined which was most accurately tuned to the attitudes of American Jews. On the issue of the war, the SLP (and *Das Abendblatt*) took a straight Marxist line: Americans, they said, were not interested in liberating Cubans, but in exploiting Cuba and driving Spain out of the Western hemisphere. The primary socialist duty was to fight capitalism at home. The *Forward*, by contrast, responded to strong Jewish feelings against Spain as the instrument of the Inquisition and the expulsion of Jews in 1492, as well as in its inhumane rule in Cuba for centuries. The *Forward* sailed with the current. At the May Day demonstration, the *Forward* section led by Barondess carried a banner "Free Cuba," while their band played "The Star Spangled Banner."

In the Dreyfus affair, the *Forward* again was more truly tuned to the aroused feelings of the Jewish people.[28] Talk of the framed accusation of treason against the French-Jewish artillery officer filled Jewish shops, synagogues, and streets. *Das Abendblatt* took its cue from the leader of the French Marxists, Jules Guesde, who declared that the Jewish aspect of the affair was irrelevant. While Dreyfus was probably innocent, Guesde said, and while racial anti-Semitism was rubbish, the whole affair was of no concern to the proletariat.[29] Eventually *Das Abendblatt* grew more sympathetic to Dreyfus as the "secret of the whole story" shaped up as class struggle, with Dreyfus a direct victim of capitalism.[30] But this devious twist could not undo the damage. Disgusted readers stopped reading the paper and its circulation declined. This steady shrinkage mirrored a similar decline in the SLP support among Jewish workers. Many writers deserted to the *Forward*, or were purged. On April 23, 1902, *Das Abendblatt* ceased publication. The *Forward* remained the sole daily Jewish labor paper.

11. New Forces, New Directions, 1900-10

In a purely organizational sense, the Jewish socialist movement could not claim any significant achievements during the first decade of the twentieth century. In 1900–1901, a wave of strikes swept the Jewish trades, and election results were disappointing until 1906. Unions in many shops were still seasonal and the chronic complaint that Jewish workers were good strikers but poor union workers was still being heard. However, important new forces outside the zone of union and political activity were at work which created a rich Jewish socialist culture in the early 1900's. Moreover, changes in socialist theory and vast dislocations in Jewish life in Russia profoundly affected the lives of Jewish socialists in the United States and altered many of their earlier ideas.

"Evolutionary socialism," [1] a reformist trend, swept all Western socialist movements in the early 1900's and weakened socialist orthodoxy. Its theoretician was Eduard Bernstein, born in Berlin of Jewish parents, a brilliant journalist and outstanding member of the powerful German Social-Democratic party. In 1881, following the promulgation of anti-socialist laws, he fled Germany and lived first in Switzerland and later in England as his party's newspaper's London correspondent. England was the main source of his revisionism. Impressed by the vigor of English political democracy, by the strength of its trade unions, and especially by the Fabian socialists, Bernstein observed that the Marxist predictions of severe capitalist crises, proletarian impoverishment, and diminishing standards of living for all classes were simply not coming true. The middle class was growing, workers were improving their lot, and parliamentary action could avert economic crises. In 1896, he began to publish a series of studies that became the classic work in reformist socialism, in which state action, not a proletarian dictatorship, was seen as the path to socialism. Bernstein also believed that the moral aspects of Marxism needed a new clarification; the "scientific" view provided no moral motivation. In order to avoid class violence and benefit society as a whole, a standard of morality was needed which would establish solidarity among class antagonists.

Although he still considered himself a Marxist, Bernstein was officially condemned by his party. However, most of the social-democratic movements in Europe accepted his ideas, bit by bit. Bernstein's theories also had a marked effect on the thinking of many socialists in America, who agreed that socialists should cooperate with those forces in society willing to fight for political democracy, pacifism, and industrial and economic reform. They admired the practical socialist achievements in Germany and followed events there closely, believing that Germany might develop the first socialist model. Russian radicals, on the other hand, could see nothing in Russia that encouraged such optimism. Revisionism, at the turn of the century, was not accepted by the Russian Social-Democratic party or by the Jewish workers in the Bund until after they migrated to the United States.

Events in Russia were of the deepest significance for Jewish socialists in America in the early 1900's. In this period Jewish radicals were subjected to a number of shock waves, which not only disturbed the certainties and dogmas of an earlier decade but which engulfed them in questions they had long since considered settled for good. The process was unsettling—many resisted looking squarely at issues—but it also uncovered a resilience and amplitude of thought among Jewish socialists that challenged socialist orthodoxy.

The first great shock was the outbreak of anti-Jewish massacres beginning with the Kishinev pogrom of Easter 1903 and the subsequent large migration of Jews from Russia. In Kishinev, the capital of Bessarabia, the ground was prepared by a local newspaper, *Bessarabets (The Bessarabian)*, which for months had been making vile accusations against Jews. It was rumored that the tsar had ordered the murder of Jews. The police helped to organize the pogrom and, then, did nothing to stop it. As the details of the barbarities became known abroad, mass protest meetings were held in England and the United States, and funds for the victims were raised. To appease public opinion, the governor of Bessarabia was replaced by Prince Serge Urussov, who made a careful study [2] of the causes of the massacre and found that it was instigated by the Minister of the Interior, Plehve.

The massacre spread to other cities in southern Russia, and in White Russia troops being mobilized for the Russian-Japanese War rioted against Jews. The subsequent disastrous defeat of Russia in 1904-1905 further incited bloody pogroms.[3] These events overlapped a surge of popular agitation against the oppressive autocracy of Nicholas II (1894-1917), which intensified during the war with Japan. The opposition to the government reached the boiling point after "Bloody Sunday," January 9, 1905, when several hundred thousand Russians, carrying icons and chanting prayers, led by the priest Father Gapon, petitioned the tsar for moderate reforms. Instead of being received by the tsar, however, the crowd was fired upon by troops, causing, in the weeks that followed, a wave of strikes and peasant disorders, and, finally, a general strike which paralyzed the country. There followed the tsar's hypocritical promise of a constitutional regime, the calling and then dissolution of several Dumas, outbreaks of revolutionary terror, and the progressive destruction of government opposition.

Jews experienced a wild, but brief escalation of hope for civil equality, swiftly followed by the nightmare of more pogroms. They again began to flee Russia in large numbers: almost 80,000 left for America in 1904, and over 125,000 emigrated in 1906, the year after the aborted revolution of 1905.[4]

The dream of revolution had been followed with panting, almost unbearable anxiety by all Jews in America, particularly by the radicals who envisioned a life's hope come true. But the dream quickly collapsed. The Yiddish dailies carried banner headlines of the massacres and detailed stories of each pogrom. Yet faith in the coming revolution did not die. "Our holy land has become sacred through the martyrdom of Russia's fighters for freedom," one *Forward* headline ran; "Siberia is our holy land." There was an immense outpouring of sympathy and financial help for the victims—not only on the part of Jews—and strong protests by the American government. In Russia, too, liberals and intellectuals commiserated with Jewish victims and courageously spoke out in their behalf. Turgenev, for example, wrote a touching letter to Sholem Aleichem: "As for my published stories, they are wholly at your disposal, and their translation into Yiddish and their publication in a collection for the benefit of the Jews victimized in Kishinev would give me nothing but heartfelt pleasure."

The Russian-speaking colony in America had shared vicariously in the struggle for a free Russia as far back as 1880, when Narodnaya Volya dispatched Leo Hartmann to the United States, to create good will for the "Russian abolitionists."[5] Hartmann and Lazar Goldenberg, Aaron Lieberman's comrade in London, founded the Russian-American National League in 1887 to protest the Russian-American Extradition Treaty, which destroyed the right of political asylum in the United States enjoyed by Russian radical exiles.[6] The memory of great events was also kept fresh. Russian-speaking immigrants marked the assassination of Alexander II as a sacred day; at annual New Year balls, they sang Russian songs, made socialist speeches, and somberly toasted the martyrs in Schlusselberg prison and Siberia. An annual memorial service paid tribute to Hirsh Lekert, a Vilna Bundist hanged for wounding, in 1902, the Vilna governor who publicly flogged Jewish and Polish workers who had participated in a May Day demonstration. In 1903, the first representatives of the Bund came to the United States, and in 1904 Catherine Breshkovskaya, fabled "grandmother of the Russian Revolution," and Chaim Zhitlovsky came as delegates of the Social Revolutionary party.

The close identification with events in Russia continued through the revolution of 1905, as hopes vaulted and fell. On December 4, 1905, some 100,000 Jews paraded up Fifth Avenue to Union Square,[7] and churches tolled their bells for Jews killed and wounded in the November massacres in southern Russia. Dozens of Russian-Jewish societies were organized to help the beleaguered Jews in Russia. But it was living contact with the new Jewish immigrants that brought the struggle close to Jewish workers. The influx of immigrants strengthened the concern for the fate of Jews in Russia, while the new immigrants felt bound to help their comrades left behind.

All points of view within the Russian radical movement were represented in the new exodus, but the Bundists predominated, particularly after the Russian-Japanese War. In this wave were many immigrants of strong intellectual bent, sophisticated cultural tastes, and broad social interests. They found a relatively settled and formed, if thin, Yiddish culture to draw upon. There existed a Yiddish press and theatre, and varied cultural institutions; some Jewish unions had already won significant gains. But Bundists were nostalgic for the ardor of their movement in Russia; they found life in America disappointing. Socialist party activity appeared tame after the bold and illegal experiences of Bundists in Russia. The tone of the *Forward* seemed melodramatic. Socialist activity in the United States was a world away from Russia, where normal political and trade-union work were impossible, and where even the purely economic struggle was illegal. Every effort there by Jews to win some small concession was handicapped by their lack of fundamental civil rights. The struggle of the Bund to awaken the Russian-Jewish worker and arm him with a strong socialist ideology had imbued the movement with great historic significance. The legality of the situation in the United States was inevitably anti-climactic. Yet adjustments were ultimately made on both sides and the weakened American Jewish labor movement of the early 1900's was revitalized by new figures, more militancy and discipline, and fresh ideas.

Zionism as well as Bundism was also revolutionizing Jewish life in Russia, and both movements challenged the current formulations of Yiddish-speaking socialists in America. Both injected the problem of Jewish nationalism into the internationalist assumptions of Jewish socialists, raising ideological ferment and identity problems where none had existed before. They also had enormous emotional force for many Jews who had sunk into a social and intellectual torpor.

A key figure in the early contacts between Jewish workers in America and Russia was the poet Abraham Liessin (Abraham Walt), who was born in Minsk, but had spent part of his youth in Vilna, where the Bund first appeared. At thirteen he was admitted to the famous Volozhin Yeshivah, but after a year was expelled for smoking and for writing poetry. He flung aside his Talmudic studies to join the revolutionary circles in Vilna, and returned to Minsk after a few years to conduct socialist propaganda among Jews, one of the few among the early Jewish radicals to concern himself with the Jewish worker. Then for a time he moved in Russian populist circles and became estranged from Jewish affairs. "Pushkin and Nekrasov, Uspensky and Zlatovratsky," he wrote, "had practically made me a Russian populist. The only stumblingblock in my mind was whether Russia could bypass the capitalist stage. While I studied this problem, Marxism became my burning faith. Besides reading the legally published populist literature, I devoured also the illegal literature . . . Marx, Engels, Plekhanov." [8] Then follows a very curious revelation:

> I do not know how the connections were made, but it happened that when I learned I was a convinced Marxist, I also discovered I was not a Russian, not just a human being (which is merely an abstraction), but a Jew. Marxism intensified my sense of reality, and the reality surrounding me was Jewish. This Jewish reality found no expression in Marxist literature or in the practical movement which this literature had fostered in Jewish communities. I realized that Geneva, the source of this literature, was as far from us as the Russian village, and that the German worker could not be our model any more than the Russian peasant. Our young minds struggled in vain to adapt the abstractions to that unfortunate Jewish reality, to our past and our future, but without success.[9]

At first Liessin tried to fight off these "sinful thoughts," as ten years earlier he had struggled with religious doubts. But the struggle was too great. He had become a nationalist, and although he had been too independent to join any socialist group, this new perception did not give him an ideological anchor.

At this time, in the mid-1890's, the Jewish social democrats who would soon become founders of the Bund, were confronting the question of how to integrate the Jewish proletariat into the revolutionary struggle. Some, like Jules Martov, a leading figure in the early years, believed that it was necessary from a practical point of view to build a special Jewish workers' organization within the larger social-democratic movement to educate the Jewish proletariat and lead it in the struggle for economic, civil, and political rights. Liessin, who sympathized with the Bund but never joined, anticipated by several years their response to national consciousness. Liessin argued that the work of the social democrats had as little meaning for the Jewish workers as the populists' work had for the Russian peasants.[10] In the late part of 1894 or early 1895, he discussed his doubts with Alexander Kremer (known as Arkady), one of the founders of the Bund. But Liessin found him "too de-Judaized to grasp the meaning of my confession. Since my inner world of Jewish experience was totally alien to him, I tried to argue with him in terms of the movement's practical aspects. I remarked that it was un-Marxist to adapt life to a pamphlet. . . . Kremer gave me a withering look and began to scold me. I, in turn, shouted even louder that the Jewish worker was a fiction, that in our towns, the worker became a petit bourgeois as soon as he married." [11] Liessin tried to convince Arkady that socialists must formulate a national program, one that would appeal to larger masses. But Arkady did not budge. Liessin's arguments "ricocheted off him like balls off a stone wall."

If his socialist comrades were assimilationist-minded, Zionists were too bourgeois and offered no intellectual haven for Liessin. He was also finding it difficult to discover anyone who shared his budding passion for Yiddish. A cousin in Vilna told him about some intellectuals who were meeting with David Pinski, who urged the use of Yiddish. Liessin became excited about the possibilities of Yiddish as the language of socialist propaganda and the possibilities of the ordinary Jew sharing in Jewish intellectual life. He met Pinski in Minsk where they argued a lot, but Liessin also read him some of his own Yiddish poems and began to realize the possibilities for creating a real literature in Yiddish.[12] Liessin soon became involved in the labor movement, one step ahead of the police, but aware that in Warsaw, where Pinski and Peretz were, "the mansion of Yiddish literature was being built from foundations to roof. The more the Jewish masses awakened, all the more would builders of our literature emerge." Liessin became a firm supporter of Jewish national culture and wanted a much more positive statement on the question than Martov had given. To the social democrats, Liessin's position at the time was much too extreme. Yet, interestingly, he could not formulate the aims of such a positive national program within the framework of international socialism.[13]

Liessin continued his contacts with the Jewish social democrats in Minsk and Vilna and perhaps would have crystallized his thinking there, but his revolutionary agitation made life too risky in Russia, and in 1897— the year in which the Bund was officially organized—he migrated to New York. When Hutchins Hapgood discovered him on the East Side, he was twenty-eight, restlessly intense in manner, given to speaking in images, and as Hapgood describes it, beset by a kind of "intellectual consumption." [14] At the time he practically lived in the East Side cafés, arguing and expounding his ideas with a rapid, impulsive flow of talk. He would earn an occasional dollar by writing a poem or article for one of the papers, then return to the cafés and intense talk until the money was gone.[15] He had lost his religious faith after his immersion in Russian literature, and when Hapgood saw him, he was unanchored, disappointed in America, and yearning for the ebullience of the Russian revolutionary intelligentsia. "Before I came to America," he told Hapgood, "I thought it would not be as interesting as Russia, and when I got here, I saw that I was right. America seemed all worked out to me, as if mighty things had already been done, but it seemed lifeless to the core. Russia, on the other hand, with no external form of national prosperity, is all activity at heart, restless longing. Russia is nothing to see, but alive and bubbling at the core." [16]

This stormy young man, writing out of his deeply Jewish and socialist convictions, began to contribute articles to the *Forward* three times a week. His poetry was inspired by the heroic lives of martyred Jews, as well as by passionate visions of social justice. He refused to make the choice between socialism and nationalism; in Liessin they were one. Thus he naturally gravitated to the Bund philosophy after the Bund had developed a positive attitude toward Jewish culture, but he found no organizational outlet in America. Nevertheless, he often wrote a round-up of the Bund's activities, which became a regular feature in the *Forward*.[17]

The first American branch of the Bund was formed in New York in 1900, and by 1904, some fifty branches were united in the Central Union of Bund Organizations, which devoted itself primarily to sending financial aid to the movement in Russia. The Bund concept of Jewish cultural autonomy was vehemently rejected by assimilationist socialists, but Bundist influence grew.[18] Some notable socialist writers in the United States even went so far as to urge the need for a separate Jewish socialist party, such as the Bund in Russia. The first to raise this question was Morris Winchevsky in 1902: "We'd be more successful in our propaganda," he said, "if we took some real interest in the problems of our fellow Jews, and did so as socialists." But there was no tangible action until 1912, when the Jewish Socialist Federation was formed.

A special relationship developed between the *Forward* and the Bundists, giving a dramatic flavor to the shifts in feeling and thinking that occurred after the Kishinev pogrom. Cahan himself, who had again resigned as editor of the *Forward* late in 1902 because of policy disagreements, resumed writing as a contributor after Kishinev. He wrote an excellent analysis of events [19] leading to the pogrom, Plehve's fears of spontaneous uprisings, and the spread of workingmen's organizations in Russia. Bundists at first shrank from the frankly popular quality of the *Forward*, but gradually their writers began to contribute to it, and personal and ideological bonds developed. Nostalgic feelings about Vilna, the Bund center, were easily aroused in Cahan and other writers, while moderate social-democratic ideas drew the newspaper and the Bund closer together. Gradually the *Forward* assumed the role of chief representative of the Bund in the United States and fund raiser.

The first delegation of the Bund came to the United States in November 1903 and consisted of Arkady Kremer and Ezra Rozenberg. Kremer stayed eight months and occupied himself with organizational work and some writing; Rozenberg, with public contacts and speaking.[20] Their main purpose was to urge the immigrants from Russia to give financial support to the Bund, but they also tried to clarify the Bund's position, which had led to a rupture with the Russian Social Democratic

Workers' party (RSDWP).[21] *Zukunft* carried a series of articles on the Bund in 1903, and Kremer, in 1904, wrote a two-part article for the journal, called "Another Critic from the Bund." Readers in America were also intensely interested in Bund conflicts with Zionists at the time.

Funds came from persons of wealth, as well as fellow socialists, and enabled the Bund to carry on its publishing and self-defense campaigns without undue financial worry. John Mill, one of the founders of the Bund, had set up a foreign committee in December 1898 which had made an inventory of the resources abroad which would be available to the Bund, and it was this committee that handled the Bund's connections in the United States. The results were quite remarkable.[22] "Thanks to the great popularity of the Bund and the moving sympathy it aroused," Mill wrote, "every appeal for help was always crowned with success." [23] Meyer London, a young Jewish labor lawyer, spoke at the first mass meeting for the Bund and was praised by Bund leaders for his "revolutionary intuition," even though he had not been in the radical movement in Russia as a youth. He emerged from this meeting as the chief American worker in the Bund's behalf. In the spring of 1906, Bundist leaders Mark Liber (Mikhel Goldman) and Gregory Maxim (Shmeun Klevansky) came to America and were given a rousing reception in New York. London dropped his law practice for several months and traveled with the men on their fund-raising tour.

Cahan, with his unappeased hunger for the old revolutionary milieu, enjoyed meeting with the Bund emissaries and often served as a welcoming committee. But his pleasure was not unalloyed. His reverence for the cause was complicated by his uneasiness with the Bund's "Jewish revolutionary nationalism," his secret satisfaction in discovering that Kremer spoke Yiddish rather poorly, and the unresolved paradoxes of his own radicalism—his sense of realism struggling with his idealization of the revolution, his guilt in not remaining in Russia to join the struggle, and the conflict between his assimilationist views and his immersion in a Yiddish paper.[24]

But the response to the Bund was much more positive for large numbers of socialist-oriented American Jews. By 1904, there were enough branches to hold a convention which featured Jacob Adler's presentation of Gordin's play *The Bundist* and a recounting of the Bund's dramatic exploits in Russia at the Grand Central Palace.[25] The Friends of the Bund, which supported Bund activities in Russia and raised money, was also founded. Bundists soon became active in Jewish unions and injected leadership, discipline, and tenacity into the movement. They transformed Jewish unions by strengthening the self-esteem of Jewish workers and creating a *Jewish* working-class identity. Bundists also made a lasting impact on the Workmen's Circle (Der Arbayter Ring).[26]

The Workmen's Circle evolved out of the needs of Jewish workers, which neither the early unions nor the socialist parties could meet: the

Jewish worker's helplessness during illness, the exorbitant costs of funerals, and the need for social fellowship and education. As early as March 1892, two cloakmakers, Sam Greenberg and Harry Lasker, were gloomily discussing the floundering state of the unions and damaging schisms which shattered personal friendships and made enemies out of friends. They hit on the idea of creating a new organization for Jewish workers, outside existing union and political affiliations, based on mutual aid, self-education, and friendship. A small group was organized and a constitution drawn up with much emphasis on educational activities.

The Workmen's Circle admitted only workers who opposed the existing economic system, but avoided taking sides with any particular political faction. This position was attractive to considerable numbers of workers, but the idea of mutual aid was much harder to promote. The weekly five-dollar sick benefits which the Workmen's Circle began to pay in September 1894 was not much of a stimulus to growth in a movement inspired by more elevated aims. A change occurred in the late 1890's, spurred by the migration of some workers to Harlem and Brooklyn. These workers did not want to travel to the East Side and decided to set up neighborhood branches. By 1900, the organization numbered about three hundred members, large enough to merit national expansion. The first general secretary, Benjamin Feigenbaum, was a popular radical Yiddish lecturer and pamphleteer. He did not have much executive ability, but through his articles and lectures popularized the Workmen's Circle. Feigenbaum reacted strongly against Orthodox religious restrictions, but championed the social laws of the Torah and Jewish ethics, especially those touching marriage and sex. He even wrote an analytical essay on Jewish dietary laws, so that every enlightened Jew could have accurate knowledge of the subject. At the second Workmen's Circle convention on March 31, 1901, the organization comprised nine branches in three states, with a combined membership of 644. In May 1902, there were 27 branches with a total membership of over 1,500. At that time, the organization was paying $6.00 a week in sick benefits for a period of twelve weeks per calendar year, $400 death insurance for a man ($200 for a woman), and funeral expenses for all members of a family. After some legal complications, the State Insurance Department of New York granted an official charter to the order.

A period of rapid development followed, partly due to the charter, but much more to the mass migration after 1903. This new wave brought many Jewish workers and intellectuals who had been in some way associated with labor or radical organizations. Some had occupied leadership positions; many had been in jail or in exile, and had served in the secret armed groups which had defended the Jewish neighborhoods during the pogroms. How many of these immigrants were Bundists is impossible to say, but the dramatic growth of immigrant societies, especially the Workmen's Circle, which was strongly Bundist in its sympathies, suggests that a considerable number came with strong socialist ideological views. The Workmen's Circle membership rose to 4,352 in 1904, and 6,776 in 1905,[27] and in 1907, Bundist groups agreed to join the Workmen's Circle en masse.[28]

Preoccupation with political events and socialist-Jewish commitments and loyalties caused serious neglects. The radicals were so engrossed in ideological activities and the vicissitudes of making a living that they had little time or interest for Jewish education of their children. This left education under the control of the old-fashioned *heder* and *Talmud Torah*,[29] where education was generally conducted under lamentable conditions by poor teachers. At first, most children of Jewish immigrants went to these schools, but under the influence of radical thought, some of these once-religious parents became anti-religious, and with the upsurge of cultural nationalism among socialists, the teaching of Yiddish and the creation of a modern Yiddish school system became essential for those who believed in a secularist Jewish culture.

The creation of Yiddish schools was enormously difficult. There were no teachers, no textbooks, and no conceptual framework for a curriculum. After several unsuccessful efforts, a way was at last found by the socialist Zionists. In October 1910, at a convention in Montreal, the Poale Zion adopted a resolution to set up a modern "national radical" school system with instruction in Yiddish. Six weeks later, the first such school, originally called the *natsionale-radicale shule* (later *folkshule*), was opened in New York. It had two primary aims: to give the children an education that would make them aware of their bond with the Jewish people and an understanding of the great social problems of the day in the socialist spirit.[30]

Labor Zionists were the first among Jewish socialists to embark on a program of Jewish secular education. A small minority in a sea of Jewish trade union and socialist opposition, they were the first radicals to realize that Jewish education could not be totally severed from Jewish religious tradition. In 1914, Hayim Lieberman read a paper at the first national conference of the Labor Zionist schools in which he said that "to play hide-and-seek with religion was impossible." How, he asked, could we explain to our children Jewish otherness if we do not initiate them into an understanding of Jewish religion? A resolution which was passed at the conference reads, in part: "National radical education must instill in the children a sound view of Jewish religion, which should be approached from a cultural-historical standpoint. The teachers should endeavor to present to the children the national-ethical and poetic aspect of Jewish religion." [31]

Bringing a secular educational system into being and stimulating other radical and labor groups to a greater consciousness of Jewish culture was probably the most important Labor Zionist achievement in America before World War I.

In 1910, the question of providing children with a Yiddish education had also been raised in the Workmen's Circle. By 1918, after years of debate, a basis was created for a Workmen's Circle school system by the levying of a special assessment on the members for school funds. Thereafter Jewish socialist schools became another arena of intense cultural activity for Jewish workers, their families, and Yiddishists of socialist persuasion.

The turn of the century also witnessed the gentle disparagement of more conventional hard-line socialist dogmas. The demands and exertions of daily life and the softening effect of experience tempered the old doctrines. America was seen to offer the blessings, as well as the evils of capitalism. For example, after his return to the *Forward* from his experiences on the *Commercial Advertiser*, Abraham Cahan defined the new socialism in scarcely recognizable terms: "The *Forward* is the workingmen's organ in their every righteous fight against their oppressors; this struggle is the body of our movement. But its soul is the liberation of mankind—justice, humanity, fraternity—in brief, honest common sense and horse sense." [32] Indeed, in October 1901, the *Forward* carried a full-page advertisement inviting readers to invest in the Utopian Land Company in California and other capitalistic ventures and offered the "capitalist" U.S. Constitution in a ten-cent Yiddish translation as "the little Torah," the "highroad to citizenship, employment and success." During a bakers' general strike in 1901, the *Forward* appealed not to class solidarity but to the sense of communal responsibility:

> It is wholly a domestic matter with us. The workmen are ours and the bosses are ours, and we alone are the customers ... Let us show the world that when a struggle like this occurs in our midst, we settle the question in a feeling of justice and human sympathy—that we settle the issue in favor of the workmen and their just demands.[33]

Following the Kishinev horrors, attacks on religion in the *Forward* were also muted. The paper pleaded for respect for the genuinely pious; even a kaftan-attired guest clasping the scroll of the Law to his chest was favorably considered for a door prize at the *Forward's* annual masquerade ball at Grand Central Palace, although "proletarian" garb was prescribed. Editorially, the paper stuck to its first concern: "We idealize the working class a bit too much," but justice and righteousness were still seen to reside with labor; workers remained "the teachers of the people."

There was a marked decrease in expounding Marxian classics and a muting of the class conflict. Some even began to look upon America as an entirely new kind of society, which demanded altogether new analytical tools. The Fabians in England, the Bernstein revisionists in Germany, and the moderate socialists in France increasingly stressed the importance of a distinct national tradition in the evolution of their respective brands of socialism. Newly awakening nationalisms in Eastern Europe and the spreading influence of Zionism also broadened and diversified ideological radicalism and made room for discussion of Jewishness and Judaism, particularly after Kishinev. The shifts in *Zukunft* were symptomatic.

When *Zukunft* resumed publication in January, 1902 (it had suspended publication in August 1897), it was no longer the spokesman for an official party or one of its factions, but was now published by the *Zukunft* Press Federation, a voluntary association of socialist groups.[34] The Workmen's Circle urged its branches to take out subscriptions for each member; similar support was given by progressive, independent Jewish societies and branches of the Bund. Changes in content reflected cultural and political shifts: there appeared more material dealing with Yiddish literature and greater awareness of the highly developed Yiddish literature in Russia. Cosmopolitan socialists argued heatedly that without religion, there was no specifically Jewish culture, but they were frequently challenged. In the January 1902 issue, we find: "That optimism which was the very spirit of the Torah had its effect on the [Jewish] people while it was yet in its infancy." This hint at a modified attitude toward the Jewish religion and the notion that religion is a private matter were attacked by orthodox socialists [35] and may have resulted in equivocal rebuttals, but the new perception of the Jewish condition could not be silenced. In 1904, the Workmen's Circle almost split over the issue, but see-sawed uncertainly. In the same year, the *Zukunft* reflected the tension of the unresolved debate: "We do not turn away religious people, or even clergymen who wish to join us; but because of this we should not weaken by a hair's breadth, not only the class conflict, but also the anti-religious and especially the anti-clerical conflict." [36] Another writer deplored "socialistically inclined" people who attend *slihot* (penitential services) and fast on Yom Kippur. But disparagers of Jewish religion were themselves disparaged. A lively exchange took place between Benjamin Feigenbaum, the former head of Der Arbayter Ring, and the writer A. Litvin, who dismissed Feigenbaum's anti-religious views as obsolete, asserting that "nowadays any schoolboy knows ... that religion has always and everywhere been an important factor in human progress.... You, Mr. Feigenbaum, may say whatever you please; I am proud that I am not a descendant of the Hottentots or Chinese, but that I am a Jew." [37] Whereupon the *Zukunft* Press Federation promptly censured Litvin, as well as the editor, for permitting him to use "such a tone" in his article against Feigenbaum.

Feigenbaum also fought the upsurge of Bundist nationalism after the pogroms, asking what kind of Jewish cultural independence enlightened socialists wanted to maintain. "To be national," someone answered, "means to possess national self-consciousness, i.e., the recognition that certain individuals belong to my nation, and that my nation is no better and no worse . . . than all other nations, and has the same right to exist as all other nations. 'National' and 'international' are not opposites, but two concepts which complement each other." [38]

The Bund's self-defense units in Russia won many admirers, but the puzzled *Zukunft* called them "a new species of humanity" who suddenly emerged after the massacre—people who evoke undefined "Jewish feelings" and proclaim that Jewish socialists must be "first and foremost Jews." *Zukunft* held them at arm's length:

> Precisely what do they mean by this? What are they to do, and toward what are we to strive as Jews? This they have never specified. They are, therefore, not to be seriously reckoned with as a separate faction, since they have no positive program in their Jewishness. It is a temporary emotion. Such cheap phrase-spouting also provides many with an opportunity to gain favor with the common Jewish masses.[39]

So the arguments rocked back and forth. But national feeling and assertiveness swelled like a rising tide which mere verbal arguments could not stem. Interestingly, even the anarchists were affected. Hillel Zolotarov, the Jewish anarchist leader, wrote his "Serious Problems" soon after the Kishinev pogrom and sounded the new theme of national and cultural regeneration. I. Kopelov, another leading anarchist wrote: "The Kishinev pogrom upset me to some degree. . . . My previous cosmopolitanism, internationalism, and similar views vanished at one blow, like the contents of a barrel with the bottom knocked out." [40]

Herz Burgin, the historian, was to write later: "This was a veritable epidemic. . . . The radicalism of the Jewish masses practically disappeared before the nationalist wave." Many were indeed swept up in sorrow, guilt, and a sudden overflowing of Jewish fervor. This shifting focus, for a time, aggravated the disarray of immigrant Jewish socialists. Still uprooted, without an alternative culture in America, they continued to define themselves in old-world radical terms even as those terms were losing all validity. When the pain of their Jewishness surfaced, the standard socialist clichés seemed more unreal than ever. *Zukunft* mourned the decline of Yiddish-speaking *genossen:* "The old generation has grown old, has died spiritually, has lost its courage, its energy, and—worst of all—its faith, its socialist convictions." [41] The anxiety of veteran socialists deepened after a debate in 1904 between Cahan and Hayim Zhitlovsky on Marxism, in which Cahan's defense of Marxism came off second best. It would take several years of philosophical groping and settling into America before a *Jewish* socialist movement defined itself.

The plight of Russian Jews after the pogroms and the hopes that were raised by the revolution of 1905 also had unexpected effects on the thinking of the leaders of Western Jewish communities.[42] The two Jews who bore the brunt of Jewish diplomatic activity at the time were the philanthropists Lucien Wolf, of England, and Jacob H. Schiff, of the

United States. Dr. Paul Nathan of Germany was also helpful, but was less independent than the others because of Germany's autocratic regime and restrictions on Jewish life.

In general, until the Kishinev pogrom, these men believed that the "Jewish question" would some day be solved in Russia itself; hence they objected to Jewish participation in Russian revolutionary movements. But the pogrom shattered this illusion and raised anxiety about renewed mass emigration from Russia. Even so, there was a lingering hope that Sergius Witte, the liberal Russian minister of finance, could break the tsarist reaction. In 1905, while visiting Russia, Dr. Nathan tried to establish contact between Witte and the Russian revolutionary parties. He asked Raphael Abramovitch of the Bund to help him bring Witte together with the Bundists and the Russian social democrats. But the Bund leaders, skeptical of Witte's intentions and doubtful of his political strength, rejected Nathan's invitation. Nathan also tried to influence the socialist leaders against boycotting the Duma. But by 1906 there was a gathering distrust of Witte and, in any case, he was dismissed that year by the tsar.

The revolution of 1905 completely changed the attitude of Western Jewish leaders toward the Russian-Jewish problem and toward the radical movements. The future of Russian Jewry was seen as being intertwined with that of all of Russia, and that meant support of liberal and revolutionary movements struggling to end Russian autocracy. Russian anti-Jewish policy was interpreted as a Russian counter-revolutionary activity and diversionary move to destroy the liberal and revolutionary movements. In their intervention in behalf of Russian Jews, Western Jewish leaders argued that the persecution of Jews forced them to ally with the revolutionary movement—an argument that was advanced without apology or regret. They favored a liberal rather than an extreme or revolutionary alternative, but soon realized that little could be expected from the Duma, and that the hopelessness of change in or from the regime would strengthen the more activist elements, such as the Bund. The Bund soon became the recipient of generous help and open admiration from Western leaders. During an interview early in July 1905, in *The Westminister Gazette*, Wolf praised the Bund highly: "Particularly interesting was the information supplied by Mr. Wolf in regard to the wonderful organization known as the Jewish 'Bund,' which is now the most powerful and best-disciplined of all the revolutionary bodies in Russia . . . nobody is more feared by the forces of autocracy in Russia today than this organization, but few realize the enormous sacrifices involved in its maintenance by a section of the population so desperately poor and mercilessly oppressed in every possible way."

The aid collected by these leaders for Jewish victims of pogroms was sent to the Bund. From time to time, it was combined with funds for self-defense units, political activity, and propaganda against loans to Russia, then under discussion. In the United States, Schiff preferred that Russian immigrants take charge of the collections, but their aid went beyond the purely philanthropic. Dr. Nathan, for example, together with other liberals and socialists, was engaged in fighting for the freedom of political prisoners in Russia; Schiff helped to organize a large Christian protest meeting in New York after the pogrom. Wolf and Nathan also took the initiative in starting several periodicals to supply the West with information about the liberal and revolutionary struggle in Russia.

Three periodicals were launched in October 1905: *The Russian Correspondence,* in London; the *Russische Korrespondenz,* in Berlin; and *La Correspondence Russe,* in Paris. Four to five thousand copies were circulated, and they became major sources of information about events in Russia. The first English edition contained a long article on "Bund Manifestoes" and information about Bund meetings in synagogues; subsequent issues dealt with other anti-tsarist groups. There were, of course, many difficulties, chiefly how to obtain reliable information (Russian Jews did this at the risk of their lives), and the support of rich contributors who disliked the periodical's tone. Eventually, Leopold Rothschild agreed to cover expenses, but only if support were limited to the constitutional parties. Unable to get other support, Wolf had to accept these terms, but by February 1906, the English paper was suspended at Rothschild's request. Undaunted, Wolf began publication again, in 1912, of a similar publication called *Darkest Russia,* a weekly carrying a concentrated attack against granting loans to Russia. This publication lasted until the outbreak of World War I.

The German and French weeklies were published from 1905 to 1914. In the United States, Schiff approved the idea of a publication and promised moral and financial support but believed it should not be a strictly Jewish concern. In July 1906, Nathan asked Schiff for a contribution of six thousand marks from the United States to aid in the distribution of propaganda materials in Russia because of Russia's repression of the liberal press. He agreed to raise the money provided Germany and England contributed equal sums. In 1907 the American Jewish Committee, in which Schiff was a prominent leader, resolved to organize a press bureau to disseminate information about Russia, but nothing comparable to *Russian Correspondence* appeared. Yet, in America, too, a number of upper-class Jews seemed ready to sacrifice their ideologies, social status, and personal economic interests in order to improve the position of Jews in Russia, even to the point of supporting a revolution.

The mood of bitter disappointment following the collapse of the Revolution of 1905 inevitably led to a decline in social literature. Writers were turning to new themes and new forms. A new audience arose which freed the Yiddish writer from the grip of a daily newspaper, while at the same time it demanded much more than sketches and vignettes of an earlier period. During this hectic transition, the large immigrant influx also swelled the number of readers of the Yiddish newspapers, theatre and lecture audiences, and membership in varied cultural societies. There were also, at the time, more than two hundred coffee houses in New York, each with its own special literary or ideological customers, who talked and argued through the night over steaming Russian tea and lemon. This great diversity was especially noticeable in the Yiddish press.

Until the early 1900's, the Yiddish periodical press largely reflected two conflicting philosophies: the religiously Orthodox and politically conservative on one hand, and the anti-religious and radical, on the other. After 1905, other trends appeared: nationalist-cultural and socialist (*Der Arbayter*, 1904); Territorialist (*Dos Folk*, 1905); socialist-Zionist (*Der Yiddisher Kemfer*, 1906); Yiddish-nationalist-socialist (*Dos Naye Lebn*, 1908); Zionist (*Dos Yidishe Folk*, 1909). Readers had more choice of reading fare and greater exposure to diverse points of view.

The early 1900's also revealed a very definite shift in the attitude of certain Jewish socialists toward expressly Jewish culture. Many of the intellectuals, particularly after the Kishinev pogrom, quite openly became interested in Yiddish cultural expression as a value in itself, not merely or primarily as a medium of enlightenment or indoctrination. Hayim Zhitlovsky, a Russian Jewish radical, formulated a theory of Yiddishism as a basis for the existence and survival of the Jewish people (published in the *Forward* in 1943).[43] He argued that it was in the interest both of socialism and of Jews that the new Yiddish literature be "a link in the chain of Jewish literatures" and live and prosper. When he came to America for the first time in 1904 as a delegate of the Russian Social Revolutionary party, he spoke out in brilliant articles and speeches for a socialist-oriented Jewish nationalism and for Jewish culture.

In January 1902, Liessin, in an editorial in the revived *Zukunft*, wrote that one of its tasks would be to make available to the Yiddish reader "the whole glowing world of science and progress, as well as the intellectual world of art and esthetic enjoyment." The latter included non-doctrinaire Yiddish literature, and *Zukunft* and other socialist journals now began to publish Yehoash's (Solomon Bloomgarden) national-romantic poetry and the work of politically uncommitted writers such as Sholem Aleichem and Sholem Asch.[44] The position of Yiddish was further boosted by the World Conference for Yiddish, held in Czernowitz, Rumania, in 1908. This conference, which was convened by I. L. Peretz, Zhitlovsky, and Nathan Birnbaum (an early Zionist leader), proclaimed Yiddish the national language of the Jewish people. This bold initiative created a furor, but heightened the prestige of Yiddish as a literary instrument and gave a certain impetus to esthetic as well as ideological argumentation.

One of the most interesting of the esthetic developments of the time centered around a small periodical called *Yugend* (*Youth*), started by young writers who had begun to write while still in Europe under the influence of the Bund and the revolutionary ferment in Russia, but who came to America after 1905, politically disillusioned and emotionally isolated. *Yugend* first appeared in 1907, and from the start, the poets were preoccupied with their individual voice, with sense impressions, and perfection of form. The leading rebels in this new poetry were Mani Leib, Zisha Landau, Joseph Rolnick, Moishe Leib Halpern, and Reuben Iceland; in prose, the main figures were David Ignatov, Joseph Opatashu and Isaac Roboy. They spent their days as poverty-stricken workers or craftsmen in the shops on the East Side. Mani Leib was a shoemaker and for a while a laundryman; Landau, a house painter; and Halpern, a waiter and jack-of-all-trades—but their spiritual world was formed by the "alien poets," as Iceland later recalled them: Baudelaire, Verlaine, Rimbaud, Rilke, Hofmannstahl, Pushkin and Blok—a strange and threatening world for Yiddish readers accustomed to poets as folk heroes, and to poetry of social protest, moral teaching and popular incitement.

Di Yunge, as they were disparagingly called, were at first mocked as upstarts and insulted by the literary establishment; no paper would publish them. But within a decade, they had revolutionized Yiddish poetry. "When we came," Iceland remarked,

> Yiddish literature was in service to ideas and movements, social and national. The poets were highly respected, but their poetry, like every servant, was disdained. We proclaimed its liberation and its right to independence. We maintained that poetry must not be bound to ideas, as it exists for its own sake.[45]

The maturing of Yiddish as a language, its refinement and enrichment by literary artists, and its strengthening by schools, scholars and journals, called forth intense ideological debates. *Yiddishkayt* (an old-world Jewishness) in America was not quite the surrogate home, the passionately held substitute for a would-be territory that it was in Eastern Europe, where faith and skepticism, tradition and the fear of losing it kept most Jews in a tense, argumentative, dialectic. But attitudes toward Yiddish in America were often equally intense.

Hayim Zhitlovsky was a fiery advocate of Yiddish, believing that it was the most powerful factor uniting the Jewish people. His great influence on the Jewish radical intelligentsia in America in the early 1900's gave special weight to those who believed that not only could socialism and Yiddish culture be fused, but that they must. Zhitlovsky [46] had a tumultuous ideological journey. The son of an affluent lumber merchant, he was a pious youngster until soon after his bar mitzvah, when he began reading Russian and German books. In the *gymnasium* in Vitebsk he became a *narodnik*, changing his name to Ephim Ossipovitch, and in 1882, he dropped his studies. Oppressed by the stultifying materialism around him, he decided to "go to the people" in inner Russia, spending about a year and a half in Tula. But instead of living among the peasants, he spent his time browsing among old books and magazines, including illegal populist literature. He was especially attracted by the articles of Peter Lavrov and seemed on his way to complete russification when his mother persuaded him to spend the summer at home. There in Ushach he struggled with his old Jewish self, unable to integrate it or exorcise it. A quite extraordinary literary experience—a chance reading of a Russian allegory called "The Old Wolf"—resolved his conflict. This experience settled his doubts and sent him, as he later wrote, "flying on a new road, not *assimilation*, not even *nationalism* in the old sense, but what appeared to me as the right and natural solution to the Jewish problem in full harmony with my socialist ideas."

The story deals with the hated wolf who, cursed by nature to be cruel and destructive, feels sorry for himself as he grows old and finally welcomes death as surcease. The imaginative nineteen-year-old Hayim instantly identified the old wolf as the "evil Jew"—the trader and money maker portrayed by the populists, but as quickly he crushed the idea. "A surge of nationalism struck my head and heart. So, we are wolves? No, we are human beings, better and more humane than all of you.... We are a people and we will live as a people, and right here in this country. Russia is as much ours as yours.... Assimilationism disappeared ... like smoke. Jewish diaspora nationalism was born in me." [47] This flashing intuition now had to be researched and clarified, for it was a "troublesome matter." Zhitlovsky then began reading huge drafts of Lavrov, Lassalle, Marx and Comte, Spencer and Mill, who had helped free him from the "intellectual chains" of the 1860's.

He was now embarked on a quest that was to engage most of his life: a formulation that harmonized socialism with Jewish nationality. Actually, this was the same quest Aaron Lieberman had pursued a few years earlier without resolution or realization, and which Liessen was also struggling with. Zhitlovsky read omnivorously, wrote poetry, supported himself by tutoring and set up a tiny library in his lodging which young intellectuals used. In this fevered summer, the final scene of Goethe's *Faust* had an overpowering effect on him. Gretchen symbolized the Jewish people, sitting in a dark prison, clutching a lifeless doll, instead of a living child, unable to accept Faust the liberator. One day he heard a wailing cry from a woman in the Jewish cemetery: "To whom have you abandoned me?" It was like a personal reproof, evoking the pledge "always to remain faithful to the Jewish people, never to abandon them, to identify with their fate, whatever befell them." Thus began his romance and obsession with the Yiddish language.

Soon after he had moved out of his parents' home, Zhitlovsky and some friends formed an underground circle of the Narodnaya Volya, but he dropped his Russian name and reverted to Hayim. At this time, he planned a Yiddish magazine and a Jewish Narodnaya Volya organization, but he was refused permission on grounds that this would lead to separatism. There followed studies on the origins of assimilation and on Jewish history in St. Petersburg; a momentary brush with Tolstoyan idealism; publication of his *Thoughts on the Historical Fate of the Jewish People*, in 1887; marriage in Berlin to a non-Jewish Populist comrade, Vera Lokhova; and a decision to move to Zurich. In Zurich, Zhitlovsky tried to interest emigré populists and Russian social democrats in publishing revolutionary material in Yiddish, but he was turned down. This period in Zurich was marked by intense discussions in the Russian colony over Marxism and populism, one famous debate lasting seventy-two nights! These "Seventy-two Zurich Nights" were the beginning of Zhitlovsky's long struggle against the "Marxist corset." At this time, he wondered if there were any necessary connection between socialism and economic materialism.

Although uncomfortable with existing Jewish religious tradition, Zhitlovsky studied Jewish religious thought at Swiss universities and received his doctorate in 1892 for a work in early Jewish religious philosophy. He then published a brochure, *A Jew to Jews*, in which he argued that the granting of civil equality to Jews would not solve the Jewish problem. Jews, he said, had a distinct national configuration and required national equality. But the populist in him was also very much alive. In 1893, he helped found the Union of Russian Socialist-Revolutionaries Abroad, out of which grew the Social Revolutionary party in 1901.

In 1897, Zhitlovsky attended the first Zionist Congress in Basel as a correspondent and wrote an article for the *Forward* analyzing his opposition to Zionism. Much more significant was his essay "Zionism or Socialism" in the March 1899 issue of *Der Yidisher Arbayter*, the Yiddish underground organ of the Bund, which he had joined the previous year. The national question was being argued by the Bund [48] during this period and the pressure to resolve it was growing very strong. In his article, Zhitlovsky said that "socialism does not intend to abolish nations, to knead them into one dough," but should provide the opportunity for every nation to develop its individuality. This right must be provided for Jews, too. Attacking Zionism as a false path, he called for the strengthening of Jewish culture through the use of Yiddish, even predicting that the future would see a system of schools and universities conducted exclusively in Yiddish.

Zhitlovsky's article drew some sharp reactions but, in fact, helped to lay the groundwork for the Bund's subsequent stand in favor of Jewish national-cultural autonomy within a socialist framework. Later, after the pogrom of 1903, Zhitlovsky inclined toward Territorialism, and in 1904, while he was in New York, he became co-editor of the weekly *Dos Folk*, which advocated a fusion of socialism, Jewish cultural autonomy within the Diaspora, and a Jewish territorial center for those Jews who had to leave their homes. His opposition to russification—Marxist or tsarist—of

minority peoples and to melting-pot theories of adjustment in America
give him a very modernist look. He advocated a socialistically oriented,
autonomous Jewish society in a commonwealth of "United Peoples of the
United States," a conceptual framework which, if difficult to reduce to
practical terms, had—and still has—great appeal to certain minds.[49]

Zhitlovsky returned to Europe in 1906 and was elected to the Second
Duma by his radical comrades, but his election was annulled by the police.
He returned to New York in 1908, a prodigy of intellectual brilliance, who
translated Nietzsche, wrote scholarly essays on Kant, Job, and Faust,
edited *Dos Naye Lebn* (1908–13), and stirred mass audiences with his
eloquence and dazzling erudition. By means of brilliant lectures, debates,
treatises, the creation of new periodicals and articles, Zhitlovsky spoke out
vigorously for a socialist-oriented Jewish nationalism, and converted
cosmopolitan Yiddish-speaking socialists into Jewish socialists. He had a
solid understanding of the importance of religious tradition in shaping the
Jewish people. But his total emphasis on Yiddish created a purely
linguistic framework of culture and made him vulnerable to attacks by
those who felt that his foundation for autonomy was much too narrow.
Nevertheless, Zhitlovsky had an immense influence on many secular and
assimilating Jews of his generation and contributed greatly to the ferment
of the early 1900's in the United States. He regularly wrote for Yiddish
periodicals and discussed ideas with depth and substance, consciously
battling against the thin popularizations of many writers and striving to
attract Jewish intellectuals. Like the Zionists, he understood the economic
deformities in Jewish life caused by centuries of persecution, and urged a
more balanced economic existence, but unlike them, he embraced the
galut. Nachman Syrkin, the socialist-Zionist leader, once pithily summed
up their differences at a meeting: "We have divided the world between us.
Zhitlovsky takes everything that exists; I, everything that still does not
exist. He has chosen the Yiddish which we have; I, the Hebrew which we
do not have. He has chosen the Diaspora which we have; I, the homeland
which we still do not have." [50]

A gradual rootedness in America was slowly to bring an understanding
of American conditions to Jewish radicals raised on Russian models, "a
broader comprehension . . . a humane relationship to one's self, to one's
own feelings," as a *Forward* editorial put it in 1909. Socialist militants
began to mellow; veteran socialists began to reject simple formulas and to
acknowledge the complexity of the adjustment to American life. A fighter
of the 1880's, Michael Zametkin, put it well: "The whole range of past
emotional conditioning, attitudes to government, nationalism, and the
relations between Jew and non-Jew, had to be relearned." Benjamin
Feigenbaum contrasted the situation in Europe, where Jews were forced to
remake themselves into another nationality, with the dignified integration
of Jewish workmen in the United States." [51] Cahan was moving toward
socialism as a secularized religion, a secularized Judaism diffused in the

glow of brotherhood and enlightenment that bathed Yiddish-reading socialists in New York at the time. From recognizing Jewish community problems as requiring cooperation among all Jews, the *Forward* went on to embrace every struggle for freedom at home and abroad as being within the appropriate concern of Jewish socialists. The Fourth of July was celebrated as well as May Day and Labor Day. The singularities of America as well as the singularities of the Jewish condition forced Jewish socialists to grope for new ways to deal with unexpected realities.

Meanwhile, the Jewish unions in the early 1900's were still floundering and still weak—wracked not only by destructive splits and personality feuds, but ideological gaps. For some, socialism was the overriding consideration, and the union, an instrument of socialist change, not mere economic improvement. Moreover, the grip of religious tradition was still strong among many workers who endured the misery of the sweatshops because it allowed them to pray and observe the Sabbath. Thus, many Jewish workers did not join unions or left after strikes to demonstrate their resistance to union leaders who were using techniques and ideological foundations borrowed from non-Jewish sources, and whose anti-religious views often shocked the ordinary worker.[52] A great deal of the intimacy, emotional involvement, and warmth which could not be found in the union was vested in the *landsmanshaften* and in the Workmen's Circle. Caught in so many cross-currents of need, tradition, and doctrine, as well as the confusing conflicts in leadership, Jewish workers in the early 1900's did not see the union as their salvation. In the second decade, however, fortified and stimulated by new immigrants and new perspectives, Jewish socialists resumed their struggle for union recognition and political power and reached many workers with an effective political and economic program.

12. Jewish Labor Triumphs:
From Zeros to Fighters

The years 1909–16 were decisive ones in the history of the Jewish labor movement in the United States, not only in terms of trade-union growth and consolidation but because of impressive cultural and political gains. The slow, unstable, strike-torn beginnings of union organization in the needle-trades industries in the early 1900's developed into a surge of confident growth and leadership within a decade, paralleling a remarkable growth in the Socialist party. The early years, however, were quite bleak, scarcely foreshadowing what was to come.

By 1900, as a result of the shift from hand sewing to machine manufacture, the ladies' garment industry had become one of the major consumer-goods industries in the country. There were large centers in New York, Boston, Chicago, and Philadelphia, with over 80,000 workers, most of whom were Jewish immigrants. Women dominated in the shops making shirtwaists, underwear, house dresses, white goods, while men went into cloak and suit making. The swift growth of the industry necessitated the formation of an international union to overcome the isolation of local unions sprouting up in new manufacturing shops. A call for such a body was issued by the New York cloakmakers on March 11, 1900. On June 3, a convention was held in New York, comprising eleven delegates from seven locals in New York, Philadelphia, Baltimore, Newark, and Brownsville, who created the International Ladies' Garment Workers Union (ILGWU).[1] A per-capita tax of one cent a week was levied, and each local union was assessed ten dollars for an operating fund. Later that month, the AFL granted a charter to the new international.

For a few years, the ILGWU made modest progress: by 1903 its membership increased to 10,000 in fifty-one locals, with more than half its strength outside of New York. But its progress was stopped by the depression in the fall of that year, by lockouts and injunctions and, in 1905, by the threat from the Industrial Workers of the World (IWW), who wanted to organize unskilled workers and merge craft unions into industrial unions. Drawing support largely from the militant Western Federation of Miners, whose bloody struggle against Anaconda Copper and Rockefeller mining interests met no response from the craft-oriented AFL, the IWW at first attracted the support of Eugene V. Debs, De Leon, and their supporters, who liked the radical, class-conscious philosophy of the IWW.

The weak Jewish unions within the AFL were unlikely targets of the IWW drive. Yet, Jewish labor was the first base in the East to attract the IWW organizing experiment,[2] and the first efforts involved several ILGWU locals. The IWW had little success in organizing new shops but raided some ILGWU locals and created rival unions, very much as De Leon had done with his Socialist Trade and Labor Alliance. Cap makers and bakery workers were also invaded, and strikes and counterstrikes were waged by the dual unions. A succession of splits within the IWW and the depression of 1907–1908 ended the IWW threat, but not before the Jewish unions were further weakened.

Unionization in the men's garment industry was even more precarious. The conservative and compromising United Garment Workers' leadership was ill-fitted to understand the acute problems of masses of Jewish tailors in the early 1900's, who were trapped in unclean shops that doubled as lodgings and worked fourteen to sixteen hours each day for unscrupulous contractors. In 1901–1904, yearly strikes were called against the contractors in several cities. The tailors demanded a fifty-nine-hour work week, and manufacturer-responsibility for agreements made by the contractors. A familiar cycle was repeated: The tailors suffered greatly during strikes, but held out until some improvements were guaranteed; then, they lost interest in their unions.

The "rise of the tailors" fascinated the muckrakers of the period—those popular writers who exposed economic and social abuses. The most famous muckraker, Lincoln Steffens, had reported on the tailors' strikes on the East Side in 1895–97. Even earlier, *Arena, Collier's, The Outlook, The Forum,* and *Evening Post* had carried articles on persecution of Jews in Russia, the special character of Russian Jews, and their life in America.[3] The muckrakers were non-Jews, but they attached special importance to the Jewish struggle for group survival and the development of social idealism in the Jewish ghettos as portending special significance for the future of the country.[4]

Almost every aspect of Jewish immigrant life came under the compassionate scrutiny of the muckrakers, but especially compelling was the idealism that seemed to overcome the struggle for existence. The Jewish tailors drew singular attention. In his autobiography, Ray Stannard Baker wrote about his ardent interest in the tailors:

No one of the articles I wrote at that time more deeply aroused my interest and sympathy than the one I called "The Rise of the Tailors," which appeared in *McClure's* for December, 1904. It concerned the effort of a number of farsighted and idealistic labor leaders to organize the most poverty-stricken, unrecognized, and undefended people in the country—masses of new immigrants who spoke little or no English, who were remorselessly exploited and cheated at every turn. . . . What thrilled me most was the extraordinary idealism and patience with which these poor men and women came to their own help. They had to suffer everything, not only the loss of their jobs, but literally hunger and cold, in forming any organization at all. They kept at it for years, they struck again and again, and when they were discharged and left homeless, other workers re-formed their lines and finally succeeded in organizing and re-creating the entire industry. The reform had come finally, as all great reforms must come, from within, from the men themselves . . . for a better life based on the organization of man's labor.[5]

This struggle, he went on, struck him as "the most remarkable exemplification of a true American and democratic approach to the solution of problems." Indeed, the Jewish tailors were prepared to risk everything, to make the dearest sacrifices for the principle of labor solidarity. But once a strike was won, they did not see any practical need for a union. Realistically, for the Jewish worker, the union did not yet—if indeed it ever did—fill all of his needed ideological and social space. *Landslayt* (old-world) ties were still strong and an employer who attended the circumcisions, bar mitzvah celebrations, weddings, and funerals of his employees could hardly be a permanent enemy. "Everything bearing the name of my native place touched a tender spot in my heart," David Levinsky in Cahan's novel had confessed. Resentment against exploitation in shops flared into strikes but did not destroy these sentiments.[6] However, class lines sharpened as these ties weakened and as new immigrants without such ties joined the ranks of workers.

Class conflict in the ghettos was partly an overflow of social antagonisms in the Pale. Bosses who had become heads of synagogues and temples in America were often men who had dominated communities in Russia. As socialist ideas began to penetrate the Jewish unions, class antagonisms came to the surface. At a time when the unions of America pursued the policy of the AFL—"a fair wage for a fair day's work"—the Declaration of Principles of the UHT in 1890 had proclaimed that "all the wealth and means of production are created through labor, and therefore the worker has the full right to enjoy the fruit of the labor which he creates." The declaration then lists the injustices of the capitalistic system, concluding that such a system must be overturned and replaced by a truly humane society. For committed socialists, peace between capital and labor was out of the question.

During the early 1900's, the capmakers were the only group in the clothing industry able to maintain a stable union. The industry itself, largely in the hands of German manufacturers in New York, was free of the evil of contracting. Earnings were somewhat better than in other branches, and the splintering of the union by De Leon's Alliance was overcome in 1900, when the factions united. The following year an international union was formed, with strong and sturdy socialists at the helm, and it became affiliated with the AFL. In 1903, all five locals boasted a membership of over three thousand, including many young women, but in 1904 the union was locked out by the large manufacturers involved in a national open-shop drive. The whole labor movement came to the aid of the capmakers, who were forced into a devastating thirteen-week strike. Pickets walked the lines in all weather; many strikers were evicted from their homes. One of the strike leaders was the fiery young Rose Schneiderman,[7] a lining maker, who had helped organize a local the previous year, and later became an international vice-president of the union. The AFL threat of taxing its membership to support the strikers finally pressured employers into a settlement.

One of the insidious problems of this strike, as of so many others, was strike-breaking. Jewish workers struggling to build unions in the East Side also had to battle against one of the most corrupt political machines in New York City history. The police and courts were also hostile, sometimes anti-Semitic. The structure and philosophy of the AFL created yet other problems. Although only about 10 percent of the total labor force in America was enrolled in the AFL, it was made up of skilled, better-paid workers who took great pride in their skills and work. But the philosophy of craft unionism found little response among Jewish immigrants. The Jewish craftsman generally found his craftsmanship superfluous in America—many learned their work after they arrived. Typically, the Jewish immigrant felt coarsened and dehumanized by his work. Socialism eventually gave him an idealized sense of labor's place in society, but this had little or no relation to crafts or special skills.[8] Moreover, the craft unions were elitist, often ethnically homogeneous and discriminatory. The UHT, which united with the AFL in 1899, was often chastised by non-Jewish labor for segregating Jewish workers in separate bodies. But if this was a legitimate complaint, the problem was aggravated by the practices of the AFL unions themselves, which, having gained acceptance, jealously guarded their new status, thus driving Jewish workers into separate unions.

The Amalgamated Painters' Union, for example, admitted about one thousand East European Jews in 1901, but subsequently, the building-trades unions barred all newcomers on the grounds that since the AFL opposed immigration, they were justified in excluding immigrants from their ranks. Jewish workers were hurt badly; many old-country carpenters, bricklayers, painters, and tinsmiths had found work in the booming building industry at the turn of the century and for the first time had a chance to work at their own trades.[9] Earnings were somewhat higher than in the sweatshops, and many educated young immigrants without a special skill could enter these fields and earn a living quickly.

Work was plentiful—new Jewish neighborhoods were developing in Brooklyn, Harlem, and the Bronx, and new Jewish suburbs were forming in Philadelphia, Boston, and Chicago. Being cheaper and easier to deal with, Jewish workers were generally hired by Jewish builders, but they soon met stiff resistance from unionized workers. Before long, the organized crafts pushed Jews out of all new building and left them with alterations on old buildings. When Jews tried to join the unions, they were blocked by high initiation fees and by examiners who simply refused to pass Jews, Italians, and other Eastern Europeans. Finally, in 1906, the UHT began to form Jewish unions of painters, carpenters, masons and bricklayers, plumbers and electrical workers. With great tenacity, the workers surmounted strikes, financial hardships and continuing AFL discrimination until they secured charters from the internationals.[10] Far from wanting to threaten the non-Jewish workers' standard of living, these Jewish workers wanted to be part of the struggle. As in the case of Jewish inside iron workers, tinsmiths, butchers, barbers, waiters, mattress and bedspring workers, the Jewish building trade workers were in the vanguard of the AFL unions once they were integrated.[11]

At the same time, the few unions in which Jewish workers had achieved status were loathe to share the job market. In 1899, for example, after a long struggle, the United Hatters admitted the Hebrew Hatters, comprising fifteen hundred members. The Hebrew Hatters thereupon made admission of newcomers difficult by charging a high initiation fee. The AFL Jewish Actors' Union did likewise, and in the slow fall season of 1904, the United Cloth Hat and Capmakers devised an examination plan to protect its members from competition.[12]

The generally gloomy picture in the Jewish unions brightened with the economic upturn that followed the depressions of 1907 and 1909 and new waves of immigration. America, not Russia, had to be the arena of struggle for Jewish workers as their hopes for the revolution in Russia died. The radicalism, zeal, and strong labor consciousness of the new immigrants revitalized Jewish unions and gave impetus to the greatest surge of Jewish trade unionism prior to the New Deal.[13] At first, there were sputterings in the 1909 strikes of Jewish bakers and pantsmakers, but the historic turning point was the "uprising of the twenty thousand." Not men, however, but young and inexperienced girls in the shirtwaist industry led the "uprising."

By the early 1900's, the shirtwaist industry in New York was the second largest in the women's garment industry, employing over twenty-five thousand workers, most of them young women. A spurt of Italian immigration brought some Italian workers into the shops, but the industry was predominantly Jewish. A small local of several hundred members existed but, because most of the young women thought of their work as an interlude before marriage, the trade was virtually unorganized. Many of the shops were in new buildings, but working conditions were oppressive. An inside contracting system kept the earnings of most of the girls, permanently classed as "learners" or "helpers," at three or four dollars a week, while employers made large profits by charging the working girls for their needles, chairs, and lockers. Supervisors harassed girls by following them into the bathroom and covering clocks so that not a minute was wasted. An intensive campaign in the summer of 1909 resulted in several strikes of workers in Local 25 of the ILGWU against two of the largest shirtwaist factories—the Leiserson and Triangle firms. The young women strikers were confronted daily by professional thugs and strikebreakers, who frightened them away from the picket lines.

The ILGWU, then numbering about eighteen hundred members, was still too weak to offer any aid; nor could the UHT.[14] However, a few of the strike leaders and Bernard Weinstein, secretary of the UHT, began to think of a trade-wide strike.[15] Committees began to agitate for a strike in other factories. On November 22, 1909, a meeting of all the workers in the trade was called at Cooper Union. Benjamin Feigenbaum, now on the *Forward,* presided. Abraham Cahan, Meyer London, Samuel Gompers, and Mary Dreier, president of the New York Women's Trade Union League, spoke. For several hours, the overflowing hall listened to speeches, when suddenly a slim girl in her teens asked for the floor. She was Clara Lemlich, a striker from the Leiserson factory who had been hurt on the picket line. "I am a working girl," she shouted in Yiddish, "one of those who are on strike against intolerable conditions. I am tired of listening to speakers who talk in general terms. What we are here for is to decide whether we're going to strike or not. I offer a resolution that a general strike be declared—now." [16] There was a great commotion in the hall, with people waving hats, canes, handkerchiefs. After a few minutes, Feigenbaum made himself heard and asked for a second to the motion. The entire audience rose to its feet. "Do you mean it in absolute faith?" Feigenbaum cried. "Will you take the old Jewish oath?" And two thousand hands rose as the oath was uttered: "If I betray the cause I now pledge, let my hand wither from the arm I now raise." [17]

The general strike [18] was on—the first large strike of women workers in America. Nearly twenty thousand waistmakers and dressmakers went out on strike, closing down over five hundred shops. The entire Jewish labor and socialist movement was drawn into the struggle, and gallant help was rendered by the Women's Trade Union League, which assigned its members to register the strikers, raise funds, and strengthen the picket lines. Stunned by this massive attack, employers used strikebreakers and the power of the police and courts to break the morale of the girls. By Christmas Day, 1909, seven hundred and twenty-three pickets were arrested and nineteen sentenced to the workhouse. One judge, while sentencing a girl, said, "You are on strike against God and nature, whose firm law is that man shall earn his bread in the sweat of his brow. You are on strike against God." When the Women's Trade Union League cabled this scolding to George Bernard Shaw, he wired back: "Delightful.

Medieval America always in the intimate personal confidence of the Almighty." [19]

A kaleidoscopic human drama was enacted during the eleven-week strike. One saw young Italian girls, who at first resisted joining the strikers, and then relented, escorted to the shops by their mothers and fathers. One could hear the fearless Esther Lobetkin, who hardly ate or slept during the strike and was arrested again and again, shouting each time from the patrol wagon, "Do not lose courage. We will win yet." There were the inspiring Switski sisters, who picketed a shop bristling with brutal private detectives. A protest march of all strikers and the Women's Trade Union League was organized on December 3 and passed City Hall.[20] Many conscience-stricken college women and social workers took turns at strike duty. One of them has conveyed the spirit of the young workers:

> Into the foreground of this great moving picture comes the figure of one girl after another, as their services are needed. With extraordinary simplicity and eloquence, she will tell before any kind of audience, without any false shame, and without self-glorification, the conditions of her work, her wages, and the pinching poverty of her home and the homes of her comrades. Then she withdraws into the background to undertake quietly the danger and humiliation of picket duty or to become a nameless sandwich-girl selling papers on the street (special strike editions of the New York *Call* and New York *Evening Journal*), no longer the center of interested attention, but the butt of the most unspeakable abuse.[21]

The strike stirred widespread public sympathy. Women of New York's social élite posted bail for arrested picketers, raised strike funds, and addressed meetings and teas. Nationally known lawyers helped Morris Hillquit and Meyer London defend the arrested pickets. Rabbis began to speak of the rights of labor. The women's suffrage movement, which had just formed a party, made the cause of the strike its own. Reformers, muckrakers, and liberal clergymen inveighed against the waist manufacturers. Led by the *Forward*, the Yiddish press poured out indignant articles and editorials; the *Forward* organized a fund-raising drive.[22] A mammoth rally was organized by all sympathetic groups early in December in the New York Hippodrome.

On December 20, the strike spread to Philadelphia, but it could not be sustained and, in fact, by this time, although Local 25 in New York had more than ten thousand members, the strike had passed its crest. Most of the small shops had gone back to work with settlements of a sort. But there was no general agreement in the industry; the large shops and the manufacturers' association refused to recognize the unions. By February 3, 1910, when the strike officially ended, 339 out of 353 firms in the manufacturers' association had signed agreements with the union. The workers won a fifty-two-hour week, four legal holidays with pay, the negotiation of wages between employer and shop committee, the abolition of charges for needles and supplies, and the employer's pledge not to discriminate against ex-strikers.[23] These terms did not satisfy the workers, but they represented some gains and, more important, gave fire to the weary, pessimistic leadership of the ILGWU and to the Jewish labor movement in general. The next objective was the cloakmakers. Their "great revolt" in 1910, like "the uprising of the twenty thousand," transformed Jewish and American labor history and stunned the public by its discipline, tenacity, and solidarity.

The grievances of the cloakmakers involved not only wages and hours, but the demoralizing practice of subcontracting which had grown worse each year. Pressers and finishers, who were especially plagued, worked sixty-five hours or more each week during the season for twelve to fourteen dollars; operators earned a little more. Those who owned their machines carried them from shop to shop; others paid for repairs and supplies, even electricity. New York was now the world's center of the women's dress industry and cutthroat competition among the manufacturers pushed exhausting demands on the workers.

With extremely thin resources [24] and a membership of no more than two thousand, a campaign for a general strike was started in the summer of 1908. Not until Workmen's Circle members began to join the union as a result of their conference in March of that year, and not until the waistmakers had built up momentum for a general strike, did the cloakmakers feel ready for a similar action. (At the height of the waistmakers' strike, New York cloakmakers in nine locals had taxed themselves two dollars to build up a strike fund.) The *Forward* gave great impetus to the campaign, and by April 1910, when the membership reached six thousand, the Joint Board published a trilingual (English, Yiddish, and Italian) bulletin, the *Naye Post*, to keep its members informed of events. Bolstered by the spirit of the waistmakers and public sympathy and AFL support, the ILGWU endorsed a general strike at its tenth convention in Boston in June 1910. Any remaining doubts were extinguished at a mass meeting of the workers on the afternoon of June 28 at Madison Square Garden. Some forty thousand people came to what the *Forward* called "the greatest Jewish labor meeting the world has ever seen." A week later, a referendum—the first of its kind—clinched the issue. The strike was called for Thursday, July 7 at 2 o'clock in the afternoon instead of the morning to deny employers and police their usual advantages. Abraham Rosenberg, who became the president of the ILGWU in the bleakest time—1908—recalled that day:

> About two o'clock some of the members of the strike committee together with some representatives of the press went to the cloak district to see how the order of the strike committee would be taken. . . . Among those who were curious to see whether the workers would respond were A. Cahan and B. Schlesinger, editor and manager of the *Forward*. Our people naturally were excited, their hearts beat fast, and every minute seemed an age to them. When ten minutes had passed and there was no worker to be seen, Cahan asked ironically: "Well,

where are your strikers?" . . . Hardly had he spoken when he saw a sea of people surging from all the side streets toward Fifth Avenue. Every minute the crowds grew larger, and all moved in the same direction. By half-past two, all the streets, from Thirty-eighth Street down and from the East River toward the west were jammed with workers. Each worker carried his tools and all moved in the direction of the halls where they were to meet, according to the instructions in the *Naye Post*. . . . Many of our most devoted members cried for joy at the idea that their lifelong labors had at last been crowned with success.[25]

That same afternoon, the *Forward* published an extra edition, jubilantly announcing the response of the workers. In a few days, the entire ladies' cloak, suit, shirt and reefer industry was shut down, involving almost seventy thousand workers. The strike was planned and managed with great care and efficiency, and worker discipline was excellent. Roll calls were held twice a day to see who was scabbing, and pickets roamed the shops to buck up those who were weakening. Each shop and meeting hall had responsible chairmen checking every detail. Morris Winchevsky was put in charge of raising money and a strike fund provided two and four dollars a week to unmarried and married workers respectively. "The great revolt" was under way. "The 70,000 zeros became 70,000 fighters," Liessen exulted.

Among the nineteen union demands, four were particularly important: a closed shop; the end of subcontracting; a forty-eight-hour week; a minimum wage for weekly workers and a minimum hourly rate for piece workers. The smaller shops signed agreements rather quickly; within three weeks over three hundred had signed. But the larger manufacturers refused to accept the closed shop. Finally the National Civic Federation, which advocated enlightened industrial relations, and Jewish leaders, who feared that the strike was tearing apart the Jewish community, prepared the way for the intervention of Louis D. Brandeis.[26] Brandeis, who later became a distinguished Supreme Court justice, was already known as the "people's attorney" but was somewhat compromised in the eyes of the strikers as an opponent of the closed shop and attorney for the Boston cloak manufacturers who had crushed the garment workers' strike with an injunction in 1907. But he was not unmoved by the idealistic leadership of the union, and had already developed an antipathy to predatory capitalism. Gradually, he began to feel that a social ethic should inform the law, and that the law should hasten needed social change. By 1910, the general strike committee of the cloakmakers was ready to listen to his "preferential union shop" (which would give preference to union over non-union member in employment). Although they did not endorse it, they authorized him to meet with the lawyers for both sides to try to conciliate differences.

Numerous conferences were held, but the main stumbling block was the issue of the union shop. The workers insisted on it; the manufacturers rejected it. Brandeis' idea did not give the workers the essential union recognition they were seeking. On August 6, the employers secured an injunction against the strikers, and many of them were arrested. Again, the UHT, the Workmen's Circle, and the *Forward* led in the mobilization of support for the strike and raised over $200,000. Eventually, Jacob Schiff and Louis Marshall, prominent and wealthy Jews, disturbed by the intra-Jewish aspects of the conflict, intervened and, after much turmoil, caused by misunderstanding over phraseology, more arrests, and another injunction, a so-called Protocol of Peace [27] was achieved. On Friday, September 2, the greatest strike in the city's history ended with a night-long celebration and thanksgiving and a festive parade the following day.

The Protocol of Peace was largely worked out by Brandeis who believed that it "would lift industrial relations out of the jungle to a civilized plane and pave the way to lasting unity and harmony." Management and labor were to create standing committees to settle grievances and forestall conflicts. While the protocol was short-lived and failed to bring peace to the needle trades, it marked the first time in American labor history that a third force—the public interest—in the form of a Board of Arbitration was drawn in to arbitrate differences between labor and management. All differences that could not be conciliated by the Board of Grievances, consisting of worker-management representatives, were to be referred to a higher Board of Arbitration, in which impartial representatives of the public would make the ultimate decisions.[28] The Protocol of Peace, despite its many deficiencies and its short life—it lasted six years in its original form—was an immense, pioneering achievement [29] in the history of American trade unionism and served as a model for subsequent labor disputes. Other important features of the settlement were the acceptance of the shop chairman as the voice of the union, agreement on the preferential union shop, a fifty-hour week, abolition of inside contracting, and minimum wage rates. Another novel feature which laid the groundwork for a comprehensive health and safety program, was the creation of a Joint Board of Sanitary Control to supervise sanitary conditions in the garment factories.

Elated by this victory, the ILGWU felt that the time was ripe for militancy elsewhere. Forty new locals were chartered in New York between July 1910 and April 1911, but the big drive was concentrated in Cleveland. A general strike of cloakmakers in Cleveland was called in June 1911 and closed practically all of the shops. However, violent strikebreaking and the subsequent terror turned much of the press against the strikers. The strikers held out, but the strike became a heavy financial burden on the International and the employers prevailed. Elsewhere, organizing drives among white goods workers, wrapper and kimono makers, and workers on children's dresses forged ahead. But it was the tragic fire in the non-union Triangle Shirtwaist Company in New York on March 25, 1911, that spurred the advance of the ILGWU and made it the spearhead of the labor movement on the Lower East Side.

The factory occupied the three top floors of the ten-story Asch Building near Washington Square. Over eight hundred workers jammed the area—most of them girls between thirteen and twenty-three, children of Jewish and Italian immigrants. Late in the afternoon, a fire broke out on the eighth floor, kindled by the bundles on tables and floor, and within minutes the whole factory became an inferno. Some were able to escape to the elevators but many died at their machines or were trapped at the locked stairway doors. Others were driven back to the windows and jumped to their deaths. One hundred and forty-six workers perished in the fire, most of them Jewish girls. For days, the Lower East Side was wracked by grief. The *Forward* printed pictures of those who could be identified above the lament: "Tears Fall Around These Pictures." A mass funeral was held for the victims and their bodies were buried in a common grave of the Workmen's Circle Cemetery. Aroused by the terrible perils surrounding immigrant workers, upper and middle-class progressives forced the legislature to set up a State Factory Investigating Commission whose work eventually resulted, in 1913, in the passage of comprehensive labor measures that won the commendation of the New York State Federation of Labor.[30]

Memories of the Triangle fire were still fresh in the early months of 1913 when strikes among dress and waistmakers and white-goods workers, mostly Jewish girls, attracted wide public sympathy and the support of influential personalities such as ex-President Theodore Roosevelt, John Haynes Holmes and Rabbi Stephen Wise. Thousands of young women who had never heard of a labor movement became courageous pickets and loyal union members. Agreements, largely based on the Protocol of Peace, were quickly reached.

The New York Factory Investigating Commission also looked into the fur trade and found shocking unsanitary conditions: lack of fresh air and dust and tiny hairs in the furs, which caused widespread tuberculosis, asthma, poor eyesight, and skin diseases. Examining doctors found that the fingers of many furriers were rotted. The UHT had organized the first furrier union in 1892, but the depression of 1893 wiped out its efforts.[31] There followed a dismal eleven-year wait until new initiatives were tried. But, besides the unsanitary conditions, there was the problem of a short season and rapid turnover: a busy season lasted only from September to Christmas, during which the speed-up became intense. After Christmas, many workers were fired or had to take a drastic cut in wages. No man could stay in a shop for more than a few years because of the toll on his health.

The entrance of several thousand younger immigrants into the fur shops had an invigorating effect, and in June 1912, the small union and the UHT called a general strike. The strike leader was Isadore Cohen, a Bund member from Vilna. Some ten thousand workers, most of them Jewish, responded and emptied the fur shops. At first, the employer representatives refused to enter the same room as the union officials, but a settlement was finally worked out in September with the help of Rabbi Judah Magnes, the well-known liberal rabbi. The union was not recognized, but the employers had to deal with the shop chairman; substantial improvements were also made in wages and hours and, as in the case of the cloakmakers, a Joint Board of Sanitary Control was set up to inspect sanitary conditions in the shops. By 1914 a very good collective bargaining agreement was signed which transformed the industry. In June 1913, an international was formed which affiliated with the AFL.

As epoch making as the great strikes of the women's garment workers in 1909–10 was the struggle of the men's clothing workers that soon followed. However, matters were complicated by the conflict between the tailors, who were militant and fully committed to the power of the strike, and their parent body, the United Garment Workers, who were conservative and unable to grasp the mentality of the radical tailors. Their past had been a long history of conflict. The United Garment Workers was mainly interested in the overall workers, most of whom were native-born women, and the importance of the union label, which carried no weight in the merchandising of ready-to-wear men's clothing.[32] The tailors thus virtually remained without a national leadership, and initiatives had to come from below. Chicago led the way.

In September 1910, some girls working in the pants shop of Hart, Schaffner and Marx, the largest men's clothing factory in the country, were handed a wage cut, setting off a spontaneous strike, which spread rapidly. Within three weeks, thirty-eight thousand tailors in Chicago left their shops. The union leadership, however, frowned on the whole action and signed an agreement with Hart, Schaffner and Marx without consulting the workers. The strikers rejected the settlement, but after hectic negotiations, an agreement was reached granting partial recognition of the union and the setting up of arbitration machinery.

The other clothing manufacturers, however, refused to settle and the president of the United Garment Workers, Thomas A. Rickert, called off the strike. Bitterly disappointed and weary, the tailors returned to work. That their morale did not totally flag was largely due to the tireless energy of a young cutter at Hart, Schaffner and Marx—Sidney Hillman, a former Kovno rabbinical student—who did much to restore the spirit of the striking tailors. Meanwhile, a new center of agitation developed in New York. There, the Brotherhood of Tailors agitated for an organizing campaign and industry-wide strike in 1912. At first, the United Garment Workers refused any help, but after months of worker pressure and prodding by the UHT, it approved a strike.

The experience of the cloakmakers signaled the importance of careful planning for a general strike, and the tailors and other locals worked for a full year making preparations and enrolling new members. On December 18, 1912, there was a vote, lasting five days, which was conducted by the

Forward.[33] The strike carried overwhelmingly, and on December 30, a general strike began. Within a short time some seventy thousand workers poured out of their shops. The offices of the *Forward* were converted into strike headquarters and its entire staff placed at the disposal of the strikers. Max Pine of the *Forward* and UHT became the chief spokesman of the strikers, [34] although official jurisdiction belonged to the half-hearted United Garment Workers.

The chief demands of the strikers were a forty-eight-hour week, a 20 per cent wage rise, and the abolition of subcontracting. Gradually, many of the smaller firms began to settle with the union, but the most important firm—that of Alfred Benjamin—was the most rabidly anti-union and held out. Suddenly on February 28, 1913, without consulting the strikers or their leaders, the union concluded a private settlement with Alfred Benjamin on less favorable terms than those negotiated by the smaller firms. The workers were resentful and bitter when news of the agreement was reported in the *Forward.*[35] The newspaper's editorial pointed out that the settlement was not as good as had been hoped, but provided an excellent foundation for the steady improvement of wages and conditions and the future of the union.

The workers, however, were in no mood to compromise. They stormed the *Forward* building and began smashing windows. The Brotherhood of Tailors, under the tireless Ike Goldstein and Louis Hollander, spearheaded the rebellious opposition. Cahan, who had urged acceptance of the compromise, tried to address meetings but was heckled. The strike resumed, while a broadened committee was formed (including John A. Dyche, the respected secretary of the ILGWU; Meyer London; Jacob Panken, lawyer for the Brotherhood of Tailors; and Fiorello La Guardia, a rising young labor lawyer, representing a new local of Italian workers) to speak for the strikers.

The strike continued for three more weeks, followed by new negotiations and a new compromise. The damage done by the premature settlement could not be entirely undone, but some improvement in terms was won: *de facto*, though not official, recognition of the union, a fifty-three-hour week, to be reduced to fifty-two hours after one year, and an increase in wages. A vote of the workers ended the strike on March 8, 1913. Meyer London served on the arbitration panel and emerged as an important political figure exemplifying moderate socialist views. For the union members, the settlement was hailed as a victory; they returned to work conscious of a new strength and dignity. The New York unions prospered, but genuine growth had to await the inevitable showdown with the United Garment Workers' leadership. At the union's national convention in 1914, many bona fide delegates of the tailors' locals were excluded.[36] The few who were admitted led a bolt from the union, and in December 1914 formed the Amalgamated Clothing Workers of America as an independent union, with Hillman as president, and Joseph

Schlossberg as general secretary. The AFL branded the Amalgamated as a dual union, but the other Jewish unions, for all their loyalty to the AFL, accepted it as a genuine segment of the Jewish labor movement.

These early struggles in the needle trades were, to a large extent, guided by the *Forward*.[37] The emancipation of labor had indeed been the cause to which the founders of the *Forward* had dedicated themselves, but the paper went far beyond the printed word in advancing trade unionism. Staff members—Cahan, Bernard Weinstein, Barondess, Feigenbaum, Hillquit, London, Schlesinger, Miller, and Pine, among others—were also organizers of trade unions. The mass movement of Jewish workers into unions of their own creation dates from the strikes of the waist makers and cloak and suit makers of 1909-10, and both were *Forward* projects. The strike of the men's clothing workers in 1913 was also almost entirely a *Forward* undertaking, although official jurisdiction belonged to the ineffectual United Garment Workers. The *Forward* opened soup kitchens and headquarters for relief services; it was to the *Forward* building that the tailors streamed to see the results tabulated on a screen, and it was there that they protested the abortive settlement. Practically singlehandedly, the *Forward* created the support and guidance that enabled exploited Jewish workers to break out into effective protest and became a kind of authority for the struggling inchoate Jewish proletariat.

As the *Forward* prospered, more and more of its resources went into the building of the Jewish unions. During major strikes, the *Forward* virtually became a house organ of the unions, neglecting all other editorial interests to help the strikers. It donated money from its own treasury and solicited contributions from its readers.[38] It emphasized not only the tactical advantage of belonging to a union but even more importantly, it justified unions morally. A union was an assertion of human dignity and the embodiment of the brotherhood of man. To *Forward* readers, trade unionism was part of a higher morality, demanding sacrifices of readers as well as members, and was invested with an almost religious fervor. Only this kind of devotion could have carried union members through long and bitter strikes, through hunger and brutal assaults by police and thugs, and readers through hectic fund raising and exhortation.

Although the *Forward* became the representative voice of American Jewish socialism, one didn't have to be a socialist to enjoy it. Its readers were not only immigrants and socialists, but also Americanized Jews who could read English papers, but who preferred the *Forward* because of their nostalgia for Yiddish and good coverage of those Jewish events overlooked by the general press. Consequently, it inspired a sense of solidarity, unseen but deeply felt, a strongly bound community in space that perhaps was the ultimate, most tangible expression of the Jewish socialist community in America, periphery as well as center. It was, of course, much more than a newspaper. New immigrants looked to it to help them cope with the terrors of a new life; shop workers looked to it for help in their struggle against sweated labor; striking workers looked to it for guidance, moral support, and financial help. It gave readers news, entertainment, political education, the flavor of literary culture, and the sense of being an active participant in dramatic experiences affecting Jews and the wider world. The *Forward* spoke intimately to its readers. Inevitably, readers looked to it for advice on personal problems. In 1906, Cahan started the *Bintel Brief* [39] (A Bundle of Letters), which carried thousands of readers' letters and editors' answers, poignantly documenting the tumultuous emotional life of *Forward* readers.

The settlement of the men's clothing strike closed the first stage of the industrial history of Jewish labor. Three decades of desperate struggle punctuated by repeated failures finally came to an end. Jewish labor ceased to be helpless. The alleged incapacity of the Jewish worker to remain a disciplined member of a union had been punctured. Neither internal explosions nor prolonged struggles with employers could now destroy the Jewish unions. [40] Having conquered the terrain of industrial conflict, Jewish workers next tackled American politics.

13. Political Struggles and Unseen Questions, 1908-17

The stormy experience with De Leon's Socialist Labor party was not the last of the political tribulations of Jewish socialists. Their subsequent affiliation with the Socialist party was patchy, incomplete, and sometimes difficult. With some, there was a yearning for a self-enclosing, ideologically satisfying milieu that the party could not provide. It lacked a Jewish ambience—which it could not be expected to supply—but which was deeply missed and, like its predecessor, it was beset by factionalism and ideological conflict. In the eye of this storm was the former youthful radical Morris Hillquit.

As soon as the *Arbayter Tsaytung* became fairly prosperous, Hillquit had resigned from the paper and gradually drifted away from the Jewish labor movement. He taught English to foreigners, studied law in his spare time, and was finally admitted to the bar in 1903. Soon he became one of the acknowledged leaders of the socialist centrist wing and attracted a number of middle-class liberals as well as wealthy individuals to the socialist cause, writing voluminously about socialism in magazines and frequently debating and making speeches.

Hillquit became a polished, successful lawyer, but he was no bland, academic socialist. He had locked horns with De Leon soon after the creation of the Socialist Trade and Labor Alliance, and led the anti-De Leon opposition movement within the Socialist party. De Leon's war against the "pure and simple" unions of the AFL was no genteel skirmish, but a civil war within the Socialist Labor party that left jagged wounds, shattered the party for years, and was fought in an atmosphere of fierce invective, purges, and even violence, in the struggle for possession of party offices. By 1897, when De Leon had broken with both Jewish and German unions, the Socialist Labor party was so honeycombed with intrigue that its national executive was forced to deliberate as though it were an underground faction working within the party.[1]

The struggle against De Leon raged wherever there were socialists, but the decisive battles were fought in New York City with Hillquit directing opposition strategy. By 1899, he had succeeded in organizing an alternate party headquarters and national executive, as well as an anti-De Leon version of *The People*, the leading socialist weekly. The revolution in New York spread and before long there were two Socialist Labor parties. By October 1899, the Hillquit-led faction had won the allegiance of approximately 45 per cent of the party's seven thousand members.[2]

There followed "rectification" of De Leon's theories of revolutionary dual unionism. All party members were urged to join the union of their trade, but with the understanding that it was not the task of the unions to fight for socialism, but to "propagate the ideas of Socialism among the workingmen."[3] For a time, the Hillquit-led SLP talked about educating the workers to "the fact of the class struggle" and the importance of leading them to effective "struggles against capital," though not for the violent overthrow of capitalism, but these phrases were soon dropped in favor of political action, which meant the election of socialists to public office. In 1900, the Hillquit-led faction held a convention in Rochester and began to plan for its merger with the numerous other local and national socialist organizations that had sprung up throughout the country, including the new Social-Democratic party. The "Socialist-unity" convention was held in July 1901—after almost two years of bitter wrangling. The new Socialist party emerged and was united structurally in a loose federation in which each state organization had a high degree of autonomy. Ideologically, however, there were few signs of unity, and although all party leaders gave lip service to Marxist "scientific socialism," there was considerable disagreement on the application of Marxist theory to twentieth-century America. By the 1904 convention, the party had already divided into three factions—right, center, and left.[4]

The right and centrist wings influenced policy and, after 1908, moved rapidly toward reformism and away from direct action, sabotage, and violent class conflict, toward which some of its elements had tended, until finally at the 1912 convention of the Socialist party, they carried a resolution banning socialists from membership in organizations advocating violent methods. The poor showing of the Socialist party in the national election of 1908 had led to major decisions affecting its subsequent philosophy and practical formulations. The party could not hope to win electoral success while oscillating between revolution and reform.[5] The left wing, led by Eugene V. Debs, demanded that the party return to its role as the organization of the working class and give up the will-o'-the-wisp of political power, but the center was convinced that the party must eliminate its revolutionary past, offer more reform than liberal Democrats, and practice a step-at-a-time socialism. A new revisionist line was hammered out, and former Marxist axioms were abandoned. Hillquit, a leading centrist, could see a socialist state "persistently filtering into the present order" [6] and American society being permeated with socialist institutions at an ever-quickening pace. Fundamental Marxist notions, such as the theory of surplus value, the class make-up of society, the role of the proletariat, and the necessity of a socialist revolution were slowly rejected as mistaken. Marx the leader, the tactician, and opportunist replaced Marx the theorist to a considerable extent.[7] The party role was to secure reforms through legislation and the election of Socialist officials to government. Its program was designed to win support from small businessmen, professionals, college students, craft unionists,[8] and liberal Christians, but it found no need to engage in propaganda or organizational work among the millions of immigrants who had poured into the country in the late nineteenth and early twentieth century.

Many immigrants had formed their own socialist organizations: Finnish, Bohemian, Lithuanian, Italian, Norwegian, and Polish. The Finnish Socialist Federation, with nearly three thousand members, continuously tried to affiliate with the party, and was finally admitted on a modified basis in 1906. But the overall process was slow. In 1910, the party constitution was amended to permit any foreign-language federations with a membership of at least five hundred to establish a national translator's office at party headquarters. This brought some of the ethnic federations into the party but did not entitle them to a full voice. Full-fledged membership entailed additional national dues and state dues, thus compelling foreign-language speaking socialists to pay more for the privilege of joining the party than English-speaking socialists. Still, the "foreign comrades" took the initial organizational steps, and by the end of 1912, Bohemian, Hungarian, Italian, Polish, Scandinavian, South Slavic, and Jewish—the smallest group—socialist federations affiliated with the national party. Altogether, the twenty thousand members of the various federations increased party strength to its peak of 118,015 members.[9]

However, most of these twenty thousand could not participate in party decisions because their branches could not afford to pay double dues; nor could they affiliate with state party organizations. In one sense, this situation exacerbated the continuing struggle within the party to determine policy because the great majority of federation members held views that were extremely critical of the center-right.[10] Yet, in another, it weakened left-wing strength in these struggles and gave the field to the moderates.

For Jewish socialists, membership in a federation loomed as a way of making their association with the Socialist party more meaningful. Just as the labor union could not fill the cultural and social needs of the Jewish worker, so the Socialist party was insufficient. Party activity did not occupy the central place for Jewish workers in America that it did in Europe. Jewish members were scattered throughout its branches, or, wherever the branch was entirely Jewish—generally for geographical reasons—it remained a unit of the party with no developed approach to the particular problems or issues facing Jews-as-socialists. A broader as well as deeper context was necessary. The labor press, the Workmen's Circle, cafés, the Yiddish theatre, and literary circles helped to answer these needs, and succeeded to some extent in creating a surrogate for an autonomous or, at least, a definable Jewish socialist community. Within the Socialist party, the Central Jewish Bureau for Agitation was set up in 1907, but it served merely to conduct party propaganda among Jews. It was dissolved after indifferent results and its place was taken by the Jewish Socialist Federation.

Jewish socialists to the left of Hillquit's centrist position organized the Jewish Socialist Federation in July 1912, largely through the efforts of former Bundists—chiefly J. B. Salutsky (Hardman), Zivyon (Ben Zion Hoffman), Baruch Charney Vladek, and M. Terman.[11] Their aim was to build a Jewish socialist movement in America that would have the same dominant position in the life of Jewish workers in America that the Bund had in Russia. This, however, assumed as intensive a Jewish community life in America as existed in Eastern Europe. Neither the federation nor any other group was ever able to arrive at a clear formulation of the goals of a Jewish socialist movement in America. Nor was such a community apt to develop, given the nature of American society. Veteran socialists attacked the federation for wanting to make a Bund in America, but it became the catalyst for educational and cultural activities that helped fill the void felt by many ex-Bundists as they strove to transplant their version of Jewish socialism and to enrich Jewish life for those who found the reiterations of socialist cosmopolitanism mechanical. Some earlier arrivals, like Winchevsky and Liessin, were also dissatisfied. They resented the *Forward's* dominating influence, Cahan's power, and the lukewarm attitude toward Jewish cultural values, and they sought new channels of expression.

The federation, like the other ethnic-based groups in the Socialist party, was an autonomous body, membership in which was tantamount to membership in the party. But not all Jewish members of the Socialist party belonged to the federation, and some of the veterans and new trade-union leaders who appreciated the existence of the UHT were opposed to a separate Jewish organization within the party [12] and had misgivings about Bundist intellectuals attempting to dominate the movement.

Although its membership never exceeded five thousand,[13] the Jewish Socialist Federation stimulated the exchange of fresh ideas and brought new zeal, as well as controversy, into the Jewish labor movement. Its weekly, *Naye Velt,* edited by J. B. Salutsky dealt seriously with political and cultural problems and even criticized the limitations of the *Forward.* Although a number of writers in the federation were on the staff of the *Forward,* relations between them were none too friendly and were aggravated by Cahan's personal animosities, although both groups cooperated more or less in the Workmen's Circle,[14] in the Jewish trade unions, in anti-Zionist activity, and especially in East Side election campaigns.

The issue of federations and the continued reluctance of the Socialist party [15] to recruit newly arrived immigrants was entangled in the new relationship emerging between the party and the AFL. Gompers had not retreated one bit from his uncompromising stand against socialist theory and political activity. With the exception of Eugene V. Debs and a few others, most Socialist party leaders accepted the AFL as the legitimate economic arm of the working class, although its conventions continued to express mild dissatisfaction over the indifference of the AFL to organizing the unskilled. The year 1912 marked the last time that the socialists ran a candidate for the presidency of the AFL against Gompers; some party members had risen to high position in the AFL itself. The desire to woo AFL votes for Socialist party candidates was an important factor that also affected the debates on immigration, which vexed unions and the Socialist party for a long time.

The American socialist movement was torn between principle and opportunism on the immigration question. Undoubtedly, its desire to win over the AFL, which strongly opposed immigration, led Morris Hillquit, the American delegate to the International Socialist Congress in 1904, to co-sponsor a resolution calling for restriction of immigration from "backward races," [16] that is, from Asiatic countries. Hillquit was again in the American delegation to the Stuttgart International in 1907, which was instructed to submit a resolution calling on all socialist parties to educate immigrants in the principles of socialism and trade unionism and, at the same time, "to combat with all means at their command the willful importation of cheap foreign labor calculated to destroy labor organizations, to lower the standard of living of the working class, and to retard the ultimate realization of Socialism." [17] However, the Stuttgart International rejected this resolution and, instead, passed one condemning all restrictions on freedom of immigration on racial or national grounds, but favoring the curtailment of mass importation of unorganized labor.[18] The center-right wings of the American Socialist party, agitated by Chinese and Japanese immigration to the West Coast and racial incompatibilities, denounced the American delegates for "permitting" the passage of the resolution.

The 1908, 1910, and 1912 Socialist party conventions debated these controversial issues with great bitterness. Hillquit, who had been unsettled by the racist slurs of some socialists, argued that immigration restrictions should be based on potential harm to the labor movement by strikebearers and contract labor. This formulation was adopted at the 1910 convention. Hillquit felt that his views were substantially a summary of the Stuttgart resolutions, but others disagreed. By 1912, inner factionalism was rending the party; attacks on the militant left-wing grew more vehement. Once more, the convention not only refused to endorse the International's position on immigration, but passed a resolution calling for the strengthening and strict enforcement of exclusion laws. These issues were intensely debated among Jewish socialists and affected the political ambitions of Hillquit.

After an absence of almost fifteen years, Hillquit returned to the lower East Side as Socialist party candidate for Congress from the Ninth Congressional District in 1906 and 1908. Eventually, in 1914, Meyer London—also from the East Side—won the first Socialist seat in Congress. But the struggle to penetrate the citadels of political power pulled many personalities and forces in Jewish radical life into a very rough-and-tumble experience. Its beginnings went as far back as Henry George's New York mayoralty campaign and, later, were spun amid the political turmoil created by the ambitions of William Randolph Hearst, the publisher of the New York *American and Journal.* Hearst had run successfully for Congress in 1902, and was a Democratic candidate for mayor of New York in 1905, but ran as an independent after Tammany Hall refused him the nomination. In a bitterly contested race, he carried the East Side but lost the election by a little more than three thousand votes. In 1906, he ran for the governorship on his own Independence League ticket. Not only was he a vote-getter, but he fancied himself a champion of the little people, especially the tenement dwellers on the East Side and, indeed, he had sent a special correspondent to Russia in 1903 to cover the Kishinev massacres. He also led a fund drive to help the pogrom victims and printed reports in Hebrew type.[19] In 1904, he published his *Yidisher Amerikaner* briefly and in his campaigns in 1905–1906, he published Yiddish campaign dailies.

Hearst's political ascent affected the politics of the Socialist party as well as the political activity of the lower East Side. There, the young party had to meet the lingering sting of the Socialist Labor party's criticism, to strengthen the position of the *Forward,* organize trade unions and, above all, challenge Tammany Hall. It had not yet acquired any national influence, but had registered some in Milwaukee and New York, where its strength was centered in the Ninth Congressional District, the most congested on the East Side and populated almost entirely by Russian-Jewish workers. Hillquit described the district as "the home of the tenements, pushcarts, paupers, and tuberculosis. It is the experimental laboratory of the sentimental moralist, the chosen prey of the smug philanthropist. Geographically, it is located in the slums; industrially it belongs to the sweatshops; politically it is a dependency of Tammany Hall."[20] This square mile of some 200,000 souls was the fiefdom of the Tammany chiefs Christy and Timothy Sullivan. Votes were openly bought and the local Republican machine worked in collusion with Tammany. Suffering from setbacks in union organization, Jewish socialists hoped for political success. In 1904, Joseph Barondess, running on the Socialist party ticket from the Ninth District, had polled over 3,000 votes, about 20 percent of the total; in 1906 and 1908, prospects seemed brighter because

of a four-cornered race among the Democratic, Republican, Socialist
parties, and the Independence League.

Hillquit, a successful lawyer, was the leading centrist figure in the
Socialist party when he ran for Congress in 1906 and 1908. Left Socialists
still opposed electioneering, but gradualist and reformist elements in the
party considered the rising tide of middle-class reform a sign of awakening
social consciousness and emphasized achieving socialism through democratic elections.[21] These elements in the AFL even abandoned efforts to
get the organization to endorse political action and concentrated on
showing workers the benefits of an intelligent use of the ballot. Middle-
class fears of revolution were quieted by explaining that "revolution"
simply meant a long series of reforms that would eventually change the
social order.[22]

These ideas and the integrity and stability of Hillquit were stressed in
the 1906 "Socialism and Hillquit for Congress" campaign. The platform
also urged protection for pushcart peddlers, improved factory conditions,
and clean tenements. However, Hillquit did not stress Jewish interests as
such in his campaign. Veteran Jewish socialists plunged into election
activity and were beginning to feel the excitement of a possible victory.
The party had gained strength since 1904, as well as the support of
distinguished personalities. The capitalist press gave serious attention and
considerable space to the Socialist program and interviewed Hillquit
frequently. Important people such as the historian Charles Beard stumped
the district for him, and thousands paraded to Rutgers Square to hear a
rousing call for Hillquit's election.[23] The *Forward* was exultant, and
Cahan welcomed the keen interest of "Americans": "The finest Americans
are interested in our congressional campaign; they impatiently await the
election of Morris Hillquit; they look upon this as the start of a revolution
in the political life of America." [24]

The *Forward* also arranged quite unexpectedly and spectacularly to
have Maxim Gorky appear in Hillquit's behalf. Gorky had come to the
United States in the spring of 1906. He was lionized wherever he went
until the press discovered that the woman he had been traveling with was
not legally married to him. Suddenly, Gorky was ostracized—except on the
East Side—finding it difficult even to obtain a hotel room.

The parades, speeches, and excitement that buzzed around the
campaign provided a good emotional outlet for socialists who were still
suffering from the failure of the revolution of 1905 in Russia.[25] On
election night, the *Forward* erected a huge screen in front of its building,
on which returns were flashed by stereopticon. Over sixty thousand
Hillquit supporters gathered in Seward Square across the street to watch
frames flashing the election count and caricatures of Tammany leaders.[26]

But Hillquit polled only 26 percent of the vote and lost the election.
As a result of a deal between Hearst and Charles Murphy, the Tammany

boss, whereby Hearst got the Democratic nomination for governorship, the Tammany candidate, Henry Goldfogle, had managed to have his name placed on Hearst's Independence League ticket as well. The socialists, who had counted on a separate Independence League candidate to divide the vote, lost.[27] They blamed the defeat on Hearst's deal, but many other factors were involved.

Hearst, a self-styled radical, cut into the Socialist vote and won the support of a number of well-to-do independent "radicals." He knew how to capitalize on the grievances against bankers and big business and used demagogic tactics in his campaign. The *Forward* warned its readers against him, but Cahan's old radical comrade Louis Miller was now at the helm of a rival independent paper *Di Varhayt (The Truth)*, which supported Hearst. *Di Varhayt* was started in 1905 by Miller, who was angered by Cahan's attack on a play by Jacob Gordin and Cahan's refusal to publish Miller's defense. This issue precipitated the break between the men. However, relations between Cahan, on one hand, and Miller, Winchevsky, Gordin, and Feigenbaum on the other, had become strained anyhow. *Di Varhayt* had attracted a number of outstanding Jewish socialists, including Winchevsky and Gordin, who were pained by the *Forward's* compromises and Cahan's cunning. On September 15, 1906, Winchevsky published an article in *Di Varhayt* criticizing Hearst's pseudosocialism. Yet the following day, the paper endorsed him. Miller's editorial began with a letter from a reader: "I have always voted for the Socialist party," the letter said, "but now, seeing the way the *Forward* people have put one over on the party by pushing through another candidate instead of Comrade Joseph Barondess, it would be a crime pure and simple to vote for the Socialists."[28] The editorial pointed out that the paper had received numerous similar letters condemning the Socialist party and urging the support of Hearst.

The following week, however, Miller learned of the deal between Hearst and Murphy over Goldfogle, which meant that Miller was endorsing the Tammany machine he had fought against for years. He was also caught in another dilemma: he railed against the dilution of socialism and mass appeal techniques of the *Forward*, yet he aspired to create an *American* paper filled with popular human-interest features and so beat Cahan at his own game. For a time, *Di Varhayt* developed a vitality and independence that threatened the *Forward*. But when Miller became hard-pressed financially and began to offer his paper to Tammany Hall for election publicity and advertising, the scrupulous Winchevsky and other supporters were repelled and left him.

In the election of 1906, Miller concentrated on the governor's race, supporting Hearst's vague radicalism and thereby alienating virtually all socialist support. This policy also flung him into common cause with the conservative *Tageblatt* and *Morning Journal*, which were anathema to radicals, and, indeed, to Miller himself. Occasional Zionist excursions were also considered politically aberrant.[29] The popularity of the *Varhayt* declined and the paper was sold to the new *Der Tog (The Day)* in 1914.

Other factors also contributed to Hillquit's defeat. Many of the socialists who had applauded speakers at Socialist party meetings were not yet citizens; others were intimidated by Tammany, while still others who identified themselves as socialists simply did not vote; nor could the Irish or German-Americans in the district be induced to vote Socialist. Yet the Socialists claimed a moral victory and braced themselves for 1908.

The contest in 1908 involved the same four political parties, with Goldfogle again running on a fused ticket. In addition, the rump Socialist Labor party ran De Leon himself with the clear purpose of ruining Hillquit's chances. Again, scores of leading socialists and intellectuals spoke at rallies for Hillquit. Debs himself made a direct appeal to the voters of the Ninth District: "The East Side," he said, "is destined to be a historic battleground. It is here that capitalism has wrought its desolation, here that it has spread its blighting curse, like a pestilence, . . . here where the victims of capitalism struggle and suffer." [30] In the two assembly districts which made up much of the area, Hillquit's running mates were Robert Hunter and James Stokes, drawn from the first echelon of the party's national leadership. The party had mounted a major offensive on the East Side, and the Ninth District offered the best chances for a breakthrough. The Jewish trade-union movement provided functionaries and rank-and-file members who were gaining political experience with each succeeding campaign. Meanwhile, Workmen's Circle membership in New York had grown to over 10,000, and highly literate, "ready-made" socialists were coming in from Russia. In the final weeks of the campaign, the party was averaging twenty-five meetings a night, with audiences aggregating 25,000.[31] Dissension and panic were reported in Tammany. Yet, when the returns were counted, Hillquit ran a distant second behind Goldfogle. His total vote was nearly one-third less than that in 1906.

The official post-mortems dwelt on the deal between the Republicans and Democrats to defeat the Socialists at all costs, Tammany terror, De Leon's candidacy, and the movement of socialists out of the East Side to Brownsville, in Brooklyn. However, in their analysis, Socialist apologists chose to ignore those issues which revolved around the Jewish interests in the Ninth District.[32] Of all the parties on the East Side, the Socialist party with its cosmopolitan and class allegiance, was least responsive to special Jewish needs, especially the overwhelming anxiety felt over kinsmen left behind in Russia. Prominent individuals, including radical intellectuals who had been passive about Jewish life, and many Jewish organizations became actively involved in the urgent cause of Russian-Jewish emigration.

This atmosphere of crisis coincided with the renewed effort to enact a literacy test as a requirement for immigration. Articles appeared in the popular press picturing the East Side as a den of iniquity and cultural backwardness, while Hillquit emphasized the need to "clean up" the area,[33] attacks which ruffled the pride of the Jewish quarter. No longer a spokesman only of Jewish workers, Hillquit pledged that he would be "the representative of the Socialist party and the interests of the working class of the country," not "the special representative of the alleged special interests" of the district.[34]

Miller's *Varhayt* pounded away at Hillquit's insensitivity, calling him a "renegade," indifferent to the tenant strike in January 1908 over rent raises and campaigns to deport immigrants.[35] "Where was Hillquit when Jews protested against the Kishinev pogrom?" Miller asked. The *Tageblatt*, too, attacked Hillquit for hiding his Jewishness and running away from his people: "If Morris Hillquit were to be elected, it would mean that New York Jewry would have no representative in the Congress of the United States." [36] *Tageblatt* also pictured the Socialist campaign as slandering the lower East Side. Despite Hillquit's disclaimers, the campaign in the Ninth District *had* been fought over Jewish interests, and Hillquit was not sufficiently identified with those interests.

In the election of 1910, the Socialist party grudgingly recognized the legitimacy of East Side ethnic loyalties. The Jewish socialists who had come in the new wave of immigration were making their presence felt within the Jewish labor movement and opposed the older, more cosmopolitan leadership that wished to merge with its American radical comrades. In 1910, the Socialist nomination in the Ninth District went to Meyer London, a man who was rooted in the district and the life of the Jewish workers.

At the Socialist Congress held in May 1910, London represented the Jewish Agitation Bureau, which had been organized a few years earlier for the purpose of recruiting Jewish workers for the Socialist party. It was suspected of Jewish "nationalistic" tendencies by the old-guard Jewish socialists, and the leadership of the Socialist party in New York was hostile toward it.[37] At the congress, when London raised the question of the voting rights of the bureau's delegates, Hillquit, who was chairman of the session, ruled that representatives of foreign-language organizations were not delegates with voting power but had only advisory status.[38] A few weeks later, London received the Socialist nomination in the Ninth District.

Hillquit moved on to national Socialist politics. The older labor and Socialist leaders on the East Side considered London's presence among them as temporary. A contemporary journalist observed: "It was expected that he would gradually attach himself to the general American movement and go into the non-Jewish sections to live. But he did not. London was drawn more and more into East Side Socialist and Trade Union activities. He remained on the East Side because his services were needed there, because his heart was there." [39] Unlike Hillquit, London had never left the East Side but lived there all his life and became a labor lawyer at a time when unions were hardly able to pay their rent. London often refused fees from his union clients and even helped them to pay the rent. He became deeply involved in the struggles of Jewish unions in the early 1890's and was sought as their legal adviser, propagandist, negotiator with employers, and defender in the courtroom. His candor, high ethical standards, and stout-hearted commitment to labor even won over the German and Irish workers who lived just outside the Jewish neighborhoods and were normally unfriendly to Jews.

London and his family were totally indifferent to material comforts; often he and his wife lived for days on coffee and bread. During strikes, he shared everything that he had with the workers and heartened them during extreme periods of want and despair. As counsel for the cloak-makers, he saw them through the great strike of 1910, and in the fall of 1910, London emerged as a popular hero of the Jewish labor movement. Not even the embittered debate on immigration at the Socialist party convention in Chicago in 1910 bruised London's image: he was known to oppose any form of immigration restriction.[40] Even the socialist Zionists, who had opposed Hillquit in 1908 because of the Socialist party's position on immigration, campaigned for London. The *Forward* was fulsome: "When Meyer London will be elected, he will be under no obligation to anyone.... The East Side has no father, or mother—no spokesman.... When London is elected to Congress, he will be the spokesman of the Jewish Quarter both in Washington and in New York." [41] The Workmen's Circle and the Cloakmakers' Union established campaign committees, and went energetically to work, stressing London's fine character and Goldfogle's dishonor. The votes of small businessmen and professionals were openly sought. London's 33.09 percent of the total vote was almost 12 percent better than Hillquit's showing in 1908 and twice as good as the rest of the Socialist slate.[42] His campaign and appeal reached well beyond the regular socialist support.

Alarmed by the possibility of a Socialist victory in 1912, the Democratic party majority in Albany changed the boundaries of the Ninth District, and the new gerry-mandered district was renumbered the Twelfth. In the 1912 election, London polled only 31.22 percent of the total vote, but in 1914 he gained almost 50 percent of the vote and won the election.[43]

London's 1914 campaign was a head-on struggle against Tammany, but by this time, the Socialists had gained not only organizational experience and political skill, but the great strength of the newly organized garment workers. The cloakmakers, ladies' waistmakers, furriers, and men's tailors—to whom London had selflessly given so much of himself—mobilized for victory. They formed committees, collected funds in the shops, and sent members who had had basic training on the picket lines to watch the polls. The Workmen's Circle, whom London represented as counsel, was again fully committed to him. The *Forward*, as it had done in the past two elections, listed the names and addresses of every one of the district's twelve thousand registered voters in its pages and plunged enthusiastically into the campaign. The English socialist daily, the *New York Call*, was also fully behind his campaign.

On election night, crowds surged toward Rutgers Square, opposite the *Forward* building, waiting expectantly for the returns. Tammany politicians tried to delay the final count, and for several hours returns were fragmentary. At eleven o'clock the conservative *Tageblatt*, located a few feet from the *Forward* building, published an extra edition announcing the victory of Goldfogle, the perennial Tammany candidate, but the crowds refused to accept the news. Then about two in the morning Tammany conceded the election, and a few hours later London himself was brought to the square to lead a jubilant demonstration. As the sun rose, Michael Zametkin hailed the light: "Perhaps the sun will shine on the East Side from now on." The following day, a Sunday, masses of people jammed Madison Square Garden to celebrate the election of the first Socialist congressman from the eastern United States [44] and the successful breaking, at long last, of the stranglehold of Tammany Hall.

Tactfully bypassing the patronizing advice offered by stunned newspapers, London remained modest, dignified, and hard-working in his new tasks, faithfully reflecting the Socialist position on issues: independence for Puerto Rico, opposition to war preparedness measures, support for child labor laws, a national unemployment insurance system, and other social legislation. As America drew closer to involvement in the war, the ranks of the socialists divided. By 1916, London, who had been re-elected, became the center of a clash over the war issue, involving various wings of the socialist movement and his colleagues in Congress. He was sympathetic to the Allied cause but continued to vote against American involvement. By 1917, however, although he voted against the declaration of war, once Congress passed the war resolution, he felt that he could not oppose any measure strengthening America's position, a view which brought down on him the vehement anger of the antiwar majority of the Socialist party.

World War I complicated positions of Jews everywhere and created painful dilemmas of loyalty as well as ideology. In the shifting search by the great powers for new alignments and support, for the first time in modern history, Jews were considered a force in their calculations—although not a force of first importance, to be sure. The growing Zionist movement and Jewish socialists began to draw the attention of politicians and diplomats.

Still gripped by hateful memories of the old country, Jews rejoiced at every Russian setback and prayed for the overthrow of the tsar. An Allied victory, they felt, would plunge Europe into medieval barbarism and utterly destroy Jewish life. As to Russia's allies, France and England, there was sympathy for them as individual nations, but outrage over the alliance—they were "doing the bloody work for the tsar." The American

Yiddish press at the time, consisting of eight dailies with a combined circulation of 634,042, had an immense influence on Jews and took a strong anti-Russian line.[45] This was interpreted by pro-Allied interests as a pro-German position. Cahan and several other Jewish labor leaders believed a revolution in Russia would be possible as a result of a German victory.

Leaders of Jewish organizations had to weave a strained line, striving to contain contradictory elements: official American neutrality, anxiety over massacres of Jews in Poland, Russian refusal to publicly reverse its anti-Jewish policies. After the United States entered the war in April 1917, there were fears of disloyalty charges as the militancy of antiwar Jews filtered into American newspapers. Most American Jews supported U.S. involvement, but those who did not were vulnerable. The government, for example, threatened to withdraw mailing privileges from the *Forward*, which continued to oppose the war even after America's entry.

The New York mayoralty election in November 1917 [46] also revealed Jewish vulnerability on the war issue and growing political complications. Hillquit ran as the pacifist Socialist candidate with the support of the *Forward*. However, most Jews, both American-born and immigrant, opposed him. They supported the government's policy and also feared raising the issue of Jewish loyalty. The AFL and pro-war socialists tried to discredit Hillquit. Anti-Semitic articles and cartoons began to appear, a disquieting portent for all Jews. It became impossible to avoid turning the Hillquit campaign into a Jewish issue.[47]

The emerging Zionist movement in America also went through a difficult political education. Prior to the war, the American Zionist movement had had little experience with American politics and no impact at all on foreign or domestic policy. However, the war, with its threat to European Jews and the Jewish settlements in Palestine, increased the numerical strength of the Zionist movement, its political awareness and, eventually, its influence. Initially, like other American Jews, Zionists were anti-Russian and fearful of the Anglo-Russian alliance. Allied—particularly British—propaganda began to cultivate Jewish opinion after 1916, using Zionism to shake pro-German feeling among Jews and rally support for the Allied cause.

When the war broke out, the Jewish population in Palestine was in a precarious—even desperate—situation, blockaded by the Allied fleet, cut off from funds, and exposed to Turkish military requisitions and arrests. By halting the expulsions of Jews in 1914–15, the Germans demonstrated their "benevolent guardianship" of Jewish interests and tried to convince Jews that *they* were restraining the Turks and would serve as a bulwark against Russian designs in the Near East. Meanwhile, toward the end of 1916, the British were expressing sympathetic attitudes toward the idea of a Jewish national home in Palestine.[48] The war was going badly for them and they hoped to tilt American Jewish opinion toward the Allied cause. A

British rejection of a German peace proposal in December 1916 had, in fact, aroused the fury of the Yiddish press in America. British benevolence was given scant credence. Until the March revolution in Russia, the Yiddish press greeted rumors of the imminent British invasion of Palestine with foreboding. Would not the Russian Cossacks follow on the heels of British soldiers? [49]

The revolution in Russia ended these fears in March, and with America's entry into the war, American Jewish pro-Allied opinion began to solidify. Middle-of-the-road and right-wing Zionists supported the war effort wholeheartedly. Socialists and socialist Zionists were split. Poale Zion officially backed the antiwar St. Louis platform of the Socialist party. "Not even Palestine is worth millions upon millions of dead and wounded," the *Yiddisher Kemfer* declared.[50] Poale Zion also supported Hillquit's candidacy despite his vehement anti-Zionist stand. The possibility that Russia might sign a separate peace treaty with Germany further strengthened the antiwar position. The peace platform of the Petrograd Soviet dangled this hope and thrilled all radicals. However, a minority in Poale Zion, led by Dov Ber Borochov, its chief theoretician, who was then in the United States, and Baruch Zuckerman, urged a prowar stand. At a Cooper Union meeting in April 1917, they hailed America's entry into the struggle in defense of "the principles of democracy and nationality." A resolution expressed the hope that these principles would be applied to the historical claims of the Jewish nation in Palestine.

The American government soon began to use the prospects for a Jewish homeland in Palestine as a way of wearing down radical Jewish antiwar attitudes. A Jewish press section was set up in the New York office of the Committee on Public Information and, among other activities, distributed sixty-five thousand copies of two Yiddish pamphlets which appealed for support of the war.[51] The anti-radical, prowar crusade was joined by Gompers' American Alliance for Labor and Democracy and a Labor Zionist affiliate, the Jewish Socialist League.

On October 6, 1917, just one week before President Woodrow Wilson approved a draft of the Balfour Declaration, in which the British viewed "with favor the establishment in Palestine of a national home for the Jewish people," the American embassy in London warned of the "great efforts" of the German government "to capture the Zionist Movement." [52] While the British were flooding Poland (under German occupation) with copies of the Balfour Declaration, trying to woo Jews away from acquiescence in the German occupation, the Germans and Turks were working out a rival proposition aimed at Jewish support.

Following American endorsement, Britain announced its position on November 2, 1917, in the form of a letter from Foreign Secretary Arthur James Balfour to Lionel Walter Rothschild, president of the British Zionist Federation. Although the Balfour Declaration was ambiguous about the meaning of the phrase "a national home" and the political character of its subsequent development, as well as question of immigration and self-government, at the time it seemed full of unmarred promise. Jewish communities from Odessa to Shanghai went wild with joy. The antiwar position of Jewish unions and radical organizations, including Poale Zion, was reversed, partly as a result of the declaration, but mainly because of the Treaty of Brest-Litovsk (March 1918), which took Russia out of the war.

An interesting change in the Jewish socialists' attitude toward Palestine now began to unfold. In May 1918, the conventions of the International Ladies' Garment Workers and Amalgamated Clothing Workers issued sympathetic statements regarding a Jewish homeland in Palestine.[53] The Jewish Labor Congress for Palestine, with delegates from over two hundred unions and labor organizations, convened in New York on June 6, 1918, thus placing support for Jewish Palestine on the agenda of the Jewish and non-Jewish unions in the United States. After Brest-Litovsk, American Jewish labor gave its wholehearted support to the platform of the Third Inter-Allied Labor and Socialist Conference held in London in February 1918.[54] One of its planks affirmed the desire to create a free and independent state in Palestine, under international guarantee, to which Jews "may return and . . . work out their own salvation free from interference."

The institutions and resources of the Jewish labor movement were not intended to serve the cause of Jewish survival but, rather, of socialist goals, meaning political activity and greater class consciousness. However, the *landsmanshaften,* the Yiddish press and theatre, East Side socialist cafés, literary societies and *fereyns,* which were so much a part of Jewish socialist culture, created an unmistakable Jewish milieu, which the shop, union, or Socialist party could not possibly duplicate. Even the class enemy—the Jewish employer—spoke Yiddish.

This compact world was far removed from the larger emerging organized Jewish community, which was already beginning to shape the main areas of its future work: synagogue, philanthropy, defense against anti-Semitism, and Zionism. To the Jewish socialists, these were typically bourgeois interests—a function of middle-class life, to which they were hostile. Yet, after World War I, there was a fast de-proletarianization of Jewish workers and movement into the middle class. The earlier style of life declined, even though certain unions still contained many Jewish workers and Jewish leaders.

In the once all-Jewish unions, the number of Jewish workers has declined sharply, and in organizations such as the Workmen's Circle, the proportion of workers has similarly declined. As these trends became discernible, the Jewish labor movement ceased to exist as an entity. Within one generation, many immigrant workers—and certainly their children—had climbed into the middle class, depleting the ranks of Jewish socialists and dissolving the once homogeneous, identifiable Jewish socialist society. Jewish workers and intellectuals either left their familiar roles and faded from public view or struggled with American realities without giving up the old rhetoric. No doubt the union experience "burned out the many isms" and helped most Jewish workers adjust to America.[55]

After World War I, they began to think more about *Jewish* issues and problems. Scope for cherished revolutionary beliefs was limited in America where most workers thought of themselves as part of the middle class. But if some Jewish socialists began to be more conscious of the need to battle anti-Semitism and support Jewish settlement in Palestine, they lacked the theoretical base needed for a new path. They had no clear conception of a secular Jewish culture for America, or for Jewish workers, nor did they have a larger philosophical frame that embraced a Jewish future based on specific values or principles. Indecisively, they moved back and forth between their familiar working-class position and middle-class American aspirations and compromises. Once the "Marxist corset" was removed, it was not replaced by any other. Interestingly, the constitutions of the great Jewish unions of the 1910-20 period—the International Ladies' Garment Workers, United Hatters, Cap and Millinery Workers, and Amalgamated Clothing Workers of America—all contained clauses pledging themselves to the abolition of capitalism. The tension between utopian vision and adaptation to American society was never fully resolved.

In sharp contrast with the veteran American Jewish labor leaders, the Bundists and Labor Zionists in America—though they differed greatly among themselves—believed that Jewish socialists had responsibilities for the Jewish future and argued for a secular Jewish culture. Their ideas certainly had some influence on the old-guard leaders, but they were not pervasive or strong enough to cause a fundamental re-orientation.

The changing attitude of the Workmen's Circle toward Jewish education during the World War I period was indicative of important changes in Jewish radical circles. Bundists and non-Zionist nationalists who joined the Workmen's Circle pressed for a more positive attitude toward Jewish culture. Chaim Zhitlovsky, who also joined, demanded that the organization set up its own schools. Labor Zionists attacked from the outside. But the old guard resisted, claiming that officially the Workmen's Circle was not Jewish, and that it could not engage in anything of a "nationalist" character. The arguments were slowly worn away, but even as late as 1920, when a school system was finally accepted, a philosophy for strengthening Jewish group life or creating conditions for meaningful Jewish survival had not yet been developed.[56]

Cahan exemplifies the paradox of a vibrant Jewish socialist culture that had no heirs. A dominant and dominating figure, living in a saturated Yiddish world, among the most receptive of the radicals to the charms and depths of Jewish religious traditions, Cahan had no faith in the future of American Jewry. Never, in the multitude of questions he tackled, did he deal theoretically or programmatically with the Jewish future in America. He was bleak about the future of Yiddish—even as he published the best Yiddish work then being written—which he felt should be used only until Jews were assimilated and understood English. Yet he was deeply stirred by Jewish suffering and committed most of his life to the struggle of Jewish workers for a better life. He reacted instantly to any threat to Jews and wrote both in Yiddish and English on pogroms and anti-Semitism. Virtually one whole volume [57] of his memoirs is given over to the tragic trial of Leo M. Frank in 1913 in Atlanta, Georgia, on a trumped-up charge of rape and murder. This case, which lasted many months and bristled with anti-Semitism, greatly agitated Cahan. Less doctrinaire than other socialists, he deplored the fanaticism of anti-religious radicals and treated subjects such as Kaddish tenderly. In the 1920s, he went to Palestine and broke the *Forward's* taboo on Zionism by opening its pages to the campaign for Jewish labor in Palestine. Yet he did not believe in an enduring Jewish life in America. He died childless and out of his then very large estate of $89,000, left no money for any social or cultural institution within the labor movement or the Jewish community.[58] Did he feel that he had left no legacy? A spiritual emptiness hangs over the echoes of the clangor, perhaps expressing the cold realism of hard-core Cahan, the inner despair of David Levinsky, the inner bleakness of American life, and the incompleteness of Jewish socialist triumphs.

After the war, Cahan and many other Jewish socialists were caught up in the Bolshevik struggle, first trying to understand it, then defending and, at last, denouncing it in bitter disillusionment. Soon their struggle moved closer to home—to Communist-dominated unions and Communist infiltration of Jewish labor and cultural institutions. These were exhausting struggles. But none of this immense effort affected the basic question of the future of Jewish existence.

There was—and is—perhaps something intrinsic in American society—in the political freedom and economic opportunity and the separation of church and state—that makes any Jewish communal life thin or problematical. In a land so young, first and second generation immigrants have had much more cultural space than elsewhere, in which to roam and slough off their old-country traditions. Jews kept theirs longer than most, but the American landscape has been seductive. The American success ethic and materialistic drive overtook Russian Jews within one or two generations, leaving the Jewish labor movement, in a large sense, without a cause and without an alternative theoretical framework. It lost its mass base and became fragmented. Socialism lost its relevance in a country where opportunity for upward social mobility was heady.

After World War I, the Jewish socialist movement, at first overjoyed by the promise of the Bolshevik Revolution, was soon convulsed by bitter debates and splits over the course it was taking. In the twenties, the struggle against the relentless Communist drive to capture the Jewish unions in the garment industry destroyed the idealism of the early movement; and in the thirties after a gradual recovery, the Jewish unions were swept into the exciting reforms and experiments of the New Deal, which stimulated their growth but also robbed them of their old ideological fire. The movement had made its way to the very center of American life.

The early Jewish socialists could not, of course, have known that their ideology could not be sustained until capitalism was destroyed, or that it would become perversely self-enclosing. Their early separateness arose from the paradox of using a Jewish language to spread the social ideal of human brotherhood, creating a distinctive culture they had never intended. Their socialist ideas also created a gulf between themselves and other American workers who were not interested in radical changes in the social order. Although Jewish trade unions joined the AFL, they never felt ideologically at home there, for the AFL did not seek a radical transformation of society, nor was it internationalist in outlook. Affiliation with the Socialist party later still left cultural and social needs unfilled; these dissatisfactions drove them further into their own milieu. Visibly separated from the larger proletariat, their sense of being *Jewish* workers deepened instead of diminished, all the while they were agitating for brotherhood. This sense of apartness was further sharpened by their rejection of general American society and non-socialist American Jewry, which included most Jews. Thus, by a strange irony, as the Jewish labor movement battled to break down barriers and create a more universalist society, it was itself becoming quite isolated or, at the very least, culturally differentiated in ways that were unintended and unanticipated. No wonder the Jewish socialists who reflected on these disturbing questions were baffled by the new challenges; indeed, most seemed to repress acknowledgment of the problem. Everything they had believed in told them there would be no distinctively Jewish future in the society they envisioned. Formally, the movement thus remained unwilling or unable to deal with the question of a future Jewish existence in America or their own role in it.

In the sense in which Ber Borochov defines a nation—that is, a group which possesses a common past and culture and a substantially segregated economy—one can speak of American Jews who had migrated from Russia before World War I as a nationality, and the Jewish labor movement as a subnation. Jewish laborers worked for Jewish employers, and the class conflicts between them were carried on in a Jewish ethnic environment in the ghettos of New York, Chicago, Philadelphia, and Baltimore. Yiddish was the language of their past life, of their *shtetl* culture, of their culture in America, and of their adjustment to a new life. The paradox of Yiddish as the lowly jargon which was the indispensable instrument of this culture and adjustment parallels the paradox of the *shtetl* dweller with no proletarian or socialist base or background in Russia, transformed into a worker who joined a trade union, which, in turn, was converted into a socialist organization. One is bound to ask how it was possible for so many Jewish workers to have made such immense emotional and cultural leaps, and whether, indeed, they had leaped too far and too fast.

Jewish workers before the migration of 1905 were catapulted into the ranks of the proletariat in America by the pressures of industrialization, with no economic or ideological preparation. Uprooted from a compact Jewish community, the immigrant worker brought with him fear of the larger state and security associated with the established Jewish community. One power was identified with government; the other, with religion. Confused and bewildered by the sudden transplanting from a ghetto in an oppressive empire to an industrialized society in a political democracy where church and state were separate, and where religion was a private matter, the Jewish worker had no time to make a gradual adjustment. The uprooting was swift. Yet, unable to forget what he had been through, many of his new experiences were filtered through the lens of bitter memories. The Jewish immigrant who became a sweat-shop worker for the first time in his life could not look to government or religion for guidance: based on his experience, one was anti-labor, the other dealt with completely different jurisdictions.[59]

Jewish socialists came on the scene to fill this vacuum and offer leadership to the floundering workers. It was they who instilled an assimilationist, internationalist philosophy into the new Jewish unions; it was they who won by default. There was no one else to guide the Jewish workers in the leap to proletarianization. Similarly, the absence of a transitional adjustment period helps to explain why "uprooted people who never saw a friendly government or a beneficial law would naturally embrace, before finding new moorings, radical programs which called for the complete revamping of the social system."[60] Thus Jewish workers without a proletarian tradition accepted militant socialism.

Jewish socialist achievements were immense, nevertheless: the transformation of degraded immigrants into dignified, socially conscious workers who became a force that altered the course of Jewish life in America and made an impact on the general labor movement and the creation of a Yiddish socialist culture that satisfied and enriched hundreds of thousands of Jewish immigrants for two generations. The Jewish labor movement also offers a model of a remarkable partnership between workers and intellectuals directed at social and political change that had no precedent in Jewish life until 1897, when the Jewish Labor Bund was founded in Russa.

The Jewish labor movement was also a pathbreaker for the general American labor movement. It introduced the principle of arbitration, which saw its greatest development in the men's clothing industry, and broke the taboo against scientific management concepts, which the general movement feared and opposed. Jewish unions believed that workers were equal to employers in managing the productive forces of society and showed this share in advancing the prosperity and efficiency of industry.[61] Ironically, advocates of class struggle became great champions of union-management cooperation. Jewish unions also pioneered the field of worker education; political action; housing, insurance, and medical benefits to union members; and protective labor legislation. Moreover, the Jewish unions led the way in their generous outreach to all liberation causes.

The Bund also had to deal with economic misery and the degradation of Jewish workers. It also had to struggle against government-sanctioned anti-Semitism and political tyranny, which the American Jewish labor movement was spared. The question of Jewish group identity confronted it as well, but the Bund faced it and groped its way toward an interesting formation that might have worked in Russia, had it been given a chance. It would not do for America, however, where a synthesis still eludes Jews with a radical bent.

III

THE JEWISH LABOR
BUND IN RUSSIA

14. The Jewish Artisan in Lithuania—White Russia

Although the pogroms of 1881–82 and the subsequent persecution of Jews in Russia created a great exodus to America, most Russian Jews remained in the Pale. There, out of conditions very different from those affecting Jewish socialists in America, a second socialist movement emerged—the Jewish Workers' Bund, which organized the Jewish masses for independent political and economic action in Eastern Europe. Jewish revolutionary activity had been urged by Aaron Lieberman in the 1870's, but he remained a voice crying in the wilderness,[1] and no organized Jewish labor movement developed from his efforts. Not until the 1890's, during a period of extreme repression under Alexander III, did a Jewish proletariat arise which responded to a small group of class-conscious workers and socialist intellectuals.

This period coincided with the economic breakdown of traditional *shtetl* life. Jews had fewer opportunities in the Pale, to which they were restricted, and fewer opportunities for a livelihood in the overcrowded towns and cities into which they were pressed. Moreover, even though there were waves of emigration in the years 1881–97, there was a net Jewish population increase of 22 percent—about 100,000 per year[2]—which meant that emigration did not solve the overcrowding. Furthermore, Jews were becoming forcibly urbanized. The so-called May Laws, promulgated in the spring of 1882 to further restrict Jewish residence within the Pale and Jewish economic activity, stopped all Jewish movement into rural areas within the Pale, while the expulsion of Jews from Moscow in 1891 further congested the permitted cities. According to the survey of the St. Petersburg committee of the Jewish Colonization Society, the urban Jewish population of the Pale in 1898 was 3,809,361, or 77.8 percent of the total Jewish population of the Pale.[3] In the northwestern provinces (Vilna, Grodno, Minsk, Vitebsk, Kovno, and Mogilev)—the area of densest Jewish population—Jews comprised almost 58 percent of the urban population. In the ten provinces of Poland, where about one-fourth of the Jews lived, almost 25 percent lived in towns of more than 10,000, and over 20 percent, in cities of 20,000 or more.[4] Thus, almost half the Jews in Poland had become urban residents before the end of the century.

Table 4. Regional Distribution of Jewish Population in Russia, 1897

Region	Jewish Population	Jewish Percentage of Total Population
Pale of settlement		
Polish provinces	1,321,100	14.1
Northwest provinces	1,422,431	28.3
Southwest provinces	1,425,618	9.7
Southern provinces	730,278	9.0
Total: 25 provinces	4,899,427	11.6
Outside the Pale	316,378	.4
Grand total	5,215,805	4.2

Source: Compiled from *Premier Rencensement Général de la Population de l'Empire de Russie, 1897.* Adapted from I. M. Rubinow, *Economic Condition of the Jews in Russia* (Washington, D. C., 1907), p. 493.

Table 5. Number of Jewish Artisans in Classified Occupations in the Pale, By Region, 1898

Occupation	Northwest Provinces	Southwest Provinces	Southern Provinces	Polish Provinces	Total
Clothing and wearing apparel	60,637	56,240	26,223	50,854	193,954
Leather goods	32,292	21,853	9,348	21,813	85,306
Food products	23,174	14,401	5,083	15,229	57,887
Wood manufactures	19,791	16,382	5,276	8,139	49,588
Metals	16,667	15,706	8,553	7,995	48,921
Chemicals	1,535	1,198	322	562	3,617
Building and ceramics	14,754	8,007	3,411	5,418	31,590
Textiles	6,993	3,422	809	7,204	18,428
Paper and stationery	3,660	3,640	2,238	2,157	11,695
Total	179,503	140,849	61,263	119,371	500,986

Source: Based on Report of Jewish Colonization Society, 1898. Adapted from I. M. Rubinow, *Economic Condition of the Jews in Russia* (Washington, D.C., 1907), p. 522.

Table 6. Russian Jews in Gainful Occupations, 1897

Type of Occupation	Jews in Pale	Jews in Russia
Agriculture	38,538	40,611
Professional service	67,238	71,950
Personal service (including hotel, restaurant and saloon keepers)	250,078	277,466
Manufacturing and mechanical trades	504,844	542,563
Transportation	44,177	45,944
Commerce	426,628	452,193
Total	1,331,503	1,430,727

Source: Adapted from I.M. Rubinow, *Economic Condition of the Jews in Russia* (Washington, D.C., 1907), pp. 500, 502.

The vast social and economic uprooting and readjustment in the urbanization process caused a fiercely competitive struggle for survival. Jewish artisans and middlemen of all kinds suffered especially and joined the already starving *luftmenshen*. Some of this misery was relieved by emigration: during 1897–1914, about 1.5 million Jews emigrated from Russia, more than half of whom were artisans. Many who remained sought work in the rapidly developing industries of Russia and by 1900, there were about 50,000 Jewish workers in medium and large-scale factories.[5] The remainder were forced to work in small factories or workshops in the traditionally Jewish occupations of tailoring, shoemaking, baking, and newer fields, such as tobacco, tanning, brushmaking, and painting.

Christians also fled to the cities for work in the new factories and workshops. At first the two labor forces remained largely isolated from each other, but in time they confronted each other as competitors for jobs and, much less frequently, as coworkers.

Other changes were also unsettling. In the past, the inner cohesion of the *shtetl* had drawn Jewish workers and employers together. Workers worked in Jewish shops; there was little social or economic distance between them and their employers. Typically, the worker was an artisan—a cabinet maker, tailor, shoemaker, or glazier—who hoped to own his own shop and become independent. Typically, the shop was small, consisting of two or three people, with the relationship between masters, journeymen, and apprentices scarcely unchanged since medieval times.[6] Jewish socialists were later to complain that the master-journeyman relationship was "paternalistic"—the object of both affection and wrath—but both maintained their solidarity through membership in craft guilds or societies called *hevrot*, which tried to ensure a decent livelihood for each master and satisfy the social and religious needs of the artisans.[7] Moreover, if there was friction, the artisan simply set up shop for himself. He might be a worker one summer and an employer the next;[8] there was no clear-cut distinction. This interchangeableness of roles—downward as well as upward—dismayed the socialists, for it obscured the class struggle.

Yet, under the battering of new economic forces, changes were taking place in these traditional patterns. The tiny shops and guilds were anachronisms in an industrializing age. Some journeymen began breaking away from the guilds and formed their own associations. As early as 1864, in Mogilev, women tailors in small shops organized an association that offered financial aid and sick and death benefits to its members and led the struggle of workers against their employers.[9] In the ensuing strikes, employers and police dealt harshly with the women. Class consciousness and planned organization were still somewhat undeveloped, but eventually, the *hevra* put an end to irregular payment of wages and established a closed shop of a sort, in which only *hevra* members were entitled to employment. A movement for separate artisans' *hevrot* in Mogilev also developed among shoemakers, jewelers and watchmakers, and tin, roof, and lock smiths.[10] By the end of the century, particularly in the shops in Lithuania–White Russia (Belorussia), the number of workers increased to ten or more per shop.[11] As the firms grew larger, Jewish artisans found it harder to improve their status. They were becoming more and more proletarianized.

The masters, too, were losing their independence, increasingly subject to stores instead of individuals for their orders. In the northwestern provinces, many artisans, facing an extremely bleak future, began emigrating to America. Of those who remained, very few left the Pale for the interior of Russia when restrictions were liberalized, because of frustrating regulations. As early as 1865, the extreme poverty of the Jewish artisans and the overcrowding of the Pale were reported by the minister of internal affairs, who charged these conditions to the legal limitations on Jewish movement. The new law accompanying this report gave Jewish master artisans and certain merchants the right to leave the Pale, but the complexity of the law and subsequent amendments made the legal position of the artisan in the interior of Russia very insecure.

A well-known textbook of special legislation relating to Jews devoted forty pages to commentaries and decisions dealing with the right of the Jewish artisan to live beyond the limits of the Pale.[12] He was obliged to have a certificate of proficiency from an artisan's guild after an examination, as well as a certificate from the local authorities; he was also prohibited from working at anything but his trade, which was strictly defined. A watchmaker, for example, could not sell any watches unless he assembled them; nor could he sell a watch fob. The police supervised these requirements closely and often forced artisans back to the Pale for infringements or demanded extortions. According to an official investigation in 1893, the number of Jewish artisans outside the Pale was estimated at considerably less than 10,000 out of a total of 500,000.[13]

As factories arose in Lithuania–White Russia, owners were extremely reluctant to hire Jews, because Jews refused to work on Saturdays and lacked technical skills. They were hired in the smaller shops or, as in the case of the Jewish weavers in Bialystok, they worked at home or for middlemen. In general, only Christians worked in the mechanized factories, even those owned by Jews. The Jewish owners wanted a homogeneous work force and wanted also to divest themselves of the entangling personal relationships with workers that had been customary in the small shops. Besides, the Christian workers were more highly skilled and less prone to strike.[14] Even in southern Russia, which was more industrialized than the northwest, Jews failed to gain a foothold in the large factories, and remained a proletariat of small shops and unmechanized plants.[15] However, Jews were employed in hosiery manufacture, tanneries, bristle-making, and tobacco—all new industries—and these workers were to play an important role in the Jewish labor movement.

Organizationally and ideologically, the northwest provinces of the Pale—Lithuania and White Russia—figure most prominently in the beginnings and development of the Jewish labor movement. Lithuania included three provinces—Kaunas, Vilna, and Grodno—and White Russia, likewise three—Minsk, Vitebsk, and Mogilev. In earlier years, Jews differentiated between Lithuania and White Russia, but in the course of the nineteenth century, the terms tended to be interchanged and "Lithuania" came to be used for the entire northwest region of the Pale.[16] During this period, Vilna was central. Geographically, Vilna was important because it was situated on rail lines to St. Petersburg and the West and was a stopping-off place for radicals enroute to and from Russia. Known as the "Jerusalem of Lithuania," Vilna was also an important cultural center for Jews. Interestingly, Polish revolutionaries also considered Vilna an important center. With its large factory and artisan population, the city became the fountainhead of Marxism and mass agitation among Jewish workers. Even when the socialist movement began to spread to Poland and the Ukraine, it remained numerically strongest in Lithuania, striking roots in the smaller towns and even penetrating the villages. Lithuania remained the organizational and ideological base of the Bund and provided its leadership up to 1919, when the movement was reconstituted in Poland.

Of all the regions in the Pale, the northwest provinces were the poorest in natural resources and the least developed industrially. Farming methods were primitive and thus limited the possibilities for trade. The Jewish *miestechkos* (the little settlements) [17] in this area, with their economic stagnation and congestion,[18] drove large numbers of Jewish emigrants to America after 1881.

Of the estimated 500,986 Jewish artisans registered in Russia, in 1898, almost two-fifths lived in the northwestern provinces, where the tempo of their proletarianization was rapid. The letters of Aaron Lieberman in Lavrov's *V'period* in the middle 1870's dealing with the workers' struggle in Vilna and Bialystok, and Pavel Akselrod's report on the large number of Jewish wage earners in the northwestern region,[19] document in great detail the economic struggle of the Jewish worker in the region in the 1870's and 1880's.[20] In this area, there was a high percentage of economically active women, and many domestic workers and unskilled workers, such as longshoremen, ragpickers, water carriers, draymen, and teamsters.[21]

Of the approximately 200,000 Jewish workers in the region, possibly as many as 90 percent were artisans,[22] laboring in small tailor, shoemaking, and carpentry shops, mainly for local markets. Only Bialystok, a major textile center in Grodno Province, stood out as an exception, but the larger factories there preferred Christian to Jewish workers.

Their large numbers also hastened the decline of Jewish craftsmen. In every city of Lithuania–White Russia, the number of Jewish artisans was disproportionately high compared with the total population.[23] Many had been forced into crafts because they could not earn a living in other fields. Jewish artisans in this area far exceeded the number of non-Jewish craftsmen outside the Pale. Mogilev had over seven times as many tailors as neighboring Smolensk; Vitebsk, over four times as many as nearby Pskov. One Russian economist pointed out that there were enough Jewish tailors to supply clothing for half the urban population of Russia!

Generally, because Jewish artisans were deprived of capital, equipment, stocks of raw materials, and cheap credit facilities, they worked for middlemen who supplied materials or acted as commission agents for manufacturers and wholesalers, or they worked at home or for sweatshop subcontractors for bigger jobbers.[24] This was especially true of *tallit* (prayer shawl) weavers in Dubrovna, tailors in Vitebsk, and knit-goods makers in Vilna.[25] In this process, the would-be independent artisan became a petty manufacturer and was completely dependent on a middleman, who bought the entire product. The ban on living in the rural villages following the May Laws forced Jewish tailors and shoemakers to seek their natural and most important customer, the peasant, in a more indirect way, at fairs. Jewish artisans frequented the many fairs visited by the peasants, but lost valuable time in the process, thus giving rise to a class of middlemen for whom artisans worked exclusively.

Members of the same family usually worked at the same trade, combining all of the objectionable features of the sweatshop and the domestic factory system, and caused by the same factors: the lack of capital, the need to borrow at usurious rates of interest, and strong competition from factory-made goods. The poor, "independent" artisan often did not have enough money to buy the material for a small private order, to say nothing of the necessary machinery that gradually forced its way into the hand trades.[26] Almost all of the work in the Jewish shops was done by hand, and although some workers were genuinely skilled, most Jewish artisans used primitive tools and turned out inferior work, making it difficult for them to compete with emerging factories or even the peasant handcraft industries.

Journeymen were expected to work "without limit," which usually meant from sunrise to sunset, but often later. On Saturdays after sunset, their work extended into the early morning. A sixteen-hour to eighteen-hour workday was common in all cities of the northwest region—a far harsher situation than the one facing the Russian factory worker, who benefited somewhat from state factory inspections and, after 1897, from the eleven-and-one-half-hour workday limit, which did not apply to the Jewish artisan-worker.[27]

Whether petty manufacturer or wage earner, master or journeyman, the Jewish artisan could not escape a proletarian fate, as the Russian government itself admitted. In 1888, when the Pahlen Commission was set up to examine legislation regulating Jewish life, it reported that "about 90 percent of the whole Jewish population ... come near being a proletariat." [28]

The situation in the northwest provinces was especially desperate. As described by Aaron Lieberman and others, the majority of Jewish workers in the cities of Lithuania–White Russia lived "in the semi-darkness of cellars or similar hovels that had wet walls and floors, and were crammed together in an oppressive, stupefying atmosphere." [29] Like their counterparts in America, they often worked and slept in a single room with hardly any ventilation. An observer in Lodz described how he found ten people living and sleeping in a single room: "There is no bed, one sleeps on the floor, winter and summer; the wretched creatures are dressed shabbily and their poverty is indescribable." [30] The Jewish press recounted the appalling situation of the artisans in Vilna and Vitebsk where people were "simply dying of hunger."

A somewhat less oppressive impression has been conveyed by a Russian writer who visited Mogilev, a town of about fifty thousand, but the overcrowding is extreme:

> The homes of the artisans are small and crowded. But no matter how small and crowded, tenants are often admitted, and there is seldom more than one room for a family. The room serves as kitchen, living and sleeping room, and workshop. And it is not unusual for a tailor to rent the same room for school purposes, so that instruction is served to a small class of private pupils in the same room where the tailor works with his apprentice; the tailor's wife cooks the food and washes the clothes, and the tailor's prolific family mingles its joyful noise with the monotonous chanting of the Hebrew teacher and the scholars.[31]

In the absence of systematic wage statistics, it is impossible to determine the average wage of the artisan-workers or the average earnings of independent artisans, but all available reports show that wages were pitifully low, often not more than a few rubles a week. Moreover, almost all Jewish artisans had seasonal work only. On ten or twelve weeks' work, they had to live for fifty-two. Estimates of earnings of male knit-goods workers in Vilna ranged from the equivalent of $38.63 to $154.50 per year; shoemakers in Grodno ranged from $77.25 to $206.00; tailors in Grodno from $77.50 to $257.50. In view of the needs of the "normal Jewish family budget in a small town"—about 300 rubles or $154.50—a vast number of artisans had great difficulty in making the minimum.[32]

John Mill, one of the early Jewish social democrats in Vilna who met workers in study groups, recalled that such Jews "didn't dream of struggling against exploitation." [33] Yet it was in the undeveloped northwest provinces, amid the impoverished artisans, that the Jewish labor movement was born and later spread to Poland and the Ukraine. So impressive was its strength, in fact, that in the 1896 Congress of the Second Socialist International in London, Plekhanov remarked that "the Jewish workers may be considered the vanguard of the labor army in Russia." [34] It was this Jewish artisan-proletariat that pioneered in the organization of embryonic trade unions that arose from the *kassy* (self-help funds), whereas Russian factory workers as late as the early 1900's had not yet been organized or even much influenced by the idea of unions. Moreover, this higher level of class consciousness among Jewish workers was well marked by employers and the Russian police. Within the Jewish labor movement itself, it was the craftsman who pioneered, and the cigarette and match factory workers who lagged behind.

This singular development of the *kassy* and their connection with labor consciousness among Jewish artisans have been the subject of considerable discussion—and even controversy—but the old tradition of self-help among Jews was clearly a factor in their separate and joint development. In the evolution of the *hevrot* (religious societies), charitable and social functions were added to the religious. Sick benefits and other forms of mutual aid were gradually added to the experience of praying together, burial rites, and ownership of a Torah.[35] The advantages of cooperative activity led to the creation of *kassy*, which, in turn, heightened class consciousness among Jewish workers. The guilds and *hevrot* gave the Jewish workers organizational discipline, a discipline which helps to explain the later remarkable organizational achievements of the Bund,[36] but which was lacking among non-Jewish workers.

Some artisans who joined the *kassy* had already broken with the old master-journeyman guilds, while others did not join a *kassa* but, rather, one of the artisan associations. A worker might belong to both the *kassa* and the *hevra*, but the *kassa* aimed to improve the economic and social lot of the member, whereas the artisan guild or *hevra* largely met religious and social needs. The *kassa* came to represent a radical departure from the past, based on class feelings. During 1888–89, *kassy* were formed by printers, tailors, carpenters, shoemakers, and jewelry workers in Vilna and Minsk.[37] The Vilna women tailors' *kassa*, which had the longest continuous existence, held its tenth anniversary celebration in 1899.

Although the earliest *kassy* were not specifically designed to aid members during strikes, with the wave of strikes by Jewish workers in the northwest provinces in the 1880's—stocking makers in Vilna and locksmiths in Minsk—the *kassy* not only aided members during the strikes but also helped to prepare for them. *Kassy* members were expected to pay weekly or monthly dues and, in return, were supported during strikes. Only workers were admitted to the *kassy*; in no case could an employer be a member. *Kassa* leaders met secretly with members, usually once a week, discussed all matters concerning their craft, and decided if and when to strike.[38] Occasionally *kassa* celebrations were held commemorating the founding of a *kassa*. After coming under the influence of the socialists, delegates from other *kassy* would bring fraternal greetings and proclaim the themes of unity, struggle, and re-dedication to the movement. Revolutionary songs were sung and funds were collected for imprisoned comrades and for continued political agitation. As with similar celebrations in the radical circles in America, a strong didactic purpose underlay these meetings and helped strengthen members in their perilous commitment.

In 1889 and 1890, these *kassy* expanded rapidly and their meetings became more militant. They were, in fact, underground trade unions [39] and the most effective of them—for example, *kassy* of the jewelry and shoemakers in Vilna—succeeded in enrolling almost all of the workers in their respective trades.[40] In Vilna in 1895, there were twenty-seven craft organizations with a total of 962 members, about 30 percent of all of the workers in these crafts; by 1899, dues-paying members increased to 1,304.[41] In Bialystok and Minsk at the turn of the century, there were about 1,000 organized workers in each city. Besides supporting comrades who had suffered, the *kassy* threatened employers with strikes and compelled them to make concessions. Even when the decline of the strike movement caused a decline in *kassy* membership, possibly as many as 30,000 Jewish workers remained under their influence.[42]

The role of the intellectuals and radical circle leaders in forming the *kassy* is not entirely clear. Some *kassy* were undoubtedly organized by the workers themselves and some strikes occurred spontaneously, but during the 1880's, some of the circle leaders also actively organized strikes. Moreover, some of the workers were also involved in circles. The stocking makers' movement of the period in Vilna is especially interesting, for it indicates that at least some socialist intellectuals were interested in "trade-union" activities at the time.[43] The young girl workers who were fairly well-educated and knew some Russian were especially susceptible. Early socialist leaders such as Lev Jogiches and Arkady Kremer made attempts to organize them, and it is possible that their leadership inspired the stocking-makers' *kassa* in Vilna. An "idealistic revolutionary autodidact" named Navaplianski is also credited with "initiating strikes of the hosiery workers" and creating an underground *kassa*.[44] (An artel of the hosiery workers was created after the strike in the winter of 1884–85, which lasted four to five months.) These early *kassy* ultimately developed into full-fledged underground trade unions that flung themselves into the economic struggle against their bosses and became workers' assemblies and councils out of which the Bund was created in 1897.

In the 1890's, Vilna became the most important center of Jewish worker concentration and radical political activity by pre-Bundist groups. These, in turn, grew out of a revolutionary circle that formed in 1885, and had adopted the program of the Narodnaya Volya: socialist propaganda among the masses; worker-artels, or cooperatives; and terrorism against the regime.[45] Charles (Khonen) Rappaport, a young Jewish revolutionary who was to play an important role in the beginnings of the Socialist Revolutionary party of Russia, and who was drawn to the revolutionary circle while a student in the Vilna *gymnasium*, has described its early meetings:

> This was the circle of Dembo and Gnatovski and in 1885–87 it was in touch with the People's Will Party in St. Petersburg. It was made up of intellectuals, particularly from the Jewish youth. They would come together, talk, discuss, drink tea, and act in a manner quite non-conspiratorial, which was not fitting for serious revolutionists. The leaders, Isak Dembo and Anton Gnatovski, however, were devoted and earnest revolutionists. The soul of the circle was Anyuta [Leybovich], a beautiful and vivacious girl around whom the youth gathered. My lodgings at that time were with the Puziranski family and their daughters also belonged to this circle. In time I became active in the group and my room became a sort of headquarters for it. Here the meetings were held and here, too, was kept the illegal literature. My room was held to be "conspiratorial." I lived in the synagogue court where there were crowds of people all day. Moreover, I was above suspicion in the *gymnasium*. The officials honestly believed that I was always studying and looked upon me as a sort of absentminded intellectual. The inspector never dreamed of checking upon my living quarters as he did with the other students.[46]

Some of the early members of the 1885–87 circle left the sphere of the Jewish labor movement for other activities; others were caught in the March 1887 political crackdowns of Alexander III and the subsequent wave of arrests. But the movement started up again later in the year with a whole new group who were to put their unique stamp on the Bund during its important formative period from 1887 to 1897.[47]

The circle—a small clandestine reading and discussion group—was still the primary radical form of expression in Russia in the 1880's where intellectuals and students of a radical bent would discuss revolutionary ideas and prospects for Russia. Several future Bundist leaders had early exposure to circles and came to Vilna with considerable experience. Tsemakh (Timofei) Kopelson had organized his own circle in Ponevezh; Arkady Kremer had been active in Riga; and his wife, Matle Srendnitsky, in St. Petersburg. Some had been arrested while still students; others had been expelled from their home towns.

In a rambling reminiscence,[48] Kopelson recalled his arrival in Vilna in 1886 and his entrance into the "Vilna organization" in 1887. At that time he met Lev Jogiches, who became a locksmith apprentice and organized a Jewish circle of locksmiths, which included Rappaport, Isaiah Izenshtat, and "revolutionaries" from Minsk. Kopelson's fondest memories were reserved for the salon of Liuba Akselrod,[49] where young intellectuals gathered, drank tea, and talked "day and night" about reaching workers and other intellectuals with propaganda, about Marxism, capitalism, terror, and the substance of the illegal literature they were reading. The group also had heated discussions in a member's country home, and in the woods as well as Liuba's salon and formed the nucleus of the subsequent Vilna social-democratic organization.

The Jewish Social-Democratic Group, commonly known as the Vilna Group, was organized in 1889 or 1890 (probably the latter) [50] and was the immediate forerunner of the Bund. According to Kopelson, one of the founders of the Vilna Group:

> In the fall of 1887 we organized a central group of three, which directed practically all revolutionary activity in Vilna. The work was divided as follows: Jogiches conducted the agitation among the non-Jewish workers, established contacts between officers and soldiers and was in charge of all other conspiratorial matters, as well as the clandestine library. I conducted the propaganda among the Jewish workers and intellectuals.[51]

This group lasted until the middle of 1888.

Other circles were formed in Minsk, St. Petersburg, and Ponevezh. Each considered itself a follower of Narodnaya Volya and stressed the importance of education, but differed in the degree of activism and nuances of ideology. Some members of the Vilna circle had gone so far as to become involved in the plot to kill Alexander III in March 1887. The effort failed, and Dembo and Gnatovski were arrested but succeeded in fleeing Russia;[52] others in St. Petersburg, including Lenin's brother, were executed. Meanwhile, a number of circle members were being influenced away from *narodovoltsy* to Marxism. Kopelson's new group called themselves "radical Marxists." No longer *narodniki*, they opposed terrorism and "subjective methods in history." [53]

In 1888, after being conscripted into the army, Kopelson was arrested for disseminating radical propaganda; his comrade Jogiches was arrested, too, and the group collapsed. But Kopelson was not easily discouraged, and after a mild punishment—he was confined to his barracks for a month—he began to form another group. One new member was Joseph (John) Mill, whom Kopelson had met while living with Mill's grandparents in Ponevezh, and whom he had urged to enroll in the Realschule (polytechnical school) in Vilna. Already somewhat familiar with the socialist struggle through radical students in Ponevezh, Mill was put in charge of the library. Under Kopelson's direction, the new group steeped itself in knowledge of the Russian revolutionaries and their struggle.[54] Kopelson commanded authority as well as influence, and the brochures and journals he shared created intense interest. "We almost swallowed them," Mill recalled. The group met with Kopelson in his room, reading and discussing Lassalle and Robert Owen, Plekhanov and Marx. Literature in Russian came from Minsk, Warsaw, and St. Petersburg; a little in Yiddish came from London.

This group—particularly Kopelson himself—was already moving away from the populist acceptance of terror toward social democracy.[55] This change began quite soon after Plekhanov, the "father of Russian Marxism," reinterpreted Marxism to explain Russian conditions in the early 1880's. Emil Abramovich, possibly the first herald of Plekhanov's ideas in Russian Jewish circles, came to Minsk from Paris in 1884 [56] and organized circles to propound the new doctrine. It was he who introduced Plekhanov's *Our Disagreements*, with its sharp criticism of *narodnik* theory, into Minsk and later, in 1886–87, into Vilna. In heated debates with the Vilna circle, he won over some of the newer members who had broken with the terrorists and founded the first Jewish social-democratic organization in Vilna.[57] Self-improvement through study and the obligation to teach others remained powerful forces in these new circles, and although the Marxism of many of the radicals still had strong tinges of populism, the young intellectuals who were to become Bundist leaders were mainly attracted by the new Marxist ideas.

Plekhanov opposed an immediate revolutionary seizure of power, convinced that there would have to be a two-stage revolution: first a bourgeois-liberal revolution, hastened by capitalism, with which socialists should cooperate; and second, a socialist revolution after Russia had become a Western-style democracy, and after the proletariat had become a fully conscious and well-organized class.[58] An immediate seizure of power as well as a rapid transition to socialism were regarded as utopian. Moreover, Plekhanov steadily abandoned the populist notion that the peasant commune could form the springboard of the revolution and placed the future of Russia in the hands of the workers. Not the peasantry, as the populists had assumed, but the urban factory proletariat, developing out of capitalism, would bring about the revolution.

The spell of the martyred *narodniki* still affected the young Jewish intellectuals, but they were skeptical of, and even disillusioned by the response of the peasants to populist agitation. Moreover, being largely from cities, they were drawn to the idea that workers of the cities would be the prime revolutionary force. Marxism was also appealing because it was cosmopolitan and had a "scientific cast." (The radical circles of the 1880's stressed the study of natural science; no fewer than eight of the thirteen youths who formed the nucleus of the Bund leadership engaged in some form of advanced technological or scientific study.) [59] Marxism also saw terrorism as essentially futile, valuing instead the role of the revolutionary teacher who understood historical processes and would awaken class consciousness among the workers and rouse them to political battle.[60] It assigned no special virtues to Russian peasant institutions or to the Russian people as such.

Ex-students of the Vilna Rabbinical Seminary (the same school Lieberman and Zundelevich had attended) and students of the Realschule provided many menbers of the first radical circles in Vilna and the Jewish Social-Democratic Group. It was also to Vilna (where there were no universities) that many Jewish students came after they had been exiled from other parts of Russia for political activity. Kept under police surveillance and ordered to refrain from political activity, they nonetheless carried on their work. Jules Tsederbaum (Martov), an early Bundist leader and later a leading Menshevik, was one such exile. The home of the director of the Vilna Talmud Torah, Shmerl Oguz, was also a meeting place of the radical intelligentsia. Rappaport himself founded a group that was to train teachers for the many students who were abandoning the oppressive atmosphere of Talmudic study for secular learning.

In 1890–91, the Vilna Social-Democratic Group was enormously enriched by new members who were destined to take it on a long and historic journey. These were the first of the pioneering spirits who, together with Kopelson and Mill, eventually created the Bund: Arkady Kremer and Matle Srednitsky, who had come from *narodniki* circles; Isaiah Izenshtat, who had already been imprisoned for radical activity, and his future wife Liuba Levinson; and Samuel Gozhansky, a graduate of the Vilna Teachers' Institute.[61] Within a few years, the group expanded to thirteen. These included the major organizers, editors, and polemicists of the "first generation" of Bundists, of whom six served on the central committee of the Bund at one time or another before 1905. They brought new life and new propaganda techniques into the group, held regular meetings, and organized new groups. Mill describes the heightened atmosphere of their presence: "It seemed as if new forces had gathered imperceptibly, gradually, and had fallen from heaven. . . . The potential material had existed, but an organized, disciplined, centralized collective, capable of giving this material form, content, and a well-worked out direction had been lacking." [62]

The new arrivals did not come from religious institutions, in the main, but from secular schools. At most they had only a smattering of knowledge of traditional Jewish subjects. From families that had welcomed the Haskalah, they grew up in the northwestern provinces and, although they had no direct experience of the pogroms of the 1880's, they were aware of the strong anti-Semitism in Russia. Indeed, most of them had been blocked personally in their efforts to enter the professions by their Jewish origin. Nevertheless, they were mainly stirred by the vast social and economic problems of all Russia and were drawn to Russian radical circles where forbidden literature was read and discussed—in Russian.

The presence particularly of Arkady Kremer brought new life into the movement.[63] Reserved almost to timidity, but inspiring deep respect, and without any taint of personal ambition, Arkady, as he was popularly called, soon became the leading figure among the early Vilna Social Democrats. His political biography, however, provides few clues to his remarkable personality. Hardly a romantic figure or spellbinding orator, he soon became the dominant figure of the movement. All of his active contemporaries and intimates—Martov, Medem, Abramovich, Kopelson, Mill, and Kosovsky—as well as later Bundist leaders acknowledge his central role in the early movement, when there was the greatest need for directing technical underground work—organizing secret groups, smuggling literature over the border, setting up secret printing presses and hectograph machines. It was Arkady's solidity, common sense, organizing ability, sternness of character, and absolute dependability that created a strong foundation for the new movement.[64]

Arkady was born in 1865 in Svencyan, in the province of Vilna, the son of a religious Jew who was also a *maskil* and a teacher in the village school. At twelve, he moved to the poverty-stricken home of his uncle in Vilna in order to enroll in the Realschule. There he met Yaacov Notkin, a pioneering figure in the early Vilna social-democratic movement who greatly influenced him. In 1885, both young men went to St. Petersburg to take examinations for the technical institute. Arkady remained in St. Petersburg for two years, then served a year in the army in Riga and entered the Riga Polytechnic Institute in 1888. It was in Riga that his revolutionary career began. Here he came in contact with Polish socialist groups, read intensively in radical literature, was arrested, and served six months in a Warsaw jail. In 1889 he was exiled to Vilna and placed under police surveillance for two years. He soon organized a circle, to which he gave his extensive knowledge of populism and Marxism, his capacity to relate easily to workers, and practical ways of integrating Marxist formulations. Soon the strong stamp of his personality was felt by all Vilna social democrats.

Kopelson, who was already a leader in the Vilna movement, has recounted how Arkady "gradually displaced me and all other workers in the movement, and assumed first place in our organization. He was then a fairly well-educated young man, wise, witty, good-hearted but often very strict, very able, and untiring. His popularity grew rapidly and practically all without exception accepted him as the leader of the organization." [65] Arkady's interest at the time was in the general Russian revolutionary movement; Jewish cadres, he believed, could be used in the larger Russian industrial centers. Under his guidance, a core of Jewish leaders held weekly meetings, drew up propaganda, set up new groups, and secured illegal literature. He was first at places of danger and often personally carried literature from one house to another. He did not often speak at meetings and actually did not possess the talents or personal inclination of an agitator. But when he spoke, his words carried great weight. Curiously, his only important writing is his pamphlet *On Agitation*, written in 1893, but it was a seminal work in revolutionary circles.[66]

Still in their early twenties, these young Vilna social democrats were faced with the problem of what revolutionary action they could take. In the late 1880's it was still futile to think of leading the working class; contact with individual workers consisted mainly of efforts to recruit them into the study circles. In Vilna and Minsk, for example, certain workers were taught how to read and write Russian; they also studied natural science, the economic basis of capitalism, and "scientific" socialism. Immediate political and social problems were largely ignored. The young founders wanted to lead the workers to socialist consciousness and train them as leaders in the industrial centers. "Small groups of class-conscious worker-revolutionaries must be founded," Samuel Gozhansky said, "and when the revolutionary movement begins, these small groups are to become leaders."

Workers also attended lectures on a wide variety of subjects. In Vilna, Leon Bernshtein spoke on the creation of the world, the "life of peoples," beginning with a study of primitive tribes and ending with the English, their Parliament and trade unions; Arkady lectured on the cooperative movement in Belgium; the brilliant revolutionary Lev Jogiches not only lectured on anatomy, but brought a human skeleton to class to illustrate his lecture.[67] Jogiches, who would soon plunge into the conspiratorial atmosphere of the Polish socialist movement and emigré politics in Zurich and Paris, was a very influential figure—"legendary," Mill writes, and "surrounded by an aura of mystery." One of the first of the socialists in Vilna with contacts in military circles, he tried to stir the workers to fight against their employers and the government. Some of the workers themselves were active in other cities such as Bialystok, Lodz, and Warsaw.[68]

As groups formed and dissolved, only Kopelson seems to have been a link between the earlier and later groups. By 1891, according to his estimate, there were 60–70 intellectuals and at least 150 workers in the circles forming the Vilna Group, with about five to ten in each circle.[69] Their thinking was at first strongly influenced by Polish revolutionaries. In the 1880's Polish socialists had begun mass agitation among the workers, and in 1889 the Union of Polish Workers, which stressed decisive action by the masses against their employers, was founded. Mill knew such Poles personally in Ponevezh: "In the Lithuanian-Polish radical intelligentsia of Ponevezh, I found not only support in my search for the truth, not only comrades-in-arms, but . . . an understanding of the special Polish approach to contemporary political problems and goals." [70] However, during this period, when the young Jewish social democrats used the term "revolution-'ary movement," they had in mind a distinctly Russian movement. Although the northwestern provinces in the Pale were open to both Polish and Russian cultural influences, the young radicals were attracted to the latter. They certainly had no interest in founding a specifically Jewish movement at this time. Yet, the circles they led were attended almost exclusively by Jewish workers. "It is not clear to many," Gozhansky admitted,

> why we began to work among Jewish laborers. Weren't there other workers in Vilna? Certainly, there were artisans ... among the Poles, Lithuanians, and Belorussians. Why were we shut up in our own world? That, comrades, is impossible to understand if one fails to recall the nature of the Jewish ghetto. The nationalities were separated by an impenetrable wall; each lived its own life, and had no contact with the other.[71]

In Minsk and Vitebsk the same traditional cleavages between Christian and Jewish workers prevailed. There were some cases of Jewish intellectuals working among Christian workers, and vice versa, but they were quite rare.

Of particular significance to the later development of the Bund was the systematic indoctrination the Vilna social democrats gave to large numbers of radically disposed youth, which the strict quotas for Jews in Russian schools produced in abundance.[72] A few of these young Jews managed to squeeze through *gymnasia* and universities, but the vast majority were rejected and turned back to the ghetto, seething with frustration. Many of those who then became externs, preparing themselves for diploma examinations through the help of private tutors, were particularly ripe for indoctrination. But unlike their tutors, they spoke fluent Yiddish, while their command of Russian was poor. They were thus much better equiped than the older Vilna social democrats to appreciate the needs and traditions of the Jewish artisans, already struggling for relief through strikes and *kassy*.

Yet the predominance of Jewish workers in the study circles did not at the time stimulate a particular interest in the Jewish proletariat or in Jewish problems as such. All hopes were entrusted to the future revolution—the identical view of the early Jewish radicals in America. Kopelson, for example, quite typically reflected their outlook at the time (1888–90): "We were assimilationists who did not even dream of a separate Jewish mass movement. . . . We saw our task as preparing cadres for the Russian revolutionary movement and acclimatizing them to Russian culture." [73]

Young Jewish radicals also looked upon their stay in Vilna as temporary and looked forward to transferring their activity to Russian industrial centers. After all, the Jewish workers they were indoctrinating were scattered in storefront workshops, whereas in Russia proper there was a genuine proletariat in the giant textile and metallurgical plants of St. Petersburg and Moscow. The circle leaders were in active contact with Russian groups from the beginning. Radical Russian student friends brought back the latest news during school vacations. Relations with St. Petersburg circles were considerably strengthened by the arrival in Vilna of Martov, an active social democrat expelled from the capital, and with Moscow circles through a non-Jew, E. I. Sponti, a founder of the Moscow Workers' Union in 1893, who at one time spent a term of military service in Vilna.

At the same time, the Jewish circle leaders, although generally assimilationist, were not dogmatically so. They did not find living in the Pale abhorrent, and did not press, as had the older revolutionaries, for assimilation as a solution to Jewish problems. Some even reacted emotionally when the first Yiddish pamphlets arrived in the Vilna circle,[74] although the prevailing feeling was to disparage the "jargon." In dealing with Jewish workers, however, the key problem was their meager revolutionary potential. Jewish artisans in small shops were not, by any stretch of the imagination, the industrial proletariat capable of the class struggle the young socialists envisioned. Yet the Jewish artisan of the late nineteenth century was actually a proletarian. Indeed, it was the drawing together of the circle intellectuals with such workers that laid the foundation for a Jewish mass labor movement in the Pale, an unlikely encounter but a real and historically significant one.

15. From Propaganda Circles to Agitation, 1890-95

One of the striking features of the Jewish labor movement was the early and close interlocking of the social-democratic intellectuals with worker groups. "The Lithuanian Jewish intelligentsia, including the radical one, had its specific physiognomy," one historian has said. It "bore a folk character, was more closely linked with the Jewish setting and manifested a profound sense of belonging to it and a responsibility for its destiny." [1] Zhitlovsky touched on this in his characterization of Russian students abroad in the 1880's, when he concluded that, compared with Russified Jewish students from the interior and south of Russia, Jewish socialists from the northwest, although externally assimilated, never lost contact with the living Jewish milieu.[2] Ideologically, they were assimilationist, but culturally they had not closed the door on all things Jewish. Nearly all understood Yiddish and were not only sensitive to the struggle of the Jewish worker but from the beginning regarded him with respect and understanding.

This social and cultural empathy may have been partly the result of the larger political situation. The Jewish intelligentsia lived in a kind of ghetto in Lithuania, where most educated non-Jews were Poles, absorbed in their own problems and working zealously to remove the Russian yoke. (Later, in fact, Jewish socialists were attacked as russifiers.) The Russian stratum consisted almost exclusively of officials who treated Lithuania like a conquered territory and kept their distance from both Poles and Jews. Consequently, the Jewish circle leaders in Vilna, Minsk, and Bialystok, although they thought of themselves as bearers of Russian culture, did not reject the Jewish world they lived in, as had other Russian Jewish radicals.

As early as 1892, the Vilna organization had contacts with Russian social-democratic groups and performed important services for them, helping fugitives cross the border and becoming a depot for radical literature smuggled from abroad, particularly for Plekhanov's Liberation of

Labor group. Vilna, indeed, became a coordinating center for the Russian movement long before the latter was in a position to do this itself. But these contacts were intermittent and fugitive; the living cultural milieu was Jewish.

In the early 1890's, Notkin, Jogiches, Luiba Akselrod and others were conducting socialist propaganda among the members of the *kassy* of stocking makers, tailors, and shoemakers in Vilna. By 1887, Jogiches had even led a strike of thirty Vilna printers. But the contact with workers remained mainly through the circles, and the purpose of the circles was to create groups of workers who would be infused with revolutionary zeal to create a new society. But not all of the Jewish workers in the circles conformed to such plans. They had ideas of their own, forcing the leaders to a basic reconsideration of their whole program.

For the Jewish workers, the educational experience of the circle was as exhilarating as the earlier Haskalah to *yeshivah* students. They hungered for new knowledge and were avid pupils. Printers, engravers, bookbinders, and tailors—the Jewish "worker-aristocracy"—flocked to the classes; however, very few factory workers came.[3] Once in the circle, the Jewish artisan came to regard his socialist "teacher" with extreme reverence. "I remember as if it were today," one of them has written, "with what a remarkable feeling of fear and awe I and other students sat on a wooden bench near a large brick oven that was hardly warm. Opposite us, at a table, sat a young man of twenty-seven or twenty-eight." The young man was Arkady, and after the lesson, the writer returned home feeling as if "a new soul had entered me."[4]

It is hardly surprising, then, that circle members began to imitate their teachers. They often dressed in a Russian-style black shirt, carried Russian books and spoke Russian or a mixture of Russian and Yiddish. Moreover, these members began to develop condescending attitudes toward the masses of uneducated workers and began to think of their education as a way of escaping their own economic misery. Some left the movement and became externs; others left for bigger cities or America or, worst of all, became employers. Such unexpected reactions led the leaders to a new approach, one supplied by the events of 1891 and the example of the Polish socialists. There was widespread hunger in 1891, and the liberal intelligentsia and the Vilna Group set up soup kitchens. Writing about the famine, Plekhanov said that workers need not be fully class conscious before they engage in the struggle for a new society, and that agitation to improve their own economic conditions is more effective in creating class consciousness than the circle-propaganda technique.[5] At the same time, Polish Marxists began to work directly with Polish workers. A new Union of Polish Workers replaced the old propaganda organization and stressed mass action. Waves of strikes swept the Polish provinces, reaching a climax in the general strike in Lodz in 1892.[6] Years later, Gozhansky acknowledged the example of the Polish revolutionaries: "Our acquaintance with the Polish workers' movement showed us that a real revolutionary movement must have its roots . . . in its own environment." [7]

Jewish factory workers at first were resigned to their lot and fatalistic. When Gozhansky first spoke to the workers at Edelshtein's tobacco factory in Vilna, their response was: "Nothing will come of this, everything you say is useless, because everything depends on fate. We poor people were born that way, and so we shall die, and nothing will improve our situation." [8] Then Gozhansky, quite by accident, found a key: the mayor of Vilna had ordered the publication of an old law issued by Catherine II in 1785, restricting the hours of work for artisans to twelve hours (with a half-hour break for breakfast and a one-and-one-half-hour break for dinner). Here was an issue that could not only rally the Jewish workers but also draw the intellectuals toward an understanding of their daily needs. Once armed with the law, the socialists found the masses responsive to their agitation. Realizing that they had a legal right to protest, the artisans were willing to fight for a shorter day. The law, Gozhansky concluded, was the basis upon which contact with workers could be established.[9]

Jewish artisans in Vilna, Mogilev, Bialystok, Vitebsk, and Brest-Litovsk now began to bombard the authorities with petitions requesting that the law be enforced. For their part, the socialist intellectuals who had limited their work to propaganda now believed that once the authorities failed to act the workers would resort to illegal means.[10] The previously inert mass of workers began to talk openly about their rights. In Vilna, small squads of workers made the rounds of the city at 7 P.M. demanding that the owners of workshops close for the day and threatening them with legal action.[11]

The authorities seemed willing to aid the workers until the mass appeals began. By 1893, owners became alarmed at the spreading movement and began to fire the "rebels." Many workers were arrested. Petitions were now discarded in favor of more direct action. The outbreak of strikes in 1893, culminating in the tailors' strike in Vilna, led the intellectuals to begin training a worker elite as future agitators. "The struggle for a 'legal' workday," Kremer wrote, "opened our eyes." [12] A new program of "agitation" for improvement of the economic conditions of the workers began to take shape during 1893–94.

Jewish workers were also becoming aware of the international workers' movement. The idea of celebrating May Day to express the solidarity of workers, which had originated with the First Congress of the Second International, reached Vilna in 1892. About one hundred workers were invited to a secret meeting in the woods. The gathering was first addressed by Kremer and Mill, and then by four workers, who spoke in Russian and Yiddish.[13] One of the workers, Fania Reznik, called for more militant action in the workshops and factories: "In order to overcome fragmentation and to further unify, we must organize frequent meetings of the workers. All must strive to found *kassy* and try to make them expand. We must organize strikes. For strikes, too, we must have *kassy*." [14] Another, sounding a note of Jewish pride, said, "We Jews need not be ashamed of belonging to the so-called disgraced Jewish race. The history of the Jews ... has also its pages of glory.... Let us—the young generation—follow in the footsteps of our forefathers and manifest our perseverance in the fight for the liberation of mankind." [15] Delighted with the performance of their pupils, the leaders asked Jogiches, who was living abroad at the time, to arrange for publication of the speeches. This was done and Jogiches wrote a foreword, with the help of his brilliant companion, Rosa Luxemburg.[16]

A Marxist conviction, which was beginning to grip some Vilna workers, was expressed at the May Day celebration. They began to recognize the importance of stirring other Jewish workers toward a sense of class consciousness, as well as agitating for immediate, practical goals. For the next two years, the Vilna Group debated the theoretical basis for such tactics; by 1894, a new formulation had crystallized. The pull to follow the workers was compelling, but the old élitist circles also had their supporters, and some opposition to the new approach developed.

The spearhead of the opposition was Avram Gordon (Rezchik), an engraver. (Engravers were a Jewish artisan élite that had supplied the circles with many of their recruits.) An outspoken, self-educated man, Gordon had created a sensation in the May Day celebration, when he gave an unscheduled speech attacking the "shameful leadership" of the intellectuals.[17] By 1893 his views, which were shared by many workers in the circle movement, were pressed with such intensity that they confronted the Vilna Group with an ideological impasse.

"Gordon," wrote Kremer's wife Matle, "operated from the assumption that knowledge is power; therefore, the workers must first of all acquire knowledge, and only then go on to fight for better economic conditions." Such knowledge can be obtained only through the educational circles; and since there is no literature in Yiddish, the Jewish workers must be taught Russian. Mass agitation would require Yiddish and would thus deprive the Jewish workers of education.[18] Gordon insisted that by replacing education with agitation, the intellectuals were denying the workers the very instrument of emancipation they themselves had set before them. They were betraying the workers; they had begun to worship false gods, and like other intellectuals before them, were leaving the workers ignorant and helpless.[19] Considerable numbers of workers who had already earned a place among the intelligentsia and looked upon the circle as their only means of educational and social uplift supported Gordon and fought tenaciously, perhaps as much to hold on to their newly won status as to fight the new philosophy.[20] A labor movement torn by strikes and mass agitation would be fatal to the intellectual order they had created.

A number of substantive issues, moreover, were debated at stormy *kassy* meetings. Some of the "advanced" workers rebelled against the use of Yiddish as the language of agitation; others, like Liessin in Minsk, ridiculed the program of agitation, calling it appropriate for a genuine proletariat but merely a struggle of "pauper against pauper" in the Pale.[21] Gordon himself had written in 1891 about the decline of Jewish crafts and the threat of extinction from industrialization and argued that strikes may be valuable for an industrial proletariat, but not for artisans who were doomed.[22] Others believed the *kassy* were pointless, that both sides of the struggle were pauperized. (Interestingly, similar arguments were used against the Bund somewhat later by the socialist Zionist Ber Borochov.) Gozhansky himself admitted that some masters were so poverty stricken that an increase in wages would force them to close their shops.

In mounting their counterarguments, the proponents of mass agitation found this point most difficult to answer. It was never refuted, in fact. The socialists admitted that they were operating under severe handicaps because of the peculiar nature of the Jewish proletariat, and hoped that eventually Jewish artisans would be absorbed into the factories.[23] Other strengths were proclaimed, however. Kremer, for example, said that artisans "are more cultured, more developed" than factory workers, and are more willing to strike.[24] Others stressed the mobility of the artisan, the fact that he could work at home, if need be, and his strong sense of organization and solidarity with the workers in his particular craft.

Jewish artisans did indeed strike in large numbers and revealed a talent for organization that far surpassed that of any other labor force in the empire. Moreover, as the *kassy* became imbued with the spirit of a spontaneous labor movement, the position of the propagandized artisan-workers who opposed agitation became weaker. Their views had no appeal to the masses of workers. The limitations of propaganda in the circles in the early 1890's were commented on by Martov:

> In my circle, I twice delivered talks on the aims and methods of socialism, but real life kept on interfering. . . . Either the members of the circle would themselves raise the question of some event that had occurred in their factory . . . or someone from another workshop would appear and we would have to spend the time discussing the conditions there.[25]

The time had come, he decided, to adopt more active methods: to assume the leadership of strikes wherever they occurred and to impart a political character to the workers' struggle for economic improvements.

As they watched this process, teachers and revolutionaries were compelled to admit that they had given circle workers the wrong advice. In 1894 Arkady Kremer, in his path-breaking pamphlet *On Agitation*,[26] declared:

> The Russian Social-Democratic movement is on the wrong path. It has locked itself up in educational circles. It should listen for the pulse-beat of the crowd and, finding it, should step ahead of the crowd and lead it. Social Democrats can and must lead the working masses because the proletariat's blind struggle

inevitably leads it to the same goal, to the same ideal, which the revolutionary Social Democrats have consciously chosen.

Taking as his text Plekhanov's assertion that "the attainment of political power is the main task of the struggling proletariat," Kremer insisted that it was only through the economic struggle that workers could be made to see the necessity of the political struggle and the impossibility of improving their lot under existing political conditions.

The central idea of Kremer's essay is that political agitation should broaden its base by a greater appeal to the working masses, that it should cease being theoretical and, instead, launch a program that would integrate political and economic goals. The working masses, Kremer said, can only become fully conscious of the need for political liberty if they can be made to see that their own economic improvement is inextricably tied up with it. "It is utopian," he wrote, "to believe that the mass of Russian workers can begin to carry on a political struggle unless they are made aware ... that such a struggle is most vital to their own interests." The economic conflicts that are apparent to them will reveal the larger class conflicts in capitalist society, which, in turn, will stimulate political consciousness:

> The struggle ... will educate workers to stand up for their demands, will rouse their courage, give them self-assurance in their own powers, the realization that it is necessary for them to unite, and ultimately, it will pose more important problems demanding solution. ... This more conscious type of class struggle creates the basis for political agitation, and such agitation then sets up the goal of transforming existing political conditions in the interests of the working class.[27]

To carry out such mass propaganda, the revolutionary agitator must maintain continuous contact with the workers and all branches of industrial production, taking as his point of departure the common daily needs of the workers, without losing sight of the ultimate socialist goal.[28]

Kremer's brochure did not deal at all with specifically Jewish problems; it was directed to the Russian revolutionary movement as a whole, but its immediate objective was to silence the arguments of those who were opposed to carrying on socialist agitation in Yiddish.[29] Kremer's views were soon accepted by the Vilna Group and accelerated the formation of an autonomous Jewish socialist organization fighting for specifically Jewish, as well as general, political rights.

On Agitation had enormous influence in all of the centers of revolutionary activity in Russia and provided a theoretical basis for a new strategy. The remarkable feature of the essay is that, although designed to meet the crisis arising out of ghetto sweatshops, its theoretical argument and practical guidelines were cast in Marxist terms and could be universally applied. A copy which Martov brought to St. Petersburg in the fall of 1894 stimulated lively discussions. Appearing at the time of factory disorders, the pamphlet gave practical guidance to social democrats who were confused by the wave of strikes. News of the Vilna technique soon spread to Kiev, Ekaterinoslav, and Odessa; the impact on the great strike in St. Petersburg in 1896 was enormous. For the next few years, *On Agitation* became the bible of rank-and-file socialist workers and changed the pace and direction of the floundering young Russian movement. The Jewish group was also transformed.

Vilna now began to send trained agitators to other Jewish communities. This sudden expansion of underground operations created a strong demand for people who could speak Yiddish and had strong feelings of identification with Jewish workers. Many Jewish artisans and self-schooled socialists now became the vanguard of such cadres: Shlome Menaker, Tsvia Hurvich, Tsila Valk, Hirsch Sarake, and Israel-Michal Kaplinsky.[30] These worker-agitators now began to replace circle intellectuals as the influential figures of the socialist movement. As spearheads in the economic struggle, they recruited members, attended many meetings, led circles, and planned strikes. They also had to understand the problems of the workers they met and realistically gauge the economic improvements that could be achieved.[31] Like the intellectual leaders of the circles, some of the agitators became figures of veneration and inspiration. They conducted their activities in special streets called *birzhes,* where workers and agitators met to discuss current problems and arrange meetings, where *kassy* members paid their dues, and where literature was distributed. The comparative safety of these streets was vitally important for the development of a mass movement in a country which denied freedom of assembly and speech. If police spies infested one *birzhe,* the groups simply moved elsewhere.[32]

The Russian movement, meanwhile, was trying to pull itself together. Until *On Agitation* appeared, Russian social democrats had largely confined their activities to secret intelligentsia-led circles on the populist model and the inculcation of class-consciousness in a small, select group of workers.[33] *On Agitation* circulated first in manuscript in St. Petersburg, then to other parts of Russia. Under its impact, Russian Marxists instigated industrial disturbances and work stoppages and began organizing factory workers—activities which culminated in the great strike of St. Petersburg textile workers in May, 1896, the first large scale industrial strike in Russian history. The spearhead of this effort was the Union of Struggle for the Liberation of the Working Class in St. Petersburg under the leadership of Martov and Lenin, which served as a model for similar groups that sprang up in 1896–97.

The Plekhanov circle in Geneva seems to have had its first contact with Lenin's Union of Struggle in the spring of 1895, when Lenin and E. I. Sponti arrived in Switzerland as representatives of Russian Marxist circles.[34] The emigrés were understandably excited by evidence of an emerging Marxist movement in Russia, but their enthusiasm was somewhat tempered by the strange and disturbing views of their visitors. With Lenin particularly, there were disagreements over socialist attitudes toward liberals. Both Plekhanov and Akselrod tried to persuade him to turn his face instead of his back to the liberals, but Lenin was not convinced.[35] These first misunderstandings anticipated the quarrels and cleavages of the next decade, as did the response to Kremer's pamphlet.

Lenin had brought with him a copy of *On Agitation*, which caused considerable dismay in Geneva. It was finally decided to publish it (1896), but with a long commentary by Akselrod, in which he argued that Arkady's program was no more or less than a reversion to the old Bakunist program, which the Marxists had long since left behind; and further, that Arkady had erred in ignoring certain tendencies implicit in the bourgeois order and in conceiving the struggle for socialism in simple terms of "exploited" and "exploiters." [36] Plekhanov also criticized the ideas in *On Agitation*. Whatever the views in Geneva, however, the work exerted a great influence on the Russian social democrats, and the methods it proposed were followed by many groups. One historian believes that "the program of agitation formulated in Vilna was the greatest single contribution the Jewish Marxists of Belorussia-Lithuania made to the general Russian social-democratic movement." [37]

Kremer's emphasis on the short-term economic struggle was later taken up and labelled "economism" by certain Russian social democrats who argued in favor of giving up long-range political goals and concentrating solely on workers' economic improvements. Lenin's *What Is To Be Done?* (written in 1902) was a sharp attack on this position, which he attributed to Kremer and the Bund, but which they, in fact, never adopted.

According to Kremer, political consciousness would inevitably grow out of the economic struggle, but need not be emphasized at the beginning. It would require time to develop. Gozhansky, in his *A briv tsu di agitatorn* (*A Letter to the Agitators*), written in 1893, had also stressed improvement of the workers' living conditions and an understanding of their economic interests. The agitator must be "aware of the slightest details affecting a worker's life in the craft;" he must know what the workers want, but also "what can and cannot be achieved." Gozhansky, of course, accepted the necessity of worker class consciousness, but urged practical involvement in everyday concerns of the workers—to connect their daily struggle with revolutionary goals. "The masses can only understand those theoretical principles with which they have direct contact," he said, "and, as we know, their lives depend entirely upon their economic condition." [38] Agitation now became the basis of the Jewish social-democratic program, and at meetings, workers discussed the improvements they wanted. This new approach won thousands of new supporters; the élitist opposition collapsed.

The Vilna Group now assumed leadership in the purely economic struggle of the workers and revised the circle training program. They now had to adopt the language of the Jewish workers—Yiddish—a step which not only changed the direction of the group, putting it on the path of an affirming Jewishness, but meant that radical literature had to be simplified and translated. Brochures had to replace scholarly books and long novels.

The lack of printed materials and the intellectuals' inadequacy in Yiddish constituted serious problems at first. The Vilna Group began to recruit new members with fluency in Yiddish and enough writing skill to produce materials that could be understood by the average worker. Fortunately there were many *yeshivah* and ex-*yeshivah* students in Vilna, as well as self-educated youths from the petty bourgeoisie, who could not attend upper or middle schools, but were very intelligent, hungered for knowledge, and read a great deal. Apart from their language ability, these "half-intellectuals," as they were sometimes called, also moved easily in the working-class environment and became the direct channel between the intellectuals and the masses.[39]

In this group of talented translators, speakers, and writers, a special place is reserved for Khaim Helfand, who used the pseudonym A. Litvak.[40] Litvak entered the movement in 1893, when friends who had already joined told him that the intellectuals wanted to meet young people with a good knowledge of Yiddish. His deep and intense love of Yiddish was nourished by his relations with Jewish workers. For Litvak, there was no way to separate Yiddish from the problems facing Jewish workers. The pride in Yiddish folk culture and the natural expression of a strong emotional tie through Yiddish was something the intellectuals had not anticipated.[41] Like their counterparts in America, in tentatively admitting Yiddish as the language of revolutionary propaganda, they were opening a dam through which rushed forces that pulled the movement in new directions, folk strengths, and invigorating pulses that were as startling in their outcome as those that shaped the early American Jewish socialist movement.

In 1893, Litvak set up a Yiddish library featuring the works of Mendele Mocher Sforim, Sholem Aleichem, and later, of I. L. Peretz and David Pinski.[42] Two years later, he became a leader of the Jargon (i.e., Yiddish) Committee in Vilna, which distributed good literature in Yiddish among Jewish workers, set up libraries, and published popular scientific books and fiction in Yiddish. Similar branches were set up in other cities. Litvak also translated into Yiddish the writings of Karl Kautsky, the German socialist, and of the playwright Sh. Ansky, a Russian-Jewish writer who was once Lavrov's secretary.

Pinsky, the well-known Jewish short-story writer and dramatist, first invited Peretz to read his poems and stories to working-class audiences. Their enthusiasm and interest led him to publish Peretz' *Yomtov-bletlekh* (*Holiday Journals*, 1894–96) which were a literary treasure trove for the Jargon committees.[43] In the search for Yiddish propaganda materials, the Vilna Group at first depended on such works by Peretz and other socialistically oriented Yiddish writers. They also used didactic stories and brochures by Gozhansky that dealt with factory conditions, Jewish disabilities in tsarist Russia, and simple expositions of Marxism.[44] Instructional pamphlets were printed in Switzerland and Germany by Jewish socialist exiles. Socialist feuilletons, both translations and original works, soon began to flow into the circles and workers' libraries.

The first effort at regular news dissemination in Vilna came in 1894 in the form of a handwritten sheet called *Nayes fun Rusland (News of Russia)*, that appeared for five issues. In December 1896, there appeared the first issue of *Der Yidisher Arbayter (The Jewish Worker)*, written and distributed in Vilna but printed abroad. As the leading editorial in this issue made clear, the Vilna Group now recognized that the movement had to spread beyond the local level and the needs of a few isolated groups. The editors would show that the *kassy* were a source of proletarian strength and that the day was fast approaching when individual, struggling groups of the Jewish proletariat would unite in one workers' socialist organization. The appearance of *Der Yidisher Arbayter* signaled a new stage in the history of the Jewish socialist movement. The journal eventually became the organ of the foreign committee of the Bund and was published until 1904. In August 1897, workers and "half-intellectuals" put out their own paper *inside* Russia, using a secret press built by one of the workers. This was the famous *Di Arbayter Shtimme (The Worker's Voice)*, which became the official organ of the central committee of the Bund until 1905.

By the turn of the century, a quite rich cultural life in Yiddish illuminated the otherwise bleak lot of Jewish workers in the Pale. In time, the cultural and educational activity of the socialist movement revolutionized the lives of Jewish workers possibly as much as did the economic struggle. *National*-political interests of the Jewish workers were also being pondered by some thinkers. In 1892, in his brochure *A Jew to Jews*, Zhitlovsky had made an attempt to combine national and socialist movements in a new theoretical framework, but the Vilna Group rejected it, ignoring the question of Jewish identity that had been touched on in the May Day celebration of that year. In 1894, the Vilna Group began calling itself the *Jewish* social-democratic group,[45] although the addition of the word "Jewish" did not mean there was as yet any desire to create a *Jewish* mass movement. Jewish intellectuals would merely be working with Jewish workers in Vilna. Except for John Mill, who was among the first of the group to feel that the Jewish component was all-important, the others tended to dismiss it. The movement was thus, at first, a movement *among* Jews, not a *Jewish* movement.

The agitation program, however, was at first a *Jewish* activity, and agitators and intellectuals had to confront the Jewishness of the workers; there was no way of avoiding the obvious. At a meeting in August 1894, leaders of the Vilna Group acknowledged that the Jewish workers suffered not only as workers but also as Jews. All forms of national oppression, they agreed, must be fought, and in the struggle for civil equality, the Jewish worker must be fully engaged. The stress on equal rights for Jews, moreover, posed the question of the future of Jews as Jews and touched on the critical issue of Jewish culture.

There were important political implications in this stress on equal rights for Jews. Would the struggle for Jewish rights isolate Jewish workers from the Russian masses? Would a specifically Jewish focus verge on the dangerous terrain of nationalism? What form could such a struggle take, and how would it affect the Vilna Group's relations with the rest of the Russian socialist movement? The Vilna Group was at a crossroads, although only a few of its members could perceive the importance of the step they were about to take. In fact, the step was seen as tactical—just as the use of Yiddish had been tactical—rather than substantive or philosophical. Moreover the Jewish socialists of Vilna were still strongly committed to the larger Russian movement and eager to fuse with it. Early in 1894, they had taken careful soundings of other Russian groups to see whether some sort of association or joint work might be feasible but, to their disappointment, they found that they were still too undeveloped and fragmentary. They had no alternative but to turn toward their own internal affairs and wait for the Russian movement to catch up.[46]

A decisive turn in these complications came unexpectedly the day after May Day, 1895, when the twenty-two-year-old Martov spoke to a small group of Vilna leaders and agitators on "The Theoretical and Practical Achievements of the Movement During the Past Year." [47] In summarizing the year's work, Martov acknowledged that the Jewish social democrats were being hampered in their efforts to establish close ties with Russian groups in St. Petersburg and Moscow because of *their* weakness, but that they were having some success among the Jewish workers. The movement had become "more democratic . . . more practical . . . and more Jewish," he said. "All of our hopes and expectations are no longer rooted in utopian theories . . . but in the capacities and possibilities of the masses." The Jewish masses have been aroused, "thanks to our economic agitation . . . We have thrown off the aristocratic and utopian style of bourgeois idealists. Now we will show what we can gain from the Jewish bourgeois intelligentsia."

Martov then exposed the Jewish bourgeois error in seeking rights and redress from the Russian government, instead of struggling for the self-realization of the whole of the Jewish people. "Life has compelled us to end this kind of tactic"—that is, dependence on an all-Russian agency. The Vilna Group, Martov believed, made a similar mistake: "In earlier years, all of our hopes were bound up with the Russian working class . . . and we yearned for union. We naturally used the Russian language . . . but we forgot to hold on to our ties with the Jewish masses . . . and paid no attention to elements of Jewish culture among the workers . . . who indeed

were already chasing after Russian culture—largely because of our propaganda. At the same time, we have raised the level of the Jewish
movement to one not yet reached by the Russian movement." The
moment of change came "when we had to take our propaganda and
agitation to the Jewish workers, [and] . . . began to give it a more Jewish
character. . . . In this process, we have learned something from the Jewish
bourgeoisie."

In an interesting and subtle modulation, Martov reached an unexpected conclusion:

> Though we remain continuously bound up with the general Russian movement,
> we must not close our eyes to the fact that it is still weak. . . . We must
> remember our democratic lesson: Everything through the people . . . but
> notwithstanding this, we must not wait for the efforts of the Russian or Polish
> movements to free the Jewish proletariat from economic, political, and civil
> disabilities. . . . The Jewish working class is building a compact organization and
> mass base . . . and will stand as a quite impressive power. . . . However, we are
> not strong enough to carry through the struggle for . . . emancipation alone. . . .
> We must remain steadfast in our ties with the Russian and Polish move-
> ments. . . . If their struggle fails, we will not be able to achieve much. But on the
> other hand, we cannot—as in earlier times—wait for the Russian movement as
> our bourgeoisie are waiting for the Russian government and bureaucratic
> liberalism to grant them their rights.
>
> The Russian working class is still facing its own difficult struggle. Concerned
> chiefly with its own needs, it may be willing to sacrifice the needs and demands
> of Jews, such as freedom of religion and equal rights.

Then he uttered the dramatic phrase that later became a rallying cry:
"That class which cannot fight its own way to freedom does not deserve to
have that freedom." In concluding, Martov called for a special Jewish
workers' organization to lead the struggle:

> We must therefore recognize quite clearly that . . . the aim of the Jewish social
> democrats working among the Jewish population is to build a special Jewish
> labor organization which will educate the Jewish proletariat and lead it in the
> struggle for economic, civil, and political liberty. . . . A working class that is
> content with the lot of an inferior nation will not rise up against the lot of an
> inferior class. . . . The growth of national consciousness must go hand in hand
> with the growth of class consciousness.

The speech was later hailed as a "turning point in the history of the
Jewish workers' movement," a virtual call for an independent Jewish
political movement.[48] But it was not so regarded at the time Martov
delivered the speech. Martov himself later admitted that he suggested the
idea of a separate Jewish workers' organization "as a purely practical
matter" because of the weakness of the general Russian movement and
because the Vilna Group had succeeded in establishing local ties and
developing closer cooperation with Jewish workers' groups in other cities.[49]
There is, moreover, a stunning irony in Martov's role at this juncture of

pre-Bundist history. Although he was a prominent Jewish social democrat in Vilna and was later credited with (and damned for) initiating a "new era in the Jewish workers' movement," by heightening Jewish consciousness in a hitherto Russian-dominated movement, Martov broke with the Vilna Group within a few years and became one of the most vehement opponents of the Bund. He became Lenin's chief collaborator in the Petersburg League and later, an important figure on *Iskra*.[50]

For those who remained in the Jewish social-democratic movement, the new style strained the old patterns of Jewish life in the Pale. Family ties were weakened under the pressure of youths yearning to discover new knowledge and new ways to live. The involvement of young women and their search for equality in the movement was a particularly wrenching experience for parents and daughters. Esther Frumkin, an early pioneering spirit, has left a poignant glimpse of the desperate intensity of the new life:

> I see them now, crate makers . . . soap workers, sugar workers—those among whom I led a circle. . . . Pale, thin, red-eyed, beaten, terribly tired. They would gather late in the evening. We would sit until one in the morning in a stuffy room, with only a little gas lamp burning. Often little children would be sleeping in the same room and the woman of the house would walk around listening for the police. The girls would listen to the leader's talk and would ask questions, completely forgetting the dangers, forgetting that it would take three-quarters of an hour to get home, wrapped in the cold, torn remnant of a coat, in the mud and deep snow; that they would have to knock on the door and bear a flood of insults and curses from parents; that at home there might not be a piece of bread left and one would have to go to sleep hungry . . . and then in a few hours arise and run to work. With what rapt attention they listened to the talks on cultural history, on surplus value . . . wages, life in other lands. . . . What joy would light their eyes when the circle leader produced a new number of *Yidisher Arbayter, Arbayter Shtimme*, or even a brochure! . . . How many tragedies young workers would suffer at home if it became known that they were running around with the *Akhdusnikes*, with the "brothers and sisters," that they were reading forbidden books—how many insults, blows, tears! It did not help. "It attracts them like magnets," the mothers wailed to each other.[51]

Comradeship in the movement helped to compensate for the loss of family affection and offered members a new set of values, a new morality, a new way to live. Not only did this new life have its own unique institutions—the *kassa*, the circle, the illegal library, and special celebrations—it also expected those who joined this new world to become "different from what they had been," to give up old habits and norms of personal behavior. "Honorable" behavior was stressed, particularly in relations between the sexes. Among the *bekante* (members of the movement), a strict moral code prevailed, approximating puritanism. Sex talk and vulgar jokes were eschewed.[52] The movement was like a temple, and those who served it had to have clean hands and pure thoughts.[53] There was, as in the case of earlier *narodniki*, a keen desire to translate a general world view into specific norms of personal conduct, to live one's personal life as part of the redemptive process. Gradually, too, new symbols and rituals replaced the old: red blouses, red flowers, and red flags were displayed proudly, and the first revolutionary Jewish hymn, "Di Shvueh" ("The Oath"), was solemnly sung with hands joined, at times around the red flag, and at times with prayer shawls and religious scrolls. Meetings opened with the singing of "The Oath" and generally closed with it. In 1902, the well-known Yiddish writer Ansky (whose real name was Shlomo Rappoport) wrote a new text for the hymn, with resounding, militant verses, calling on comrades to swear "to strive for freedom and right against the tyrant and his knave," to "wage the holy war . . . until right triumphs over wrong," and "the humble is equal to the strong."

Such involvement in revolutionary activity produced a crisis not only of cultural but also of personal identity. Young Jewish revolutionaries were defying the traditions of their own communities and threatening the methods Jews had customarily used to buffer the harshness of government power: appeals, prayer, and bribery. Such rebels also had to work out conflicts within themselves: they were leaving a compact, tightly webbed, restrictive community that was secure if suffocating, and plunging—often after a traumatic break with parents—into a small illegal movement where everything had to be created: means and ends, principles, values, new friends, and a way of life.[54]

The break with tradition also involved a rebellion against the accepted prestige of teacher and rabbi. Together with the young rebels who yearned for secular learning, there were some who wanted to take up a trade—by choice rather than necessity. Moreover, young women who struggled for equality in the radical community found great difficulties—both social and economic—in some of the *kassy* where men did not wish to mix with women, and in some shops. Kremer, for example, mentions the tension between men and women workers in tailor shops where women's clothes were made. And yet, there was also a certain continuity. Not only was Yiddish a binding force between the generations, but many of the circle workers and "half-intellectuals" still prayed and went to the synagogue regularly. The calendar of Jewish holidays was adhered to well into the Bund period and the use of the Torah scroll and prayer shawl was common in movement ceremonials.

Gradually, the political group began to fill the emotional void. Commitment to the group's program and aspirations gave members hope for a better future and a sense of purpose that compensated for all that had been given up or lost. The cohesion and solidarity of the Jewish social-democratic movement, out of which the Bund was formed in 1897, were very strong and gave members a feeling of intense involvement. Often they referred to the movement as their only real home. Personal ties were fused with abstract beliefs, creating an intense, compelling sense of identification that aroused the deepest loyalties among comrades and the deepest hostility toward political opponents.[55]

16. Jewish Workers Organize, 1895-97

The budding socialist movement, with its militant secular philosophy, created great strains within the organized Jewish community, challenging established religious and social beliefs and institutions. Traditional Jewish society was already experiencing severe stress and erosion from earlier poundings, but the danger from the socialist movement was of a radically different order. From an economic point of view, the vehemence of the class war, which made employers and employees irreconcilable adversaries, threatened the harmony of the community, making it more vulnerable to attack from the outside. Employers, in anger and desperation, began to look to the state to intervene in their behalf, or called on rabbis to condemn the workers. The Jewish socialists deepened these divisions, lashing out at religious leaders for supporting employers, as well as at the employers themselves.

A dramatic incident during a strike at a Vilna tobacco factory in 1895—the largest of its kind in Vilna up to that time—exposed the antagonists in a new and frightening light.[1] The police had urged a *maggid* (preacher) to speak to the strikers, but instead of appeasing them, he made matters worse by openly criticizing them in the synagogue for breaking the law and harming the Jewish people. Because of the strikers, he said, the government would now consider all Jews seditious.

In an unprecedented display of defiance, the workers shouted him down, causing great commotion in the synagogue and among Vilna's Jews. The Vilna social democrats considered the episode so important, they put out a pamphlet written by Gozhansky called *Der Shtot Maggid (The Town Preacher)*.[2] Gozhansky called the attack on the workers for the benefit of the employers "a humiliation for the temple," but also asserted the reality of class enmity, which does not stop "even for the strength and cruelty of the all-powerful police." These were harsh words from young Jews; their counterparts in deeds shook the unity of the community and, increasingly, drew the mockery and criticism of other Jews. In Vilna, they were called "philosophers" and in Bialystok, "the weaver patriots," but elsewhere they were called "roughnecks" and worse.[3] Retaliation from employers could be quick and punitive: obstreperous, striking workers were fired or police intervention was sought, further sharpening class divisions.

The Russian police also began to deal with the rising movement as a dangerous threat. Police spies were used to ferret out agitators, infiltrate meetings, and make detailed reports of revolutionary groups. The arrest rate jumped sharply in 1896. The advent of agitators, leaflets, and linked strike attempts revealed the functioning of a collective effort which the government watched closely and began to perceive as an organized danger to the status quo.

However, these multiple threats to Jewish workers did not stop the momentum of agitation, organization, and striking. By the end of 1895, the Jewish social democrats had organized almost 2,000 Jewish workers in Vilna and Minsk, many of them in the small tanning and bristle shops. In Vilna, the 850 organized workers represented 27 trades and about 30 percent of all workers in these crafts.[4] In Minsk in 1895–96, 15 *kassy* were organized. There was also a *kassa* in Kreslavka, an important center of the *bershter-bund*—the bristle workers who had conducted strikes as early as 1890. In 1891, they organized *kassy* in Vilna and other cities and in 1895, delegates from these *kassy* met in Vilna and issued a pamphlet stressing the interdependence of all bristle workers. A few years later they established a union of bristle workers in Poland and Lithuania and created their own news organ. Writing about them later, Vladimir Medem, a Bund leader, called them *di smetene*—"the cream" of the movement. Many worked in small towns on the Prussian border as smugglers of illegal literature and revolutionary fugitives. As a group they were considered extremely intelligent and highly developed socialists. In Minsk they had the highest literacy rate of any single proletarian group,[5] and a Jewish Colonization Association study spoke of them as "more cultivated than their colleagues in other industries."

Intensive organizational work was also carried out in Warsaw and Bialystok, and in the summer of 1895 two hundred tobacco workers struck the Edelshtein factory.[6] This first strike of factory workers in Vilna at the largest factory marked a new stage in the labor movement there. A program of agitation was also carried by activists to Gomel, Vitebsk, Grodno, and Kovno, resulting in a wave of strikes. Workers in some of these cities had conducted sporadic strikes and built temporary organizations earlier, but they lacked direction until the socialist intellectuals entered the movement and became the catalysts of organization. In Bialystok, for example, virtually the whole textile industry was shut down by a strike of some 12,000 workers, including 3,000 Jewish workers, in 1895. This was a massive strike which the workers themselves conducted. Yet a year later, there were only 1,000 organized workers in Bialystok, showing the falling off of discipline and holding power. Not until activists from Vilna came into these cities was a permanent, well-grounded organization established. The institution of the *kassy*, which had taken root in Vilna and Minsk, spread to other cities and became the organizational backbone of the new campaign.[7]

Members were expected to pay dues to the *kassy*, in return for which they would get financial support during a strike. Admission was selective: a member had to be a worker who understood the conflicting interests of workers and capitalists, and who would not refuse to strike if a majority of the members so decided. The *kassy* were variously known as *skhodkes* ("assemblies"), or *fakh komisies* ("craft commissions"), or *ferayns* ("unions"). Members of *kassy* elected representatives to an all-craft or "agitation" assembly. Supervising the movement from above was the local committee, at first made up mainly of the socialist-intellectuals who seldom met with the workers for security reasons and because they could not, as yet, speak Yiddish.

The organizational structure of the embryonic movement operated in such a way that very often the various components did not know of each other's existence. Agitation assemblies, for example, might be unaware of the existence of a local committee. In Minsk, Vladimir Medem, a member of the local committee, was forbidden to take part in mass agitation.[8] Workers generally did not know the real names of intellectuals, who used pseudonyms. This compartmentalization made it virtually impossible for intellectuals to take an active part in labor agitation. In time, certain workers met with the intellectuals in joint councils. Council meetings were political in character, and the workers who attended these meetings, although regarded as representatives of the *kassy*, were not elected, but were chosen "from above." [9]

The members of the *kassy* realized that the movement was being guided by some inner circle—unknown to them—and their desire to penetrate it led to the establishment of a central, elected workers' *kassa*. Its function was to help strikers with men and money, to lead strikes, publish proclamations, and maintain contact with other cities to ward off strikebreakers. In the period from 1895 to 1897, the "inner circle" was slowly penetrated by some workers.[10] Quite naturally in the early years, the conspiratorial nature of the movement caused misgivings among many workers, but after the Bund was created, policy initiatives were frequently taken by the workers themselves. The top level of the hierarchy was linked to the councils through the city committees. These, consisting of both elected and appointed members, met secretly—a kind of "holy of holies" of the movement. The committees provided propagandists for the workers' circles, supplied literature, made contact with other cities and foreign countries, and obtained funds.[11]

From 1894 to 1897, when the Bund was organized, the number of politically conscious Jewish workers grew rapidly, and Jewish social-democratic organizations spread throughout the Pale. This activity was given impetus at a meeting in August 1894, when the Vilna social democrats decided to develop "closer cooperation with Jewish workers' organizations in other cities." [12] This activity, known as "colonization," drew Vilna activists to Warsaw, Bialystok, and Minsk, and other centers. An important step toward closer coordination took place in June 1895, when delegates from Vilna and Minsk met in Minsk to discuss strikebreaking, but then went on to consider a united policy, organizational links, and the possibility of an organ. According to John Mill, there seemed to be some sense that a purely Jewish political force was in the making.[13] But such intimations (which he was among the first to perceive) were outweighed by other considerations: the need to organize more workers and the state of the Russian movement.

The drive to improve the lot of the workers—shorter hours, better pay and working conditions—stimulated the growth of organized Jewish labor, especially in Vilna and Minsk, where by 1897, fifteen hundred and one thousand workers respectively were enrolled in *kassy*. As the struggle for the legally sanctioned twelve-hour day failed, workers increasingly resorted to strikes in the trades with strong *kassy*. In 1894–97, there were over fifty strikes in Minsk, and fifty-six in Vilna for the two-year period, 1895–96.[14] Most of these strikes were successful—at least temporarily—in achieving shorter hours, higher wages, and more hygienic working conditions. Moreover, there was growing solidarity among workers; worker groups helped each other with funds and moral support during strikes. The response to organization among Russian workers was less positive.

The Jewish social democrats at this time were actually more cohesive than the Russian movement, and their achievements were freely acknowledged. Yet they slowed down their own momentum toward a single organization because of their conviction that their own fate was tied to the whole Russian working class. When the great strike of 1896 occurred in St. Petersburg, *Der Yidisher Arbayter* in its first issue rejoiced that the Russian workers had finally joined the "great struggle for liberation from the yoke of capitalism, which the Polish and Jewish workers were already waging." [15] In the same issue, the intention of the Jewish social democrats to join the future Russian party—as soon as it was organized—was made clear.

During this period, the Jewish movement was close to developments in the larger Russian social-democratic movement—still largely in exile—and hoped a party would soon be formed. When a group in Europe formed the Union of Russian Social Democrats Abroad late in 1894 to arrange for the printing of propaganda materials, the Jewish groups established ties with them. In early 1895, Kopelson went to Europe and became the primary link between the two movements. Russian emigrés in Plekhanov's Liberation of Labor Group in Geneva were also urging organizational ties among all social-democratic groups scattered throughout the Russian empire. At the Socialist International in London in 1896, Plekhanov proclaimed the building of a united organization as the chief aim of the Russian social democrats in the immediate future. At the same time, he also praised the staunchness of the Jewish social democrats in their "struggle with their exploiters" and their "keenness in understanding the socio-political tasks of the contemporary workers' movement."

The assimilationist orientation among some Jewish social democrats was still very strong, and those who left Vilna to "colonize" elsewhere in Russia were often envied. Tsive Gurvich, an activist during this time, said that "we envied those who left for work among the Russian proletariat" and disclaimed any signs of "nationalism," to which he and other Russianized workers were opposed.[16] Several times in 1895–97, Vilna broached the question of coordinating efforts, and carried on negotiations with Russian groups in St. Petersburg, Moscow, and Kiev. Some Jewish workers said that the only thing that kept them from settling in Moscow or on the Volga was the difficulty in getting residence permits. Russian-educated leaders also looked beyond the Pale. Martov, for example, when his term of exile was over in the fall of 1895, returned to St. Petersburg; Isaiah Izenshtat settled in Odessa to revive a group recently broken up by the police; Kopelson resettled in Warsaw and later in Berlin to facilitate the flow of propaganda material into Russia.[17]

Some artisans who succeeded in getting residence certificates also "emigrated." Out of a group of locksmiths whom Martov guided, one moved to the Volga region while others joined Gozhansky in "colonizing" Bialystok, where Jewish and Russian textile workers joined forces in the strikes of 1895. Another pupil of Martov, a bookbinder named Moshe Dushkan, settled in Ekaterinoslav with a dedicated group of tailors and locksmiths to spread the gospel of agitation. Dushkan helped set up a secret printing press for *Rabochaya Gazeta (The Workers' Newspaper)*, an organ sponsored by the Kievan social democrats to advance the cause of unity.[18] These "colonizers" never returned to the Vilna movement and never felt themselves to be anything but Russian.

In these early years Vitebsk also became a Jewish socialist center and then a dispersion point. Rather typical of the Vitebsk wave is the attitude of Abraham Ginzburg, who later became a key member of the Odessa Committee of the Russian party: "I chose Ekaterinoslav out of definite party considerations. I decided to devote myself to agitational work among the Russian factory and industrial workers, which in my eyes, had incomparably more interest and prospects for success than work among the artisan Jewish workers." [19]

In the south of Russia, especially in Odessa, Kharkov, Tiflis, and Kiev, many first-generation Marxist intellectuals were of Jewish origin but chose to work within exclusively Russian groups. After a period of "wandering" in the Russian movement, Ginzburg returned to become a prominent activist in the Jewish movement. Other Vilna-trained Jews who had been oriented toward the Russian revolutionary movement remained in the south and helped to establish Russian organizations.

Yet another pressure tugged at the frail Jewish socialist movement— indicative of the later exposure of the Bund to strong exertions and difficult, sometimes indecisive moves. In the early 1890's, the issue of nationality was thrust upon the Jewish social-democratic leaders by the Polish Socialist party (PPS).[20] More developed than the Russian movement and struggling for national rights and an independent Poland, the PPS was raising difficult and embarrassing questions, pressing the Jewish movement to define their socialism more precisely. Why, the Polish socialists asked, did Jewish workers need to know Russian? In following a policy of russification, were not the Jewish social democrats giving aid and comfort to the enemy—the oppressive Russian government—and isolating their own movement? How could their cosmopolitanism be reconciled with reliance on Russian culture and the Jewish workers' cultural separatism? Did they not grasp the fervor of the desire for Polish independence? The Vilna leaders, of course, did not see Russian culture as an extension of tsarist policy; rather, it was an opening to the wider world, and in their shrinking from support for the Polish national cause, they believed their demand for the liberation of all inhabitants of the Russian Empire was a worthier, more universalist purpose. Closest of the Vilna Group to the Polish socialists, Mill admitted that relations between them were "negative" because of the Poles' mistrust of Russian socialists, their doubts about the possibility of a revolution in Russia, and their "chauvinistic language."[21]

Kopelson also noted the pressure from the PPS—intimidating pressure from one of its leading figures, Joseph Pilsudski (later the president of the Polish republic), who told the Vilna Group to adopt the Polish language and intimated that there would be pogroms by Polish masses if the russifying policy were not abandoned. But the Vilna Group did not yield, although shortly after Pilsudski's attack, they switched to Yiddish for practical reasons. They did not believe an independent Poland offered any solutions to the problems of Jewish workers. As Mill put it, liberation of the Jewish masses did not rest on a Polish victory, but only in "the victory of the united revolutionary and socialist forces of all Russia, including Poland."[22] Yet the existence of a Polish socialist movement committed to national liberation narrowed the revolutionary horizon and troubled the premises of socialism. Threats of anti-Semitism raised other doubts— memories of pogroms, which earlier revolutionaries had done nothing to stop.

The formation of another national grouping—the Lithuanian Social-Democratic party—in 1893, was further evidence of national consciousness raising among socialists. These things were known to the Vilna Group and gave them new worries. Martov's speech, it will be recalled, did not light nationalist fires in their midst. It expressed a new, logical political goal for an organization that was already struggling for economic goals and a growing sense of self-confidence and dignity among Jewish workers.[23] However, the dreamed-of Russian movement stood as the overarching purpose and aim of all their work. Yet they could not sit back and wait until it materialized. A choice might soon have to be made.

One indication of the state of the Vilna Group's development on the issue of a Jewish organization was Abraham Liessin's talk with Arkady Kremer early in 1895. It will be recalled that Liessin, an activist in Minsk, was groping for a synthesis of nationalism and socialism but could not formulate a program. He discussed his dilemma with Kremer but left feeling that Arkady hardly understood what he was talking about. Martov had given the movement a new task and a new definition, but this did not change its basic orientation. The national overtones that were read into Martov's speech came later. But an important change had already taken place—perhaps unconsciously—when the Vilna leaders recognized that *Jewish* workers could be mobilized in the pursuit of economic goals. It was only a short step to the realization that they might be mobilized politically as well—a perception already developed by Arkady and Gozhansky.[24]

Martov had set forth "independent" tasks in his 1895 speech, and the idea of a special Jewish workers' organization was a practical one in view of the weakness of the Russian movement. The Vilna Group had been establishing contacts with Jewish groups in other cities, holding meetings and discussions. Jewish workers were demonstrating their readiness to join the revolutionary struggle. The imperceptible, but qualitatively important progression to the idea of a Jewish workers' *political* struggle was inescapable. As one of the workers at the 1892 May Day rally had put it: "If the struggle is imminent for the Jewish worker as well as for all other workers, who will fight for him if he will not fight for himself?" [25] Increased Zionist activity and concentration by the Polish and Lithuanian socialists on the national question further heightened the Jewish consciousness of some elements among the Jewish social democrats. Forces were gathering that gave momentum to the formation of a separate Jewish socialist organization.

Moreover, the use of Yiddish propaganda forced the Jewish social democrats to work together—they had nowhere else to go for revolutionary literature. Their "colonization" efforts also involved close personal ties, a strong sense of common purpose, and a focal point in Vilna. Already enjoying a practical, functioning hegemony in the Jewish movement, Vilna socialists were reluctant to surrender this position to the uncertain vicissitudes of a wider party organization. The handwritten and hectographed efforts at dissemination of news in Yiddish in 1894–95 within the scattered movement also revealed the need to link the parts of the movement. This was finally achieved with the publication, in 1896, of *Der Yidisher Arbayter* (*The Jewish Worker*), which was printed abroad in editions of one thousand copies, and, by Russian revolutionary standards, marked the beginning of a highly coordinated organization. The Vilna Group now recognized that the movement had to spread, that workers had to understand that their *kassy* were a source of general proletarian strength, and that their struggle was part of a mighty struggle of all workers. There was also the inner momentum of sheer numbers: Thousands of Jewish workers had joined *kassy*; thousands of others who were involved in strikes and read movement literature were sympathetic.

Vladimir Akimov (Makhnovets), a non-Jewish Russian socialist, who observed the Jewish movement with great interest and admiration, believed that it was the workers themselves who demanded the introduction of a "political" element into the agitation, whereas some of the leaders seemed to hesitate. He uses the appearance of the *Di Arbayter Shtimme (The Worker's Voice)* in August 1897 as an example of political activity initiated by workers who had become tired of waiting for the revolutionary organization to meet their needs and undertook the publication of a political journal of their own.[26] Nor was it the first. As consciousness of political rights increased among individual workers, leaders responded by "shorten[ing] the birth pangs of the new ideas by propaganda, by incitement, and by leadership in the mass struggle."[27] Most significant of all for the history of the Bund was the consolidation of the alliance between workers and intellectuals during the years 1894-97. The spirit of solidarity among the organized Jewish workers and the growing awareness of the intellectuals of their needs and traditions was creating something altogether new.[28]

Security considerations and the innate cautiousness of the Vilna leaders held back the formal creation of a united Jewish labor organization. Police surveillance, threats of arrest, and detention of strikers were multiplying. The Vilna leaders had been frankly shocked at Martov's openness with them when he first arrived in Vilna, and when Lenin stopped briefly in 1895, they apparently suspected him of being a provocateur.[29] After the Minsk conference in June 1895, a wave of arrests caught several of the most active leaders including Gozhansky, Liuba Izenshtat, and Dushkan in Bialystok. Two years elapsed before the Bund was formally organized.

Undoubtedly, the reluctance to move ahead alone, without the larger movement, also inhibited the Jewish social democrats. Yet, paradoxically, the possibility that the larger movement might soon be formed hastened the founding of a separate organization. In May 1897, as Arkady Kremer remembered it, he went to Geneva as a representative of the Vilna social democrats and the St. Petersburg movement.[30] During the visit, in a discussion with Plekhanov, Vera Zasulich, and Akselrod on the question of their becoming official representatives abroad of Russian social-democratic movement, Plekhanov asked, "How can we represent you if you yourselves are not united? As yet there is nothing to represent formally." The remark made a strong impression on Kremer, and when he returned home he discussed the matter with Mill in Warsaw and others in Vilna. They decided to organize a congress of Jewish social democrats quickly. (Mill, however, recalled that Kremer made his trip in 1896, indicating—as does other evidence—that the idea of a united Jewish movement was mulled over earlier than 1897. In 1896, Mill was working very hard with a small group of Jewish social democrats in their struggle against the PPS. "No other group," Mill wrote, "was as interested at that time in the founding of the party as the Jewish workers of Warsaw.") [31]

Kremer himself, before he left for Switzerland, observed that "the creation of a general party, not only a Jewish one, is being considered . . . and will be decided in the near future." [32] Furthermore, in the spring of 1897, the social democrats of Kiev circulated a plan to unite all social-democratic groups, further prodding the Vilna group to hasten the formation of a special Jewish organization or, at least, make a decision. Thus, at the very outset, the innate, never quite resolvable duality of the Bund was revealed: its desire to struggle for the freedom of Jewish workers within a separate Jewish organization, and its desire to struggle for the freedom of all workers as part of the larger movement. One force would always tug at the other.

The founding congress of the Bund was low-keyed, practical in every aspect, and exceptionally careful about security arrangements. Kremer was apparently ready to call off the meeting even as delegates were arriving in Vilna because of the stepped-up vigilance of the police, but was dissuaded by Mill.[33] Several delegates were informed of the time and place of the meeting in coded messages in newspapers. Only thirteen delegates were invited by the Vilna group—activists in Minsk, Bialystok, Warsaw, Vitebsk, and Vilna itself.[34] The sessions were held in a small house, far from the center of town, on October 7–9, 1897. The time coincided with the Jewish high holidays and was chosen so that delegates would seem to be traveling to see friends. Although no official records were kept, Kosovsky took notes for *Di Arbayter Shtimme*. At no time did all of the delegates meet at once.

The six Vilna delegates, including three workers, dominated the meetings, and Kremer's plea for unity among Jewish socialists was the dominant note. For all practical purposes, he said, Jewish workers and social democrats in a number of cities were now bound together in a common struggle; all that remained was to "pour this existing unity into a mold so that it will have a definite form." The government, he added, was threatening these bonds by attacking Jewish workers and arresting leaders. A central organization was urgently needed—one that would function without dealing directly with the workers, thus avoiding police attacks and keeping the cities from becoming isolated. Moreover, political rights for Jews had to be pressed:

> A general union of all Jewish socialist organizations will have as its goal not only the struggle for general Russian political demands; it will also have the special task of defending the particular interests of the Jewish workers, carrying on the

struggle for the civic rights of the Jewish workers and, above all, carrying on the struggle against the discriminatory anti-Jewish laws. This is because Jewish workers suffer not only as workers but also as Jews, and we must not and cannot remain indifferent at such a time.[35]

As to the question of a general Russian socialist party, Kremer said such a time was drawing near, that the Jewish working masses would share in that movement, but that they could not enter the party divided into separate groups. He urged the use of Yiddish as a practical expedient to assure effective development of a segment of the Russian proletariat. National issues were to be treated functionally, not ideologically; Jewish autonomy was essential but only to serve practical revolutionary needs. The language of the meeting, interestingly enough, was Russian, rather than Yiddish, and although the delegates reserved the right to make all decisions on Jewish matters in the forthcoming all-Russian party and enter as an autonomous group, Jewish problems as such were bypassed.

A central committee was formed consisting of Kremer, Kosovsky, and Abram Mutnikovich (all from Vilna), with *Di Arbayter Shtimme* as its official organ. After much debate, the name "The General Jewish Workers' League in Russia and Poland" [36] was adopted—a concession to those who felt that the words "social democratic" would frighten some workers. However, local committees could use that designation if they chose. The popular name *Der Bund* (The League, or Alliance, in Yiddish) was soon widely used.

Kosovsky, whose real name was Nahum Levinson, was the outstanding theorist and publicist of the early movement. He did much of the writing and editing of *Di Arbayter Shtimme*, guiding the workers and "half-intellectuals" who created the paper, and writing many of the Bund's publications. Later, he became a leading proponent of the Bund's program of national-cultural autonomy. Mutnikovich had belonged to Narodnaya Volya in Kovno. He was expelled from school for his revolutionary activity and went to Berlin in the 1880's to study and become acquainted with the German labor movement. He was expelled from Germany and returned to Russia—to Ponevezh—where he was soon arrested. From 1894 on, he was one of the central figures among the Vilna social democrats. (In 1896 he wrote an important detailed report of the movement's activities for the Socialist International held in London that year.)

The emergence of a separate Jewish social-democratic movement and the founding of the Bund in 1897 did not signify any break in former sympathies. The Bund was certainly never conceived as a breakaway from the Russian movement; rather, its founding was intimately connected with the forthcoming First Congress of the Russian party. Tsoglin (David Katz), who participated in both, insists that the major considerations were of a practical, not ideological, nature. He also adds the interesting point that the Russian social democrats were considered too lax in matters of conspiracy, and that it was therefore considered safer for the Jewish organizations to be related to the party indirectly through their own leadership rather than through individual membership.[37]

The founding congress of the Bund joined together Jewish workers and intellectuals in a common acceptance of the mission of the Jewish proletariat. An organization had been forged which, if it lacked a thoroughly worked out ideology, bound the movement and the members to each other in a strong commitment. In the beginning, the Jewish socialists found themselves deeply involved in a predominantly Jewish movement. Yet, as Kremer recalled, "in no sense did the initial founders carry on extensive work among the Jewish masses; they wished merely to create a few more developed workers, to make them class-conscious socialists, to prepare them for agitation in Russia, in the industrial centers among the Russian working class." Yet a separate organization of Jewish workers and socialist intellectuals had been formed. A structure now existed to give form and direction to a movement seeking freedom and dignity for Jewish workers. This initial grounding of the Bund in particular Jewish conditions was to complicate its subsequent relations with the larger Russian movement and create certain tensions and vacillations, as well as strengths, in the whole of its life as a movement.

17. The Early Years of the Bund, 1897-1901

The first central committee of the Bund functioned for ten turbulent months. It swiftly established formal relations with local committees and the scattered Russian and Polish socialist groups, operated an active, secret press—moving first from Vilna to Minsk, then further southeast to Bobruisk—smuggled illegal literature into Russia, and made important political decisions. From the start, for the sake of security, the three members of the central committee deliberately isolated themselves from other members and left Vilna, disappearing in Minsk, where even Minsk members were unaware of their presence.[1] *Di Arbayter Shtimme* became the central political organ.

The new organization also quickly attracted the attention of the non-Jewish revolutionary world—not all of it admiring. At first Mill was enthusiastic about the response in Warsaw to the founding of the Bund and concluded that the admiration must be quite general throughout Poland.[2] But this was far from the case in the Polish provinces or elsewhere. Some social-democratic groups were openly opposed to the organization of a separate party of Jewish workers; others objected to strike agitation. Kremer tells of his night-long arguments with resisters.[3] The cities of Gomel and Grodno were especially recalcitrant and did not join the Bund until 1900. In Riga and Lodz, however, the formation of the Bund seemed to sharpen the direction of loose, existing groups.

In Poland, the reaction of the PPS was vehemently hostile. In November 1897, at its own Fourth Congress, it attacked the Bund's goal of joining the Russian socialists as "the denial of solidarity with the Polish and Lithuanian proletariat in their struggle for liberation." It also criticized the Bund as an offspring of the bourgeoisie that had prevented an alliance of Jewish and Christian workers, and predicted that its program would fan anti-Semitism. Kosovsky wrote a strong counter-blast,[4] meeting each charge incisively and rubbing in the inconsistencies and confusions in the PPS attack. He asked what the PPS had done for Jewish workers in areas where they were weak, chided it for not fighting the anti-Semitism of Polish workers and exposing its own anti-Jewish prejudice by raising the spectre of anti-Semitism. In the following year, the central committee also issued a strong rebuttal, reaffirming the Bund's connection (by 1898) with the new all-Russian party, in contrast with the narrow nationalist position of the PPS, and the necessity of Jewish workers fighting for equal civil rights.

The problem of forming this all-Russian socialist party involved the Bund even more; nothing had greater importance for them, and they became prime movers in its formation. It was for this purpose, indeed, that the Bund was founded. Building on earlier contacts with social democrats in St. Petersburg and Kiev, Kremer visited both cities soon after the Bund founding congress to discuss the matter of a general party.[5] Technical arrangements, requiring complete secrecy, were made by the Bund, which not only served as host but also provided machinery and type for the press. Nine delegates, representing four cities and the Bund (which sent three delegates, including Samuel Katz, the only worker who attended) met on March 1, 1898, in Minsk and deliberated for three days over many of the same practical problems that had faced the Bundists: the need for unity and an organizational network to effectively mount a struggle against the regime.[6] After considerable debate, a name was chosen—the Russian Social Democratic Workers' party (RSDWP)—and a central committee was created, on which Kremer represented the Bund. In all problems related to Jewish workers, the Bund was given full autonomy; no one objected. This question would later become a burning issue for the Russian movement, but at the moment the Bund had all the autonomy it wanted, namely, the freedom to handle its own literature and conduct the economic and political struggle on behalf of Jewish workers.

The RSDWP was a fundamental step toward uniting Russian Marxists, but it was a fragile base of perhaps no more than a few hundred individuals in scattered cities. Moreover, it lacked the organizational cohesion and discipline of the Bund. Personal ties were not as strong as those within the Bund. Large segments of the movement were not present for various reasons, and as if to foreclose all promise of a future, its frail beginnings were soon wrecked. No sooner had the first RSDWP congress ended than a wave of arrests all but crushed both it and the central committee of the Bund. The actions of the government had made clear that the workers could not hope for reforms, but must prepare for revolution. Frightened by the increasing use of workers' funerals and demonstrations to protest intolerable working conditions, the government cracked down with call-ups of army recruits, deportation of political prisoners, and arbitrary arrests.

In 1897 a new colonel of the police named Vasilev was appointed in Vilna. When he declared that it was already too late to stop the movement, S. V. Zubatov, head of the Moscow Okhrana (secret police), was dispatched to Vilna to study the situation. His agents had already made inroads in the Moscow labor movement and followed the trail of some of the RSDWP delegates to Minsk, which led them to Kremer and other Bund leaders. In March, 1898, a wave of arrests felled the RSDWP and in July, Kremer, Mutnikovich, Kosovsky, and many other Bund activists as well as the press operators, were arrested [7]—seventy in all. Many important links were destroyed. Curiously, the Bund knew it was being watched and trailed but was busy with "pressing problems," including work for the RSDWP, and felt strong enough to resist Zubatov,[8] but miscalculated his patience and cunning. The Bund central committee was wiped out and the vital presses in Bobruisk and Minsk were seized without which, it was said, "we would become dumb."

The Bund reeled back, but as the first shock of the losses wore off, solid reserve forces among organizers, agitators, and technicians in the local centers came forth to create a new center. David Katz, a member of the Vilna committee, began to reestablish addresses, contacts, and codes, and started routine work. Within a few months a new Bund congress was convened, and illegal literature and *Di Arbayter Shtimme* began reappearing.[9] A new group of leaders emerged—Katz, Leon Bernshtein, Sendor Zeldov, Bainish Mikhalevich, and Tsvia Hurvich—who had strong roots in the movement and were by now toughened agitators. Younger, largely self-taught, and Yiddish-speaking, they were quite different from the first group of leaders. They also seem to have had a more natural access to workers and looked upon the working masses as a natural focus of activity.[10]

One of their first efforts involved the convening of a Second Congress—this time in Kovno, in September 1898. Besides the six towns that were represented, there was a representative from the Bristle Workers' Union. A highly developed movement, the "Jewish Bristle-Workers' Union in Poland and Lithuania" was established earlier in 1898, the only example at the time of an organized trade union of workers in a single trade encompassing several towns and cities. Such a pioneering effort was made possible by the nature of the industry, which was extremely well-organized and employed mobile but homogeneous work forces in various cities. The workers organized largely in border areas (incidentally rendering valuable service to the Bund's smuggling of literature into Russia) and in Warsaw, Bialystok, and Smorgon as well as Vilna.[11] At first preoccupied with the struggle to improve economic conditions, by 1898 the Bristle Workers' Union declared its allegiance to the Bund and joined the struggle against the regime. By 1900 the union claimed a membership of eight hundred workers.

The Second Congress of the Bund deliberated for three days, discussing local conditions, the economic struggle, aid for arrested comrades (they had all been sent to Moscow), illegal literature, relations with other revolutionary parties, and the naming of a new central committee.[12] The arrests had not disrupted the local groups; indeed, delegates reported a growing political consciousness among Jewish workers and increased growth in Lodz and Warsaw. Strikes were spreading, but fewer of the strikers were formally organized in *kassy*, a situation that required the dissemination of literature to the non-*kassa* worker.

The question of disseminating major socialist works also drew the attention of the delegates, many of whom were self-educated workers. Cheap editions of the *Communist Manifesto* and Kautsky's *Erfurt Program* were published in Yiddish. The shortage of literature encouraged the development of local organs to supplement *Di Arbayter Shtimme*. Minsk, Warsaw, and Bialystok soon followed the example of Vilna's *Der Klasen-Kamf (The Class Struggle)* and the Bristle Workers' Union started its *Der Veker (The Awakener)*.[13]

Although the RSDWP was all but defunct, the Bund deferred to it on the still troublesome question of the PPS. Continuing its cautious and pragmatic approach to problems, the Second Congress also urged restraint in the use of strikes and took a position against terrorism. David Katz, Tsvia Hurvich and Sendor Zeldov were elected to the new central committee. Thus despite the arrests and wiping out of the experienced leadership, the Bund held fast, mending and reforming where it had to, restarting the press, finding funds, looking to security. The new leaders had to acquire false papers and learn to live as illegals; they also had to throw over qualms they may have had about living on party funds. Katz and the others were not as well-educated or as confident as the earlier leaders, but they were every bit as dedicated, and soon enough gained confidence, experience, and balance.[14] The recovery of the movement from what might easily have been a mortal blow was both admired and envied by the Russian revolutionaries. It soon strengthened itself even more with a counterpart movement abroad.

As Katz and his comrades began rebuilding the Bund in Russia, Mill, who had left earlier to set up a press in Geneva and contact Jewish student colonies in Europe, organized vital support from the outside. Amazed by the resilience of the new leadership, Mill was inspired to work long hours and carry the burden of the work in the West. He set up a foreign committee—a kind of extended central committee—made up of emigré revolutionaries and enlisted expatriate students and sympathizers to contribute funds to the cause.[15] In an atmosphere of greater freedom and wider horizons, the intellectual radicals abroad were intensely interested in ideological issues, and the literary output of the foreign committee, helped by talented Jewish students in Berne, had a decided ideological cast. This literature was decisive in meeting the needs of the Bund in Russia. Of the twenty-two pamphlets published by the Bund between July 1898 and July 1900, fourteen came from the press in Geneva, totalling 52,000 copies.[16]

Publication, in fact, became the committee's chief activity; in 1899, it took over *Der Yidisher Arbayter*, making it virtually a journal, with Mill as editor. Mill also arranged for Vorwärts, the publishing house of the German social democrats, to transfer material from Switzerland to Russia, often in false-bottomed suitcases. Moreover, the foreign committee became a clearing house for distributing funds to political prisoners and their families and a repository of materials dealing with the Jewish workers' movement in Russia—the foundation of a Bund archive.[17]

Local Bund committees, meanwhile, were weaving their organizational course between the force of local needs and the guidance of the central committee, for the first few years working almost autonomously. Inasmuch as many Jewish workers were still not aware of the Bund's activity, or did not approve of a separate organization or of strikes, the work of reaching new workers and organizing them was the main task of the local committees. Personal contact was best, of course, but increasingly, organizers resorted to leaflets, mass meetings, and, occasionally, the presentation of a play. The Vilna May Day demonstration of 1899, involving only Jewish workers, seems to have been the first open, independent political expression of the all-Jewish movement, and this was a local responsibility.[18]

Considering the difficult problems facing local Bund groups, the growth of the movement was quite impressive: by 1900, it had at least 5,600 members and some loosely organized worker-circles.[19] Yet worker militancy frequently was carried on outside the framework of the Bund. Only the most courageous and dedicated were willing to risk membership in an illegal organization, but many new workers were newly recruited to the agitation program and, like their counterparts in America, waged strikes fearlessly.

The strike movement was naturally dominated by artisans, but gradually the more backward workers of the large cigarette and match factories were drawn into it.[20] In Vilna, the first strike by factory workers occurred at Edelshtein's cigarette plant in 1895, three years after the artisans had begun their organized drive.[21] In 1899, eight hundred women went on strike in Shereshevsky's cigarette factory in Grodno, and in the same year there was a strike—the first—in the Zaks' match factory in Dvinsk. The strike wave spread from the shops to the factories, and from the large centers to the smaller towns. Worker-agitators, some of them from the Bund, generally from larger centers, would spark a strike action. Once launched, a local strike movement could count on help from the nearest local Bund committee.[22] But in the provincial towns of Lithuania–White Russia, it was generally the workers themselves who initiated strike actions. Bund committees could exercise only a degree of control over the strike movement but their leadership was directive. The Jewish labor movement was not synonymous with the Bund, but "where the Bund committees did not exert some degree of influence, the Jewish labor movement of 1897–99 consisted largely of sporadic and local responses with no general aim and no real direction." [23]

Strikes, at least up to 1900, were usually successful, but only briefly so. Cuts of two to four hours per day and wage increases of one to two rubles a week were common and other grievances received some degree of redress. In a statistical study of the Jewish labor movement, Ber Borochov, a leading socialist Zionist, estimated that between 1895 and 1904, at least 2,276 strikes were conducted in the Pale by Jewish workers; between 1900 and 1904, there was an average of more than one a day, leading him to conclude that the strike movement of the Jewish workers in the Pale was of far greater intensity than any in the Western world.[24] (He considered the Jewish class struggle in Russia as essentially hopeless because of the poverty-stricken labor movement and the general decline of Jewish craft industries. As a Zionist, he thought that the Bund economic program was doomed to failure.) But this readiness to strike—so similar to the militancy of Jewish workers in America—was not due to any innate aggressiveness, but rather to the fragmented nature of the Jewish economy. The typical strike occurred in small shops,[25] where workers were more apt to risk the consequences of a strike than workers in a large factory and where, in fact, they struck time and time again—generally for a reduced workday. Statistically, their strikes counted as much as strikes in larger factories, but there was more desperation than promise in their struggle. The position of the small shopowners was almost as precarious as that of the workers. Many of them could not bear any increased labor costs and could not compete with the newer mechanized plants, often selling out to them or disappearing. Unemployment broke the spirit of many workers in the small shops, especially as they were rebuffed by the factories in their search for work.

The Bund committees played a considerable role in many of the strikes, contributing money, direction and literature, except where *kassy* and *skhodkas* were strong, in which case the Bund did not take a direct hand.[26] This was the case, for example, in Bialystok, where strike leadership came directly from the ranks of the workers. As yet, there were very few workers' organizations to deal with the larger firms. The Bund also had to face the increasingly serious problem of violence. The beating of strike breakers, the use of police spies, and employer recourse to the police were quite common, particularly in Dvinsk, despite the Bund's stand against political and industrial terror. In the embittered atmosphere of frustration and tension, the Bund, with its secret committees, also faced demands for greater organizational democracy, especially in Minsk, where the worker-committees controlling each trade opposed the local Bund committees.[27]

However, the most critical problem besetting the Bund at this time was the close collaboration between employers and government. Employers not only blacklisted "troublemakers," but refused to hire any worker suspected of belonging to the Bund, and frequently turned strike leaders over to the police.[28] Reprisals were heavy: between 1897 and 1900 almost one thousand people in the movement—workers and intellectuals—were arrested.

The use of Christian strikebreakers also posed serious dilemmas. If Jewish strikebreakers were employed, workers felt less inhibited about using strong-arm methods. Violence against Christians could easily lead to violent outbreaks of anti-Semitism and damage to the hope of international labor solidarity.[29] Such a double standard, however, naturally embittered most Jewish workers, the more so as Jewish employers persisted in using the tactic of employing Christian strike-breakers. Moreover, the gap between Jewish and non-Jewish workers remained virtually unbridgeable; anti-Semitism among Russian and Polish workers was rife.

Meanwhile, the Bund was under both external and internal pressure to confront the question of Jewish national needs. The publication of Herzl's *Judenstaat* in 1896 and the meeting of the first Zionist Congress in Basel in 1897 had sent shock waves throughout Jewish communities in Russia as well as Western Europe. The northwestern provinces were somewhat less aroused, but events elsewhere forced the Bund to consider the national question at its Third Congress in December 1899. Mill, who anticipated the strength of the national question as an issue for the Bund, interpreted Herzl's *Judenstaat* as a crucial moment:

> . . . After *Judenstaat* appeared and the idea of a Jewish state in Palestine began to spread gradually . . . it became clear that the Bund could no longer ignore the new movement. If not today, then tomorrow [Zionism] would appear among the Jewish masses in socialist dress to express the new aspirations among the Jewish petit bourgeoisie.[30]

The ideas of Zhitlovsky, Ahad Ha-Am, and Simon Dubnow also began to influence and provoke some Jewish socialists. Moreover, a very strong influence was exerted by large student groups in the universities and technical institutes of Switzerland, Austria, Germany, France, and Belgium. All of the Russian and Jewish revolutionary parties sought to recruit followers among the Jewish students from Russia. The largest groups were those of the Bund, and Bundist students in Berne, Berlin, Vienna, Zurich, and Geneva devoted a great deal of time studying and declaiming on the "Jewish Question" and national needs.[31]

One state in particular was the subject of the closest study, namely, Austria-Hungary, a classic example of a multi-national state, in which two famous social democrats, Karl Renner and Otto Bauer, were evolving concepts of national autonomy and "nonterritorial autonomy." The idea of a Jewish nationality deserving at least cultural autonomy was, however, rejected even by Bauer, who of all socialist theoreticians did most to make intransigeant internationalists accept the claims of oppressed nationalities to independence. "To contend that the Jews are not a nation," Bauer said, "is perhaps to go too far today, even in Western and Central Europe. But one may well contend that they are ceasing to be a nation." [32] The assimilating Jews of Western Europe seemed no longer to constitute a national group, but this was not the case with the large masses who could not break out of the Pale. Was this cultural-religious community, which had enjoyed a certain measure of autonomy under the most adverse conditions *not* a national minority group, entitled to self-determination like other national minorities? Though moribund in theory, Jews were very much alive in fact, and existed in Russia as a community *sui generis*, which even under tsarism had enough strength to develop cultural institutions, schools, and a labor movement. Should they not be accorded "nonterritorial autonomy"?

These ideas were discussed among Russian-Jewish student and intellectual circles in Switzerland and Germany with great intensity. In December 1899, the *Yidisher Arbayter* reported enthusiastically that the Brunn Congress of the Austrian Social-Democrats had organized their party along federal lines and declared that this "is already almost an answer to the national question." Stimulated by the two main ideas outlined, namely that the proletariat should be concerned about allowing national cultures to develop, and that even a people without a land could demand national rights, the editors admitted that the Bund, too, must give an answer to the national question. "What that answer will be, we do not know yet. But an answer there must be and the sooner the better." The idea of nonterritorial cultural autonomy was thus planted.

At this juncture, Mill was a key figure. As a representative of the new foreign committee, he brought to the congress a heightened interest in theoretical questions through close contact with many emigré radicals from Western Europe and with Polish socialists struggling for national independence. Moreover, as editor of *Der Yidisher Arbayter*, he published an important article by the revered Karl Kautsky, a leading German social democrat and Marxist exegete, dealing with the nationalities problem in the Austrian Empire. He also ran an article by Zhitlovsky, actually attacking Zionism, but raising the whole question of Jewish national feelings and rights, insisting that Jews indeed had a national culture.[33] Zhitlovsky's article drew an editorial comment claiming that the Jewish nation, like other nations, had to have equal political, economic, and national rights.

The problem of national rights and a national program for minority people was new to the international socialist movement and to Marxist theory, but Kautsky's insistence on grappling with the question forced radicals to take a fresh look at it. Kautsky believed that national feeling was natural, that diverse ethnic and cultural groups could live together peaceably, and that the proletariat need not be hostile to such movements. For the many nationalities within the Austrian Empire who could not acquire territory, the solution, in Kautsky's view, was cultural autonomy. Moreover, he insisted that the proletariat was not only not an enemy of such national movements, but wanted to see such movements continue to develop. A sense of national identity, he felt, was not at all inconsistent with internationalism.

The very name of Kautsky made discussion of the national issue important. The Russian social democrats were great admirers of German socialism, and few German socialists had more prestige than Kautsky. The delegates to the Bund Third Congress, however, were afraid that fully opening such an explosive question would divert the attention of the proletariat from class to national interests. Mill, however, insisted on putting it on the agenda and proposed that the Bund, acting on behalf of the Jewish proletariat, demand equal *national* as well as civil rights. But his proposal was strongly opposed. Some delegates were doubtful about the merits of dealing with national rights at all; others feared that national demands would hurt worker-solidarity. There was some fruitless debating, but it was agreed that there would be a full discussion at the next congress. Mill then opened *Der Yidisher Arbayter* to a further discussion of the question.

The congress took place in May 1901, by which time the Austrian social democrats had formally supported the notion of a union of equal national cultures in the Austrian empire. The weakening of the territorial principle and the emphasis on culture as an expression of national identification seems to have helped Bundists—especially the older leaders—accept the principle of cultural autonomy.[34] Much more than the veteran pioneers, a new crop of Yiddish-speaking members were also deeply concerned with Jewish national rights. Mill, meanwhile, had been using the services of Jewish students abroad, especially the Berne Group, to write and translate articles for *Der Yidisher Arbayter*. These various currents led Mill to say that "One could feel and see that the new tendencies had already won, and that the Bund was for a change in its program in the area of the Jewish question."[35]

By 1901, the issue had become more urgent and a finer articulation of the question was advanced. Between 1899 and 1901, many other changes, both internal and external, pushed the Bund to re-shape its positions on several other issues and change its tactics. The Bund also became a more self-conscious Jewish revolutionary organization during this period, putting it on a course both broader and narrower, and certainly more complicated than its early quite simple formulations heralded.

Within the Bund itself, the earlier intimacy among a small circle of comrades had given way to greater formality as police surveillance, organizational problems, and the rivalry of other socialist and national parties grew. The party's cohesion became more difficult and decisions could no longer be made by informal consensus.[36] Moreover, the relations between the local committees and the central committee became more complicated because of new problems and stretched lines of communication.[37] Yet at no time, apparently, did the central committee issue orders; rather, it made recommendations and suggestions to the local committees. The question of "rights" was not raised, and although there were many differences and conflicts, they appear to have been resolved on the "fundamental principle . . . that the movement be run on a basis of mutual trust and moral influence." [38] This pervasive mutual respect was probably the Bund's greatest strength.

During 1900-01, the Bund leadership recovered substantially from the effects of the arrests of 1896 and 1898 and showed impressive growth. Kremer, Kosovsky, and Mutnikovich, who were released from exile pending sentencing, fled Russia to Switzerland, which now became the site of the central committee, and rejoined the others. Another comrade, Noah Portnoy, escaped from exile in Siberia and was coopted to the central committee. He quickly became the single most important figure in the leadership left in Russia. In terms of organizational growth, the Bund added only seven new groups during this period, but it began to penetrate new areas in the southwest from Gomel to Berdichev and Zhitomir, following the migration of Jewish workers seeking work, and to Kiev, seeking to attract Jewish students there.[39] In the summer of 1900, some of these students began to organize Bund groups among Jewish workers in Kiev.

As organizers moved south, they found social democratic groups with a large Jewish composition in Kiev and Odessa. Some which were purely Jewish and preferred a separate organization joined the Bund; others preferred the RSDWP and were encouraged to remain, with the Bund providing Yiddish literature. The Russian party was still fragmented and weak, less a party than orbiting groups seeking a political star. Yet the Bund, though much stronger, continued to defer to it as a higher authority and did nothing to challenge or compete with it. The founding congress of the RSDWP had not placed any geographical limitations on the work of the Bund in dealing with problems affecting Jewish workers, but the Bund was very circumspect in its attitude toward an essentially nonexistent political parent. Within a short time, however, the scattered Russian movement was to feel the abrasive, brilliant force of Lenin, with fateful consequences both for it and for the Bund.

Another important Bund organizational drive during this period was directed at the tsarist army. The need for revolutionary propaganda in the army became acute as soon as the army was used against Russian workers in the first large-scale strikes. It became vital to explain to the Russian soldier, who was a worker or peasant in uniform, that the government was forcing him to attack his fellow Russians. Traces of such activity by Jogiches and Mill can be detected as early as the 1880's.[40] By 1899-1900, revolutionary agitation was fairly widespread in the army and numerous arrests were made. In Vitebsk, for example, in 1899, six workers were arrested during a demonstration protesting the induction of recruits—the first of its kind reported in the Bundist press.[41]

By 1900, the Bund was conducting systematic propaganda in the army. Revolutionary literature was disseminated in garrisons and some materials even appeared in officers' quarters. Inspired by the effectiveness of the propaganda distributed to the German, Swiss, and Belgian armies, the Vilna Bundists in May 1901 issued a proclamation "To the Officers," [42] distributed by disguised postmen to all officers of the 27th Infantry Division:

> We appeal to your intellect and heart. We wish to open your eyes to the full disgrace of your position, the baseness of your role—hangmen in the service of the police. . . . We ask you to reflect on the events about you and we are certain of the direction your sympathies will then take.

This was followed by an appeal to army recruits and a condemnation of Russian militarism and the treatment of Jewish soldiers:

> The dreadful days are approaching when hundreds of thousands of young people all over Russia will be wrested from their homes, friends and occupations and sent for four years to dingy, stuffy barracks. . . . Worse than any other is the Russian brand of militarism. The Asiatic despotic regime, which has 135 million in its iron grip, which suppresses every free word, every original impulse, which satisfies no one but a handful of bureaucrats—this regime could not last a day without the help of militarism.
>
> The Jewish soldier is treated with far greater brutality than all the others. Mockery and degradation are our lot even when we fulfill our duty to our sovereign and country. . . . What is the remedy for this military plague? Socialism! [43]

The proclamation ends with a rousing call to all soldiers to rally around the socialist banner together with other suffering Russians to end slavery and exploitation.

In 1902, the year of the great strikes, revolutionary agitation among soldiers was intensified by all revolutionary organizations throughout Russia. Numerous bloody clashes broke out between soldiers and workers where there was resistance. In setting forth guidelines [44] for this struggle, the Bund first urged workers to try to persuade soldiers not to shoot at them. There were also precise instructions on conduct during demonstrations and the technical organization of resistance, particularly the importance of disabling or killing commanders of units sent against demonstrators. This militant charge and a similar one by Lenin in his famous brochure *What Is To Be Done?* sparked the beginning of military revolutionary organizations in Russia and prepared the way for massive defections during the Russo-Japanese War of 1904–05.

This new activity and the widening work of "colonization" were quite substantial marks of Bundist influence, but the best energies of the movement in the early 1900's were spent battling a force that became known as "police socialism" or Zubatovism,[45] named after the head of the Moscow secret police. A one-time circle-member turned informer and policeman, and the man responsible for the Bund arrests in 1898, S. V. Zubatov aimed to destroy the workers' attachment to the Bund by luring them with economic benefits and legal trade unionism under the official shield of the government. All those he arrested were subjected to his lectures and harangues on the futility of illegal political activity in contrast with the concrete gains to be won through legal trade unionism. Shrewdly, he exploited the ongoing debates among Bundists and other radicals over the political versus the economic struggle. By appealing to the workers' economic self-interest and driving a wedge between workers and intellectuals, Zubatov hoped to divert the strike movement from its revolutionary path. By 1901, he had succeeded in promoting a "Jewish Independent Labor Party" in Minsk. Its manifesto stressed Zubatov's line: the Jewish working class demanded nothing more than "bread and knowledge" and rejected political ideas which were foreign to its aims.

Zubatovism gained followers in several cities but took root particularly in Minsk, the second most important city of the Jewish labor movement, where the Bund first came to Zubatov's attention. In the Minsk police chief Vasilev, he found a ready ally in his campaign; both men gave or promised funds and worked especially to win over shop assistants. Workers, attracted to the goals of legal trade unions, went over in large numbers to Zubatovism. By August 1901, there were six "independent" unions in Minsk—those of the carpenters, tinsmiths, bristle workers, binders, masons and locksmiths.[46] Committed as they were to improving economic conditions, these unions, ironically enough, were engaging in strikes supported by the police at a time when social democrats were laying more stress on the political struggle. In some instances, Vasilev went so far as to threaten shop owners: "You exploit the workers! You force them to labor to the point of exhaustion. You employ foreign labor.[47] You tell the workers that they are rebelling against the government! I am the guardian of governmental order and I demand that you satisfy the workers immediately!"[48] No Bundist agitator could have put the matter more pungently.

The materials and agents' reports gathered at the time of the Bundist arrests in 1898 had led the police to conclude that they were dealing with an important, well-disciplined political organization. Unproductive talks then with Kremer and Kosovsky led Zubatov to observe that "the Jewish movement produced an impression of some kind of mighty, almost unassailable force." Still, he tried to woo them. After Kremer was released in April 1900 (pending sentencing), Zubatov wired him asking him to come to Moscow for a talk; a little later he intimated that Kremer could influence the fate of his comrades.[49] Kremer fled the country; the Bund leadership could not be swayed. But Zubatov claimed that he had had "brilliant successes" with some of the prisoners. In 1900, a number of newly arrested young and inexperienced radicals were taken in by Zubatov's arguments and defected from the movement.

Zubatovism created a serious crisis for the Bund because it threatened the movement at a time when there was a severe economic depression in Russia and great reluctance to strike. Workers could be readily taken in by small concessions and the safety of legality. Zubatov's support of educational and cultural activities—especially the utilization of Yiddish literature and need for greater "democracy," and his deliberate strategy of casting suspicion on intellectuals—all seemed to offer a viable alternative to the Bund. The Bund fought back, but it was not easy to differentiate between someone who was working with the police and someone who merely agreed with the Zubatov line. The resort to legal processes to gain a twelve-hour day was, after all, an objective the Bund itself had recently endorsed. Moreover, the economic misery of Jewish workers complicated the problem. As more and more shops became mechanized, owners of small shops simply could not afford to make concessions. The economic struggle seemed self-defeating. The delegates to the Fourth Congress of the Bund in May 1901 had to admit that in some trades "economic improvement . . . can go no further under present conditions of production," and sought to reassess the value of an economic struggle that required great energy and effort without producing significant results.[50]

Moreover, an effort to shift to the political struggle could not be sustained. From April 1900, when Portnoy took over the *Di Arbayter Shtimme*, he had emphasized the importance of the political struggle and the state's role as enemy of the working class. Other Bund intellectuals expressed similar views, encouraging participation in demonstrations. Obviously, there was far less opportunity for mass participation in political activities than in the strike movement. The risks were much greater and the commitment to a political goal had to be much stronger. On May Day 1901, the Bund in Bialystok decided not to sponsor a demonstration because the city was swarming with police spies; after years of worker struggle in that city, the most that the Bund could organize that year was a demonstration on the occasion of a funeral of a bristle-worker. Some three thousand people attended—both Jews and Christians—and workers sang revolutionary songs and shouted, "Down with autocracy!"[51] Secret meetings commemorating the abolition of serfdom or the assassination of Alexander II were generally held in the forests where great precautions had to be taken to avoid the police. In the main, however, Jewish workers were opposed to political activism, their feelings ranging from apathy to outright hostility. They preferred "legal" strikes at this stage and were thus susceptible to Zubatovism. A cleavage threatened the unity of intellectuals and workers, creating a serious crisis for the Bund. Defectors began to agitate for a legal labor movement.

In the summer of 1900, the central committee distributed a leaflet, written by Portnoy, warning the workers against Zubatov: No true revolutionary could have any dealings with "such scum," and those who did, hurt the workers' cause and must be considered traitors and provocateurs.[52] The state's record of mass arrests was exposed as well as the government's fear of the workers' struggle for political power. It was apparent, the Bund argued, that the state feared the Bund so much it had to take over part of its program to destroy it. Autocracy was the mortal enemy of the working class; their interests were fundamentally incompatible. If Zubatov failed, where could the workers go?

But there were difficulties for the Bund. Clearly, not everyone who agreed with Zubatov was a provocateur or informer. Moreover, a large gap had been developing between the politically oriented intellectuals, some of whom were already thinking of the Bund as a political party,[53] and workers who saw it only as an instrument of the economic struggle. The existing Bund structure had not yet succeeded in welding together both top and bottom levels, and both economic and political tools, nor had the Bund's political definition of itself been precise enough. Zubatov's campaign forced the Bund to reexamine these questions at a time when the emphasis on economic activity threatened its revolutionary ideology.

The crisis over Zubatovism came at a very difficult time for the Bund. The economic struggle, having produced certain results, was, in a real sense exhausted. To many trades, as one historian has put it, "it no longer applied at all because what improvement was possible had already been attained; the funds [*kassy*] had lost their trade union character and in the absence of the constant stimulation of strikes, their existence was largely nominal—the masses had ebbed away from them, only their 'political members' remained . . ." [54]

The workers who were Bund members of course worried over the question whether they were dealing with provocateurs or honestly misguided people. Some also seem to have been genuinely convinced that they were fighting for the "independence" of the labor movement from the revolutionary struggle, with which they were not yet identified, even as they were aware of the oppressiveness of the regime and the protection of the gendarmerie they hated.

At the Fourth Bund Congress in April 1901, trade union funds were scarcely mentioned, and the decision to refrain from strikes was formulated—a decision that was unpopular with many Jewish workers. In the following year, Lenin's *What Is To Be Done?*—with its pressure on every revolutionary organization to "declare its independence from the economic movement" and stop diverting forces from the socialist struggle—created an anti-union orientation within the Bund. One member, M. Rafes, who worked in Vilna in 1902, critically analyzed the disruption this caused in the Bund:

> The whole summer passed in restructuring the organization. We started from the idea that separate trades—cobblers, let us say—if left to themselves and organized within trade limits, did not have a chance to come in contact with

Social-Democratic politics and were doomed to follow the line of trade-unionism. . . . *The economic organization was simply broken up.*

The politically more mature vanguard was torn from the economically organized mass and artificially regrouped. The six to seven hundred Jewish workers who comprised the tightly knit political organization of the Bund proper were broken up into groups *regardless* of their trades or, rather, *against* them: every group had to include different trades—cobblers, joiners, tailors.[55]

The resulting separation of the vanguard from the masses led the Bund to carry out a hasty reorganization that left the *kassa* as the base, but added an elective political council. This council included the experienced leaders of the economic struggle who continued the work of political agitation. At the time, however, these efforts were not very effective.

The problem of relations between Christian and Jewish workers was also a thorny one. In urging Jewish workers to struggle against Jewish shop owners, Bundists had to crush a deeply embedded notion of Jewish unity—a difficult enough task. But in their efforts to overcome the barriers separating Jewish and Christian workers, age-old, burnt-in hatreds had to be broken. Occasionally this was achieved through the initiative of Jewish bristle makers and tanners, but non-Jewish workers in the great Jewish socialist centers such as Vilna and Minsk were not generally drawn into the orbit of Bundist propaganda or agitation.[56] Centuries of hostility and the exploitation of this hostility by employers and police made it impossible to organize a multi-national labor movement in the Pale. Moreover, it was in this very area that Christian workers did not even respond to Russian or Polish socialists, whereas the level of class-consciousness among Jewish workers was high. There were scattered occasions of worker solidarity—in strikes, demonstrations and at funerals of dead comrades, but no potentially strong mixed labor base ever developed in the northwest or elsewhere.

A vivid experience recounted by Leon Bernshtein in a talk with the Polish socialist Feliks Dzierzyński shows how great the gap was. Dzierzyński (who later became the head of Cheka, the Bolshevik counterintelligence organization) was in close touch with Bundists and, wanting to make contacts in Kovno, asked Bernshtein for help. A meeting was arranged with the remarkable Liza Epstein and her husband.[57] Liza was a self-educated, resourceful Bund organizer and activist who worked as a tailor. As Bernshstein and Dzierzyński left the Epsteins, Dzierzyński admitted ruefully that he would not have been able to meet Bernshtein in the home of the most devoted Christian socialist workers, for the best of them were still afflicted with anti-Semitism. "To succeed in our mass agitation," he said, "we have to avoid certain questions."

Zionism was also making inroads among Jewish workers and pressing the Bund further to define itself. The political blurring among Jewish workers was so widespread that as late as December 1900, the official Bund paper *Der Minsker Arbayter (The Minsk Worker)* was insisting that there ought not be any hostility between social democratic and Zionist workers, since Zionists also participated in the economic struggle.[58] Actually, this was not so strange, because Zionism was beginning to appeal to some workers. Socialist-Zionist groups were already forming in Russia in 1900–01 and Syrkin's and Zhitlovsky's essays began to stimulate discussion of the possibility of fusing socialism and Zionism. In Minsk particularly, where Zubatovism was already strong, the Bund also felt attrition from Jewish workers who were joining socialist-Zionist groups.

For the Bund, a labor-oriented Zionism—no matter how limited its influence at first—posed a new challenge and need for further political definition. There was now an alternative to the Bund where none had existed before. On a much less vehement note than was to be true later, Bundists carried on debates and discussions with Zionists, and Zionism became an increasingly conspicuous subject in Bundist publications. However, Zubatov's wooing of Zionists in *his* fight against the Bund gave a bitter edge to the intensifying conflict and drove Bundists and labor Zionists further and further apart. By 1901, at the Fourth Congress, the Bund banned all Zionists from its organizations, signaling an unceasing ideological struggle.

Meanwhile, largely under prodding by Mill, who had a natural inclination to confront the "national question," the Fourth Congress took an important incremental step in defining itself as a *Jewish* organization. For fifteen months prior to the congress, local committees had discussed the national question in all its aspects. This was to be the central question before the Congress, the outcome of which marked a major ideological shift for the Bund, although at the time it was seen only as an incremental step, a progressively logical development of what had gone before. The new formulations of the Austrian social democrats at their Brunn Congress [59] also played a role in this change. By 1900 Austrian socialists were proposing the concept of a federated union made up of culturally autonomous nationalities as a solution to the problem of the diverse empire and its numerous minorities. Why, then, not grant equality of national culture to Jews? Kremer raised the possibility of writing on Yiddish schools, which a new member, Ben-tsion Hofman (Zivion), took up in *Der Yidisher Arbayter*. Another new member, Mark Liber, debated the question of Jewish national rights in Berne in 1900 and soon became one of the Bund's strongest advocates of national autonomy. The Bund's foreign committee also began thinking of the Bund as having a *national Jewish* image.

Like their Austrian counterparts, the Bund delegates to the Congress agreed that in addition to economic, civil and political rights, each nationality has *national* aspirations.[60] They also agreed that the concept of nationality applied to the Jewish people. Moreover they felt that the principle of self-determination, as announced by the RSDWP in 1898, had to be elaborated. The territorial solution was categorically rejected;

national autonomy was seen as the only guarantee of national rights. Beyond these points, however, there was wide-ranging disagreement. Liber wanted practical work to raise Jewish national consciousness to begin at once. Others like Pavel Rosenthal believed that the national question was actually "alien to the masses at the present time," that Jews must be drawn out of their isolation toward cooperation with the Christian proletariat and parties, and that "national self-consciousness" verged dangerously on "bourgeois" nationalism. Other delegates took a middle position. At the end, a statement of principle, rather than a demand, was written into a resolution and adopted without discussion, thus moving the Bund further along in its historic course toward an independent Jewish radical party. The resolution affirmed that:

> It is against the sense of the social-democratic program to allow for the oppression of one class by another, of citizens by the government, and also of one nationality by another and one language by another. The conference holds that a state such as Russia, consisting as it does of many nationalities, should, in the future, be reconstructed as a federation of nationalities with complete national autonomy for each nationality, independent of the territory in which it is located. The conference holds that the term "nation" is also to be applied to the Jewish people. In the light of existing circumstances however, it is still too soon to put forth the demand for national autonomy for Jews and hence . . . for the time the struggle is to be carried on only against all discriminatory laws directed against Jews . . . [and] against any suppression of the Jewish nationality, but at the same time care must be taken not to fan national feeling into a flame, for that will only obscure the class consciousness of the proletariat and lead to chauvinism.[61]

Meanwhile, relations with the still fragmented, and weak but surviving Russian party (RSDWP) were moving the Bund toward more explicit self-definition, unintended independence, and sharpened conflict with the mother party. A curiously ambivalent attitude toward the RSDWP developed—partly self-assertive, partly deferential, out of step with the wished-for guiding force, unable or unwilling to stop its own development, yet pulled back by the asymmetry of a potentially great but weak parent party and a much stronger, better disciplined, and more developed constituent.

The Bund's drive for support abroad and growing popularity in American radical circles drew it into what was considered perverse competition with Russian social democratic forces. Pavel Akselrod complained bitterly to Lenin over the small amounts of money coming in. At the same time, the Bund, feeling that it had become a real force in the Russian revolutionary movement, pressed for a large delegation to the forthcoming International Congress in Paris (September 1900). "We have the right to be represented by a large delegation," wrote Mill, "which would reflect our strength, our work and our real significance. . . ."[62] Eleven Bund delegates attended the congress—the largest single group in the Russian delegation—with twice as many votes as the Liberation of Labor Group (which had represented the whole Russian social democratic movement in 1896). Self-confident and proud of their achievements, they submitted a report on the struggle being waged by Jewish workers in the Pale and an account of the Bund's history. Akselrod and the Liberation of Labor were also infuriated by this assertiveness of the Bund, further chilling relations that had grown very cool between the Vilna Social Democrats and the Plekhanovites even before the Bund was formed. Personal relations were not cordial, and the publication of Kremer's *On Agitation* had dragged on for several years. But besides this, the Plekhanovites thought that the Jewish social democrats were not doing anything to secure political allies for the political struggle, and, in fact, were placing too much stress on the economic struggle and delaying or subverting the deep revolutionary elements of Marxism. Believing that the political struggle developed out of the economic, and that both were indeed part of an organic process, the Bund did not tear itself apart over this question as did the Russian social democrats [63] and never gave the Plekhanovites the support they wanted within the "Russian" movement. Undoubtedly, the Plekhanovites were also envious of the head start the Jewish social democrats had achieved through their own press, literature, and influence over thousands of workers. These hostilities were open, but the Bund did not spend any of its energies in theoretical or tactical controversies with its Russian comrades. This very neutrality turned the Bund upon itself, its own organizational problems and the needs of Jewish workers—all of which strengthened its habits of independence, its view of itself as a single mass organization, and its divergence from the Russian movement. Meanwhile, developments of great significance for the Bund and the Russian revolutionary movement were beginning to unfold, imperceptibly at first. The hatching-ground was the Siberian exile of Lenin.

During his four-year exile, Lenin had read omnivorously, studied, written, and argued sharply over interpretations of Marx and watched with dismay the disintegration of the RSDWP. During the last year of his sentence, in 1899, together with his fellow exiles Martov and Alexander Potresov, he began to make plans for a united, disciplined revolutionary organization and a new revolutionary paper. Early in 1900, he settled in Pskov, near the Estonian border; the others joined him there later and organized agents for the distribution of the new paper. Eventually, one by one, they made their way to Geneva, with Potresov obtaining funds from wealthy relatives. In Geneva, where they sought Plekhanov's collaboration, there were difficulties. Plekhanov, Akselrod, and Zasulich were by now old-guard Marxists, removed from the day-to-day life in Russia. Lenin, Martov, and Potresov were young, more rigidly doctrinaire and opposed to any watering down of orthodox Marxism, but Plekhanov still enjoyed a unique authority as the theoretician of the party, which Lenin, as yet unknown, was slow to challenge. However, with the founding of *Iskra* (*The Spark*), designed as a central party organ to make the workers conscious of their importance, Lenin pressed ahead with his ideas and single-minded plans. Plekhanov, Akselrod, and Zasulich, together with Lenin, Martov, and Potresov formed the first editorial board, but Lenin very quickly emerged as the ideological pacesetter. He knew exactly what he wanted: an accepted body of revolutionary doctrine capable of uniting the fragmented groups and an organized revolutionary party. *Iskra* was designed to give "a definite physiognomy and organization" to the scattered social democratic groups. Moreover Lenin was determined to be at the center of the rebuilding of the party.

Iskra was printed in Germany in tiny type on thin cigarette paper and financed by a variety of sources—a Russian bookseller, German social democrats, and Russian exiles. The first issue appeared in December 1900, but never reached Russia; it was seized at the border by the police. But soon a network of underground smugglers perfected their craft and became the organizational network of a party that did not as yet exist. Inside Russia, *Iskra* came to have an almost mystical importance; here was the spark that would ignite the revolution at last. Contributors—especially Lenin—became familiar and inspiring names.

The *Iskra* group at first had good relations with the Bund, and Lenin himself was critical of Plekhanov for his attacks. The first issue of *Iskra* had even pointed to the Bund as an efficient organization the Russians would do well to emulate. Plekhanov objected to such "glorification," but was overruled. But soon Martov began criticizing the Bund's neglect of political work and its narrow concentration on Jewish workers instead of the Russian masses.[64] The Bund leaders became uneasy; Portnoy, the Bund's chief organizer in Russia, was frankly alarmed. Kosovsky feared dictatorial tendencies in *Iskra*. This new quarter of controversy—and later, hostility—further plunged the Bund into a more precise definition of itself as a Jewish workers' party even as it battled to be part of the general Russian socialist movement.

18. *The Struggle with Lenin*

Open conflict between the Bund and the Iskraites flared after the Fourth Congress passed the resolution on Jewish cultural autonomy. Its growing concern with the national question led the Bund to reexamine its relationship to the still-fragmented RSDWP. Some delegates considered the Bund's autonomous status inadequate and proposed a federative plan for consideration by the next congress. It was also decided to create new Bund organizations in southern Russia to serve the needs of Jewish workers who were not being reached by Russian groups, without in any way hurting the Russian movement.[1]

When these resolutions appeared, the Iskraites challenged them, with Martov leading the attack. He criticized the growing "nationalism" among the Jewish social democrats and asked mockingly if there would be "self-ruling communes" wherever the Jewish population formed a majority of the population. The main evil choking the Jewish masses, he held, was the regime; by moving toward nationalism, the Bund was making a great political error and weakening its ties with the general workers' movement. The Bund replied in a letter to *Iskra* (August 1901) that its concept of Jewish national autonomy referred to national expression in language, education, and art, not territorial independence; that once a nationality is aware of itself, it must acknowledge itself openly and permit for Jews what is considered just for all nationalities.[2]

Other Iskraites frankly doubted that Jews had a national culture or that present differences justified future self-determination—as acknowledged in the party manifesto of 1898. Lenin himself accepted in principle the right to self-determination, but only conditionally. Such support, he said, must be subordinated to the struggle of the proletariat. Plainly, the Iskraites had no alternative to the Bund proposals for Jewish autonomy. Their chief concern was a united party organization, and they were determined not to allow anything to deflect them from their course. Clearly, they did not want any competitors.

Russian sympathizers interviewing Jewish victims of the Kiev pogrom, 1881.

...tle page of Abba Braslovsky's Yiddish transla-...n of Karl Marx's *Wage-Labor and Capital*,...blished in 1888. Note the stamp of the...ddish-speaking Branch No. 8 of the Socialist...abor party. (*New York Public Library, Jewish...ivision*)

Title page, in Yiddish, of the constitution of the United Cloth Hat and Capmakers of North America, 1901.

Striking shirtwaist makers selling copies of *The Call*, New York socialist daily. (*Munsey's*, 1910)

A commentary on the Triangle Fire, 1911. Cartoon titled "Harvest of Death" in the New York *American*.

Fellow Workers!

Join in rendering a last sad tribute of sympathy and affection for the victims of the Triangle Fire. THE FUNERAL PROCESSION will take place Wednesday, April 5th, at 1 P. M. Watch the newspapers for the line of march.

צו דער לויה שוועסטער און ברידער!

די לויה פון די הײליגע קרבנות פון דעם טרייענגעל פייער וועט זיין
מיטוואך, דעם 5טען אפריל, 1 אזהר נאכמיטטאג.

קינער פון אײך מעך ניט פערבלײבען אין די שעפער! שליסט זיך אן אין די רייהען
פון די טרויער-לעװאנד! דרוקט אויס אײער סימפּאטיע און טרעגט בעדיינערג אין אייר דעם
נרויסען פערלוסט װאס די ארבײטסקלאסע האט געהאט

נעכיינען די קנפ – כים ציטעתעטע הערצער זעלען מיר פירהען אונזעתע בהיינתע
ספאקטע צו זייער לעצטער רוה.

וועמט די דייפונגען דורך װילכע מיר וועלען לעזען וויסען וואו אייזר קענען זיך
צוזאמעו קומען.

צו דער לויה פון די הײליגע קרבנות,
סאמע שוועסטער און ברידער!

Operai Italiani!

Unitevi compatti a rendere l'ultimo tributo d'affetto alle vittime dell'imane sciagura della Triangle Waist Co. IL CORTEO FUNEBRE avrà luogo mercoledi, 5 Aprile, alle ore 1 P. M. Traverete nei giornali l'ordine della marcia.

Call to the funeral procession for the victims of the Triangle Fire. (*ILGWU, New York*)

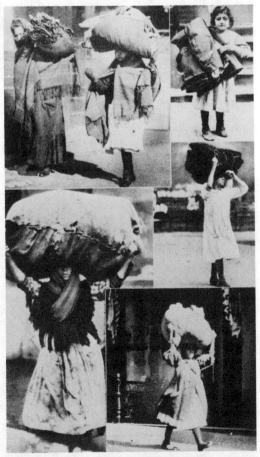

Carrying cut goods for work at home on New York's Lower East Side. (*YIVO Institute for Jewish Research*)

Typical sweatshop in a contractor's apartment. (*Jacob A. Riis Collection, Museum of the City of New York*)

United Garment Workers in Union Square, New York, March 1, 1913, protesting a settlement made by union leaders.

Selling wares on the Lower East Side, New York. (*YIVO Institute for Jewish Research*)

e Forward Building, 175 East oadway, New York City, erected 1912. (*YIVO Institute for Jewish search*)

Jacob Gordin

Abraham Liessin. (*YIVO Institute for Jewis Research*)

Abraham Cahan. (*Jewish Daily Forward*)

Morris Hillquit. (*Jewish Daily Forward*)

Morris Winchevsky. (*YIVO Institute for Jewish Research*)

Chaim Zhitlovsky. (*YIVO Institute for Jewish Research*)

Sketch of Morris Rosenfeld by Jacob Epstein, 1901. (*YIVO Institute for Jewish Research*)

Vladimir Kosovsky. (*Bund Archive*)

Arkady Kremer. (*Bund Archive*)

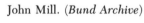

John Mill. (*Bund Archive*)

Vladimir Medem. (*Bund Archive*)

Noah Portnoy. (*Bund Archive*)

Aaron Lieberman (seated, third from right) and the Vilna circle. (*YIVO Institute for Jewish Research*)

D. Gordon. (*Zionist Archives and Library, New York*)

Ber Borochov. (*Zionist Archives and Library, New York*)

Arthur Ruppin. (*Zionist Archives and Library, New York*)

Nachman Syrkin. (*Zionist Archives and Library, New York*)

Degania Aleph, 1910

Martov also criticized the Bund for carrying its organizational expansion to the south, where Jewish and non-Jewish workers were known to be working together and where the Iskraites were also organizing. The Jewish workers, they said, would not respond sympathetically to the Bund's "national passion." The question of a federated party, which had also been raised by the Bund, was interpreted as if the Bund had presented the party with a *fait accompli*. Other misunderstandings made contacts abrasive or at best, cool. The fundamental problem seems to have been one of contrasting development. The Bund was already carrying on all or most of the activities it wanted to see undertaken by the all-Russian party, whereas other parts of the social-democratic movement were much weaker. The Iskraites were afraid the Bund position would shatter what was already, in Lenin's words, in a "deplorably weak state." Akselrod described the Iskraites as "a talented literary group . . . devoid of the slightest following or operational basis abroad," while, by contrast, the Bund was active and effective. But Lenin saw far beyond the mere problem of contrasting development. The Bund was blocking his vision.

The Bund's close ties with the Union of Russian Social Democrats Abroad (and the Bund's foreign committee's autonomy on Jewish matters within the Union Abroad) also rankled the Iskraites. When the Iskraites broke with the union and demanded that the Bund do likewise, the Bund refused. Speaking for the Bundists, Kremer reminded the Iskraites that the union was still the official representative of the RSDWP and that the Bund would remain in it until a congress decided otherwise.[3]

These open quarrels ended temporarily in the summer of 1901, but there was no reconciliation of views. Then, in March 1902, the Iskraites sabotaged plans for the convening of an RSDWP congress to put an end to the party's disunity. Somewhat defensive and eager to anchor itself in an all-Russian movement, the Bund had searched for the elusive unifying key for the social democratic movement. Feelings of discouragement and even isolation were commonly expressed. Finally, late in 1901, the Bund itself made arrangements for an RSDWP congress in Bialystok. The Bund foreign committee and the Union Abroad made the necessary contacts in the West. The Iskraites, however, regarded the proposed meeting with distaste. Lenin's wife Krupskaya wrote that "no one was taking the Bund's attempt to convoke a congress in Bialystok seriously." A small delegation responded and met in April 1902. Knowing that the Iskraites were still too weak and unprepared to build a party, Lenin used this meeting to plan a later full-scale congress which he could control, and sent a delegate, Theodor Dan, to read a statement pronouncing the meeting premature and insufficiently planned.

The meeting was inconclusive, but the *Iskra* delegate succeeded in having a committee set up to plan another congress later. A wave of arrests, which hit the Bund particularly hard, played into Lenin's hands. The Iskraites began to staff the new organization committee exclusively with their own people. The Bund, now hurt by the arrests, Zubatovism, the call for vengeance against the police, and the rising challenge of socialist Zionists, could not give this matter the importance or attention the Iskraites gave it, and the subsequently reconstituted planning committee was strongly pro-Iskraite.[4]

Meanwhile, the giant long-frozen body of Russia was stirring: "The air is heavy with ominous things; every day we see the glare of fires on the horizon; a bloody mist crawls over the ground," wrote a landowner in Voronozh in 1901. Demonstrations ceased to be little forlorn affairs managed only by fervent intellectuals; workers jammed the squares, hurled stones and curses at the police, and reformed after troops had passed through. There was animated talk among liberals and professionals; a Social Revolutionary party had formed to give leadership to the peasants. Even among civil servants, there were some who drew up illuminating and alarming reports urging reforms. The long-silent universities again rang with student speeches and strikes. Rich men began contributing to revolutionary movements. Even a few ministers to the tsar, like Sergei Witte, stopped at the foot of the throne. A weak despotic tsar was increasingly dominated by a narrow-minded, superstitious tsarina, and she, in turn, by the dissolute monk Rasputin—all of them obsessed with the survival of the hemophiliac male heir to the throne.

The level of unrest among workers and students had risen throughout Russia, pushing the government to drastic measures. Landlords had to account for their tenants' whereabouts at night; secret trials were held in military courts; anyone suspected of belonging to a secret organization could be held by the police for three months. Terrorism spread, fed by frustration and government repression.

The Fourth Bund Congress dealt directly with the issue of terrorism. Individual workers had retaliated against police and strike breakers for beating up their comrades, but the Bund, as an organization, rejected both defensive and political terror as inappropriate and inopportune. The use of terrorism, the resolution read, "blunts workers' social democratic consciousness, worsens their material situation, and discredits the labor movement." [5] Did this leave individuals free to work off their need for vengeance? The increased importance of demonstrations also meant that violence might erupt at Bund gatherings. This question became entangled in the tragic episode involving Hirsh Lekert, a Vilna shoemaker, which aroused Jewish workers to a fervent emotional pitch, and led to a firm position by the Bund.

In Vilna, a new governor, Viktor von Wahl, had inaugurated a savagely repressive policy toward political prisoners and suspects. His troops broke up the Bund's May Day celebration in 1902 and on the following day, six Polish and twenty Jewish workers who had been arrested were publicly whipped. Shattered by this blow at worker dignity, which the Bund had worked so hard to elevate, the Vilna committee of the Bund joined other social democratic organizations in drafting and distributing a leaflet which warned against the unleashing of popular vengeance and hatred: "We fight with peaceful means . . . but patience has its limits. It will not be our fault if popular vengeance, hatred, and resentment take on violent forms— Wahl himself has pointed out the path." [6] Listing the names of the major officials involved, the leaflet ended ominously: "Vengeance shall fall on each of you, and your names will be damned." On May 18, Lekert fired twice at Wahl, wounding him superficially. He was caught immediately and hanged on May 28.

In a movement that discouraged all symptoms of personality cultism and heroics and where anonymity prevailed, Lekert became its one martyr, a folk hero, and symbol of Jewish proletarian courage. His action was justified by the atmosphere of anguish and outrage. "Lekert is a Jew, Lekert came from the ranks of the workers . . . *for light wounds he had to pay with his head.*" Nevertheless his defense of a Jewish worker's honor came dangerously close to an act of defensive terror, which the Bund Congress had repudiated. Among workers, vengeful feelings rose. Some workers believed the assassination attempt would have succeeded had the Vilna committee itself organized it. The Bund now had to weave its way between condemning attacks on police and authorities in the populist terrorist tradition and defending organized acts of vengeance against officials who abused workers.

The central committee called a conference in Berdichev in August 1902 to thrash out this dilemma. Gozhansky came with a revolver; several delegates had recently come back from exile in Siberia. Strong passions overcame customary restraint. "It is absolutely clear," the delegates declared, "that we must protest with all our strength against such barbaric acts [those of Wahl]. . . . The honor of a revolutionary party demands revenge for the oppression of its members. . . . It would be a mistake to think that this kind of revenge has any relation to terror. . . . The aim of such acts is only to wash away the stain on the party, to take vengeance for a shameful insult." [7] As a precaution, the Bund took upon itself the sole right to organize such acts of reprisal.

Abroad and far from the seething events in Russia, the Bund foreign committee was openly critical of these views. Medem felt that there was little difference between organized revenge and organized terror and that such tactics would cause the degeneration of the movement.[8] Kosovsky, the most severe critic, warned that violence would become self-feeding and impossible to control. As a movement, he maintained, the Bund could not adopt the rules and goals of individuals answering insults; its answer to insult lay in the struggle to liberate the masses. Individuals had to defend their honor; the movement had to strengthen their sense of dignity and confidence and destroy the basis of terrorist feelings.[9]

At its Fifth Congress in June 1903, the Bund accepted Kosovsky's analysis and conceded that the Berdichev position was wrong. With hardly any debate on the question, the delegates rejected the principle of organized revenge as a form of terrorism, but their paper resolutions hardly settled the matter. Workers were bitter at this cool dismissal of a burning issue. Some left the Bund; others took to terrorism and were attracted by the pro-terrorist anarchists and the Social Revolutionary party, which had been founded in 1901. Ex-Bundist terrorist groups formed in Riga, Lodz, and Bialystok and provoked official denunciations from the Bund.[10]

The Bund, meanwhile, was a continuous target of abuse by the mass of traditionally orthodox Jews who shunned any political action. Their attitude is reflected in the irate proclamation issued by the Rabbi of Minsk after the attempted assassination of the governor of Vilna by Lekert. "A shudder passes over us," he wrote

> when we hear the terrible story of what happened in the theatre. How do we Jews, who are likened to a little worm—the worm of Jacob—come to get messed up in such matters? How do we Jews, who, according to all sense and reason, are always obligated to pray for the well-being of the sovereign power, without whom we would long since have been swallowed alive—how do we Jews dare to climb up to such high places and meddle in politics? Oh, beware, Jewish children! Look well what you are doing! God only knows what you may bring upon our unfortunate nation, upon yourselves, and upon your families. Our people always were proud of one thing—that they never had any rebels among them; and now you desire to wipe out this virtue too. We hope you will think well about all this and you will not wish to place in jeopardy the happiness of our whole nation, your own fate and the fate of your parents and families.[11]

Meanwhile, the struggle against Zubatov's achievement, the Jewish Independent Workers' Union, wore on. For a time, the union gained a substantial following and at one time in Minsk may have had more members than the Bund. The government permitted it to hold discussions and lectures which Vasilev himself attended. A recruiting drive was started by the union in Vilna in the summer of 1902, at a time when all of Vilna's Jews were agitated by Lekert's death. But Vilna's workers fought back with boycotts, charges of "political prostitution," and the raw facts of the state's repression. In Minsk as well, the union's position deteriorated with spreading unemployment. Police refused to support Zubatov-fostered strikes in Odessa, which got out of hand; moreover, they were having second thoughts about their own role.[12]

Trade unionism "pure and simple" had nothing to offer unemployed workers and many left the Independents during the widespread depression of 1902–3. Above all, the terrible Kishinev pogrom in April 1903 forced Jewish workers everywhere to see how vulnerable they were to government-incited anti-Semitism, how treacherous the Zubatov solution had been. In June 1903, the Jewish Independent Labor party of Minsk announced that its activities were at an end.

Meanwhile, the events of the spring and summer of 1902 convinced many Bund leaders that organizational and ideological changes were urgently needed more than ever. A shift to the political struggle had to be made. Faced with intensified police repression, the fear of open or even secret demonstrations, the limitations of the strike movement and *kassy* in meeting the revolutionary demands of the time, the Bund now attempted to energize the masses to act politically and to remodel its own structure which had rested on the *kassy*. In an important article in August 1902, *Di Arbayter Shtimme* concluded that the *kassy* had outlived their usefulness and were hindering further revolutionary work. What was needed now was "broad political agitation among all the masses" and "support of every protest against the present political order." [13] The Bund's most pressing task was "to free our revolutionary institutions from their old foundation— from the professional [trade union-*kassa*] movement."

This fundamental change in emphasis and direction was not achieved quickly or easily. In Vilna during the summer of 1902, efforts were made to shift to workers' political organizations, but they were partly thwarted by the struggle against the Minsk Independents. In Pinsk the reorganization was hastened by the visit of Mark Liber, a representative of the central committee, and later by two party professionals, who created a *birzhe* which channeled political agitation and cut through some of the old *kassa* loyalties.[14] When the Fifth Congress met in June 1903 in Zurich, with the local splitting of economic and political organizations still in process, the powers of the central committee were increased, resulting in greater centralization and control of local organizations. The central committee could now coopt political activists into local committees and make whatever organizational changes were necessary. It did this at a cost but without destroying the strong inner cohesiveness of the movement.

In a study of the Bund structure made in 1904 by Vladimir Akimov after the so-called break-up period, Akimov concluded that "the proletarian character of the Jewish movement was already so far advanced that the newly formed organizations did not destroy the trade councils but acted as a highly important adjunct to them." [15] He also stressed the continuing tradition of mutual trust at all levels in the Bund. These revolutionary groups of fifteen to thirty people were made up of the most advanced workers who dealt with questions related to ideology and the political program. Their activities were generally guided by the local committee and their composition was quite fluid.[16] The formal Bund committee structure seems to have been careful not to move too far ahead of the workers.

Political demonstrations, despite the hazards, increased, posing a greater challenge to the regime than strikes. In a Bund report to the Second Congress of the RSDWP (dated October 1903), which covered a two-year period, there were 30 street demonstrations, 260 protest meetings at schools and theatres, at which all of the urgent problems of Russian and Jewish life were set forth—involving about 50,000 people—and miscellaneous other meetings and May Day demonstrations. The state responded by cracking down not only with police but with cossacks and other military units.

With greater centralization and politicization of the Bund, many local journals fell by the wayside while publications of the central and foreign committees grew substantially and carried an ever heavier political content. The local committees began to issue increasing numbers of handbills and directed them to Polish and Russian as well as Jewish workers. Between the summer of 1901 and the summer of 1903, the Bund put out 101 handbills totaling 347,150 copies.[17]

With its broadened program in place of a simple call for economic struggle, the Bund also undertook to attract those Jewish intellectuals who had been hostile, indifferent, or estranged from the Jewish masses and afraid of the class character of the movement. Pavel Rosenthal, one of the few of the older generation of Bundists who completed his professional education in Russia (he studied medicine), a veteran in the movement, and now a member of the central committee, particularly berated those alienated Jewish intellectuals who ignored or fled from the struggle.

The fateful struggle, however, was with Lenin.[18] By 1902, Lenin was already fully exerting his capacity for single-minded concentration on organizational matters. In the middle of the year, *Iskra* set before its readers a draft party program that represented a careful mixture of the views of the more moderate and cautious Plekhanov and those of the bolder and more decisive Lenin. Lenin contributed many of the articles in *Iskra* and took on many antagonists in rough polemical exchanges, but the clearest statement of his views at the time are to be found in his pamphlet *What Is To Be Done?* which appeared in the summer of 1902 and paved the way for Bolshevism. This work, which contains a sharp and violent attack on "economism," reflects two propositions to which Lenin returned again and again and conveys his strong sense of the nature of the Russian state and existing Russian conditions.[19] The first proposition was that "without revolutionary theory there can be no revolutionary movement." To lead such a movement, Lenin called for a party of intellectuals, developing independently of the spontaneous growth of the workers' movement. Contemporary socialism, he said, was born in the heads of individual members of the bourgeois intelligentsia. He had only contempt for purely workers' literature, purely economic struggles, and spontaneous mass workers' movements. True, Russia's rapid industrial development had provoked a wave of strikes against intolerable misery, but such protests, Lenin believed, were not guided by any revolutionary consciousness or theory. "Consciousness" was thus opposed to "spontaneity"—a catch-word of the Economists, whom Lenin excoriated. Such consciousness, according to Lenin, could come to the workers only from without, from a revolutionary élite which would then lead them to overthrow tsarism.[20]

Lenin's second proposition argued that the nature of the Russian state precluded the formation of any kind of socialist or democratic party on a Western model and drove every such movement into secret and conspiratorial activities. Thus revolutionary groups of workers and students led by well-meaning amateurs were isolated from each other and fell easy victim to the tsarist police. The making of revolution in Russia, then, in Lenin's view, was a task for professional revolutionaries—a small, compact party under a strong central leadership to act in the name of the proletariat as the spearhead of the revolution. Such men do not think or feel politically in shades of gray, only in black and white. Bukharin said of him in later years: "Lenin is a strategist of genius. He knows that it is necessary to strike the principal enemy and not eclectically weave shade upon shade." This was the man who could not and would not accommodate the complications of the Bund positions.

Lenin's political cunning at the time of the Bialystok conference called to plan the Second RSDWP Congress was a foretaste of what was to come. The fate of the organization committee had great significance for the Bund and the future of the RSDWP. Kremer had documents from the conference, but when he offered to give them to the Iskraites together with a personal report, they declined.[21] A police spy had arrested all of the members at the Bialystok meeting except Portnoy, and Lenin quickly arranged to have *Iskra* agents replace them. To an agent in Samara he wrote on May 23, 1902:

> And so your task now is to create *from your own selves* a committee to prepare the Congress, to admit a Bundist into the Committee (after sizing him up *from all sides*—note this well), and to push your own people on to as many committees as possible.[22]

To another agent in St. Petersburg he wrote on June 22:

> I just gave the Bund your contact address. This concerns the Congress. . . . Act with authority, but with *care*. Take upon yourself the responsibility for as much territory as possible in making preparations for the Congress . . . and let the Bund for now limit itself to its own bailiwick. . . . The make-up of the committee must be as favorable for us (perhaps you could say the committee has already been organized and you would be happy to have the Bund take part). . . . In short, make yourself master of this undertaking.[23]

A month later, he gave more specific instructions: "With the Bund, be extremely careful and firm. Don't show your cards; leave it to manage its own affairs and *don't allow it to poke its nose* into Russian affairs. Remember that it is an unreliable friend *(if not an enemy)*."[24] Meanwhile, organizations abroad were planning a foreign section of the so-called organization committee, but Lenin maneuvered to sweep aside such a group which would contain opponents. He worked to put the Iskraites in control of the committee, referred to as the O.C., before its existence became public and was particularly determined to exclude the Bund.

Delegates from Iskraite organizations began to assemble in London in the summer of 1902, but their arrival was not made public. Lenin's wife Krupskaya admitted that "for the time being, the O.C. will be considered as not established, and no one but us knows it. It consists exclusively of our people." Meanwhile, groups persisted in trying to organize a foreign section of the O.C., as proposed at the Bialystok Conference. Kremer represented the Bund. But Lenin rejected any role for potential opponents and when the O.C. was finally organized in November in Russia, he instructed his agent P. A. Krasihov to see to it that the work abroad remain unimportant.[25]

The meeting reconstituting the O.C. took place in Pskov and consisted of only three of the seven organizations that had been at Bialystok. All three were committed to the Iskraite position. A new O.C. was created, without Bund participation, and the Bund reacted angrily. But recognizing it could not undo what happened at Pskov, the central committee nevertheless stood ready to join the O.C. after the Iskraites admitted blame for the failure of the Bund to receive an invitation. Portnoy was named the Bund representative in new negotiations. The unilateral formation of the O.C. was a flagrant violation of the Bialystok arrangements. Disturbed by a *fait accompli*, the Bund strove to gain support for its plan to broaden participation of all social democratic organizations, including national organizations, in the forthcoming RSDWP Congress and to propose federation.

In Lenin's mind, the issue of the Bund was indeed uppermost. He accepted the Bund in the planning of the Second Congress, but only on his terms, and was fully prepared for a struggle that might mean the expulsion of the Bund from the party. To one of his supporters on the O.C. he advised that he be "correct and loyal to the Bund formally (no open kick in the teeth), but at the same time quite cold," and to "press them mercilessly and hourly on a legal basis without fear of going to the limit. . . . Let the Bundists leave if they want to, but we must not give them the slightest excuse . . . to make a split." [26]

Once in the O.C., the Bund tried to make the forthcoming congress more broadly representative and to redefine its relationship to the new party in a "federative alliance." Lenin vehemently rejected both ideas, insisting that the Bund's "nationalist passion" would have to disappear, that the nationalities would be invited after a "basic nucleus" was formed. Kosovsky then led a counterattack, charging that *Iskra* was demagogic for suggesting that the Bund was fighting the party: "You are striving," he said, "not only for theoretical, but also for organizational hegemony. The Bund is hampering you by its separate existence, by its independence, and for this reason you fight it." [27] Lenin's followers, Kosovsky charged, were already saying that "the task of the Second Party Congress is to destroy the Bund." Why couldn't Jewish social democrats have the same cultural autonomy permitted the Armenian social democrats?

Kosovsky also urged opening up the discussion of the national question and federation in the party, arguing that the development of a class conscious proletariat in any nationality strengthened the whole. Besides, the RSDWP had failed to mark the ongoing struggle of the Bund against the government, employers, and the Jewish bourgeoisie. Nor had it done anything to check the anti-Semitism of Russian workers. In order to ensure the movement the greatest amount of revolutionary energy, he wrote, every national social-democratic organization had to have equal rights. Moreover, the more the Bund grew, the more new workers would be drawn into the movement, while the Bund's principle of federation would create an *all-Russian* social-democratic movement instead of a *Russian* party.

Polemical warfare raged in leaflets, newspapers, and journals. Ironically, it was the same Martov who, in 1895, had called for a Jewish workers' organization to struggle for economic, social and civic equality for the Jewish worker, who now aided Lenin in attacking the Bund, claiming it was too narrow and isolated to understand the need for unity.[28] A separate party was not needed by Jewish workers. Yes, the *Iskra* group was striving for hegemony, Martov admitted, but only for the sake of unification of the movement. Those who wanted control were not enemies of the Bund, but wanted the Bund to give up its "parochialism."

One historian concedes that "The importance of his contribution to *Iskra's* campaign against the Bund is difficult to overestimate," but believes that "Martov was not so detached from his own people as to play his role against the Bund without pain or misgiving. . . . What did distinguish him from many a Jewish socialist was his personal involvement in the struggle against anti-semitism . . . he never abandoned that struggle and to that extent he remained true to his Vilna days and the family tradition of his grandfather Alexander Tsederbaum." [29] As a child Martov had lived through a pogrom in Odessa, which obliged him to recognize that identification with the masses was not sufficiently comprehensive to deal with persecution of the Jews. At the same time, his own Jewishness lacked substance, for his parents had denied its value. In explaining Martov's later hostility to the Bund, one writer has concluded that "Jewishness was to become in Martov's mind a weakness in his armor, a handicap with no compensatory rewards." [30]

The last words in this early phase of the Bund-*Iskra* debate were made by Kosovsky in a pamphlet published for the foreign committee in April 1903. In it he upheld the Bund's qualifications and achievements as a party of revolutionaries, and deplored *Iskra's* attitude as a continuation of the old image of the Jewish masses as inert and incapable of radical change. In order to generate maximum revolutionary energy, every national party had to have equal rights, Kosovsky argued, but the Iskraites were unable to understand this or the significance which the Jewish movement had for itself and Jewish working masses. The Bund was no mere regional organization, but a class organization that could act in behalf of Jewish workers wherever they were. The first RSDWP had, in fact, endorsed this idea. The Bund was thus the party of a distinct nationality which must be acknowledged in the only possible form uniting *all* organizations—namely federation.[31]

Lenin's attack on the Bund had centered on the issue of "nationalism," but more fundamentally, it was the existence of an autonomous Jewish social democratic organization in Jewish districts alongside a Russian one and the untidy, not to say threatening, consequences of autonomy that Lenin could not accept.[32] For some time before the congress, *Iskra* committees had been working to break up and absorb Bund organizations, and Lenin's correspondence shows that before 1903,[33] he had determined to force the Bund into the wilderness, for it not only might block his path to absolutist control of the party, but had already demonstrated the effectiveness of its organization and program at a time when the Russian movement was weak and fractious. It also had drawn on workers, not only intellectuals, in its leadership, whereas the Russian movement was still largely a stirring among intellectuals. In every way, the Bund was clearly well ahead of the Russian movement at the time.

Some Bundists now began to feel that the Iskraites were determined to destroy their movement. There was also a sharpened awareness that the interests of the Jewish proletariat were being ignored or trivialized. Their fears were well founded: In March 1903, in a confidential letter to the editors of the Russian paper *The Southern Workers*, Lenin wrote: "We want you, privately, to prepare everywhere and everyone for a fight with the Bund at the Congress. The Bund will not give up its position without a stubborn struggle, and we can never accept its position. Only the foremost resolve on our part to see this through, even to the expulsion of the Bund from the party, will force it to yield." [34] Krupskaya herself found it necessary to criticize certain Iskraite comrades for assuming good will on the part of the Bund.

The rules for the Second RSDWP Congress were formally established at a meeting in February 1903. The two Bund representatives, Portnoy and Izenshtat, tried to protect the Bund's position but failed on almost every point. Nevertheless, the Bund was willing to swallow a great deal to remain in the O.C. and thereby again assert its commitment to the unity of the whole social-democratic movement. Portnoy especially was conciliatory and tactful. Meanwhile, the Bund's own official stand at the RSDWP Congress had to be hammered out at its own Congress—the Fifth—which was held in Zurich in June 1903.

The central and foreign committees had already endorsed federation, and in the first Yiddish articles on the idea in *Di Arbayter Shtimme*, "national independence and international solidarity" were upheld as the desired basis for uniting the organizations of the RSDWP.[35] A few members, notably Pavel Rosenthal and David Katz, disagreed, but they were out of step with the prevailing views. A preliminary conference of leading Bundists in Geneva in June thrashed out the question of the tasks of national social-democratic organizations and the responsibility of the RSDWP. The news of the Kishinev pogroms in April 1903 broke in the midst of these discussions.

Vladimir Medem came to these sessions from Munich, where he had spent days in libraries poring over the literature on anti-Semitism. He wrote of the "shuddering impact" of the pogroms on the Bund, arousing reaffirmation of the revolutionary struggle and the formation of Bundist self-defense groups.[36] During this time, in a heated discussion among Russian social democrats in Karlsruhe, Medem tilted with Trotsky on the Jewish question. At one point, Medem turned to Trotsky and said:

> "As for your own person, you cannot ignore the fact that you belong to a definite nation. You consider yourself, I take it, to be either a Russian or a Jew." Trotsky shot back quickly: "No you are wrong! I am a social-democrat, and that's all." [37]

When Medem arrived in Geneva he found a number of people from the foreign committee and other Bundists living outside Russia there: Kremer (who had escaped from the police after the 1902 arrests in Bialystok), Mill, Kopelson, two former friends from Minsk (Genia Hurvich and Boris Frumkin), and two rising young men in their twenties, Mark Liber and Raphael Abramovich. Liber, who was to play a leading role at the forthcoming RSDWP Congress, is described as a nervous, energetic man with flashing dark eyes and black beard, high-tempered, deeply devoted to the Bundist cause, and a polished eloquent speaker. He had made contact with the Lithuanian social democrats while still in secondary school and from 1900 on was active in the Bund. Abramovich was described by Medem as a young man of twenty-four of "iron will and patience, of deep philosophical bent." [38]

The two big questions facing the group were the national question and relations with the Russian party, both of which were discussed with great care and deliberation. Medem, who made the final report, recounted the many hours he and Abramovich worked in a Geneva garden over the proposals to the congress, word by word. The group finally concluded that federation was the only way to safeguard the interests of nationally oriented groups such as the Bund and the Polish Social-Democratic party. Proposals on the Bund's prerogatives, jurisdiction, and status within the party were also made. Medem made the report of these deliberations in Russian, which Liber later translated into Yiddish.

The Bund's Fifth Congress had been scheduled to meet in Russia, but Liber succeeded in having the site changed to Zurich because of security considerations and the need to deliberate away from the tense atmosphere in Russia. The debates, particularly on the national question and the Bund's formal relationship to the party, were heated and prolonged; in fact, the debate on the national question, which split the delegates about half and half, was not reported until 1927–28, in *Unzer Tsayt,* [39] which appeared in Warsaw. Medem also recalled a strong "assimilationist" position (led by Kopelson); he, Liber, and Kosovsky took a more positively national approach.[40] One of the delegates, Aaron Weinstein, stated the issue bluntly: "Either the Bund is a national party, in which case it must have its national program, or the viewpoint of *Iskra* is correct."

Unable to get off the horns of this dilemma, the congress was deadlocked. The sessions, however, did provide a rising new Bund thinker—Vladimir Medem—with an opportunity to deal more incisively with the national question which, he said, social democracy had to confront. Kosovsky and Mill agreed with him. Medem's solution, which came to be called "neutralism," [41] lay midway between the extremes of nationalism and assimilation. Neutralism to Medem meant that each group should work out its own path to national development in its own way, and that social democracy guarantee to every nationality the freedom to find its own way. National identity per se was not important. As far as Jews were concerned, he believed that a Jewish culture existed, that it had validity in the past, and that the Jewish masses would probably retain their specific identity. But he did not believe that the Bund—or any other social-democratic party—should influence the process of expressing or encouraging this identity. Medem later devoted his best talents and energies to a further analysis of the national problem, but the essential polarity of the traditional national-Marxist juxtaposition made clear resolution impossible, and Medem remained a Marxist, at least until 1917.

Medem's close identification with the Jewish masses in Russia and later in Poland is in striking contrast to his family background and his own early life.[42] He was born in Libau in 1879 into a completely assimilated Russian Jewish family; his father was one of the first Jews to graduate from the St. Petersburg Military Medical Academy and spent his mature years as an army doctor in a totally Russian environment. Both of Vladimir's parents converted, as had most of his aunts and uncles. The older children were baptized into the Lutheran Church and Vladimir, the youngest, into the Orthodox Russian Church. His childhood was happy, but there was a pervasive shame about the family's Jewish origins and the use of Yiddish. When an old Jewish woman Leykeh spoke to his mother in Yiddish the six-year old Vladimir was sick and upset by his mother's replies in Yiddish.

The dark gold pictures, glowing candles, richly colored vestments, and splendor of the choir of the Orthodox Church services at first overwhelmed the young boy, but by the time he reached his second year in the *gymnasium* of Minsk (where his father was stationed), he became more critical and he and his circle slowly and imperceptibly began to recover a sense of their Jewishness. (In his memoirs Medem admits that he has no clear recollection of how he came to return to Jewish life.) [43] His closest friends were Jews and in some of their homes he heard Yiddish—no longer painful to him—and saw Jewish customs observed.

In 1897 he enrolled in the University of Kiev, soon switching from medicine to law, meeting Marxists and *narodniki* and studying political economy. Besides Marxism, Medem also decided to study Hebrew at the time, mostly to enable him to read the Bible—which he had never considered a Jewish book!—in the original language. These efforts were not very successful, but Medem did learn the Hebrew alphabet, which later gave him the key to Yiddish. He also became a student activist and met more Jewish students whose group solidarity and warmth aroused a certain yearning. Friendship with an older Jew, Isaac Teumin, who took him to a synagogue in Minsk on Yom Kippur also made an overpowering impression on him. The torrent of individual cries to God contrasted dramatically with the ordered majesty of the Russian Orthodox service but stirred Medem profoundly. Walks with Teumin on Friday nights through the quiet streets of the Jewish quarter glowing with Sabbath candles also affected him deeply. The Zionists, he said, would call his feelings typical of the *galut* (exile). The palm trees and vineyards of Palestine were alien to him. The streets of Minsk, the huddled houses and Sabbath lights, the warmth of a living community in his midst aroused and compassed his sense of Jewishness.

In 1899, Medem was expelled from the university for political activity and ordered to return to Minsk, where he soon made contact with the Bund and began working for the movement. Early in 1901, he was arrested and when asked his nationality by the police, without hesitation wrote "Jewish" on the form. After several subsequent arrests he went to Berne, where he became involved in the controversies between Bundists and Iskraites and began his long involvement in the national question.

Medem's views stimulated a lively, sometimes contentious debate at the Bund congress in 1903. In several exchanges, the future of the Bund itself was mooted, with some delegates like Kopelson believing that the Bund would disappear once Jews achieved full equality, while others believed that the Bund would help advance Jewish national culture and that national development was a positive process in the strengthening of class consciousness. Izenshtat believed that neutralism and autonomy were incompatible. Kosovsky believed that the Bund was fostering national autonomy by its very activities; to him, Jewish national culture sprang from the masses and was being nurtured by the Bund. Other delegates considered Kosovsky's idea Zionistic.

Such wide-ranging differences made a decisive vote impossible, and the call for national cultural autonomy did not win enough support to pass. The resolution of the Fourth Congress—militant in demanding civil rights for Jews, but cautious in asserting autonomy—was upheld by the Fifth. Thus, Lenin's charge of "nationalism" was wide of the mark.

There was heated discussion on a number of other issues, but in the end, a twelve-point resolution was passed, including the following major provisions that were to have significance at the forthcoming RSDWP Congress:

1. The Bund is a federated part of the RSDWP.

2. The Bund is a Social Democratic organization of the Jewish proletariat, unrestricted in its activity by any regional framework, and enters the Party as the sole representative of the Jewish proletariat; moreover, any activity in the name of the whole proletariat in an area where the Bund as well as other Party organizations is active, is permissible only with the participation of the Bund.

3. The Bund elects its own representatives to the Central Committee, the Foreign Committee, and the congresses of the Party.... The method of representation must be based on principles that are alike for all contracting sides.[44]

The congress accepted the RSDWP party program as its own, but hoped to supplement it with the above points raised by "the specific conditions of the Jewish proletariat in Russia."

The Bund congress did not insist on a federative party structure, but described itself as "a federated part of the RSDWP," thus avoiding the issue of the status of other parts of the party and the party as a whole. The delegates also revealed their flexibility—and anxiety—over the coming party congress by retreating to a line of minimum conditions. These were irreducible positions beyond which the Bund could not go short of leaving the party.[45] (These conditions, too, remained secret for a time and enraged Lenin when he learned of them.) Basically, they left the Bund substantially independent in the sense of being the sole representative of the Jewish proletariat. The Bund was allotted five delegates[46] to the forthcoming party congress: Liber, Portnoy, and Izenshtat, representing the central committee, and Medem and Kosovsky representing the foreign committee. As a member of the first RSDWP central committee, Kremer was an honorary delegate with an "advisory voice," but no vote.

Lenin meanwhile had been making painstaking preparations for the party congress itself—packing local committees, greeting, sounding out, and persuading early delegations, and working on the documents, arguments, and resolutions he intended to present. "How Vladimir Ilyich longed for this Congress!" Krupskaya wrote many years after it had taken place. This congress was not only historically important for the Bund, but marked a crucial turning point for the Russian social democratic movement. Eventually, its most serious result—the Bolshevik-Menshevik split— had profoundly serious consequences for the history of Russia and Jewish life there.

The first delegates, mostly from emigré colonies, arrived weeks before the congress opened, overrunning the hotels in Brussels, meeting with Lenin, and waiting for delegates from Russia, some of whom didn't arrive until after the congress was over. The sessions finally opened on July 30,

1903, in a large flour warehouse draped with red cloth, with Russian and Belgian police swarming in nearby alleys and streets. The Belgian police followed delegates to their lodgings and into parks and restaurants, searched rooms, intercepted letters. One woman delegate was deported; several others were given twenty-four hours' notice to leave the country, after which the whole congress packed up and left for London, where they met in a "socialist church" in the midsummer heat from August 11 to August 23.

From the outset, Medem recalled, the Bund delegates found themselves in a hostile atmosphere: "We felt as if we were among our worst enemies. . . . Privately, there was no one to talk to but each other." The *Iskra* people, he wrote, "had been instructed." [47] Kosovsky wrote that the Bund "was isolated and encircled by a host of enemies." Officially, there were forty-three delegates, some of whom, like Lenin and Martov, had two votes each, having secured mandates from Russian and emigré organizations. Representatives of twenty-five social democratic groups attended, only four of them workers. This preponderance of intellectuals and their intense identification of individual with ideological "truth" may explain the strained intellectualism and ferocity of the debates. Of the fifty-one official votes, thirty-three—a clear majority—were held by *Iskra* supporters. As long as the Iskraites remained united, the only real opposition came from the five votes of the Bund and three of *Rabochee Delo (The Workers' Cause)*. This was the organ of the "Economists" and chief rival of *Iskra*. It had widespread support throughout the movement, but lacked the driving force of Lenin. Their delegates were Vladimir Akimov, his sister Lydia, and A. Martynov. The rest of the delegates Lenin contemptuously called "the Swamp" because they had not lined up predictably on the issues.

Plekhanov opened the congress with a moving address, the delegates sang "The International," and hopes for a revived, united all-Russian Social-Democratic Workers' party were high. But Lenin's steam roller soon crushed their transient euphoria. He insisted on an all-Iskraite presidium, winning over Martov's suggestion for a representative one. He then very quickly tackled the agenda with the purpose of smoking out the Bundist desire for federation. From first to last, each draft agenda constructed by the Iskraites made the Bund's place in the party the first order of business.[48] It was clear to Lenin that the Bund's desire for federation threatened his plans for a centralized party. His strategy, then, was to declare the congress a "successive" one, thus keeping statutes of the First Congress (1898) in force. But what did this mean? For the Bund, it meant autonomy in Jewish matters and a federated party. For Lenin, it meant nothing more than limited autonomy. "It is impossible," Lenin insisted, "for the Congress to begin harmonious work until these differences have been settled." For the Bundists, since the earlier congress had failed to make a clear definition, there was nothing in the earlier granting of autonomy to prevent what they considered its logical extension, namely, federation. Liber, who became the Bund spokesman, argued this inter-pretation. But the Iskraites felt just as free to argue theirs, insisting meanwhile that the whole question of the Bund's relationship to the party be discussed as a separate item on the agenda.

This issue was voted, and at the fourth session, the first full-dress debate of the congress took place on "The Place of the Bund in the Russian Social Democratic Workers' Party." It was obvious to the Bundists that an organized fight had been planned.[49] Liber again reminded the delegates of the vagueness of the 1898 resolution regarding the Bund and the need for a more precise form. A federated party, he said, would give the Jewish proletariat a chance to participate in the work of the entire movement. Autonomy separated national needs from the center and from general questions, isolating Jewish workers, whereas a federation would break down that isolation and bring greater centralization. He then offered the rules worked out at the Bund's Fifth Congress as the logical development of the principles of 1898.

But the strength of the anti-Bund bloc was quickly grasped, and the Bund began a swift retreat virtually to its minimum position "in order not to increase the hostile frame of mind toward the Bund and so as to increase the possibility of agreement." This included removing the paragraph declaring the Bund "a federated part" of the party. "We have done everything possible for unification," Liber said, "we are not in a position to go further on this. Without the remaining points the very existence of the Bund is impossible."

The Iskraites, seeing a weakening in the Bund position, pressed ahead aggressively. Martov argued that the Jewish proletariat did not need an independent political organization to represent its interests; it was intolerable for a part of the party to represent one stratum of the proletariat—if other groups did this, the result would be disorganization. He then introduced his own resolution, rejecting federation and permit-ting the Bund to remain an autonomous part of the RSDWP, "the limits of whose autonomy should be fixed by the working out of general Party rules." Martov also urged that the Bund's proposal not be considered since it brought the Bund to the congress as an independent entity. One could use the difficult position of the Jews to argue for autonomy, but this resulted from "unfortunate historical conditions," which no "heroic resolution" could change. Martov's resolution passed, and new Bund proposals were referred for consideration to the discussion of party organization. No sooner had Martov finished than Trotsky quickly rose to inform the delegates that twelve Jewish comrades, all members of the RSDWP, were signing Martov's resolution and still considered themselves representatives of the Jewish proletariat. This maneuver stung Liber to reply that those who signed were representatives of a Jewish proletariat "among whom they have never worked."

Debate ran on for days, from the fifth through the eighth sessions. Lenin spoke little. A few delegates were moderate or conciliatory; the vast majority were hostile toward the Bund. Portnoy also joined the debate, stressing the issue of historical conditions: the Bund, he reminded the delegates, had been formed under abnormal conditions. Had conditions for Jews now become normal? The congress had said nothing about the Kishinev pogrom. Liber then argued that the Bund's position was the same as that of Rosa Luxemburg, who had demanded that the German social democrats grant the Polish social democrats the right to concern themselves with all matters involving Polish workers living in Germany. Why did the opponents of the Bund dwell on the isolating effects of its work, instead of recalling the solidarity of Jewish workers with other workers? Moreover, without recognizing the fact of nationalities, the party's claims to be all-Russian, i.e., multi-national, were empty. But the opposition did not relent. Trotsky put it laconically for the Iskraites: The Bund was either "the only representative of the interests of the Jewish proletariat in and before the Party" or a "special organization of the Party for agitation and propaganda among the Jewish proletariat." Which was it to be?

The debate raged until, at the seventh session, on August 3, the Bund again moved to a new position. Liber offered a new set of proposals, revising and removing all clauses which implied federation until the Bundists found themselves clinging to the ill-defined autonomy of the 1898 congress. But bit by bit, even this position was chewed away by the hard-line Iskraites, led by Martov and Trotsky, who viewed autonomy in terms of agitational tasks, dictated by peculiarities of language and custom. "From our point of view," Trotsky declared, "the autonomy of the Bund is in principle no different from the autonomy of each committee." Liber tried to rescue the former basic guarantee of independence for the Bund in all questions that specifically touched on the Jewish proletariat, but the voting went strongly against the Bundists.

They could and perhaps should have left the congress at that point, but instead, as they explained later in their report, they "decided . . . to wait, since the congress had not expressed its opinion of our rules [in their changed form]." The last fateful stage for the Bund did not come until the twenty-seventh session on August 18. Meanwhile, a startling realization had struck the Bundists: the party congress had not the least interest or understanding of their problems or achievements. They were completely isolated during the debates on the Bund's place in the party and, although they received some support on national rights issues in the party program and on regional as against purely local self-rule, whenever Bund or Jewish interests were involved, there was a very negative tone, indeed a bias.

The party resolution on nationality simply affirmed "the right of self-determination for all nations in the state." Medem moved an amendment "to establish institutions guaranteeing full freedom of cultural development" to national minority groups with no specific territorial framework, but the congress voted overwhelmingly against it. Yefrem Levin, a spokesman for the anti-Bundist majority, who was on the committee on by-laws as well as the party program and was considered a moderate, made a sharp retort:

> So far as the national question is concerned, our demands can only be negative ones, that is to say, we are against all restrictions imposed on nationalities. But whether this or that nationality will be able to develop as such, is none of our business as Social Democrats. That will be decided by an elemental and spontaneous process.[50]

A second Bund amendment, less unequivocally phrased than Medem's, urging that freedom of cultural development be guaranteed, as well as the right of self-determination, was also overwhelmingly defeated. Yet the congress had approved a proposal of the Polish social democratic delegation that was almost identical—a response that greatly embittered the Bund.

The Leninist approach to the national problem could already be glimpsed in the budding pre-Bolshevik faction's opposition to the demand for "broad local and regional self-government," proposed by the committee on the party program, and especially pushed by Izenshtat. Lenin immediately moved to strike out the words "and regional"—a possible limitation on the power of the future central government. His motion was defeated, but among the Bolsheviks the principle of centralization later acquired the sanctity of tradition. It became an essential element of the party's "democratic centralism" and determined in advance its views on national problems and the governmental structure of a multi-national state. At the congress, most delegates opposed autonomy for areas inhabited by minority nationalities and limited their acceptance to Martov's amendment advocating "regional self-government for those border areas in which the way of life and composition of the population differ from those in genuinely Russian areas." [51]

When a paragraph guaranteeing freedom of "conscience, speech, press, assembly, strikes and unions" was discussed, Liber proposed the insertion of "language," referring to the right to use a language other than the state's. This point brought some of the closest balloting at the congress. A tumultuous debate—and eighteen separate votes—raged over the question of national language rights, with the delegates finally affirming the right of a people to acquire an education in its mother tongue, to use it in public meetings and in all public agencies.

The strategy of battering the Bund position and, indeed, its existence, shifted to a larger context: Lenin's plan for a highly centralized party structure and the development of a party of professional revolutionaries committed "not just for an evening meeting, but for a lifetime." These questions were set forth at the fourteenth session, on August 11, when the organization of the party was reached on the agenda and when Lenin presented his plan for a highly centralized structure.

Lenin was fiercely single-minded about what he wanted—control of the party by the *Iskra* group and his personal control of the group. He is described during those days as being in a fever of planning, scheming, maneuvering, of wanting to have his own way, scarcely eating or sleeping. With a razor-sharp perception that a tight party organization depended on the strict discipline of members within the structure, he pushed through a motion which set up a presidium consisting entirely of *Iskra* men, with Plekhanov as chairman, and he as one of the vice-chairmen—a move he later described as wielding the "iron fist" against all social democrats who resisted *Iskra*'s control of the party.[52] A number of speakers were called, but before the Bund could be heard on its proposed rules on organization (as Martov's resolution had promised), discussion was closed.

Martov tried to assure the Bund that no "trap" was being set for them, but the Bund delegates had seen and heard too much to be soothed. Medem spoke out. The Bund did not reject centralism in principle—its own central committee exerted some control over local organizations. But Lenin's idea of centralization was "monstrous," a power so great that it could destroy local organizations rather than guide them. Brushing aside Martov's soothing disclaimer, Medem said that Lenin wanted prior acceptance of his plan so that the position of the Bund could be determined by his principles, without any consideration of the Bund proposals. The central committee of the party could then "alter the composition of the central committee of the Bund ... dissolve it ... repeal the decisions of the Bund congresses, etc." Medem told the delegates how serious this moment was: "If our proposals, which represent the minimal conditions for the continued existence of the Bund, are rejected, then the question of the Bund's departure from the party will have been decided." [53]

The final confrontation came on August 18, when Martov brought up that part of the Bund proposal that claimed unlimited territorial rights and sole representation of the Jewish proletariat. Liber put the Bund case eloquently before the final dénouement. Reminding Martov of his speech of 1895, Liber declared that the Bund's position had not changed at all since the First RSDWP Congress of 1898 and that its need for autonomy was simply a natural and legal outgrowth of conditions and problems of that time, not the nationalism it was accused of. Rather, it was the Russian comrades who had changed. Otherwise, why had they not noticed these "harmful" views until now? The truth, Liber continued, was that the Bund had grown in Poland and Lithuania without the help of the Russians. "Let our Russian comrades not forget that if this question of the Bund is for them the first page of history, for us who have lived through almost the same struggle with the PPS, the struggle with the Russian comrades is the second page of our history." [54] He chastised the Russians for their ignorance of the Bund's achievements and then went on to defend the Bund's minimum proposals.[55] These were the two crucial points: the right to be sole representative of the Jewish proletariat and the exercise of this right without territorial limitations.

There was almost no discussion. Both proposals were voted down overwhelmingly, forty-one to five, making it impossible for the Bund to remain in the RDSWP. Liber, speaking for the delegation, said that the proposals voted down were the minimum necessary conditions for affiliation. "The Bund," he said, "is leaving the Russian party." [56]

Everyone remained quiet while the Bund walked out, Medem recalled. "It was a dramatic moment. Even on our opponents, it made a deep impression. It was much heavier for us. . . . We all knew that the separation was a severe blow to both sides. We took our step with a heavy heart. It was a catastrophe, tearing the ties that must bind Jewish and Russian workers. It was as if a piece of living flesh were being torn from a living body. . . . Our unity had been a sacred thing. But we had no choice. Fanatics with a Caesar-like centralization complex wanted to choke the Bund. . . ." [57] Later, Medem also saw in the tragic events a component of Jewish self-hatred, inasmuch as those who led the attack on the Bund—Martov and Trotsky—were themselves Jews.

19. 1905: *The Bund at Its Zenith*

Besides the departure of the Bund, the Second RSDWP Congress also marked the beginning of the rift between the groups that eventually became the Bolsheviks and Mensheviks. The irritant that later became an ideological inflammation grew out of the Martov-Lenin difference over the wording of the rules defining party membership. Martov was willing to admit all who had accepted the party program and gave the party "regular personal cooperation under the guidance of one of its organizations." To Lenin, a party member was "any person who accepts its program, supports the Party with material means and personally participates in one of its organizations." This seemingly trivial distinction in fact concealed far-reaching differences on the nature of revolution, revolutionary conscious-ness, and the role of the "bourgeois revolution." Lenin lost this contest over definition but won on the rest of the statute which involved the setting up of a centralized party. The core of this was the *Iskra* board.

Besides the five Bund delegates, two others had left the congress: Akimov and Martynov from the Union Abroad, after the Iskraites recognized a pro-*Iskra* foreign group and disenfranchised the union. The withdrawl of seven delegates who had voted with the "soft" bloc on membership qualifications thus had the result of shifting the balance in favor of the "hard" bloc and gave Lenin power over the party organs—*Iskra* and the theoretical journal *Zarya* (*The Dawn*). The growing split between Lenin and Martov now became ugly and acrimonious. Lenin's proposal to appoint himself and Plekhanov (two "hards") and Martov (one "soft") to the *Iskra* board (which would actually control the party) though it passed, drew vehement opposition. Martov's charge that "martial law" was taking hold of the party and that "exceptional laws" were arrayed against certain groups was the first skirmish in the protracted struggle between the Bolsheviks (Lenin's majority supporters) and the Mensheviks (Martov's minority).

Plekhanov, who had stood firmly behind Lenin, was soon shocked by his ruthlessness in dealing with the Mensheviks, most of whom were Plekhanov's old comrades. Trotsky, too, began to attack Lenin for his dictatorial methods. Soon the Mensheviks took the offensive and Lenin, defeated and isolated by the barrage of criticism, resigned from *Iskra* in 1904 and was evicted from the party machine the congress had placed within his grasp. Still undaunted and superbly self-confident, he retreated to Geneva, called together twenty-two Bolshevik stalwarts to serve as the nucleus of a new Bolshevik force, and founded a new journal *V'period (Forward)*.

Mensheviks in those years were clearly the majority movement, representing the Western-oriented rationalistic strand in Russian Marxism. They waited for the first-stage Marxist prediction of a bourgeois-democratic revolution, and while they waited for conditions in Russia to ripen, Lenin seized the whirlwind. Though he was momentarily off center-stage, he was shaping the forces that have shaped much of twentieth-century history, and predetermined to a large degree the fate of Russian Jewry after the Bolshevik Revolution.

It is significant that in his controversy with the Bund, which continued well beyond the Second RSDWP Congress, the rejection of the Bund's proposal for a federated party was a crucial step in the formation of the Leninist party and Leninism.[1] The conflict with the Bund molded the highly disciplined, monolithic Leninist party and decisively established it as a cohesive, tightly controlled apparatus. "Factions" were not technically outlawed until 1921, but Lenin's formulations of 1903 created an ideologically tough Bolshevik model and made an ultimate union with the Mensheviks impossible.

Interestingly, Akimov, who admired the Bund very much and wrote a study of it in 1904, attributed part of the growing divergence between the Russian factions to the Bund's lack of a theoretical framework. At the Second Congress of the party, he wrote,

> the Bund delegation did not even try to contribute to working out the program, which it accepted as submissively as did the rest of the delegates. Although it instinctively sensed that its own organizational principles were in sharp contradiction to those of *Iskra*, it proved incapable of formulating its opposition to *Iskra* in clearly defined terms. The Bund delegation thus showed itself unable to crown the Bund's historical services to the Party and to assume the leadership of the Party's purely proletarian wing. The Jewish proletarian movement is moving along the highway in exactly the right direction. Yet, lacking theoreticians, it is powerless to point the way to others. It moves forward itself, but it does not lead.[2]

The Bund leadership, however, despite its break with the RSDWP, continued to see itself as a part of that larger movement, with which it would be re-attached at some future time. It never saw itself as leading the movement ideologically or politically because of its long-held position of awaiting the development of the Russian party, of standing by while it coalesced. Moreover, the Bund was clearly a *Jewish* movement, whose reach for leadership would surely have been smashed by non-Jewish socialists. Perhaps even more significant were the uncertainties and ambivalences within the Bund itself as to how far it could go in being a Jewish movement. A political movement undergoing identity conflicts cannot release the energy and confidence needed for the control of contrary ideas or struggling social forces. The Bund had defined itself sufficiently to leave the RSDWP Congress, but it was left in ideological limbo, isolated and attacked not only by other Russian socialists, but increasingly by Zionists. The Russians were pushing, while the Zionists were pulling, creating an inner vacillation which was never altogether resolved.

Opinions as to how to define and apply the principle of cultural or national autonomy varied greatly. Some, like Liber, who differentiated between "national" and "nationalist," wanted immediate autonomy, which he insisted would not harm social-democratic consciousness; others strongly opposed taking any immediate steps, pointing to the dangers of any sensitivity other than the consciousness of national oppression. Still others believed that national agitation (as carried on by the Zionists) was harmful to class consciousness. But Zionist inroads on worker sympathy had left the Bund somewhat defensive and wanting on the national question, making a mere call for self-determination insufficient. The duality of socialism and national autonomy eluded precise formulation at the congress held just two months after the Kishinev pogrom. Not until the Sixth Congress of the Bund in 1905 was the demand for national-cultural autonomy for Jews made a definite part of its program, but there were no concrete proposals for its implementation until the Eighth Congress in 1910, when, for the first time, the deliberations were held in Yiddish.

The Bund's groping for a socialist framework that gave scope to Jewish national culture was undoubtedly pressed by the growing appeal of Zionism and, more especially, by socialist Zionism, which had appeared spontaneously in several forms between 1901-03.[3] The theoretical foundations of the movement were shaped largely by the work of Nachman Syrkin and Ber Borochov. Both were socialists who, like the Bund, recognized class conflict in Jewish life, but unlike the Bund, found Jewish problems so singularly insoluble in the Diaspora, that they could see no alternative but national independence in a Jewish homeland. Syrkin lashed out especially at those Jewish socialists who had forsaken their own national heritage for alien cultures and were now advocating a "cultural autonomy" based on an Austrian concept and a jargon—Yiddish—which could never become a genuinely national language and was associated with a past of degradation.

The Bund became increasingly worried about the appeal of labor and socialist Zionists, who, after Kishinev, could not be content with the goal of a socialist Palestine but who also plunged into the social struggle in Russia as a worker-oriented movement, and thus clashed with the Bund from a common class base. Both movements appealed to Jewish workers and socialists, but with different perspectives and programs. Despite the split at the Sixth Zionist Congress in 1903 over territorialism—a movement devoted to finding an alternative territory to Palestine and a highly charged issue which the Bund believed might redound to its benefit—labor Zionist groups multiplied.

The perspectives of the two movements were poles apart. The Bund saw a hopeful future for the Jewish worker in a transformed society and viewed his bitter lot as the result of legal restrictions that would eventually be removed. Similarly, the Bund saw Christian-Jewish antagonism as an outgrowth of a distorted society, whereas Zionists felt that Jews could never achieve full economic and physical security in a society permeated with Christian anti-Semitism.

The Kishinev pogrom sharpened existing hostilities between the Bund and all branches of the Zionist movement and, to a certain degree, aggravated conflicts within Russian Jewry. Class and national loyalties tugged at each other, creating opposing solutions and competing appeals. The General Zionists still believed in obeying the government and in the possibility of getting its help in securing a charter for Palestine.[4] They condemned the Bund for defending Russian workers who participated in the pogrom and for engaging in activities that cast suspicion on all Jews. Most Jews, still politically inert, despaired of their future.

The ominous shadows of the Kishinev pogrom hung over the Bund delegates to the RSDWP Congress. For Medem, the trauma also became the occasion for condemning the Zionist movement, which, up to the time of the pogrom, had "made a big thing not only of its loyalty to Russia, but to the Russian government—the same government under whose shield agents carried on the pogrom." The pogrom, he said, was "the birthday of the socialist stream of Zionism," and the beginning of Zionist political protest in Russia. For the Bund, by contrast, it re-affirmed the rightness of its revolutionary course. It also led the Bund to form self-defense groups, "not something apart from the Bund's earlier revolutionary struggle, but, indeed, an integral part of that struggle and a role which strengthened its influence." [5]

The pogrom shattered Jewish life in the Pale and wracked many Jews with shame and helplessness, Medem among them. Yet his almost instant reflex was to attack Zionism and defend the Bund position. Coming from the Bund leader who struggled most to resolve the socialism-Jewish nationality dilemma, and who most influenced the working out of the Bund position, his response reveals a belligerent defensiveness.[6] Had the Bund really come to grips with the complications of radicalism-and-Jewishness? Medem was to become the most vehement of the Bund critics of Zionism, relentlessly hostile, as he himself struggled to reconcile Marxism with Jewish cultural autonomy. One set of feelings perhaps drove the other.[7]

The barbarities of the Kishinev pogrom were without precedent in Russia.[8] Some Jews had nails driven into their heads; others had their eyes put out. Little children were thrown from garrets to the ground and women had their stomachs ripped open or their breasts cut off. Many were raped. Drunken mobs broke into the synagogue and tore the Torah scrolls to shreds. Fifteen hundred houses and stores were looted and demolished. For two days the butchery continued as police and passersby looked on, as wagons moved through the streets carrying the dead and wounded. A Jewish deputation begged the governor to intercede, but he replied that he could do nothing since he had received no instructions from St. Petersburg. The liberal press in Russia and the foreign press were outraged by these events and accused the government of inspiring and guiding the pogrom and refusing help to the victims.

The Bund reacted swiftly to the crisis. Jewish self-defense groups were formed in a number of cities and spread even though they were declared illegal by Plehve. The Bund's first self-defense unit had been organized after the pogrom in Czestochowa, Poland, in August 1902, but the response to Kishinev was much broader and more thorough-going. The Fifth Congress in June 1903 legitimized the use of armed resistance at the first signs of an impending pogrom and thereby made the Bund a protective shield for the whole Jewish community. A successful model was created in Dvinsk, where about eighty physically strong men divided themselves into squads called "tens," each with its own leader, who alerted the group in emergencies and supplied it with weapons and quarters.[9] During the Easter season in 1903, this group was enlarged to about two hundred armed with knives, clubs, axes, and revolvers and bombs, and stood ready for an expected attack. A fight that might formerly have swelled into a pogrom never materialized; the peasants took to their heels and the police stood apart. In August in Gomel, where Jews formed half the population, government troops served as cover for the mobs that vandalized Jewish homes and shops. Where self-defense units and pogrom-raisers clashed, the Jewish fighters, aided by about thirty Christians, dispersed the mob. Some labor Zionists also helped the Bundist fighters.

The Bund interpreted the spirit displayed at Gomel as a new phase in the social and revolutionary history of the Jewish people and a vindication of their philosophy. Their units protected meetings and synagogues and, as their reputation spread, pogromists were deterred. In the Pale, Jews were divided: many were proud of the ability of Jews to fight; others were frightened by the prospect of confronting the powerful state at a time of growing government persecution. The Bund's influence affected Jewish liberals as well as workers and far exceeded its numerical strength at the time—about 30,000. Jewish liberals became particularly sympathetic to the Bund's self-defense efforts and contributed money. Maxim Vinaver, a well-known Jewish lawyer and member of the First Duma, met Raphael Abramovich, who was sent by the Bund to St. Petersburg on a money-raising mission after the pogrom. "What do you want?" Vinaver asked open-heartedly. "We are, actually, all Bundists." [10] Occasionally, Bundists were also invited to fund-raising banquets. Later, the migration of Jews to the United States provided a continuing source of funds for the Bund, giving it an enviable financial position for a radical organization.

Plehve, the Minister of Interior, was bent on repressing the spreading liberal and revolutionary forces in Russia. The Bund itself suffered from the high arrest rate. Over two thousand Bundists were arrested between April 1901 and June 1903, and more than twice this number between June 1903 and July 1904.[11] House searches were common, and meetings and demonstrations were attacked with great fury. The ensuing violence was blamed on the revolutionaries. Sometimes the Jewish self-defense policy boomeranged: when police were asked to defend streets in the Jewish quarters against mob action, they sarcastically advised Jews to go to the Bund. Many Jews thus caught in the toils of anti-Bundist agitation no longer could afford its protection.

The Russo-Japanese War, which broke out in 1904, also posed new problems and dilemmas for the Bund. A classic Marxist interpretation of the war and a strong antiwar position could not comfort either workers who lost their jobs in the economic dislocations caused by the war, or Jewish recruits facing anti-Semitic soldiers and the bleak prospect of fighting for a regime that itself was steeped in anti-Semitism. Moreover, a clear call to avoid service or desert would expose the whole Jewish population to the charge of treason. Soon after the war broke out, certain anti-Jewish measures were temporarily suspended and Jewish communal leaders urged Jews to support the war. In this predicament, the Bund decided to concentrate on intensifying its agitation within the army and head off military suppression of demonstrations.

At the time of the draft in October 1902, the Bund had issued a proclamation instructing recruits not to fire at workers' demonstrations and recommending separate revolutionary-military organizations. In 1903–04, twenty-five thousand copies of the proclamation were issued and distributed to recruits in Bialystok, Berdichev, Vitebsk, Gomel, Zhitomir, Ponevezh, and Riga.[12] The proclamation cited Kiev, Rostov and Tiflis, where soldiers were compelled to fire at workers' demonstrations and called on Jewish recruits to join or organize revolutionary military organizations. During 1903 there were frequent meetings of recruits and departure-demonstrations. On the eve of the war, the effects of the revolutionary agitation began to be felt in many areas of the military, and arrests of soldiers became frequent. The momentum of protest led to strikes in the army in Kiev, Moscow, and Riga against excessive production quotas and inedible food.[13]

In those areas where the Bund was active, the army was particularly vigilant. Barracks were raided and searched at night, and commanding officers vehemently attacked revolutionary propagandists, singling out Jews for special attention and inciting soldiers against Jews. Jewish soldiers receiving letters in Hebrew and Yiddish were punished arbitrarily. But the Bund went ahead with its agitation in the military and summarized this phase of its work for the Fourth International in Amsterdam in July 1904.

The Bund believed that the war would doom the regime through economic dislocations, an incompetent army, and demoralization as a result of military reverses; in such an extreme crisis an autocratic government might make opportunistic concessions—as happened after Plehve's assassination—but was incapable of genuine change. Government corruption and inefficiency contributed to and were glaringly exposed by the immediate military defeats. The war had no popular support. From the government's blundering policy in Manchuria and Korea, through Japan's surprise attack on Port Arthur, to the recurring stories of humiliating reverses and heavy casualties, there was mounting criticism of "the system," of tsarism. Normally passive and acquiescent, Russians began to clamor for radical reform: for political liberties, a constitution, representative government, vast social and economic change, and an end to the war. Spreading industrial unrest, protest meetings and attacks on the police gripped the country, which was now, it was said, passing through a "revolution." Many of the revolutionaries, however, who had ardently looked forward to such a time and debated ways of bringing it about were themselves taken by surprise. A deceptive lull followed Plehve's assassination in July 1904, during which his successor Prince Mirsky revoked a number of repressive edicts, including censorship regulations. The press became more optimistic and *zemstvo* (local assembly) leaders, students, and professional groups demanded reforms. The police were instructed not to break up their meetings.

Spontaneous meetings of Russian middle-class intelligentsia, liberals, and *zemstvos* took place in November and December, demanding a constitution and civil and political rights. These activities began to interest social democrats, but created predicaments. How should they deal with these enemies of their enemy? How support this opposition movement *only* on condition that it range itself on the side of social democracy and expose the bourgeois forces within the opposition? The Bolsheviks backed off completely, waiting for the "decisive blow" that would overthrow the regime. Very possibly the first miscalculation stemmed from the tendency common to most radicals to treat the war not as an opportunity for revolution, but as something extraneous to the struggle against autocracy. Lenin, for example, virtually ignored the war throughout most of 1904, and when he did comment, it was merely to say that Russia's defeat was desirable and would hasten the revolution. The great fear, grounded in socialist doctrine, was the possible compromise between the regime and the liberal opposition, which could then thwart the revolution. This view was translated into a rigid opposition to any liberal-socialist alliance, even after the liberal forces showed unexpected strength against the regime in 1905–06.

The Mensheviks tried to bring their segment of the movement out of the underground and involve at least some workers at meetings and demonstrations. Bolsheviks accused them of "opportunism," while the Mensheviks denounced the Bolsheviks for "creating a state of seige." Akselrod's articles in *Iskra* treated Bolshevism as "center fetishism" and "an organizational utopia of a theocratic nature." [14]

Toward the end of 1904, fine-spun intra-party arguments filled the pages of *Iskra*—"the wrangling of intellectuals," as the more advanced workers saw it. But the diffuse unrest that was longing for unity and organization was ignored. Menshevik groups increased at the expense of Bolshevik committees, which were reporting shaky, precarious, and depleted ranks.[15] According to a Bolshevik account, the Bolshevik St. Petersburg Committee was in "an extremely sorry state" in January before "Bloody Sunday." Workers' feelings toward the committee were hostile to the degree that Bolshevik agitators were beaten up and their leaflets destroyed.[16] Not a single worker was on the committee. A veteran RSDWP member of the old active Kiev Committee wrote of "a strange dearth of people in the organization, a meager organizational life. . . . In the Party . . . were gathered mostly callow youths, hotheaded and resolute, but weakly linked to the working masses. . . . The old Social-Democrats among the workers . . . for the most part stood aside." [17] There was a painful lack of contact between the RSDWP and the turbulently rising workers.

Then on Sunday, January 9, 1905, led by a Russian priest Father Georgy Gapon, large crowds of workers from St. Petersburg and their wives, some of them bearing icons and singing hymns, set out for the Winter Palace to present a petition of their grievances. Without warning they were fired on by troops guarding the palace; over fifteen hundred men and women were killed and wounded. "Bloody Sunday," as the day came to be known, had a profound effect on Russian workers and gave the social democrats, stunned by events, an unexpected opportunity to expand their influence. For Bloody Sunday unleashed a wave of strikes and social unrest that opened the first phase of the Revolution of 1905, forcing the revolutionaries to examine their relations with these new forces and attempt to grasp their direction.

The petition of January 9 was naive and trustful, beginning with a plea to restore three workers who had been fired from the Putilov metallurgical works, and moving to a demand for peace, for a constituent assembly, an eight-hour day, and the freedom to form unions. "We, workers of St.

Petersburg," the petition asked humbly, "have come to Thee, Sovereign, to seek justice and protection. . . . Do not refuse to aid Thy people." The social democrats had scarcely any role in this dramatic episode; in fact, they dismissed Gapon as a Zubatovite agent because his Assembly of Russian Factory Workers had been organized with the sanction of government officials. The St. Petersburg workers, indeed, were not in the least a class-conscious proletariat in the Marxist sense, but followed Gapon because his assembly promised some improvement for them through legal means. At first, in January, when social-democratic agitators attended meetings called by the assembly, they were tolerated as long as they confined themselves to criticism of existing social conditions, but once they began to shout "Down with the Autocracy" and unfurl their red banners, there were jeers and catcalls.[18] Gapon himself was eager to keep the movement from losing its nonviolent, nonpartisan character and he finally prevailed on the social democrats to march at the rear of the crowd and maintain a low profile.

Gapon was not a simon-pure spiritual leader, although he undoubtedly thought he was.[19] In his early thirties at the time of Bloody Sunday, he had impressed Russian workers as sincere, intelligent, and seriously interested in their welfare. Earlier, at the Poltava seminary, he came under the influence of Tolstoyans, who testified to his kindness toward the working poor and solicitude for their condition. While still in the seminary, he composed and forwarded to the government a lengthy memorandum outlining a plan for setting up a network of work houses and colonies for the poor. The movement he eventually founded was related indirectly to Zubatov's. Gapon attended some of the meetings Zubatov had organized in St. Petersburg late in 1902, but was repelled by the too obvious dependence on the police. The type of organization he envisioned was a cultural and mutual aid association with religious overtones and, although he was loyal to the authorities, he valued worker initiative and did not want too much official interference.

Gapon at first borrowed trade union literature from Zubatov and seemed to be under his influence, remaining personally loyal to him after he was relieved of his duties in August 1903. But soon Gapon went his independent way. In the fall of 1903 he asked for formal legalization of his tearoom-reading clubs to foster self-education and self-help activities among factory workers. Early in 1904, his Assembly of Russian Factory Workers of St. Petersburg was approved. The movement began as a "loyal" undertaking of edifying uplift for workers, but it changed as more politically sophisticated workers and radicals began to crowd assembly meetings. The wartime rise in the cost of living as well as the campaign to legally improve the conditions and life of the workers soon drew virtually all workers and some socialists in the huge Putilov locomotive works and machine shops in St. Petersburg into Gapon's league. Yet hostility was directed much more at employers than at the tsar, and "God Save the

Tsar" was sung fervently at each meeting. When moderate demands on Putilov resulted in the firing of leading members of Gapon's league, the priest went over the heads of his own superiors in the Police Department and Interior Ministry and took the workers' petitions directly to the tsar.[20] On the eve of the planned procession, Gapon even wrote a confidential message to the tsar, urging him to stand before the people and humbly accept their petition.

The bullets and bloodshed swept away all vestiges of trust in the regime. The minds of the workers were now more susceptible to democratic and socialist ideas and the power of independent action. With the help of social revolutionaries, Gapon fled abroad and sent one more note to the tsar, without any respectful salutation:

> The innocent blood of workers, their wives and children lies forever between thee, oh soul destroyer, and the Russian people. Moral connection between thee and them may never more be. . . . Let all the blood which has to be shed, hangman, fall upon thee and thy kindred! [21]

While unknown men of the masses were leading strikes, peasant riots and mutinies in closest cooperation, the emigré radical factions wrangled. When Gapon reached Geneva, he tried to unite all of the revolutionary parties "and to begin the business of armed uprising against tsarism. . . . The first aim is the overthrow of the autocracy." Lenin was much taken with him; Gapon, according to Krupskaya, helped him understand the peasant as a concrete revolutionary force and the shortcomings of piece-meal concessions to the peasants on the land issue.

Lionized by a variety of visitors in Geneva and the recipient of large sums of money, Gapon eagerly met with representatives of a number of socialist parties on April 2 and thought of himself as their leader in the struggle against tsarism. Medem, who was one of the Bund delegates to the conference, has left an interesting vignette of Gapon.[22] The "cream of the revolutionary movement" was present at Ansky's house where the conference was held. Medem had to be persuaded to go—he was only twenty-four and felt overwhelmed by the veterans. Yet he was very observant. He and Gapon—"in a gray tunic, with a red beard and small brown eyes and uninteresting face"—were alone for a few minutes. Gapon, the speaker who had gripped thousands of workers with his inspiring words, could not find anything to talk to Medem about. "Are you married?" Why are you so pale? Are you sick?" was all that he could muster. Then, when he began to address the whole group, he fumbled and hesitated so, the embarrassed delegates had to avert their eyes. "We felt pity for him. When he mentioned the Amsterdam Congress, which had passed a resolution calling for the unity of all socialist parties, he could not even pronounce the name of the city properly."

The parties soon fell to petty quarrelling. The Lettish delegate, who scarcely had a party to represent, wanted to lead the drive for unity. Lenin caviled at the absence of the Finnish social democrats. "Why were they not invited?" When it was explained that they were invited through friendly liberal contacts, he bristled at *that*. The only point the delegates united on, Medem recalled, was the purchase of some things which they bought jointly, but which never arrived in Russia.

After the attack on the workers on January 9, both Mensheviks and Bolsheviks at least had agreed that the revolution had begun, that soon there would be an armed uprising of class-conscious masses, with the party working to develop this consciousness by fomenting strikes and anti-government demonstrations. The Bolsheviks, directed by Lenin, favored an insurrection controlled by the experienced party élite. Their attitude toward unions remained negative, or at most, equivocal. Indeed, radical politics ravaged by factional controversy, assumed the proportions of verbal civil war at a crucial time in Russian history. For the first time, mass fury with the oppressive state was exploding. A wave of strikes spread throughout St. Petersburg after Bloody Sunday—414,000 men in January, 291,000 in February, and 72,000 in March—and then fanned out to other cities. Martial law was declared. In the western and northwestern border provinces and in Transcaucasia and Georgia, violence was endemic. These were ethnically non-Russian areas where national animosities inflamed existing unrest. In several episodes, the Bund took a leading role, sometimes alone, sometimes in concert with other social democratic groups.

During this period there were intermittent contacts between the Bund and the RSDWP groups, but no sustained cooperation until the dramatic "October days." After the Bund's break with the party in 1903, such contacts bristled with mutual recrimination. In 1903–04, the RSDWP began to campaign among Jewish workers in the northwest provinces, which was Bund territory, and even tried to win over Bundists. But the gains were very slim and, in fact, were nullified by intra-party conflicts. These conflicts were generally described as "organizational," or matters of "tactics," but the growing cleavages in basic orientations were the fundamental cause of all the disputes between Bolsheviks and Mensheviks in 1905. It was only in the crucible of the revolution of that year, in the face of a largely uncontrollable mass movement, that the contradictions and tensions that had beset the Russian social democrats from the beginning exploded. Both Bolsheviks and Mensheviks were then forced to articulate and act out their often unspoken assumptions about their roles as spokesmen of the Russian workers.

Against this gathering storm within the RSDWP, the Bund in 1904 found not only re-affiliation but practical everyday working relationships impossible. The nationality problem, which concerned the Bund, was considered politically distracting to an RSDWP still struggling for socialist unity and organizational energy for initiatives. The fullest contacts were with the PPS, but the Bundists were still unwilling or unable to formulate a new policy on Polish independence. The Bund saw the PPS as the RSDWP saw the Bund: divisive and nationalist! Despite its involvement in the national question, the class war still came first for the Bund, as it did for the RSDWP.

In June 1904, the Bund finally made an overture to the RSDWP, admitting that unification was impossible because of the great differences in organizational principle, but suggesting a *"temporary* alliance for a special *temporary* task." [23] The RSDWP hesitated because of its weakness and fear that the Bund initiative might lead to federation under Bund domination. "It would be better to take that initiative upon ourselves," Martov said, a remark that reveals much about the insecurity within the RSDWP.[24]

The Russians, however, finally decided on a preliminary conference of all social-democratic organizations, including the Bund. The Bund responded eagerly. Representatives met in the late summer while they were preparing for the Amsterdam Congress of the International. The Bund wanted to discuss a proposal to bring together all parties opposed to tsarism; the RSDWP wanted only to react to a Finnish proposal. There followed a bitter dispute between the Bund and the RSDWP over representation to the International in September, resulting in a vehement polemic between Plekhanov and the Bund,[25] which, incidentally, aroused great interest in student and emigré circles and in the Yiddish press in America. Still pressing for possible accord, the Bund again, in November, urged all social democrats to come together and drew up an agenda. But the RSDWP Council wanted only to introduce its own proposals.[26] A conference was finally held, but by then Bloody Sunday had already erupted.

Before 1905, the Bund's most harmonious relationships were with the national-minded Latvian social democrats, with whom the Bund shared mutual claims to exclusive representation of a national group. In Riga, both groups mobilized more than 20,000 workers in a mass demonstration on January 12, 1905. On the next day, the crowd increased to 60,000. Shots fired by the troops into the crowd killed over thirty and wounded seventy more. On January 15, the RSDWP joined the special strike commission created by the Bund and Latvian socialists. Their objective was to bring everything to a halt in Riga.[27] Within a few days they shifted to economic aims: an eight-hour day and better pay. Employers began to make concessions. In Vilna a general strike was called on January 11 and lasted several days. A similar strike was called in Kovno. In the small industrial towns of Smorgon and Krinki workers completely controlled affairs briefly. In Krinki, the Bund captured the post office and police station for a day and took arms. But in Warsaw, an important workers' center, the PPS rival SDKPiL (Social-Democracy of the Kingdom of Poland and Lithuania) and the Bund were divided over strategy. When the general strike was finally called on January 14, it was quickly put down by troops.[28] Workers were unable to build barricades; many demonstrated without leadership. The failure in Warsaw was felt acutely.

The conference of Russian social democrats, which had met in January in Riga, devised political goals, including an end to the war, universal suffrage, a constituent assembly, creation of a democratic republic, guarantees of the basic freedoms and basic rights for workers, but it had no joint strategy for dealing with the unravelling social order.[29] Immediately after the conference Mensheviks and Bolsheviks began to battle each other anew.

Their disputes centered on a crucial relationship that the Bund had already worked through, namely, the respective roles of the socialist intelligentsia and the workers. Had they solidified this fundamental partnership as effectively as the Bund, the Russian Revolution of 1905 might have achieved the great transformations that were on the verge of realization. But, tragically, the RSDWP was torn by opposing theories of the role of the worker. These conflicting ideas were argued in *Iskra* with a weirdly unreal intensity on a rarified, theoretical level, while the Russian working masses were explosively coming to political life. Yet, however labored and excessively attenuated the arguments seem, they expose the incapacity of the RSDWP to lead the masses when they were ready.

The basic thesis of the Bolsheviks had already been propounded by Lenin in *What Is To Be Done?*—namely, that only the bourgeois intelligentsia is capable of working out a socialist ideology, that workers are incapable of developing a socialist consciousness by themselves, and that such consciousness must be brought to them from without. Workers, according to Lenin, will tend to gravitate toward a bourgeois ideology as they create their own trade unions; only the socialist intelligentsia can neutralize or change this progression. The task of the socialists, then, is to bring labor under the wing of revolutionary socialism, to bring workers a socialist ideology *from without.* Coupled with his conviction that, under Russian conditions, this ideology could be transmitted only by the party, and that the party machine *had* to be directed at all levels by tested "professional revolutionaries," no role at all remained for independent workers. Moreover, the social composition of the leadership of the RSDWP was entirely bourgeois; there were no workers in policy-making positions.

The Mensheviks, on the other hand, were struggling to encourage workers' independent activity, wherever possible, and give them a share in party life. As Martov put it, the RSDWP was "only an organization of leaders of the proletarian struggle, not an organization of struggling proletarians." [30] Akselrod, too, in a letter to Kautsky on June 6, 1904, wrote that the party must be transformed into a "true proletarian class party" before the "struggle with absolutism" can be joined.[31] As late as

July 1904, despite his antagonism to the Bund, Martov was full of praise for the Bund's habit of discussing matters with workers.[32] In the second half of 1904, these conflicts led to the formation of Menshevik "groups" in places where Bolshevik "committees" already existed, causing wasteful overlapping, rivalry and confusion among workers.[33]

Lenin's conception of the dictatorship of the proletariat and Lenin himself as the embodiment of the revolutionary spirit at first won over most of the radical youth, for whom the Mensheviks, by contrast, were fuzzy, complex and cautious. Later, many of them were repelled by the Bolshevik-controlled party committees' denial of the workers' strivings for independent activity and organization, first in the form of independent trade unions, and then the soviets.

But even the Mensheviks could not fully satisfy the workers' wish to make the party their own. The most active workers, realizing that they were not considered full-fledged party members, frequently expressed bitterness toward the party intelligentsia. For example, in a pamphlet published by the Menshevik press late in 1904 and signed "A Worker," the author accused the intelligentsia-leaders of preventing workers from influencing local party work and systematically blocking independent activity from the bottom up.[34] In March 1905, Martov accused the Bolsheviks of having dismissed "organized proletarians" for the past year. By contrast, he said, Menshevik "groups" were becoming stronger than the Bolshevik "committees." [35]

Following Bloody Sunday, an experience unprecedented in Russian history, involving St. Petersburg workers in an elementary kind of collective bargaining, strengthened the Menshevik group there over the Bolshevik committee and gave the Mensheviks their first realization that living ties could be made with workers. This came late in January 1905, when in a conciliatory gesture, the government decided to appoint a special commission to determine the causes of and cure for the unrest. A so-called Shidlovsky Commission was to be created, made up of elected representatives of *workers* as well as manufacturers. No police, factory inspectors, or foremen were to be present at the elections of workers. The government plan was for workers to elect electors who would then elect deputies to the commission. Instead, the electors themselves became workers' representatives in the factories. A number of remarkably gifted workers came to the fore in the dramatic elections and began to press long-suppressed demands upon their employers and on Senator Shidlovsky, the commission chairman, as well.[36]

The elections in February were the first basically free elections ever held in Russia by workers and aroused enormous interest not only in St. Petersburg but in Kharkov, Kiev and Odessa. Altogether about 160,000 workers from over 250 factories in St. Petersburg took part in this remarkable mass voting.[37] Neither Mensheviks nor Bolsheviks directed them; in fact, they were uncertain about how to react. At first skeptical, they tentatively decided to participate in the elections, but rejected participation in the commission. The Mensheviks eventually saw the commission as a "platform for agitation," bringing workers to consciousness as a proletariat and creating unity among the workers. The Bolsheviks changed their position from day to day, but their prevailing view was to boycott the election campaign. The proletariat was ready for the crucial "uprising," they maintained.

The four hundred worker-delegates, of whom about 20 per cent were social democrats, insisted on meetings to discuss freedom of press and assembly, unions, workmen's insurance, and an eight-hour day. They also demanded that eleven local unions which had been closed down after Bloody Sunday be reopened, that all workers arrested since January 1 be released, and that members of the commission have complete freedom of action. A general strike was threatened if the response from Shidlovsky was unfavorable.

This was entirely too much for the regime. The resolutions died stillborn and the commission was disbanded. A wave of strikes and arrests followed, crushing hopes for an organized labor movement. The fiasco of the commission, however, had created the model of a workers' representative organization that later helped pave the way for a workers' soviet. This whole experience drove Mensheviks and Bolsheviks further apart.

The Bund, meanwhile, like all social-democratic groups, had been electrified by the revolutionary possibilities of Father Gapon's march and had commissioned Raphael Abramovich to draft a leaflet immediately. "The great day has come!" he wrote exultantly. "The revolution has come.... Comrades in all towns, take up the battle!... Arm yourselves.... Let every street become a battlefield! Break into the arsenals! Seize rifles, revolvers...." [38] The leaflet also called for action to create a democratic republic. Over 100,000 copies were printed, but there were no detailed plans to guide the local committees. The Bund, too, was waiting for the signal for an uprising. It was proud of its own achievements, its discipline and response to events during the January upheavals in contrast with the other social democrats in Russia, yet it could not muster the leadership missing in the other groups. In true form, it undertook a reevaluation of events at a conference in Dvinsk from February 11 to 17.

The Bund's own weaknesses and the failure of the non-Jewish revolutionaries to lead a proletarian movement were analyzed. The Bund acknowledged its thin ties with the non-Jewish masses and called for an organizational drive and strengthening of leadership.[39] It also urged more armed resistance to police and troops. The general strike was underscored as the most potent weapon against the regime. United action with other social democratic groups was urged, but not at the cost of organizational independence. The primary aim was to reach and radicalize the masses. A new, intense wave of strikes involving Jewish workers in Vilna, Dvinsk, Minsk, and Bobroisk unrolled in February and March.

The leaders of the RSDWP, meanwhile, mainly in exile, were miles away from the farms, factories, peasants, and workers about whom they were theorizing. Lenin was planning an all-Bolshevik congress. Martov was busy editing *Iskra.* Plekhanov and Akselrod were ill. Doctrinal schismatics destroyed the needed perspective on events. Local committees were adrift without leadership from the center, their composition constantly changing as a result of arrest or shifts in assignment. Estrangement from workers was a recurring theme. In May 1905, a typical complaint was made by a dissatisfied group of workers at Cherkassy on the Dnieper:

> Even now we see that all the higher posts are occupied by intellectuals. One has to hunt for workers with a lamp. . . . When a worker, even if an "advanced" one, suggests some means of improving the agitation, he is told to mind his business and do as he is told, so that the voice of every worker in this so-called "workers' party" is reduced to nil.[40]

Paradoxically, the men on the committees came to lose touch with reality. Living on false passports, frequently changing addresses, and requiring an elaborate network of passwords, codes and secret addresses, the committee men were enwrapped in a revolutionary fantasy nourished by underground life. They lived in a self-invented world that helped bolster their felt exercise of power but deceived them as to the extent of popular support, confusing the actual circumstances that confronted them with the imaginary situation they dreamt about. One historian of the movement has commented: "This tendency to indulge in fantasy was less common among the rank and file, and does much to explain the tension between them and the intellectuals." [41] The mystique of the conspiratorial life also strengthened the position of the intellectuals in the party, who controlled the links between the rank and file and the outside world. In this respect, the Bund had achieved a much better balance and perspective than other social democratic groups.

These committees poured out a torrent of propaganda from their secret printing presses, agitated among workers, and set up militia units armed with knives and guns. But the lifeline to the masses was missing. Theorists had had interminable discussions about the so-called "organization question," but there was no practical guidance as to how the party could exercise control over movements that sprang out of mass needs. Both segments of the party were reacting to instead of creating events.

In keeping with their old attack on Economism and spontaneous strikes, the Bolsheviks considered strikes for economic demands the weapon of a still-backward proletariat. Only *political* mass strikes together with an armed uprising were considered effective in the struggle against tsarism, although Bolsheviks were sometimes drawn into strikes in areas where they made up most of the party organization. This was true of the general strike in Ivanovo-Voznesenk in May–June, 1905, one of the most important before the great general strike of October 1905.[42] But this activity was unusual for the Bolsheviks, and during the important strike movement in September-October 1905, the Bolsheviks remained passive.

For the Mensheviks, strikes came to mean an important way of "unleashing the revolution," and striking workers became a source of new strength for the movement. Later, the element of subordination was removed and Mensheviks helped to create trade unions. The Bolsheviks fought the Mensheviks on this issue, too, remaining almost to the end of 1905 a captive of Lenin's ideas of 1902: to fight the spontaneous development of the labor movement. When it became politically embarrassing to openly oppose the formation of trade unions, the Bolsheviks settled for those subordinated to the party. Such an idea was offensive to the Bund and to Latvian social democrats especially in Riga, where their own organizations had much more influence among the workers than the Bolsheviks or Mensheviks.[43] The characteristic refusal of the Bolsheviks to bend dogma to reality made their role in the labor movement of 1905 insignificant.

A new complication entered the Marxist strategic underpinning of the events of 1905 with Lenin's new perception of the peasant. Both Bolsheviks and Mensheviks agreed that the coming revolution would not be a socialist but a bourgeois one, and that the proletariat would have to ally itself temporarily with the bourgeoisie. But who were the bourgeoisie in Russia in 1905? Loyal to traditional doctrine, the Mensheviks identified them as the urban middle class. The Bolsheviks, however, added a new component. Stimulated by a Russian-born Jew named Parvus (A. L. Helphand), who had an outstanding reputation as a Marxist theoretician in the German socialist movement, Lenin began to perceive the peasants as an important—if temporary—ally of the industrial proletariat instead of the traditional bourgeoisie, whom he excoriated. He began to extol the peasantry as a "bulwark of the revolution and the republic" with as much fervor as he denounced the urban middle class.[44] Even the kulaks (the prosperous peasants), he argued, were more interested in seizing private estates than in upholding the principle of private property.

For the Mensheviks, Lenin's discovery of the revolutionary potentialities of the peasant was a reversion to *narodnik* heresy, an argument underlined by the experience of 1848, numerous passages from Marx and Engels, and later, by the experience of 1905, when, as Trotsky said, the proletarian revolution was broken "on the bayonets of the peasant army." For Lenin, the idea was purely tactical, to ensure maximum development of the revolution, and speculative, growing out of debates with the Mensheviks, but not at all related to the actual state of existing social relationships in Russia.[45] Despite considerable misgivings, the third "Party" Congress (all-Bolshevik) in April 1905 in London (the Mensheviks met separately) committed itself to full support of the peasants and an immediate armed uprising. The alliance was to usher in a revolution leading to a revolutionary provisional government that would eliminate the old regime, introduce essential democratic reforms, and organize elections to the constituent assembly—in a word, complete the bourgeois democratic revolution. Once this was achieved, since the peasantry as a whole would not support the proletariat in its advance toward the socialist revolution, it would be necessary for the proletariat to split the peasantry against itself and enlist the support of the semiproletarian elements—the poor and landless peasants—against the rich peasants who would have profited most by the division of the landowners' estates. In this struggle, the European proletariat would come to the aid of the Russian proletariat.

Far from the turmoil in Russia [46] and estranged from most of the leaders in the original party, Lenin elaborated these ideas during the summer of 1905 in his *Two Tactics of Social-Democracy in the Democratic Revolution*. He also harangued the St. Petersburg Committee to

> go to the youth . . . and workers. Let them arm themselves immediately with whatever weapons they can obtain—a knife, a revolver, a kerosene-soaked rag for setting fires. . . . Some can . . . assassinate a spy or blow up a police station, others can attack a bank to expropriate funds for an insurrection. Let every squad learn, if only by beating up police.[47]

The emigré Mensheviks were likewise preoccupied with mental constructs, but more loosely knit than the Bolsheviks and lacking a counterpart to Lenin, they spoke with several voices. In general, they were more cautious than the Bolsheviks and more orthodox in their Marxism. At their conference in May 1905, when prospects in Russia were still very promising, they hinged success there to the spread of socialism to Western Europe. And impressed by the strength of the liberals, they gave up the concept of proletarian "hegemony" and urged socialists to collaborate with them in the common struggle. "March apart, but strike together!" Plekhanov had urged. Martov and Dan, editors of *Iskra*, wanted to push the liberals as far as possible to the left, pulling up the roots that had nourished them until they fell under the party's influence. As to the composition of the provisional government, the Mensheviks did not visualize any role in it for the social democrats. It was not their responsibility to establish a new bourgeois order; rather, they were to be the "party of extreme revolutionary opposition."

The debates in *Iskra* and *V'period* were often bitter, even ferocious, taking at least some force from the psychological needs of the combatants, their isolation from events, and the very abstractedness of their thinking. Of all the leading Russian social democrats, only Trotsky played a conspicuous part in the actual events of 1905. In February he returned to Russia as an active revolutionary, by now belonging to neither faction but lacking the support of any regular following. He soon became the ideological leader of the first workers' soviet in St. Petersburg, organized in October 1905. On issues of doctrine, he was fairly close to Lenin, but on matters of organization, he identified with the Mensheviks and despite other differences, often allied with them, especially in their conception of the party. In later years, as the rift between them grew wider, he was tireless in his efforts at conciliation.

In sharp contrast with the ruptured RSDWP was the Bund, which in 1905 was a genuine mass party in the Pale with a tradition of mass worker action, socialist consciousness, and broad worker support. Moreover, the Bund had impressive numerical strength. At the beginning of 1905, the entire Russian party (not including the Poles and Letts) numbered only 8,400, while the Bund, representing Jewish workers alone, could claim a membership of 30,000.[48] Its leading groups were not invariably composed of intellectuals, but substantially of workers. This balance and the Bund's numerical strength as well as its reputation for discipline and organization aggravated the abrasiveness between its members and the Bolsheviks. Moreover, although the area in which the Bund functioned was not of decisive importance, its agitation during 1905 was effective, and the involvement of Jewish workers during 1905 was on an unprecedented scale.

As in January, in the period from February to October, 1905, the provinces where the Bund was strongest were the areas of great strikes: Lodz, Riga, Vilna, and Bialystok. Bund agitators attended all strike meetings, distributed literature, organized meetings and demonstrations, and helped the striking workers financially. Petrokow province, incorporating the city of Lodz, led the country in a number of strikes (2,316 as compared with 1,861 in St. Petersburg), with 95 per cent of its workers participating.[49] In the northwest provinces of Kovno, Vilna, and Grodno, where the Bund was strong, the average participation was over 80 per cent.

The influence of the Bund grew and the Bund name was magnetic enough to commend it to unorganized workers. Employers faced with boycotts organized by the Bund frequently sued for a settlement. The *birzhe* continued to be an important outlet, and at *birzhe* meetings—some attended by up to a thousand people—and street markets, large throngs of workers brought a new dramatic intensity and glamour to Bund activity.[50] For thousands of Bund members and sympathizers, "the exhilaration of political revolution, open and visible, and the personal participation in a heroic struggle made those few short months their moment in history." [51] This period marked the peak of Bund influence among workers.

Careful preparations were made for May Day celebrations in 1905. With police swarming and the Black Hundreds threatening pogroms, the Bund organized well-armed defense units. Yet, local groups were directed to observe May Day with peaceful strikes. Many Jewish workers participated, but in spite of the cautious preparations, violent clashes with the police broke out in Warsaw, Lodz, and Kalisz. There were some disappointments, but they were far outweighed by accomplishments. Scores of meetings and celebrations were held in streets, synagogues, and factories, with the Bund press reporting events in eighty towns and cities.[52]

Warsaw virtually came to a halt. More than 20,000 workers celebrated May Day in six cities in the Pale. Leaders predicted "an end to political slavery" in the coming year. In Jewish communities the Bund was becoming something of a legend.

"When I went into one of our towns," wrote Raphael Abramovich, "I used to feel like the representative of a great power that was well-loved and supported by the working masses and the intelligentsia alike." The Bund was consulted on divorce matters, dowries, quarrels, swindles, family disputes—all manner of questions normally referred to rabbis. "It was regarded as some kind of mystical being," Litvak recalled, "with fear and hope. It could achieve everything, reach everyone. . . . The word of the Bund was law; its stamp of approval was hypnotic. Wherever an injustice, wherever an insult, even when it had no relation to the workers' movement . . . one came to the Bund. It was legendary." [53]

This was also a time for romantic figures in a movement that was characteristically sober, cooly rationalistic, and disdainful of heroics. One of the most colorful of the young Bundists at this time was Baruch Nachman Charney (later Vladek),[54] who was sent by the Bund to help organize a general strike in the spring of 1905. Charney learned much of his revolutionary theory and tactics in tsarist jails. After his release in September 1904, he led a group of factory workers in the outskirts of Minsk back to the city across an open plain when they were suddenly attacked by Cossack horsemen who lashed them with whips and swords. Charney—then only nineteen—was left half-dead in the snow. After his recovery, he was sent to Vilna, where he became known as a stirring public speaker and was affectionately called *der tsvayter Lassalle* (the second Lassalle). He was arrested in Vilna too, and after spending six more months in jail, was sent by the Bund to Poland, where he had hair-raising experiences in Warsaw, Lublin, Lodz, and many smaller towns, slipping past the police, impersonating a Russian gentleman to get a police escort to a train, and using his excellent Russian to keep a bored but menacing Russian officer in relaxed conversation.

The inevitable political reaction, already forming, would soon shatter such heightened moments as well as the hopeful promise of a better life felt by Jews and non-Jews alike in midsummer 1905.

20. *Reaction and Introspection, 1906-10*

The reaction was at first carefully disguised and slow to emerge. On February 18, 1905, stung by the assassination of his uncle the Grand Duke Sergei, one of the most detestable of the Romanovs,[1] yet intimidated by waves of revolutionary unrest, the tsar had called on all "well-intentioned persons" to struggle against "the internal sedition." In a rescript to Bulygin, the new Minister of the Interior, the tsar also announced his intention "to invite the worthiest men . . . to participate in the consideration of legislative projects." Both supporters and opponents of the regime could find comfort in this ambivalent formulation. Pent-up progressives, including Jewish groups, now began to deluge the government with resolutions and declarations demanding a parliamentary government. But Jewish hopes were quickly cut down by counter-forces, one of the most vicious of which were the government-backed armed thugs called the Black Hundreds, who were unleashed against the liberal intelligentsia and Jews. Pogroms could now be "patriotic"; revolution could be exposed as the work of Jews; the unwillingness of the "people" to abolish autocracy could be dramatized. A wave of pogroms struck Bialystok, Melitopol, Zhitomir, Troyanov, Minsk, and Lodz; threats arose in many other cities and towns.

Actually, the cycle of pogroms and pogrom-agitation involved four periods: the spring of 1904, and February, March-April, and the summer of 1905.[2] For the Bund, these periods were a kind of barometer of revolutionary activity. After the pogroms in Kishinev and Gomel, the Bund realized the counter-revolutionary political nature of government-protected pogroms. The great surge of open, vigorous activity in the spring and summer of 1905, including waves of strikes and demonstrations and involving Jewish and Christian workers, as well as peasants and soldiers, was offset by counter-waves of anti-Jewish agitation inflamed by private societies and police in the Black Hundreds. Leaflets and agitators accused

Jews of murdering Sergei, of inciting the Russian people to revolution, of corrupting students. A flood of pogrom rumors spread through Kishinev and Kreslavka after the tsar's February call to put down sedition; during the dangerous Easter season, the agitation swelled, resulting in several pogroms, the worst of which occurred in Zhitomir. In the late spring and summer, new outbreaks of violence followed Russian military defeats in the war against Japan.

The Bund's self-defense units mobilized all possible forces against the Black Hundreds to defend Jewish homes and shops. Their own armed groups were conservatively estimated at about 1,100, with perhaps another 8,000 to 9,000 in reserves.[3] Appeals for arms were made to Jews in America [4] as well as in Russia. Besides guns, bombs became an important weapon after threats to the Jewish population increased in the summer of 1905, and chemists and students were drawn into the making of explosives. These weapons were now used by the Bund in a two-front war: to defend Jewish life and property, and to protect meetings, demonstrations, and strikers. The Bund boasted that "we were the first to acquaint the Jewish street with revolvers and knives." [5]

The expectation of further struggle with the state made the issue of armed insurrection vital during 1905. What plans had to be made in case of the expected uprising? There were discussions of military objectives, logistics, tactics, and other technical considerations, but the Bund leaders were also anxious that their own armed units not become independent (as were the social revolutionary armed units),[6] and shear away from the parent movement. Moreover, the Bund looked to the broader movement to signal the moment and form of "the last decisive struggle." In June, a bloody outbreak in Lodz, in which over 1,500 people were killed or wounded, led the Bund to develop plans for the construction of barricades and other military contingencies and anticipate the breakdown of military discipline. They hoped the spirit of revolt would cause soldiers to desert and join the struggle against the regime.

Late in June, Lodz was in the grip of mass meetings, strikes, and demonstrations. One Bund activist, A. Tschemerinsky, wrote excitedly that "the whole town was living in *birzhes*." [7] The streets were full of striking workers, and Jews and Christians felt new ties of solidarity. Morale was high and the Bund, which was strong in Lodz, forged into a leading role. Its speakers were used by other social democratic groups, even though they had fought the Bund in unions. All languages and all national groups seemed to fuse in a great show of unity. An intoxicating camaraderie seems to have filled the whole city for a time. Polish and Jewish workers kept returning to the streets to demonstrate with increasing enthusiasm.

Then, in the last week of June, some members of a Bundist youth group were peacefully demonstrating when they were suddenly shot down. The whole city trembled with shock and rage; the police refused to give up the bodies of the youths. Barricades arose. "We collected everything,"

Tschemerinsky recalled: "big stones, ladders, wagons, poles. We dragged everything from street to street, making barricades and everyone grouped around the barricades—men, women, children, old people.... On the second day, the barricades were strengthened and made higher. But there was no plan, no overall political or military strategy.... The soldiers came shooting at the barricades from all sides." [8]

That was on June 23. Then cavalry moved in and police and soldiers seized stores of arms. Many wounded workers who had to be carried under the hail of bullets died. The resistance was quickly crushed. At one point, after a street was emptied, an old Polish worker was seen tearing off his clothes, spreading out his hands and crying to the soldiers, "Shoot!" [9]

The unequal struggle in Lodz brought home the realization that workers at the barricades were no match for professional soldiers. From this experience, the Bund concluded that no popular revolt could possibly succeed, but that "the revolutionary organizations, with strong discipline and firm control, must lead the final revolt." [10] They would intensify the struggle, it was believed, until the army itself would crack and come over to the side of the workers. Special groups set up to agitate among soldiers pressed on with their work especially during the dramatic October days.

The Bund also had to deal with accelerating changes within Jewish life in 1905 and develop strategies for meeting new forces among a politically awakening Jewry. Sometimes their goals converged; often they clashed. By February, both the liberal opposition to the regime and the revolutionary movement had stirred Jews in the Pale as well as outside. Alternating between fear and unyielding stubbornness, Nicholas II had appointed a council to draft a constitution and permit groups in the population to submit their recommendations. Jewish groups emerged and began debating resolutions of varying degrees of vigor, some very mild, verging on self-abnegation, others, more demanding.

A small Jewish Democratic Group formed in St. Petersburg, advocating civil and political rights for Jews. The Bund praised this step as "progressive," but found the appeal to Jews *as a whole* repugnant. Moreover, the group did not make any social demands and left the question of a new government untouched. Although the Bund itself was far from having clarified its own position on the Jewish nationality question, it criticized the group for leaving the matter of cultural self-determination to private initiative instead of positive action from the state.[11]

In the third week of March, Jewish liberal intelligentsia—many of them lawyers who had defended Jews in the trials following the Kishinev and Gomel pogroms—met in Vilna to form a nonparty federation to fight for equal rights. Under the skillful leadership of Maxim Vinaver, one of the founders of the Constitutional Democratic party (Kadets), sixty-seven delegates from diverse organizations formulated a program to secure "to the greatest degree possible the civic, political and national rights of the Jewish people in Russia." Conspicuous by its absence, the Bund attacked the "slavish psychology" of such Jews who still had not gone beyond the despised practise of petitioning the Russian state, yet it admitted that the resolution was a step forward. The delegates, indeed, met as if they were revolutionaries. To forestall a police raid, they held closed meetings in private homes and changed places several times. Yet they were in an exhilarated mood for such meetings were unprecedented. They talked at length about Jewish representation in the prospective Russian Duma, voting systems, parliamentary factions, and the meaning of cultural autonomy. Simon Dubnow, the eminent Jewish historian, read a paper on Jewish national rights, which dealt with communal autonomy, recognition of Yiddish, and a Jewish educational system, issues which elicited the most heated debates.[12] A compromise was finally agreed upon and the organization was re-named The League for Equal Rights for the Jewish People in Russia.

The growth and activity of such groups sharpened the Bund's dilemma of wanting to carry on a revolutionary struggle for long-range goals while recognizing the advantages of short-term cooperation with liberal organizations. For the moment, it kept its revolutionary position.

The great surge of hope and release felt even by the submerged Jews of Russia was soon darkened by the Easter wave of pogroms, especially the massacre at Zhitomir. The Bund, meanwhile, was propelled by its own troubled introspection and sorrow to give more attention to the national elements of its program. The Sixth Bund Congress (October 1905) incorporated national-cultural autonomy into its "Program-Minimum." This congress in Zurich, originally planned as a full-scale review of tactics and unsettled questions of principle, was drastically changed by the revolutionary tumult in Russia, including preparations for a general strike. Although a number of delegates decided to remain in Russia, thirty attended the congress. Some still held negative positions on the national question, but a large majority supported the principle of national-cultural autonomy [13] as well as full civil rights for Jews and the right to use Yiddish or Hebrew in all courts and other government agencies.

The congress resolution re-affirmed the government's right to determine general educational standards, but insisted that all cultural matters, including schooling, be removed from the jurisdiction of the state and transferred to special local and central institutions staffed by people representing nationality groups and chosen by universal, secret voting.[14] (Medem, the Bund's chief theoretician on the national question, noted in his autobiography that the congress' endorsement of national-cultural autonomy had already been anticipated by a central committee pamphlet distributed in December 1904. He believed that the committee acted as it did because it sensed how much the sentiment for full national rights had grown since the previous congress and quite fully expected ratification of its views.) [15]

During the summer of 1905, meanwhile, discussions of the coming Duma dominated Russian political circles until Bulygin revealed his plan on August 6, 1905. The Mensheviks were groping for ways of mobilizing "revolutionary self-government" for the conquest of a constituent assembly modeled on the transformation of the French Estates General of 1789 into the Constituent Assembly and then the Convention with full powers.[16] To achieve this, they urged the formation of semilegal, agitation committees of workers to work with Menshevik groups and "elect" their own representatives to the Duma concurrently with "legal" elections. Lenin dismissed such ideas as opportunistic—a renunciation of the uprising, which to him had to come first and lead to a revolutionary provisional government. The Mensheviks believed that victory would come by way of "revolutionary self-government," with or without an uprising.[17] Both Bolsheviks and the Bund, at this time, proposed "actively boycotting" the coming elections—that is, demonstrating in front of electoral meetings, breaking them up, and staging a general strike on the day the Duma opened.

Finally, on August 6, the "Bulygin Constitution" was announced. It provided for a truncated Imperial Duma with a complex system of indirect voting and representation based on class qualifications. Its powers were trimmed to advisory functions. The Constitution granted Jews the right to vote and be represented, but barred other rights no less important, such as the right of residence outside the Pale and the right of free movement. Russian liberals pressed the government for a truly representative body. Many Jewish liberals were disappointed but saw Bulygin's announcement as a valuable first step toward basic reforms. The Bund attacked it contemptuously. Meanwhile, as news of military defeats poured in, congresses of *zemstvo* men became increasingly militant. The actual offer of a Duma, however, no matter how restricted, was to achieve one of the chief aims of the regime, namely, to divide the opposition. Dissension over the agrarian question and rights of national minorities, as well as basic freedoms—questions which had never had a public airing in Russia— strengthened the hand of the government, as did the conclusion of the Treaty of Portsmouth (August 29), which finally brought the war to a close. There would now be large numbers of troops to deal with mounting internal opposition.

At the same time, the social democrats were finally able to exert significant influence over the Russian workers. In October 1905, after a September lull in strike activity, almost half a million workers went out on strike following the announcement of the ratification of the Treaty of Portsmouth. The loyalty of the armed forces, no longer strained to support the regime, would swing to the workers, it was hoped.

The revolutionaries now had the ears of the workers. A pervasive frustration had spread through the country. What had the sacrifices achieved? How could the people cope with rising prices, food shortages, police repression, disappointment over long-deferred liberties, which the promise of a Duma did nothing to remedy? The circulation of the radical press rose by leaps and bounds. A "provisional regulation" of August 27 giving students the right to hold meetings and a measure of autonomy was later described by Witte as "the first breach through which the revolution, having matured underground, emerged into the broad light of day." [18] The Mensheviks had suggested that Moscow University students call off their strike, in progress since February, return to school, and throw open lecture halls to the people. An epidemic of meetings spread to university centers, with crowds of workers and intellectuals responding with great enthusiasm—becoming "transformed," Trotsky said—as they listened to social democrats and felt stirrings of class solidarity. Even Moscow, which had consistently resisted the radical agitators, began to rouse itself.

The chief impetus came from the railway workers, who had the "veins of capitalism" in their hands. Slowly but surely, strikes of railway workers affected nearly every public service. Electricity, transportation, and communications broke down and paralyzed economic life. Moscow and St. Petersburg lay in an eerie stillness as city employees, druggists, actors, physicians, lawyers, and students joined the strike movement. The support of professional men and a large segment of the middle class could not help but impress the conservatives.

The railroad strike that began in Moscow on October 8 soon spread to other parts of the country, leading almost everywhere to general strikes. The St. Petersburg junction, where much of the impetus and organizational energy was provided by the Soviet of Workers' Deputies, was struck on October 12.[19] On October 10, the St. Petersburg Mensheviks had debated how to channel the revolutionary mood of the proletarian masses. Here was an opportunity to use the idea of "revolutionary self-government." They decided to revive the workers' committees already familiar since the days of the Shidlovsky Commission. Appeals went out to workers to organize committees and plan for a general strike.

For the Bund, the October wave of strikes was the long-awaited revolutionary spark that would hopefully ignite an uprising. But food shortages, occasional clashes with patrols, and casualties in various places revealed that the weapon of the general strike was limited. In several towns, moreover, the Bund faced potentially ugly situations. In Vitebsk, for example, the police and military created a pogrom mood in order to forestall strikers.[20] In Gomel, where the strike was about to collapse because Christian shopkeepers refused to close on Saturday, violence broke out as workers battled soldiers. News of the tsar's manifesto, however, temporarily foreclosed further conflict.

Powerless for the moment to assert his authority in the face of national paralysis and in virtual isolation, Nicholas II finally issued the constitutional manifesto of October 17 and proclaimed an amnesty for political prisoners—a turning point in the 1905 revolution and a landmark in Russian history. The October Manifesto was largely the work of Count Sergei Witte, the tsar's chief minister, who had urged a more liberal policy, to which Nicholas grudgingly consented. The manifesto reaffirmed the principle of a Duma as a major factor in the legislative process and indicated that voting rights would be extended to new groups. Freedom of speech, assembly and association were seemingly granted. At first some Bundists, especially those returning from the Sixth Congress, could not believe that any real change had taken place and thought that the manifesto was a trick to flush out revolutionaries. Yet there was no doubt of the government's weakness. As to the manifesto, if it did not herald revolution, it did seem to promise a constitutional regime with opportunities for developing new strategies and ways of testing the new freedoms and expanded suffrage in the coming elections to the Duma.

The Bund began making some basic decisions. It decided to keep its organizational apparatus secret, but to openly publish a Yiddish daily in Vilna called *Der Veker (The Awakener)* and a Russian-language weekly, *The Jewish Worker*, in order to ascertain the government's intentions. (The underground publications *Di Arbayter Shtimme* and *Der Bund* ceased publication in September and November 1905, respectively.) The illegal presses were shut down and a new experience with government censorship (which was not ended by the manifesto) and technical problems was about to start.

The question of workers' organizations was an urgent, immediate problem. Workers now had the right to form trade unions. Yet all revolutionaries, including the Bund, had serious reservations about the capacity of nonpolitical unionized workers to bring socialism to Russia. In the northwest provinces, the RSDWP, the socialist Zionists, and the PPS supported the development of neutral, i.e., non-political, trade unions, but the Bund did not. Arguing from the experience of Jewish workers in the Bund, where economic and political development had been parallel, and fearing that neutral unions would come under the control of bourgeois liberals, the Bund committed itself to party-led unions, which they felt would be part of the ultimate class struggle.[21] The "free days" following the manifesto were being enjoyed, but the Bund was not modifying its ultimate goal. Russia was in transition but social democrats were not yet able to carry on their political struggle openly. Only a class-conscious proletariat led by a party could create socialism; there could be no such thing as a non-party political struggle, the Bund maintained.

The government, weak, but far from collapse, soon recovered some of its old power. Mass violence had increased in the cities, among peasants, and in the armed forces, creating near-anarchy. The most serious shortcoming of the government was its failure to clearly define the rights and freedoms that Russian citizens were now supposed to enjoy. What was meant by "the immutable foundations of civil liberty?" If everyone had the right to join or form political organizations and hold meetings, what powers remained to the authorities whose power was being challenged? The uncertainties of the time were complicated by arguments between liberals, who were inclined to adhere to "legality" and hope for reform in the coming Duma, and socialists who opposed "mere" constitutional democracy. As this conflict became more polarized, the right-wing opposition reassembled itself and frequently vented its violence on Jews, who were accused of being the root cause of revolutionary agitation. Toward the end of October, the Black Hundreds, leading the counter-revolution, instigated a ferocious wave of pogroms, some with official connivance. In Odessa and Ekaterinoslav there were bloody outbreaks against Jews; murderous mobs also attacked intellectuals, agitators, and students outside the Pale. Terrorist attacks struck prominent leaders in the "opposition" movement. Very quickly, all political middle ground dissolved and the struggle, in the minds of the socialists, became one between "reaction" and "revolution."

The mutiny of sailors at the Kronstadt base, waves of peasant risings, and the increasing strength of the St. Petersburg Soviet signaled a quickening crescendo of revolutionary momentum; on the other hand, there were ominous signs of reaction. Medem and other leading Bundists who were stuck in Zurich, nervously switching from congress sessions to reading about the extraordinary events in Russia, wrote:

> We sat on needles. . . . News from Russia was coming in, exciting us more and more. Then, suddenly, we read the first telegrams about the pogroms. After the first came the second, then the third . . . as if everything were drenched in a torrent of Jewish blood. . . . The counterrevolution was manifesting itself in its most frightful, most shameful form.[22]

Later, as some delegates were making their way home from Zurich, they met refugees from pogroms in Ekaterinoslav and Odessa and felt nagging doubts about the Russian masses.

Yet the Bund did not despair. Despair, wrote Medem, was the basis of Zionism, but could never be the force motivating the Bund. "A movement cannot be built on a foundation of despair; one builds only on a basis of faith." The Bund leaders quickly realized that although it looked as if revolutionary forces had shredded the regime, real power was still in the old hands. "A bitter struggle still lay ahead. . . . We have only climbed the first mountain and seen the first peak," Medem noted sadly.[23]

The massive strikes continued in November and December, but revolutionary leadership was not forthcoming. In many other parts of Russia—the Baltic provinces, the Ukraine, the Caucasus and even in Siberia—there were disturbances in which social democrats exercised momentary control, but vast distances, thinned-out cadres, and fatal hesitations beset the revolutionaries. Urban intellectuals were shocked by the realities of life in the villages, where loyalty to tsar and church, anti-Jewish impulses, and sullen indifference to the plight of city workers coexisted with half-digested revolutionary slogans and solemn pledges "to stand for the people's cause." *These* masses were hardly bearers of the revolution. Yet, the revolutionaries tried to overcome their periodic black moods. *Der Bund* of November 22 predicted that a general uprising "could become a fact at any moment." The manifesto, it believed, would establish a "constitutional autocracy." What was required was a constituent assembly, which could be brought about only by an armed uprising.

A great source of sustained worker strength lay in the St. Petersburg Soviet. Maximum representation was reported in November, when 562 worker-deputies were selected, representing 181 factories and sixteen trade unions.[24] The Mensheviks, Bolsheviks, Social Revolutionaries, the PPS and the Bund, (which appointed Abramovich) also sent representatives,[25] but it was the Bolsheviks who ultimately set the tone in the soviet and made their influence felt through its executive committee. On another level, Bolsheviks and Mensheviks seemed ready to mend their differences. After the announcement of the October 17 Manifesto, the pressure for unity as well as democratization of the party was strong.[26] On October 18, the St. Petersburg Mensheviks and Bolsheviks formed a Federative United Council to plan and direct the political actions of the St. Petersburg proletariat, a breakthrough that rank and file party members greeted joyfully.[27] The process of mending the rift by direct local merger seemed likely. Then in November, new nonpartisan "workers' clubs" and "political unions," initiated mainly by Mensheviks, began to appear in St. Petersburg. These constituted new areas of conflict.

At first the Bolsheviks were mistrustful, viewing the idea of workers' committees as a "new intrigue" of the Mensheviks, but because of their already tenuous contact with the mass movement, they had to reverse their stand—at least until the strike was over. In the interim, the soviet managed the strike. The Bolsheviks admitted its indispensable value for the strike struggle, but feared that the soviet might become the germ of an independent labor party, opposed to the RSDWP.[28] Trotsky, who had become the Menshevik leader in the St. Petersburg Soviet, said the attitude of the Bolsheviks continued to be negative until Lenin arrived in Russia in November.[29] Until then they wanted—and expected—the soviet to dissolve in the party (Bolshevik wing). But even after the strike was over, the soviet continued as a strong proletarian force.

Lenin actually had a great deal of doubt about the prevailing Bolshevik position and for a time even thought that the soviet might become the nucleus of a provisional revolutionary government, but he reversed himself and began to regard it as a rival to the party.[30] Later he changed his mind again, but by then the soviet had been crushed.

In practical terms, the chief aim of the soviet was to maintain the impetus of the strike, which many social democrats, including Bundists, believed would lead to revolution. The soviet's strategy involved a two-fold struggle: one against employers, the other against government. Its campaign for an eight-hour day paralleled the formation of armed groups. Some middle-class elements and workers, however, were alienated by the threat of an insurrection, and the call for a general strike by the soviet in November drew a limited response. Professionals, tradesmen, and even some railway workers remained aloof; popular sympathy began to diminish.

Witte later wrote that he "never attached any particular significance to the soviet." This was an exaggeration, but the soviet as such was not an immediate threat to the security of the regime.[31] In early December, in the midst of plans for leading an armed insurrection, almost two hundred members of the soviet were arrested, including all of the principal leaders. The expected working class revolt never developed.

In Moscow, meanwhile, the Mensheviks had also been trying to organize a soviet during the general strike. Workers' committees were created in several factories early in October, but the Bolsheviks impeded the creation of a soviet until late November.[32] All of the factories were on strike by October 15; the city had no electricity or transportation. Even after the October 17 Manifesto, strikes continued elsewhere. Between 350,000 and 400,000 Russians took to the streets in November and December. There were also army and navy mutinies in Moscow in December. Both Bolsheviks and Mensheviks led in the call for a general strike and won considerable support in the city, but neither knew how the general strike was to transform itself into a popular uprising, or how to seize the centers of power while the insurgents had the initiative. Working-class families began to leave the city after a few days, and militia bands soon melted away. By the middle of December, the momentum of resistance had ebbed.

For the Bundists, the Moscow outbreaks were at first construed as part of the mounting tide of revolution, and they continued to think in terms of an armed revolt. The first issue of *Der Veker* referred to the government shooting its last bullets at the proletariat. Autocracy was under seige. The only remaining question was "what kind of order will be founded in its place"—a limited monarchy or a true democracy. In this continuing belief in the future of the revolution, the Bundists rejected the newly projected Duma, particularly after a new electoral law was announced on December 11. This decree added a fourth *curia* (for industrial workers) to the three previously envisaged by Bulygin, (for landowners, town dwellers and peasants), but excluded, among others, those who worked in enterprises with fewer than fifty male workers, a restriction that excluded large numbers of Jews. The tsar's ministers were convinced· that property qualifications for voting would pit Jewish proletariat against Jewish bourgeoisie, a situation the Bund perceived at once.

Except for the Mensheviks, who did not boycott the Duma, the revolutionary parties refused to believe that the October Manifesto was anything more than a camouflage for the regime's recovery of power. The liberals were not happy with the December electoral law but, once elected, planned to change it and summon a new Duma based on universal suffrage. The revolutionaries did not trust them, but unexpected developments changed their views, or at least their tactics.

The liberal composition of the First Duma—including 12 Jews, Constitutional Democrats (Kadets), and some left-wing delegates (*Trudoviki*), including Mensheviks—which met at the end of April 1906, persuaded the Bund that, although it rejected the Duma and must continue to expose its inadequacies, it could be used as a forum for revolutionary propaganda. (At the Bund's Seventh Congress in August–September 1906, the Bund officially ended its boycott strategy; it sent representatives to the Second [1907–12] and Third [1913–15] Dumas, both markedly more conservative and restrictive than the First.)

By early January 1906, almost all of the insurrectionary violence in Russia had been suppressed. The surprisingly resilient government quickly strengthened its authority as the opposition began to fragmentize. In St. Petersburg alone, at the end of 1905, there were over a dozen left-wing parties and groups. Hopes for extending the suffrage and creating a democratic assembly were dashed when the tsar dissolved the Duma on July 8, less than three months after it convened. Even earlier, he had dismissed Witte and replaced him with I. L. Goremykin, a reactionary of the old school.

There had not been a word about Jews in the October Manifesto, but the question of Jewish civil equality assumed great importance in the deliberations of the First Duma and was accepted on principle by the liberal Kadets and the *Trudoviki*, who together commanded a large bloc. The pogroms in 1905 were also brought sharply into focus in the Duma sessions, and government complicity was documented. The Duma had addressed a question to Stolypin on May 9 on the role of the police in the printing of inflammatory literature, but before he replied, news of the terrible pogrom in Bialystok (June 1–3) reached the assembly.[33] A number of delegates demanded immediate action to halt the attacks. Stolypin promised to act quickly, but did not. The deputies expressed their revulsion and recalled the government's complicity in pogroms in the past. Unwilling to rely on the government, the Duma launched its own investigation. Resolutions of protest and expressions of sorrow and indignation poured in from many quarters, and relief for the victims was organized.

At the suggestion of the central committee of the Bund, a joint conference was called together with representatives of the Russian and Lettish social-democratic parties and the Social Revolutionary party to discuss the pogrom. The conference resolved to propagandize the masses against anti-Semitism, declaring that the enemy of the people was not the Jews or any other nationality but the tsarist autocracy. One means of preventing the recurrence of such outbreaks was the general arming of the people for self-defense and the organization of a civilian militia. The Duma was urged to take strong measures.

Stolypin minimized the charges against the police, but Prince S. D. Urussov, governor of Bessarabia, refused to allow the whitewash. Citing names and addresses, he described in detail the operations of a printing press in the police department at St. Petersburg which was turning out inflammatory pamphlets. First came rumors of an impending pogrom, then the distribution of leaflets, then the appearance of strangers in the community, and then the pogrom itself.

Debate on the pogrom raged through the remaining days of the Duma; the Duma Commission report concluded that the pogrom was neither spontaneous nor the result of national and religious hatreds, but that it had been organized in advance. A Duma resolution called on all those responsible to be brought to trial. On July 6, the Duma denounced the government's "policy of oppression, frightfulness, and extermination" and called on the tsar to dismiss his Cabinet. Two days later, the deputies found the Duma building closed and the Duma dissolved, allegedly for encroaching upon a domain outside its jurisdiction (land reform) and for investigating acts (pogroms) of authorities appointed by the tsar.[34]

Immediately after the Duma was dissolved, about half the deputies assembled across the border in Viborg, Finland, where they issued an eloquent manifesto calling on the Russian people to resist the government until the Duma was restored. But there was no response. Many of the delegates were subsequently arrested or went into exile. Revolutionary terrorism, which had subsided during the sessions of the Duma, now broke out anew. Attempts upon the lives of high officials, expropriations, and strikes erupted, intensifying government oppression. In the course of five months (September 1906–January 1907), a political court-martial sentenced over a thousand people to death, many of whom were Jews.

Reaction was soon again in the saddle. The theory that insurrections in the cities would arouse the peasants and soldiers to join the revolutionary tide had collapsed. Moreover, the revolutionaries themselves had made no effort to seize the government, while their mistrust of bourgeois liberals was too ingrained and unyielding for compromise. The Kadets as a whole were anxious to maintain good relations with the socialists, but their calls for solidarity were icily rejected. They were judged less by their actions than by the rigid preconceptions Marxists had of them. Once the "bourgeois-democratic revolution" had been achieved, the Marxists insisted, liberals would turn against their former allies and crush them. On their side, the liberals had overestimated the willingness of the tsar and his advisors to carry out the pledges made in the manifesto. Nor had they taken into account the reserves of popular support that helped the conservatives recover lost ground.

All of the social democratic factions, singly and together, had failed in their efforts to lead Russians to a new political threshold in 1905. Both the Bolsheviks and Mensheviks had had opportunities to test some of their ideas in practice, but nowhere had they been successful. Evidently, something was seriously wrong with their approach to politics, with their appraisal of actual political forces, and with their strategic concepts.[35] A root cause of their trouble was the party's inherent weakness. Not only did it suffer from the Bolshevik-Menshevik split, but it lacked a natural organic bond between its leaders and Russian workers. "We measured the temperature of the proletariat by our own pulses," one social democrat complained afterward. Riveted to ideas formed by ideological dogma, they—with too few exceptions—had distorted perceptions of the social and political turbulence of the time.

Most of the popular movements had caught the revolutionaries by surprise. In the genuinely spontaneous popular upsurge of hope for change and belief in the possibility of fundamental reforms in Russia, the words of socialists were received almost as a new revelation. But these freshly released energies were not harnessed by the RSDWP of the time, for in 1905 it was basically a propaganda and agitation agency, with little understanding of the complex issues raised by the building of a new order.[36] The party could not even work out realistic attitudes and relationships with non-party organizations such as the trade unions and the soviets. Both of these were used to gain recruits for the party and to advance the party's interests. Consequently, trade unionists who wished to remain politically independent or concentrate on economic matters found the policy of the party unattractive. Schisms within unions as well as factional schisms within the party resulted, with Lenin insisting that wherever they infiltrated, Bolsheviks maintain control, secretly when necessary. The Mensheviks had begun this process of relating to workers more realistically but did not have time to fully develop the contacts.

Lenin, meanwhile, was working out a strategy for the post-1905 period. Mensheviks and Bolsheviks had technically reconciled their differences at the so-called unity congress in Stockholm in April 1906, but this congress had a Menshevik majority and Lenin was determined not to let the idea of unity "tie a noose around our necks," as he told one of his lieutenants, Anatole Lunacharsky, or "let the Mensheviks lead us by the rope."

It was at this congress that the Bund was readmitted to the RSDWP. Medem wrote that there was the same hostility, the same blindness about the Bund as before, especially among the Mensheviks.[37] Lenin had not changed his mind about the Bund either, but he needed allies in order to outvote the Menshevik majority on the question of boycotting the Duma. At that time, the Bund was very close to the Bolshevik position in strongly favoring a boycott; the Mensheviks had a somewhat more qualified position. Lenin hoped that in the squabbling, the Bund—a large organization with many votes—would vote with him. "That the Bund was 'nationalistic' . . . 'chauvinistic' did not matter. . . . One draws whatever meaning one needs and hides the other under the table."[38] Thus the Bolsheviks made it relatively easy for the Bund to rejoin the party, whereas most Mensheviks voted against readmission. Within the Bund, however, discussions on the question went on the entire summer in conversations, at meetings, and in the Bundist press. Thus, although the political center of gravity was in St. Petersburg, revolutionary leaders were preoccupied elsewhere.

Medem wrote a series of articles on the question of unity in a new Bund journal called *Nashe Slovo (Our Word)*, which the Bund began publishing in Russian early in 1906. Abramovich was its driving force and spirit, although he wrote very little. Most of the writing was done by Medem and three young students from Kiev, all talented writers: David Zaslavsky, M. Haylikman, and A. Zalotariev. Zaslavsky was a gifted humorist and satirist, Haylikman wrote on Jewish questions, and Zalotariev wrote political articles.[39] The historian Dubnow's daughter contributed literary essays. Medem wrote on a wide range of topics, and together with Abramovich and Liber took a "soft line" in advocating reunion with the RSDWP. "The movement toward unity is too strong to resist," Medem wrote. "We will have to wait until the time of the Messiah for Russian members to come to the Bund position."[40]

Increasingly mindful of the national question, he maintained that the Bund position had not changed. "We enter the party," he said, "to struggle. . . . The Bund was not, is not, and never will be the translator of Russian Social Democracy into Yiddish. The Bund is the organized and conscious expression of the decisive, broad, and powerful currents in Jewish life. . . . The national program of the Bund cannot be changed from above." The congress disposed of the old nagging question by evading it: "The question of the national program remains open in view of the fact that it was not re-examined."[41] On the question of re-unification, there was strong opposition led by Litvak and Slawek Grosser, but a resolution approving re-unification was passed by a large majority at the Seventh Bund Congress in the fall of 1906. The party, however, was still a very frail anchor.

Differences soon ruptured the thinly patched unity. The semiconstitutional regime of 1906 presented a partially salvageable situation for some socialists and opportunity for some legal activity. A group of Menshevik and Bundist leaders who remained inside Russia became convinced that these opportunities must be used to develop worker consciousness and activity. The members of this group, which was led by Alexander Potresov, one of *Iskra's* founders and a once-close supporter of Lenin, were vehemently condemned by Lenin as "liquidators"—those he said, who wanted to liquidate underground revolutionary activities. He fiercely opposed every accommodation to existing legal conditions and demanded direct revolutionary action.

The Bund debated the issue, and a majority agreed with the Mensheviks—in fact the Bund was of considerable influence on them—advocating the maximum use of legal means, but not the liquidation of illegal party cells. No social democrat in the Russia of 1906–07 could possibly have favored this. Bundists and Mensheviks were far from being the peace-loving evolutionists Lenin accused them of being, but they were, in fact, repelled by the kind of party he was trying to create, with its conspiratorial intrigues, splits, and harsh attacks on all who disagreed with him. Bolshevik fund-raising methods also became questionable. As financial aid from bourgeois sympathizers trickled away after 1905, certain Bolsheviks seized funds from public and private sources, a habit which almost imperceptibly slipped into terrorism. These practices later alienated many social democrats.

With the collapse of the revolution, political and social reaction and economic depression witnessed widespread political disillusionment and depletion in the ranks of all socialist parties. Many Bundists went to the United States, to prison and exile, and as the movement began to decline, it was challenged by other Jewish groups.

Until the beginning of 1906, the Bund was not only the dominant but also the only Jewish political force engaged in the struggle of the Jewish masses for basic rights. Within a few short months, the situation changed; many non-socialist political groups emerged, and socialist Zionists began winning support among Jewish workers. Six of the twelve Jewish deputies in the Duma had been Zionists, indicating a political awakening that was changing the Zionist position. Prior to the 1905 Revolution, Russian Zionists were consistently apolitical, but in November 1906, at an all-Russian Zionist convention in Helsingfors, Finland, a new comprehensive and imaginative "Helsingfors Program" brought Russian Zionists into the struggle for civic and national rights in the country as well as the building of the Jewish homeland in Palestine.

Moreover, the failure of the 1905 Revolution aroused a widespread feeling among Jews that the sacrifices of the Jewish revolutionaries had been futile. Even the limited right to vote had now vanished. Besides, anti-Jewish feeling was being heated up by pogroms for which the revolutionaries had no satisfactory answer. As the mood in the Pale became increasingly nationalist, the Bund had to move with the prevailing winds.

Medem and Kosovsky both contributed greatly to the formulation of the Bund's national program, but it was Medem who devoted his best energies and talents to a thoroughgoing analysis of the national problem: the interrelationships between Marxism and nationalism, nationalism and internationalism, and nationalism and the Jewish problem. The evolution of Bundist thought on the problem of Jewish nationalism was greatly influenced by Medem, who himself underwent intellectual changes during a lifetime of study and analysis. Yet he remained a confirmed Marxist, and in his writings, the class struggle looms as the basic principle of social development. Marxist assumptions formed the bedrock of his thought and remained so. "My views," he wrote in 1917, in a foreword to a series of articles, "are grounded in scientific socialism and my literary work in that field always aimed at harmonizing the national question and Marxist thought." [42] Despite his sympathetic treatment of the national question, it is never allowed to dominate "the supreme criterion of the class struggle," a view which remains consistent in Medem from 1904, when his first important work on the subject "Di Sotsial-Demokratie un di Natsionale Frage" (Social Democracy and the National Question) first appeared. "Solidarity of the entire nation," he wrote in that essay, "means giving up the class struggle, means peace between proletariat and bourgeoisie, means spiritual and material enslavement of the proletariat." [43] Thus, the only fundamental solution to the Jewish problem will come with the overthrow of capitalism and the creation of a socialist society.

In his earliest writings on the national question, Medem refused to discuss any concrete national program for the Jews. "What are the tasks and the goals of a nation? In what direction should the course of national development be steered? Such questions no more exist for us than do the class interests that posit them." Yet Medem persistently fought for a positive recognition of the importance of the national question at a time when most leading Marxists (the two exceptions were the Austrian Marxists Karl Renner and Otto Bauer) brushed it aside. "We have long since become alien to the mood of cosmopolitanism . . . but we are also no idolatrous worshippers of the national idea," he said.[44] Medem accepted the legitimacy and reality of national differences but did not identify them with nationalism; rather, he believed they were merely the national forms in which the class struggle goes on: "A national culture as an independent entity, as a closed circle with its particular content, does not exist at all. . . . The content of cultural life, which is generally the same all over, takes various colors and various national forms, as soon as it enters into different groups with different social relationships. These relationships involving social tasks, conflicts and intellectual developments place a national stamp upon culture." [45] Thus it is the class struggle that takes on various national forms; nationalities are realities which cannot be ignored, yet are subject to universal laws of social development.[46] However, culture is so much a matter of form that each nationality must have autonomy in cultural matters.

Medem excoriated assimilation as strongly as nationalism (including, of course Zionism), viewing it, among Jews, as a product of a money-greedy Jewish bourgeoisie. He sarcastically contrasted the free, emancipated, non-

Jewish bourgeois citizen with the insecure, weak Jewish bourgeois who tries frantically to get rid of his Jewish past—religion, language, customs, clothing, manners—in order to be accepted and become part of the established bourgeoisie. The nationalism of the frightened petty-bourgeois takes on the aspect of a weak and depressed group, captured by ultra-modern business enterprise and big capital, "who loses the very foundation under his feet." [47] "Nowhere does this striving to assimilate," Medem said, "bloom so greatly as among Jews." Blaming the Jewish bourgeoisie for assimilation, he accused them of giving up their own identity in order to approximate the position of the non-Jewish bourgeoisie and find favor with them as well as keep their improved economic position. Using scathing language, Medem invents the thinking of the hated Jewish bourgeoisie: "We must get for ourselves a piece of the 'leviathan' and a place in this market. . . . We must not only break down the walls, but must not allow a trace of any of the differences to remain. Everything that can possibly reveal the Jew under the cosmopolitan exterior must be forgotten. . . ." [48]

Yet his attack on Jews who deny their ancestry, who ridicule anything Jewish and "deny that the Jews are not a nation but a religious association," is not to be misconstrued as an affirmation of Jewish nationality in the ordinary sense. Medem condemned that, too. Personally, he rejected traditionalism, religious values, the Hebrew language and literature, and any activity intended solely to develop Jewish national consciousness—all of those elements which, in one form or another, provided the basis for Zionism and Diaspora nationalism.[49] He believed strongly that the development of national consciousness can never be an end in itself for any social movement, that it is, indeed, only the other side of assimilation: "The ideology of assimilation is the same as that of nationalism, only the other side of it. The assimilationist strives for a stranger's nationality and tries to make it his own. . . . While the [Jewish] nationalist tries to put his nationalist stamp on everything possible." [50]

In the struggle against the Zionists, Medem took an aggressively leading role. He opposed Zionism on the grounds that it neglected the real interests of Jews and offered them only fantasy and illusion. Like other nationalist movements, Zionism's emphasis on national solidarity was viewed as the antithesis of the proletarian struggle and an escape from the struggle for Jewish rights in the lands where Jews live. To him, this was an abandonment of the masses. Medem saw Zionism as a philosophy of surrender to a dream—in essence, an ideology of weakness. The Zionist, he wrote, "cannot look life straight in the eyes, he is too weak, tired, terrified, fearful of life. . . . He waxes eloquent with nationalist phrases, masking . . . his own weakness and political bankruptcy." [51] And in an interesting if disquieting analysis of the psychologically complex motives that animate Zionists, he concluded that "over and above all these many-colored streams, there is one main current, one dominant mood, one main feeling—the feeling of a man ... who senses his loneliness and isolation and who is pushed aside from the main stream. ... It is a sort of chosen-people idea turned inside out." [52]

The national consciousness that Medem made room for was the consciousness felt by a social group (the proletariat) for realizing certain national tasks. Whoever stops with the goal of developing national self-consciousness "remains standing in the middle of the road. The chief question remains unanswered, i.e., for what purpose is such national consciousness to be developed? The entire character of the movement depends on this 'for what purpose?' " [53]

Medem struggled with these questions for many years. On a theoretical level, he worked out a concept which he called "neutralism" to resolve the seeming contradiction between recognizing the existence of a Jewish nationality but rejecting assimilation, and the raising or strengthening of Jewish national consciousness. Neutralism basically meant a refusal to take a stand—and therefore political action—on the question of the future of the Jewish nation, a refusal to do anything one way or another to influence the existence or continuation of a Jewish national will, and thus the national survival of Jews.[54] All forms of national oppression, including enforced assimilation, are to be vigorously fought, in Medem's view, but one cannot predict the future course of the Jewish people and therefore one must do nothing to create a national will that aspires toward continued national existence.

This position was based on a certain submission to the blind forces of history and, philosophically, on materialistic determinism. Only history, Medem believed, could determine the fate of the Jewish people; complex historical processes can be studied and analyzed but cannot and should not be interfered with. Within the straitjacket of this rather tendentious reasoning (particularly for a man very much involved in a directive movement), both assimilationists and nationalists are condemned for "interfering" with the forces of history, for confusing outcomes with goals by assuming *a priori* that history is moving in a definite direction and making this direction their goal. Whether the Jewish nation will survive in the future or assimilate depends on multiple, complex forces about which no one can make definite predictions, according to Medem. Thus the course of Jewish national development cannot be directed. If it is the destiny of the Jews to become assimilated, one should not act to oppose the process. Nor will he act to foster assimilation. If, on the other hand, the historical process is tending in the direction of the development of Jewish culture, he is neutral toward that, too.

The Bund officially adopted neutralism, which helped mute opposing nationalist, cosmopolitan, and assimilationist tendencies within the movement. However, Medem himself began to retreat from the neutralist position in 1910 with the publication of his essay "Natsionalizm oder

Naitralizm," when he began to recognize the need for a positive attitude toward the national future of Jews. Even so, his thinking still wavered.

In the light of his theoretical position—at least up to 1910—one may indeed wonder at Medem's consistency in championing the cause of national cultural autonomy for Russian Jews in the early 1900's, a position which may have responded to existing Jewish needs, but which also created them. He was not only unwilling to allow the blind forces of history to overtake the living actuality of Jewish national-cultural expression, but laid the basis for the Bund's program of Jewish national-cultural autonomy. It was on this very question that Medem and the Bund were locked in an ideological struggle with Lenin and the *Iskra* group from 1901 on. This conflict did not abate after the Bund rejoined the RSDWP in 1906 but grew in vehemence, creating an unbridgeable gap that conditioned a whole generation of Russian Bolsheviks and fatefully affected Jewish life in Russia after the Bolshevik Revolution.

Medem had pointed out that in a multi-national state such as Russia, guarantees of individual freedom are not enough. In the cultural field, where national differences are great, a violent struggle between nationalities will develop if all cultural problems are left to the central government. Only juridically recognized bodies of the nationalities themselves, he maintained, can avoid such conflicts and guarantee real equality of rights.[55] In his "Social Democracy and the National Question," Medem developed an elaborate critique of the territorial view of nationalism, showing how any purely territorial identification of nationality is untenable since it always leaves minorities subject to dominant majorities.[56]

On the more abstract, theoretical level, there was an obvious struggle going on in Medem's mind as he thought and fought his way to neutralism, even as he defended Jewish national-cultural autonomy. His detached search for a rational position for a Jewish socialist movement has none of the emotional intensity or commitment of a Zhitlovsky and offers no program of action for a political movement, but the groping for an orientation discloses a much more profound awareness of the problem of national Jewish existence than was true in the American Jewish labor movement, where no comparable analysis was undertaken.

Medem's thinking moved toward a more active involvement in Jewish cultural life, especially after the evacuation of Poland by the Russians in 1916.[57] He made a strained, even tortuous effort to reconcile socialist doctrine with Jewish realities in the intervening years. One is bound to admire this struggle, but one must also mark Medem's failure to see the contradiction between his deterministic conception of the historical process and·his rejection of directive actions as intruding upon this process. Yet are not these forces, in themselves, part of "the blind historical process"? One also feels in Medem's neutralism a sense of resignation, submission, or plain inhibition, to act decisively and take initiatives during the "October days" in 1905, not only on the part of the Bund, but also on the part of both Mensheviks and Bolsheviks. All were governed by Marxist dogma. This belief in the inevitability of "historic forces" very possibly prevented the collapse of tsarism in 1905.

The assimilationist trend within the Bund was never fully developed theoretically, but those members who had assimilationist views through personal conviction, or who felt vulnerable to RSDWP charges, were steadily eased out of leadership positions or joined another segment of the RSDWP. This was more true of older members of the Bund, but some of the younger generation—for example, Moishe Rafes (Borisov), who was active in Gomel and Vilna after 1905—also warned against the bourgeois nature of the "national tide which floods the Jewish working mass." Some of these members ultimately joined the Communist Bund and the Communist party.

Among the younger members who took a strongly nationalist position was the romantic idealist and talented writer Esther Frumkin, who by 1906 began to become known merely as Esther. She made flaming speeches on Yiddish and Jewish education, trying to spark national consciousness among the Jewish intelligentsia and masses. In 1909 she proclaimed that "The task of the conscious proletariat is to ... show the people the way to the struggle for the rights of the Yiddish language, of the Jewish school." [58] Yiddish must be used in special Jewish schools for the Jewish child as a link to the past and to the Jewish nation. He must receive a new, concentrated proletarian-national education.

> When we speak of education in a proletarian spirit, we do not mean that children should recite part of the Erfurt Program instead of the "Shema," or a chapter of the Communist Manifesto instead of the "Modeh Ani.". . . But when we say "proletarian upbringing" we mean that Marxism is not only a political program but a *weltanschauung* . . . and in such a form it is never too early for a proletarian child. What a child now feels he will later understand.[59]

The intense social visions of the Jewish prophets were perceived as earlier manifestations of the Bund idea and thus easily comprehended by the Jewish child. Jewish kindergartens, libraries, language courses, plays, holidays—all were to be instruments of a rich Jewish national-proletarian culture which the Bund must develop for the masses; they, in turn, would pass it on to the assimilated intelligentsia. In one brochure Esther wrote about religion as a necessary element in the raising of a "folk-child" and was eloquent about the positive educational value of religious customs such as the blessing of the candles. Interestingly, there seems to have been no thought of expelling her from the Bund for her national-religious "deviation."

The political reaction that followed the collapse of the Revolution of 1905 created a radically new situation for the Bund, challenging it not only to set new directions and purposes but to undergo a process of halting, stumbling self-education, for which there were no precedents, signposts, or ideological guides. A remarkable network of cultural institutions for which there was political justification slowly began to develop: "In trade unions, educational societies and courses—everywhere we must build our islands ... saturated with Social-Democratic ideas, with the Social-Democratic spirit." [60] Fear of Zionist and liberal influence on Jewish workers also contributed significantly to the new "feeling for reality." It has even been suggested that Jewish cultural activities helped to keep the Bund a viable movement after 1905, at least in part, "because what the members were doing was consistent with their traditional way of life, and because cultural aspirations were as valid as revolutionary goals." [61] Like its counterpart in America, the Bund could not escape its Jewish character, and despite all its efforts, could not reintegrate itself into the all-Russian movement.

21. Reassessment and Decline, 1907-10

Before the next RSDWP Congress in London in 1907, recriminations had broken out again between Bolsheviks and Mensheviks. Lenin accused Menshevik leaders of making a bargain with the liberals over elections to the second Duma. Meanwhile, although the Menshevik majority at the 1906 RSDWP Congress [1] in Stockholm carried a vote against expropriations such as raids on banks, government offices, and merchants "for the revolution," Lenin never accepted such a policy. He got the congress to agree to set up a military-technical bureau, which, ostensibly, was to fight the Black Hundreds, but which, under his direction, revived the expropriation raids and used some of the money to win over new Bolshevik recruits and start a newspaper of his own. In fact, Lenin's control of the military-technical bureau became an extra-legal Bolshevik center, which, together with an illegal secret finance and military affairs committee of three (Lenin, Alexander Krassin and Leonid Bogdanov), was more powerful than the party's central committee with its Menshevik majority and non-existent treasury. [2] Lenin controlled funds, which as Martov was later to write, manufactured a majority at the 1907 London Congress, funds that were acquired by expropriation and confiscation and that helped pay delegates' expenses for their journey to the congress. [3] In his reminiscences, Medem writes about the demoralization in the movement caused by the "ex-es" (expropriations). [4]

Lenin's plans were made very carefully. Although he remained in Finland, two very able associates, the physician Bogdanov and engineer Krassin stayed behind in Russia leading double lives and keeping the Bolshevik cause very much alive. Lenin himself worked assiduously to prepare for the new party congress in the spring of 1907 and a test of strength. At this congress, the Bolsheviks outnumbered Mensheviks, though the balance was held by smaller groups. Hostilities were still intense.

Before the first session, Lenin had written an article sharply criticizing Dan and other Mensheviks in the St. Petersburg organization for making a bargain with the Kadets over the Duma elections, which he denounced as "selling workers' votes." He was summoned, on the charge of slandering comrades, [5] to a party court which included a judge named by the Bund. In a remarkable speech in his own defense, Lenin acknowledged that he had used "language impermissible in relations between comrades in the same party," but held that "one may and must write in that strain about a seceded organization." [6] The Menshevik "split," he said, justified carrying confusion into the ranks of the proletariat; such political enemies require "a fight of extermination." [7] These were fateful words.

Interestingly enough, Lenin had reversed himself suddenly and completely in January 1907 and advocated fusion slates—a Left bloc—for the Second Duma election campaign. The Mensheviks had already decided on a bloc with the Kadets and leftist parties, a position which Lenin interpreted as a fresh split in the party. His trial came to an abrupt end when, at the London Congress, he achieved a scant majority and the new central committee dropped charges against its now dominant figure. This breach embittered the Mensheviks all the more, particularly when Lenin was elected to the presidium of the congress.

The 1907 congress was contentious and inconclusive, but stands out because of the colorful array of talented men who attended and the support for Lenin from a new group of Bolsheviks who were destined to play a leading part in the 1917 revolution: Bogdanov, Kamenev, Zinoviev, Voroshilov, Litvinov, and Yaroslavsky. Over 300 delegates representing 150,000 members attended, 196 listed as intellectuals and professional revolutionaries (118 delegates were "living at the expense of the Party"), and 116 workingmen. At first they assembled in Copenhagen, but the Danish king, the tsar's uncle, said he could not permit a congress of Russian socialists in Copenhagen, and they were forced to leave.[8] They straggled to London, where the British socialist Ramsey MacDonald managed to obtain the use of the Brotherhood Church, which belonged to a religious sect known as the Christian Socialists, in the east end of London. The arrangement was that the Russians could meet for three days, but three weeks later the Christian Socialists were still pleading for their guests to leave so that they could have their Sunday prayer meeting.[9]

The newly "united" party consisted of five delegations: Bolsheviks, Mensheviks, Polish social democrats, Lettish social democrats and the Bund. Trotsky, recently escaped from Siberia, and three other delegates were technically unaligned, but on most issues these four votes went to Lenin. There were 91 Bolsheviks and 89 Mensheviks at the congress. The Bund sent fifty-five delegates, of whom Abramovich and Liber were elected to the central committee; the Polish social democrats, led by the frail, brilliant Rosa Luxemburg and her companion Jogiches, sent forty-four. The venerable but still vigorous founders of the movement were there—Plekhanov, Akselrod, and Deutsch—as well as younger disciples such as Martov and Dan, the founders of the Bund, the student Angelica Balabanoff (future secretary of the Communist International), the writer Maxim Gorky, Caucasians in sheepskin hats, and bearded workers in Russian blouses. Ten deputies from the Second Duma were among the delegates.

Medem reported that the presence of Maxim Gorky, the "guest" of the Bolsheviks (he had arrived from self-imposed exile in Capri, where he conducted a school for Russian revolutionaries), created a "sensation." [10] A profitable American tour by Gorky in 1906 had raised considerable funds for the party, and Gorky's wife had been left a large legacy by a Moscow textile manufacturer, a millionaire who dabbled in radicalism. Some of the needier delegates were supported by these funds and by money raised among English friends. A 3,000 pound loan was also given by Joseph Fels, wealthy manufacturer of Fels-Naphtha soap.

Lenin's words to Gorky at the beginning of the congress foreshadowed the wrangling and polemical hostilities of the sessions: "So glad you've come," he said. "I believe you're fond of a scrap? There's going to be a big scrap here." [11] The congress was a tumultuous one, in almost continuous uproar. It was opened by Plekhanov and the entire first week was taken up in electing a chairman of the presidium, with Lenin narrowly edging out Plekhanov. Medem's impression was of strong and disciplined delegations and especially good whips among the Bolsheviks and Polish social democrats who drove their delegates into line, in contrast with the Bund and Mensheviks, who had no whips.[12] The very slight edge of the Bolsheviks over the Mensheviks gave the Bundists, Poles, and Letts the power to break deadlocks, lending special intensity to speeches, resolutions, and compromises. There were strenuous efforts to win over pivotal votes.

During the second session, Medem conducted a sitting that was relatively quiet, but very quickly the deep underlying conflicts between the Bolsheviks and Mensheviks broke out with great bitterness, dividing all the delegates into one camp or the other. The Mensheviks were eager to expose Lenin for terrorism, gun-running, notorious robberies, and expropriations,[13] and for inspiring or controlling (sometimes with the help of the social revolutionaries) professional smugglers and thieves. But they could not substantiate their suspicions. Debates raged on these matters and the delegates—including a majority of Bolsheviks—reaffirmed the Stockholm decision to dissolve armed bands and stop the expropriations. Lenin, taking advantage of his position as chairman at the time, did not vote, and when the delegates shouted from the floor, "What does Lenin say? We want to hear Lenin!" he only chuckled, "with a somewhat cryptic expression." [14] Expropriations, however, did not stop.

With their westernized socialist outlook, their influence in Russian trade unions, and eagerness to surface from the underground and join forces with Kadets and Liberals in the struggle against tsarism, the Mensheviks argued for legal activity. Debate on this issue rocked back and forth inconclusively. Lenin and a few Bolsheviks (many opposed him because they favored a flat boycott of the Duma) argued against a "nonrevolutionary" use of the Duma, but refused to boycott it. Lenin's tactic was a purely revolutionary one—he wanted to "unmask the counter-revolutionary Kadets" and call the masses to prepare again for armed revolt. The Bund was close to the Mensheviks on this issue.

After the Revolution of 1917, documents found among the archives of the secret police revealed that the Okhrana had instructed its agents to give the Bolsheviks a free hand in their campaign against the Duma. Okhrana agents were penetrating revolutionary newspapers, meetings, and smuggling rings, and were ordered to create and aggravate splits—a process which assumed the proportions of a huge fifth column inside the revolutionary movement by 1912. Stolypin, the Interior Minister, in looking for an excuse to dissolve the Second Duma, was rendered invaluable service by the Bolsheviks, who were insisting that the social-democratic deputies use their immunity to organize a revolt. The Bolshevik military organization began organizing delegations of soldiers and sailors to press these demands. A woman Okhrana agent in this center established collusion on the part of the deputies (all Mensheviks, ironically) and helped draft an incriminating resolution, a copy of which was subsequently used in a treason trial of the deputies. This frame-up gave Stolypin the pretext he needed to dissolve this Duma on June 16, 1907.

The quick end of the Second Duma shattered Jewish as well as liberal hopes and social-democratic strategy. In contrast with the first Duma, in which there were twelve Jewish deputies, the second contained only four, one of whom was the Bundist Raphael Abramovich. The Duma had spent itself largely in the struggle between the Left and Right; the question of Jewish emancipation was left hanging in committee. A new electoral system arbitrarily decreed by the tsar, in preparation for the Third (often called "Black") Duma, created segregated national class curias, barring the most progressive and democratic elements of the empire and disenfranchising Jewish and other workers. Many so-called dangerous nominees were arbitrarily arrested on framed political charges and were unable to run for office. The Black Hundreds, meanwhile, continued their destructive rampages. Only two Jewish deputies managed to get into the Third Duma, which was made up largely of political reactionaries and anti-Semites. Torrents of abuse against Jews filled the Duma chamber, while outside a hail of decrees expelled whole Jewish communities from their homes, slashed school admissions of Jews, made Zionism illegal, and destroyed many Jewish and other ethnic literary and educational societies.

The Bund suffered from waves of arrests, executions, emigration, and defections from its ranks as the tide of repression came flooding in.

Stolypin had not ceased hounding radical and liberal leaders. By May 1907, some six hundred constitutionalists were sentenced to hang by tsarist tribunals—the infamous "Stolypin neckties." Hopes for Jewish emancipation lay buried, and thousands of Jews now began to make preparations to leave Russia. Nearly 230,000 left for the United States in 1905-06. Determined to crush the revolution, Nicholas II persuaded Stolypin that it could be best "drowned in Jewish blood." Stolypin set loose the Black Hundreds and intensified legal assaults against Jews. Repression, however, was only part of his policy. He skillfully combined it with a strategy for enlisting the peasants on the side of the government, arguing that they could be used to defeat the revolution by freeing them from communally shared land and permitting them to acquire property. By 1909, over half a million peasants acquired land of their own—an unpleasant process in terms of Marxism, which had counted on a discontented landless rural proletariat. These attempts at agricultural reform as well as punitive expeditions against radicals had the effect of squeezing revolutionaries out of certain villages. Stolypin's land program also created allies for the tsar later when Lenin was struggling for the support of the peasants.[15]

Stolypin, for his part, was not a purblind reactionary. He had neutralized the peasants by making land reforms; he was also determined to make Russia into a modern state and fought off the tsar's efforts to eliminate the Duma completely. Russia, he insisted, would at least have a quasi-parliamentary regime, but revolutionary activity was to be crushed, as he made clear in his famous declaration to the socialists in the Second Duma: "What you want is upheavals, what we want is a great fatherland."

In the interests of modernization, a law of 1906 permitted the legal—if limited—chartering of trade unions, mutual aid societies, and cooperatives. This loop and the experience many social democrats had had operating openly and publicly in 1905-06 were soon to further undermine the "unity" of the party at Stockholm and tear it asunder. The Mensheviks and most Bundists were favorably inclined toward trade unions, the mass organizations, and a broadly based party; the Bolsheviks preferred a secret, conspiratorial underground, armed fighting units, a vanguard élite to work for the workers and lead them to a rising. These differences were to become irreconcilable. The lessons each drew from the events of 1905-06 also differed markedly.

The Mensheviks still held to the basic Marxist notion that only the development of a strong proletariat could produce the socialist revolution, but that this would happen only after Russian capitalism had developed, that is, after a bourgeois revolution. As Akselrod had put it rather pessimistically after the Stockholm Congress:

> Social relations in Russia are as yet ripe only for a bourgeois revolution; and the impulse of history drives the workers and revolutionaries themselves with much greater force towards bourgeois revolutionism ... than towards [socialist] revolutionism.[16]

The Bolsheviks accepted this essential Marxist line, but argued that the Russian bourgeoisie was too weak to complete the bourgeois-democratic revolution and, fearing the proletariat was already becoming counter-revolutionary, Lenin argued that the Menshevik policy of delay would make bourgeois resistance all the more stubborn, that only the proletariat was the consistently revolutionary class that would not only go on "to the end," but would also complete the bourgeois revolution.[17]

Lenin had gained control of the central committee at the London Congress in April 1907 and had profited from the frame-up of social democratic deputies to the Second Duma, which led to exile in Siberia for a number of leading Mensheviks. By midsummer of 1907, however, he had abandoned hope for an imminent armed uprising and from Finland called on his comrades in Russia to participate in the elections for the Third Duma. The revolutionary movement was demoralized and in decline. Yet the Bolshevik center continued to raise money from armed raids, including a hold-up of the Tiflis post office in June that netted over 300,000 rubles. Scandals soon rocked the Bolshevik faction because of evidence of counterfeiting and the use of Okhrana informers. Many leading Bolsheviks deserted Lenin at the time, among them Gorky, Bogdanov, and Lunacharsky. Lenin was virtually alone.

Throughout the rest of 1907, Bolsheviks fought him on the issue of boycotting the Duma, but one by one they yielded to his "uncanny ability to appraise Stolypin correctly and to adapt his tactics to the hard realities of revolutionary decline." [18] At the central committee meeting of the RSDWP in the summer of 1908, the conflict still smoldered within the Bolshevik faction. Lenin voted against the boycott, together with the Mensheviks, Poles, and Bundists, but all of the other Bolshevik delegates voted for a boycott. This must surely have been one of the lowest, most depressing periods in Lenin's political career. Yet he ultimately prevailed.

Incited by its growing closeness to the Menshevik positions, his attacks on the Bund resumed with the old vehemence. "From the first signal," Medem recalled, at the RSDWP central committee meeting in Geneva in 1908, one constantly heard the cry, "Save the Party from the Liquidators!" Medem angrily told Lenin that the word [liquidator] was "inflammatory and unworthy." Lenin did not answer back. "He shot a sharp glance with his small dark eyes and remained quiet, as if he were not the issue at all." [19]

Factions within the Bolshevik and Menshevik groups also "grew like weeds after a rain, breaking the party into pieces" over the question of the social-democratic delegation to the Third Duma. There was even a group among the Mensheviks called the "recallers," who wanted the deputies to resign.[20] Liber, who together with Medem formed the Bund delegation to the RSDWP committee, tried to bring all the factions together, but failed. Medem himself felt that the splintering was a symptom of a disease in the Russian party that could not be healed from the outside. Only after the creation of a mass movement would it fade.[21]

Medem was soon replaced in the RSDWP central committee and began to devote himself entirely to Bundist matters, especially its foreign committee and newspapers. He dreamed of regular work on "a great daily paper." And the "national question" continued to absorb him.[22]

Meanwhile, the Bund had been making big readjustments. At the time of its reconciliation with the RSDWP in 1907, its membership stood at about 26,000,[23] but during the next few years, the movement declined and its political activity was seriously limited by dwindling numbers and the harsh reactionary climate. The Bund now began to devote much energy to semilegal activities—cultural, literary, and musical societies; evening courses; drama circles; and an ardent campaign for the use of Yiddish. Bundists began to participate in general Jewish cultural activities— activities that would have been unthinkable just a few years earlier—such as the Society for the Promotion of Culture Among the Jews of Russia. They also began to meet with Jewish communal leaders, demanding greater autonomy, secularization, and democratization of organized Jewish life.

Yet despite the disillusionment and decline after 1906, when the organizational structure and leadership of the Bund were severely tested, there was surprising continuity in the leadership. Among the twenty-three top leaders of the 1907–17 period, all had joined the Bund before 1907 and all but five had served at the same level before 1907; two had served in second-echelon posts.[24] This top leadership had been diminished by about half, but had not withered or drastically changed. Turnover in second-echelon posts was very marked, however.[25] The continuity in policy-making leadership was very significant: it ensured the Bund's commitment to the Russian revolutionary movement and sustained the traditional balance and interaction between intellectuals and workers that had characterized the movement in the past.[26] There was greater readjustment at second echelon levels but, on the whole, although greatly reduced, the movement maintained organizational stability and a sense of solidarity among members, strengthened by the opportunities for "legal" practical work. As in the past, the Bund adapted its course to changed conditions.

However, some Bund leaders who had been revolutionaries for over a decade and could not accept any concessions by a tsarist regime or rely mainly on "legal" measures left the Bund. Others, like Arkady Kremer, changed their relationship to the organization. Kremer was arrested in 1907, and after his release in 1908 ceased his professional association, but continued to serve the Bund in other capacities. Abramovich edited various Bund journals in 1908–09 and taught school; Bernshtein lived in France and helped Bund groups abroad; Gozhansky left active political work; Litvak did important literary work for the Bund and visited the United States in 1908; Tsvia Hurvich, who had been arrested several times and exiled, returned to Vilna in 1907 and became active in the RSDWP in St. Petersburg; Izenshtat became chief editor of the Bund's first legal daily from 1906 to 1912; Kopelson headed the Bund publishing house in Vilna until 1908; Kosovsky wrote and edited Bund and later Menshevik publications; Mill remained abroad working for the foreign committee.

At this juncture in Bund history—which historians of the Bund mark as the dividing line between revolutionary political struggle and the subsequent role of the Bund as an instrument in the development of Yiddish culture—Yiddish was strengthened as the primary tool of a mass Jewish cultural uplift and the main force in the drive for national cultural autonomy. After 1907, many members and leaders were involved in Bundist reading circles and libraries, and in journalistic and literary work. Those with an educational role maintained close personal ties with Jewish workers and were able to attract new workers who had cultural aspirations and interests—a field which now was as valid for the Bund as revolutionary political goals.[27]

This new perspective and commitment not only helped the Bund resolve the problem of legal versus illegal activity, but saved it from the savage factional splitting of the rest of the social democratic movement. In cities and towns throughout the Pale, a great variety of societies was formed, officially nonpartisan, but often under Bund direction. *Harp*, a musical dramatic society founded in Lodz in 1908, was typical of many others.[28] Only Bundists served as officers in the *Harp*. But the government became suspicious of a revolutionary undercurrent. Meetings were frequently raided and the *Harp* was eventually closed down by the police. The same thing often happened when Bundists became active in projects started by others. The Central Yiddish Literary Society was founded in St. Petersburg in 1908; by 1911, Bundists became so visibly active that the organization was closed down and some of its members were arrested.[29] In 1906 the Polish Society to Spread Education was started with a Jewish section led partially by Bundists. In 1910, the librarian, a Bundist, was arrested for keeping illegal literature and other Bundists were dismissed from the Society.[30]

The advancement of Yiddish as the instrument of a Jewish cultural renaissance had predated the founding of the Bund, but the movement was much advanced by the Bund's efforts to have Yiddish recognized as the national language of the Jewish people and—as had happened in the Jewish labor movement in America—to have it used as a literary tool by Bund writers and sympathizers. The daily life of Jewish workers as well as political and literary themes became the appropriate and legitimate content of literary work. However, the increased emphasis on Yiddish also plunged the Bund into new dilemmas: there was the danger that the movement for Yiddish and cultural development was drawing bourgeois support, threatening the class struggle and the Bund's role in that struggle. This problem was perceived with disquiet by the Bund's most politically oriented representatives at the Czernowicz language conference in 1908 and again at a second conference in Kovno in 1909.[31] When the four

Bundist delegates reported on the Kovno conference, they noted that of the 120 delegates, only 25 to 30 could be characterized as "social activists"; the rest were well-to-do bourgeoisie who rejected the political aspects of culture. The Bund introduced a resolution that would have given the conference the task of "spreading enlightenment among Jewish workers," but it received only eight votes.[32] A similar divergence in outlook also separated the Bund from those whose interest in cultural development was rooted in a commitment to Hebrew and religious tradition, who feared that wide use of Yiddish would lead to secularization. These complications added stress to the Bund's problem of coping with new competitive forces in Jewish life.

The urgency of these pressures was noted in the September 1909 issue of *Voice of the Bund:* "our democratic intelligentsia . . . are making every effort to put their particular stamp on the cultural movement. The Zionists and bourgeois intelligentsia in general are doing the same. . . . In the struggle of ideas going on, our opinions regarding these questions must be placed on the scale if we do not wish the workers to fall under the influence of other points of view." [33]

As in America, the Yiddish press played an enormous part in creating and stimulating a literary culture and cultural diversity. It also created a mass readership, which broadened knowledge of social and political issues and raised cultural consciousness but also, inevitably, battered Jewish unity and exposed cleavages. The cleavages, in turn, expressed a certain vitality in the pervasive gloom, but the Bund lost its early predominant role. Whereas between 1894 and 1900 it had sponsored 13 of the 15 periodicals started, between 1901 and 1915, when all Yiddish publications were suppressed by the government, it was responsible for only 54 of the 261 Yiddish journals started.[34] Problems which had been purely academic and theoretical now became explicit and practical not only for the Bund but for other Jewish groups and organizations. Differing approaches and solutions cracked old structures and oligarchies.

For the members still left in Russia, the question of legality and the so-called liquidators agitated many discussions, as it did the Bund conference in the spring of 1910. Although thousands of government regulations negated or handicapped the legalization of unions, cooperatives, and certain cultural activities, [35] some of the delegates believed that the Bund must take advantage of whatever legal loopholes there were without giving up the underground aspects of its work. There were stormy clashes of opinion at the conference and sharp exchanges, possibly reflecting the low spirits of the delegates as well as different approaches. This was the "bitter heritage of the years of reaction," Medem recalled. The most divisive arguments were over the question of legal versus illegal possibilities for the Bund in the new situation. "The illegal activities would have to be undertaken by only a limited number of the most trusted comrades, in whose hands must be found the direction of and integration with legal activities. The strongest supporters of this policy were Liber and Abramovich. . . . The second group viewed legal activity with great skepticism . . . and kept stressing the importance of illegal work." [36] Izenshat was the chief defender of this position. The arguments were often vehement, even bitter, but ultimately the Bund tradition of mutual trust, good will, and unity prevailed.

The conference proclaimed that Jewish social democrats should not only lead the struggle against assimilation and against the Hebraists who were opposed to Yiddish, but that they should involve themselves in the restructuring of the *kahal* by placing it on a secular basis and replacing the rabbis and traditional leadership with leaders of the proletariat. The conference also directed the Bund to form all sorts of unions—legal, illegal, and neutralist. In keeping with its decision to make maximum use of legal means, the Bund also issued directives to its local organizations to proceed with the active development of all kinds of legal associations, such as trade unions, cultural clubs, dramatic and literary circles, and choruses. It was at this conference that all discussions were carried on in Yiddish for the first time.

These developments reflected the changes brought about under the semiparliamentary regime. Such questions as Jewish communal activity, Jewish schools, and the election of Jewish representatives made practical decisions necessary, and these decisions had a bearing on the Jewish future as well as the present. Out of these social and political circumstances came the change from "neutralism" to a more positive affirmation of the Jewish future.[37]

Medem began to retreat from his earlier position in his essay "Natsionalizm oder Naitralizm," published in 1910. He admitted that the word "neutralism" may have been an unfortunate choice because it was misunderstood to mean that the Bund had no interest in Jewish cultural activity or in Jewish survival. But, unlike the assimilationists and nationalists, who were sure of their prognoses, Medem refused to be swayed by false optimism or a mystical belief in the future of Jewry. He thought their predictions cavalier and glib, not at all consonant with the complex forces in history. "We don't know what will happen to the Jewish people in the future," Medem reflected. "Shall we make of this observation a principle? We can have a position without making a prognosis, but we have to delve more deeply than we have to find new approaches. . . . However, it is not a question of faith or belief, but of existing needs" [38] He maintained that "Our neutralism is a thousand times more honest than mystical nationalism." Yet "neutralists" are not indifferent to the fate of the nation—if the Jewish masses have cultural interests, the Bund must concern itself with them; if no such interests exist, the Bund should not stimulate them. "For us, the most important thing is the actual interest of the working class . . . for [the nationalist], nationalism is an end in itself and its existence does not depend on any interests." [39] Human efforts can influence the inexorable historical process only when such efforts serve life-needs and life-interests. Later, when Medem became involved in the practical problems of the Yiddish language and Yiddish schools, he claimed that he was not interested in some abstract Judaism, but in the real needs of Jewish workers.

Medem was no kinder in dealing with Diaspora Jewish nationalists like the historian Dubnow, who believed that Jews throughout the world shared common cultural and historical traditions and formed a *Kulturgemeinschaft*, than he was with Zionists. Instead, Medem perceived a deep gulf separating various Jewries, undergoing different experiences, lacking a common Jewish environment and open to varying destinies. He also rejected the idea of a world Jewry and the use of traditional religion or the Hebrew language to infuse the idea with meaning. This was, he believed, another form of romanticism that led to neglect of the practical needs of the Jewish masses.

These ideas were shared by most Bundists through the political vicissitudes of the Bund in the years up to the Bolshevik Revolution—when the bulk of the movement passed into Poland—and in Poland, through the most destructive years of the Holocaust. Even while Polish masses helped the Nazis exterminate Polish Jews, the Bund for months held to its sense of solidarity with the workers of Poland in the struggle against the common enemy and refrained from making common resistance with other Jews in the ghettos. Once it decided that the Poles were not going to help, it joined with other Jewish groups and became a leading resistance force, but it delayed that decision. Medem, who died in 1923 in the United States, would probably have supported this position. One may wonder, however, if he would have been as relentless in his subsequent analysis as he had been in his analysis of Zionism. Would he have understood the Bund position to have been extravagant romanticism in the guise of a socialist mandate during a time of Jewish national catastrophe?

Not until 1916, when the evacuation of Poland by the Russians opened the way for the development of a large-scale national program in the Jewish communities, did Medem shed the last vestiges of "neutralism." [40] During the German occupation of Poland, the issue of Jewish secular schools became a practical matter and Medem took the lead in organizing schools and children's homes, in developing textbooks, and in laying the foundation for the educational program which later developed into the large network of Yiddish schools in Poland known as Cysho. Medem was also among the first Bundists to call for active involvement by the Bund in the *kehillot*, and action on the question of the Sabbath day of rest.

Medem's sensitivity to the nationality question was also evident at a conference of the International in 1910 in Copenhagen, which he attended as a delegate (the other delegates from the Bund were Izenshtat, M. Nachimson, and Anna Lifchitz, who became famous as an orator at the time of the Potemkin incident in Odessa in 1905). In contrast with the International at Amsterdam, there was no controversy over the Bund's voting rights—it had received two as the result of a special decision of the International Bureau. Ten votes were given to the Social-Democratic party (half of all those given to Russia). Medem found the Amsterdam Congress more interesting, but became engrossed in one question in Copenhagen: the matter of Czech unions.[41] The Austrian party was divided by differences between the Czech and German positions. The party itself had ratified the idea of a federative union of six national organizations, but the Czech delegates wanted separate unions and clashed bitterly with the German delegation. Medem deplored the fact that Plekhanov, "who had no interest or sympathy for problems of national minorities and came from a powerful nation," chaired the special commission discussing the question and wrote the report. Medem tried to introduce a resolution recognizing the special needs of the Czech unions, but the conflict had already become a split which shattered the Austrian union and the political movement as well.[42]

Other more serious arguments portended. At the Copenhagen International, Lenin remained adamant—and alone—in his refusal to make peace with the opposition, which now included defectors within Bolshevik ranks. He was accused of ignoring the will of the party and of suppressing all independent opinion. At the time, the entire social-democratic movement was weakened by political and personal schisms and defections as well as by Stolypin's repressive policies. Yet, Russia had moved forward in certain ways since 1905. Besides the 1906 law regarding trade unions and mutual aid associations, after 1910, certain new newspapers were permitted. If the censor banned a paper, it often reappeared under a new name. Mensheviks, Bundists, and, indeed, many Bolsheviks were now convinced that an underground party honeycombed with spies and government agents was no longer useful. Mensheviks were devoting their main energies to organizing trade unions and were having marked success. Lenin regarded this trend with alarm. Workers were withdrawing from underground activities. The party, he believed, was in danger of becoming an emasculated arm of the legal trade union movement. Yet while he continued to attack these socialists for seeking to "liquidate" the Social-Democratic party, he tried to gain control of some of the unions and use them as bases of Bolshevik power.

Politically, the work of the Bund at the time was largely limited to raising funds to cope with strikes and lockouts that had broken out in some parts of the Pale. Jewish union activity did not cease, nor did the Bund's involvement. Between 1909 and 1910, the Bund led strikes in ten cities, but to a large extent, these were costly, time-consuming, and hardly the basis of a revived movement. By 1910, legal trade unions, limited to printers and several other highly skilled trades, were found in only four cities—Bialystok, Lodz, Riga, and Vilna.

The Eighth Conference of the Bund in Lemberg in 1910 had revealed the dimensions of its decline. There were actually only nine functioning Bund organizations (in Bobruisk, Bialystok, Grodno, Dvinsk, Warsaw, Vilna, Lodz, Pinsk, and Riga) representing 609 members, most of whom were in the Polish cities of the empire.[43] Only two centers in Belorussia, one in Lithuania and one in Latvia were represented. Medem recalled that the entire socialist movement in Russia had all but collapsed at this time, but that the Bund "didn't stop existing or working for a minute." It underwent and surmounted its severest crisis; at this conference, he wrote, "We roused ourselves and began a new era of work." [44]

In the summer of 1911, several members of the foreign and central committes met to discuss the possibility of publishing a legal Bund weekly from Warsaw, with articles written in Krakow or Vienna because of police surveillance in Warsaw. In the spring of 1912, Litvak, Abramovich, Grosser (Slawek), and Medem met in Vienna to start work. Medem describes Vienna with immense enthusiasm: "One quickly loses one's sense of being a foreigner and feels at home.... The mixed population creates a broad tolerance, even toward Jews, and Jews themselves, accustomed to the mixture of peoples, have a more tolerant outlook." [45] However, the Germans, he recalled, wanting to keep the "German character" of the city, took up a fight against "strangers," protesting especially against Czech meetings and concerts. He noted also the anti-Semitism of the dominant Christian Socialist party, but observed that it was felt very little in daily life. "As compared to the Jews in Russia, the Jews in Vienna lived like trees in a winegarden."

The newspaper *Lebensfragn* (*Living Questions*) was launched in May from Grasser's shabby, meagerly furnished room. Every day the editors met, discussed topics, and wrote and edited articles that were then sent to Warsaw. Administrative work and correspondence there were directed by Moishe Rafes, who joined the Communist party after the Bolshevik Revolution and became a fiery antagonist of the Bund. The paper aroused great joy among subscribers; the Bund had its own organ again after four and a half years. But a new blow soon struck. Medem did not as yet know how to write Yiddish, and wrote his articles in transliterated Latin letters. The Polish police became suspicious, confiscated the second issue, and said threatingly, "We know this is a Bundist paper!" The whole administrative staff as well as a correspondent from Lodz were arrested.[46] It was clear that the paper could no longer be published from Warsaw and after several months, a shift was made to St. Petersburg, where the climate was somewhat freer and where there already existed a socialist press. The paper was renamed *Di Tsayt* (*The Times*).

A severe crisis gripped the Russian party from 1907 to 1912. Former activists deserted it en masse and arrests further depleted its ranks. By the summer of 1909, not more than five or six of the Bolshevik underground committees were still functioning regularly. It seemed pointless to think of rebuilding an illegal party on such a crumbling foundation, yet Lenin held fast to his notion of the illegal élitist party as the instrument of revolution and stubornly resisted any thought of reconciliation. When the United Central Committee of the party met in Paris in 1910, the Bolsheviks claimed control by virtue of their majority at the 1907 congress. But the Mensheviks and Bundists refused to yield. In order to forestall the opposition, Lenin, now living in Paris, sent his agents into Russia to mobilize a "general party convention" of his sympathizers. Such a meeting, consisting of delegates hand-picked by Lenin, was held in Prague in January 1912. They asserted that they represented the entire Social-Democratic party and denounced all others as "Menshevik liquidators."

Lenin also attacked the position of the Mensheviks and Bundists on the new Duma, the Fourth (convened November 1912). They believed that the social-democratic delegation (7 Mensheviks and 6 Bolsheviks) offered opportunities for creating a broad leadership for the reviving labor movement and the formation of a progressive bloc against the tsar. For Lenin, however, the Duma was merely another platform for arousing the masses to revolutionary action. It was this Duma that provided the setting for the dénouement in RSDWP affairs. At the center was the bizarre case of Roman Malinovsky, double agent extraordinary.[47]

Malinovsky had met Lenin at the Prague conference in January 1912. He was a talented, vigorous metalworker whose expensive tastes had led him to serve the Moscow Okhrana for 50 rubles a month, while his revolutionary ardor led him into trade unionism, Menshevism, and then Bolshevism. The police had ordered Malinovsky to do as much as possible to deepen the split in the party—the same aim as Lenin's. (It will be recalled that the all-Bolshevik Conference in Prague contained only Lenin's hand-picked delegates.) A number of police had already gained important positions in the Bolshevik underground, but Malinovsky was the key figure. He was much admired and liked by Lenin, who coopted him to the new central committee as chief of the Russian bureau, and promoted his election to the Fourth Duma. During this period, he also became the Okhrana's highest paid spy, with a salary of 500 rubles a month. The donations he made to the Bolshevik cause were charged to his police expense account.

The Bolsheviks and especially the police worked zealously to get Malinovsky elected to the Duma, where he became head of the Bolshevik delegation. At first the thirteen social-democratic deputies formed a united block, much to Lenin's displeasure. Even the Bolshevik daily *Pravda* at first carefully avoided controversy with other socialist groups in order to gain a solid reputation among workers and a large circulation. It even censored or supressed articles by Lenin that sharpened the fight against Mensheviks and Bundists. Lenin raged. The editors, he said, "must be kicked out. . . . They praise the Bund . . . and their attitude toward my articles is monstrous." He decided on a strategy which Malinovsky spearheaded: to condemn the Mensheviks for not representing the working class but "a lot of Siberians." A new editor-in-chief was found for *Pravda* (also a police agent, it turned out), and Stalin too was enlisted to help carry out the split, until he was arrested on March 13. Malinovsky, for his part, led the attack on the "liquidators" in speeches in the Duma written or amended by Lenin, Zinoviev, and Kamenev. He attended highly confidential meetings called by Lenin and even went on joint lecture tours with him. The police received full transcripts of everything—Lenin's decisions, secret plans, and moves. Arrests were timed to avert suspicion from Malinovsky. But eventually, rumors that he might be an agent provocateur spread, and when he suddenly resigned from the Duma, the Menshevik leaders Martov and Dan demanded an investigation by a party tribunal—a situation fraught with possible disaster for Lenin. But, instead of a broadly representative tribunal, the Bolshevik central committee set up an investigating commission; no Mensheviks were included. The subsequent exchanges over this affair split the two sides irrevocably. The maneuvers of Lenin and Malinovsky had smashed all possibility of unity in the social democratic delegation. The Mensheviks were violently attacked as "malicious slanderers." Lenin raged: "If Martov and Dan, plus their concealers, the Bundists . . . the August Bloc people, etc., directly or indirectly invite us to a common 'investigation,' we answer them: We don't trust Martov and Dan. . . . We will deal with them only as common criminals."

The Bund also had to endure the revelation that one of its own members, Israel-Michal Kaplinsky, had become one of the most notorious provocateurs in Russia at the time. Kaplinsky—later known as Azev—had built the press which printed the Bund's first paper, *Di Arbayter Shtimme* in 1897. A victim of the mass arrests of Bundists in 1898, he became a police agent under pressure from Zubatov. His complicated life had yet another identity: he also became the leader of the Social Revolutionary party's dread Terror or Fighting Section. These roles enabled Kaplinsky to permit as well as betray planned assassinations by comrades and take funds from both revolutionaries and police. He apparently wanted to be both a terrorist spying on the government and a police agent spying on revolutionaries.

The Bund learned of his double life in 1909 through Vladimir Burtzev, a vigilant one-man tracker of spies. Burtzev was in Paris at the time, with access to Russian police documents that had been brought to Paris by an Okhrana agent named Mentschikov.[48] Burtzev wrote to the central committee of the Bund, naming Kaplinsky as a provocateur. There was great shock at first and shame, but also relief that the highest ranks of the Bund were clean. Medem described Kaplinsky as "clever and cold-blooded," involved in conspiratorial work, yet apparently working "dutifully" for the Bund for many years. It was recalled that he "hung around" the central committee and "knew the members of the central committee and important correspondence like his five fingers."[49] Yet he never informed on members of the Bund. He went into hiding after his exposure and was shot by the Soviet regime in 1918 or 1919.[50]

With the end of the limited collaboration of Mensheviks and Bolsheviks in the Duma, following the all-Bolshevik conference in Prague, the two factions became irrevocably split. The Bolshevik deputies gave the Mensheviks an ultimatum to accept Lenin's program. The Mensheviks refused (August 1913), and the two factions separated. The fortunes of the Bund thereafter were bound up with the Mensheviks.

Meanwhile, the Russian labor movement was bestirring itself. After 1910, there was an economic upturn in the country following a protracted economic depression, and some recovery within Russian labor ranks. Trade unions multiplied and many strikes were called. Of special significance to the revolutionary movement was the strike called at the Lena River gold mines in Siberia in April 1912, following a clash between workers and owners. Soldiers who were called out shot at the strikers, injuring and killing hundreds. In a few days, because of the brutality of the soldiers, spontaneous demonstrations and strikes swept nearly all the industrial centers in Russia, creating the greatest mass disturbances since 1905. Summoned by the Bund, Jewish workers also joined the protests. A May Day (April 18) work stoppage involved six-thousand Jewish workers in Warsaw and several hundred each in Vilna, Minsk, and Bobruisk.[51] This was the first mass demonstration of Jewish workers following the years of reaction and augured some promise for the future of the labor movement.

During this time, two other matters had occupied the Bund: plans for its ninth conference (in Vienna) and the campaign for elections to the Fourth Duma, which embroiled the Bund in intractable Polish anti-Semitism. In Congress Poland, elections to the Duma intensified Polish nationalism. Polish economic anti-Semitism was inflamed by slogans to Polonize the economy—to take economic positions away from Jewish artisans, merchants, and traders. In 1909–10, an anti-Jewish boycott was started. Bundist and other Jewish efforts to achieve cultural autonomy also clashed with the intense Polish nationalism of the time. In the elections to the Fourth Duma in 1912, Jewish electors decided to support Eugeniusz Jagielle, a Polish socialist, whose position on Jewish rights was clear and unqualified.[52] The nationalist Poles then threatened economic reprisals, violence, and pogroms. The Jewish national bloc, including Zionists and Bundists remained firm, however, though quite fully aware of the consequences. The gifted writer and editor and Zionist leader Nachum Sokolow, who had spent his youth in Poland, wrote of the unusual role of the Jewish bourgeoisie in the election: "We will vote for the man who favors full civic equality. Even we, the Jewish bourgeoisie, will vote against our economic interests for a Polish socialist because of something higher:

Jewish honor." [53] But common Jewish action drew ugly reactions. Jewish support of Jagielle became the pretext for continued economic warfare against the Jews in Poland, and a portent for all Jews who feared the nationalism of the Poland to come.

The election posed a further dilemma for the Bund. Because there were two rival socialist parties in Poland—the SD and the PPS—the question of the choice of socialist deputies was a very heated one. The Bund wanted to create a bloc with both, and after complicated negotiations a fusion was agreed upon, but it was short-lived. The SD, which the Bund was closer to, bolted from the bloc, but the Bund stayed with the PPS—Medem said "they had no choice"—and chose Jagielle, who won the election.[54]

Medem also perceived the ominous shadow of Polish anti-Semitism when, in 1911, Polish workers in shoe factories in Warsaw began to force Jewish workers from their machines.[55] Earlier, something similar had happened among weavers in Bialystok until an agreement was worked out dividing the work equally among Jewish and Christian workers. What should the Bund do about these intensifying conflicts in Poland?

Medem said that an understanding with the Polish socialists was essential but could not be achieved. Some of them objected to the fact that Jews kept themselves "apart"; others, that they spoke Yiddish and had to become "civilized." The PPS "showed more understanding but didn't have the skill or desire to resist the spirit of the masses." [56] Medem also wrote a very controversial article in one of the Bund almanacs dealing with the problem and suggesting that only after a struggle between both sides could there be any understanding; by struggle, he meant resistance by the Jewish workers. When he sent the article to Russia to be translated, the central committee thought it "harmful" and asked him to recast it, but he refused.[57] At the Vienna conference, however, a resolution was passed that Medem could endorse. It called on Jewish workers to consider Polish workers who push them out of factories in the same class as strike breakers and requiring the same kind of struggle.[58] This problem foreshadowed only one of the many battles to come.

When Poland was reconstituted as an independent state in 1918, it inherited a serious nationality problem. Poles were, at best, a bare majority among millions of Ukrainians, Germans, Belorussians, Lithuanians, and Jews,[59] all of whom had nationalistic aspirations. The Bund insisted on cultural autonomy for the more than 3 million Jews who came under Polish rule. Its position—as in Russia—separated it from other Jewish parties and from all the Polish socialist parties.

The progressive involvement of the Bund in anti-Semitic actions also drew it into the Beilis case. In 1911, Mendel Beilis, a Jewish manager of a brick factory in Kiev, was arrested and accused of the ritual murder of a young boy. Almost as soon as the body was found, the Kiev cell of the Black Hundreds organized demonstrations and outbreaks against Jews.

Stolypin saw in the situation a perfect opportunity to divert unrest with an anti-Semitic campaign and directed the Kiev district attorney to exploit the murder. Medical professors were bribed to say that the child had been drained of blood while still alive; police and criminals were used by the government to frame Beilis. By 1912 liberal journalists and lawyers began to shred the government case and expose it as a political maneuver of a reactionary regime. Liberals and socialists stepped up their anti-tsarist propaganda. Mass strikes and protest meetings again began to involve many thousands of Jewish workers. The ninth Bund conference, held in Vienna in August 1912, protested vehemently against the Beilis trial and demanded the abolition of the Pale of Settlement.

Marking the 300th anniversary of tsarism in Russia, 1912 was also the year of political amnesty for many political exiles who now returned to Russia, some to resume work interrupted by the failed revolution of 1905. In 1912, moreover, the Mensheviks began to look more favorably on the principle of national-cultural autonomy. The August 1912 conference of right-wing Mensheviks took the first steps in the direction of a national program, which the party had heretofore lacked. It asserted in its resolution that "national-cultural autonomy was not contrary to the party's program guaranteeing national self-determination." By 1917 the entire Menshevik party, which had many Jewish members and which, by then, was politically linked with the Bund, incorporated national-cultural autonomy into its official party platform. Mark Liber, Raphael Abramovich, Isaiah Izenshtat, Tsvia Hurvich, and Vladimir Kosovsky were among leading Bundists who became actively involved in Menshevism as the two movements drew closer together. Unfortunately, in this historic crisis Menshevik leadership was no match for Lenin. Under Martov, the Mensheviks drifted uncertainly, unable to chart a clear program for Russian workers or make the necessary alliances with other movements that might have toppled the regime. No such weakness attacked Vladimir Ilyich.

22. The End of the Bund in Russia

Lenin remained adamant on the national question. Until he moved to Austrian Poland in 1912, his polemics on nationalism had been directed almost exclusively against the Bund. But in that year in Cracow, amid the nationalisms erupting out of the Balkan War, the struggle between Pilsudski's and Rosa Luxemburg's Polish socialist parties, and the views of the Austrian Marxists on the national question, Lenin expanded his targets and intensified his attack. As in 1904, he had seized control of the RSDWP by convening a rump Bolshevik congress in Prague in 1912, which "elected" a new central committee consisting solely of his followers. Henceforth the Bolsheviks were not merely a faction within the party but the party itself. The excluded factions and individuals, among them, Plekhanov, Akselrod, Martov, and Trotsky, were indeed the variegated substance of the social-democratic movement. They called counter-congresses to try to block Lenin's coup d'état, and, despite Trotsky's efforts at conciliation, soon fell to fierce quarreling among themselves and factionalism.

However, their short-lived union against Lenin, the so-called August Bloc, led them to blur differences on all matters except party unity. In order to include the Bund, for example, they found it expedient to adopt a resolution stating that the Bund's "demand for national-cultural autonomy is not incompatible with the point in the Party platform concerning the right of nations to self-determination." [1] Logically, then, it was up to each people to determine for itself whether it wanted national-cultural autonomy or separation. When the Georgian social democrats adopted the same resolution, Lenin saw the opportunity to carry his war into the most powerful stronghold of Menshevism.

Before the RSDWP split in 1913, the Bund and Georgian Mensheviks tried to press acceptance of national-cultural autonomy upon the RSDWP. Lenin was infuriated at what he saw as one more manifestation of "liquidationism." His experiences in Austrian Poland redoubled his hostility to the idea of cultural autonomy. To his amazement, he found the views of Austrian Marxists, influenced by Renner and Bauer, markedly opposed to his.[2] Anticipating the empire's federalization rather than its liquidation, with equal national, cultural, and administrative rights for all the nationalities within it, and anxious to counteract the disruptive nationalistic forces within the Dual Monarchy, the Austrians stressed the very values Lenin excoriated—national-cultural autonomy and federalism. Lenin's intense feelings about the Austrian Marxists can be gauged by a letter he wrote to Gorky, at the time in which he reassured Gorky that in the Caucasus, Georgian, Armenian, Tartar, and Russian social democrats had worked together in a single organization for more than ten years. "That is not a mere phrase, but a proletarian solution of the national question. The only solution. So it was in Riga, too: Russians, Letts, Lithuanians; *only the separatists* split away: the Bund. ... *No, such vileness as in Austria will not appear among us.* We won't permit it." [3]

The Transcaucasian organization, uniting revolutionaries of Georgian, Armenian, Russian, and other nationalities, could be used as a model. Koba (Stalin), who had arrived in Cracow at this time, was known to have opposed local nationalism in the Transcaucasian revolutionary movement.[4] His visit was welcomed by Lenin, who later wrote to Gorky: "About nationalism, I fully agree with you that we have to bear down harder. We have here a wonderful Georgian [Stalin] who has undertaken to write a long article ... after gathering *all* the Austrian and other materials. We will take care of this matter." [5]

To help him prepare materials for his critical essays on the national question (1913–14), Lenin sent this same Georgian Bolshevik, Koba Djugashvili, who had craftily carried out certain expropriations in the Caucasus, to Vienna. The result was Josef Stalin's "Marxism and the National and Colonial Question," published in a party journal in the spring of 1913, an essay which repeated Lenin's attacks on cultural autonomy and remains the standard work in party literature on the subject. Stalin defined the nation as a "historically evolved stable community of language, territory, economic life and psychological make-up manifested in a community of culture." [6] The Austrian definitions of a nation as "a cultural community no longer tied to the soil" or "an aggregate of people bound into a community of character by a community of fate" (Bauer), were sharply condemned on two counts: one, for limiting the rights of nations and blocking the right of self-determination by maintaining the multinational state and substituting equality of cultural rights for sovereign political rights; and, two, by perpetuating national prejudices and treating the nation as a fixed and permanent category, so that the Austrian perception of the future socialist order would "divide humanity into nationally delimited communities."

Overlooking the fact that the activities of the Bund were mainly concerned with a linguistically homogeneous Jewish population in the Pale, Stalin asks:

> What ... national cohesion can there be ... between the Georgian, Daghes-
> tanian, Russian and American Jews? ... if there is anything common to them
> left it is their religion, their common origin and certain relics of national
> character. How can it be seriously maintained that petrified religious rites and
> fading psychological relics affect the "fate" of these Jews more powerfully than
> the living ... environment that surrounds them.[7]

Moreover, very few Jews live on the soil and do not constitute a majority in any province in Russia. Interspersed as national minorities in areas inhabited by other nationalities, they serve "foreign" nations as manufacturers and traders and as members of the free professions, naturally adapting themselves to the "foreign nations." All this, taken together with the increasing reshuffling of nationalities characteristic of developed forms of capitalism, inevitably leads to the assimilation of the Jews, according to Stalin.[8] The abolition of the Pale will hasten this process.

Stalin accepted the principle of cultural, i.e., linguistic, rights but attacked the Bund's aim of securing special Jewish rights, such as Saturday as the day of rest:

> It is to be expected that the Bund will take another "forward step" and demand
> the right to observe all the ancient Hebrew holidays. ... The maintenance of
> everything Jewish, the preservation of *all* the national peculiarities of the Jews,
> even those that are patently noxious to the proletariat, the isolation of the Jews
> from everything non-Jewish, even the establishment of special hospitals—that is
> the level to which the Bund has sunk.[9]

The duty of the Social Democratic party, in short, was to agitate against such harmful institutions and other demands of nations, in the interests of the proletariat. For national minorities, especially in backward areas, Stalin proposed regional autonomy.

Regional autonomy was acceptable for the Transcaucasus because it would help backward areas there to cast off the shell of small-nation insularity. But *national-cultural* autonomy would work in the opposite direction, shutting up these nations in their old shells. Regional autonomy was also recommended for areas such as Poland and the Ukraine in order to break down rather than strengthen national barriers and make way for division according to class. Jews, of course, being scattered, could not merit regional autonomy.

Stalin undoubtedly benefited greatly from the discussions with Lenin in Cracow. In a conversation with the Yugoslav dissenting communist Milovan Djilas in 1948, Stalin said that he had expressed Lenin's views and that Lenin had actually edited his work.[10] There has been considerable disagreement among scholars as to the degree of collaboration or originality. The concept of regional autonomy was clearly Stalin's. In any case, Lenin was pleased by the results. He wrote to Kamenev, for example, on February 25, 1913: "The article is *very good;* the issue is a fighting one and we will not surrender one iota of our principled opposition to the Bundist trash." [11] Later he wrote, "Koba has managed to write a big article on the national question. Good! We have to fight for the truth against the separatists, the opportunists from the Bund and from among the liquidators." [12] In an editorial somewhat later, he wrote that Stalin's article "stands out in first place." [13]

Lenin himself did not deal with the Jewish question systematically, but in numerous, scattered references. In the spring of 1913 he wrote several polemical pieces on the national question. In two articles in *Pravda*, he condemned the Czech social democrats in Austria as separatists "clinging to the coat-tails of liquidators and Bundists," and wrote a draft platform for Latvian Bolsheviks (to bolster them in their struggle against the dominant Menshevik Latvian social democratic movement), in which he again attacked national-cultural autonomy and federation.[14] The "Theses on the National Question" were written for lectures delivered in July 1913 in various Swiss cities and propounded the right of self-determination (including secession) for all nationalities while urging the proletariat to ally only with other workers of all nations in *their* struggle—a double harness that caused great confusion in socialist ranks later. The "cultural-national autonomy slogan" is described as having been followed "only by Jewish bourgeois parties" and "uncritically followed by the Bund." [15]

In August Lenin wrote a scathing attack against a government proposal for creating special Jewish schools, linking this with the Bund's notions of national autonomy. Later, in an article in December, he ridiculed the idea of giving Russia's many national minorities their own national school programs but insisted on their right to have lectures, books, and language teachers for appropriate cultural activities.

In the autumn of 1913, Lenin made a report on the national question at a conference of the party's central committee, where all of the foregoing ideas were adopted. After the conference, he started work on "Critical Remarks on the National Question." This includes a summary of the Leninist juxtaposition of bourgeois-national and proletarian-internationalist culture and serves as the text from which the standard Bolshevik formulations on the nature of Jewish culture have been derived. The elements of democratic and socialist culture, Lenin declared, are present in every national culture, but every nation also possesses a dominant culture—the culture of the landlords, the clergy and the bourgeoisie. Those who wish to serve the proletariat must unite the workers of all nations and fight bourgeois nationalism, both domestic and foreign. The same struggle applies to the

> most oppressed and persecuted nation, the Jews. Jewish national culture is the slogan of rabbis and bourgeosie, the slogan of our enemies. But there are other elements in Jewish culture and ... history as a whole. Out of ten and a half million Jews throughout the world, *about one-half* live in a civilized world,

under conditions favoring *maximum* "assimilationism," whereas only the oppressed and wretched Jews of Russia and Galicia, deprived of legal rights and downtrodden by Purishkeviches,[16] live under conditions favoring *minimum* "assimilationism" and maximum segregation. . . . In the civilized world, the Jews are not a nation. . . . In Galicia and Russia, the Jews are not a nation; there they are unfortunately (not through any fault of theirs, but through that of the Purishkeviches) still a *caste*.[17]

Thus, argued Lenin, Jewish reactionaries and Bundists who oppose assimilation are "turning back the wheel of history." Bourgeois nationalism and proletarian internationalism are "irreconcilably hostile," and those, like the Bund, who advance the idea of national culture are guilty of "the most refined, most absolute and most extreme nationalism."

Anyone directly or indirectly putting forward the slogan of Jewish "national culture" is (whatever his good intention) an enemy of the proletariat, a partisan of the *old* and the *castelike* in the Jewish group. . . . Contrariwise, those Jewish Marxists who merge with the Russian, Lithuanian, Ukrainian, and other workers in international Marxist organizations, contributing their share (in both Russian and Yiddish) to the creation of an international culture of the labor movement—those Jews carry on (in defiance of the separatism of the Bund) the best Jewish tradition when they combat the slogan of "national culture." [18]

Stalin had ridiculed the Bund for proposing autonomy "for a nation whose future is denied and whose existence is still to be proved." Lenin attacked national cultural autonomy as divisive, yet he insisted that the rights of national minorities be guaranteed although it was "inappropriate and impossible to define particulars in a program." [19] He also maintained that "in every national culture there are *elements* of a democratic and Socialist culture" which Marxists must take from the dominant national culture of the landowners, priests, and bourgeoisie.[20] The Bundists, he said, leave this basic Marxist truth "in the shade, and in practice oppose the opening up of the class gulf in society, instead of exposing and explaining it." After yielding that "the Marxist fully acknowledges the historical legitimacy of national movements," Lenin warns that "it is necessary to limit" this acknowledgment "most strictly to that which is progressive in these movements—so that this recognition should not obscure proletarian consciousness with bourgeois ideology." [21]

A murky zone is then described—which subsequently caused great bewilderment among the party faithful—in which the Marxist struggle against national oppression overlaps the danger of betraying proletarian internationalism:

To overthrow every feudal yoke, every oppression of a nation, every privilege, for one particular nation or one language, is the undoubted duty of the proletariat as a democratic force, undoubtedly to the interest of the proletarian class struggle, which is confused and retarded by class strife. But to assist bourgeois nationalism *beyond* this limit—rigidly determined and placed within a definite historical framework—means betraying the proletariat and taking the side of the bourgeoisie. . . .

A struggle *against* all forms of national oppression—unquestionably, *yes!* A struggle *for* every kind of national development, *for* "national culture" in general—unquestionably, no! . . .[22]

Many questions were left in limbo by this dialectic: Would the right of self-determination and secession be forfeited if Russia were to become ripe for a *socialist* revolution? How could workers know when the struggle *against* national oppression shaded into a struggle *for* national development? What guideposts could resolve the dilemma of the Polish and Ukrainian proletariat, indoctrinated in the goal of the "fusion of nations," suffering under Russian oppression, struggling to break out of the yoke, and confronting secession and the creation of yet another nationalism? Was not a certain measure of national development necessary to awaken the masses to the "struggle against national oppression of any kind?"

One of the last direct exchanges between Lenin and the Bund on these questions took place in the fall of 1913. The Bundist Peisakh Liebman (Liebman Hersh) published an article in *Tsayt* charging that "self-determination" was much too vague to have any real political meaning. "When the Jewish working class . . . began to work out the specific content of this concept, the master theoreticians of Russian Social-Democracy cried out, 'Nationalism!' . . . Every attempt to give clear and concrete expression was attacked as a petite-bourgeois heresy against Marxist doctrine." Liebman argued that

Anyone in the least familiar with the national question knows that international culture is not non-national . . . ; non-national culture, which must not be Russian, Jewish or Polish, but only pure culture, is nonsense. International ideas can appeal to the working class only when they are adapted to the language spoken by the worker, and to the concrete national conditions under which he lives. The worker should not be indifferent to the condition and development of his national culture, because it is . . . only through it that he is able to participate in the "international culture of democracy and of the world working-class movement." This is well known, but V.I. turns a deaf ear to it all.[23]

Lenin denounced these views with contempt and accused the Bund of "spreading faith in a non-class national culture," of being "propagators of bourgeois nationalism in the workers' ranks." When he shifted to "concrete examples," the meaning became obscured:

Can a Great-Russian Marxist accept the slogan of national, Great-Russian, culture? No, he cannot. . . . Our task is to fight the dominant Black-Hundred and bourgeois national culture of the Great Russians and to develop . . . the rudiments also existing in the history of our democratic and working-class movement. Fight your own Great-Russian landlords and bourgeoisie, fight their "culture" in the name of internationalism, and in so fighting, "adapt" yourself to the special features of the Purishkeviches . . . that is your task, not preaching or tolerating the slogan of national culture.[24]

What precisely does it mean for the proletariat to "adapt" to anti-Semites while fighting bourgeois culture? It sounds ominously as if some of the techniques will have to be borrowed from them. Yet Lenin vehemently opposed all manifestations of anti-Semitism.

His views on self-determination were also complicated by qualifications and push-pull pronouncements. Above all, a centralized party loomed. In contrast with the West, where the pattern of one-nation, one-state had already developed, the backward, multinational Russian and Austrian empires were in need of a "bourgeois-democratic revolution" and national self-determination struggles to free the oppressed nationalities. But *inside* the empires, the proletariat of all nationalities must be united—regardless of national origin—into a single, centralized party. Thus, Lenin maintained "we require an item in our program on the *right* of nations to self-determination." But this right of self-determination, he wrote to his Transcaucasian comrade Suren G. Shaumyan in December 1913, is an *exception* to the general premise of centralism.

Not only a centralized party, but rigid opposition to federalism are also revealed in the letter, which, incidentally, was not published until 1922:

> We are in principle against federation—federalism weakens economic ties, it is an impossible arrangement for a state. You want to secede? To hell with you, I say, if you can succeed in breaking the economic ties—or, to be precise, if the injustices and frictions of "cohabitation" are such as to *spoil* and ruin economic relationships. You don't want to secede? Pardon me, then; don't make up my mind *for* me, don't think you have a "right" to a federal union. . . .
>
> The right of self-determination is an *exception* to our general thesis, which is centralism. This exception is absolutely necessary in face of the Black-Hundred type of Great-Russian nationalists. . . . But a broad interpretation may not be made of an exception. There is *nothing*, absolutely nothing here, and must be nothing here, but the right to secede.[25]

The right to secession, however, was complicated by the many hedges, expedients, and explosive national emotions the idea aroused. Lenin did not give the principle much elasticity: "This demand" for self-determination, he wrote, "is by no means identical with the demand for secession, for partition, for the formation of small states. It is merely the logical expression of the struggle against national oppression in every form. The more closely the democratic system of state approximates to complete freedom of secession, the rarer and weaker will be the striving for secession in practice."

Lenin's views on cultural autonomy and on the rights of self-determination and secession were compressed into several resolutions passed by a joint conference of the central committee and officials of the RSDWP in the fall of 1913. This was the first official party pronouncement on the national question and echoed Lenin's ideas. The right of self-determination was further defined: it must "under no circumstances be confused with the expediency of a given nation's secession." The latter question is decided by the party "exclusively on its merits in each particular case in conformity with the interests of social development as a whole and with the interests of the proletarian class struggle for socialism." [26]

Expressive of Lenin's strongly felt view that Jews were the most persecuted group in Russia, and that all Russian workers must join in protesting this oppression, he pressed the social democratic bloc in the Fourth Duma to introduce a bill in March 1914 abolishing all disabilities affecting Jews and hoped to have the bill backed by tens of thousands of signatures and declarations. A paradox is suggested immediately: Lenin believed that such a measure would eliminate the barbarous conditions under which Jews were forced to live and would lead to assimilation. Yet equality of rights meant employment of teachers of Yiddish and Jewish history in areas where Jews wanted such cultural expression. This freedom would *sustain* Jewish identity, however, and defeat assimilationist trends. Lenin, however, never resolved this contradiction, believing, as did Kautsky, that the persistence of the Jewish people throughout history was solely the result of anti-Semitism. The men whom Lenin knew best— Zinoviev, Trotsky, Martov, and Kamenev—were wholly russified, and represented prototypes of the Jew-to-be.

Lenin never departed from the Marxist idea of national differences and antagonisms as "vanishing ever more and more" with the approach of socialism, but his conditional acceptance of self-determination and tantalizingly ambiguous formulations created a storm of polemical counter blasts within the party. The outbreak of war provoked further controversy and complicated positions. The blurred lines between the "bourgeois" and "socialist" revolutions were now to be criss-crossed by inflamed nationalisms, confusing loyalties, and opposing interpretations of nebulous formulations. By March 1919, after the Bolsheviks had seized power, the nation's "will to secede" in Russia became the right of the "toiling masses"—that is, the prerogative of the Communist party. And by an ironical turnabout—so much a feature of Soviet Russia—Stalin eventually adopted the concept of cultural autonomy as a proud achievement of the Soviet Union but shriveled it to mean little more than the right to disseminate centrally issued directives in many languages, euphemistically phrased: "national in form, but socialist in content."

In 1917, the national question became urgent. The war had intensified national aspirations, and separatist tendencies among the Poles, Ukrainians, Lithuanians, Latvians, Estonians, and Armenians became explosive. The Bund's program of cultural autonomy now acquired great popularity among non-Jewish socialists who sought to save the unity of the Russian state through concessions to national minorities. At the first Congress of

Soviets in June 1917, Mark Liber and Raphael Abramovich were the official spokesmen on the national question. In elections to the Constituent Assembly in November 1917, the Bundist principles of territorial self-determination and extraterritorial cultural autonomy were made part of the platform of the Social Democratic party.[27]

However, Leninist views on the national question were to condition and then control Soviet policy toward Jewish cultural aspirations. Although one can find improvisations such as the Birobidjan project and the Jewish Anti-Fascist Committee, which seem to conflict with Lenin's insistence on the ultimate disappearance of Jewishness, these were opportunistic innovations or tactics that did not basically alter the officially required end: assimilation. Moreover, during those periods when Yiddish literature was promoted, it was always yoked to propaganda needs and "socialist realism." When it did not meet these criteria, the writers suffered; many were killed in the purges of 1936–38, and during the "Black Years," 1948–53.

The Bundist view, which preserved and stimulated certain aspects of Jewish culture, had to create a framework that kept workers free of bourgeois influence and interests. The Bolsheviks held that in doing this, the Bund glossed over the interests of the proletariat. But the Bolsheviks, in wanting to abolish all ethnic inequalities, did little to stimulate or preserve national cultures. Their impatience with any obstacles to the unity of the proletariat and the cosmopolitanism of their more articulate leaders ultimately had a leveling force that destroyed the possibilities of rich cultural diversity and created a powerful, centralized, and repressive state.

World War I, which ultimately catapulted the Bolsheviks into power in October 1917, raged through the whole of the Pale of Settlement and devastated Jewish life. To this havoc was added government persecution of the Jewish population. Jews were accused of spying for Germany, and hundreds of thousands were forcibly hounded out of their homes. Very early in the war, Germany occupied Congress Poland, Lithuania, the Baltic states, and part of Belorussia and aggravated the hostility of the Russian government by professing friendship for the oppressed Jews in the German-occupied territory. The German press meanwhile played up Germany's role as liberator of the East. General Ludendorff did indeed repeal tsarist anti-Jewish legislation and issued proclamations of friendship—"An Meine Libe Yiden in Poylen"—in choice Yiddish, but the ravages of war in the German areas drove Jews to desperation. Many subsisted on cooked weeds and grass.

On the war itself, Russian socialists were divided. Some believed that workers must take an active part in the defense of the country; others like Rosa Luxemburg and Lenin believed that the crisis of war must be exploited to hasten revolution. Some socialist leaders in Germany began to preach the "socialist meaning" of Germany's war aims. Burtsev, the foremost exposer of police agents in the revolutionary movement, called on all socialists to support the Russian war effort. Social Revolutionary party leaders became advocates of "defensism." Plekhanov, the father of Russian social democracy and a leading exponent of "orthodox Marxism," became a passionate defender of the Allied cause and recruited volunteers among Russian emigrés in Paris for the French army. Even Bolsheviks were split on the war issue; a number volunteered to serve in the Russian army. The International Socialist Congress, called for August 9, 1914, was shattered by the elemental force of nationalism when the strongest section of the International, the German Social Democratic party, voted unanimously for war credits. A stunned Lenin exclaimed: "The Second International is dead." A war fever took possession of the masses, including the class-conscious workers organized into trade unions and socialist parties. International working class solidarity was exposed as a myth.

At first most Bundists supported a majority of Mensheviks, who took an antiwar internationalist position; the social democratic deputies in the Duma voted against military appropriations. This was the prevailing attitude of the Bund until after the Revolution of March 1917, when the tsar, faced with colossal human losses, troop mutinies, and food riots, was forced to abdicate. By April 1917, many leading Bundists had moved to the "revolutionary defensist" position advocated by leading Mensheviks. The "revolutionary defensists" argued that the war had to be prosecuted, not for social patriotic reasons, but in order to preserve the revolution from destruction at the hands of imperialist Germany. Within the Bund, this position was pressed by Henry Erlich and Mark Liber, who were also in the Menshevik leadership, and by Esther Frumkin, among others. At this time, Raphael Abramovich was the only internationalist left in the central leadership of the Bund, but his position was supported by Bund activists such as Vladimir Kosovsky, Benjamin Kheifitz, and Victor Alter, who were returning to Russia at the time.[28] The Menshevik "defensists" favored socialist participation in the Provisional Government that supplanted the tsar, but at the April 1917 conference in Petrograd, the Bund voted against such participation [29]—a decision that almost caused a split between the Bund and Mensheviks. Abramovich expressed the dangers of such a split: "We knew that were we to leave Menshevism, we would have to unite with the Bolsheviks. Are we ready to do that? No, because a great abyss separates us! Therefore, a split in the Menshevik party would mean only a weakening of the working class because we would have to build a *third* party." [30]

The stresses and strains in the Bund, cautiously alluded to by its leaders, at times threatened its own unity. Workers, uprooted and scarcely surviving, were sick of war. Their needs were stark and practical—on quite a different level from the principles established by the Bund leadership in Russia. Moreover, the organizational structure of the Bund was greatly disrupted by the war, and the composition of its membership changed substantially after the March 1917 revolution.[31] Large numbers of Jewish workers, in fact, were now outside the Pale and in need of basic relief.

The Germans tolerated and even encouraged labor organizations, including the Bund, which undertook the organization of public kitchens, cooperatives, and shelters for children. Jewish schools were also started and some political work was permitted. In February 1916, the Bundist *Lebensfragn* was started again, edited once more by Medem, who had been imprisoned, maltreated, and even chained, and then released from prison by the Germans. In the summer, the Bund and other socialist parties participated in elections to city councils in Poland. Bundist and other trade unions were permitted. The first—but still illegal—convention of the Polish Bund was held in December 1917.

Meanwhile, the war had thrown a sharp light on the problem of Jewish persecution and disabilities, and Jews in Europe and America were determined to bring the issue before the coming peace conference. The Bund, at its conference in Kharkov in May 1916, had put its views on this question forthrightly:

> Whereas under present war conditions the Jewish question to some extent assumes international significance . . . this conference deems it necessary to draw the attention of the workers of the world to this circumstance, so that the demands for equal civil, political, and national rights for Jews be incorporated in the peace program of the Socialist International.[32]

The Bund also asserted that the Jewish question "must be considered as an international question" and must be solved "not in one country, but in all countries in which Jews live."

The terrible slaughter of 1914-16 shocked the revolutionaries, but did not cause them to lose their taste for disputation. Often in exile and far from the fighting fronts, they conducted war strategy at a high pitch. Some defensists now feared a Russian defeat or a separate peace with Germany and the destruction of the revolutionary movement. Lenin, in Switzerland, hostile to all the European socialists parties because of their patriotic line, wanted the spread of civil war, chaos, and world revolution; later, he was prepared to deal with Germany to hasten the revolution. The Mensheviks and Bundists, as a whole, were opposed to a German victory. They believed that a revolution was inevitable but feared the dismemberment of the empire if the revolution was premature.

In Russia itself, the Provisional Government, in one of its early acts (April 4, 1917), issued a historic decree granting full rights and national recognition to the Jews in Russia. For the next nine months, Russian Jews thrilled to the promise of genuine freedom and creative independence and an astonishing proliferation of ideas and organizations blossomed forth.

But these possibilities were soon struck down by the Bolshevik seizure of power in October 1917.

Some Bundists had scoffed at the Bolshevik claim that the time was ripe for revolution; others had warned that the great discontent with the war made the masses ripe for Bolshevik demagoguery; yet others feared that militant opposition to the Bolshevik coup would allow reactionary forces to split the revolutionary movement. There followed a great struggle of Bundists and Mensheviks to contain the Bolsheviks by socialist coalitions in local soviets, revolutionary councils, and in the Constituent Assembly. Bund papers carried the slogan, "The Constituent Assembly Is the Only Hope," and the Bund campaigned actively in elections to this body. The assembly did, in fact, have a non-Bolshevik majority, but it was weak and ineffectual, and was forcibly dispersed by the Bolsheviks in January 1918.

The hurtling events following the Bolshevik coup could scarcely be grasped; Trotsky had called it a "revolution by telegraph." By no means secure, the Bolsheviks had aroused fierce antagonisms within the socialist movement, but none of the other parties could withstand Lenin's ruthlessness and the revolutionary terror that was quickly unleashed. The swift descent to a Bolshevik dictatorship shocked moderate socialists like Pavel Akselrod, who had believed that Marxism could be a genuinely liberating force only if it allowed the masses themselves to agitate, organize, and participate in the process of government. Although he never lost faith in Marxism, by the end of 1917 he knew that the revolution would not accomplish its purposes. On December 20, Lenin instructed Felix Dzerzhinsky, whom the Bundists once knew as a member of the Lithuanian Social-Democratic party, to organize an Extraordinary Commission for Combating Counter Revolution and Speculation—the dread Cheka.

During 1917, Akselrod also confronted once again the Jewish question that he had never quite put to rest. On November 25, the Jewish Press Bureau in Stockholm asked leading socialists to comment on "The Impending Peace and the Jewish Question." In his statement, Akselrod no longer hesitated to strongly and publicly condemn anti-Semitism. He urged the "international proletariat"—especially in Poland, Galicia, and Rumania—to intervene in favor of persecuted Jews and urged that Jews be granted not only full citizenship but the right of "national self-determination" and of "national autonomy on a personal basis." [33] This last point was not elaborated, but he had clearly abandoned his idea of assimilation and his long-standing opposition to the Bund's contention that the Jews constituted a nation.

His views on Zionism were even more revealing. On the one hand, he thought it "a pity that the Jews exert so much energy in colonizing Palestine. But in view of the hard facts of reality, of the pogroms, and of all the various forms of Jewish persecution, there stirs within me sympathy for Palestine and a wish to see in the realization of the Zionist goal a refuge for that unhappy people." [34] There was no doubt in his mind that the "concrete demand" of the Jewish socialist organization Poale Zion for unimpeded Jewish colonization of Palestine was "absolutely justified." [35] Obviously the intensity of his feelings over Jewish suffering from 1882 on, though perhaps intermittent, could not be altogether quenched. He also came to doubt a Marxist axiom—that a laborer was necessarily, or even potentially, the embodiment of all socialist virtue—and his subsequent struggle with the Bolsheviks led him to conclude that even a movement that considered itself Marxist was not, by that fact alone, beyond moral reproach.[36]

The momentum of the Bolshevik drive for complete power pushed on in 1918. A large bloc of the Bundist movement was already part of a rising Poland; the rest, in Russia, began the tortured road of splitting and capitulation. In March 1919, an all-Russian conference of the Bund (the eleventh), after heated and passionate debate, decided to accept the "platform of a Soviet Government," but the delegates condemned the terrorist practices of the Communist party and called for democratization of the soviets and freedom of speech and press. At the next conference in April 1920, in the midst of the horrors of civil war, the criss-crossing of foreign armies, news of pogrom-wracked Ukraine, and Bolshevik Cheka terror, a majority of the diminished Bund half-heartedly accepted the Bolshevik program. But their request to join the Communist party as an autonomous organization was rejected. Some individual ex-Bundists joined the Jewish Sections (*Yevsektsia*) of the Communist party. In 1921, a special committee of the Communist International ordered the Bund liquidated as an autonomous party. A minority of Bundists, including many of the old leaders—Litvak, Liber, and Abramovich—withdrew from the 1921 conference and formed the Social Democratic Bund. It struggled to maintain itself as a legal party in the Soviet Union, but was soon liquidated together with all other political parties.

The center of Jewish socialist and labor activity now shifted to Poland, which became an independent nation in 1919. Here, the Bund began the struggle "to defend the interests of Jewish workers in Poland and the interests of Poland in the hearts of the Jewish workers"—a tumultuous, difficult, and gallant struggle, in which it refused to dissolve into the Polish Communist party (as other Polish socialist parties did), give up its identity as a Jewish workers' party, or concede that Jews would be better off if they left Poland for a less hostile home. Even after the destruction of the Warsaw Ghetto and almost the whole of Polish Jewry during the Holocaust, the tattered Bund remnants were able to somehow summon up their indestructible faith in Polish workers. On May Day 1944, they proclaimed:

In keeping with our glorious tradition, we are bound to the working people of Poland and other lands through our common destiny in the common struggle against our common enemy for our common ideals of liberty. These ideals are today the slogans and the postulates of our common labor holiday, the First of May.[37]

For the sober, rationalist Lithuanian Jews in the Bund, these are impassioned words, expressing a passionately held faith in humanity perhaps no less blind or romantic than that of the Zionists they held in such contempt, who had an equally intense but different faith.

IV

SOCIALIST ZIONISM

23. Nachman Syrkin:
Precursor and Visionary

"Moses Hess," wrote Nachman Syrkin in the introduction to his Yiddish translation of Hess's *Rome and Jerusalem*, "is not the founder of Zionism ... but he is the founder of Socialist Judaism, the reviver of the Jewish revolutionary culture idea, whose consequence is also political." As such, Syrkin concluded, Hess "inevitably became the founder of Socialist Zionism." Hess's work (published in 1861) indeed bases Jewish regeneration on the dual forces of nationalism and socialism, rooted in the Jewish prophetic vision of social justice and a moral order, but it did not create a political movement, and in fact was neglected for many years. As a crystallized national and social ideal and as a theoretical basis for a political movement, socialist Zionism had its beginnings in 1898, with the appearance of Syrkin's pamphlet *The Jewish Question and the Socialist Jewish State*, originally published in German as *Die Judenfrage und der sozialistische Judenstaat*. This effort, too, was all but still-born. Political Zionism as launched by Theodor Herzl was only a year old and treading gingerly on the vast and complicated world diplomatic scene, while socialism was dogmatically rejecting special national needs of Jews. A marriage of the two was improbable.

The young man who was not daunted by obstacles of this order was the bold and irrepressible Syrkin, born in Mogilev, Russia, in 1868 to prosperous, middle-class parents.[1] His father was a gentle, retiring scholar, but his mother, who had a particularly strong influence on Nachman, was a proud, energetic, self-taught woman, literate in Yiddish, Russian, and very probably French, as well as an able businesswoman. Nachman went to the local *gymnasium* for secular studies, and a rabbi came regularly to the house to supervise his Jewish education. High-spirited, rebellious, and mischievous, Nachman was expelled from the *gymnasium* for objecting to a teacher's anti-Semitic remarks.

In 1884 the Syrkins moved to Minsk, where Nachman completed his high school education and came under the influence of the Hovevei Zion movement and revolutionary circles. He also became active in local Zionist groups; at 19, he was writing for the Hebrew journal *Ha-Melitz* under the pseudonym Ben Eliezer. He was jailed briefly for radical activities, lived for a time in London where he wrote for the Yiddish theatre with limited success, and then returned to Minsk. Problems of social injustice, including the scandal of a few plutocratic families who opposed Jewish emigration from Russia, tormented the youth quite as much as the special wretchedness of Jews in Russia. By the time he was twenty, Syrkin was boldly seeking a synthesis of Jewish nationalism and socialism. When Shmarya Levin, the brilliant Zionist leader and publicist, met him in Minsk, he "spoke both as a fiery socialist and as an ardent Jewish nationalist. He already defended at that time the point of view which subsequently became the philosophy of his party: that nationalism was a necessary and logical corollary of socialism, and that socialism necessarily and logically led to nationalism, while true Jewish nationalism, as preached by the ancient prophets, necessarily led to socialism." [2] Other contemporaries recalled with great relish Syrkin's fiery temperament, incessant activity, enthusiasm, and great store of traditional Jewish knowledge.

Like other Russian Jewish youths barred from Russian universities, Syrkin mastered German, enrolled in the philosophy department of the University of Berlin, and plunged into the economic and social controversies of radical Russian student circles. These groups lived an intense life of their own, quite apart from German Jewish or German students. Large colonies of Russian Jewish students in Berne, Geneva, Zurich, and Munich, as well as Berlin, drew together rebels of one sort or another, driven by persecution and intellectual starvation. Children of middle-class Jews, they were rather vague about their future, but passionately absorbed by radical ideas. Women students were almost as numerous as men. The Jewish socialist students had their own organization, but had to be very careful of police surveillance because they were subject to Russian law. Their precious residence permits could be withdrawn.

By contrast, students interested in Zionism were much better off—the Russian government was not yet concerned about Jewish nationalism. They formed the Russisch-Judisch Wissenschaftliches Verein—The Russian-Jewish Scientific Society. Chaim Weizmann has left a marvelous vignette of that life:

> We held our regular Saturday night meetings at a café, and mostly it was the one attached to a certain Jewish hotel—the Hotel Zentrum on the Alexanderplatz, because there, during lean periods, we could get beer and sausages on credit. I think with something like a shudder of the amount of talking we did. We never dispersed before the small hours of the morning. We talked of everything, of history, wars, revolution, the rebuilding of society. But chiefly we talked of the Jewish problem and of Palestine. We sang, we celebrated such Jewish festivals as we did not go home for, we debated with the assimilationists,

and we made vast plans for the redemption of our people. It was all very youthful and naive and jolly; but it was not without a deeper meaning. At first I was greatly overawed by my fellow-students, among whom I was the youngest. Fresh from little Pinsk, with its petty Zionist collections and small-town discussions, I was staggered by the sweep of vision which [Leo] Motzkin and Syrkin and the others displayed.[3]

But Weizmann, eager to work in the real world, had his share of the life of the Verein,

a curious world, existing, for us Jewish students, outside of time and space. . . . In part this was due to our tacit fear of destroying our own refugee opportunities. But it sprang mostly from the sheer intensity of our inner life. . . . If we constituted a kind of ghetto . . . it was to a large extent because most of us were practically penniless. I, with my hundred marks allowance a month . . . was among the well-to-do. But I think I can safely say that during all the years of my sojourn in Berlin I did not eat a single solid meal except as somebody's guest. We lived among ourselves because we could not afford to live separately.[4]

Among the "definitely underfed" was Nachman. At the beginning of every month, he would turn up at Weizmann's lodgings for a loan, which Weizmann "pinched off" from his allowance. Toward the end of the month, he would ask for a "pledge"—that is, something that could be pawned, a cushion or Weizmann's chemist's weights. This recourse to the pawnshop was, indeed, an intermittent feature of Nachman's later life.

As a student in Berlin, Syrkin lived on what Levin described as the "absolute minimum." [5] The demands of five other children who had to be educated strained the family resources. When Levin himself came to Berlin, he was met by Syrkin and together they went to Syrkin's lodgings on the fifth floor of a typical workers' tenement. Syrkin paid 15 marks (about $3.75) a month for a large, decently furnished room and a simple breakfast. On Saturdays, he had two white rolls without butter. Half-famished, he hit on the idea of writing for samples of sausage, herring, cheese and cereal. An industrious correspondent, Nachman figured, could probably feed a dozen indigent students. But the results were disappointing—the portions were just samples, insufficient even for himself.

The Verein met on Saturday nights, but the recruiting of members— Levin called it the "catching of souls"—took place during the day, among the enrolled students and new arrivals:

Every morning the train would bring into Berlin, from the eastern frontier, new unsuspecting students; and Socialists and Nationalists lay in ambush for them. These newcomers were green; for the most part they did not know where their sympathies lay, and their future would be decided by the first contacts. The competition was fierce. The agents of the two parties would be standing in the station before sunrise, under the flickering arc light. The Jewish student coming from Russia was easily recognizable, if not by his appearance, then by his marvelous collection of bundles and baskets and packages. . . . From a fourth-class carriage a student creeps out, dragging his packages after him. Two young men detach themselves from the crowd and make for him: each claims the honor of leading the newcomer to his lodgings. There they stand, the three of them, gummy-eyed from lack of sleep. The newcomer is in a stupor; in the land he comes from Jews are accustomed to receiving blows; here he sees people coming to blows over a Jew.[6]

The Verein turned into a rallying center for socialists and antinationalists, who came to sharpen their arguments against the nationalists, often bringing along a battery of famous figures in the German Social Democratic party to crush the arguments of "chauvinists" and "reactionaries." Their fiery debates, polarizing the antagonists into two bitterly hostile camps, often attracted several hundred spectators. One of the deadliest on the socialist side was Parvus (Alexander Helphand), a Marxist theoretician who could describe the class struggle as if barricades were rising in the streets at the moment. One night, while thundering against the meaninglessness of nationalism, he grabbed hold of his own coat and described the geography of its parts: wool from Angora, thread spun in England, buttons from Germany, and so on. He was winning over the crowd when, suddenly, while pulling his own coat too tight, he ripped the sleeve. Syrkin, who was bursting with rage, shouted, "And the rip in your sleeve comes from the pogrom in Kiev!"[7]—a retort that undid Parvus's argument on the internationalism of labor.

Syrkin quickly made a reputation as a brilliant, formidable debater—he could wither each side—but as yet had no adherents of his fused philosophy. Students would enjoy his satire, his invective and repartee, but did not take his serious views seriously. Both movements engaged in perpetual literary and political polemics, and a steady stream of converts and penitents flowed back and forth as personal needs and perceptions of solutions to the Jewish problem changed. But Zionism and socialism were largely viewed as antithetic and irreconcilable. Against the stream, Nachman nurtured his socialist Zionism, and often argued it, knowing full well that he was thought ridiculous. People began to call him *Nachke der Meshugener* (Crazy Nachman). But he had a sublime confidence in his revolutionary vision.

After studying with the philosophy faculty at the Berlin University for a few years, Syrkin switched to the medical school and then left to continue his studies in Berne. In 1896, his first published work, *Observations on the Philosophy of History*, appeared in German. In it he attacked the prevailing dogma of historic materialism, reasserting the important role of human will in shaping history—a force in which Syrkin ardently believed throughout his life.

Berne swarmed with Russian Jewish students and Russian radicals of all colorations in exile. Most were cosmopolitan and assimilationist; Zionist circles, by comparison, were tiny. Into this student ferment, which reflected the larger scene, came Herzl's tract *Der Judenstaat* (*The Jewish State*), published in 1896. It came, in Weizmann's words, "like a bolt from the blue. We had never heard the name Herzl before . . . *The Jewish State* contained not a single new idea for us. . . . Herzl made no allusion . . . to his predecessors in the field, to Moses Hess and Leon Pinsker and Nathan Birnbaum. . . . Apparently Herzl did not know of the existence of Chibath Zion; he did not mention Palestine; he ignored the Hebrew language. Yet the effect produced by *The Jewish State* was profound." [8]

With Herzl, Zionism as a political movement was born. The First Zionist Congress met in 1897, in Basel, the same year the Bund was founded. Herzl's approach in this early period was to persuade rich Jews to give money to the sultan of Turkey, who was always in debt, so that he in turn would let Jews go to Palestine, then under Turkish control. He also felt that the Great Powers—England and Germany especially—had to be persuaded to exert pressure on Turkey. If this strategy was flawed, Herzl's energy, passion, and organizational skills were used to good effect in conceiving the Zionist Congress—the galvanizing of a mass Jewish movement. No longer would Zionists have to meet furtively and fearfully; they would come together in public and address their appeals and demands to the world.

Curiously, a few years before the First Zionist Congress, a meeting of students in Syrkin's room in Berlin had pondered the possibility of convening a congress, but the idea perished "for lack of stamps." At about the same time (1892) Shmarya Levin recalled that Nachman even permitted himself a political jest: "Without consulting any one of us, he calmly went to the Turkish ambassador and proposed the purchase of Palestine, naming one hundred million francs as the sum. The ambassador listened earnestly, and counselled Syrkin to apply to the Grand Vizier in Constantinople. . . . Syrkin, even in later years, always liked big, sweeping propositions. Money, he used to say, is a purely technical question." [9]

Herzl's call for an organized Jewish movement to create a Jewish homeland and the inspiration of his own personality gave all the fragmented Zionist circles and societies a much-needed rallying force. But strains were soon felt among the diverse representatives to the congress, including the few socialist nationalists who attended, Syrkin among them. There were too many rabbis and bourgeois elements in charge, he thought, and mincing deference to the figures of the kaiser and tsar. Herzl's diplomatic strategy shocked the radicals as much as his view that Zionism was one way of stopping the drift of Jewish youth into radicalism.

Vague sproutings of a fusion of Jewish nationalism and socialism had appeared among some intellectuals in Switzerland, influenced by Zhitlovsky and Syrkin, but Syrkin alone pressed ahead with a clear formulation:

> A guiding instinct and a deep conviction gave me the courage at that time to start preaching Socialist-Zionism and to place myself in opposition to the entire Jewish intelligentsia. If the idea of a Jewish homeland and the idea of a Jewish revolution could unite harmoniously in the mind of one man, why could it not

become a living, creative concept for both the Jewish intellectuals and the Jewish masses? . . . So I undertook the thankless task of being a socialist among Zionists, and a Zionist among socialists. Naturally, each side attacked me violently and sent me packing to the other.[10]

Syrkin's synthesis was worked out in an 1898 lecture delivered in German in Zurich before a Zionist group called Hessiona. As the meeting was attended mostly by curious German anarchists and Russian-Jewish students who did not understand German, the response was largely bewildered silence. In Berne, however, where he repeated the lecture, he was met with cries of "bourgeois!" [11] There, a very large colony of Russian-Jewish students were under the heady influence of Plekhanov, Lenin, and Trotsky, who treated with contempt any Russian Jew who concerned himself mainly with the sufferings and fate of Jews. A tiny group of Zionist students, including Syrkin, Ansky, and Weizmann, could hardly cope with the glamor of Siberian exile and the legendary authority of Plekhanov. For a time they were swamped by the Russians until they decided to organize a Zionist society, the first in Switzerland, called Ha-Shahar (Dawn).[12] They held their first meeting in the back room of the Russian colony's library and had to meet standing up, because the "others" had removed the furniture from the room. Two gifted young Zionists from Germany, Martin Buber and Berthold Feivel, were invited to speak at a meeting in a beerhall that lasted for two days and three nights. The first real breach in the ranks of assimilatory revolutionists was made at that meeting: 180 students enrolled in the Zionist society.

Plekhanov was furious. He approached Weizmann afterward and asked angrily, "What do you mean by bringing discord into our ranks?" To which Weizmann answered, "But Monsieur Plekhanov, you are not the Czar!" [13]

Syrkin's lecture was expanded and published as a pamphlet called *Die Judenfrage und der sozialistische Judenstaat (The Jewish Question and the Socialist Jewish State)* [14] under the name of Ben Eliezer. Except for a few items in the German press and some correspondence with a German pastor on Christianity, this essay, which remains a path-breaking Zionist work and formed the philosophical basis for the socialist Zionist movement, was at first largely ignored. Syrkin challenges both traditional Zionists and Jewish socialists. Beginning with an analysis of the unparalleled historical situation facing Jews—the life of a nation without a land—he traces the dream of national rebirth as a force of genuine power giving direction to the life of the ghetto. He then analyzes the bourgeois struggle for freedom—freedom of religion, conscience, unlimited rights of property and social mobility—which resulted in the accidental and sudden emancipation of Jews, especially its strongly individualistic character and acquisitiveness. But bourgeois society has been vitiated by great contradictions that will lead to its breakdown, according to Syrkin. The values of the ghetto clashed with those of the new bourgeois order and gave way, but "the splendor of the solution lasted only as long as the reign of liberalism," and quickly, the individual and class economic struggle betrayed the principles of liberalism.

Moreover, modern anti-Semitism, based on race, has replaced the old religious anti-Semitism and is often promoted by bourgeois elements. Jews still remain strange and hostile to non-Jews; they are viewed as torchbearers of capitalism, exploitation, usury, and instability. Syrkin sees these attacks as a mirror-image of the characteristics of bourgeois society as a whole and a reaction to the economic struggle against Jewish competition. With uncanny vision, he also sees the most intense expression of anti-Semitism in declining classes: the middle class, endangered by capitalists, and the peasant class, endangered by landowners. "They stand between the capitalist class and the proletariat and live in constant fear of falling into the latter. The more wretched their positions become, the fiercer their internal conflicts." They sink deeper and deeper, into a semi-underworld, devoid of any principles or ideals, but still hold on to the tail of the ruling classes. As class antagonisms become sharper, all classes will unite in their common attack on the Jew, and the dominant elements of society will seek to use the religious and racial struggle as a substitute for the class struggle.

A classless society *and* national sovereignty, Syrkin concludes, are the only means of solving the Jewish problem. "The social revolution and cessation of the class struggle will also normalize the relationship of the Jew and his environment. The Jew must therefore join the ranks of the proletariat ... striving to make an end of the class struggle and to redistribute power on the basis of justice." The Jew thus must become the vanguard of socialism, but a socialism that has nothing in common with the sinful assimilationism of current socialism. Instead of first crying out as Jews and then raising their protest to the level of the universal, "with peculiar Jewish logic, they [the assimilated Jews] did the contrary. . . . The assimilated bourgeoisie turned away from Judaism because the Jewish people was weak and there was no economic advantage in being a Jew; Jewish socialists turned away from Judaism, because, for them, socialism was not the result of a moral protest against the world of the oppressors, but a last haven for the Jew whom liberalism had betrayed."

Syrkin then goes on to excoriate those who use the term "internationalism" falsely, especially those who conspire to suppress or destroy the national character of a people. The socialist movement strongly supports all attempts of suppressed peoples to free themselves. There are no socialist leaders in any national group who deny their own nationality and preach assimilation to a dominant nationality. "Only the bourgeoisie of oppressed nations deny their own nation and abandon it, and in the case of the Jews, the socialists have inherited assimilation from the bourgeoisie, although they preach national emancipation for all other people."

Jewish national existence may be a poor thing today, Syrkin continues, but that is no reason for rejecting it. Enemies of the Jews have *always* considered them a nation; and their continued existence, which has involved a bitter struggle for survival, symbolizes the battle for human rights. Moreover, Jewish life must be freshly endowed with "significant national content," and Jewish socialists must acknowledge the Jewish protest as its basic motif. Jewish socialism must be placed on the same level as proletarian socialism: both have a common source in the oppression of human beings and the unjust distribution of power. In this process, it can be guided by the healthy Jewish proletariat that has fought off assimilation and developed personal and national self-respect.

But because the lot of the Jews in modern society is unique, Syrkin believes neither socialism nor the class struggle can help much. In fact, anti-Semitism is nourished by the class struggle, and the lot of the Jewish bourgeoisie and intelligentsia is made worse by it. Nor does the Jewish proletariat (which includes small merchants and peddlers) benefit. Economic development in Eastern Europe, where the mass of the Jewish proletariat lives, will not quickly change its depressed state. Acutely aware of the indifference—or worse—of socialists and others to anti-Semitism, Syrkin predicted that the condition of Jews "will not be radically altered through an overthrow of the present political regime." The only immediate remedy for Jewish suffering in Russia is emigration and Zionism.

According to Syrkin, Zionism is not a utopian solution but is rooted in the economic and social realities of the Jewish condition. The socialist argument that Zionism conflicts with the class struggle is foolish. Why should the Jewish proletariat reject Zionism merely because other classes of Jews have adopted it? "The class struggle does not exhaust all the expressions of social life. When a people is endangered, all parties unite to fight the outside enemy. . . . Zionism is a creative work of the Jews . . . and, therefore, stands, not in contradiction to the class struggle, but beyond it."

Turning to contemporary political Zionism, Syrkin argues against the trend to establish a Jewish state based on the rights of private property. A new autonomous state cannot be created on a basis of social inequality, for that would be tantamount to entering into "a social contract of servitude." Conscious social action must transform the status quo. Syrkin foresaw the perils of laissez-faire: "Since the entire effort of colonization will be taking place in an undeveloped country, wages will be depressed far below any level of subsistence that a European Jew could find acceptable. Most of the workers will, therefore, be recruited from the native population because they will work for less. Colonization will thus increasingly become a business venture; Jewish immigrants will be forced to leave, and the groups intending to follow will be stopped by fear. The entire movement will disintegrate almost before the beginning."

The land first to be considered by Syrkin for the establishment of a Jewish state was Palestine, the ancient Jewish homeland. It would be purchased from Turkey by a Jewish national fund or bank, or obtained through diplomatic pressure or movements of liberation in the Turkish empire. If the effort to secure Palestine failed, the purchase of neighboring areas or a tract in Africa might be considered. Specific and detailed recommendations were made regarding work, the work day, defense, and communal stores. The administration was to be solely concerned with regulating the economy, and a federation of social and economic groups was to be developed until they created "a huge industrial village in which industry and agriculture meet." Like Hess's socialism, Syrkin's is not Marxist, but ethical and humanistic, based on the striving for a new universal order which both men believed was the essence of the Jewish national spirit and the unique contribution of Judaism to the world. "The guidelines of the new Jewish state," Syrkin declared, "must be justice, rational planning, and social solidarity. . . . The hope for a Messiah, always the basic sentiment of the Galut Jew, will be converted into political fact." [15]

Syrkin had no intention of launching a separate movement through this essay, but it became a starting point for controversial discussions in the Zionist and Jewish socialist press. He and other radicals who attended the First Congress thought they would be able to work within the general Zionist movement, but by the Second Congress in 1898, there "gathered in Basel fine gentlemen from the round-about resorts, silken young rabbis, Hebrew writers, doctors and lawyers—all uninfected by socialism." [16] The congress had opened in an atmosphere of awe aroused by news of Herzl's forthcoming meeting with the kaiser, but the young radicals were bitterly opposed to negotiations with "tyrants." The tsar had also convoked a peace conference, and when Herzl proposed that a telegram of appreciation be sent, Syrkin's violent protests caused a disturbance which threatened the congress. Syrkin also demanded that workers be represented on committees; he spoke passionately about building Jewish life in Palestine on the principle of cooperation and objected to the domination of rabbis on cultural committees. He was often hissed and shouted down, but remained undaunted and unintimidated. Herzl quieted the session and suppressed publication of the incident fearing that it might hurt Russian Jews. However, the episode touched off stormy disagreements between the radical youths and "the Jewish bourgeoisie, which walked hand in hand with bloody regimes." At the Third Congress in 1899, Syrkin was asked to expound his ideas at an open meeting, after which Herzl with his customary geniality and wit, said, "You socialists, come to the Seventh Congress and drive me out." [17] By that time, there was indeed a large socialist bloc, and the congress hall was hung with large red placards announcing socialist meetings.

Meanwhile, Zionist and socialist Zionist ideas were taking root in the Pale. *Yeshivot* students were raging against teachers and rabbis who persecuted students with Zionist leanings and searched rooms for modern

Hebrew books. Ahad Ha-Am's thin green literary monthly *Ha-Shiloah* was spreading underground. Visitors came to little towns and described the splendor of the Zionist congress. During their summer vacations, Weizmann and other students returned to Russia to persuade Jewish communities to elect delegates to the Zionist congresses. In Zalman Shazar's tiny village of Steibtz, the young boy, already a Zionist, was asked to invite the dressmakers of the town to meet in the home of a member of the girls' Zionist society, Bnot Zion.[18] Someone was coming to speak to them on "The New Way in Zionism," which he had learned about in Pinsk. The "new way" was the fusion of Zionism and socialism, making it desirable to organize Jewish female workers. The few smiths, tailors and shoemakers in the town were already members of the Bund.

The actual Jewish settlement of Palestine was unsteady, unorganized, and variously motivated. The Alliance Israélite Universelle had established an agricultural school in 1871 at Mikveh Israel, but this was pure philanthropy, with no national purpose. Of the 30,000 Jews in Palestine in 1881, many were supported by the *halukkah*, or charity distribution system. Only 2 percent worked on the land; the little colonies at Motza and Petach Tikvah were weak. Stirred by the pogroms and disabilities of 1881–82, about 7,000 more Jews had gone to Palestine, but most of them opened shops or became artisans. These migrations were what one might call pre-Zionist. The small stream of Biluim [19] who went to Palestine in 1882 had a strong Zionist consciousness and pledged themselves to work on the land and only along cooperative principles. Some of them hoped to receive financial support from a sympathetic English writer, Lawrence Oliphant, but the aid never materialized. They left for Palestine with only a few hundred rubles, and on the way issued a naive and touching document expressing the hope that "the interests of our glorious nation will rouse our national spirit in rich and powerful men, and that everyone, rich and poor, will give his best labors to the holy cause. Greetings, dear brothers and sisters. Hear, O Israel, the Lord our God, the Lord is One, and our land, Zion, is our only hope." [20]

They were totally unprepared for life in Palestine and, although they left their stamp on later *aliyot*, Biluim utopian visions were crushed by the brutal reality they found. Without any conditioning for manual work, yet desperately in need of work, they dug ditches for 12 hours a day at Mikveh Israel and Rishon le-Zion. At last, after a number of Biluim had abandoned the group, they were given a fresh start in 1884 by Yechiel Pines, a representative of one of the Jewish colonizing societies. Pines came with some money, bought a parcel of land, and in December 1884 the cooperative colony of Gederah was founded. But it could not sustain its cooperative character and became a private colony.

The few colonizing groups of the time were composed of independent enthusiasts committed to the idea of Jews working on the land, but they had no practical farming experience and little money. Often they were ignorant of one another's existence. Some of the new settlers had been Russian university students caught up by the idealism of Russian populism and Zionism. One such pioneer, discussing works by Herzen and Chernyshevsky, noted in his diary: "So agitated were young Russian revolutionaries by these books, that they decided to 'go to the people' and cause a revolution in their lives. The Russian people exist and live on native soil; [Jews] must re-create everything from scratch: the work, the land, the people and the society." [21]

Many forces besides the pogroms contributed to this historically important trickle: age-old prayers and yearnings for a restored Jewish nation; the historical investigations of Nachman Krochmal, Solomon Rapoport, and Samuel David Luzzatto, who reacquainted Jews with their national heritage; the early *maskilim* like Mapu who not only depicted the glories of ancient Palestine but insisted on reviving Hebrew as a living language; the force of contemporary nationalism; and possibly most significant, the trenchant essays and tracts of several Russian-Jewish writers of the time. One of the most influential of these was Peretz Smolenskin.

Smolenskin knew intimately the sorrows and stunted life of the Pale. As a child he saw his oldest brother snatched for the army. His father died when he was ten. While studying at the *yeshivah* in Shklov, he cultivated an interest in Russian and other secular subjects. Persecuted by the townspeople for this "heresy," he had no choice but to run away. His years of wandering are vividly described in his autobiographical novel, *Hatoeh Bederekh Hahayyim* (*The Wanderer in Life's Ways*), the most widely read book in modern Hebrew literature in the 1870's. While still in his teens, Smolenskin eked out an existence in various towns of the Pale by singing in choirs and occasionally preaching in synagogues. At twenty, he hopped a freight train to Odessa, the great Black Sea port and intellectual refuge for Jews seeking the modern world. Here he earned a living teaching Hebrew while he studied and began his literary career.

In 1868, he went to Vienna and realized his long-cherished dream of founding a Hebrew-language literary monthly, which he called *Ha-Shahar*. Installments of his novels, in which secular humanist characters were described as thinly veiled assimilationists, appeared in its issues. Rounding out his realistic evocations of Jewish life in the Pale were characters drawn from *yeshivot* and saturated in Talmudic learning, to whom Smolenskin attributed unusual spiritual fervor. In his novels and essays, Smolenskin both accepts and criticizes the desirability of modernizing Jewish life: Modernization is necessary but will not lead to the acceptance of Jews in general society. As early as 1869, he sounded the countertheme of cultural nationalism and eventually called for the end of exile and emigration to Palestine as the only solution to the dilemmas of Jewish life.

In 1872, *Ha-Shahar* featured Smolenskin's essay "Am Olam" (Eternal People), one of the most important weapons in the battle against assimilation and a strong defense of Jewish nationalism. "Like [the other nations]," he wrote, "let us treasure and honor the language of our people! Just as other subjugated nations are not ashamed to hope for their national redemption, neither is it a disgrace for us to hope for an end to our exile." [22] Reaffirming the national-religious identity of the Jewish people and skeptical of emancipation, Smolenskin believed that hope in a return to Palestine was essential. Although he did not formulate a practical program for the reconstruction of Palestine, Smolenskin did much to inspire the idea of settlement in Eretz Israel.

Another powerful tract was written by an assimilated Jew, a passionate Russian patriot who was shattered by the pogroms of 1881. This was Leo Pinsker, who, after a thoroughly Russian education, received a medical degree from the University of Moscow and became a leading physician in Odessa. Pinsker became interested in Jewish affairs after 1860, but went far beyond other *maskilim* by insisting that Russian culture should completely dominate the inner life, even the religion, of the Jew. The Odessa pogroms of 1871 shook him, but did not deflect him from his assimilationist course. Then came the mob violence of the pogroms of 1881, when the connivance of the government and the horrors, which he witnessed, could not be ignored.

In *Auto-emancipation*,[23] Pinsker attempted to analyze the causes of anti-Semitism "scientifically." Hatred of the Jew, he declared, was permanent, a psychopathological phenomenon, because the Jews, though dead as a nation, continued to exist as a people without a land, without unity, yet undoubtedly existing—a phantom presence in history without parallel, creating fear and Judeophobia. Since the Jew is nowhere at home, he remains an alien everywhere. Emancipation is a chimera and can never solve the Jewish problem. Pinsker scored Jews for lacking a national consciousness, thus exposing themselves to perennial contempt and abuse. The only means of liberation is the creation of a Jewish national state—not specifically Palestine—but a land of their own, where they can regain national self-respect and equality with other nations.

Published anonymously in German, Pinsker's pamphlet was at first greeted with vociferous opposition. Orthodox Jews regarded the author, whose identity was soon enough known, as irreligious; assimilated liberals, in and out of Russia, attacked him as a traitor to the doctrine of humanism and brotherhood. The personal prestige of Pinsker, however, and the intensity of his changed attitudes made *Auto-emancipation* the first clear-cut appeal to Jewish nationalism as an answer to anti-Semitism. It also placed Pinsker in the midst of the ferment boiling around the embryonic Lovers of Zion movement and the arguments that raged over the question, "Whither Russian Jews: Palestine or America?"

Smolenskin's *Ha-Shahar* and *Ha-Melitz*, in Hebrew, and *Razsvet*, in Russian, became the literary vehicles of nascent Zionism, but Pinsker needed a practical instrument for the colonization of Palestine. He joined forces with Lovers of Zion, a loose and fragmentary movement that formed in 1882 in many communities of the Pale to promote agricultural colonies in Palestine and assist settlers there. Its adherents collected money, conducted courses in Hebrew and Jewish history, and organized self-defense units called Maccabee clubs. Their meetings, of course, had to be conducted secretly and were often disguised as wedding parties. Following the pattern of Russian-Jewish students in German universities, who were unhampered by police and had financial and cultural contacts in the West, they held their first convention in 1884 in Katowice in Upper Silesia, then part of Germany. Pinsker was elected president of this, the first Palestine conference of modern times. But internal dissension, the intrigues of opponents, and the sheer physical difficulties of surviving in Palestine at the time, as well as the precariousness of living in a Turkish land without status, plagued the early movement.

Russian radicalism had a strong influence on some of the new colonies. An early manifesto by the Kiev Lovers of Zion, reminiscent of the Am Olam experiment in America, denounced private ownership of land as the greatest evil of civilization and warned the settlers against building Palestine on the "rotten basis" of the old world order. One charter forecast extreme collectivization. But none of these ideas could take root during the "first *aliyah*." The students grew hungrier and leaner; many were forced to return home or drifted into colonies owned or subsidized by Baron Edmund de Rothschild.

Rothschild was not under the pressure of any social ideal or of Zionist hope, but rather was moved by philanthropy. In October 1882, he responded to a plea by the colony at Rishon le-Zion for a modest loan of 25,000 francs for the extended digging of wells. He did so as an "experiment," to see if it was possible to settle Jewish farmers in Palestine. The colonies soon became his main charity, and between 1884 and 1900 he spent an estimated million and a half pounds [24] on the purchase of land, machinery, houses, livestock, and training for Jewish settlers. He considered the colonies his domain and exercised tight control over them through tough, suspicious overseers from France. Although he later changed his mind, at the time he considered Zionism "dangerous" because it exposed Jews to the charge of being unpatriotic. When a delegation of Russian Zionists called on him to discuss needed reforms, Rothschild was in his usual autocratic form: "These are my colonies, and I shall do what I like with them!" Just before World War I, his attitude toward Zionism mellowed, and Weizmann quoted him as saying, "Without me, Zionism would not have succeeded. But without Zionism, my work would have been struck dead."

Rothschild's style derived in part from the prevailing nineteenth-century plantation colonialism: The economy of the colonies was based on cheap Arab labor and the profit motive. The colonists, moreover, were guaranteed a certain minimum income. There were a few idiosyncratic twists: Rothschild insisted that the colonists strictly observe Orthodox religious laws—though he did not—and dress in the local Arab style. His domination of Jewish settlement in those early years offended Zionists, but he provided some sort of economic base against which later settlers could rebel, and his experiments proved that Jews could indeed become farmers. It was a first stage in Jewish land settlement, without which it would have taken the Zionist movement another two decades to create settlements. A survey taken in 1900 revealed that there were 473 Jewish workers in the twelve existing colonies.[25] Seven of them, involving 360 workers, were subsidized by Rothschild.

These were, of course, not the stuff of a national revival, nor the foundation of a movement. The initiative of the farmers was blocked by overseers who made all the decisions and by dependence on Rothschild's generosity. Some may have been inspired by the idea of a Return, but they were thinking, above all, of their own needs. Yet Jews *were* living on the land. By 1902, there were about 5,000 of them in twenty-two colonies, a few of which were self-supporting. Meanwhile, new forces were stirring in other places.

The ideas of Hibbat Zion, which had been limited in Russia to support of settlements in Palestine and cultural work, spread to Central Europe and became more politicized. This evolution was greatly stimulated by waves of anti-Semitism and the advent of Christian socialism. In Vienna, particularly, Jewish students came face to face with social and physical anti-Semitism. Student bodies began to expel Jewish members. The earlier hope for liberalism and assimilation began to fade; Jewish youths yearned to defend Jewish honor. They needed action and involvement which they could not find in Ahad Ha-Am's "Lo Ze Ha-Derech" (This Is Not the Way), with its inner-directed call for redemption of the spirit before rebuilding the country. Ha-Am's insistence on quality before quantity had an elitist, almost priestly, overtone that weakened his influence and made it impossible for him to lead a large-scale movement. With the coming of Herzl, these youths found a leader of vision who gave Jewish national aspirations political form. Some of them also began to respond to Syrkin's ideas.

By 1901, Syrkin himself moved to organization—albeit on a very small scale. He founded Hessiona,[26] a society consisting of four members in Berlin, including his friend Mirkin and Mirkin's two-year-old child. In the following year Herut (Freedom) was formed, this time with ten charter members and two branches, one in Berlin and one in Zurich. Letters and postcards began coming, reporting that small groups of kindred spirits were forming in various cities of Russia, Germany, Austria, and Switzerland. Without money, without a propaganda apparatus, without paid organizers and speakers, a small movement developed. Plans for new societies were drafted. Innumerable requests for articles poured in. A comrade in Russia, writing in Hebrew, chided Syrkin for not using the language and asked him what to tell *yeshivah* students who "have Zionist impulses and yet believe in a collectivist program." He also discussed organizational problems involving groups in Kiev, Minsk, Smolensk, and Odessa. "Let us not indulge in visions," he warned, when he thought Syrkin's plans were too extravagant.[27]

In 1901, Syrkin also published his first popular work, *A Call to Jewish Youth*,[28] originally given as a lecture to Hessiona. Published in Russian to keep the German police at bay, it was widely read in Russian student colonies, then copied and smuggled into Russia where it was read with great excitement. Here, at last, was a call to action based on a socialist Zionist analysis of the unique suffering of Jews in Russia, Rumania, and Austria. In this essay, Syrkin proposed a two-way struggle: one for economic and political rights in the countries where Jews lived, and one for emigration to Palestine, where an "autonomous Jewish center" can be created to stop the purposeless wandering, the nonproductive work and spiritual maiming of Jews. For these objectives, Syrkin suggested that two independent but cooperative organizations be established to deal with differentiated tasks and win support from different sources: a Jewish social democratic group with support from the local working class, and a socialist Zionist group from the bourgeoisie. (Within a few years, he gave up his two-plan theory and accepted the concept of a single movement.)

Syrkin reaffirmed his faith in the spiritual gifts of Jews, now choked by oppression, but capable of fresh expression. He called on socialist Zionism to bring light to the darkness caused by "orthodox obscurantism and Talmudic idolatry" and blamed the antinationalism of the Jewish bourgeoisie for alienating progressive Jewish youth by discrediting the idea of a Jewish national renascence. Furthermore, in an argument similar to that of the Bund, Syrkin pressed the idea that the Jewish proletariat—including petty traders—were not yet class conscious, and in their desire for a new life were succumbing to answers "in terms of the pathological, slavish psychology" developed through the centuries. This failure of Jewish workers to be stirred by class awareness—not the class interests of the Jewish bourgeoisie—was responsible for the reactionary character of contemporary Zionism.

Syrkin then castigated Jewish socialists, who had misinterpreted the origin and essence of Zionism, who had not led the movement into socialist channels, and who had evaded responsibility for dealing with the problem of Jewish national revival. As to the charge of "utopianism," he held that it was not the cooperative colonization of Palestine that was utopian, but the dependence on the whim of the sultan and faith in diplomacy—an obvious swipe at Herzl and other "political" Zionists. Finally, Syrkin called on enlightened Jewish youth to fight in the struggle against petrified tradition and reactionary Zionism, to prevent the doom of Zionism by changing the nature of Jewish colonization [29] from a capitalist to a socialist basis.

A Call to Jewish Youth actually marks the beginning of socialist Zionism. Some sections, indeed, are still seriously relevant to the problems of modern Zionism and the state of Israel. Written in a popular militant style, this was the "first Poale-Zionist manifesto," in the words of Ber Borochov, another leading socialist Zionist thinker, and circulated widely among Jewish student groups in the West. Ideas that a few years earlier had caused only limited discussion among a few intellectuals now had an electrifying effect. The time was now riper for socialist Zionist thinking.

In Russia itself, socialist Zionist groups began to sprout in 1900. Borochov himself organized one of the first in Ekaterinoslav.[30] But the groups were scattered, with no common literature or platform. Moreover, the beginnings in Russia had no relationship to Syrkin's work abroad.[31] His ideas were developed independently. He had almost no success, however, in the immediate arena of political activity. There were no Jewish workers in Berlin or Zurich to respond to his call. In Russia and Austria, Zionism was still in an embryonic stage. The political organization of Russia and Galician socialist Zionists was not destined for Syrkin. "By a matter of a few years and a boundary or two between him and the rise of the popular movement he led, it was Syrkin's fate to begin his historic career as a precursor. . . . He was [the] guide and beacon [of Poale Zion groups] but not their organizer." [32]

Yet he was irrepressibly energetic and optimistic. By 1902, his Herut group in Berlin made plans to launch two magazines: *Der Hamon* (*The Proletariat*) in Yiddish, and *Ha-Shahar* in Hebrew, both largely written by Syrkin under a variety of pseudonymns.[33] Each journal lasted only one issue, but the purpose and content of each reveal a great deal about Syrkin's vision and anticipate some of Borochov's strictures against the social structure of Jews in the Diaspora. *Der Hamon* was not actually designed as a popular journal for the masses, but underscored the primary role of the masses in the fulfillment of Zionism. In the leading article, "Zionism and the Masses," Syrkin makes a bold analysis of Jewish workers, observing that the "Jewish masses consist chiefly of a proletariat which does not live from labor." Since its functions "are no longer essential in contemporary society, it must bear the whole yoke of the 'slave of slaves,' the 'proletariat of the proletariat'." This class, which he says has been led astray by the Bund, comprises the miserable shopkeepers, peddlers, *luftmenschen*, tailors, and shoemakers who may be helped momentarily by emigration and the securing of equal rights in Russia, but not in the long run. Syrkin here becomes prophetic and warns against the coming restrictions on immigration, even in democratic countries. "Zionism," he argues, "must become a movement of the masses, of the millions of Jews who have no land, no rest, no work, no language, no culture; who, as workers are oppressed more than other workers. . . . These great Jewish masses are bound to Zionism through the very conditions of their lives." [34]

Another article inveighed against the Jewish Colonization Association

(ICA) founded by the philanthropist Baron Maurice de Hirsch. Hirsch believed that the solution to the Jewish problem lay in an occupational redistribution. He invested huge sums of money to transfer Jews from Eastern and Central Europe to other countries—particularly Argentina—and settle them on the land. Syrkin attacked Hirsch not only for dispersing Jews instead of concentrating them in one territory, but for misusing what he called "national capital," [35] although it was donated by private Jewish philanthropists. For the philanthropy of the rich Jews, Syrkin had only contempt: They wanted to smother anti-Semitism by smothering the Jewish problem and assimilating it out of existence—and embarrassment.

In contrast with *Der Hamon, Ha-Shahar* was aimed at learned Hebraists who had been led astray by Ahad Ha-Am or by Bundist visions of civil emancipation and had to have their concepts of Jewish nationalism widened and deepened. Syrkin believed that the problems of Judaism, with which Ahad Ha-Am wanted to deal, cannot be separated from the problems of Jews and their daily life, while in his attacks on the Jewish bourgeoisie and intelligentsia, he tried to pierce the illusion that civil rights would solve the complicated problems of Jews. The nonproductive nature of the Jewish middle classes—a subject with which Borochov dealt at great length—troubled him greatly. It could be overcome only, he believed, by his socialist Zionist fusion.

In the meantime, other developments of significance for the future of socialist Zionism were taking place in southern Russia, where scattered Poale Zion [36] (Workers of Zion) groups were forming under the leadership of the brilliant young Ber Borochov. In 1900–01, Borochov belonged to the Ekaterinoslav branch of the Russian Social Democratic party, which issued an illegal paper, *The Southern Worker*, agitated among Jewish and Christian workers, and distributed radical literature. "My duty," recalled Borochov later,

> was to read Bogdanov's popular book, *Principles of Political Economy*, with the workers, explaining it to them in simple words and by concrete illustrations. I do not remember what made me change my ideas. It must have been after a chance joint meeting of Jewish and Christian workers that the truth of Socialist-Zionism dawned on me. The committee then discovered that I had a bad influence on the workers—I was teaching them to think for themselves. I was accordingly expelled from the Russian Social Democratic Party. . . .
>
> What can an expelled Russian Social Democrat do when he becomes a Zionist "unbeliever"? I joined a large educational club [about 150 members] of Jewish students and made them the first Poale Zionists in Russia. Menachem Mendel Ussishkin, head of the Ekaterinoslav Zionist region, was a man of steel and iron. He boasted of living at the corner of "Iron" and "Stiff-necked" streets. (The streets were really named that way.) Ussishkin sternly and categorically declared, "I will not tolerate such new-fangled ideas!" Dr. Shmarya Levin was also against our socialist endeavors and in his fine and cultured manner attempted to influence us through friendly argumentation. He came personally

to the same educational club and delivered a series of lectures against Socialist-Zionism.

Youth, however, did not follow its elders, and the club adopted my motion to call itself the "Zionist Socialist Labor Alliance." [37]

Borochov was then only nineteen.[38] His background was somewhat different from Syrkin's, but like Syrkin, he was nourished by both socialist and Zionist influences. He was born in 1881 in the Ukraine, in the small town of Zolotonoshi, of cultured parents for whom education was a paramount value. The year 1881 was a year of destructive pogroms, especially in the Ukraine, and the family was forced to move. They settled in Poltava, which, like Vilna, was chosen by the government as a place of exile for Russian revolutionaries. It was also one of the first centers of Zionism in Russia. A branch of Hovevei Zion was established there, and Borochov's father was an active member. An avid reader of everything he could lay his hands on, the young Ber especially loved travel stories. Inspired by them and by the Zionist atmosphere at home, the ten-year-old boy and a playmate decided to leave for Palestine. They stole out of their homes early one morning, but were brought back late that night by strangers who found them on the outskirts of the city.

Ber entered the *gymnasium* at eleven, with a perfect command of Russian, and achieved a brilliant if undisciplined mastery of Greek, Latin, Sanskrit, philosophy, and economics. Once, having escaped punishment in school, he decided for a second time to leave for Palestine. When he reached Nicolayev penniless, he turned to the local rabbi and asked for help. But the rabbi convinced him to return home. An exile and wanderer most of his short life, Borochov was never to realize his dream of seeing Palestine.

The presence of radical intellectuals in Poltava came to exert great influence among the local youth, especially the young Jews in the *gymnasium* and *Realschule*. There were numerous opportunities to hear lectures on economic and political topics in private homes, schools, and synagogues. Jewish cultural activity was also varied. It was in this milieu that Borochov grew up. Political exiles helped him master socialist ideas, while his interest in the Jewish national movement came naturally from his family and Jewish life around him. But neither orientation by itself seemed completely satisfying. The Kishinev pogrom of 1903 was a profound shock to the Jewish youth of the time and compelled a searching examination of the Jewish national question. Borochov's own talks and lectures stimulated probing discussions and exerted a deep influence on them.

Borochov's socialist Zionist activity in southern Russia developed independently of Syrkin's struggle. There were other scattered socialist-Zionist groupings, also called "Poale Zion," in Russia, whose only distinction from the General Zionists was their working-class character. Yet they denied the connection between the Jewish proletariat and the socialist revolutionary movement on the grounds that the revolution could not solve the problem of Jewish poverty, which they said sprang from the Galut.[39] Later they held that a struggle for socialism in the Galut was impossible because there was no Jewish ruling class and no healthy Jewish proletariat. They did, however, concern themselves with economic issues and conducted trade union work.

By contrast, Borochov's groups based their ideology on a unity between socialism and Zionism. The first public appearance of the first group in Ekaterinoslav was, according to his own account, the organization of a self-defense group during a pogrom at Passover 1901; its second was during Sukkot in a strike of men's tailors, the first strike of Jewish workers in the city.[40] An Odessa Poale Zion group formed in 1902, and in the same year the scattered groups issued their own illegal paper.

Meanwhile, Herzl's pursuit of great men, princes and rulers who would "give" Palestine to the Jews, attracting as it did the support of rich and conservative Jews, aroused misgivings among liberal, nonrevolutionary Russian students like Weizmann. They also believed that the growing Zionist establishment was excluding Russian Jews from the leadership and established a democratic faction within the Zionist Congress to offset the pull of both the Right and Left, thus attracting Jewish liberals who might have moved toward Syrkin's position.

In Russia, at the time, the revolutionary mood was growing stronger and antirevolutionary measures fell heavily on the Jewish population. At first the government thought it could use Zionism to its own advantage: Zionist activity would distract Jews from the struggle against the tsarist regime and conditions within Russia. But when Russian Zionists turned their attention to educational and cultural work and to improving the conditions of the Jewish masses in Russia itself, the secret police began to regard Zionism as a potential menace. In order to observe these changes more closely, permission was given to Russian Zionists to hold a conference in Minsk in August 1902—the first and last to be sanctioned by the authorities.[41]

Previous gatherings had all been illegal; the police had known about them, of course, but had done nothing to stop them. All shades of opinion were represented at the Minsk conference—religious Zionists, Weizmann's democratic faction, youthful socialists, and representatives of Jewish workers whom Zionism had attracted away from the Bund. They supported Herzl's policies, but did not rest content with political and diplomatic activity. Most of the delegates urged a positive attitude toward Jewish settlement in Palestine combined with intensive educational and cultural work.

In fact, Ahad Ha-Am, who had not taken any role in Zionist political work since the First Congress, was invited to attend and spoke on cultural matters. The need for such work was not challenged, but the conference divided bitterly over the efforts of the religious minority to put a religious stamp on the movement. Most of the delegates were secularists but not antireligious, and at last a compromise, proposed by Ahad Ha-Am, was accepted: There would be a two-track Zionist educational and cultural program, religious and secular.[42] This eventually paved the way for three separate trends—religious, secular, and socialist—all within a united Zionist framework.

The Minsk conference confirmed police suspicions that the Zionist movement was not concerned merely with emigration, but was a large, popular movement now grappling with the sufferings of a whole people and pervaded by a new and—to Russia—threatening nationalist spirit. Zionism in Russia was now indeed ranged against tsarism, and Minister Plehve ordered fresh restrictions. There was as yet no persecution such as the revolutionary movements had to endure, but the question of going underground was raised. Youth groups had sufficient strength to do so and wanted to, but the rest of the movement demurred. Instead, Herzl was asked to intercede with the Russian government on its behalf.

Herzl had for some time been seeking an opportunity to establish contact with the government because of its influence at Constantinople, but without success. By midsummer 1902, he had come to the end of the line with Turkey. He had had several talks with the sultan and his aides amid long processions of soldiers, eunuchs, pashas, and other dignitaries, somehow managing to keep afloat in what he called the swirling "sea foam" of Turkish bureaucracy and *baksheesh*-snatching at the palace entrance.[43] The Byzantine indirection and evasiveness at these meetings did not take the Westernized Herzl in completely, but he seemed to believe that if only he could raise the 85 million pounds the sultan needed to cover his enormous debts, he could have a charter, Palestine, and unlimited immigration of Jews.

These may not have been fantastic ideas.[44] Turkey's sources of revenue were not merely pawned, but supervised by foreign creditors. European loans were followed by intervention, then occupation of Egypt and Tunis and eventually Tripoli. The expression the "public debt of Turkey" appeared in newspapers of the time day after day. Turkey was even ready to invite the Russian navy and army to put down any internal threat. Moreover, the notion of a state-supported charter, with political, judicial, and fiscal guarantees for settlers in Asia and Africa, was widely accepted at the time. Perhaps Herzl was more naive in believing that he could raise great sums of money from wealthy Jews. "Fire and brimstone must rain from heaven before those stones are softened," he wrote in a letter in 1901 to his friend Dr. Mandelstamm. "It is something utterly unheard of, and 50 years from now people will split the graves of these men for the fact that I should have been held up because I could not get the miserable money." [45]

By July 1902, terms of a possible arrangement with Turkey had shifted too far to be considered. The sultan was prepared to open his empire to Jewish refugees, but they would have to become Ottoman subjects and settle in provinces *other* than Palestine. A Jewish syndicate would consolidate Turkish debts. Herzl left Turkey empty-handed, having escaped, as he later wrote, "from the murderers' den and the robbers' country." Besides, he later learned that the Turks were merely using him as a pawn to squeeze out a loan from a large French consortium.[46]

Yet he did not despair. In the fall of 1902, his efforts shifted to England. There, public opinion was becoming aroused by an influx of Russian Jews. Herzl saw a chance to explain his views. Projects in Cyprus, Sinai, and El Arish were mooted, but nothing came of them. When the Colonial Secretary, Joseph Chamberlain, mentioned Uganda in East Africa, Herzl at first brushed it aside. Jews would have to be near Palestine, he said. But within a short time, events forced him to consider all possibilities, including East Africa.

It was during this period that Krushevan's anti-Semitic paper *Bessarabets* was poisoning the air of Bessarabia. The press of St. Petersburg and Kiev were also extremely provocative. Then the ominous signs of violence materialized in the Kishinev pogrom in April 1903. Overwhelmed himself by the calamities visited upon Russian Jewry, Herzl redoubled his efforts at a quick diplomatic breakthrough, even if it meant talking to the Russian government about speeding up Jewish emigration. Given the outcries against the pogrom in Western Europe and America, Herzl believed the government might want to create a better image of itself by offering some concessions and even exerting pressure on Turkey to absorb some Jews.[47]

Much to the consternation of many of his colleagues and Russian Jews, Herzl talked with the notorious Plehve several times in August 1903. The minister showed himself astonishingly well informed about Russian Zionist affairs, aware even of the opposition to Herzl. He agreed to let the Zionist movement organize an exodus of Jews from Russia, but absolutely opposed Jewish nationalistic propaganda. Herzl also met with the foreign minister, Witte, who had a reputation for being a friend of the Jews. According to Herzl, however, Witte was much more negative and hostile than Plehve. Nothing came of these talks, although Herzl later said that Plehve told him that without his (Herzl's) intervention, Zionism would have been banned in Russia.

The controversy surrounding Herzl's talks with officials of the hated tsarist regime was bitter and its results much disputed. The young progressives and radicals hated Plehve, "the butcher of Kishinev." Weizmann felt that Herzl's humiliating talks were pointless and unrealistic: anti-Semitism was a necessary instrument of Plehve's policy. "Unreality could go no further; anti-Semites are incapable of aiding in the creation of a Jewish homeland." [48] The socialist Zionists were even more inflamed because Herzl had allegedly promised Plehve, who complained that most Jews were revolutionaries, that Jewish socialists would no longer attack the tsarist government. In an address to the Jewish leaders in St. Petersburg, Herzl warned Zionists against harboring radical elements in their midst.[49]

Yet such was the despair and blind hope of the Russian Jewish masses that Herzl's passing through the Pale took on an almost messianic character. Tens of thousands shouted *Hedad* as he passed. In Vilna especially—the Bund center—there was a tumultuous outpouring of the population that moved Herzl to tears. The squalor and destitution in the ghettos were a horrifying experience and goaded him to accept reluctantly the tentative British offer of Uganda in August 1903 as an emergency measure, a *nachtasyl* (refuge for the night). One week after his Russian trip, Herzl was in Basel for the Sixth Zionist Congress.

He read the cautiously worded but generous British proposal to the delegates and, while admitting that "Uganda is not Zion," suggested that the congress send a commission to investigate the territory. The delegates were at first electrified by the news—this was the first time in all the centuries of exile that a great power had officially dealt with the elected representatives of the Jewish people. But as soon as the substance of the offer was analyzed, vehement and bitter differences almost broke the Zionist movement. Symptomatic of the passions aroused was the action of a young woman delegate who, when the first session was suspended, raced to the platform and angrily tore down the map of Uganda that had been hung in place of the map of Palestine.[50] Later she exclaimed to Herzl, *"Monsieur le President, vous êtes un traitre!"*

Medem was on his way from London at the time and stopped in Basel to observe the congress.[51] Even his strong antipathy to Zionism could not completely crush his curiosity and sense of the unfolding drama, but his tone is sarcastic. "The audience," he wrote, "was intoxicated with Herzl." Delegates "screamed" and applauded thunderously whenever he spoke—"a typical picture of mass-hypnotism." Medem himself was stirred by the figure of Herzl: "He was like a king, proud, reserved, with a face of rare beauty." But his "shameful political maneuvering" agitated all people of stout heart. According to Medem, only Syrkin, whom he described as a "comic figure," genuinely protested the visit with Plehve. The democratic faction merely demurred in a "very diplomatic manner," saying that "some words were said which would have been better left unsaid."

At the Seventh Congress in 1905, the Uganda offer was officially rejected. After the vote, Syrkin rose to announce the withdrawal of most of his faction from the congress (twenty-eight delegates of the Socialist-Zionist Workers' party) and delivered a blistering attack against the remaining delegates. They were limiting Zionism to Palestine, he raged, contrary to the interests of the Jewish masses, who urgently needed a territorial base, and were distorting Zionist national consciousness. His group then allied itself with the Socialisti-Sionisti (SS), a socialist territorialist party that clung stubbornly to the Zionist name (see pp. 407-08). The Anglo-Jewish writer Israel Zangwill also left, and together with some general Zionists established the Jewish Territorial Organization. (Syrkin returned to Zionism in 1909; Zangwill, not until 1924.) This split was also reflected among Poale Zion groups in Russia, America, and Western Europe.

Herzl had died suddenly on July 3, 1904, and the center of gravity in the Zionist movement thereafter shifted to Russian Jewry and the practical necessity of steady piecemeal settlement in Palestine. When Herzl died, there was no longer any real hope that the Zionist movement would gain a firm foothold in Palestine before the disintegration of the Ottoman Empire. Herzl had laid the foundation without which there would have been no Zionist political movement and mass response in Eastern Europe, but the time for hectic diplomacy was over.

Syrkin had greeted the idea of Uganda with enthusiasm. He thought it might indeed be a turning point in Jewish history and believed that all progressive elements in Zionism would welcome the idea. Claiming to be practical and eager to have a concentrated place of settlement immediately, he was seized by the vision of a fertile land and Jewish masses farming it. But, like Herzl and those who became territorialists, Syrkin was not attuned to the deepest longings of the Jewish masses in Russia. These men were astounded by the intensity of their fixation on Palestine and rejection of Uganda and settlement anywhere except in Eretz Israel. A resolution was passed urging the beginning of practical settlement activities as quickly as possible. Even the delegates from Kishinev were against Uganda. After the Russian Zionists left the Congress, they departed for Kharkov, called together their own conference, and fastened themselves exclusively on the idea of Palestine. In England, too, public opinion was against turning "rich" Uganda—actually a desolate wilderness—over to the Jews. The few white English settlers already in Uganda would surely oppose a Jewish influx into their territory. The British government made a graceful withdrawal.

24. Rejecting the Galut:
From Gordon to Borochov

Among the places Herzl had visited in the Pale was the small market town of Plonsk in Russian-controlled Poland, about 40 miles from Warsaw. David Gryn (later David Ben-Gurion), a youth at the time, remembered Herzl's visit vividly: "When he appeared in Plonsk, people greeted him as the Messiah. Everyone went around saying 'The Messiah has come,' and we children were much impressed. It was easy for a small boy to see in Herzl the Messiah. He was a tall, finely featured man whose impressive black beard flowed wide down to his chest. One glimpse of him and I was ready to follow him then and there to the land of my ancestors." [1]

His generation, young David believed, was ripe for Zionism. His father's generation had talked and dreamed about "the land of Israel"; some had joined Hovevei Zion. Then Herzl came and galvanized young Jews into thinking that Palestine was achievable. Anti-Semitism in Plonsk was muted, but the town sent a high proportion of Jews to Palestine. In David Gryn's case, two books that he read as a small boy seemed to fuse in his mind: Mapu's *Ahavat Zion* (Love of Zion), vividly describing the life of Jews in biblical times, in Hebrew, and Stowe's *Uncle Tom's Cabin*, in Russian. Although a frail child, and all but crushed by the death of his mother when he was only ten, by the time he reached fourteen he "suddenly emerged from this tunnel to throw myself heart and soul into the Zionist movement." [2]

He and his close friend Shlomo Zemach, who later became a well-known Israeli writer, created a small-scale *ulpan* in Plonsk, called the Ezra Society, to supplement the *heder*. The first pupils, generally from the poorest families, began to teach other children and finally reached the parents. Soon virtually everyone in Plonsk achieved fluency in Hebrew. David planned to study engineering, but in 1904, he decided he had to come to grips with "the land" itself. His friend Zemach, a few years older, left first, writing faithfully every week in great detail but without despair of the harsh realities he found. Labor was a burning issue. Zemach returned to Plonsk for a visit in the summer of 1906 and the two friends eagerly planned to leave together.

Two arrests intervened: David was picked up by a policeman in Warsaw on suspicion of being an anarchist—he wore his hair too long—and later he was thrown in jail while attempting to resolve a quarrel between two rabbis. The local officials accused him of undermining Russian justice, confiscated his papers, and talked ominously of sending him to Siberia,[3] but he was released both times.

While waiting in Odessa for a ship to Jaffa, David and Zemach visited the Russian Zionist leader Menachem Ussishkin. They were astonished to find him annoyed because they were leaving for Palestine without consulting his committee! He warned them that the Turkish government did not want mass immigration. Doctors and agricultural engineers were needed first, Ussishkin insisted. But the youths were not deterred. After a fourteen-day trip on a filthy freighter, fourth-class, they arrived in Jaffa, a poor, run-down port at the time with one main street lined with stalls and shops. From there they walked to Petach Tikvah and tried to get work as day laborers.

Many of the Jewish farmers in Petach Tikvah were sons of the idealistic pioneers of the 1880's, but they preferred Arab workers to newcomers without any farming experience. At Petach Tikvah, David Gryn almost starved. He began wandering from settlement to settlement, taking work when he could get it: carting manure, digging irrigation ditches, moving rocks and boulders. As soon as the rainy season started, he fell ill with malaria, but he hung on grimly, refusing any help from his father as a matter of principle. "When I left Poland," he said, "I believed something I continued to believe, which is that everything we had in Palestine should be created from the beginning. I knew how fundamental was our historical claim to the land. But I also knew that if we were to call it truly ours again, it must be earned with our toil. So living on handouts from my father, no matter how welcome, would not have suited my mission here." [4]

Indeed, as the young Gryn and other Jewish pioneers were waging individual and social struggles, the very institutions and practices they were attacking were themselves going through critical times. Officially, the Zionist movement at the time was turning away from Palestine and considering settlement in Uganda. The Sixth Congress had dispatched an expedition to look into possibilities there. Colonization funds for Palestine had virtually dried up. The Russian Zionists, though part of the congress, had retained a certain amount of autonomy in the Odessa Committee,[5] which had given funds to the Biluim, had established the settlements of Haderah and Rehovot, and provided support for several others. But their funds were also meager. Moreover, Ahad Ha-Am's criticism of "practical" activities and stress on the need for a "spiritual center" brought about an intensification of cultural activities, but could not form the basis of an *aliyah* or settlement movement. Ahad Ha-Am had made several trips to Palestine in 1891 and found the colonization activities "unsystematic and groundless." Colonization languished until the so-called Second *Aliyah* (1904–14) wholly changed the direction of Zionism and Jewish settlement in Palestine.

The impetus for this migration came from the pogroms of 1903 and the failure of the Revolution of 1905 in Russia, but the immigrants were far from homogeneous, politically or otherwise. Some were Marxists, including former Bundists; others were social idealists and romantics who despaired of the Diaspora and regarded Palestine as the last hope for Jews. Some were, of course, ardent Zionists. The first wave of this *aliyah* was a small group from Homel—most from self-defense units—that arrived in Palestine in January 1904. Slightly more than 1,200 came in 1905, and almost 3,500 in 1906, mainly from White Russia, eastern Poland, and Lithuania.[6] These Jews, almost all of whom were young and unmarried, had grown up in a traditional Jewish environment, spoke Yiddish, and knew at least some Hebrew.

Other groups which came from southern Russia were largely assimilated, spoke Russian, and were influenced by socialist ideas and the revolutionary movement. They had come to Zionism in reaction to the pogroms and the failure of the Revolution of 1905. Nourished on socialist ideas, the young men and women of this *aliyah* were, so to speak, resurrected Biluim: proletarian or collectivist in outlook, of middle-class origin, hating the helplessness, misery, and stunted life of Jews imprisoned in Russia. But between the first Biluim and their successors, changed conditions created a new opportunity for testing the Bilu ideas. This was a riper time, but the main difference lay in the single-mindedness, greater numbers, and persistence of the Second *Aliyah*—at least of its enduring segment.

The first group of Poale Zion worker-immigrants arrived in Palestine in 1904. No land was made available to them for settlement; thus, there was absolutely no prospect of creating mass immigration or remolding those who came in the image of a Jewish worker who could till the soil, end the unnatural hired-labor situation, and build a cooperative Jewish society. The process of Jewish national development could not begin until the struggle of the newcomers to obtain work in the colonies of Petach Tikvah, Rishon le-Zion, Rosh Pinah, and elsewhere had run its course, compelling them to start afresh, out of ideological conviction and a commitment to achieve specific national goals.

When the newcomer first came to a colony, he found a European private farming model, with an Arab *fellahin* population existing at the most primitive cultural level and willing to work at extremely low wages because generally the *fellah* already had a house and some land of his own.

For the Arab, in sharp contrast with the Jewish worker, outside work in a Jewish settlement was often a secondary occupation.[7] Moreover, the Arab worker, already acclimatized and used to farm work, proved more suitable than the untrained, urbanized Jewish worker. The older settlers themselves, none too well off and depending on support from the Jewish Colonization Association [8] and Baron de Rothschild, when there was a bad harvest, cattle plague, or other crisis, decided that only the Arab worker was suitable for farm work in Palestine. If they had ever had any visions of Jewish *national* revival in the land, they had now lost this hope. The well-intentioned paternalism of the Rothschild system had sapped their initiative and the struggle to stay on the land had led them to make compromises. Worse, they saw their children leaving the land and going to the cities, or returning to Russia.[9]

The high moral tone of the newcomers irritated those who had survived the early struggles to become farmers. It was also guilt-provoking, because the oldtimers had themselves once been idealistic. Strikes, demonstrations, and picketing erupted; there were even riots and arrests by police. The economy of Jewish plantation managers and landlords, in fact, was vulnerable not only because of the extensive use of Arab labor and doubts about its permanence and stability, but also because there was an unbridgeable gap—as in all plantation colonies—between workers and the thin stratum of overseers who lived in an atmosphere of boredom and nostalgia for the life they had left behind. A return to Zion was certainly not possible where there was no organized Jewish community, and the plantation colonies did not provide one. Jewish labor had to fight for its right to work and create decent conditions for both Arab and Jewish workers if the character of the colonies was to change.

This system offered nothing but frustration to the newcomers. Ousted from hired labor, they were also outraged by the stifling and exploitative nature of mean profit-taking. The private farms could give no scope for their intense social and national idealism.

At first the land itself was intoxicating: "I smelled the rich odor of corn," David Gryn wrote. "I heard the braying of donkeys and the rustle of leaves in the orchard. Above were clusters of stars, clear and bright against the deep color of the firmament. My heart overflowed with happiness, as if I had entered the land of a wonderful dream." [10] But reality crushed these first delights. Like so many others, David and Shlomo Zemach trekked wearily from one farm to another. Eventually they found work at 8 piasters a day, a few cents, just enough to buy a meal and rent a bed. The experiences at Petach Tikvah had a profound and lasting effect on the personality and philosophy of the young Gryn. He never lost his deep resentment of the "rich Jewish squatters," a carryover from Diaspora ways.

David and Shlomo toiled in Judea for a year. Hunger was a frequent companion:

It would stay with me for weeks, sometimes months. During the day I could dismiss it somehow, or at least stop thinking of it. But in the nights, the long racked vigils, the pangs would grow fierce, wringing the heart, darkening the mind, sucking the very marrow from my bones, demanding and torturing, and departing only with the dawn. Then shattered and broken, I would drop off to sleep at last.[11]

The hostility of the colonists toward Jewish workers reached a climax of sorts in the boycott of Jewish workers in Petach Tikvah in 1905, some of whom had held a memorial meeting in honor of the self-defense units that had fallen during the pogroms of 1905. Orthodox colonists were doubly offended because workers of both sexes attended the meeting together.[12] All possible measures had been taken to prevent the commemoration from taking place. Some of the more fanatical men even forbade the colonists to give workers lodging. After this struggle, the workers left Petach Tikvah.

Many of the young men and women who came from Russia between 1904 and 1906 were the sons and daughters of lower middle-class families, driven by a passion to regenerate the nation and solve the perennial Jewish predicament by creating a new socialist society in the ancient homeland on the basis of *kibbush avoda*, the conquest of labor. Manual labor became the mystique of the Second *Aliyah*. It was invested with a moral fervor that fused *hagshama* (self-realization) with national redemption. The conquest of the Jew for labor and the conquest of labor for the Jew would provide a strong economic base for the Jewish nation established on the land tilled by Jews. The embodiment of this idea was Aharon David Gordon, possibly labor Zionism's greatest teacher, a legend in his own lifetime.

Gordon was born to a family in Podalia related to the baronial Günzburgs. His childhood and youth were spent amid the fields and forests of an estate which his father managed for the Günzburgs and in the study of the Talmud and European and Hebrew literature. A child of rather delicate health, Aharon nevertheless became a person of vigorous will and self-discipline. After his marriage, he too became an official of one of the leased Günzburg estates and for the next twenty-three years (1880–1903), patiently worked at his duties and stoically endured personal disasters—of seven children, only two survived. His devotion to them and interest in their education overflowed to young people in the nearby town, who were drawn to him. Soon he became the intellectual center of Jewish life in the area, creating a library, arranging lectures and readings, and preaching in the synagogue about Hibbat Zion. But none of this prepared him for the drama soon to come.

In 1903, the lease of the estate he managed ran out. He was already forty-seven, with a wife and two grown children, and now had to find a new job. After months of indecision, he followed the pattern of the aged Tolstoy's flight to Yasnaya Polyana and went to Palestine in 1904.

Physically weak, he insisted on being a laborer on the land and working out on his own aging body the painful but necessary transformation he demanded of a whole people. For several years he worked as a day laborer in the vineyards and wineries of Petach Tikvah and later, after he brought his wife and daughter to Palestine, in the Jewish colonies near Jaffa, working in the fields and citrus groves with great joy and devotion. The figure of this aging man, with his enormous beard and Russian tunic, wielding pickaxe and mattock side by side with the young men, fighting physical exhaustion, malaria, and often despair, was a great support to them, as much by his personal example as by his writings.

In his essays, often written by candlelight in the very early hours of the morning, Gordon expounded on the "blessed glow of labor." "One works," he wrote,

> at rough, hard tasks. Yet, at times, one feels that which cannot be better expressed than by saying that one works oneself organically into the work of nature herself, that one grows into her life and creation. Something seizes one, something large as the world, wide as the heavens, deep as the lowest abyss; and it seems to a man suddenly that he, too, is nourished by the rays of the sun, that he, too, like the grasses and bushes and trees, is merged more deeply into nature, more greatly into the great world.[13]

This sense of melting into the cosmos through labor is wholly new to the Jew and growing weaker everywhere as more and more of the world becomes ready-made, according to Gordon. The Jewish people, cut off from nature for two thousand years, are in dire need of physical labor to bind them once more to the earth, without which there can be no national life. The Talmudic saying that when the Jews do God's will, their work will be done for them, must be replaced by a healthier, more normal involvement in labor. "In Palestine we must do with our own hands all the things that make up the sum total of life," Gordon insisted. "We must ourselves do all the work, from the least strenuous, cleanest and most sophisticated, to the dirtiest and most difficult. . . . Labor is our cure." [14]

The Jewish people, accordingly, stand in need of the spiritual uplift produced by physical work. Conditions of exile have impoverished Jews as individuals and as a nation. Returning to the homeland will be of little consequence unless it means release from those conditions and habits and a wholly different way of life rooted in regenerative labor. Nothing less than a thorough transformation of the individual Jew can regenerate Jewish life. This task of revival, of creating a new man, must be experienced within each man. Gordon did not believe that the class struggle and a socialist revolution, or any other social transformation, would produce a better and more just society. Only individual ·change really mattered. Gordon's return to nature did not mean loosening the bonds of behavior imposed by civilization or a return to the primitive, but the development of a high discipline and responsibility. "We are engaged in a creative endeavor," he wrote, the like of which is not to be found in the whole history of mankind: the rebirth and rehabilitation of a people that has been uprooted and scattered to the winds. It is a people half dead, and the effort to re-create it demands the exclusive concentration of the creator on his work. . . . We must not ever, even for a moment, let our minds wander from it [Palestine]. We must shun political activity as destructive of our highest ideals; otherwise we become unwitting traitors to the principle of our true self, which we have come here to bring back to life. Nor must we tie ourselves to the world proletariat, to the International, whose activities and whose methods are basically opposed to ours. . . . We must draw our inspiration from our land, from life on our own soil, from the labor we are engaged in, and we must be on guard against allowing too many influences from outside to affect us.[15]

Thus, there is no social blueprint in Gordon; socialism as a doctrine is eschewed as resting too much on technique and action, on the external life, on the improvement of the social system, instead of the regeneration of the human spirit. Gordon also found socialism deficient because in their battle against capitalism, socialists concentrated on the exploitation of workers instead of the exploitation of all people. "By this act," he wrote, "it [socialism] robbed labor of its vital content, of its national strength and made of it a mechanical force in wake of capital as though . . . it had no national or human account. . . . Not in vain was socialism based on materialism and the class struggle. This factor alone—that the founders of socialism relegated all life and the entire conflict in human life to one side—shows clearly how deeply it is impregnated with technical thought." [16]

Nor is man sacrificed on the altar of nation. For Gordon, the individual is not a spoke in the wheel of historical necessity. Nor may individual creativity and fulfillment be at another's expense. "[The] struggle against exploiters and oppressors will not be a class struggle, but the struggle of the nation against its parasites." [17] Thus, Jewish national regeneration is not restricted by specific plans for a new social order or ideology. Yet Gordon's concept of land, labor, and individual fulfillment laid the foundations for that vital stream of socialist Zionism that led to the development of *kibbutzim*, in which individuals are renewed by their individual labor "for the renewal of life . . . with the members of the community who labor for the renewal of life of a renewed people." Gordon himself searched for this continuously renewing cycle in Degania, the first Jewish collective in Palestine, formed in 1909.

The small group of Poale Zionists who had left Homel in January 1904 firmly believed that they were the vanguard of a great mass movement. But within a year or two, they bitterly realized how wrong they had been. Indeed, half or more who did come left within a few months to return to Russia or go to America.[18] The harsh land, the loneliness, the impossibility of finding work, malaria, and culture shock were too much for all but the hardiest in body or spirit. Many, like the young radicals in America, could not slough off memories of the Russian landscape. The young Ben-Gurion was typical of those who grimly held on. "There is no going back to the old life," he wrote his father in 1906, returning 10 rubles he had sent. "Zionism is a struggle and one can only feel sorry for those who flee the battlefield blaming conditions here. . . . You know I won't leave the country." [19]

Was it reasonable, under the circumstances, to encourage further immigration? Yosef Witkin, a Russian Jew who was a teacher in Palestine, issued a call to Jewish youth in Eastern Europe to come to Palestine and strengthen the Jewish struggle to work the land: "You are necessary to the land as air is to breathing," he proclaimed. "Know that you must create a new epoch in the land. . . . Be prepared for a battle with nature, sickness and hunger, with people—friends and foes, strangers and brethren, enemies of Zion and Zionists. Be prepared for the animosity and cruelty of your own brethren who see in you a dangerous competitive force. . . . Be ready for the worst—but also for victory! Your victory will be the victory of the people!" [20]

This call was at variance with the official position of the Poale Zionists, influenced as they were by Borochov's prediction that they should not artificially stimulate immigration, but rather wait patiently for the natural, even inevitable processes which would bring both capitalists and workers to Palestine. The ranks of the socialist Zionists, in fact, were badly fragmented after the Seventh Zionist Congress in 1905. Syrkin referred to this time as "the period of theoretical chaos."

Most of his followers had left the formal Zionist movement over the Uganda issue and joined the Socialisti-Sionisti, a socialist-territorialist party which clung to the name Zionist. Yet they were also Marxists, who together with all Russian social democrats of this period believed that the development of capitalism was increasing the ranks of the proletariat at the expense of the petty bourgeoisie. However, there was a corollary: Because of the special oppression of Jews and the competition of non-Jewish fellow workers, it was impossible for the declassed Jews to become proletarians. The capitalistic system could be overthrown only by the industrial proletariat, but the class struggle of the Jews was helpless and self-defeating. The revolutionary tendencies of the Jewish proletariat are attributed not to its place in the scheme of production "but to ideological motives and particular tendencies to abstraction." [21] Haphazard emigration leads to similar dilemmas, according to the SS, but must be directed to lead to class consciousness and efforts to settle the Jewish masses in a free territory where the class struggle will be given normal expression. Territorialism was thus seen as complementing the class struggle. The growth of Jewish emigration in the early 1900's, in fact, strengthened the

SS movement, especially in Minsk. The southern Russian socialist Zionist groups, influenced by Borochov, retained their identity with Palestine, although they too had a strong Marxist underpinning.

In August 1905, still another movement among socialist Zionists arose—Vozrozhdeniye (Renaissance)—which stressed the possibilities of Jewish national rebirth in the Diaspora. The intellectuals working out its ideology, which resembled that of Zhitlovsky, criticized both the indifferent attitude of Jewish socialists to the fate of the Jewish people and the blindness of Zionists who ignored the needs and possibilities of the Galut. It had no objection to Palestine as a national home, but concentrated on a "national renaissance."

Later developments, however, took this group quite far from its original position. One of its important offshoots was the Sejmist party (Jewish Socialist Workers' party, or SERP), which stressed national development through federations of representatives of different nationalities. This striving for full self-development through deepening of national consciousness was similar to the nationalist emphasis in the socialist revolutionary movement. Each nationality, including Jews, would have its own Sejm, or parliament, in which the proletariat would clamor to have their interests supported. The Sejmists became Galut-orientated and concentrated on the class struggle, Yiddish, cultural work, and efforts to secularize the kahals. They believed that by normalizing conditions for Jews in the Galut, it would be easier to build a national territorial center.[22]

In the prevailing competition for supporters, the SS was the most energetic of the socialist movements among Jews and for a time actually became the strongest competitor of the Bund, claiming a membership of 27,000 throughout the Pale in 1905. Poale Zion had about 16,000 members at the time and the SERP, about 13,000. The SS lost its position to the Poale Zion in 1907, when the unity of the party was achieved as a result of Borochov's strenuous efforts.

At the same time, a quite different development in labor Zionism took place in Austria, centered in Galicia. There, socialist Zionists formed trade unions, mutual aid societies, and Zionist clubs of workers, clerks, and salesmen. Besides their Zionist allegiance, which embraced all Jews and transcended class interests, they stressed the need to democratize the Jewish community. In 1904, a convention of these varied groups met in Cracow and formed the Jewish Socialist Party–Poale Zion of Austria. Considering itself an integral part of the Zionist movement, it negated the socialist solution and the materialistic interpretation of history unless it was combined with an autonomous Jewish territory. It also maintained that the position of the Jewish worker was different from that of the non-Jew inasmuch as he had to face both exploitation and discrimination. Mass migration to Palestine was also pressed as a way to quickly establish a Jewish national home.

Poale Zion groups in other countries followed either the Russian or

Austrian models. In 1907 a worldwide convention was called at the Hague, resulting in the Jewish Socialist Workers World Confederation Poale Zion. Technically, this became an autonomous federation within the Zionist movement in the same year, but underlying ideological differences could not be wholly resolved and many of the Russian members, influenced by Borochov, who believed that participation in the general Zionist movement was a kind of class collaboration, withdrew from the congress in 1909. For a time, they even refused to work for the Jewish National Fund and set up their own Palestine Workers' Fund.

Yet within specific countries, and in Palestine, the Poale Zion movement, loosely united though it was, realized very significant achievements. In Russia, it pioneered with the Bund in the armed self-defense movement. It also energetically conducted trade union activities, elections to the Duma and local bodies, and an open fight against anti-Semitism, particularly rife among Polish workers. It was actively involved in the cultural revival of Yiddish, especially after the post-1905 reaction. Its bitterest struggle, however, was against the self-proclaimed monopoly of the Bund.

Many memoirs of the time disclose the tension and hostility between the two movements, which were adversaries on almost every level except self-defense. Zalman Shazar, third president of Israel, who was among the early Poale Zion members in the little town of Steibtz, recalled the first "battleground" there—the library—during the period of the Russo-Japanese War:

> When the struggle became particularly intense, the library was split in two, they taking the Russian section, which was "theirs," and we taking the Hebrew, which was "ours." My older sisters helped with the Russian books, assisting the town teacher of Russian and one or another student or extern or girl student from Bobroisk. Alter, the Hebrew teacher, took care of our books and I helped him, but our faction had no students of its own. When the atmosphere grew even more hostile and the Poale Zion movement was about to be established, we brought a Russian teacher of our side to the town. A brilliant young extern, dazzling theoretician and orator, he instructed us in socialist Zionism.[23]

This young man, with wavy black hair and impeccable manners, was a vegetarian (he refused to allow the youths to hang flypaper in their meeting room), and an idealist who rejected Marxist materialism. By day he gave lessons to externs and by night he taught the doctrines of labor Zionism. His friend, the town beauty Vera Yakovlevna, arranged for a performance of Goldfaden's play *Shulamis* to raise money for the library. Rehearsals lasted all winter and the performance was a great success, raising the status of the Poale Zion group. Then during Shavuot, the groups arranged a secret assembly in the Zadvoriya woods:

> "Patrols" lined the paths to point the way to the meeting place. There among the trees we staged our first ideological debate, with some of us impersonating

our opponents. This intellectual fencing was intended to give our members practice in answering the arguments of our many antagonists. The teacher directed the "performance"; he had given me the role of a Bundist spokesman and taken it upon himself to answer for Poale Zion. I had diligently gathered the most telling arguments against Zionism, building a towering structure out of what I learned from my sisters and their friends, teachers and visitors, as well as what I could gather from reading and reflection. When our teacher got up after I finished and eruditely tore down every inch of my structure, leaving nothing at all, I was triumphant.[24]

The Poale Zion group marched with flag unfurled for its first public "demonstration" and a confrontation with the Bundists, who were by far the larger group—they had the workers with them, the sons and daughters of the wealthy families and the best of the intelligentsia. The Poale Zionists sensed disaster, but their singing of the party hymn was loud and clear; Vera Yakovlevna outsang everyone and almost the entire town followed her all the way to the Poale Zion meeting room.

Most of the confrontations, however, were not so mild or romantic. As the socialist Zionists gained strength, they began to take the offensive against the Bund. In *Der Hamon* in 1903, Syrkin attacked the Bund's doctrine of cultural autonomy as totally inadequate for a national minority. Without territory, he argued, there was no foundation for political and civil laws, and without their own laws, a people could not have genuine autonomy. Under the Bund conception, Jews would still be governed largely by alien laws. Syrkin also railed against the Bund's bent toward Yiddish, which he regarded as the language associated with Jewish degradation, claiming that true independence would come about only through Hebrew.

Bundists perceived the threat from socialist Zionists particularly after the Kishinev pogrom, when the latter realized how distant a national home was and began to engage in the existing struggle in Russia. This change in direction took them right into Bundist political territory. Labor Zionist and socialist Zionist circles and groups grew in 1903-04 and made the problem of socialist Zionism and Zionism generally an issue of great concern to the Bund, as evidenced by the stream of articles in the Bundist press and a continuing concern with the national question.[25] The Bund had to take the position that the Russian land belonged to Jews as rightfully as to any other people, that it was, in fact, their "home"—a dubious and ironic claim.

A favorite and somewhat vulnerable target of the Bund was the labor Zionist movement in Minsk, which had not severed its connection with the general Zionists.[26] The Bund accused it of being a totally bourgeois group. Why did they even bother to form a separate party, the Bund asked. On the other hand, most embarrassing for the Bund was its split with the RSDWP, which Zionists called another example of anti-Semitism. As they saw it, the Russian social democrats had wanted to use the Jewish workers to their own advantage, and when they refused to be so used, the Russians rejected them. The arguments were pressed relentlessly, and in 1905–06, Borochov trenchant analysis of Jewish economic misery gave the Bund tough new material to cope with.

In 1904, Borochov's close friend from Poltava, the young Itzchak Ben-Zvi, made his first visit to Palestine. After he returned, he had long talks with Borochov, who asked many questions about the country, particularly its working-class elements. Undoubtedly, these talks strengthened his views against Uganda or any territory other than Palestine.[27] Borochov developed into an excellent speaker and skilled debater, and traveled through many cities and towns of Lithuania, the Ukraine, and Poland discussing national and economic questions with the masses of Jewish workers. These experiences spurred him to formulate a socialist Zionist synthesis that had been working on his mind for some time. He returned to Russia from the Seventh Zionist Congress (1905) as waves of pogroms swept the country and plunged into the work of consolidating the scattered groups of Poale Zion.

Meanwhile, the socialist Zionists who retained a pro-Palestine orientation had held a conference in Kiev in July 1905, at which a Jewish Social-Democratic Poale Zion party was constituted. Soon afterward, it sent forty-seven delegates to the Seventh Zionist Congress and selected a central committee. But the Sejmist influence was already strong and a split occurred in December 1905 at a dramatic conference in Berdichev.[28] A month earlier, Borochov delivered an address at the district conference in Poltava and took an active part in drafting a specifically Jewish socialist program. This conference was a turning point in the history of the party. It formed a new strategic center against Sejmism and founded its own organ *Yevreiskaya Rabotchaya Chronica (The Jewish Labor Chronicle)*, which Borochov edited during 1905–06.

After the Poltava conference, Borochov and Ben-Zvi attended the district conference in Berdichev as delegates from the Poltava meeting and met delegates from party groups in the provinces of Kiev, Podolia, Volnynia, and Bessarabia. This conference, Ben-Zvi recalled, "was held under highly adverse conditions, for Cossacks were rampaging in the streets and it was dangerous to be out in the evenings. We spent days and nights in meetings and discussions in a small room illuminated by candlelight." [29] The Sejmist supporters left; the rest made plans for a nationwide congress.

This historically significant All-Russian Organizational Convention of the Jewish Social-Democratic Labor Party Poale Zion was held on Purim eve, February 1906, in Poltava. Thirty delegates met furtively in a Jewish bakery on the outskirts of the city. "For seven days and nights," Borochov recalled, "we sat and slept there, not taking a step outside for fear the Tsarist police would notice us. The profoundest theoretical questions and the most difficult organizational problems were courageously and enthusiastically dealt with in that uncomfortable environment." [30] Later, Borochov related other details of that meeting: Twenty-seven pounds of dynamite and seven finished bombs were buried in the courtyard of the bakery in case of a pogrom or uprising. (Twenty pounds of dynamite and all the bombs were found by the police.) Finally, the police began to suspect the activities in the bakery and the delegates had to hurry away to a hotel in the center of the city. Borochov further recalled:

> Our "retreat" took place in perfect order, so that the enemy was unable to capture any prisoners of war. Our small army quite peacefully continued its deliberations in the hotel which we had forcibly captured by sternly warning the proprietor not to accept any other guestsm But the police discovered us even in our new abode, and two prisoners fell into their none-too-gentle hands; but the minutes and other documents were carried to safety in time. We hastily finished the most important organizational work, elected the first Central Committee, and appointed a commission to draw up the Party platform.[31]

The commission, on which Borochov was to play a leading role, hid itself in a small town outside Poltava, where again two comrades were arrested. The others fled to Simferopol, where Borochov wrote preliminary reports on nationalism and internationalism, nation and class, autonomy for Jews in the Diaspora and Palestine, and socioeconomic analyses of proletarian movements among Jews. These reports were discussed in sessions that lasted for three weeks. Borochov then prepared the final draft of "Our Platform," which appeared first in Russian, since at the time many members of the party used Russian exclusively. Later, in 1907, parts of "Our Platform" were translated into Yiddish by the sixteen-year-old Shazar (then Rubashov) who had recently joined the party. This document formed the official position of the Poale Zion until the Bolshevik Revolution.

There is a curious omission, indeed a fundamental one, in Borochov's impressive edifice: Although the party had already made contact with some of the early *halutzim* in Palestine who had come from Poland, Lithuania, and Russia, and whose letters were printed in party publications, there is no acknowledgment of the efforts of these groups or projection of their role in the future of Palestine in "Our Platform." Borochov's Marxism simply didn't find room for them—as yet.

Borochov himself had already resolved the burning issue of Palestine or Uganda (or any territory other than Palestine) in "On the Question: Zion and Territory," published in Russian in 1905. In his essay Borochov developed a new theory that was to become the foundation of Poale Zion and a central plank in its 1906 platform. In this work, Borochov raised the level of discussion against the Uganda scheme to one of fundamental principle by applying a materialist analysis to the Jewish problem and establishing Zionism as an elemental force produced by the anomalies and insecurities of Jewish experience. In the same year he wrote his pathbreaking "The National Question and the Class Struggle."

At the Poltava conference, the young party was still torn by splits and ideological conflicts. Nevertheless, Borochov's insights and formulations guided the tiny Poale Zion group in Palestine in 1905–06 (it later deviated from Borochovism), and helped greatly to finally consolidate the re-cycling fragmentation of the party as a whole.

Borochov's task in "The National Question and the Class Struggle" was exceedingly difficult not only because of the intractable subject matter, but because his theory of nationalism based on dialectical materialism was developed in the teeth of socialist opposition to the force of nationalism in the class struggle. Marx had failed to deal with social problems arising out of national differences, leaving many questions unresolved or answered dogmatically. Borochov had to work out a new approach to nationalism without sacrificing socialism, as well as a rationale for Jewish survival in Palestine and the Galut, and a theory of the role of the Jewish proletariat.

Marx had analyzed the clash between the *forces* of production, that is, labor, and the existing *relations* of production, on which legal and political superstructures are based. To the Marxist concept of relations of production, Borochov added what he called the *conditions* of production, including the geographical, anthropological, and historical conditions under which production takes place, and which create distinct entities called nations.[32] This concept furnishes the basis for Borochov's analysis of the problem of nationalism and national struggles. As society develops, the social and historical conditions of production assume greater importance than the natural conditions and result in differentiated economic structures and the subsequent struggle between social entities. One body seeks to annex the field of the other or to defend itself against the other, and a national struggle ensues: "The national struggle is waged not for the preservation of cultural values but for the control of material possessions even though it is very often conducted under the banner of spiritual slogans."

In dealing with nationalism, Borochov defines it as "the feeling of kinship created as a result of a common historic past, the roots of which arise from the common conditions of production." It is a product of bourgeois society, developing with the end of feudalism and the rise of capitalism. Among all the material and spiritual resources of a nation, the most vital is territory, on the foundation of which rise all other conditions of production. For the great landowners, territory is valuable as their chief source of income, namely, rent. For the "great bourgeoisie," it is a base for seizing the world market, and for the middle class and petty bourgeoisie, territory is a market for consumer goods.

For the proletariat, in Borochov's view, territory is important as a workplace and arena for the class struggle. The proletariat, too, is divided by conditions of production and competition. This situation is the reason for the lack of class consciousness and the presence of nationalistic sentiments among the masses in search of work, as well as among natives defending their jobs against foreign workers. Thus, as long as workers of a given nation have not yet made their place of work secure, the problem of work is much more important to them than the class struggle. Class consciousness is often obscured by national consciousness when the proletariat is forced to defend its national place of work. For example, the constant immigration of new workers into England and the United States threatens the security of the places of work of English and American workers, heightening their national consciousness and deterring the development of class consciousness.

In discussing the nationalism of oppressed nationalities, Borochov pointed out that the conditions of production to which they are subject are abnormal because they are deprived of territory, political independence, and cultural development. Cultural aspects assume great importance and all individuals affected begin to clamor for national self-determination. But the chief protagonists of genuine national emancipation are the progressive elements of the masses and the intelligentsia who aim at normalizing the conditions and relations of production for the entire nation, which means assuring the proletariat a normal base for its labor and class struggle.

Borochov's theory of landless and oppressed nations is applied to the situation of Jews in "Our Platform." [33] In a trenchant and forcible analysis, he shows how Jews, lacking a territorial base, are an "expatriated nation," forced to adjust economically to the demands and whims of the majority among which they live. Not permitted to enter agriculture or the basic industries, Jews are tolerated only in commerce and in the last levels of production. To Jewish capitalists, economic interests in the Galut are their main concern; only the fear of anti-Semitism and philanthropy toward poor Jews create any sort of bond with other Jews. The middle-range Jewish bourgeoisie can drift into assimilation or sharpened national consciousness, but cannot be counted on to radically reconstruct Jewish life. The Jewish proletariat too (including the declassed petty bourgeoisie) suffers from the abnormality of the economic distortions in Jewish life. When the Jewish worker goes on strike against the industry that exploits him, he does not appreciably disturb the equilibrium of the country; his demands have to be sought with the support of non-Jewish workers. Thus, according to Borochov, since "his difficulties are based on national factors, he must be . . . interested in nationalism."

Borochov then develops the idea that intensified national competition under capitalism aggravates the Jewish problem, making assimilation impossible and driving Jews to seek their solution in emigration. Emigration, in turn, forces Jews into concentrated areas to ease adjustment, but condemns them to retain their old economic traditions and habits—the manufacturing of consumer goods. "Thus the need of the Jews to develop their forces of production and to become proletarianized remains unsatisfied." A territorial solution to the Jewish problem is required, but migration must not continue to be a "confused and scattering process." Besides, eventually all nations will bar Jews, Borochov predicted. Emigrating masses must be organized and directed through the realization of what he called "Proletarian Zionism."

Proletarian Zionism comes about in two stages: resolution of the social conflict (economic oppression) and resolution of the much more complex national conflict, involving a radical change in the conditions of national existence. For the Jewish proletariat, the national problem arises because its strategic base is unsatisfactory both economically and politically. "If we were the proletariat of a free nation," Borochov declared, "which neither oppresses nor is oppressed, we would not be interested in any problems of national life." But as this is not the case, a territory for Jews will enable the Jewish proletariat to engage in the primary levels of production and conduct a class struggle against a "mighty bourgeoisie which organized the production of the country."

This point of view excludes a general program for the Jewish people as a whole. In Borochov's view, "the anomalies of the *entire* Jewish nation are of interest . . . only as an objective explanation of the contradictions in the life of the Jewish proletariat." At the same time, he assumed that a large part of the Jewish people, including workers, would always remain in the Galut as a national minority. Thus, for the Galut, national political autonomy was proposed only as a palliative, but one "placing the Jewish proletariat in the political arena face to face with the Jewish bourgeoisie," enabling them "to create and shape their own destiny" within the circumscribed conditions of the Galut.

In defining the land targeted for Jewish immigration, Borochov, in his earliest writings, disregarded all moral or spiritual considerations, or any other forces that were not clearly materialistic. A concept such as the collective will of the Jewish people to settle its historic land, or the burning idealism of the early pioneers, had no place in his early theorizing. Palestine became his choice because he believed that sheer economic necessity dictated it. Unlike the territorialist SS, which claimed that the proletarianization of Jews in the Galut would meet the competition of the local population, Borochov believed that Jewish workers would not take their places in basic industry, but would be forced into light industry and backward branches of production.

In Borochov's view, the need for new lands of immigration increases as Jews are expelled from their occupations. But Jews cannot emigrate to lands in order to serve commercial and industrial interests (because there would be no room for their petty capital and no local markets), or in order to become farmers, because as city-bred people, they cannot compete with experienced farmers in the world market. Rather, Jews must emigrate to a country where petty Jewish capital and labor can be utilized, where the Jewish worker can work in basic industries or transfer from industry to agriculture without great difficulty. Such a land must be semi-agricultural, thinly populated, and not particularly attractive to other immigrants. It must be a country of low cultural and political development. It must, then, be Palestine.

As opposed to the free choice of territory of the other socialist territorialist theoreticians, Borochov propounded his interpretation of Palestine as the land of future Jewish immigration through what he called a *stychic* [34] process, that is, the working out of spontaneous, inevitable, automatic processes—the migration of Jews to Palestine and the Jewish proletariat's search for a base from which to conduct the class struggle. In terms of economic development, Borochov theorized that Jews in Palestine would produce for the native population, but not be dependent upon it, as in the Galut; they would also produce for the external market of the surrounding countries of the Mediterranean. The question of the Arab population is not touched on in these early writings.[35] Later, Borochov (who never went to Palestine) believed that the Palestinian Arabs would eventually be culturally assimilated. Finally, he clearly differentiated the tasks of bourgeois as against proletarian Zionism: To the former he assigned the "creative" role of the organization of capital and the development of production, including colonization methods; to the latter, he assigned a "liberating" role—the process of democracy and the class struggle, which he predicted would be a "bitter" one. The conclusion of "Our Platform" links the struggle of Jews for cultural autonomy in the Galut with the struggle in Palestine in a historic process that unfolds simultaneously. "Which we shall obtain first," he wrote, "does not matter," but each process strengthens the other. Although his materialist analysis led him to Zion, he simultaneously taxed Zionism with the task of normalizing the Galut. "The dream of Zion," he wrote,

> grew out of material conditions, out of the growing divisionalism which matures and grows throughout the entire Jewish nation. The dream of Zion is the full answer to the divisional processes, to the process of integration, to anti-Semitism and Jewish nationalism. In Zion is found a means to the normalization of the Galut.

At a later period in his life, Borochov reformulated some of his views, and by softening his stringent Marxian dialectics, found room for Jewish historical aspirations as a basis for socialist Zionism. After 1914, undoubtedly influenced by his life in America, he became more of a pragmatist, calling himself "a Marxist without 'matter' and a critical empiricist opposed both to materialism and idealism," ready and willing to cooperate with all forces opposed to capitalism and involved with the whole Jewish people in the building of the national home. He even began to use the term *Eretz Israel* instead of the colder *Palestine*.

But all of this came later. In the earlier period, he formulated an original theoretical framework that strongly appealed to radically minded Jews who had Marxist leanings, but who could not accept the prevailing socialist views on the Jewish question. Those ideas did not provide answers comprehensive enough for the anomalies of Jewish life, or clear a way to the liberation of the Jewish people. These young doubters and rebels could not accept the indifference of most socialists to the uniqueness of the Jewish predicament or the sweeping dogmas that pulled Jewish fate into the churn of mighty forces. They observed that it was not only Russian reactionaries, but workers and even revolutionary intellectuals who condoned or participated in pogroms. (Borochov himself had been propelled into Zionism by the proletarian variety of Russian anti-Semitism.) They also realized that industrialization, which according to Marx should turn artisans and petty bourgeoisie into proletarians, did not have this effect on Jews, who instead became a rootless mass of middlemen without fixed commerce, or laborers in the most insecure and declining parts of the economy. The inexorable economic pressure combined with political and social oppression that drove them to emigration certainly saved many Jews, but, from a socialist's point of view, also took them out of the revolutionary arena. Indeed, the Jewish socialist Zionists saw with chagrin that neither the problem of the Jew nor his role in the coming revolution mattered very much to the other socialists, for Jews were not considered historically essential.[36] They might help in Russia and Poland, but they had no genuine role themselves and would disappear as a distinct group, according to socialist predictions.

Bundists, of course, were socialists who cared deeply about the Jewish proletariat, but the cardinal question—the anomalous Jewish economic situation with its peculiarities and all of its implications—was not dealt with directly. (The Bundists Kremer and Gozhansky at first conceded that the unusual nature of the Jewish worker-artisan class greatly handicapped socialists. Later they reconsidered their revolutionary potential and were much more positive.) The basic premise of Borochov (and the brilliant young socialist Zionist economist Jacob Lestchinsky) was that the Jewish artisan class was doomed to extinction.[37] Its failure to enter the great factories was not a temporary phenomenon, but a symptom of an abnormal position which no social revolution would change. The Bund could never refute its own admission that the class struggle for Jews would be "pauper against pauper," though it continued to hope that Jewish artisans would eventually be absorbed in factories. The Jewish class-conscious proletarian struggle in Russia involved many thousands of workers in strikes and economic and political agitation, but this activity was a palliative rather than a cure for their misery. In the Diaspora, Borochov argued, Jewish workers were a class without a future.

This new approach, differing sharply from the mystical and messianic Zionism of an earlier period, created a materialist Zionism that challenged the Bund on its own terms. Moreover, Borochov charged the Bund with dogmatism and lack of historical realism, and called cultural autonomy a theoretical hybrid and a politically expedient doctrine. Bundists were often pessimistic about the future of Jewish life in the Pale. How, then, could they turn the values of Diaspora life into a positive nationalist doctrine? Borochov also condemned the Bundists and other territorialists like the Sejmists for having turned the problem of national Jewish independence into a bread-and-butter question instead of elevating it, as Zionists did, to a more positive realm. That is to say, "materialist-territorialism was based solely on Jewish misery, while Zionism went beyond, to a more positive approach." [38]

In creating a new theoretical economic base and a new revolutionary situation for the Jewish masses while keeping the Marxist dialectical framework, Borochov was able to overcome the abnormal economic situation of the Jews in the Galut, which isolates them from the basic productive process and forces them into the crevices of national economies. In his formulation, a normal socioeconomic structure can be developed only in a Jewish nation. Only there can the necessary class struggle take place. Only there can the struggle against marginality and exploitation be waged and won.

Borochov (and Lestchinsky) thus joined Syrkin in examining the particular social and economic conditions affecting Jewish workers. Their subsequent justification for Zionism was based on this analysis, as was the conclusion that the anomalies of Jewish economic life in the Diaspora were irreparable. Convinced by their studies that the determining force behind the Jewish national movement was the reality of misery of the broad Jewish masses, "they were to become the first Jewish economists and sociologists." [39]

By giving Zionism the force of Marxist determinism and developing a class analysis that made a return to Zion a historic necessity, Borochov was able to rebut the charges of utopianism and desertion of the Galut flung against many socialist Zionists. There were tasks aplenty for socialist Zionists in the Galut. In Russia, the movement battled for Jewish rights, conducted strikes, formed Jewish trade unions, created Jewish secular schools, and fought for the creation of a strong Yiddish culture. At times, Poale Zion activity in Russia seemed to neglect Zionism and Palestine.

By recasting Marxism to fit the objective Jewish situation, Borochov was singularly original. His theories even found some adherents among Ukrainian, Finnish, and Armenian social democrats.[40] On the evening of June 3, 1906, after the tsar had disbanded the Duma, Borochov was arrested. In prison, he founded a "People's University." Many of the Ukrainian prisoners were social democrats who fell under the spell of his theories of nationalism.[41] Later, a number of social-democratic Ukrainian groups even called themselves "Borochovists."

The question of how much effort to invest in the political and economic struggle in Russia was a particularly difficult one for socialist Zionists. They ruled out a Diaspora solution to the Jewish question, but from a practical point of view, especially after the collapse of the Uganda scheme, it was apparent that large Jewish masses would remain in Russia for a long time. A tension between the claims of Palestine and the Diaspora—very much like the tension in the Bund between the claims of general Russian socialism and the particular needs of the Jewish workers— existed. Nevertheless, the rising storm of 1905 could not be ignored, and Zionist socialists, as well as Bundists, became activists on the Russian scene. Indeed, the Poale Zionists, the Zionist Socialist Workers' party (the SS), the Sejmists—all claiming to represent the economically and culturally deprived Yiddish-speaking workers—often overlapped in their activities. All championed national cultural autonomy for Jews in Russia, a stand also eventually taken by the Bund, and all cooperated in the establishment of Yiddish schools, which were seen as the main force in the creation of Jewish national autonomy. The Jewish socialists in Palestine, however, had to grapple with a wholly different set of problems.

25. Ruppin and the First Kvutzot

Jewish socialists from Eastern Europe were notoriously disputatious, and socialist Zionists in Palestine no less so. In 1904–05 the small Poale Zion groups were struggling to conquer labor, experiment with collective ideas, and make massive personal adjustments, but they did not ignore ideological issues. Indeed, ideological controversy flared early. In July 1905, about forty Jewish workers gathered in the hut of Ezekiel Chankin, who had inspired the organization of Jewish self-defense groups during the pogroms of 1903, to establish a Jewish Workers' Organization. Some in the group were already committed Poale Zion party members—Marxists who had a well-developed theoretical orientation based on the ideas of Borochov. Others were less doctrinaire and frankly opposed to a deterministic socialism, placing their whole emphasis on *kibbush avoda*, the conquest of labor by Jews. By October 1905, the more moderate group (generally the younger, more recent arrivals) formed a "party" called Hapoel Hatzair (The Young Worker). Within a month, a separate Palestine Poale Zion party was also formed.

Hapoel Hatzair was greatly influenced by the philosophy of A. D. Gordon, whose "religion of labor" and intense belief in man's need to restore his bond with the land and nature eschewed the class struggle or radical overthrow of existing institutions. Emulating Gordon, Hapoel Hatzair believed that Jews had become alienated from nature, but that the new Jewish worker, in fresh contact with labor and the soil, would pioneer a national renaissance. Thus, in contrast with Poale Zion, which was a thoroughly ideological party in the pre-1914 social democratic tradition, Hapoel Hatzair was pragmatic, non-Marxist, and opposed to doctrinal formulations or disputes. It had come into being *in* Palestine and did not have to struggle with the ideological straitjacket of a parent movement.

Its policy was set forth in the sentence which, at the time, appeared in every issue of its paper: "The necessary condition for the realization of Zionism is conquest by Jewish labor of all occupations in the country." [1] Later (in 1908) they declared that "Hapoel Hatzair must unite under its flag all the healthy forces in the country, irrespective of their field of activity [i.e., whether or not they were workers] provided they accept the principle of 'conquest of work' and are prepared to help in some way in implementing this principle." [2] It was therefore essential to increase the number of Jewish workers as quickly as possible and to improve their working and living conditions. But uppermost was the conquest of agriculture. Hapoel Hatzair realized earlier than Poale Zion that Jewish workers in Palestine were facing a situation totally different from that of any other labor movement [3]—hence their opposition to "foreign" ideologies, although there were traces of Russian populism, anarchism, and social revolutionary ideas in their thinking.

A certain amount of antagonism was inevitable between these two small groups. Being a Marxist party, Poale Zion did not want to concentrate exclusively on agriculture; the urban proletariat also demanded attention. Its rival was referred to as a pleasant kindergarten for the sons and daughters of lower middle-class parents (as were their own!), too much preoccupied with cultural problems, Hebrew and Zionism, and isolated from the "masses." They also carped at Hapoel Hatzair for refusing to celebrate May Day. At first, they also criticized the strained emphasis on the "conquest of labor," arguing that there were not enough Jewish workers on which to base a movement. But the realities of Palestine at the time drew the groups together within a few years. Hapoel Hatzair also underwent change. At first its concept of "conquest of labor" foreclosed permanent settlement (Wouldn't becoming permanent settlers mean becoming owner-farmers? Wasn't the conquest of labor more important than the conquest of the land?), but this view gradually gave way. Moreover, Hapoel Hatzair soon shed some of its exalted notions and became involved in politics.

The tiny Poale Zion group in Palestine, after its split from Hapoel Hatzair in the winter of 1905, consisted of about 60 members. Hapoel Hatzair had 90 out of a total of 550 workers. [4] (Five years later there were no more than 500 members in both parties.) Both groups took themselves very seriously as political parties, with their solemn speeches, "periodicals," and "historical missions." They also set up work exchanges, cultural and social clubs, and sickness funds.

The political program of the Palestine Poale Zionists was hammered out by less than a dozen members at a clandestine meeting in a Jewish guesthouse in the Arab town of Ramle in 1906. It was almost an exact replica of the platform of the Russian Poale Zion, based on Borochov's thesis that Jewish capitalists would eventually invest their money in Palestine, that a Jewish working class would come into being, and that a class struggle would ensue. Among those working on the draft was David

Gryn, who personally scorned idealistic Zionists trying to settle in Palestine on the basis of a Marxist social philosophy and battled for the use of Hebrew and Jewish national content in the Ramle program. But class warfare and historical materialism remained its dominant themes.

Yet nagging questions persisted in the face of raw experience: What if capitalists did not build up Palestine? How could Borochov's "strategic base of the Jewish worker" be created if Jewish employers refused to hire Jewish workers? How could the land be developed without capitalist initiative? There were also growing doubts about the Russian Poale Zion's involvement in Russian matters. Who needed another Bund? Hesitantly at first, but more boldly later on, the Palestinian Poale Zion, under the leadership of young Gryn, Itzchak Ben-Zvi, and Israel Shochat, took an independent path that brought them into conflict with the Russian party.[5] The Palestinians reached the conclusion that the building up of Palestine could not be left to the remorseless processes of history. Like the impatient young Rachel Yanait (later Ben-Zvi), who had asked Borochov, "And *when* is the inevitable stychic process going to start?" they had grown tired of rarefied theory. Contrary to Borochovism, which left all economic development to the capitalists, they founded cooperative settlements, and in contrast to the world Poale Zion movement, which published much of its literature and conducted meetings in Yiddish, the Palestinians also began the long, arduous process of transforming Hebrew into a living tongue. This, too, was outside Marxist doctrine. There had already been a great efflorescence in Hebrew literature in Russia in the late nineteenth century, but this was a far cry from natural daily use by Jewish farmers, city workers, and schoolchildren. To the torments of exhausting work in the fields and swamps, the new pioneers added the trial of learning and speaking Hebrew when it would have been so much more comfortable to lapse into Yiddish or Russian.

David Gryn had left Sejera in 1910 and gone to Jerusalem to become one of the editors of *Achdut (Unity)*, the Poale Zion periodical published in Hebrew. He had no more faith in journalism than he had in the Zionism of conference rooms and congresses. Rootedness in the land was the real meaning of Zionism. But he decided to become an editor out of his love of Hebrew and faith that the revived language would bind the nation together. The paper was to express what was unique in the movement: work on the land, based on the cooperative idea, self-defense, the revival of Hebrew. Four issues appeared in 1910, aided by funds from Poale Zion abroad. (It was during this time that Gryn changed his name to David Ben-Gurion.) Like others with the same zeal for the language, he suffered many bitter quarrels and setbacks. At the Poale Zion congress, about two months after the first publication of *Achdut*, Ben-Gurion gave a speech in Hebrew to the general consternation and anger of the delegates, most of whom spoke Yiddish. They left the room, but Ben-Gurion continued talking—to a virtually empty room. Only three delegates remained: Ben-Zvi, his brother, and the young Rachel Yanait who was on the staff of *Achdut*.

Other ideas of Ben-Gurion were conveyed with the same determined vigor. In the first article he wrote, he pointed out the great social and cultural gap between new immigrants and older residents and called for a reform of outdated social structures. He expressed this idea with great vehemence at the World Congress of Poale Zion in Vienna in 1911, to which he and Ben-Zvi were delegates. When the discussion shifted to consideration of the Workers' Bank that had been established in Palestine, Ben-Gurion declared: "It is not for the World Congress to decide on the Bank's policy, but the Jewish workmen in Palestine."

The Palestinian party also began to think and write about a socialist *Jewish* nation in Palestine, although none of its members thought this was likely in the near future. Feudalism in Turkey would have to be overcome and Jews abroad inspired to make *aliya*. Contacts with Bulgarian and Armenian workers' organizations in the Turkish empire had to be made. Practically, like Hapoel Hatzair, the movement had to deal with the "conquest of work" and the problem of defense—*hashomer*.

The older colonists used Arab or Circassian guards on their property; having never known the experience of Jewish policemen or guards, they never thought in terms of *Jewish* guards. But the Arabs and Circassians were not prepared to risk life and limb to defend Jewish property, and at times acquiesced in looting by nearby villagers or herdsmen. The colonists realized that Jewish guards would be more reliable, but strongly doubted that Jewish boys could handle guns, manage horses and stand up to defend themselves. Besides, there was great hostility between the old colonists and would-be-*shomrim*. Nevertheless, the issue of using mercenaries was faced at first not in the old colonies, but in the workers' settlement at Sejera in 1909. There were no overseers there, but the village was guarded by Circassians, who were considered hard, even cruel men. To arm Jews would provoke them as well as the Arabs and inevitably cause bloodshed. The villagers resisted the idea of arming Jews; the farm manager was especially dubious. But the young Ben-Gurion, who worked in Sejera at the time, was thoroughly aroused and led the fight for Jewish guards.[6]

He and Ben-Zvi had walked to Sejera from Petach Tikvah, where they had been repelled by the haughtiness of the overseers and the humiliation of the Jewish workers. "After Judea," Ben-Gurion wrote, "Sejera had almost the same effect on me as Petach Tikvah after exile. I had at last found the atmosphere of a real homeland. There were neither shopkeepers nor speculators, mercenaries nor parasites. All in the settlement were workers ... farm workers, peasants, smelling strongly of manure and the fields, with faces tanned by the sun." [7]

Sejera, which was to become the first colony to use *shomrim* (guards), was in the middle of the struggle between the old and new approaches to Jewish farming. ICA had started a farm training school at Sejera, but held to the old views. Those who finished their training were given small parcels of land and the necessary capital, to be repaid on easy terms. Thus, a new group of individualist Jewish farmers was created, once more under conditions that discouraged the employment of Jewish labor. Elsewhere, ICA had reorganized the colonies and put them on a more self-sustaining basis. New settlements were started in lower Galilee and more extensive plots were cultivated, but the results were not very impressive. Agricultural programs as well as economic conditions improved somewhat, but settlers still complained of the overbearing, bureaucratic overseers. The over-extended investment in vineyards (wine was often subsidized and sold at less than cost) gave way to cereal and citrus culture. There was even some experimentation, but over the whole enterprise loomed the anxiety to quickly establish an independent farmer class. A common experience of newcomers looking for work in these colonies was the complaint: "Look, I'm not a Zionist. I'm a farmer. I have nothing to do with national causes!" Or, "Madman! Why have you come here? Go back to Russia, or move to America!" As yet, a national purpose was sorely lacking.

One person who helped strengthen the will for cooperative colonies worked by Jewish farmers and changed the direction of Sejera was Manya Shochat, one of the stormiest and most colorful of the early revolution-aries.[8] Manya had been an activist in the Russian social revolutionary movement. Her brother Nachum Wilbushevich, a young engineer, had gone to Palestine in 1903, filled with dreams for the industrialization of the country. Manya was in Berlin at the time, part of a group planning the assassination of the hated Plehve. Worried about her dangerous involve-ment (several of her comrades were later caught by the police and shot), her brother persuaded her to come to Palestine by pretending that he had suffered a great misfortune. Soon after she arrived, she accompanied Nachum, who wanted to make a study of the country's resources, on a horseback tour of the country. With Mendel Chankin, the brother of Joshua, as their guide, they rode ten hours a day through the whole of Palestine, from Dan to Beersheba. The trip lasted six weeks, in the course of which Manya developed a "deep and passionate love for the country." In the spring of 1904, she learned of the commune in Rehovot and decided to gather statistics on all the Jewish colonies. For a year she sent out and collated questionnaires covering the economic side of colony life, particularly details of income and the employment of Arabs. When she was in Petach Tikvah and told the Jewish workers, who were getting 5 piasters (25 cents) a day, that they ought to demand houses and public buildings, they replied that this would be "philanthropy"—a renewal of the evil of *halukkah*.

Manya had already had some experience with a collective in Minsk. Her first encounter in Palestine was with an urban cooperative. Having learned carpentry in her brother's factory in Russia, she raised a loan to start a carpenter's cooperative in Jaffa and worked out procedures on the basis of the Russian artels. After three months, however, the cooperative fell apart over internal dissensions. But her zeal did not diminish.

In 1905, she went to Paris and urged the ICA to buy land in the Emek Jezreel for workers' colonization. She also spoke to French colonization experts, but what she had in mind "was not to be found anywhere." The experts considered agricultural collectivism "ridiculous." At the same time, she also raised money for Jewish self-defense against the pogroms in Russia, reentered Russia illegally, and worked with the Jewish resistance in Shedlitz. Toward the end of 1906 she returned to Palestine, but could not as yet find a way to organize collectivist colonies. Restless as ever, she went to the United States and South America, visiting cooperative experiments, and returned to Palestine in 1907, convinced that what was needed was a "substitute for the religious enthusiasm which had made these settlements possible"—namely, socialism.

Manya joined the group at Sejera, where she worked half time on the books and accounts, and the other half in the cow barn. She finally prevailed on ICA to give Jewish labor a chance to work on its own and wipe out the farm's deficit. Three other young women were admitted in time under Manya's prodding, and a collective of eighteen worked in the field and dairy, setting up their own division of labor and meeting regularly with the manager for lectures on agriculture. They agreed to turn over one-fifth of their total harvest in return for livestock and seed and a small sum of money. The "collective" had excellent relations with the other workers on the farm and organized a communal kitchen where all workers ate. After a year and a half, it paid the farm one-fifth of the harvest, returned in full the money that had been advanced, and demonstrated that a collective economy was possible for Jewish farmers in Palestine. Sejera for a few crucial years was the focal point for Jewish workers in Galilee. It was at Sejera that the first Jewish women workers were taken in, and the first attempt made to organize the Jewish land workers in Palestine through Ha-Horesh (the Ploughman). It was also at Sejera that an organization of Jewish guards was founded.

A Jewish nation had to be created in this country, Ben-Gurion argued, and it could not depend on the guns of mercenaries. The opposition was finally worn down and some rifles were bought near Haifa. Ben-Gurion and his friends then staged an attempted robbery to test the reaction of the Circassians. They did nothing to protect the village and were dismissed. An all-Jewish guard was then trained to guard Sejera. During Passover 1909, three Jewish workers were attacked by armed Arabs on their way from Haifa to Sejera. The Arabs were driven off, but one was wounded and later died. Armed Arab horsemen roamed the village, and a Jewish *shomer* named Israel Korngold was fatally shot. A Jewish carpenter named Shimon Melamed was also killed. "From that moment at Sejera," Ben-Gurion said later, "I felt that conflict was inevitable. What happened that day in my village was child's play compared with the dangers that the future had in store for us." [9] Ben-Zvi became a *shomer*, but Ben-Gurion was rejected for being too much of an "intellectual."

Ben-Zvi in fact had met with Israel Shochat and Alexander Zeid in Jaffa in 1907 and formed a secret society called Bar Giora, the fore-runner of *Ha-Shomer*. Their tiny group were mostly from Homel, where Jews had fought off the Black Hundreds in 1904. On the initiative of Ben Gurion, a broader organization called *Ha-Shomer* was created in April 1909 at Meschah. The group by then numbered twenty-six. Rigidly disciplined and functioning like an elitist new order, they accepted members only after long training and proof of complete reliability and loyalty.[10] Their standards were very high. To join, a man or woman had to have, besides the physical and moral qualifications, a strong commitment to a Jewish national renaissance.[11] Candidates were trained to shoot, ride horseback, and master military tactics; adventurers or dilettantes were rejected. As with all élites, the *shomrim* dramatized themselves with creative rituals and a touch of mystery and secretiveness. A new member could be accepted by a two-thirds vote of the entire group, but punishment, including expulsion, could be voted by a simple majority. The *shomrim* had a very serious view of their mission and a strict code of conduct, especially in their relations with Arabs. They believed that whatever could be achieved by patience and friendliness should not admit force. Self-defense was to be coupled with self-restraint (*havlagah*), not revenge—a guiding principle of the Yishuv (Jewish community) in later years.[12] There are many accounts of demands for vengeance—a life for a life—made by the families of murdered *shomrim*, but the stern response was that once begun, a vendetta perpetuates an endless cycle.

Gradually, the privately operated colonies—at Meschah (Kfar Tabor) Rehovot, Bet Gan, Bet Shemen—were compelled to ask for *shomrim*, to turn to them when Arab or Circassian guards proved unreliable. The *shomrim* always drove a hard bargain, but not with respect to "pay" (generally they received all their pay in kind), or even conditions of service. They demanded that Jewish workers be given employment in the colonies and that their organization be recognized as the sole body functioning in the defense of the colonies. Gradually, they won the respect of both colonists and Arabs and took on the character of a general militia. Often changing his post a dozen times a year, the *shomer* had to remain footloose, ready for duty in any place.[13]

One of the chief triumphs of the *shomrim* was taking over the protection of the large settlement of Rehovot, where conditions had become intolerable. The guards were lazy and dishonest and poaching on Jewish land was commonplace. When the *shomrim* came, they first cut the number of guards in half and then set about showing the local Arabs that a new regime had begun and that the lawless old days were over.

At first, Hapoel Hatzair refused to participate in the formation of the *shomrim* because of its pacifist orientation and Gordon's influence. Later, however, its attitude changed and Hapoel Hatzair became involved in the *shomrim* program.

In December 1912, Shochat drew up a document that is the most explicit, firsthand statement of the time concerning the aims, problems, complaints and demands of *Ha-Shomer*. Its function had not been limited to training a small group of young Jews to guard the settlements, Shochat declared, but "to inculcate in the farmers and workers the feeling . . . that they, and only they, can defend themselves and their property." The Turkish government and the Arabs have become accustomed to the *shomrim* and are no longer suspicious. He deplores the meagerness of the movement and the lack of official Jewish interest in security needs and then modestly describes *Ha-Shomer*'s achievements. With rare insight, he foresees the need for flexible mobilization of the whole Jewish work force: "Our ideal is that in time of danger all the farmers and workers who are able to bear arms will participate actively in defense. . . . In each and every settlement a local defense association must be organized which will include all able-bodied and eligible farmers and workers, in order to prepare and train them. . . . Our goal is not an ephemeral one, born at a moment of crisis, it is rather a great historical goal, the value of which is timeless." [14]

Meanwhile, other workers' groups sprouted between 1908 and 1909, going their separate, nonpolitical ways: Ha-Horesh aimed at creating physically and mentally strong farmers in cereal production, who would supply basic foodstuffs; Ha-Avoda had a common fund for the earnings of its members and functioned on communist economic principles. Later, there were several hundred workers of Yemenite origin who stayed out of the violent and often incomprehensible quarrels of the Jews from Europe. Eventually, however, partisan quarrels had to fade before the harsh realities of life in Palestine. The conjunction of several factors—the persistence of young Jews who wanted to control their farms as well as work them, the imagination and faith of Arthur Ruppin, and some accidents—set colonization efforts on a collective path and led to the creation of an autonomous workers' economy which forms the most strikingly original aspect of modern Israel and interesting models of non-Marxist socialism.

The sporadic, uncertain settlement activities in Sejera and Kinneret—and later at Merchavia—actually marked the beginning of the *kvutza* (commune), which has become the single most significant feature of the Jewish labor movement in Palestine. The communal idea, of course, had had a long and checkered history. It was generally scorned by "scientific socialists," although the *narodnik* tradition of sharing among comrades and selfless commitment to the cause still influenced the new immigrants. In the official Zionist movement, the practical possibilities of cooperative settlement were first broached by the well-known Jewish economist and sociologist Franz Oppenheimer, who published a comprehensive work in 1896 on the problem of producers' cooperatives. Oppenheimer believed that from the earliest times to the development of capitalism, the accumulation of wealth and power, and hence the gross inequality among men, originated in social conflict. The central evil has been the monopolization of land, which forces the rural population into urban areas. If this process could be replaced by agrarian cooperatives, independent farmers would emerge and a "liberal socialism" would be established.

Oppenheimer's interest in Zionism and Jewish affairs began in 1902, when he was introduced to Herzl. The following year, when El Arish was being considered for Jewish settlement, Herzl proposed to Oppenheimer that he work on the creation of a model cooperative colony. Herzl's own ideas in his utopian novel *Altneuland* (Old-New Land) come very close to those of Oppenheimer, with whom he had been in frequent contact before he finished the novel. The economic order in *Altneuland* is described as "mutualistic"—a cooperative order midway between individualism and collectivism. Oppenheimer was invited to present his ideas at the Sixth (1903) and Ninth (1909) Zionist congresses.

Meanwhile, the *halutzim* were struggling to win support for the Sejera idea. At the World Conference of Poale Zion in Cracow in 1909, the delegates from Palestine were dismayed by the distance between the delegates from The Land and those from the Galut. Rachel Yanait, who was to lecture on "The Agricultural Laborer in Palestine," was mocked when she reported that there were only 500 workers in all the villages. "How dare you compare *Galut* workers with our *haverim* in the villages?" she shouted. "They are working hard to create a new life, and if conditions are difficult and their numbers are few—you all are to blame!" [15] After much debate, it was agreed to raise the question of cooperative settlement at the forthcoming Zionist Congress.

Here, too, the Palestinians felt estranged by the speeches that proclaimed the "ultimate aims of Zionism" but had no actual contact with the land. Rachel Yanait spoke sharply in Yiddish: "It is so hard to speak here about the Jewish workers in Eretz Israel. They have not even been mentioned in the addresses of the . . . Executive. And yet they constitute the most important subject the Congress can discuss. They represent . . . the most vital interests of the whole Jewish people. They are the laborers . . . the guards . . . the defenders. To bring Jewish workers in large numbers, the Jewish National Fund must establish cooperative settlements. . . . If the delegates think that such practical work in Eretz Israel is unrealistic—then there is no need for a Congress!" [16]

This congress, after a long debate, established a settlement company and special fund for a cooperative project, and the Jewish National Fund bought 3,500 dunams of land at Merchavia for this purpose. This decision was influenced by the serious crisis in Jewish agriculture in Palestine. The private colonies were producing much more wine than they could sell. The situation in the grain-growing colonies of Galilee was no better, while the results of farming were so meager that settlers had to try to find other sources of income. Arab farmers were also suffering. The only farmers who seemed at all prosperous were those in the two German colonies near Jaffa, which concentrated on dairy products.

The decision of the Ninth Congress was a great concession to the "practical" Zionists, members of Poale Zion, and Jewish workers in Palestine, who were united in their opposition to the "commercial" approach to settlement activities. This congress met a year after the revolution of the Young Turks in an atmosphere of hope that the new Turkish government would remove its restrictions on immigration and land purchase. The shift toward settlement had been foreshadowed at the Eighth Congress in 1907, when the "practical" Zionists came to the fore. They insisted that settlement activity in Palestine not be delayed until after the granting of a charter. It was at this congress that Weizmann made his famous speech on "synthetic Zionism," merging political with practical activity. "We must aspire to a charter," he said, "but our aspiration will be realized only as a result of our practical work in Eretz Israel." In keeping with this new approach, the Palestine Office was founded in 1908 to direct the work of agricultural settlement for the World Zionist Organization. A young German Jew named Arthur Ruppin was appointed to head it, and his own rather remarkable experiences as a young man gave the socialist Zionist movement an unheralded ally.

Ruppin [17] grew up in Magdeburg where his family, once comfortable, lived in great poverty, either supported by relatives or barely eking out a living selling in stalls or peddling. Four of the children died from undernourishment. When Arthur was fifteen, he became an apprentice to wholesale grain merchants for three years. By the time he was nineteen, he was head clerk and traveled to see important customers. He gave virtually his whole salary to his family, but it scarcely covered their needs. Not until he became managing clerk, when he was twenty, did the family actually have enough to eat. Ruppin had left grammar school in order to go to work, but did brilliantly in matriculation examinations at a *gymnasium* and developed a passion for all forms of learning. He saved enough for further studies and went to the University of Berlin, reading avidly and finally obtaining a doctorate in political economy in the Faculty of Law. While serving in various legal and judicial capacities, he dealt unflinchingly with a steady stream of anti-Semitism, even to the point of a pistol duel to protect his integrity as a Jew.

In 1904, Ruppin went to Berlin to manage the Association for Statistics of the Jews and edit its *Journal for Demography and Statistics of the Jews*. Although his closeness to Jewish religious tradition had diminished, Ruppin had a strong intuition "that anti-Semitism would one day make it impossible for me to remain in Germany." Many youthful diary entries comment on widespread anti-Semitism in Germany. Some are chillingly prophetic. On February 25, 1893, he noted that "Anti-Semitism is growing by leaps and bounds," that "Jews may one day be *thrown* out of Germany." [18] On March 22, 1897, he wrote: "There are imponderable aspects of the German national character of which we Jews, with our sophistry, are unaware, or at least we are quite incapable of understanding them." [19] He had heard of Jewish national and Zionist aspirations for the first time while he was still a business apprentice. As his interest mounted, he attended meetings and lectures and corresponded with a Russian Zionist, Sarah Rabinowitz,[20] who had written a doctoral thesis on the Russian Jewish working class. The sufferings of Russian Jews under tsarism pained him, as did the Dreyfus Affair in France.

One evening in December 1898, while he was reading, he was suddenly seized by a desire to write on a massive theme: "The Jews in the Past, the Present and the Future." While the project buzzed in his mind, he came across a book of statistics on contemporary Prussian Jews and found it so absorbing that he wrote an article on the social conditions of Jews in Prussia—probably the first article on Jews to employ statistics and appear in a general scientific publication. He discarded his materialistic view of history and decided to use the article as the basis for a book. Realizing that he had no personal knowledge of Jewish life in Eastern Europe, he decided to fill this gap by traveling to Galicia. He was given a month's leave of absence by the court in which he worked and left for Vienna on May 9, 1903, admitting in his diary that, "from a practical point of view, the journey is, after all, a rather aimless adventure, but a sort of psychological need drove me to it." [21] He was also curious to meet Sarah Rabinowitz, who was traveling in Galicia on behalf of some Jewish society.

Ruppin saw Jews in the small towns of Galicia in all their poverty and strangeness. He asked searching questions of Jewish workers and sought out wonder-working *rebbes*, who were besieged by Jews from far, straining to touch them and hear their words. Ruppin was struck by the prevalence of arranged marriages between children, refuse in the streets, and the crowding of little alleyways with large numbers of children. New aspects of Jewish experience were revealed. In Galicia, " 'being Jewish' did not mean loosely belonging to a 'confession,' as it did in Germany, but being firmly related to a certain ethnic and cultural group." He also saw the "differences between the upper classes, tending toward assimilation, and the masses, who were still firmly rooted in tradition." These impressions were strengthened by visits to Jewish sections in Amsterdam, London, and Liverpool. The result was not only a slow change within Ruppin himself, but a new kind of work on Jewish life: *Die Juden der Gegenwart* (The Jews of Today).

Ruppin's work was published in the spring of 1904 and marked a departure in the literature on the Jewish question. There are no apologetics, no special pleading, only a marshaling of information, independently observed and objectively presented. This statistical basis transformed the sociological treatment of Jewish life in all later studies. At the time, Ruppin was still ambivalent about Zionism, but had already concluded that the diplomatic Zionism of Herzl was "hopeless and unrealistic." However, the fate of the Jewish people was close to his heart, and in his systematic survey of Jewish life, he was obviously concerned about rescuing and preserving the "Jewish nation."

The Jewish problem and its solution thereafter became Ruppin's own problem and preoccupation. He never freed or divorced himself from it, and all of his later works were variations of the first. A transfer to Berlin brought him into the circle of "practical" Zionists, who demanded immediate Jewish settlement in Palestine, and transformed the whole course of his life. The advent of Ruppin also revolutionized the course of Jewish settlement in Palestine.

Besides his duties in the court in Berlin, Ruppin directed the Association for Jewish Statistics and wrote most of the articles for its journal. In Berlin he also met the youthful Jacob Thon from Lemberg, who became his lifetime friend and collaborator. It was Thon who was largely responsible for Ruppin's decision in 1907 to make a journey to Palestine in order to study conditions there.[22] Ruppin had officially joined the Zionist movement in March 1905, when he paid his *shekel,* and that summer he attended his first (the Seventh) Zionist Congress. He was very critical of the party politics and of some "vain and empty-headed" delegates, but he wanted to see the start of actual settlement and therefore bore the sessions stoically. "I see no opportunity here in Germany," he noted in his diary, "which would allow one to be of active assistance in the matter. But, if I could go to Palestine, it might be possible to do something there." [23] He was already thinking in terms of training Jewish farmers in Europe as a prerequisite for systematic settlement in Palestine.

At the time, Thon was secretary to Professor Otto Warburg, a renowned botanist and member of the Zionist Inner Actions Committee. Through Thon, Ruppin became acquainted with Warburg, who encouraged his interest in going to Palestine. Early in 1907, Warburg and David Wolffsohn, the president of the movement after Herzl's death, asked him to undertake a mission for the Zionist movement and report on economic conditions there. Ruppin's decision to go to Palestine at this juncture in his life seemed reckless and quixotic. He had just passed his final law examinations, had gained a doctorate in political economy, and was a published author. A brilliant career lay ahead in Germany, but this prospect did not interest him as much as the possibilities of Jewish settlement in Palestine. Besides, he had the feeling that no matter how much he would achieve, he "would encounter hostility and be regarded as an outsider." [24]

One of the first things he tried to do after his arrival in Jerusalem was to visit all of the Jewish institutions and undertake a census of the Jewish population in the city—probably the first since the days of Emperor Augustus. He enlisted the help of some students and divided the city into twenty-four districts, assigning several to each student. Some were soon arrested; others were told they needed the sultan's permission. Ruppin then went up and down the country, visiting settlements and sweating out an attack of typhoid fever in a "hospital" that lacked running water and was filled with the night noises of numerous cats. He also was slowly evolving a personal decision to settle permanently in Palestine. "I had got to know the country, and the people," he wrote in his diary, "and although I found many faults, it seemed to me that there was a possibility of large scale settlement." [25] During his visits to the colonies, he was particularly struck by the fact that Jewish farm workers were not trained for farming and that most Jewish colonies relied entirely on a single product, resulting in seasonal work and likely failure of the colony. These colonies, he believed, must turn to mixed farming—that is, grain growing in addition to cultivation of oranges, almonds and grapes—so that Jewish workers would have year-round work.[26]

Ruppin returned home after five months and told Wolffsohn and Warburg that he planned to emigrate. This decision meant a rupture in his family life, but it was outweighed by duty and conscience and the call of an important task. Warburg and Wolffsohn asked him to head the newly founded Palestine Office of the Zionist organization, and in December 1907 his proposal for the creation of a financial instrument that would be legally responsible for land purchase and settlement was accepted by the Zionist Actions Committee, though not enthusiastically.[27] The agency was called the Palestine Land Development Company (PLDC), with a share capital of only 10,000 pounds (about $50,000), but Ruppin was determined to reduce or liquidate the *halukkah* system, establish new settlements, increase landholdings, and consolidate those already existing. A systematic colonization effort by Jews (Ruppin later called it "preparation for colonization") was now to begin in Palestine under the hand of this modest, unspectacular man of astonishing foresight, initiative, integrity. Like so many others, Weizmann, who had met him in Haifa in 1907, was taken aback by Ruppin's correct, reserved, almost Prussian manner, but soon came to admire his judgment, ability, and "passionate attachment to his people." [28]

Ruppin himself soon became familiar with the hardships confronting the young pioneers, as described in his report to the Eighth Congress (1907):

> It was customary in the old colonies to let most of the work be done by paid Arab laborers. These conditions were fatal to the young Jewish workers who had been immigrating in small numbers. They could not compete with the Arab laborers because they were inferior to them in agricultural knowledge and staying power, because they suffered much more from the climate and diseases

of the country, and because they could not descend to the primitive level of the Arab peasant.[29]

The struggle of Jewish laborers against this system of plantation-colonies began very early. Since there was no agency to help them, some of the young workers decided to try to solve the problems they shared. Hapoel Hatzair created a committee to contract all available jobs and distribute them among the members, newcomers and oldtimers alike; other committees were set up to receive new arrivals, find housing for them, promote cooperative kitchens and housing, and set up an unemployment-sick fund.[30] But their vision far outstripped existing opportunities and facilities. Available land to work was one of the most serious gaps, and the struggle against the colony system seemed foredoomed. Rothschild, however, was loosening his grip. In 1899, he had transferred the direction of his Palestinian enterprises to the Jewish Colonization Association (ICA). He was still a long way from accepting Zionism, but he was already aware of the inadequacy of his private philanthropy. Moreover, he was in poor health. By turning over his colonies to a quasi-public body, he relaxed to some extent his personal pressure on administrators and farmers for quick independence for individual farmers.

Until Ruppin's coming, the Jewish National Fund, which had been founded a few years earlier for the purchase of land as the inalienable property of the Jewish people, "was little more than a charity-box collection," [31] collecting less than a quarter of a million dollars in six years. Moreover, it had not provided for the settlement of the land purchased. Between 1905 and 1907, it had acquired plots rather haphazardly near Tiberias, Lydda, and along the Jerusalem-Jaffa railway, called Hittin, Dalaikah, and Um Juni (today Kinneret and Degania), Beit Arif (Ben Shemen), and Huldah.[32] It was up to Ruppin to find some use for these areas and to safeguard them against *mahlul*—expropriation of the land by the Turkish government if the land had not been worked for three years. But this was far from easy. The Hittin area of 2,000 dunams (500 acres) consisting of several hundred separate large and small lots, had no water and was totally unsuitable for any sort of settlement, at least for the time being.[33]

The second area in Dalaikah and Um Juni consisted of 6,000 dunams and had the advantage of being all in one piece and possessing an ample water supply, but Ruppin had grave doubts about using his limited funds for establishing a settlement there. He mentioned these doubts to an agronomist M. Bermann, who had once been an agricultural inspector in Russia. Bermann worked out an estimate of probable income and expenditures—even food for a watchdog—showing the farm making a profit of 11 percent during its first complete year. Ruppin was skeptical, but had the calculations checked and confirmed by several other agricultural experts. In 1908, Bermann was engaged as manager and was authorized to establish a farm at Kinneret for Jewish workers, with all the necessary building and stock. This was the first Zionist farm. It attracted about thirty Jewish workers and soon evolved into the prototype of all *kvutzot* in Palestine.

Small, modest experiments in communal living and sharing expenses were also being carried on in *moshavot* (villages) in Judea. There was, for example, a *kommuna* in Rehovot, revolving around the Hankin family, made up of immigrants from Homel, Russia.[34] Though the members of this group worked in various places, they turned their earnings over to a common treasury, which was used for their joint maintenance. The Hankin family eventually moved to Petach Tikvah, and the others to Galilee, where they again organized a short-lived commune.

Another small group from Romni, in the Ukraine, is of greater historical significance. Four young people from Romni were joined by several others on the boat bound for Palestine in December 1907. A *kommuna* of stonecutters in Jerusalem had refused to accept them, so they went to Petach Tikvah. There was considerable unemployment during their first five months, which overlapped the rainy season, but the members were considered competent workers and able to compete with Arab workers. They suffered less than individual workers because they had joint living and eating arrangements and enjoyed generous credit.[35] Their house became a center for nearby Jewish workers, containing one large room, with a table and long benches in the center, and beds, made of planks on kerosene cans, lining the walls. Miriam Baratz, one of the founders of Degania Aleph, who was working as a hired worker in a nearby citrus grove, visited the group frequently and volunteered to serve as housekeeper during her spare time, but the group considered this "unreasonable exploitation."

At the time, at nearby Ben Shemen, a forest of olive trees was being planted by the Jewish National Fund as a memorial to Herzl. Much to the resentment of Jewish workers, the supervisor (Bermann) employed Arabs for the work. The Romni group reacted vigorously. They uprooted the saplings and planted them again—without any charge—as a protest. This episode created something of a scandal, but a reconciliation with Bermann followed and the group went to the training farm at Kinneret.

Ruppin's plans for national land settlement envisioned an apprenticeship of three years under a qualified expert, followed by a division of the national farm into small holdings to be owned and worked by qualified trainees. Work at Kinneret began in the spring of 1908. Each worker received 5 Swiss francs per month, plus food. (The Romni group pooled their earnings.) At first, their enthusiasm overcame all difficulties—malaria, the harsh work, and Bermann's arbitrary style. But they soon found fault with his management of the farm (the first year closed with a large deficit) and bitterly resented his high-handed dismissal of their opinions. Accustomed to the Russian model of obedience of the workers and the wide social gulf between manager and workers, Bermann remained rigid and friction intensified. Ruppin visited several times to try to reconcile differences, but the trip from Jaffa took almost a week and could only be made every few months.[36] In December 1909, the Romni group left after a strike which climaxed conflicts with Bermann.

In 1910, the surviving workers struck again over conditions that caused the deaths of a sixteen-year-old girl and an older man. The workers had demanded that a sickroom be built and that a surgeon's assistant be employed at Kinneret, but Bermann refused. As the man lay on his deathbed in a hospital in Tiberias, the workers asked for transport and time to visit him. Even though the weather was rainy and work was at a standstill, Bermann refused. The workers went anyhow and found the man already dead. Bermann was dismissed, but so were the workers for taking strike action on a national (JNF) farm.[37]

Kinneret was technically a failure, but it illuminated the problems of an outside manager and new approaches to colonization. A few years later, Ruppin assessed his "error":

> But if I had not made this error with regard to [its] paying possibilities . . . at the beginning, I would probably not have had the courage to found the farm; and then the shore of Tiberias would have remained waste and empty till now. . . . If the Kinneret farm had not shown . . . the way, neither Degania, our finest Palestinian farm, nor the girls' training farm of Kinneret, nor the purchase of Merchavia, would have followed. If there is in Lower Galilee today a freshness of life which distinguishes it from Upper Galilee, much of the credit must be assigned to Kinneret. . . . I hope that long after the deficit of the first years of operation will have been forgotten . . . Kinneret will be remembered and appreciated as the first step toward the revitalization of our stagnating colonization work.[38]

Ruppin also became involved in difficulties at Ben Shemen, where an agricultural school had been started for orphans of the Kishinev pogrom. By 1909, the school had to be closed for lack of funds, but there remained the problem of the buildings and 2,000 dunams of land belonging to the JNF. Yitzhak Wilkansky, who had completed a course in agriculture at the University of Königsberg but lacked practical experience, was put in charge by Ruppin. Wilkansky introduced mixed farming, experimenting with new fodder crops, importing milk cows, and combining milk production with poultry.[39] It was difficult to establish such a farm successfully with Jewish workers, for nearby was the German Templars' settlement, Wilhelmina, which used cheap Arab labor. The experiences at Kinneret and Ben Shemen convinced Ruppin that the establishment of Jewish farm settlements was going to be an uphill struggle. "That I did not despair," he wrote, "but . . . stubbornly persisted with the work . . . was entirely due to the enthusiasm and the devotion of the Jewish workers, which continued to carry me along."[40]

On the occasion of the first strike in Kinneret in 1909, Ruppin had long discussions with the workers (among whom was the young Berl Katzenelson, later an important labor leader and editor of *Davar*). They complained repeatedly about the intolerable burden of the manager's bourgeois standard of living, in contrast with the miserable condition of the workers. Referring to an experiment being tried by the ICA at Sejera, they suggested that the manager be eliminated and responsibility for the farm be placed in the hands of a committee they themselves would choose.[41] Ruppin was very much impressed by their seriousness and sense of responsibility. Handing over the whole farm seemed too risky, but he agreed to let six specially chosen experienced workers manage independently, in a sort of joint tenancy, the area of Um Juni on the opposite side of the Jordan. They were allotted 1,600 dunams to cultivate in the first year. Two of the six were selected as managers and a brief contract—in German—was drawn up. In the autumn of 1909, the six workers and a woman, Shifrah Sturman, who joined them (members of Hapoel Hatzair and Poale Zion and one member of the Romni *kommuna*) settled in Um Juni, which they later called Degania.[42]

The select seven accepted responsibility for one year. Their monthly wage was 50 francs from the Palestine Office. At first the group lived in miserable conditions in a barrack and mud huts left there by the former Arab owners. Without neighbors, perpetually thrown on each other's company, they began experimenting with a democratic and cooperative way of life. The results were astonishing. At the end of the year, in spite of the group's inexperience and illness, the farm showed a surplus.

Ruppin did not fully realize the importance of this undertaking at the time, but he had a hunch that "major consequences might follow from this minor beginning," and wrote about it to the Palestine Land Development Company in Berlin on December 10, 1909. "The farm," he said, "will remain our property. . . . [but] we have granted the workers a great deal of independence and a stake in the farm through arranging to pay them a high percentage of the profits and through appointing the manager responsible for the enterprise from among the workers, according to their own suggestion." [43] In keeping with the wishes of the group, Ruppin urged the PLDC not to draw public attention yet "to this first modest experiment of a cooperative settlement in Palestine."

It then became necessary to replace the occupational group with a settled group; Ruppin appealed to the Romni *kommuna*, then in Hadera, a primitive place shared with several Arabs where Mrs. Baratz had helped the group find housing. Individual members had had to find work on nearby farms, and their struggle against malaria was unceasing. But a vision of a new kind of society animated them:

> We said this is the way the society in Israel will be built. This was not a theoretical approach. We had not yet read about *kommunas* in action. We had no examples as yet in Israel, though in the town *kvutzot* were founded and then

split up. I remember that this approach emanated out of love of the country, love of work and a desire to create something more just and more social. This aspiration and belief in the future helped us overcome the difficult working conditions . . . unlimited hours, no running water in the house.[44]

Meanwhile, Ruppin sent word to Yisrael Bloch, one of the founding members of the Romni group, asking that it settle permanently on the Um Juni land. Fascinated by the proposal, the group debated it heatedly. Yosef Bussel, its gifted leader who became the farm manager, suggested that they settle down and develop a particular site, and not move on from place to place preparing the land for others. Developing an area permanently, he said, was also a "conquest of labor." [45] Some of his comrades were horrified—to settle was not pioneering; it meant becoming owners, a hated class. Some remembered their conflict with Bermann with great bitterness; others were drawn to Merchavia, which was ready for settlement. At first the group rejected the offer but later Bussel's arguments prevailed. Everyone would continue working as before and the land would be owned by the whole group. Arab labor, of course, was forbidden. Mrs. Baratz, who joined them, recalled:

[We] started on a tour of the moshavot in Judea and on the day after Sukkot we moved to Um Juni, greeted cordially by every community we passed. Everybody felt that something important was being formed somewhere on the other side of the Jordan. We were the emissaries for the labor sector of that period, though it was not clear what would be the form of the group which was being settled permanently.[46]

On October 28, 1910, ten men and two women took over the inventory from the occupation group at Um Juni. Six men worked with draft animals; two were on guard duty; one became manager; one was in reserve for any eventuality.[47] The two women were housekeepers, at first not doing any work in the fields. Besides food, housing, and laundry, the members received the equivalent of $2.50 per month. The fatigue and bouts of malaria were temporarily relieved by frenetic dancing and fervor. "We were intoxicated with labor," Shmuel Dayan wrote, recalling the first days of Degania:

Labor filled every recess of our souls. The whole long day—from two hours before dawn to two hours after dark—had no other content for us. We had cast out the earth and the fullness thereof from our hearts. . . . We confined ourselves within the framework of a life of labor . . . and focussed our gaze upon one point so that we might see it truly. . . . Only in this way, we thought, could we achieve self-conquest.

. . . During the hours of the long day we gradually worked off our pent-up, turbulent energies . . . [and] the farm implements became like playing balls in our hands. We worked with peculiar ease, as if engaged in games or sport. Sometimes, even after the long day's work . . . we would ride our mad kicking she-mules, or work on the threshing floor. We would pile up heaps of grain in preparation for the threshing sledge. Heavy sheaves of wheat would fly about the place, or be thrown many meters into the air, like feathers. We looked upon the pitchfork as a light, precious, pleasure-giving instrument. There were times when we had no desire to leave off work, and then we would continue for hours by the light of the moon. This often happened when favorite tasks like winnowing had to be performed . . .

Sometimes . . . one man would burst out singing. A second promptly took up the melody, and soon all were singing. About us stood the sheaves, in tens, hundreds, thousands. . . . A man would fall upon a heap of straw or corn, and his comrades would come after, falling one on top of the other. And the air was filled with laughter.[48]

The group was fiery in its commitment to all-Jewish labor and threatened to destroy anything built by non-Jewish labor. Arabs did indeed prepare the foundations but the members insisted on preparing their own. Supplementary wage labor, though Jewish, also created a dilemma. Would the members become employers and managers? Bussel assured them that the workers would be treated as members with equal rights and obligations. Members also thrashed out the problem of women workers. Bussel, especially, wanted to change the pattern of the economy so that female workers would be freed from the narrow confines of housework. A pattern of mixed farming helped to overcome this problem.[49]

Degania Aleph passed through spiritual, social, and economic crises [50]— as have all other *kvutzot*. Meetings were frequently punctuated with self-criticism, self-doubts, conflicts between individual and social impulses, anxiety about the departure of oldtimers, deficits, and the arrival of newcomers who were not attuned to the *kvutzah* philosophy. Every member was paid 50 francs a month from the Palestine Office. Some members paid the whole amount into a common fund, others kept some back for clothes and shoes. Shmuel Dayan's suggestion that no one should marry during the first five years was not taken seriously, but the birth of the first child caused intense discussions over details of child care and housing. Bussel pressed for the principle of communal care of the children at the expense of the whole group, in order to free the mother for other kinds of work and expose the child to a cooperative way of life. This question was discussed for several years, and although Bussel's views were adopted in August 1915, several more years passed before they could be implemented. There was inevitable bickering and gossip as well as the straining after noble ideals, arguments over the economy, efforts to brace depressed spirits, impairment of the early intimacy and mutual trust, fear that a managerial regime would become necessary as the *kvutzah* expanded. For a number of years, there was a magic belief in a small commune of only twelve. Yet in spite of the ebb and flow of mood and energy, the deficits, and the changing composition of Degania, the story of the experiment excited many Jews and gave socialist Zionism a new dimension.

Moreover, as the years passed and the success of the first communal settlements spread, a *kvutzah* ideology developed: The commune (generally consisting of twelve to fifteen members until after 1919, when, with the arrival of many new immigrants, the idea of a large *kvutzah* began to spread) was not just the way to reach a certain end, but was an end in itself. It was a microcosm of the future, a preview of a more humane, progressive, and socially enlightened society. Some, of course, simply regarded it as the most rational form of agricultural settlement which should be expanded. But there was also growing awareness that it was significant not only in the framework of Palestine, but that it constituted a specifically Jewish socialist contribution in the search for a new society.[51]

Degania became a prototype for later *kvutzot* in Jewish Palestine and a fundamental force in socialist Zionism. Much hung on the outcome of the experiment. Of the 20,000 new settlers in the country when Ruppin arrived, only about 1,000 families were engaged in agriculture, and their circumstances were very unsatisfactory.[52] It was important to expand this small beginning as quickly as possible if the experiment was to be taken seriously. Ruppin himself kept a steadfast faith in the settlers, but he was badly handicapped by lack of funds and the doubts of JNF directors, even including Oppenheimer.

Ruppin believed that the cooperative at Degania was a realization of Oppenheimer's own proposals, but Oppenheimer demurred, saying his plans called for joint ownership of a large-scale enterprise, the employment of an expert manager, and a scale of payment to workers based on their output. To these ideas, the Degania group objected. They distrusted outside managers and felt that any differential in wages would destroy the comradeship on which the success of the farm depended.[53] But when Degania was not financially successful in its second stage, exceeding its budget by 40 percent, Oppenheimer argued that a capitalist bank could not accept responsibility for the debts of an enterprise over which it had not the slightest influence.[54]

Ruppin, nevertheless, though plagued by a lack of money, did not lose faith in the *kvutzot* idea. For a time he tried to raise private capital for agricultural as well as urban settlements and published two pamphlets in 1909: *Land Purchase in Palestine* and *Establishing Plantations in Palestine*. But the main thrust of his work was to establish Zionist settlements modeled after Degania.[55] The experience at Merchavia in Emek Jezreel strengthened his resolve.

The acquisition of the Emek Jezreel—the largest fertile plain of Palestine—for colonization had been the object of Jewish efforts for many years.[56] Following the pogroms and expulsions of Jews in Russia in 1890–91, Hankin had reached an agreement with wealthy Arab *effendi* for the purchase of 160,000 dunams. But before the agreement could be consummated, the Turkish government prohibited Jewish immigration entirely and the whole project dissolved. Two decades passed before another attempt was made.

In 1910, Hankin resumed his negotiations, this time for 9,500 dunams in Fuleh, later Merchavia, in the Emek. Part was purchased by the ICA, part by the Palestine Land Development Company, and 3,500 dunams by the JNF for the cooperative colonies. Even so, some Turkish officials refused to authorize the sale. The governor in Nazareth fought the purchase against the orders of his superior, the district governor in Akko. An appeal was then made to the governor general in Beirut, where Hankin and Ruppin cooled their heels for two weeks. Finally, approval was given by authorities in Constantinople.[57]

The 3,500 dunams in Merchavia were set aside by the JNF for cooperative colonies as Oppenheimer understood the concept. He believed that, in agriculture, it was necessary to combine the immense technical advantages of a large-scale operation with the involvement of worker-comrades bound together in a cooperative plan, caring for stock and equipment, and eventually becoming co-owners.[58] While Merchavia was being prepared for settlement, it was under the direction of an agronomist administrator, S. Dick, who planned it as a large collective, taking in a thousand workers at a time, but also allowing for settlement by individuals. The large collective was to own a mill, bakery, and varied workshops in common with the individual settlers. Great difficulties soon developed. There was friction between the workers and Dick, made all the sharper because the workers did not constitute a homogeneous group, but had been drawn from all parts of Europe. Moreover, because the planting of large areas of summer fruit, which required a large labor force, proved expensive, Dick gave orders to employ cheap Arab labor.[59] The Jewish workers balked and a workers' co-administration with limited rights was conceded. Dick treated them as apprentices, and resentment grew. Eventually compromises were worked out, but the workers refused to hire seasonal Arab labor.

Oppenheimer had forecast the failure of Degania on the ground that it lacked the prerequisite training period, the expert guidance and incentive which his managed farm at Merchavia provided, but whereas Degania yielded a profit during the first year and for several years thereafter, the Merchavia farm showed a loss. Degania's balanced budget seemed to prove that the difficulties resulting from shortages of food and raw materials, from epidemics, raids, and military exactions were better met by the *kvutzah*, a closely knit group propelled by a sense of shared values and a common goal. In Merchavia, these hardships aggravated the chronic friction between the workers and the manager, while the wage differentials, which often netted a higher income to the bachelor than to the head of a family, were an added source of internal discord.

During the war, the outside administration system was given up in Merchavia and the workers elected their own manager. Ruppin later called the *kvutzah* "the cradle of the Jewish agricultural working class in Palestine." It did not emerge as a deliberate social experiment or the specific aim of the three Zionist funds (JNF, the Palestine Land

Development Company, and the Olive Tree Fund). Colonization, in general, was not the function of any of these institutions, and the founding of the first Zionist farms in Kinneret, Degania, and Merchavia, grew out of improvised arrangements and the pressure from Jewish workers who opposed Arab labor and saw in the Zionist farms their only hope of living with their principles and obtaining agricultural training.

Within a few years, similar experiments were carried out on the JNF land at Huldah and Ben Shemen, and although by 1914 hundreds of Jewish workers were employed on Zionist farms, thousands were still waiting. Ruppin decided on several new measures: He determined to make it cheaper for the Jewish workers to live and thus compete with Arab labor by building large hostels for unmarried workers with communal kitchens in Petach Tikvah and Hadera.[60] JNF supplied the funds. Small houses with one dunam of land for married workers were also built, providing cheap accommodations and a plot for home gardens at Petach Tikvah, Hadera, and Rishon le-Zion. Ruppin also made a special effort to attract Yemenite Jews, who were used to a hot climate and a relatively low standard of living, to the Zionist farms.

These ideas were moderately successful, and by the Eleventh Zionist Congress in 1913, Ruppin was able to report that the number of Jewish farm workers had risen to more than 1,000—not a large figure in itself, but a growing and dynamic force that was beginning to influence other Jews. For example, Ruppin told the congress about the effect of these new workers on the twenty-year land the JNF had bought in the old colony of Kastinieh, which was failing. Ruppin wanted to sell off parcels of land to buyers but few came, so eight Jewish workers were sent to work the land. Within six months, more buyers were available and Ruppin wanted to withdraw the workers, but the entire Kastineh council implored him to leave the workers in the colony. For the first time, the council said, they were learning what work really was—all their previous work had been a "joke." [61]

In meeting criticism from some Zionists who believed that colonization in Palestine had to be undertaken by private initiative, or those who questioned the need to colonize at all, Ruppin reacted strongly:

> A Jewish culture in Palestine cannot be the forerunner, but can only be the consequence of a Jewish development. . . . It can emerge only if Palestine has acquired a considerable Jewish population which has become firmly rooted in the soil.[62]

He hammered away at the importance of subordinating profit "to the higher demands of our national movement. To me the training of workers or . . . the revitalization of a colony . . . are assets of the highest value. . . . I am at a loss to understand how . . . the occupational restratification of the Jews and their transformation from city dwellers into landworkers can be decided by considerations of dividends. We might just as sensibly demand that our schools be run at a profit." [63]

Ruppin also began to take seriously the problem of training women farmworkers. Some time in 1910 a shy young girl named Hannah Meisel (later Shochat-Meisel) came to the Palestine Office and met Ruppin.[64] She had just qualified as an agronomist at a French university and had come to Palestine to devote herself to training girls in agriculture. No one had given much thought to the training of wives of Jewish farmers, although a German farmer at Sarona had warned Ruppin that the help of women on the farms was absolutely essential to their success. From the first, Ruppin was extremely sympathetic to Hannah but had no farm at his disposal. Yet he was not willing to give up the idea. Early in 1911 he obtained a few rooms and a small piece of ground on the Kinneret farm and the Verband Jüdischer Frauen für Kulturarbeit in Palästina in Berlin provided a little money to establish and maintain a school there.[65] Thon's wife Sarah was very active in enlisting the support of the women in Berlin. In the spring of 1911 Hannah Meisel was able to move to Kinneret and begin the training of five girls. The number soon increased to twelve, but they were far from welcome. Bermann, who was still the manager when she arrived, had agreed to the experiment with great reluctance. Once, when Ruppin walked with him across the fields in Kinneret, the girls were working in city clothes completely unsuitable for farm work. Bermann pointed to them and said angrily, "Look at them playing! One tomato produced by them will cost one *medshidy!*" (a Turkish coin worth 5 cents).[66] The atmosphere eased when Bermann left the farm, but the financial situation became more difficult. Hannah and Ruppin held fast, with Ruppin repeatedly drawing attention in articles and reports to the necessity for the wives of settlers to have some training in agriculture.

Vegetables were the chief crop at Kinneret, but a dairy and poultry run and a nursery for ornamental trees were also started. By the third year, there were twenty-two girls. Like the young men in *kvutzot*, they allowed themselves nothing but the bare necessities. When the Verband in Berlin sent some furniture for their room, they rejected it as a luxury. Gradually, other temporary girls' *kvutzot* were established in Sarona, Metullah, Tiberias, and Ekron. In time they became havens for unemployed young women as well as agricultural training schools. Later, during World War I, they had an uphill struggle to obtain sites from the Palestine Office that they could manage themselves. Members insisted on doing all of the work themselves, and the girls' farms became known as centers of revolt. Ada Fishman, one of the early pioneering figures of the time, has described the Jewish women's struggle to wrest a place for herself on the land:

> They [the girls] would not permit a single man to work on the farms for fear that management would pass into his hands. They never tired of assuring themselves that sole responsibility for the management was educational and

stimulating and that it brought out the practical abilities of the members. They were equally extreme and meticulous in their views concerning the output of the farms and never counted the hours in their long working day.[67]

Instead of Isaiah's prophesy: "Behold, these shall come from afar . . . and they shall bring thy sons in their arms, and thy daughters shall be carried upon their shoulders," these *haluzot* set their hearts on working shoulder to shoulder with their male comrades in re-establishing Jews on the land and in transforming the values of their personal lives.

26. The Cooperative Model

The period of the Second *Aliyah* marked the foundation of a cooperative agricultural economy, one of socialist Zionism's most persistent and influential traditions and a chief force in the nation-building process. However, cooperative ideals inspired the thinking of Jews interested in Palestine long before the Second *Aliyah*.[1] When Sir Moses Montefiore paid his second visit to the country in 1839, he carried with him plans for a cooperative village near Jerusalem to replace *halukkah*. In 1868 Zeev Kalischer, one of the founders of Petach Tikvah, developed a plan for a religious *kvutza* for 3,000 Jews in Jerusalem who wanted to become farmers, in which all property and income were to be communally shared. It is believed that the first agricultural commune in Palestine was organized in Petach Tikvah in 1880 by the Shabath family. In 1883, middle class immigrants from Bialystok who had purchased land in Petach Tikvah organized a cooperative fund called Achava V'Avoda (Fraternity and Work) for the joint purchase of agricultural equipment. Regulations prohibited the use of wage labor as long as the farmer and his family could do the work. Members had to look after their own livestock, but had to consult with each other about labor requirements and the purchase of equipment.

Despite the individualist strain observed among Eastern European Jews, they were familiar with cooperatives before they emigrated to Palestine, chiefly with credit cooperatives which the Jews in Russia started in the 1860's and which the Jewish Colonization Association did much to encourage. This experience has undoubtedly contributed to the dominance of the cooperative philosophy in Israel today, and for a time, to the reliance on cooperatives as a cure-all for all economic troubles in the country. Undoubtedly the physical desolation of the land and the scarcity of water created tasks that were too difficult for individual enterprise and required the organized efforts of many hands. But it was primarily the Bilu idea of the 1880's that did most to crystallize principles which were embodied into a *kvutza* credo or ethos, even though the Bilu commune experiment failed. The failure of large numbers of Jews to follow the Biluim as well as their own severe economic hardships and internal conflicts was a setback to the communal idea, but their burning idealism and commitment to the national, spiritual, political and economic revival of the Jewish people made a lasting imprint on the colonization process.

Even though the private farms of the time outnumbered the cooperatives during the Second *Aliyah*, the *kvutzot* and *kibbutzim* helped to diffuse the principles of an egalitarian social system throughout the Yishuv and prepared the way for later socialist Zionist institutions that have made a strong imprint on the state of Israel. From 1904 to 1914, the important thing was the model and the commitment to enlarge on it. This period also witnessed the beginnings of a unified trade union organization, at first involving agricultural workers and later workers in cities and towns.

The first of these, the organization of agricultural workers in Judea, took place in 1911 in Ein Ganim, near Petach Tikvah. Shortly thereafter, a similar conference of agricultural workers of the Galilee was held in Um Djuni. Both groups were somewhat inactive at first, but in time they dealt with pressing problems: the need to expand the network of cooperative settlements, housing and working collectives to take charge of planting on the piecework system, and organization of workers' kitchens and clubs. A Sick Fund (Kupat Holim) was also created at the second (1912) conference and developed rapidly, but the question of party affiliation was hotly debated, particularly since many of the workers were themselves "nonparty." [2] This issue remained alive in the postwar period. Nevertheless, the need for an agricultural workers' trade union was accepted and in 1914, the agricultural workers of Samaria were also united within a single organization.[3]

Beginnings were also made toward organizing urban workers and laborers in the private colonies. Carpenters and construction workers waged a bitter struggle for the most elementary workers' rights. Then the idea of a federated union began to be discussed, but too many conflicts were still unresolved when the war intervened. The more developed of the 1,200 Jewish agricultural workers in Palestine had strongly formed attitudes toward political as well as social issues. There was not merely the question of being politically neutral or committed when the war broke out, but the question of whether the two workers' parties had the right to exist. The nonparty workers demanded that the trade union take over all colonization and cultural and even political tasks, such as relations with the Zionist organization.[4] The two parties resisted such a comprehensive extension, but the nonparty view prevailed in the founding of the cultural commission of the Ha-Histadrut Ha-Klalit shel Ha-Ovdim (General Federation of Labor) and publishing activity. Later, when all workers were organized under the umbrella of the Histadrut in 1920, it included those affiliated with political parties, without neutralizing them.

A first attempt to establish a branch trade union occurred in 1912, when engine workers employed in the orange groves of Petach Tikvah were called to set up an accident fund. The movement of such workers from place to place and then the war aborted these efforts, but they are important historically and indicate the changes in thinking and the piecemeal process that eventually led to organization based on occupational differentiation as workers became more closely bound to their work places.

Ironically, a serious stumbling block in the early period was the existence of the Palestine Workers' Fund, set up by Poale Zion in 1912 to give financial support to the cooperative movement. It was financed by contributions from Jewish workers in the Diaspora and created the only important link between Jewish workers in both societies. The agricultural organization in Judea, under the influence of Hapoel Hatzair, at first opposed collaboration with the fund because it was a party-controlled institution. But after protracted discussion, it was agreed to collaborate with the fund "in the same way as with other information offices." [5] Despite the fact that it was a party office, the Workers' Fund worked on behalf of the interest of Jewish workers as a whole and developed rapidly as an economic and colonizing force. Its chief aim was to help workers to emigrate and settle in Palestine, but it also organized cultural projects, loans, and labor exchanges. It began the first mobile work-contracting groups, such as a mobile group of five carpenters who did the woodwork at the Haifa Technion and became the nucleus of the cooperative Carmel, and a group of machinists who formed the Amal cooperative. Much of the fund's budget was used for public works to relieve unemployment and for organizing workers' clubs and libraries. Workers from Poale Zion and Hapoel Hatzair tried to organize cooperative workshops for carpenters and shoemakers and canteens and consumer stores, but the work of the decade from 1905–15 was generally sporadic, lacking in initiative from the bottom, and short-lived. Unity between the political factions was not achieved until 1920.

Joseph Trumpeldor, the legendary soldier-*halutz* who was killed in 1920 defending Tel-Chai against Arab attacks, was among those who urged unity of all workers after the war. He recalled:

> When I left Palestine at the beginning of the war, there were two labor parties: Hapoel Hatzair and Poale Zion. A battle raged between them, yet to general questions it was possible to find a general answer. There existed a unified agricultural workers' organization, a common sick fund. Now there is not a single endeavor. Hapoel Hatzair has its labor bureau, and Achdut Ha-Avoda [Labor Union] [6] has its labor bureau; there exist two sick funds; two agricultural workers' organizations. Why all this? . . . There exists a basis for cooperative work, and common institutions can be created! [7]

The evolution toward unity took many years, finally creating the basis for a substantial workers' economy in present-day Israel that controls segments of industry, agriculture, marketing, housing, credit, health, cultural activities, and trade union matters. Over a million persons, including 40,000 Arabs, are members of the Histadrut, embracing about 60 percent of the adult population and representing all labor parties.

The beginnings of trade union organization in industry in the prewar period were much slower than in agriculture and required large-scale immigration to give it the necessary impetus. Moreover, the early Jewish socialist movement in Palestine—even Poale Zion, which wanted to organize urban workers—was committed to the fundamental importance of Jewish farmers working the land. Jews, long alienated from the land, had to reestablish that bond before they could refashion a Jewish society. Consequently, most Jewish workers were on the land, not in the towns or cities. Town life at the time attracted virtually no capital and held few attractions or challenges. Contrary to Borochov's predictions, most Jewish immigrants went not to Palestine but to America, and no Jewish capitalists at the time established factories in Palestine, ruling out the anticipated class struggle. In 1909, Tel Aviv was still largely under sand dunes; Jerusalem was largely in the grip of *halukkah*; industrial stirrings in Jaffa and Haifa were very slight and living conditions were primitive. A few scattered schools of the Alliance Israélite Universelle, the Bezalel arts and crafts school, and Hebrew grammar schools in Jerusalem and Jaffa did not greatly brighten the generally bleak educational landscape in the cities.

Thus, the development of an urban proletariat—the keystone of doctrinaire socialist Zionists—was very slow. Prior to 1914, even Poale Zionists saw Jewish workers on the land as fundamental to the national-socialist struggle. The first organized effort of Jewish workers to protest their conditions may have been among the printers of Jerusalem. This trade was closely bound up with the Orthodox population, whose prayer books and other religious writings required the existence of a variety of printing shops.[8] Many of the workers themselves, observant Jews, were flung into a conflict between their religious loyalties and daily economic conditions. Nevertheless, a printer's union was organized in the spring of 1897 to protest a 12-hour day's work in cellars and pay of 12 francs a week.[9] Many of the workers and their families were forced to subsist on *halukkah* aid. They were much too weak to hold out, and within a few weeks the union collapsed.

A second union of printers dispersed throughout the country was formed in 1902. They demanded a 10-hour day and an end to night work. After a strike that lasted three weeks, the dispute came before a rabbinical arbitration court. The owners conceded a 10-hour day, but they demanded the end of the union; the rabbis who talked about the harm of any "secular organization" dissolved the union as well as the printing shop owners' association. Again in 1907, a third union was organized. This time, the newly formed labor parties joined the dispute and became involved in clashes with the police and strikebreakers. The rabbis once more issued a ban against the union, and the workers' struggle was blunted.[10]

With the founding of Tel Aviv in 1908 and the beginning of construction of the Polytechnic Institute and the Jewish area in Haifa (Hadar Hacarmel) in 1911, new elements—construction workers—began to enter the labor force. Once more, the struggle involved Arabs who worked cheaply and expertly in stone, against Jews whose experience in Russia had been with bricks. At first, a local Jewish union in Tel Aviv demanded the right to take charge of building about two hundred houses on the outskirts of Jaffa, on land which had been bought by Ahuzat Bayit (Jaffa Building Company). This actually marked the beginning of a new town subsequently called Tel Aviv. Ruppin, who saw the enormous possibilities in the Ahuzat Bayit interest, was later to comment: "Tel Aviv became the training ground for Jewish skilled and unskilled labourers in the building trade. Although there were a few bricklayers among the Jews . . . the usual building material in Jaffa was a rough, porous sandstone *(debbish)*. The Arabs had been familiar with this stone for generations and knew how to use it. Therefore, until Tel Aviv began to be built, it was the rule in Jaffa . . . that all the masonry was carried out by Arabs. It was extremely difficult to introduce Jewish labourers into the building trade." [11]

But the local union soon dissolved. Soon the more aggressive workers became entrepreneurs themselves and refused to hire Jewish construction workers because they were "expensive and bad." In Haifa, there was a different kind of struggle. There, the Technion was mainly built by Jewish workers, but non-Jewish workers demonstrated and demanded priority in employment.

Jewish building workers as a group were stronger than other urban workers, but they could not make any headway in the prewar period. There was as yet little support upon which the Jewish worker could rely. Scattered workers' clubs existed before 1914 and in Haifa and Jaffa workers' booklets were issued. During the prewar construction of a girls' school in Jaffa, there were efforts to set up cooperative builders' groups.[12] Near Tel Aviv, after the first houses were built in 1909, Ruppin, finding some additional land for sale along the beach, handed over half of it to a group of workmen who had formed a cooperative to build houses there.[13] Construction workers, indeed, seemed the most promising group susceptible to organization, but trade unions were not the first area of Jewish worker autonomy in the towns and villages.

In his comprehensive report to the Eleventh Congress (1913), Ruppin analyzed the reasons for industrial underdevelopment, pointing to lack of government interest in transportation enterprises, the simple needs of the Arab population, the absence of an internal market, and the lack of basic raw materials, especially iron and coal. Above all, he stressed the 6 to 1 population ratio (100,000 Jews in a total population of 700,000) between

Arabs and Jews, necessitating the Jewish settlement of a few points, "the creation of a Jewish milieu and of a closed Jewish economy . . . in the vicinity of the towns, in which there is already a large Jewish population . . . to provide an economic hinterland for the town Jews." [14] Much more promising than direct industrial activity at this time were the development of tourism and the attraction of Jewish students to the Hebrew Gymnasium in Jaffa and the Technion in Haifa, and "in years to come, a Jewish Lausanne founded in Jaffa, Haifa and Jerusalem," [15] none of which would involve a rapid increase in population.

Yet worker consciousness was stirring in the towns. The May Day celebrations in 1911 and 1912 were attended by about fifteen hundred workers. The organizing principle was the same one already at work in the Zionist agricultural colonies, namely, the cooperative. One of the earliest transfers of this idea to the private sector involved the workers in the Petach Tikvah colonies.

In the fall of 1913, the workers at Petach Tikvah founded the Achvah (Brotherhood) group in an attempt to deal with inadequate wages and the special disabilities of women workers. The old problem of using cheap Arab labor in the citrus groves, vineyards, and fields left many Jewish workers out of work. A group of Jewish workers decided to negotiate with the citrus growers and take charge of all the work on an annual contract basis.[16] This would save the wages of the foremen and manager and leave the workers with more than the usual wage rate. For some time, Poale Zion had discussed the organization of a *kvutzah*, and this form became the internal structure of the group.[17] The members pooled their tools and organized a cooperative without a loan or grant from the Palestine Office.

The group made a fair showing financially: the accounts for the first year's work showed that each worker was paid 0.17 francs per day in addition to the 2 francs ($.50) daily wage rate. At the beginning, Achvah was a *kvutzah* for joint production, and the earnings were distributed pro rata, according to a member's work days. The *kvutzah* bought several draft animals and ploughs and when there was no work, the animals were used to plow the land that had been leased. The *kvutzah* was quite large, at one time reaching two hundred, and the farmers in Petach Tikvah soon realized that anyone who worked in Achvah knew how to work.

With the outbreak of war, members saw the need of living as well as working together. A house was rented and earnings were pooled. Then a joint kitchen and laundry were set up and clothes were sewed and mended cooperatively.[18] The *kvutzah* also started to raise its own vegetables and grain. During the war when Turkish soldiers began molesting Jews in Petach Tikvah, most of the Achvah group went to Mikveh Israel near Jaffa and Judean villages. With the arrival of the British, most of the members joined the Jewish Legion. (After the war, Achvah members founded the *kibbutz* Yagur near Haifa.) Other similar communes known as Amal, Atid, Ezra, and Achim were formed during the prewar period, signs of a search for collectivist, voluntary, autonomous forms beyond producer and settlement collectives.[19]

The founding of a workers' central buying and selling cooperative—Hamashbir (The Supplier)—proved to be especially significant. Hamashbir was set up in 1916, when economic conditions in Palestine were severe. The war threatened to destroy everything that had been built up. Soaring prices and shortages led to profiteering and hoarding of cereals, petrol and sugar. Hungry workers conceived the idea of founding an organization to buy cereals, fruit, and other staples at harvest time, when they were comparatively cheap, and sell them at cost during periods of shortages to avoid speculation.[20]

A managing body for Hamashbir was elected in 1916 in Galilee. Some money was raised by the workers themselves, and a loan of 13,000 francs was granted by the Palestine Office.[21] By the second year, the entire cereal crop of the *kvutzot* was bought up. More shares were sold to workers and new loans were obtained. Soon a variety of foods was being sold through Hamashbir: jam, oil, salt, and clothing went from Judea to Galilee; peas, wheat, and other farm produce went from Galilee to Judea. The cooperative was quickly able to enlist the support of almost the whole Jewish working community of Palestine, demonstrating that the principle of cooperative economic activity was superior to private enterprise from a social as well as national point of view. Later, Hamashbir was to play a vital role in the development of the trade union movement and the agricultural settlements.

Although World War I struck the Jewish population of Palestine with particular harshness and demoralized many workers (Ben-Gurion and Ben-Zvi were expelled from the country by the Turkish government and many others were persecuted and arrested), four new colonies were established in upper Galilee: Kfar Giladi, Ayelet Hashachar, Mahanayim, and Tel-Chai. *Shomrim* were particularly attracted to these unknown northern frontier areas.

Meanwhile, a pioneering youth movement called Zeire Zion (Youth of Zion) arose in Russia and Poland in the early 1900's, in response to Yosef Witkin's 1905 appeal to Jewish youth to come to Palestine. Members were called upon to undergo agricultural training to prepare themselves for pioneering assignments, and *hachshara* (training) sites multiplied. Zeire Zion was, at the outset, non-socialist, even non-political, emphasizing personal redemption through *aliyah* and thus creating an alternative to the existing parties. Zeire Zion also rejected Marxist determinism and the intense involvement of the various Jewish socialist parties in the Diaspora. Their members believed that Zionism would be built not by "objective forces" but by an ardent personal commitment and a style of life governed by a strict code of social ethics. Later on, Zeire Zion was given its theoretical foundation (*Volkssozialismus*) by Chaim Arlosoroff when, after

World War I, it expanded all over Eastern Europe and became one of the main reservoirs of *halutzim*.

During the war, another pioneering youth group, Hashomer Hatzair (Youthful Watchman) was founded in Galicia by middle-class Jewish youth seeking to find a way between the Polish world that rejected them and the Jewish bourgeois existence they found so distasteful. They, too, turned, not to Marxism or party organization, but to personal self-fulfillment through a remaking of themselves into productive workers building a just society in Palestine.[22] Frequently quite assimilated and removed from Yiddish folk culture, they gravitated to Zionism not through a searching analysis of the plight of Jewish masses but through a personal struggle to achieve spiritual and cultural fulfillment. They were very much influenced by the German youth movement and Martin Buber.

The Hechalutz (Pioneer) movement was dramatically advanced by Joseph Trumpeldor, who inspired a whole generation in the Diaspora to prepare themselves to be anonymous and selfless servants in the cause of building up Jewish Palestine. Trumpeldor was a man of great physical and spiritual courage, strength of will and love of life. A complicated man, he combined interesting paradoxes—a passion for Russia and Russian literature; a deep Jewish consciousness, though he was often far from Jewish life; a capacity to plunge into the immediate situation and commit himself to it utterly, while yet dreaming of a new society based on Tolstoyan communes in Palestine; a thirst for action and danger contrasted with a love of repose and commonplace pleasures. After his tragic death in an Arab raid on Tel Chai in 1920, the writer Joseph Brenner, during the last months of his own life, devoted much time to reading and translating Trumpeldor's letters, which remain the fullest and most expressive revelation of his rich and disciplined spirit. He was, as Brenner said, "a complete man." Everything in life had its value for him.

Trumpeldor [23] spent his childhood and youth far removed from Jewish life in Piatogorsk, in the northern Caucasus, the son of a man who at eight was taken away for twenty-five years to serve in the army of Nicholas I, where most Jews perished or converted. Joseph's father had never been *bar mitzvah* and could not even follow the prayers in the synagogue, yet he persisted in remaining a Jew—as did Joseph, despite the pressure of his mother and brothers to convert. Joseph attended a religious school for a few years and then went to a government school, but he could not circumvent the restrictions against Jews at the *gymnasium*. He apprenticed himself to a dentist, and with the help of a tutor began a round of studies that kept him abreast of his *gymnasium* class.

He absorbed everything—mathematics, French, philosophy, poetry— and came under the influence of Tolstoy (there were Tolstoyan settlements near his home) and Leo Pinsker. In Trumpeldor's mind, the Tolstoyan ideal of communes became intertwined with the Jewish need for a homeland. At eighteen, he too was drafted into the Russian army, and two years later, in 1904, after the outbreak of the Russo-Japanese War, he was sent to Port Arthur where he distinguished himself for unusual bravery under fire and won the highest decoration in Russia, the Cross of St. George. Throughout the ordeal of living with anti-Semitism as well as the hardships of war, he proudly identified himself as a Jew. He was also a proud Russian, and even after being severely wounded and having his left arm amputated, he insisted on going back to the front.

Port Arthur was finally taken by the Japanese, and Trumpeldor spent a year in a prisoner of war camp in Japan. Among the prisoners were nearly five hundred Jews among whom Trumpeldor organized workshops, self-help services, and reading classes in Russian. He borrowed a hand press and printed a basic Russian grammar, lectured to his comrades on history and politics, and organized a library. He even managed to collect some money for the Jewish National Fund and founded a Zionist group and weekly newspaper. A Yiddish play staged by the Jewish prisoners was so successful that Trumpeldor translated it into Russian and presented it to the Russian prisoners.

It was during these days that Trumpeldor resolved to leave Russia for Palestine with some of his fellow prisoners. In October 1905, he wrote to his parents:

> I have already written you that eleven of us have banded together to form a settlement in Eretz Israel.... As long as I was under obligation to defend Russia, the land of my birth, I have spared neither my life nor my safety. But if you think for a moment about our situation as Jews in Russia, what could be more miserable?... We have nothing but crushing servitude, an unbearable burden which has hindered our proper development. The time has come when we must stand on our own feet as a people.... Now, I believe, the time has come to begin solid, practical Zionist work.... My group is a good one; almost all of them are craftsmen—honest fellows who know how to work. We shall come back to Russia, try to find the necessary resources (about two or three hundred rubles per head) and then go out to work in Eretz Israel.[24]

The camp was liquidated soon after the peace treaty was signed and Trumpeldor was cheered and feted by over a thousand prisoners—Jews and Gentiles—whose spirits had been buoyed by his activity. On the long train ride to St. Petersburg, he was preoccupied with details of housing and the special skills of his comrades. He assigned one of them the task of compiling a Russian-Hebrew dictionary after he had learned Hebrew! Upon arriving in St. Petersburg, he was acclaimed as a great Russian hero and invited to see the empress, who gave him an artificial arm as a gift. In 1907, he was commissioned an officer in the reserves—the first Jewish officer in the history of the Russian army. When at last he was able to visit his parents in Rostov, the Jews of the town held a special Sabbath service in his honor.

His visit with his parents was very brief, marred by the familiar, unpleasant pressure from his mother to ease his way to the university by converting. In prison, Trumpeldor had thought long and hard about what skills he would bring to Palestine. He decided that a formal university education would provide him with the best training, but he refused to convert. In the winter of 1907 he became a student at the University of St. Petersburg, studying at home and supporting himself by tutoring. He continued to dream about communal settlements in Palestine but warned against romantic lapses: "For a long time . . . we shall give to Eretz Israel, receiving nothing in return, for in every respect she is meager and poor." [25]

In 1911 he and his friend Zvi Schatz held a conference in Romni to discuss their projected communal colony in Palestine. Seven members attended. In 1912, the group, which had grown to eleven, arrived in Migdal—a barren, windswept piece of desert that had been bought by a Jewish agency. They suffered greatly but would have persevered except for the presence of a manager who insisted on using hired Arab labor. The commune fell apart. Trumpeldor then went to Degania, working happily and deeply influencing those who came in touch with him. In 1913 he tried in vain to persuade the Eleventh Zionist Congress to permit only Jewish labor at Migdal.

When war broke out, the workers at Degania decided to accept Turkish citizenship in order to remain on their land, but Trumpeldor left the country in his old army uniform. In Alexandria he met Ze'ev Jabotinsky. Both men wanted to use the outbreak of the war to liberate the country and pressed for the creation of a Jewish fighting force to help the British conquer Palestine. After prolonged negotiations, the British consented to the formation of a Jewish labor battalion of mule drivers. Trumpeldor hoped that the "Zion Mule Corps" would become the kernel of a Jewish army fighting in Palestine, but the corps was fated to fight in the Dardenelles as a transport unit. Jewish volunteers carried water, supplies, and ammunition piled on mules up to the fighting lines, often under heavy fire. After a few months, the corps suffered great losses in the disastrous Gallipoli campaign and was disbanded after the remnant refused to fight to quell a rebellion in Ireland.

Jabotinsky, meanwhile, was traveling all over Europe trying to get support for a Jewish legion.[26] Trumpeldor met him in London and the two men campaigned for a Jewish fighting force. During their time together, Trumpeldor had ample opportunity to explain his concept of Hechalutz:

We shall require people who are everything . . . he said, "everything that Palestine will need. A worker has his worker's interest, a soldier has his ideas about caste, a doctor or an engineer, his habits. But among us there must arise a generation which has neither interests nor habits. A piece of iron without a crystalized form. Iron from which everything that the national machine requires should be made. Does it require a wheel? Here I am. A nail? A screw? A girder? Here I am; I have no features, no feelings, no psychology, no name of my own. I am a servant of Zion, prepared for everything, bound to nothing, having one imperative: Build! [27]

"There are no such people," said Jabotinsky.

"There are," Trumpeldor replied simply.

The first reports of the upheavals in Russia reached Trumpeldor in London. After the destruction of tsarism, he saw the chance to raise an army of Russian Jews who would fight their way to Palestine over the Caucasus through Armenia and Mesopotamia. From these ranks, he hoped, would come a strong nucleus that would remain and establish communal settlements—the road by which "humanity can reach a secure material existence and spiritual wholesomeness." He returned to Russia and submitted a detailed memorandum to the Kerensky government, requesting permission to recruit a Jewish army, and spoke to several cabinet ministers, but Kerensky's consent was needed, and he was at the front.[28]

In the meantime, Trumpeldor moved untiringly from city to city, inspiring the spread of the *halutz* movement, meeting with young people, writing pamphlets, and helping to prepare *hachshara* sites. The young men and women who joined the movement felt that a profound revolution had taken place in their lives. "All these fields in which they now did agricultural work," wrote an observer, "had formed part of the environment in which these young people had been born and brought up. And yet they had not noticed their existence until this man [Trumpeldor] came, opened their eyes and showed them that the solution to the riddle of their lives, which they had sought in vain in thick volumes and complicated theories, was to be found near them and in their midst." [29]

In his efforts to organize the dispersed movement, Trumpeldor enlisted the support of the Russian Jewish writer Ansky, and together they organized the Nationalist-Socialist Group, whose program combined ideas from the Russian Social Revolutionary party and socialist Zionists. Then in July 1917, the shaky Kerensky regime was threatened by the tsarist general Kornilov, who had raised an army and was marching on Petrograd. Trumpeldor, asked to lead a counterforce, defeated Kornilov and the grateful Kerensky government approved his plan to raise a Jewish army of 120,000 men. However, the idea of a Jewish Legion to fight the Turks on the Allied side, fell together with the Kerensky government. The Bolsheviks drove out Kerensky and took Russia out of the war.

In the confusion of the early period of Soviet rule, Trumpeldor nevertheless struggled to make the Hechalutz movement in Russia the creator of the Third *Aliyah*. In early 1918 he wrote and published a pamphlet called *Hechalutz—Its Principles and Immediate Tasks*, with two appendices—a proposed constitution and a questionnaire.[30] A new political opportunity had arisen, he said, as a result of the Balfour Declaration. But speedy action was imperative. Trumpeldor pressed for a conference of all the *halutzim* in Russia to create an organization uniting all Jewish workers and those ready to live a life of labor. The organization, as Trumpeldor conceived it, would be nonpartisan, and would prepare its members to lay the foundation in Palestine of "a free Jewish commonwealth of labor, living on its own work and supplying its own needs."

By the summer of 1918, Zionist organizations were already being closed down in Russia and the Yevsektsia (Jewish Sections of the Communist party) were denouncing the "counter-revolutionary essence" of Zionism. Trumpeldor realized that time was closing in. One bitter winter night in a Moscow attic, he sat talking to three youths, trying to persuade them to call a Hechalutz conference before it was too late. The surviving resources of the movement must be organized. The youths were full of doubt—contacts with the branches had broken down, the railways had collapsed, and the organization was no longer legal. But Trumpeldor prevailed and a conference of thirty representatives met in Communist Petrograd. Trumpeldor, the chairman, insisted that it was necessary to begin agricultural and military training and preparation for *aliyah*. The organization, moreover, must be independent of the official Zionist organization. Trumpeldor himself was appointed the Hechalutz representative to Palestine to look into possibilities for settlement and establish contact with workers there.

In the prevailing chaos and pogrom-ridden atmosphere, Trumpeldor also tried to organize a military force to protect the Jewish population, but his plans were smashed in the ensuing civil war. He was accused of being a counterrevolutionary and arrested by the Bolshevik Cheka.[31] Luckily, several Red Army militiamen—Jews who had been in his *halutz* movement—claimed him and gave him forged papers. Before he left for Palestine, Trumpeldor managed to organize self-defense units and a *halutz* training farm in Simferopol. He made his way to the Crimea, where he met many of his followers—without proper documents, money or plans— but bent on reaching Palestine. Wild rumors of imminent salvation for Jews were rife at the time—overheated hopes that clashed with actual danger from White armies and Bolsheviks. In the midst of these swirling forces, Trumpeldor obtained permission from the government Commissar for Agriculture to organize agricultural "communist" groups. These groups were called "Hechalutz," in Russian letters, with a period after each letter, so as to look like the initials of some slogan or the name of some organization.[32]

In the middle of August 1919, Trumpeldor embarked at Yalta for Constantinople, where he organized a relief program, several workshops, and an information office for Jews struggling to reach Palestine. Three months later, he sailed for Palestine but continued to maintain an active correspondence with all the centers he had established.

In Palestine he found the Jewish workers weary, dispirited, and still disunited. Achdut Ha-Avoda had just been set up, but the union was not complete. Without labor unity, Trumpeldor could see no hope for the future. When new *halutzim* arrived, they found two labor offices, two agricultural federations, and many workers' kitchens. A fierce struggle was going on between two groups of railway workers. "Why should all this be?" he lamented, in a fervent appeal for unity. "I have many old friends in the ranks of both parties; together we have worked and suffered from fever, together we have faced danger, here or over there in Gallipoli. Together we have loved this land, our own land, without any calculations. I love and respect my old friends in both camps . . . but now they cannot speak to each other without anger. Why should this be? . . . We need a united effort of all the workers. Every moment is precious. Every Jew who comes in is being delivered from certain death or a life of shame. Every moment of delay is a crime. Therefore I beg of you to try to emerge from the circle of party strife." [33]

His appeal produced some results: Discussions were opened with a view toward cooperation. Then disturbances in the northern part of upper Galilee claimed his attention and, tragically, his life.

The Sykes-Picot agreement signed in 1916 between England and France provided for definite boundaries between English- and French-administered zones in Palestine. In the north, the Jewish settlements of Tel-Chai, Hadera, Kfar Giladi, and Metulla fell under French rule and were separated from the rest of Palestine. But both nations, seeking to keep the region within their sphere of influence, were directly and indirectly inflaming local Arabs and dividing them into hostile groups. Both the tribes that lived in the area permanently and the Bedouin were well-armed. At first Arab Christians who were friendly to the French were attacked; then the French troops and Jewish settlements were harassed. At Metulla, the defenders, led by Trumpeldor, were surrounded by armed Bedouin and stripped of all their clothes and weapons. Wrapped only in sacking, they made their way to Tel-Chai. The tiny garrison there could not withstand the intensified Arab attacks and the settlement went up in flames. Trumpeldor and several comrades died in the attack in February 1920. His dying words were: "It is good to die for our country."

Trumpeldor's death gave the fledgling Yishuv and Zionists everywhere their first heroic legend, and the Trumpeldor Labor Brigade created in the early twenties provided many members of *kibbutzim* and political leaders in later years. His death in the midst of Arab hostility and violence in the upper Galilee also dramatized the growing tensions between Arab and Jew.

27. The Arabs in Palestine: The Unresolved Question

Following the announcement of the Balfour Declaration in November 1917, Zionists were heartened at first by expressions of Arab sympathy, especially those of the Emir Faisal in May 1918. It was also noted that two leading Arab newspapers in Cairo took a positive stand on the Jewish Homeland. But these reactions proved to be qualified, contingent, and highly volatile. The Arab world was in a state of restive uncertainty after the war. Rival leaders were pressing to fill political vacuums, win promises from both the French and the British, and play upon *their* rivalry in the struggle over the Turkish empire. A final treaty with Turkey was not signed until 1923, contributing to the restiveness and even giving rise to Arab hopes for deliverance from their former Turkish oppressors! By that date, seven new Arab states had been created; yet the Arabs grudged Jews the "small notch" in Palestine, as expressed by Balfour, "being given to the people who for all these hundreds of years have been separated from it."

Few pledges or statements of British Middle Eastern policy have been so thoroughly examined and deliberated upon as the Balfour Declaration.[1] All of the important public figures involved in its drafting fully accepted British responsibility to facilitate the development of "a home for the Jewish people" in Palestine. Public and press opinion at the time in Britain and the United States reflected and supported the earnest intent of the pledge. The Declaration subsequently gained international validation from the Allies and the League of Nations. Emir Faisal accepted it in his agreement with Weizmann on January 3, 1919. Yet it was to become the inflamed core of the subsequent Arab-Jewish conflict in Palestine.

For many years the document has been subjected to relentless textual analysis: what precisely did the phrase "a home for the Jewish people" mean? Admittedly, the phrase was and is ambiguous. There was, moreover, no precedent for its use. However, at the time, it was interpreted and

understood by the men who shaped it to have quite specific meanings.[2]
The Declaration was made to the Jewish people as a whole, not to the
actual Jewish population in Palestine. Behind British policy was the
recognition of the principle of Jewish nationality: every Jew in the world
had the right to return to his National Home. Well aware that the Arabs
outnumbered Jews in Palestine, the British nevertheless believed that the
Jewish claim, grounded in history, tradition, urgent current needs and
future hopes, was greater than that of the Arabs. On February 19, 1919,
Balfour wrote in this vein to Lloyd George, acknowledging that because
Palestine is "absolutely exceptional," the principle of numerical self-
determination for the Arabs was being rejected. It was understood that
Arab civil, economic and religious rights in Palestine were to be assured,
but political rights were not implied or recognized. The British accepted
and encouraged Arab national aspirations outside Palestine, but not
within it. The Arabic-speaking population in Palestine was to remain
undisturbed and protected but the British intention was to encourage
Jewish immigration and colonization so as to create a Jewish majority. It
was expected that Palestine Jews would gradually be transformed from a
minority into a majority (as the British also intended for Greater Armenia)
and that ultimately this would mean Jewish self-government and sovereignty. The actual pattern of Jewish-Arab relations was only vaguely
surmised.

In subsequent years, to conciliate Arab opinion, the British government denied that it had intended to establish a Jewish State, but this was
surely not precluded, and in the minds of a number of important figures,
was clearly envisioned. Lloyd George recalled that during the deliberations
on the Balfour Declaration, the government wished to consult the
Palestine Arabs, but found it impossible because they were fighting against
the Allies. Moreover, Palestine did not constitute a separate administrative unit and its Arab population was not a recognized national entity.
Observing that Palestine Arab national history, tradition, and sentiment
were virtually non-existent, the British believed that Jews had an
inalienable right to the land independent of Arab wishes. In 1921, when
the merits and demerits of the Zionist policy were discussed in the British
Cabinet, it was pointed out that "the Arabs had no prescriptive right to a
country which they had failed to develop to the best advantage." The
overriding consideration at the time was that Jews had a stronger claim,
and that Palestine was a *sui generis*. The original sponsors of the
Declaration had no regrets. They assumed that the two people would co-
exist harmoniously, that the Arabs would benefit greatly from Jewish cooperation, and that in view of their own large gains of territory and
independence after the war, they would not "grudge that small notch" to
the Jews. Naive assumptions and muddled thinking, perhaps, but nonetheless, those ideas prevailed.

The Declaration was the occasion for great rejoicing and thanksgiving on the part of Jews everywhere. In Russia and Rumania especially, it had an electrifying effect. The formerly weak and powerless Zionist movement was now suddenly transformed to a world political force. It had gained national rights for the Jewish people and recognition of the concept in international law. More than ever, it now bound all of its hopes for fulfillment of the restoration to the good will of Britain. Inevitably, Zionists had been influenced by the British perception of the future of Palestine as it had been expressed in the Declaration. This meant a somewhat naive optimism regarding relations with the Arabs and specifically, an inclination to attach great importance to Faisal's agreement with Weizmann (which the British had sought), in which Faisal renounced any claim to Palestine. "Prince Faisal is an eagle," Weizmann had said in a exultant moment. "He has a bright future." But that was hardly the case.

The British understanding of the Declaration and the Arab acceptance of it—if briefly—conformed to Zionist prewar hopes for harmonious coexistence. After the war, these illusions were quickly blasted. Faisal was willing to concede Palestine if he secured Syria, but the French did not take kindly to his self-coronation there and dethroned him. Faisal then made a determined bid for Palestine and repudiated his earlier stand. Moreover, when the Arabs realized that the British military administration had no intention of implementing the Declaration, they began to protest openly. Early in 1919, leaflets were distributed in Jerusalem and Jaffa calling on Arabs to resist the "Zionist danger." A small Arab terrorist band called the Black Hand fomented anti-Jewish attacks. In the spring of 1920 came the raid on Tel Hai, soon followed by the shocking riots in Jerusalem. Arab leaders began to demand the annulment of the Balfour Declaration.

It has been suggested that the pattern of postwar Arab opposition to Zionism was prefigured in the attitudes and activities of Arabs before 1914.[3] But one must be cautious in pressing this argument too far. There are some strands that bind both periods, but there are also qualitative differences of great magnitude that make close interweaving of the periods risky. The roots of the contemporary Arab-Israeli conflict are far too complex to be disentangled by reference to the forces at work in the pre-1914 period alone. The war itself was a catalyst that changed everything, and the subsequent violence of Arab opposition to Zionism in the 1920's and 1930's grew in response to certain postwar changes: the collapse of the Ottoman Empire, the association of Zionism with a European power, the controversy over the McMahon Correspondence and the Balfour Declaration, the pro-Arab bias of British administration of Palestine under the Mandate, the spreading poison of the Protocols of the Elders of Zion, and the fateful leadership of the Arab world by Haj Amin al-Husseini, the Mufti of Jerusalem. Later came the destruction of European Jewry and the desperate need for one place in the world where Jewish survivors could go, a catastrophe that forced upon Zionism a completely new task and character and made Palestine a Jewish imperative of great urgency. Early socialist Zionist social visions have also been shattered by the globalization of the Palestine issue and the antipathy of the Third World and communist satellite states to Jewish national survival.

In 1917, all of this history was yet to unroll. Inevitably, the configuration of the present struggle overshadows the more blurred picture of the past, investing it with projections that were far from inevitable at the time. The pre-1917 period indeed witnessed some Arab-Jewish conflict, but no hardening of positions. Arab nationalism itself was problematical. Some Arab nationalists before the war saw the confrontation between Jewish and Arab nationalism as crucial for an Arab revival. At the same time, others were sincerely interested in collaboration and concord. At critical moments, the interposition of Turkish power—as later, of British power—distorted relations and skewed possibilities of an understanding. An examination of the cross-currents of the prewar period and the state of "The Land" which had been Palestine is necessary in order to keep the two periods separate and to try to understand the pre-1917 perspectives of the Arab and Zionist movements, including the particular orientation of socialist Zionists.

Before World War I, there was no Palestine as such, but a hodgepodge of *sanjaks* or subprovinces, ruled from both Damascus and Constantinople (see map, p. 461). Administrative confusion was further compounded by the presence of several large religious minorities, some of whom enjoyed extraterritorial privileges. Before World War I, the whole area that is now divided into the states of Saudi Arabia, Jordan, Syria, Iraq, Lebanon, and Israel was governed by Turkey. The present divisions did not exist, nor did most of their names. After the Romans suppressed the last Jewish rebellion in A.D. 135, Judea was renamed Syria Palestina. Thereafter, Palestine was not to be found in any map of the world until 1920. Much of the land had been desolated by centuries of warfare and neglect, with both Bedouin and *fellahin* contributing to the ruin of the countryside. Most significantly the *fellahin* had been sinking ever deeper into grinding poverty, hopelessly indebted from generation to generation to landowners, tax farmers and moneylenders.

After the 1880's, when a new type of Jewish immigration began, mainly from Eastern Europe and inspired by the vision of a renewal of Jewish life, a new force that became identified with the "Zionist invasion" converged on a feudal society just beginning to undergo the ordeal of modernization. Islamic hegemony had declined under the spreading power of Western Christianity, and by the late nineteenth century, educated Arabs (many of them educated in Christian schools) began to realize that the West had forged ahead while the Arab world had stagnated. It is quite astonishing, for example, to realize that the printing press was not introduced into the Arab world until the 1830's, when American and European missionaries

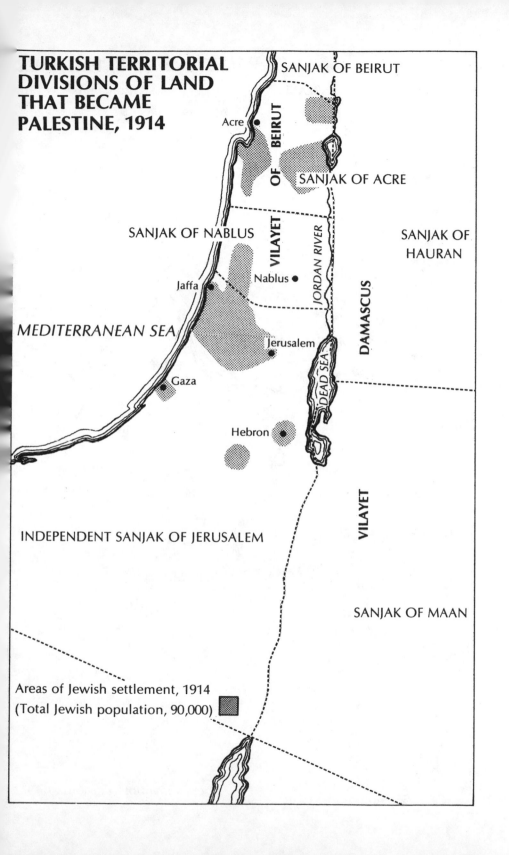

TURKISH TERRITORIAL
DIVISIONS OF LAND
THAT BECAME
PALESTINE, 1914

SANJAK OF BEIRUT

Acre

VILAYET OF BEIRUT

SANJAK OF ACRE

SANJAK OF NABLUS

VILAYET

JORDAN RIVER

SANJAK OF HAURAN

Jaffa

Nablus

DAMASCUS

MEDITERRANEAN SEA

Jerusalem

DEAD SEA

Gaza

Hebron

VILAYET

INDEPENDENT SANJAK OF JERUSALEM

SANJAK OF MAAN

Areas of Jewish settlement, 1914
(Total Jewish population, 90,000)

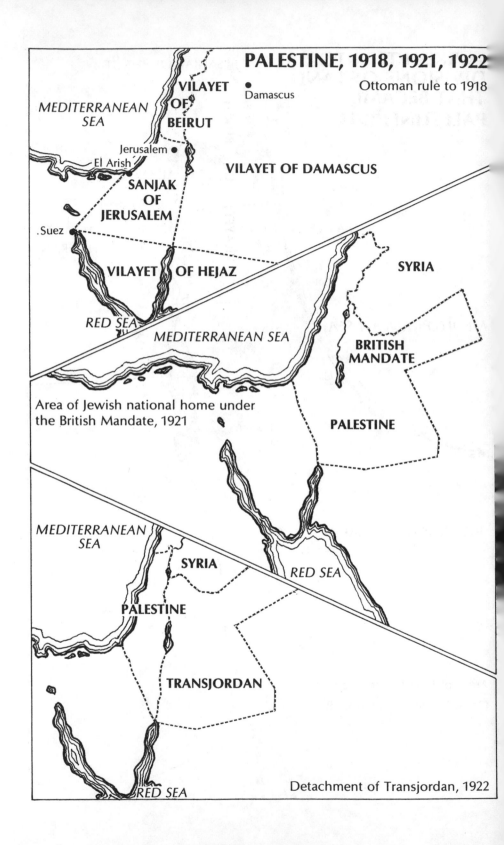

PALESTINE, 1918, 1921, 1922

Ottoman rule to 1918

MEDITERRANEAN SEA

VILAYET OF BEIRUT

• Damascus

Jerusalem •
El Arish

VILAYET OF DAMASCUS

SANJAK OF JERUSALEM

.Suez •

VILAYET OF HEJAZ

SYRIA

RED SEA

MEDITERRANEAN SEA

BRITISH MANDATE

Area of Jewish national home under the British Mandate, 1921

PALESTINE

MEDITERRANEAN SEA

SYRIA

RED SEA

PALESTINE

TRANSJORDAN

Detachment of Transjordan, 1922

set up presses to print the Bible in Arabic. Somewhat later the German Lutheran Templars, after vehement opposition from the sultan, established several settlements and introduced wheeled vehicles and roads on which they could operate. Arabs began to react to westernization, as European political and religious pressure and economic exploitation made inroads on a stagnant society. By the 1880's, Syria itself had become a focus of Russian, French, German, and British imperialist designs. Elsewhere in the Turkish empire, the more firmly European ideas and institutions implanted themselves, the more hostile Arab reaction became. Nor was this rejection of Europe confined to the conservative, traditionalist elements of the Muslim elite. It was also found in the "westernized" elite as well and expressed itself in an "obdurate, repressed hostility which ... became stronger and more articulate as 'westernization' spread and increased." [4] Europe was both coveted and spurned, respected and despised, wanted and rejected.

The Russo-Turkish War (1877-78) brought home the fact that the Ottoman Empire could be penetrated militarily and defeated and that its fate would be henceforth decided in Europe. The subsequent occupation of Tunisia by France and of Egypt by England gave proof that Europe was no longer a "civilization" but a threat which no longer evoked strictly religious reactions but involved new secularized elements: lawyers, journalists, teachers and army officers.[5] Zionism overlapped and reinforced this rejection process.

Jewish immigration was coming out of the West, composed of Jews who had mastered some of the magic of the West. They were perceived by the Arabs as a threat to existing realities. In the tangled skein of forces that have strangled Arab-Jewish relations in what was to become Palestine, the Arab perception of the immigrant Jew as a danger has worked particular mischief. An Arab-Israeli journalist, a man from both worlds, has put it this way:

> The ruling classes tried to divert the anger of the people against an obscure phenomenon in society and to put the blame on those "foreigners, the Jews," and whoever was among the minorities. They were accused of stealing the peoples' share of land, their resources, and of betraying the general welfare. These ruling classes succeeded in misleading quite a large ratio of the people who rid themselves of their drowsiness in order to divert their anger toward the Jews.[6]

Arab leaders told the masses that these "foreigners" intended to conquer their land and eject them from it. The pioneers of the Second and Third *Aliyot* were shocked by such a formulation. They had come to build a new, just, socialist society in their ancient home, seeking to "conquer" only labor—that is, to re-create Jews who would master physical labor. Their chief preoccupation in their first contacts with Arabs was to avoid and remove exploitation of Arab labor. They sincerely believed that there was enough room in the land for both Jews and Arabs, that both people could live together peaceably. In the 1880's Russian Zionists expressed confidence that Jews and Arabs could live together side by side, and in *Altneuland*, Herzl envisioned harmonious relations and ultimately great benefits for the Arabs with the introduction of modern methods of land cultivation. A future of raging conflict was unthinkable to the early *halutzim*. Yet some Jews did see early portents of trouble.

Ben-Gurion first perceived the seriousness of the Arab problem in Palestine in Sejera where he worked as a day laborer in 1907–09. He had already engaged in the struggle for Jewish labor in Petach Tikvah and Rishon le-Zion, where most of the laborers were Arabs. Sejera had attracted him because all of the work was done by Jews. "But Sejera had its full share of Arab enmity," he observed. "It was surrounded by aggressive armed Arab villages like Lubiya and Kafr Kana, and by the Zabuah tribes, and here, for the first time, we all saw Jews being murdered—it was on the last day of Passover 1909—simply because they were Jews." [7]

Other Jews, even earlier, had also foreseen a struggle between the two peoples for the land. One was Simon Dubnow's brother Ze'ev (Vladimir), who reached Palestine with the second Bilu group on September 21, 1882. In a letter to his brother, he wrote: "The final goal is eventually to gain control of Palestine and to restore to the Jewish people the political independence of which it has been deprived for two thousand years." [8] Besides the founding of settlements and factories so that the land will be in Jewish hands, Ze'ev conjectured that "it is necessary to instruct young people and the future generation in the use of firearms (in free, wild Turkey, anything can be done), and then . . . the glorious day will dawn of which Isaiah prophesied." [9]

Writing out of his belief in "spiritual Zionism," Ahad Ha-Am, in an article in *Ha-Shiloah* in 1891, following his visit to Palestine, reminded readers that the land was not an empty territory: "We are in the habit of thinking that all the Arabs are wild men of the desert and do not see or understand what goes on around them. But that is a great mistake. The Arabs, especially the town dwellers, see and understand what we are doing and what we want in Palestine, but they do not react and pretend not to notice, because at present they do not see in what we are doing any threat to their own future. . . . But if ever we develop in Palestine to such a degree as to encroach on the living space of the native population to any appreciable extent, they will not easily give up their place." [10]

What Jews wanted in Palestine was far from clear at the time, and this warning could hardly have had any practical meaning as long as Turkey was in control of the country. After the establishment of the Zionist Organization, Herzl spoke no longer of a Jewish state, but of a "publicly and legally assured home in Palestine and a Charter." He and other "political" Zionists were primarily concerned with the ruler of the land, not its inhabitants. The "practical" Zionists, on the other hand, would not wait for a charter and demanded settlement activity. But they ignored or minimized the problem of how Jewish immigration and settlement would be possible in a country not under Jewish control.[11]

It could hardly have been otherwise. Zionists in Russia had only the vaguest ideas about Arabs living in Palestine, while those who came in the First and Second *Aliyot* lacked any clearly defined political goal. They did not expect to have to confront an Arab question. Even the purchase of land was at first haphazard and undirected. Technically, Turkish law prevented the sale of land to Jews, but Arabs who owned it were willing to sell it. "We merely went ahead," Weizmann wrote, "in a small, blind, persistent way. Jews settled in Palestine, and they were not expelled. . . . Between *baksheesh* and an infinite variety of subterfuges, the first little colonies were created." [12] The ban on Jewish settlement in Palestine was announced in 1882, and inasmuch as it was aimed primarily at the entry of Russian and Rumanian Jews (other nationalities were not interfered with), it was aimed at the most oppressed Jews in Europe. The edict was clearly in violation of the Capitulations, which assured foreign nationals unrestricted travel in the Ottoman Empire (excluding Arabia). The sultan apparently feared the possibility of nurturing another national problem. Moreover, the Russian government, worried about any possible disturbance of the status of the Holy Places, had put pressure on the Porte to prevent mass Jewish immigration into Palestine. Several of the powers protested against these restrictions in 1887, but official Turkish prohibitions against mass Jewish immigration from Russia lasted until 1917. However, protests by European consuls, who insisted on their Capitulatory rights, the venality of Turkish officials, and Arab willingness to sell land rendered the ban somewhat less than airtight.

Ahad Ha-Am's observation about the native Arab population was penetrating, indeed even prophetic to a degree, especially in the light of events since 1948. Yet these intuitions of later conflict do not mean that Zionists ignored the Arab presence in Palestine. They may have known too little about Arab customs and at first not understood the importance of learning Arabic, in their preoccupation with their own struggle. They may not have comprehended the implications of the first stirrings of Arab national feeling and may not have foreseen the possibility of a clash of national forces, but they were certainly aware that several hundred thousand Arabs lived in Palestine and that they constituted a majority of the population.[13]

The texture of Arab-Jewish relationships at the time was uneven, a patchwork of varied strands often creating quite strong human ties: In the old Sephardic community, the use of Arabic made relations more comfortable; some Jews were in business with Arabs, others were good neighbors and even friends; *shomrim* often went out of their way to make friendly contacts with nearby villages whose *fellahin* were known to have warned settlements of attacks and even helped them. However, like other subjugated people who have been long exploited, *fellahin* developed certain traits that made them difficult neighbors for the Jewish settlers: They could be cruel, cunning, and treacherous in their dealings with those they had not accepted as friends or allies.[14] Moreover, in the settlements where Arab guards had been replaced, *shomrim* took on a paramilitary character and showed Jews in a wholly new role that aroused suspicion and fear. The few *kvutzot* hardly dominated the character of Jewish settlement at this time, but the communal style of life, the fairly strident sexual equality and freedom, and the intense ideological rigor of the communes were certainly disturbing to some Arabs who had any experience of them. There was also a preexisting Muslim disdain, verging on contempt, for religious Jews who had been living in Palestine. They taunted cowards among their own ranks with the epithet *siknag*, a distortion of "Ashkenazi" and a term of great abuse. The newer settlers were not greeted by the Arab villagers with any great show of neighborliness, but then they were not well disposed toward any strangers. Those Arabs who worked in the ICA colonies were comparatively well-paid and seem to have been reasonably content working among Jewish overseers and workers. Tensions developed and violence was intermittent but cannot be ascribed to a single cause or even pattern: In some cases, there was hostility where Jews became *shomrim*, or if *fellahin* were displaced as a result of land sales, or when an all-Jewish work force was introduced. Early manifestations of Arab peasant opposition to Zionism seem to have been largely economic and social, rather than religious or political. After 1908, however, when there were a few nationalist organizations and papers, there was a political overtone. Anti-Zionism, indeed, became one of the mainstays of Arab politicians in the Ottoman empire who wanted to win favor with the Turkish authorities or win seats in the parliament.[15] It was also a line often encouraged and incited by the Turkish government itself.

Early Jewish colonization efforts were mainly in the south, on large uninhabited tracts of swampy and sandy land which owners were glad to be rid of. In the north, however, *fellahin* were sometimes displaced as a result of sales by Arab landowners who often demanded and got high prices and sold without any thought for the *fellahin*, who were their tenants or sharecroppers.[16] At times Arab moneylenders acquired land from *fellahin* who were in debt and sold it to Jews, aggravating their resentment. To make matters worse, Jews were inevitably in the hands of land-agents, since they were unfamiliar with land laws and the byzantine obscurities of the language in which the contracts were written.[17] These agents received their commissions from the seller and, zealous to conclude sales, did not care if Jews bought land which wiser buyers would have shunned. Initial resentments were probably never entirely rubbed away, but once a Jewish colony was established and assumed a more or less permanent form, a *modus vivendi* was struck. Day-to-day relations were generally harmonious, especially as most colonies employed five to ten times as many Arabs as Jews.[18] In the towns, the rich landowning families rejoiced at the eagerness of Jews to buy land at almost any price. The large class of uneducated Arabs seems to have been indifferent to the newcomers, but the predominantly Christian small businessmen and professionals had apprehensions about possible economic competition. It was they who organized the first Arab protest against Jewish immigration in 1891.[19]

As to the Jewish socialist workers, they had come not as conquerors but as workers, to return to the land and redeem the Jewish people from the curse of landlessness and homelessness. From their perspective, cheap Arab labor was an evil they struggled to overcome. They believed in working-class solidarity and, as socialists, endowed the *fellah* with as much dignity as anyone else, but saw him as part of the economic backwardness and neglect of the country that must be reversed. In the early years, the struggle to sustain the few *kvutzot* (five in 1914) was an all-consuming task—the problem of the *fellahin* scarcely concerned the *halutzim*. Later, many socialist Zionists expected the Arab working class (after it had become organized) to join them in the struggle against the *effendi*, who were considered both the national and class enemy.

Arab society was controlled by a few families who had large land holdings and heavy economic interests in the cities. (These were the same families who did much to inflame anti-Jewish feeling among the Arab masses, especially after World War I.) Arab society was also rigidly polarized, and more than 30 percent of the rural population had no land of its own.[20] Land purchases by Jewish settlers sometimes involved the *fellahin* and occasionally caused their displacement. Generally, Zionist land-buying policies concentrated on unpopulated land and involved compensation or alternate employment for the displaced *fellahin*—a practice which, by the way, Jews introduced. Under Turkish law, tenants had no protection. As a matter of record, the number of *fellahin* dispossessed was small, even in later years when the Arabs made a great outcry over alleged eviction.[21] (It was found that between 1919 and 1932, when Jews had acquired 115,000 acres, only 664 Arabs could be classified as evicted tenants, of whom only a hundred or so took advantage of resettlement opportunities offered by the British administration.) [22] Moreover, only a tiny percentage of the land acquired by the Zionists was bought from small-scale peasants. Most of it came from large land-owners.[23] One-quarter of all Jewish land in Palestine (the Esdraelon Valley) was in fact acquired from a single absentee landlord—the Christian Arab Sursuq family, who lived in Beirut.[24] (Even the virulently anti-Zionist Haj Amin el-Husseini, the mufti of Jerusalem, had to admit to the British Peel Commission in 1936 that at no time had there been anything approaching a forced sale by Arabs to Jews.) [25]

The economic benefits to the Arabs that flowed from Jewish investment and labor were often cited by Zionists in arguing their case, as Arab opposition mounted, but these, although considerable, were not sufficiently strong to stop Arab nationalists once they began attacking the Zionist "invasion." Jews in their colonies used novel methods and machinery and provided work for the *fellahin*. They also provided a market for local Arab produce. Medical care and schools and general improvement in living conditions as a result of Jewish settlement actually increased Arab migration to Palestine between 1919 and 1936.[26] But these benefits were discounted.

Difficulties for Jewish settlers were also sharpened by the spread of multiple Christian interests and the increase in the Christian population throughout the Turkish Empire during the nineteenth century. Churches, schools, hospitals, orphanages, missionary societies, and settlements were established by all sects and appropriately supported by the power of protective states—Russia, France, England. They were often in turbulent political as well as religious conflict with each other, but together quite consciously promoted non-Muslim westernizing influences. Anti-Jewish feeling was also spread by the churches in Palestine, and the Eastern Christians, who had traditionally vied with Oriental Jews in the Ottoman Empire as clerks, bankers, and merchants, fanned this rivalry by religious prejudice. In 1847, Greek Orthodox Arabs had charged Jews with the blood accusation libel. Before World War I, Arab nationalist newspapers were in Christian hands, and Christians were numerically strong and active in the Arab national societies. Interestingly, Zionists found much more sympathy among Christian Arabs outside Palestine, who feared Muslim domination.[27]

Security for the Jewish settlements was the overriding concern of the Yishuv in the pre-1914 period. Turkish rule for decades had been marked by venality and incompetence; after 1876 the empire lay under the subtle and oppressive tyrant Abdul Hamid, who opposed the slightest hint of any reform except the modernization of his army. Local government, such as it was, involved a bewildering proliferation of jurisdictions: pashas, European consuls, patriarchs, and bishops; tax collectors, Bedouin sheikhs, and a council of Arab notables. British interest in the Jews residing in the Turkish dominions—especially in Palestine—was first expressed by Lord Palmerston in 1839, when he instructed the British vice-consul "to afford protection to the Jews generally." (Palmerston and others in England were then interested in establishing a Jewish state in Syria and Palestine to serve as a buffer between Turks and Egyptians and enhance British influence.) Later, other European consulates were established. They offered slightly more security to Europeans than had existed before, but the Turkish government refused to give any satisfactory guarantee of overall security for the Jewish settlements. The northern territory especially was overrun by warring clans and brigands. For its part, the Turkish government was indifferent to the welfare of its own subjects, concerning itself almost exclusively with the collection of taxes and exploiting where it could the interests of other countries in the area. Arabs, as a whole, did not regard Turkish rule as alien, despite linguistic and cultural differences, and regarded themselves as Muslim subjects of a Muslim empire.[28] Beyond this general acceptance was the social and economic hierarchy: the *effendis* were concerned with their land holdings and local power; the *fellahin*, struggling for subsistence, remained ignorant and downtrodden; women existed solely to serve men; the Bedouin persisted in their millennial nomadic ways.

Several of the Balkan states had broken away from Turkey in the late nineteenth century, but national sentiment, in the usual sense, elsewhere in the empire was virtually nonexistent up to 1914, except in very narrow circles. In the main, the people living in Palestine had no real feeling of belonging to any wider unit than their village, clan, or confederation of clans.[29] The language spoken was one or another of the many Arab dialects, though only the Bedouin at the time thought of themselves as Arabs. (Studies of the *fellahin* by scholars in the nineteenth century disclosed that many of them were not "Arabs" in the sense of having entered the country with or after the conquerors of the seventh century, but had been there already when the Arabs came.)[30] Islamization was a continuing process right into modern times.

Neither the Turkish governors nor the sultan elicited any feelings of loyalty on the part of ordinary villagers—only the local sheikh or clan, or unusual personal leader such as Abu Ghosh, created any sense of specific affiliation. The empire itself, called "the realm of the sultan," had no meaning at all for the villagers, and political or territorial boundaries, often shifting under the movement of Bedouin and warring sheikhs, further militated against expressions of solidarity or unity.

In such a landscape, there were only glimmers of Arab national consciousness flickering in the darkness of Turkish oppression, a consciousness difficult to perceive and more difficult to evaluate. Before the fall of the sultan Abdul Hamid in 1908, any open Arab nationalist expression was forbidden. No political activity at all was officially permitted in the empire. The earliest furtive beginnings of unrest can be traced to the University of Beirut in 1875, when a group of five Christian students formed a secret society with revolutionary aims. They made contact with friends in Damascus and Tripoli, but government spies made it unsafe for them to remain in Syria or the Vilayet of Beirut and they moved to Egypt. Their activity was mainly directed against Turkey.

In the early 1880's, when Russian Jews began coming into Palestine, the total population of the Jewish colonies, no more than 1,000, were known only to their immediate Arab neighbors. Jews were unaware of the Arab custom of sharing natural pasturelands, and quarrels and skirmishes arose out of unintentional Arab incursions. Restrictions on Jewish immigration and land purchase had been somewhat relaxed in 1889, and the small, predominantly Christian class of tradespeople and professional men had apprehensions about the probable economic competition that would follow.[31] The first protest against Jewish immigration was organized in 1891. On June 24, 1891, a petition was sent to Constantinople demanding the renewal of restrictions. They were reinstated a year later, and land purchases were radically curtailed until 1900, when there was some loosening. Between 1897 and 1900, inquiries about Jewish immigration were channeled from the provincial administrations in Jerusalem and Beirut. Restrictions were reimposed after the First Zionist Congress in 1897. Finally, in 1900, Jews were permitted to acquire state land in Palestine, and Jewish pilgrims were permitted to stay in Palestine for three months. There was some grumbling among Arabs and occasional fights between Jews and Arabs, but nothing of consequence.

Interestingly enough, the First Zionist Congress was simply mentioned in the Arab press among other news items. No special attention was paid to it.[32] Some months later, incipient national feeling can be discerned in an attack on the indifference and disunity of Arab Muslims. Rashid Rida, the Syrian editor of *al-Manar* and a fervent believer in Islam, commenting on the Jewish national revival, was both affronted and inspired by what the "weak and penniless" Jews were doing and called on Arabs to understand that they were being restricted "in the rights of your homeland," urging them to organize and unite like Jews.[33] At this stage, Zionism for Rida was more of a model for an Arab awakening than a menace.

Another interesting response to Jewish colonization was made in 1899 by Yusuf Diya al-Khalidi, a former president of the Municipal Council in Jerusalem. A "sacred obligation of conscience" compelled him to write to the Chief Rabbi of France that Zionism was "completely natural, fine and just. Who can contest the rights of Jews to Palestine?"[34] But Palestine was now part of the Ottoman Empire, he warned, and although the Turks and Arabs were generally well-disposed toward Jews, a few were infected with hatred. Moreover, there were Christian "fanatics" who inflamed hatred between Jews and Muslims. Zionists must find another territory, he concluded; otherwise, there would be a popular movement against Jews in Palestine.

Among the Arab national expressions that drew the attention of the European press and several Zionists prior to 1908, when the stirrings of a "movement" began, the most important was a book by a Christian Arab Négib Azoury, who had previously assisted the Turkish pasha in Jerusalem. In his *Le Reveil de la Nation Arabe*, published in 1905 in Paris, Azoury demanded the establishment of an independent Arab empire from the Nile to the Euphrates. He also pointed to the lurking danger of the revival of the ancient Jewish state and warned that the two rising movements "are destined to continually struggle until one overcomes the other."[35]

An article on the Arab movement ("The Veiled Question") devoted largely to an analysis of Azoury's book appeared in the periodical *Ha-Shiloah.*[36] The author discussed "the Arab movement that had just come to light," pointing out that although there was as yet no real Arab nationalist movement, if one should develop that is "both nationalist and popular," it will pose a danger to Zionism; for "even if the Arabs cannot say that Palestine is their country historically, they form the majority of the population and, most important, are tillers of the land." In the same year (1905), during the sessions of the Seventh Zionist Congress in July, President Max Nordau saw even more in the sporadic signs as reported in the European press. He referred to a "movement" which "has taken hold of a large part of the Arab people" and "can easily take on a direction that will affect Palestine." [37]

These Arab expressions were still largely those of individuals harkening back to the days of past Arab glory, often from outside the Turkish empire. Zionism was the irritant. Fear of Zionism as a threat to the existing status quo was the counterpoint of those Arabs who saw Zionism as blocking the way to a great Arab empire. Moreover, the Turkish example of opposing Zionism also influenced some Arabs and reinforced their opposition. However, clear signs of an "Arab national movement" were still not visible.

During this period, Zionists were still largely caught up in the struggle between the "practicals" and "politicals," and one segment of the socialist Zionist movement—Poale Zion—was itself split over Uganda. At the Seventh Congress, the territorialists and supporters of Syrkin withdrew from the congress and the Zionist movement. Otto Warburg, who was to become the moving spirit of practical Zionism, made his first appearance at this congress, emphasizing the political value of limited settlement. The Arab question was obviously not in the foreground of Zionist thinking. However, a young agriculturalist then studying in Switzerland, Yitzhak Epstein, was extremely sensitive to the issue and interpreted it from the point of view of some of the new Zionist settlers.

Epstein spoke earnestly to a closed meeting at the congress,[38] declaring that the Arab question was the most important of all problems facing Zionists and urging them to enter into an alliance with the Arabs. He dwelt upon the rights of the *fellahin,* calling on Zionists to buy only such land as was not being cultivated. Epstein also believed that Zionists should give full support to Arab national aspirations, even to the point of becoming more fully aware of the psychological difficulties of Arabs and helping them find their own identity. He also urged Jews to make an immense effort to raise the economic and educational standards of the Arab people.

Epstein's analysis provoked a reply,[39] in which it was argued that the *fellahin* had been exploited not by Jews, but by Arab landowners and moneylenders; that the more Jews tried to ingratiate themselves with other people, the more they were hated; and that the severity of the struggle of Jews in Palestine at the time made large-scale aid for the Arabs unrealistic and impossible. It was also argued that, unlike the Arabs, who had not been persecuted and had never ceased to be a people, Jews desperately needed to reconstitute themselves in their historic homeland.[40] These opposing positions in the continuing argument on the Arab-Jewish conflict have remained essentially the same to this day. In terms of the realities of Jewish life in Palestine at the time, Epstein's demands (made from remote Switzerland) that Jews help Arabs find their own identity have a strained, perverse intellectuality that presses too hard on credible human behavior.

The Jews in Palestine in 1908 had no sense whatsoever of being a Yishuv; there was no autonomous Jewish authority or recognized leadership. Many of the early idealists had given up the struggle and left the country. The remaining *halutzim* were groping physically and ideologically to find socialist Zionist forms of life free of abstractions and dogma. Contact between Jews and Arabs did not follow a pattern; some were friendly, others hostile. Zionist agencies, also without power and far from the land, were dealing with an unfamiliar political as well as physical terrain. At the Seventh Zionist Congress, it was suggested that a political commission be appointed to determine "our attitude to the movement of the Arabs so that everyone will not hold forth according to his inclination." But the issue did not come into sharper focus until the revolt of the Young Turks on July 23, 1908. In the months just prior to the revolt, Zionists were involved in one of their customary negotiations with the Turkish government, which was in the midst of one of its perennial financial crises. Zionist bargaining power, such as it was, involved making a loan in return for immigration and land-buying rights. This time the demands were fantastic. The government insisted on a loan of 26 million pounds at a time when the annual budget of the Zionist executive was a mere 4,000 pounds! One land agent demanded 1 million francs to revoke the ban on immigration. While the bargaining was still going on, the sultan was deposed by the Committee of Union and Progress (CUP), a group of army officers known as the Young Turks.

The revolt of the Young Turks aroused great enthusiasm among Zionists—the manifestos of the new regime, in fact, with their talk of decentralization and constitutional assembly, at first encouraged all minorities. At the celebrations in Jaffa, Zionists carried their blue and white flag and asked that they be represented in the new assembly to press for autonomy. But the Young Turks were fundamentally out to Turkify the empire, not liberalize it, and both Arab and Zionist hopes for greater independence were blocked. Arab frustrations spilled over into more vehement anti-Zionist activity. Zionists tried to follow the pitch of events following the 1908 coup.

Immediately after the revolution, Dr. Victor Jacobson, a Russian-born Zionist who managed the Beirut branch of the Anglo-Palestine Bank, was sent to Constantinople to carry out Zionist diplomacy and quietly cultivate support for the movement in official and unofficial circles, but he made no headway. "There is no one to talk to," he concluded. In February 1909, the faction that wanted more decentralization was ousted from the government by the more nationalistic elements in the CUP. Jacobson became quite despondent about what concessions Zionists might now expect.[41] The ban on Jewish immigration was not lifted and, indeed, negotiations with the Turks ceased for the next two years. The Zionist movement during this politically fluid time had to assess the shifts and maneuvers of the government, the forces at work in the new Ottoman parliament, and the meaning of intensified Arab hostility toward Jewish settlement, both in action and word.

For nationally conscious Arabs, the revolt of the Young Turks spelled *hurriyya*—liberty—and pent-up emotions coursed freely in the press and parliament, in which Arabs held about one-quarter of all the seats. New Arab newspapers voiced radical demands and made Zionism a target for their fulminations. Leaflets calling on Arabs not to sell any more land to Jews and demanding that Jewish immigration be stopped were widely distributed.[42] There was also a sharp increase in armed attacks on Jewish settlements and on individual Jews. It was during this time that a series of raids on Sejera culminated in the murder of two Jews. Old regime functionaries and other malcontents insinuated themselves into the CUP branch at Tiberias and persuaded peasants in villages close to Sejera to challenge boundaries that had been agreed upon a decade earlier.[43] When this failed, a series of raids was begun on the settlement itself.

A steady perspective on these events was extremely difficult, particularly since the signs of a clearly political Arab movement *in Palestine* were missing. Even the early Arab nationalist Azoury, who had returned from Paris to campaign in the 1908 election to the Ottoman parliament, did not use the Arab nationalist program as his platform; his speeches were couched in the most general terms.[44] The Arab political parties at the time were very small, involving only several dozen people—hardly representative and hardly offering organized channels of contact. An Arab political leadership was as yet non-existent. There were individual Arab notables, but they were still trying to squeeze whatever profit and power they could out of the old Turkish system.[45] The Arab movement in Egypt was clarifying its direction and goals, and Arab nationalist societies were forming in Constantinople and Paris, but there was no evidence of a recognizable national movement in Palestine. Moreover, there were none of the elements out of which national movements had arisen in Europe, such as a developing national consciousness among the Arab masses, a national literature that could arouse a political revival, an economic or social program, or a call for a popular uprising. There were not even signs of a movement for popular education directed at arousing national consciousness.

Yet, after 1908, there was unquestionably more Arab hostility toward Zionism. Individual Zionists as well as officials of the movement tried to fathom its meaning. The analysis of evidence of increased tension stressed the incidents themselves, rather than the possible greater force animating them. "Official" Zionist opinion was inclined to view the pillaging, infiltration, and occasional murder by Arabs as a nomadic tendency or a reflection of the lawlessness rife in the Turkish empire, not an index of popular Arab feeling. Vested interests, such as Christian Arabs and Arab landowners who wanted to fan bad feeling between Arabs and Jews, were also blamed.[46]

A Poale Zion delegate to the Tenth Zionist Congress (1911), Shlomo Kaplansky, differentiated between the animosity of such interests and the community of interests of Jews and Arabs as a whole and was convinced that an understanding with the "democratic forces" in the Arab world was possible.[47] This essential identity of interest was a major theme in the ideology of members of Palestinian Poale Zion, although its substance was not elaborated. The Tenth Congress urged two general guidelines to promote this understanding: the establishment of contact and a neighborly relationship with the Arabs, and an informational program for the Arabs describing Jewish intentions and the intentions of those from the outside who incite Arabs against Jews.[48] This was not an incisive or clearly defined policy, but the delegates were largely Diaspora Jews, far removed from actual events and well aware of their political powerlessness and limited financial means. Moreover, they were chiefly concerned with propaganda and fund raising and with getting political support for their struggle. The power to redress, they believed, was still in the Turkish government. Jews in Palestine were in a much better position to assess Arab activity as it developed, but they too inevitably had *their* angle of vision, and the bare facts of the Jewish presence in Palestine as they saw it could scarcely be considered "threatening."

Just before the beginning of World War I, Jews owned a little more than 100,000 acres, or 2 percent of the land in Palestine. The vast majority of the 90,000 or so Jews in the country belonged to the old religious rather than to the new nationalist movement while the number of Jewish farm workers was about 2,000, or 10 percent of the total hired labor employed in Jewish farms and villages. There were three *kvutzot* struggling to survive and the faint beginnings of trade unions and cooperatives in the towns. Objectively these were very meager results after thirty years of struggle to create a society based on Jewish labor and hardly the elements of a "threat." Yet some Arabs perceived Zionism—particularly its future, undefined goal—as ominous. Jewish farms, schools, newspapers, the use of Hebrew, strange new methods of working the land, the air of purposefulness and progress aroused envy and anxiety. What were they planning? The Zionists, of course, had no clear ideas of what the future would hold, but the Arabs were drawing their own conclusions: They were sure that the Zionists intended to come in ever larger numbers, buy up the land, and push them out or take over the country, Turkish power notwithstanding.

A few Zionist officials began to express some misgivings about socialist Zionist activity, thinking that this might be a clue to the growing hostility. On April 24, 1908, S. D. Levontin, director of the local Anglo-Palestine Bank (set up by the Zionist Organization), wrote to Wolffsohn that Poale Zion members "increase the class struggle and preach verbally and in their organs against giving work to Arabs. They thus sow hatred against us in the heart of the local population." [49] A clash between Arab and Jewish workers in Jaffa about the same time led Levontin to further complain that the young men from Poale Zion were largely responsible for the growing tension. They had been walking around, some armed with sticks, some with rifles, behaving antagonistically toward Arabs and creating suspicions about Zionism by urging that cheap Arab labor be replaced by Jewish labor.[50] Yet in December 1907 Levontin had also noted that the hostility to the Yishuv was fanned by the *mutasarrif* (subgovernor) in Jerusalem and his counterpart at Jaffa.[51] Ruppin, who later became a champion of binationalism, viewed the Jaffa violence as "an accidental brawl such as occurs daily in countries ... [that are] culturally or religiously heterogeneous. Instead of being surprised that disturbances had occurred in Jaffa, one should rather be surprised that the relations between Jews and Arabs here in Palestine are so peaceful, notwithstanding all differences." [52]

Those in Poale Zion who still clung to their Marxism were caught in an ideological dilemma: On the one hand, they could not accept the idea that Jewish colonization might involve them in a conflict with the indigenous population; on the other hand, their Marxism preached that the brotherhood of workers applied only to a proletariat already secure in their employment, not to a potential proletariat such as the Arab *fellahin*. The men involved in land purchases—Ruppin, Thon, and R. Benyamin—were very sensitive to Arab suspicions and were later among the founding members of Brit Shalom, a movement that regarded Arab-Jewish understanding as the main task of the Zionist movement. Less than a month after the Young Turk revolution, Ruppin commented on the consequences inherent in the change of regime. He perceived the vital importance of creating good relations with the Arab population. Special rights for Jews, he believed, could possibly be granted and even defended with the state's power. However, as long as the Jews in Palestine constituted a negligible quantity numerically and economically, "even the best will of the central government in Constantinople cannot help the Jews to procure political power in the country. Arabs and Christians would soon make any Jewish privilege illusory." [53] Rubbin desired to foster a more favorable view of Zionism by starting an Arabic newspaper in Jerusalem and by other informational devices. But mainly he stressed the need for tact in the purchase of land. He, too, had some reservations about the doctrine of all-Jewish labor in Jewish settlements, although he supported the *kvutzot*.

In 1910, Ruppin wrote to the representative of a Russian Zionist group that proposed the purchase of land on the east bank of the Jordan, explaining that it could not be immediately colonized by East European Jews because it was too far from the other Jewish colonies and because "the Arabs in the Zarqa area have as yet had no acquaintance with Jewish settlement and . . . therefore it is necessary to be especially careful in the first years of intercourse with these Arabs. Unpleasant incidents between Arabs and Jews in Palestine keep occurring simply because the Jew understands neither the language nor the customs of the Arab and the Arab views with animosity what has in reality to be ascribed to the Jew's ignorance." [54] In order to avoid misunderstanding and hostility, Ruppin urged that the land be first settled by Jewish workers who knew Arabic and Arab customs.

Ruppin wrote in a similar vein to representatives of Jewish workers' groups: "We need laborers who know Arabic for they must live in peace with Bedouin neighbors"; in connection with the first settlement in the Negev (Ruhama), he wrote that six to ten laborers were needed "who know Arabic, the Arab's way of life and traits and how to live peacefully with their neighbors." [55] Yet he also fully realized the importance of "giving work and bread to our own poor brethren. Insofar as Jewish laborers seek employment in our farms, we shall give them preference, but it would be very dangerous to reverse the axiom and . . . give employment only to Jews." [56]

In his administration of the Palestine Office, Ruppin used the services of men with an intimate knowledge of local conditions, particularly Joshua Hankin and Albert Antébi, director of all Palestinian institutions of the Alliance Israélite Universelle. He also initiated and encouraged the immigration of Yemenite Jews, who were close to Arabs culturally, to take up work in the agricultural settlements. But it fell to East European Jewish socialists and Gordonists to put their stamp on the character of Jewish settlements. Ultimately, their passionate commitment to Jewish manual labor and opposition to cheap Arab labor were among the forces that destabilized Arab-Jewish relations and seemed to confirm Arab suspicions about Jewish separatism and sovereignty. Driven by a sense of the righteousness of their mission and self-abnegating social idealism, totally lacking, it has been said, "the cement of hypocrisy," they were too preoccupied with their vision, their perpetual striving to refashion their lives, and the religion of labor to see the possible complications of creating a separate economic sector. They believed they were earning their historic birthright through the bitter sweat of their brows, but their islands of *Avoda Ivrit* (Jewish labor)—won at such great cost—were creating the beginnings of a separate society, in danger of becoming alienated from the larger society.[57]

Moreover, none of the ideological guides—Borochov, Syrkin, Marx, and Gordon—foresaw conflict in the way it developed, or oversimplified the way in which it was to be resolved. Marxists among the Poale Zion, who were doing the most menial work at the lowest pay, were sure *they* were not exploiting Arab workers; if there was no exploitation of Arab labor, they reasoned, how could there be antagonism? Nor did the *halutzim* look down on the *fellahin*. Generally, except during raids, they were admired, even romanticized and emulated, because they were genuinely rooted in labor on the land. With tragic irony, this scrupulous avoidance of Arab exploitation drove the already separate cultures further apart.

By 1914, there were about 1,600 Jewish workers in Palestine, several hundred of whom were identified with Poale Zion or Hapoel Hatzair. The few hundred Yemenite workers did not affiliate with either party. It will be recalled that at first Poale Zion had been a strongly ideological Marxist party, but existing realities in Palestine forced the movement to accept the importance of Jewish agricultural communes. At the second Poale Zion world conference in 1909, Borochov still held to his Marxist views, arguing that the class-conscious proletariat (only a factory proletariat was authentic) in Palestine was still very weak and that any diversion into farming would weaken it further. But Poale Zion members from Palestine disagreed; by 1911 they accepted in principle the idea of cooperative agricultural settlements. The members of the nondoctrinaire Hapoel Hatzair were struggling to overcome the shame of parasitism in Jewish life in the Diaspora and become simple tillers of the soil. It was left to Poale Zion in the prewar period to articulate the socialist position with respect to the *fellahin*, and it took a conventional Marxist stand: The *fellahin* would have to organize a class struggle against *their* oppressors—the *effendis*—and become "proletarianized" before there could be Arab-Jewish worker solidarity. As to the spread of Western ideas and techniques, Poale Zionists regarded these as "progressive." There was nothing in socialist doctrine, as they interpreted it, which dictated that their settlements should remain poor and unproductive and that Palestine should remain backward and infertile.

As for Hapoel Hatzair, one can hardly imagine a more idealistic or peaceful movement; its members at first even refused to be *shomrim*. They insisted that Arab rights not be violated in the least way, but also strongly upheld Jewish rights. "We shall find a way," Gordon declared, "for a life in partnership with the Arabs, for cooperative life and work, destined to become a blessing to both people." Jewish relations with Arabs should neither be "submissive" or "arrogant." [58]

Refusing to see any distinction in the nature of the rights involved, Gordon maintained that though the Arabs were in the majority, "the land we bought and redeemed by our own labor belongs to us. No majority can invalidate our title to it, or take from us what is ours by right of labor and of our creative powers." He then argued that "quantity was not the main factor," but quality, that is, growth and self-sacrifice: "Whoever works harder, creates more, gives more of his spirit, will acquire a greater moral right and deeper vital interest in the land." [59] As to the argument that

Arabs may be the "actual masters" of the land, Gordon claimed that the Arabs had forfeited this right, first to the Turks and then later to the British, who became the real rulers. Barring the rights acquired through living and working on the land, the Arabs, like the Jews, have a historic claim, but in this regard, the Jewish claim is stronger in Gordon's view.

In buying land, Gordon urged the most scrupulous care: "There must be no infringement upon the human rights of the Arabs nor any dispossession of those who actually are working on the land." Rather than wrong them in any way, Jews must be ready to pay many times the value of the land to compensate "the real owners fully—those who live and those who work on the land." [60] As to the future, Gordon believed that neither the violence of Arab propaganda nor destructive action would avail against the life forces Jews were creating, that eventually "a human attitude" would develop between Arabs and Jews and both people would rise to higher levels of life and human association.

These observations were written after the war, when Zionists were still discussing the question whether there was or was not an Arab national movement. Socialist Zionists shared Gordon's views. But on one important point, he took issue with them. Sensing that the Arab masses could not be drawn away from their leaders, he warned: "They delude themselves and us who wish to persuade us that the Arab masses are or will be on our side and against the effendis. Such men overlook the fact that the Arab mass is not a detached body to be likened to our own proletarians who call themselves masses. The Arab mass is part and parcel of a living people." [61] Gordon also pointedly observed that in their attacks on Zionism, the Arab leaders never mentioned the "Jewish nation." This concept for Arabs today is still largely avoided or evaded or rejected. It has been, indeed, the "veiled question" for Arabs."

Ruppin had recognized the possible dangers in the socialist Zionist position, but was also aware of other complexities. For example, he observed strong resistance to Jewish colonization from *effendis* and rich Christian Arabs in Haifa and Nazareth, who loaned money to Arabs at usurious rates, who were under Russian influence, and who were "the best starting-point for Russia's advance into Palestine." Moreover, he had no doubt of the benefits to both Arabs and the Ottoman government from Jewish settlement. In a memorandum which he wrote together with Levontin, he stressed the high wages paid by Jews to Arab laborers, the high value of Jewish agricultural methods as an example to the *fellahin*, and the fact that Jews purchased the worst land.[62] The Palestine Office went to great pains to demonstrate that Jewish land purchase was not only inconsiderable but beneficial to the local population and prepared a detailed analysis of the various tracts of land that had been purchased since 1880. Ruppin also understood that the weakened role of the Turkish government played into the hands of anti-Jewish elements who could not yet demand Arab autonomy and vented their anger on the Yishuv. Indeed, general security deteriorated sharply in Palestine after 1908, and Jews were not the only victims of the spreading lawlessness.

Increased hostility against Jews in 1911–12 was marked by people who were not alarmists generally,[63] and by the Palestine Office, which had been surveying the Arab press. Arab nationalists fulminated against Jews in the newly founded papers *Falastin* and *Al-Muntada*, published in Palestine, and *Al-Muqtabas*, printed in Damascus. Both had to be suspended by the authorities for their inflammatory tone.[64] The Palestine correspondent of *Ha-Olam*, the central Zionist organ, warned that "the greatest force in Palestine is the Arabs," who have been neglected by the Zionists and who have been left wide open to anti-Zionist propaganda. "They are afraid lest the Jews should drive them out of the country. We should have been prepared for such an attitude." [65] The "greatest enemies" are identified as Christian intellectuals among the Arabs.

An unusual meeting of representatives of all Jewish organizations and villages was called by the Palestine Office on February 6, 1911, to discuss the increased tempo and bitterness of anti-Jewish feeling. Many agreed that practical steps toward positive and friendly relations with Arabs were essential. Ruppin himself said that nothing was more important to Zionism and the Yishuv than the goodwill of the Arabs, but no one knew how to channel this concern or deal with the elements provoking violence against Zionist colonies. No one dreamed that the Turkish empire would soon collapse, yet it was difficult to decide how much effort to invest in keeping the government from becoming hostile. For their part, the Arab deputies in the parliament began attacking the ruling party (CUP) for its pro-Zionist sympathies! They denounced Jewish aspirations as contrary to the Ottoman state and Arab interests. The Arabs were listened to with a mixture of unconcern, irritability, and impatience, and given assurances that the government would enforce existing regulations.[66] The dangers of Zionism were being exaggerated, the CUP supporters said. Ruppin believed that the Turkish government was "not unfavorably inclined toward the Jewish colonization in Palestine, even considering it a barrier against the growing Arab danger. Yet it does not dare to come out openly against the Arabs." [67]

The February meeting of Jewish representatives created a provisional committee to deal with the important issue of strengthening approaches to the Arabs. Yet, as Ruppin himself admitted, it was impossible "at the present embryonic stage of party relationships in Turkey to determine a certain role for Jews." [68] Zionists now had to weave uncertainly between Arab and Turkish forces, trying to win at least a remission of antagonism. A steady, unswerving course for a diplomatically and financially weak movement was clearly impossible.

The Turkish-Italian war in 1911 and the Balkan war in 1912 further weakened Turkey and gave fresh impetus to Zionist activities. There was greater willingness—and need—to listen to Zionist requests as long as the Turkish treasury was bankrupt. There was even talk of *une alliance islame-juive.* Restrictions on immigration were partly lifted and it became easier for foreign citizens generally to buy land in Palestine. Had the Zionist movement had more money at its disposal, various economic concessions that were for sale could have been acquired.[69] Then, in the midst of these shifting forces, in another sudden switch, certain Arabs began to woo the Zionists.

By the spring of 1912, the Zionist Executive seems to have achieved a new perspective on the turbulent political events of the time and determined that an understanding with the Arabs was the overriding consideration: "The governing party in Constantinople comes and goes, but the Arab population of Palestine stays where it is. . . . We are even more dependent on concord with the Arab population in Palestine than on the goodwill of the government." [70] The Arab nationalists, meanwhile, had been spurred by Turkish defeats and began to talk openly of autonomous rule in Turkey or secession. Their growing assertiveness made it urgent for the Zionists to strengthen their position by purchasing more land and bringing in more Jewish workers to cultivate it. By the same token, the Arab nationalists needed to strengthen their position by seeking allies. In the winter of 1912–13, two new Arab nationalist societies were formed: the Decentralization Party in Cairo and the Committee of Reform and Defense of Syrian Rights in Beirut, both of which turned to the Zionists for some sort of understanding. On February 19, 1913, the editor of the usually anti-Zionist Cairo daily *al-Ahram* wrote a surprising postscript to an anti-Zionist polemic: "It is absolutely imperative that an entente be made between the Zionists and the Arabs, because the war of words can only do evil. The Zionists are necessary for the country; the money which they will bring, their knowledge, their intelligence and the industriousness which characterizes them will contribute without doubt to the regeneration of the country." [71]

At the beginning of April, Salim Najjar, a Syrian Arab and one of the leaders of the Decentralization party, wrote to Sami Hochberg, the editor of *Jeune-Turc* (a Zionist-sponsored daily published in Constantinople) warning that it was to the interests of Zionists to cooperate with his party and urging an Arab-Jewish entente. Hochberg reported the news to Jacobson; he in turn recommended that the Zionist Executive send Hochberg to meet with the Arabs. Hochberg was an excellent choice: He had many important political contacts and was closely associated with members of the Zionist Executive but was not an official. Moreover, he spoke fluent Arabic and knew many Arabs, including Najjar, who had worked on the staff of *Jeune-Turc.* He went to Cairo with the blessings of the Zionist Executive.

Hochberg met a number of Arab nationalists in both Cairo and Beirut. On the matter of Jewish immigration, he observed that there was "anxiety or at least uncertainty," but since no official position had been adopted by either the Decentralization party or the Beirut Reform Committee, these views were still personal. He was surprised to find some Arab Christians who were conscious of *their* minority status in Syria even favoring a Jewish *majority* in Palestine and autonomy that would buffer *(tiendrait en deux)* the Muslim mass that populated vast, contiguous regions. A number of the Muslims present were willing to accept Jewish immigration without any reservation; others wanted to limit it as well as land sales. Of the twenty nationalists Hochberg met, only two were openly opposed to Jewish immigration, and they because Jews represented a European element "which would break the compact Arab mass whose force derived from the very unity of its language and customs." [72] In general, Hochberg gained the impression that both nationalist groups wished to come to an understanding with the Zionists. He, in turn, indicated to them that the Zionists would probably be willing to enter into such an arrangement if the Arabs integrated Zionist demands into their program.

Considerable optimism was felt by all parties. Final decisions awaited the coming Arab Congress in Paris in June, but a verbal understanding was reached between Hochberg and the Decentralization party whereby the latter agreed to "tone down statements in the Arab press and elsewhere prejudicial to Jewish immigration which has hindered a rapprochement between Arabs and Jews." [73] In return, *Jeune-Turc* would support the Arab movement to the degree that would be compatible with the integrity of the empire and would publish sympathetic accounts of the Arab movement and encourage similar accounts in the European—especially the British—press. The president of the Decentralization party prepared a special statement for the press urging the acceptance of Jewish help for "the development of our provinces," and Salim Najjar undertook a series of articles on the Arab-Zionist entente.[74] Hochberg then went to Beirut, where the verbal understanding was accepted by the Reform Committee. By July, the Palestine Office in Jaffa, which followed the Arab press closely, reported that the tone of articles on the Zionist issue had become noticeably more moderate. Public opinion could be changed.[75]

At the Arab Congress, the question of immigration was handled rather gingerly. Most of the delegates opposed *Turkish* immigration into the Arab provinces but were afraid of angering the government by a specific resolution. Nor was there anything unfavorable to *Jewish* immigration. Hochberg observed the same attitudes he had encountered earlier in Cairo and Beirut. A resolution was ultimately passed favoring such immigration as would benefit Syria economically. The chairman of the congress told Hochberg that he and his colleagues believed that Jewish immigration should be encouraged so long as the immigrants became Ottoman subjects and so long as Arab peasants were not displaced. He also disclosed that nationalist leaders as yet did not enjoy authority in the Arab world, and could not until the government met Arab demands. He then admitted that at this stage it would be injudicious for Zionist and Arab leaders to conclude an official agreement. For the moment, a secret entente would have to suffice.[76]

The Zionists now seemed finally to have found an organized channel through which to make contact with the Arab "movement" and reach a possible accord. Yet the leaders of the movement were handcuffed—as were the Zionists themselves—by the regime. Moreover, the leaders of the nationalist societies had no popular base, were in no way "typical" of the Arab masses, or of most Arab leaders and notables.[77] (Some scholars estimate that the three main societies had among them only 126 known members by October 1914. Only twenty-two were Palestinians, of whom perhaps only twelve were truly committed.) [78] This was admittedly a tiny yet potentially important group for the Zionists to deal with. Moreover, there were no others available. While waiting for instructions from Berlin, Hochberg obtained an extremely sympathetic, if vague, statement from several representatives at the congress, describing the Jews of the world as "Syrian emigrés . . . homesick for their native land. . . . We are sure that our Jewish brothers . . . will furnish their support to help achieve our common cause." [79] This was published in *Le Jeune-Turc* on July 16.

Jacobson came to Paris late in June and reported to the Zionist Executive that an entente with the Arabs would probably not be discussed; instead, he hoped to obtain a declaration from some of the Arab leaders in Paris, which could then be used to influence the government to relax its restrictions. However, the Arabs also had to deal with the vulnerable Turkish government—as did the Zionists—in their seesawing for accommodation. By September, they had already succeeded in winning certain promises and no longer seemed to feel that an entente with the Zionists was necessary. For its part, the Turkish government then put pressure on Zionists to make an entente with the Arabs before *they* could expect any relaxation of restrictions. The Beirut Committee hedged, waiting to see how far the government would go toward implementing promises. During the winter of 1913, in Constantinople, both Hochberg and Jacobson went through "entente pleasantries." In Cairo, however, the more radical Arab nationalists were dissatisfied with Turkish concessions and wanted full independence. For this end, Zionist backing was still sought.[80]

Zionists tried to comprehend these shifts and switches. The executive summed up the situation as it stood in November 1913:

> The national-autonomist efforts of the Arab population of Syria and Palestine have recently acquired a much more explicit character. . . . It is not possible to ascertain exactly how organized and strong the Arab movement is yet. Even if it does not seem strong at present, its future development cannot be anticipated. We must, of course, take this movement into account much more than do the Turks. . . . [We must try] to form an agreement. The means at our disposal are personal relations with influential circles . . . influence on the press, public

institutions which are accessible to the press (as for example our Banks and Health Bureau), specific agreements with the spokesmen of the Arabs. . . . [We] have already been working in this direction. Now this work has to be conducted systematically and on a larger scale.[81]

It was anticipated that Nahum Sokolow, a member of the executive, would be able to advance the efforts of Hochberg and Jacobson.

As for concessions to the Jews, toward the end of 1913, the three-month restricted permit for Jewish pilgrims was abolished, and three of the most virulently anti-Zionist papers were closed down for a short time. Transfers of land were quietly authorized. Once again sporadic anti-Zionist violence broke out and new anti-Zionist societies were founded in Jaffa and Haifa. Early in April 1914, Sokolow came to Jaffa. Among other tasks, he was to make a comprehensive examination of Arab-Jewish relations. On the tenth, an interview was arranged with a correspondent of *Al-Muqattam.* Sokolow urged Arabs to regard Jews as fellow-Semites "returning home" and made the point that if Jewish immigration were hindered, the land would remain waste and be of no use to anyone. Emphasizing the need for an Arab-Jewish understanding, he said that the Arabic language and literature would be taught in Jewish schools, that social services would be expanded, and that banking services would be opened for Arabs. In responding to the interview, Rafiq Bay, head of the Decentralization party, complained that Sokolow's words were "very nice," but that Zionists were seen as an economic threat and the vanguard of a Great Power invasion. To prove their intentions, they must cooperate economically with the local population and become Ottoman citizens. Other exchanges also followed, especially in the Cairo press. The Decentralizationists were disillusioned with the Zionists, it was said, but the need for further meetings and an Arab-Zionist understanding was expressed.[82] A perceptible shift in Arab interest was obviously going on.

Certain Arab leaders had been attacking those nationalists who had urged an entente at the Arab Paris Congress and had not taken a stand against Jewish immigration. Press attacks against Zionists intensified and in the April 1914 parliamentary election campaign, anti-Zionist statements were rife. Rashid Riad, the uncompromising Moslem theologian and publicist, said there were two choices: an agreement to settle differences, or a movement of opposition, including the formation of armed gangs. He used the word "cauterization." [83] Riad's threats were undoubtedly colored by his intense dislike of Europeans and his Pan-Islamic fervor.[84]

When Sokolow reported to the Executive in June, he wrote that "the question of settling *our relations with the Arab population has become acute.* . . . The reasonable Arabs . . . stress one common Semitic origin, are aware of our importance in Palestine as a stimulating and instructive element, and appreciate the advantages of Jewish cultural activity as against Christian, of which they were always afraid. At the same time, they do not conceal the fact that a *force* has now appeared," which, though numerically small, they "do not feel capable themselves of opposing." They now want further steps. "They want our schools to be put at the disposal of their children, that Arab be taught intensely in them, that we care for the fellahin, that Jewish, and not Christian, capital implement the large concessions, etc. There can be no question, but that these wishes absolutely correspond with our own interests." [85] But how to find the necessary means? Zionism is no great power, Sokolow lamented, and cannot conduct colonization activity with the means at a great power's disposal. Otherwise, "we would, in our interests, proceed in precisely this fashion."

Certain Arabs had apparently realized that they had been unduly optimistic about possible concessions from Turkey; some such as Nasif Bey al-Khalidi were also disturbed by the mounting anti-Zionist activity. Nasif Bey was the chief engineer in Beirut, on friendly terms with Kalvarisky, the administrator for the ICA, and a strong supporter of an Arab-Jewish understanding. Kalvarisky introduced Sokolow to Nasif Bey and other Arab leaders in Beirut and Damascus who expressed an interest in a high-level conference.[86] At the end of May, Sokolow instructed the Palestine Office to prepare a list of delegates for a preliminary meeting. On June 19, the office invited ten Arab delegates to meet with the Zionists on July 1 at Brummana, near Beirut. Nasif Bey had indicated that a meeting would take a long time to organize—prominent Palestinian notables would have to be won over, he said. Toward the end of June, his list was not yet complete, but he indicated that the editors of *Falastin* and *al-Karmal* might be present.[87] The Zionists were asked to supply "documentary evidence concerning the aims and methods of Zionism," following which the Arabs would "formulate their demands."

The editors named had, of course, been among the most vociferous of the anti-Zionist baiters. Afraid of unproductive, acrimonious sessions with such men, the Zionist Office requested the names of the delegates in advance of the meeting. The Turkish government, meanwhile, through the person of the governor of Beirut, opposed the meeting, saying it was unnecessary, and that he did not know in whose names Nasif Bey and the others were authorized to speak.[88] Moreover, he, the governor, was ordered to protect the Jews. Neither Nasif Bey nor Thon, who was by then involved in the negotiations, wanted to jettison the idea of a meeting. Nasif Bey cautioned Thon that "Governments are transient and fluctuate; the people are the constant factor, and one must come to an agreement with the people." [89] For their part, the Zionists wanted to maintain contact with the Arabs, but they were reluctant to negotiate with those whom Nasif Bey had nominated: Of the ten named, only three were thought to favor an Arab-Zionist entente. *Not a single Palestinian notable of any real standing was on the list.*[90] The Zionists feared that a meeting under these conditions would make matters worse. They sent a small delegation to meet with Nasif Bey the first week in August to find an acceptable way of postponing the meeting. Within a few days World War I broke out in Europe. Its results revolutionized the Arab world, dramatized Jewish insecurity, and precipitated new forces in the Middle East. The prewar configuration could never again be reconstructed.

From this brief analysis, it is obvious that between 1908 and 1914 both Zionists and Arabs were involved in a very complex web of shifting threads, making it difficult for an observer to see emerging patterns clearly. Forces appeared, were eclipsed, then reappeared, only to be fragmented, or modified, or nullified. Before the war the *halutzim* in Palestine had neither the power nor comprehension of events to set upon a political course leading to Arab-Jewish rapprochement. They could not possibly have foreseen the coming war, the collapse of the Ottoman Empire, or the ways in which Palestine would be drawn into the war's vortex. In 1910, the perception of Ben-Gurion and Ben-Zvi, socialist-Zionist leaders, was that they must learn Ottoman law, so they went to Constantinople. When they first heard rumors that war had started, they expected a general strike of European workers to stop it. As good socialists, they were shocked by the collapse of the Socialist International and the murder of Jaurès, dreamer of world brotherhood. Once Turkey entered the war, many Jews adopted Turkish nationality and volunteered to join the national militia, but the Turkish government rejected the idea. Socialist-Zionists wanted to organize a joint militia with the Arabs; the government said no. Soon after Turkey declared war, it took a very harsh line with Jews in Palestine, imprisoning and deporting many, including the Shochats and Ben-Gurion and Ben-Zvi. These anti-Jewish actions worsened relations with the Arabs, who began to eye Jewish property covetously, and made the problem of Jewish defense urgent. In 1915, there were not yet 100 *shomrim*, and Jewish settlements were falling. Hunger, attacks by locusts, malaria, and the unyielding land in Palestine also crowded the frame of reference of socialist-Zionists. Nor were the victims and Jews endangered by Russian pogroms forgotten; as remnants made their way to Palestine, they were cared for. Toward the end of the war, the exposure of the Jewish NILI organization as an arm of British intelligence and the terrifying news of the Armenian massacres escalated fear to a dread of the total annihilation of the Jewish presence in Palestine. When the war ended, except for the brief hope of reconciliation, the clash of Jewish and Arab interests erupted with new ferocity.

It is sometimes suggested that the beginnings of an Arab "national movement" can be identified after 1908. If that is so, was the nascent movement born with a built-in antipathy to Zionism? Was it, indeed, defined by that antipathy and fated forever to regard Zionism as an incubus? In helping to answer these questions, the following points are suggested for consideration:

1. The Arab fear of the Zionist movement was largely economic and
    social, partly overlapping the fear of the European presence, of
    modernization, and the uncertainties of change. It was intermixed
    somewhat with the traditional Muslim contempt for the religious
    Jew and fed by the refusal of a small, landowning class that
    dominated Arab society to care about the day-to-day life of the
    fellahin. Zionists were a threat because they were solving economic
    and social problems that created a better life which was denied the
    fellahin. Rather than draw the *fellahin* into a massive land-reform
    program, it was easier for the *effendis* to call on the tribal loyalties
    of the peasants in a common attack on the "foreigner."
2. A few years before the war, Arab nationalist societies had *political*
    goals, but these groups were splintered and had no popular base.
    They often functioned at cross-purposes. Like the Zionists, they
    had to appease the Turkish government, causing shifts and
    maneuvers in their tactics and inevitable ambivalence and murki-
    ness in their dealings with each other. Their apparent desire for
    entente with Zionists in 1913–14 may have been opportunistic, but
    the complications of their negotiations are not entirely explained
    by "opportunism." Some Arab leaders were clearly interested in an
    understanding with Zionists, some because Zionists were bringing
    prosperity to Arab society, others because they were sympathetic to
    the Jewish longing to return to Palestine and believed Zionists
    could help Arabs achieve independence.
3. The Zionist movement, being largely a movement of the Diaspora,
    lacked a realistic understanding of Arab fears, but a number of
    leading Zionists were acutely aware of the "Arab problem" and the
    necessity of working out an understanding with the Arabs. Despite
    myths to the contrary, the Zionist movement lacked both the
    wealth and power as well as manpower resources to meet Arab
    cultural and financial demands. The movement was often weak-
    ened by inner divisions and factions that pulled and pushed to
    disunity. Moreover, before 1914, it had no clear political goal,
    which led the Arabs to imagine the worst, namely, that the Zionists
    aimed to conquer the country. The socialist Zionists, intent on
    ridding themselves of Diaspora abnormalities, plunged into the
    most demeaning work in order to become "natural" laborers and
    avoid exploitation of Arab labor. The Arab *fellahin*, they believed,
    would have to first become an organized proletariat before a
    brotherhood of workers could be achieved.
4. It can be argued that the pre-war Arab national movement was
    essentially reformist, not separatist, in character.[91] The name of the
    Decentralist party denoted its purpose: administrative rather than
    political. Their quarrel with the CUP leaders was a domestic issue,

concerned with the way in which the empire was governed. Riad, one of the founders of the party, continually stressed Arab loyalty to the Ottoman state, which was, after all, the embodiment of Islam, and accused European imperialists of fomenting Arab separatism. Those societies that preached the necessity of breaking away from Turkey did not get a response. Moreover, the Arab revolt on which the British pinned so much hope during the war never materialized. Moslem solidarity proved much stronger than British-sponsored Arab nationalism.

5. Both Jews and Arabs were frustrated by the duplicity and corruption of Turkish politics, yet both had to deal with the reality of Turkish power. A fruitless cycle developed: As long as the Arabs were hostile to Jewish settlement, the government would not relax its restrictions against Jews. At the same time, continuing restrictions had a perverse effect on Arab-Jewish relations. Zionists had no political leverage whatsoever in Turkey, whereas Arabs controlled one-fourth of the seats in Parliament. The government would stop at nothing to compromise the Yishuv if Arab opposition required it; yet the danger of an Arab-Zionist accord also posed a threat to Turkey, and in the 1913–14 contacts, Turkey intervened and, in effect, stopped them. Many of these excruciating balancing acts, feints, tentative and substantive signs of an Arab-Jewish rapprochement are also to be found during the period of the British Mandate.

6. Despite its weakness and limited resources, the Zionist movement could have done more, as Ruppin and others believed, to encourage Jewish settlers to become Ottoman subjects, to learn Arabic, and to develop greater sensitivity to Arab customs. There was, it is true, some talk of a "joint Semitic spirit," of Jews and Arabs together building a great Palestinian civilization, even assimilation of Jews to Arab culture. But the European cast of mind could not be unmade. Nor could the passion of Jewish national feeling. Being so absorbed in their own national revival, perhaps it was humanly impossible for Zionists to identify with the aims of Pan-Arabism. Even if that had been possible, it is likely that Arabs would have continued to oppose Jewish immigration and settlement.

The conflict may have been inevitable. If those who say that no struggle for national liberation has ever been achieved without bloodshed are right, then no possible alternatives would have mattered. The two national movements may have been on a collision course in 1914, but the evidence is not conclusive. After the war, however, the vociferous demands of extremist Arab nationalists drowned out the voices of moderation and made reconciliation impossible. The war and its consequences, the vagueness of British promises to Jews, Arabs, and the French, the pro-Arab sympathies of the British administration in Palestine, the extremist Arab leadership, the impact of Nazism and the Holocaust on the Jewish consciousness and the desperate Jewish need for Palestine widened and deepened the differences which the agony of four wars has yet to heal.

Notes

CHAPTER 1: THE LONG JEWISH NIGHT IN THE PALE

1. The existence of Jewish communities in the Caucasus and in Transcaucasia can be traced to a time soon after the destruction of Jerusalem in 586 B.C. By the end of the fourth century B.C., cities in Armenia had large Jewish populations. Later, there were settlements in the Crimea, where, by the eighth century A.D., Jews comprised the single largest ethnic group. This area became the center of conversionist activity by Jews, Christians, and Muslims, particularly among the Khazars, a powerful people of Finnish-Turkish origin. Most of the Khazars, including the king and nobility, converted to Judaism. The account of this conversion, which occurred sometime between the seventh and eighth centuries, was related by medieval Arab travelers.

During the reign of the Jewish kagans, the Khazar kingdom rose to great power and prosperity. Jews were esteemed by the inhabitants, and many Jews fleeing persecution in Western Europe found refuge in the Khazar kingdom. Sometime during the tenth and eleventh centuries, the Khazar kingdom was conquered by the Russians. Louis Greenberg, *The Jews in Russia* (New Haven, Conn., 1965), 2: 1–4.

2. By the twelfth century, Greek Orthodoxy, which had become the state religion of Russia after a conversional competition, looked upon Judaism as a dangerous rival. Jews were hated and feared, but in spite of growing intolerance, their position was much better than it was in Western Europe, largely because the power of the church took several more centuries to consolidate. The Judaizing heresy of the late fifteenth century resulted in many apostasies from the church, and in 1478, Ivan III's court included government officials, high-ranking clergy, and his daughter-in-law, who had converted to Judaism. Within ten years, Judaism became so strong an influence that only Inquisition-inspired methods could crush it.

3. The root of tsarist Russia's anti-Jewish policies undoubtedly stemmed from fear of this early Jewish influence. Another interesting view is suggested by James H. Billington, in his rich and suggestive work, *The Icon and the Axe: An Interpretive History of Russian Culture* (New York, 1970), pp. 72–73:

The anti-Jewish fervor in the sixteenth century bespeaks an inner similarity between the ancient claims of Israel and the new pretensions of Muscovy. A newly proclaimed chosen people felt hostility toward an older pretender to this title. The failures and frustrations which might logically have caused the Muscovites to question their special status led them psychologically to project inner uncertainty into external fury against those with a rival claim to divine favor. . . . Like Israel, Muscovy was more a religious civilization than a political order. All of life was hedged with religious regulations and rituals. Like Old Testament prophets, ascetic monks and wandering fools saw Russia as the suffering servant of God and called its people to repentance.

Moscow was referred to as "Jerusalem" and "the New Israel." Like the early Jews, Muscovites dated their calendar from creation, celebrated their New Year's Day in September, wore beards, and had elaborate regulations regarding the preparation and eating of meat. Too, Ivan IV, defended his right to absolutism as a leader of a chosen people.

4. An exception to this policy was a sect called the Karaites, who believed in the supreme authority of the Bible and rejected the Talmud. They were not subject to anti-Jewish measures or persecution in tsarist Russia and apparently remain immune under Soviet rule as well.

5. Israel Friedlaender, *The Jews of Russia and Poland* (New York, 1915), p. 97.

6. Simon Dubnow, *Nationalism and History* (Philadelphia, 1958), pp. 9–10.

7. Solomon Maimon, *An Autobiography* (New York, 1967).

8. Supporters of assimilation often claim Mendelssohn as one of their own, while opponents of assimilation tend to denounce him. Dubnow warns of the danger of such "a great historical error." Mendelssohn fought vigorously for the separation of church and state, but rejected the separation of Jewish nationality from the synagogue. He did not consider Jews to be a secularized cultural nation, nor did he create the notion that Jews are a religious group capable of merging with other national groups. In his philosophy as well as his own personal life, he viewed the Jews as a religious nation that would never be merged with other nationalities, but would develop closer relations with other people with the advance of culture and education. See Dubnow, *Nationalism and History*, p. 366.

9. Jacob Raisin, *The Haskalah Movement in Russia* (Philadelphia, 1913), p. 189.

10. Edward Hallett Carr, *The Romantic Exiles* (London, 1949), pp. 145–46.

11. Simon Dubnow, *History of the Jews in Russia and Poland*, trans. I. Friedlaender (Philadelphia, 1918), 2:134.

12. Those who paid at least 1,000 rubles in taxes annually in any city, provided they had formerly been First Guild merchants within the Pale for at least five years.

13. In 1879, all categories of persons with a higher education.

14. Samuel Lieb Citron, "A Pilgrimage to Peretz Smolenskin," in Lucy S. Dawidowicz, *The Golden Tradition* (Boston, 1967), pp. 140–41.

15. Lionel Kochan, *The Making of Modern Russia* (Baltimore, 1962) p. 169.

16. Ibid., p. 173.

17. Jacob Lestchinsky, "The Economic and Social Development of the Jewish People," in *The Jewish People, Past and Present* (New York, 1946), 1:375.

18. I. M. Dijur, "Jews in the Russian Economy," in Jacob Frumkin, ed., *Russian Jewry (1860-1917)* (New York, 1966), p. 127.

19. Dubnow, *History of the Jews in Russia and Poland*, 2:366-67.

20. Ibid., p. 191.

21. Ibid., pp. 192–93.

22. Speech of the Hon. Samuel S. Cox, July 31, 1882, "On the Persecution of the Jews in Russia," *Congressional Record,* 47th Cong., 1st Sess, Appendix (Washington, D. C., 1882), pp. 651–58. A detailed list of anti-Jewish outbreaks is included.

23. Greenberg, *The Jews in Russia,* 2:24.

24. Dubnow, *History of the Jews in Russia and Poland,* 2:312.

CHAPTER 2: THE JEWISH *NARODNIKI*

1. The best single work in English on Russian populism is Franco Venturi, *Roots of Revolution: A History of the Populist and Socialist Movements in Nineteenth Century Russia,* trans. Frances Haskell (New York, 1960). Chapters 9–16 in Avrahm Yarmolinsky, *Road to Revolution: A Century of Russian Radicalism* (New York, 1962), are also excellent.

2. Venturi, *Roots of Revolution,* pp. vii–viii. Some writers have defined the term more narrowly. Billington takes an intermediate position, concluding that "by the end of the late sixties, a reasonably coherent tradition of radical protest had come into being inside Russia, which can legitimately be called populist. It was an anti-authoritarian movement dedicated to a radical transformation of Russian society." See James H. Billington, *The Icon and the Axe* (New York, 1970), p. 745.

3. Billington, *The Icon and the Axe,* p. 386.

4. Venturi, *Roots of Revolution,* pp. 223–24.

5. Yarmolinsky, *Road to Revolution,* p. 107.

6. Billington, *The Icon and the Axe,* p. 391.

7. Ibid.

8. Ibid., p. 393.

9. "Young Russia" was written by a 19-year-old student, Pyotr Zaichnevsky, son of a retired colonel, while he was in jail in Moscow for agitating villagers to take the land. All of his life he clung to the idea of enforcing socialism by means of the dictatorship of a revolutionary party—the notion later adopted by Lenin. Yarmolinsky assigns Zaichnevsky a place in the genealogy of Bolshevism.

10. Yarmolinsky, *Road to Revolution,* pp. 114–16.

11. Ibid., p. 24.

12. Billington, *The Icon and the Axe,* p. 397.

13. Yarmolinsky, *The Road to Revolution,* p. 209.

14. A. L. Patkin, *The Origins of the Russian-Jewish Labour Movement* (Melbourne, 1947), p. 80.

15. Leonard Schapiro, "The Role of the Jews in the Russian Revolutionary Movement," *Slavonic and East European Review* 40, no. 84 (December 1961): 149. "International" was the name given to the International Workingmen's Association, organized by Marx and Engels after their arrival in England. See note 3, chapter 7, for a fuller account of its activities.

16. Ibid.

17. J. L. Talmon, *Israel Among the Nations* (New York, 1970), p. 41.

18. Eliahu Tscherikover, "Yidn Revolutsionern in Rusland in di 60er un 70er Yorn," *Historishe Shriftn,* YIVO, 3 (Vilna, 1939): 89–90. (Subsequent references in this volume will be referred to as *Historishe Shriftn,* 3).

19. Ibid., p. 152; Yarmolinsky, *Road to Revolution,* p. 265.

20. Venturi, *Roots of Revolution*, p. 507.

21. Greenberg, *The Jews in Russia*, 2:146.

22. Ibid., 1: 83.

23. Ezra Mendelsohn, *Class Struggle in the Pale: The Formative Years of the Jewish Workers' Movement in Tsarist Russia* (Cambridge, 1970), p. 29.

24. See N. Myzel, "Layzer Tsukerman," *Roiter Pinkes* 1 (Warsaw, 1921): 93.

25. Those grounded in Talmudic Judaism also succumbed, as is shown by the comparatively large number of rabbinical students who also became deeply involved in the revolutionary movement. Greenberg suggests that "indoctrination of humanitarian Talmudic training predisposed them to the idealistic aspects of the revolutionary movement." *The Jews in Russia*, 1: 68.

26. Lev Deutsch, *Yidn in der Rusisher Revelutsye*, tr. from Russian by E. Kerman (Berlin, 1923), p. 20.

27. A. Litvak, "Aaron Zundelevich," *Roiter Pinkes* 2 (Warsaw, 1924): 83.

28. Deutsch, *Yidn in der Rusisher Revelutsye*, p. 20.

29. See Chapter 3.

30. *Historishe Shriftn*, 3: 159–60.

31. Stepniak [S. M. Kravchinsky], *Underground Russia: Revolutionary Profiles and Sketches from Life*, trans. n.c. (London, 1883), pp. 201–3. In 1878–79, the press regularly printed proclamations, small brochures, and five issues of the *Zemlya i Volya*.

32. Zundelevich was one of the accused at the first trial of the Narodnaya Volya in October 1880 (the so-called Trial of the Sixteen Terrorists). In court he professed pride in being a Jew and a revolutionary, declaring that he had been opposed to assassinating the tsar because "the tendency of the Christian world is to ascribe to the entire Jewish nation sins that are committed by one of them. In this case, the accusation would easily fall upon all the Jews." Zundelevich wanted to avoid these consequences. Another defendant at the trial, L. Tsuckerman, was also a Jew, a former *yeshivah* student from Mogilev who worked on Lieberman's *Ha-Emet* in Vienna and later returned to St. Petersburg to manage an underground printing press. Both he and Zundelevich were condemned to hard labor in Siberia. Zundelevich was later freed during the revolution of 1905 and went to England.

33. Deutsch, *Yidn in der Rusisher Revelutsye*, p. 33.

34. Stepniak, *Underground Russia*, p. 23.

35. Several Russian emigrés pioneered in establishing socialist parties in foreign countries. One was Anna Rosenstein, popularly known as Signora Kuleshov, who tore up her diploma in Zurich, signifying her rejection of the status quo and simultaneous entry into the revolutionary movement. She expounded anarchism in France and Italy, then shifted to socialism. She and her husband, A. Turati, founded the Italian Socialist party in 1891–92. *Historishe Shriftn*, 3:162.

36. Venturi, *Roots of Revolution*, p. 33.

37. Stepniak, *Underground Russia*, p. 111.

38. *Historishe Shriftn*, 3: 158.

39. Ibid., pp. 162–63.

40. Pavel Akselrod, "Pogromen un di Revelutsyonere Bavegung mit 43 Yor Tsurik," *Zukunft* 29 (1924): 550.

41. Ibid.

42. Ibid.

43. *Historishe Shriftn*, 3:164.

44. Quoted in Salo W. Baron, *The Russian Jew under Tsars and Soviets* (New York, 1964), p. 166.

45. Yarmolinsky, *Road to Revolution*, p. 218; *Historishe Shriftn*, 3:135-36.

46. *Historishe Shriftn*, 3:158.

47. Ibid., p. 159.

48. Ibid., pp. 136-37.

49. Venturi, *Roots of Revolution*, p. 577.

CHAPTER 3: AARON LIEBERMAN PERCEIVES THE JEWISH WORKER

1. The historian Dubnow obtained a copy of the Pahlen Commission report from which these statistics were taken. The report, which was printed for circulation within the Russian administration only, is discussed in detail in his *History of the Jews in Russia and Poland* (Philadelphia, 1918), 2: 363-69.

2. Mark Wischnitzer, *A History of Jewish Crafts and Guilds*, (New York, 1965), p. 275. In 1806 Napoleon created the semi-independent Duchy of Warsaw out of Prussia's share of Poland. After the Congress of Vienna in 1815, most of this territory was attached to Russia and became known as Congress Poland.

3. Ezra Mendelsohn, *Class Struggle in the Pale: The Formative Years of the Jewish Workers' Movement in Tsarist Russia* (Cambridge, 1970), p. 24.

4. Ibid., p. 25.

5. Ber Borochov, "The Jubilee of the Jewish Labor Movement," in *Nationalism and the Class Struggle*, ed. Abraham G. Duker (New York, 1937), pp. 174-75.

6. On the early strike movement in general, see Abraham Menes, "Di Yidishe Arbayter-bavegung in Rusland fun Onheyb 70er bizn Sof 90er Yorn," *Historishe Shriftn*, 3: 9ff.

7. Cited in Mendelsohn, *Class Struggle in the Pale*, p. 28.

8. Quoted in ibid., p. 18.

9. Ibid.

10. Ibid., p. 22.

11. Menes, *Historishe Shriftn*, 3: 11.

12. Quoted in Mendelsohn, *Class Struggle in the Pale*, p. 28.

13. Quoted in ibid.

14. Material on Lieberman is based on *Aron Liebermans Briv*, ed. Kalman Marmor (New York, 1951); Eliahu Tscherikover, "Der Onheyb fun der Yidisher Sotsialistisher Bavegung," *Historishe Shriftn*, 1: 512-32; and Ber Borochov, "Aaron Lieberman," in Duker, ed., *Nationalism and the Class Struggle*, pp. 169-73.

15. This circle is described in Tscherikover, *Historishe Shriftn*, 1: 470-532.

16. Eliahu Tscherikover, "Peter Lavrov and the Jewish Socialist Emigrés," *YIVO Annual* (New York, 1952), 7:132.

17. Ibid.

18. Quoted in A. L. Patkin, *The Origins of the Russian-Jewish Labour Movement* (Melbourne, 1947), p. 96.

19. Lloyd P. Gartner, *The Jewish Immigrant in England, 1870-1914* (London, 1960), pp. 99-112; Peter Elman, "The Beginnings of the Jewish Trade Union Movement in England," *Transactions of the Jewish Historical Society of England* 17 (1953); Eliahu Tscherikover, "London un Ir Pionerishe Role in der Bavegung," *Geshikhte fun der Yidisher Arbeter-bavegung*, YIVO (New York, 1945), 2: Ch. 2.

20. Ibid.

21. Tscherikover, *Historishe Shriftn*, 1:542–43. Samples of Lieberman's hand-writing appear on plates following p. 544.

22. Elman, "The Beginnings of the Jewish Trade Union Movement," pp. 58–59.

23. *Jewish Chronicle*, No. 39 (September 8, 1876), p. 364, quoted in Gartner, *The Jewish Immigrant*, p. 104.

24. The list of members, statutes, and minutes was published in *Historishe Shriftn*, 1:538–94.

25. Tscherikover, *Historishe Shriftn*, 1: 517–18.

26. Lieberman's proclamation was modeled after Lavrov's appeal to Russian radical youth, which had appeared earlier.

27. Samuel Lieb Citron, "A Pilgrimage to Peretz Smolenskin," in Lucy S. Dawidowicz, *The Golden Tradition* (Boston, 1967), pp. 139–40.

28. Tscherikover, *Historishe Shriftn*, 3: 519.

29. Borochov, "Aaron Lieberman," p. 172.

30. Ibid., p. 173.

31. Marmor, ed., *Aron Liebermans Briv*, p. 82.

CHAPTER 4: JEWISH RADICALS AND THE POGROMS OF 1881–82

1. From the acronym BILU (Bet Ya'akov Lekhu U-nel-ekha—House of Jacob, come, let us go). See *Bilu Manifesto* (1882) in *The Israel-Arab Reader*, ed. Walter Laqueur (New York, 1969), pp. 3–4.

2. The first BILU group was formed in Kharkov in 1882, consisting mostly of university students who, like the members of Am Olam, aimed at establishing cooperative colonies.

3. Joel S. Geffen, "Whither: To Palestine or to America, in the Pages of the Russian Hebrew Press: *Ha-Melitz* and *Ha-Yom* (1880–1890)," *American Jewish Historical Quarterly* 59, No. 2:179–208. See also Louis Greenberg, *The Jews in Russia* (New Haven, Conn., 1965), 2:62–72. *Ha-Melitz*, the first European daily, stressed Palestine as the only solution; *Ha-Yom* dwelt mainly on possibilities in America.

4. Abraham Menes, "The Am Oylom Movement," *YIVO Annual* (New York, 1949), 4:12.

5. Abraham Cahan, *Bleter fun Mayn Leben* (New York, 1926–31), 2: 17. The first two volumes have been translated and edited by Leon Stein et al., *The Education of Abraham Cahan* (Philadelphia, 1969).

6. Menes, "The Am Oylom Movement," p. 15.

7. Ibid., p. 16.

8. I. Kasovich, *Zekhtsik Yor Leben* (New York, 1919), p. 214.

9. The first was a colony of thirty-four families from Elisabethgrad who settled on Sicily Island, Louisiana.

10. George M. Price, "The Russian Jews in America," *Publications of American Jewish Historical Society (PAJHS)* 48, no. 1 (September 1958): 312.

11. Menes, "The Am Oylom Movement," p. 29.

12. Price, "The Russian Jews in America," p. 41.

13. Cahan, *Bleter*, 2:297–303.

14. Joseph Brandes, *Immigrants to Freedom: Jewish Communities in Rural New Jersey Since 1882* (Philadelphia, 1971), p. 41.

15. *The Jewish Daily Forward*, January 31, 1900; February 22, 1901.

16. Cahan, *Bleter*, 2: 305.

17. Simon Dubnow, *History of the Jews in Russia and Poland* (Philadelphia, 1918), 2:327.

18. Quoted in ibid.

19. Quoted in Greenberg, *The Jews in Russia*, 2:56.

20. Aaron Antonovsky, *The Early Jewish Labor Movement in the United States*, ed. and trans. from the Yiddish (New York, 1961), p. 37.

21. Ibid., pp. 35–36.

22. Ibid., pp. 36–37.

23. Greenberg, *The Jews in Russia*, 2:162.

24. Abraham Ascher, "Pavel Axelrod: A Conflict Between Jewish Loyalty and Revolutionary Dedication," *Russian Review*, 24, no. 3 (July 1965): 251.

25. Antonovsky, *The Early Jewish Labor Movement*, p. 37.

26. Ascher, "Pavel Axelrod," p. 251.

27. Ibid., p. 252. See also "Zichroines fun Grigory Gurevich," *Historishe Shriftn*, 3:224–43.

28. Ibid.

29. Quoted in Eliahu Tscherikover, "Peter Lavrov and the Jewish Socialist Emigrés," YIVO Annual (New York, 1952), 7:133.

30. Based on excerpts from Ascher, "Pavel Axelrod," and *Zukunft*, which is summarized in English in Lucy Dawidowicz, *The Golden Tradition* (Boston, 1967), pp. 405–10.

31. Ibid.

32. Ascher, "Pavel Axelrod," p. 256.

33. Ibid., p. 259.

34. Akselrod's manuscript was published in *Iz Arkhiva P.B. Akselroda, 1881–1896*, ed. V. S. Woytinsky et al. (Berlin, 1924), and is abridged in *Zukunft* 29 (September 1924): 550–55.

35. Ascher, "Pavel Axelrod," p. 260. Cahan's little-known novel, *The White Terror and the Red* (New York, 1905), deals with this negative, not to say destructive, attitude of Jewish revolutionaries toward the pogroms and toward their own origins. The novel is set in the 1870s and early 1880s and explores the dogmas, doubts, and conflicts besetting young Jewish revolutionaries of the time. The dilemmas of Akselrod are expressed by the figure Elkins, but unlike Akselrod, Elkins works his way toward an affirmation of his Jewishness. He leaves his comrades and decides to join other Jews going to America. Like Cahan himself, he joins a group very much like Am Olam. Cahan's own ideological passage, oscillating from socialist-assimilationist to concern for specifically Jewish issues, can easily be inferred from the issues raised in the novel.

36. Ibid.

37. Stepniak, *The Career of a Nihilist* (New York, 1889), p. 47.

38. Quoted in Yarmolinsky, *Road to Revolution*, p. 310.

39. Antonovsky, *The Early Jewish Labor Movement*, p. 41, states that all attempts at self-defense are found in the Russian police file on the pogroms, a copy of which is in the Simon Dubnow Collection of the YIVO Archives.

40. Greenberg, *The Jews in Russia*, 2:160. The Odessa account that first

appeared in Russian in 1882 was expanded later. The expanded version was reprinted in *Ha-Olam,* nos. 20–24 (March 1939).

41. Antonovsky, *The Early Jewish Labor Movement,* p. 42.

42. Quoted in ibid.

43. Greenberg, *The Jews in Russia,* 2:55–56.

44. Quoted from Mordecai ben Hillel Hakohen, *In mame-loshn* (Vilna, 1935), p. 216.

45. Antonovsky, *The Early Jewish Labor Movement,* p. 43.

46. Cahan, *Bleter,* 1:500.

47. Antonovsky, *The Early Jewish Labor Movement,* p. 40.

48. Lev Deutsch, *Yidn in der Rusisher Revelutsye* (Berlin, 1923), p. 10.

49. Quoted in ibid.

50. Tscherikover, *Historishe Shriftn,* 3:124. A secret report of the "Third Section" (secret police) which surveys the revolutionary propaganda between 1873–75, contains the first account of the Jewish participation in the revolutionary movement. Of 1,054 persons brought to trial within this period, 67 were Jewish (6½ percent). Dispersed throughout the report are the personal comments of the writer on the large number of Jews, such as, "The number of Jews is deserving of particular attention," or "The Jews are extremely dangerous." The Vilna circle (1876), according to the report, is the second largest of such groups and is mainly Jewish.

51. Figures based on official data from tsarist archives, cited in Greenberg, *The Jews in Russia,* 2: 149.

CHAPTER 5: THE UPROOTING: JEWISH RADICALS COME TO AMERICA, 1881–83

1. Aaron Antonovsky, *The Early Jewish Labor Movement in the United States* (New York, 1961), p. 56.

2. Mary Antin, *From Plotzk to Boston* (Boston, 1899), pp. 11–12.

3. Antonovsky, *The Early Jewish Labor Movement,* p. 61.

4. Estimates of the number of immigrants from Russia differ considerably. Wischnitzer's figure of 25,619 seems reasonable. See Mark Wischnitzer, *To Dwell in Safety: The Story of Jewish Migration Since 1800* (Philadelphia, 1948), p. 66. For a discussion of mass migration to America, see Eliahu Tscherikover, ed., *Geshikhte fun der Yidisher Arbayter Bavegung in di Fereynigte Shtatn,* (New York, 1945), 1: chaps. II, VI, X, and XII; and Zosa Szajkowski, "How the Mass Migration to America Began," *Jewish Social Studies* 4, no. 4 (October 1942).

5. Leon Simon, ed, *Essays, Letters, Memoirs of Ahad Ha-Am* (Oxford, 1946), p. 329.

6. *Jewish Messenger* 50, no. 19 (November 18, 1881): 5, 6.

7. Eliahu Tscherikover, "Jewish Immigrants to the United States, 1881–1900," *YIVO Annual* (1951), 6: 160.

8. *Ha-Melitz,* July 13, 1882; quoted in ibid., p. 163.

9. Antonovsky, *The Early Jewish Labor Movement,* p. 59.

10. Abraham Cahan, *Bleter fun Mayn Leben* (New York, 1926–31), 2:67–68.

11. Emma Lazarus, "The Schiff Refuge," *American Hebrew* 12, no. 10 (October 20, 1882): 114–15.

12. Antonovsky, *The Early Jewish Labor Movement*, p. 113.

13. Peter Wiernik, *History of the Jews in America*, 2nd ed. (New York, 1931), p. 29.

14. Following biographical sketch based on Cahan, *Bleter*, vol. I.

15. In the story *Uncle Moses*, Sholem Asch vividly recounts the story of Jews from the little town of Kusmin who work in Brooklyn for one of their *landsmen*, a manufacturer, Uncle Moses. All of them, from the rabbi to the leech-applier, sat all day long sewing trousers.

16. Morris Hillquit, *Loose Leaves from a Busy Life* (New York, 1934), p. 32.

17. This episode is described in Ronald Sanders, *The Downtown Jews: Portraits of an Immigrant Generation* (New York, 1969), pp. 56–59.

18. A copy of the handbill is in the YIVO Archives.

19. Cahan, *Bleter*, 2: 102–03.

20. Ibid.

21. Ibid., pp. 105–06.

22. Ibid., pp. 104–05.

23. Khaim Spivack, *Yubileum-shrift tsu Ab. Cahan's 50tn Geburtstog* (New York, 1910), p. 33.

24. Leon Stein, ed., *Education of Abraham Cahan* (Philadelphia, 1969), p. 237.

25. Bernard Weinstein, *Di Yidishe Yunyons in Amerike* (New York, 1929) pp. 101–02.

CHAPTER 6: SOCIALIST INTELLECTUALS ENCOUNTER JEWISH WORKERS, 1881–87

1. Quoted in William Leiserson, "The Jewish Labor Movement in New York," B.A. thesis, University of Wisconsin, 1908, p. 13 (MS. in YIVO Archives).

2. Louis Levine, *The Women's Garment Workers* (New York, 1924), pp. 32–33.

3. New York *Tribune*, August 25, 1885, p. 8.

4. Quoted in Levine, *The Women's Garment Workers*, p. 39.

5. Mary Beard, *A Short History of the American Labor Movement* (New York, 1920), p. 117.

6. See Eliahu Tscherikover, ed., *Geshikhte fun der Yidisher Arbeter Bavegung in di Fereynigte Shtatn* (New York, 1945), 2: ch. 6, for a full account of the JWA.

7. Cahan, *Bleter*, 2:237.

8. One of their leaders, Jacob Schoen, who had emigrated from Hungary in 1879, became a presser in the ladies' garment industry. By 1883, he had organized a dress and cloak makers' union, whose pressers' local became affiliated with the Knights of Labor. Schoen became a member of the Socialist Labor party and was involved in efforts to organize Jewish workers in the shoe and tobacco, as well as the garment, industries.

9. Herz Burgin, *Geshikhte fun der Yidisher Arbayter-bavegung in Amerike, Rusland, un England* (New York, 1915), p. 109.

10. Bernard Weinstein, *Fertsik Yor in der Yidisher Arbeter-bavegung* (New York, 1924), p. 51.

11. Chester McArthur Destler, *American Radicalism, 1865–1901* (New York, 1966), pp. 12–13.

12. In 1882, the CLU had nominated their own candidates for Congress, the state assembly and board of aldermen, but the workers did not turn out to vote for them. For the next four years, the CLU kept out of politics altogether.

13. Samuel Gompers, head of the young AFL, was generally skeptical of labor parties, but was swept along by the enthusiasm of the time. He even participated in the large torchlight parade that took place the week before the election.

14. Selig Perlman, *History of Trade Unionism in the U.S.* (New York, 1922), p. 103.

15. *The New York Times*, November 3, 1886.

16. Cahan, *Bleter*, 2:274.

17. Weinstein, *Fertsik Yor*, pp. 106–07.

18. Ibid., p. 110.

19. *American Hebrew* 36, no. 11 (October 19, 1888), p. 175.

20. *Folkstsaytung*, January 14, 1887.

21. Aaron Antonovsky, *The Early Jewish Labor Movement in the United States* (New York, 1961), p. 232.

22. Morris Hillquit, *Loose Leaves from a Busy Life* (New York, 1934), pp. 20–21.

23. Jacob Magidow, "Recollections of an Old Associate," in H. Laing and M. Feinstone, eds., *Gewerkshaftn*, issued by the United Hebrew Trades on the occasion of its fiftieth anniversay (New York, 1938), p. 30.

24. Many pushed themselves to exhaustion trying to save money for families left behind in Russia and were often blamed for unbearable conditions in the sweatshops.

25. Hillquit, *Loose Leaves from a Busy Life*, p. 23.

26. Ibid. On the formation of the UHT, see also Weinstein, *Fertsik yor*, pp. 143–50.

27. *Folkstsaytung*, October 5, 1888.

28. Described in Hillquit, *Loose Leaves from a Busy Life*, pp. 23–24.

29. Antonovsky, *The Early Jewish Labor Movement*, p. 301.

30. This was the first time that American Jewish workers were represented at an international conference.

31. *Arbayter Tsaytung*, March 24, 1890.

32. Described in Hillquit, *Loose Leaves from a Busy Life*, pp. 24–26.

33. Ibid., pp. 25–26.

34. Ibid., p. 26.

35. Ibid., pp. 26–28.

36. Ibid., pp. 28–29.

CHAPTER 7: THE JEWISH QUESTION AND THE SOCIALIST INTERNATIONAL

1. *Arbayter Tsaytung*, October 10, 1890.

2. Ibid.

3. The other Jewish organization represented was the Jewish Socialist Workers' Union of London, represented by Phillip Krantz. The First International was a loose federation of small socialist and trade union groups (rather than parties) which infused the working class with a sense of international solidarity. Many

currents of thought were represented at the First International: Mazzini-style nationalism, trade unionism, German socialism, extension of suffrage, anti-slavery protest. In one of his rare conciliatory periods, Marx was able to prepare a program that momentarily satisfied everyone. This came in the form of an inaugural address, in which, after describing the debased economic conditions of the English workers, he stressed the need for factory reform and worker conquest of political power—peaceably where traditions and custom would so dictate. But, inevitably, great cleavages developed. The interests of farmers clashed with those of the industrial workers; some wanted the overthrow of Napoleon III, others did not; some strongly supported the cause of Polish nationalism; others did not. Moreover, between 1865-70, there were serious splits among socialists, and between anarchists and socialists. Bakunin was thrown out after a violent fight between his followers and those of Marx. Finally, in 1876, the First International collapsed in Philadelphia.

4. Edmund Silberner, "Anti-Semitism and Philo-Semitism in the Socialist International," *Judaism* 2, no. 2 (1935): 117.

5. Ezra Mendelsohn, "The Jewish Socialist Movement and the Second International, 1889-1914: The Struggle for Recognition," *Jewish Social Studies*, no. 3 (1964), p. 131.

6. On his way to Brussels, Cahan stopped in London where Marx's daughter Eleanor brought him to see the old Friedrich Engels who, unlike his famous colleague, was sufficiently interested in the young Jewish labor movement in America to learn enough Yiddish to enable him to read the titles and subtitles of the articles in the *Arbayter Tsaytung*. Cahan was delighted to see his paper on Engels' desk.

7. Eliahu Tscherikover, "Di Ershte Yidishe Delegaten oif di Kongresen fun Sotsialistishen International," *Historishe Shriften*, 3: 791-92.

8. Abraham Cahan, *Bleter fun Mayn Leben* (New York, 1926-31), 3:162.

9. Silberner, "Anti-semitism," p. 118; Tscherikover, "Di Ershte," p. 788.

10. Cahan, *Bleter*, 3:166. Text of Cahan's speech appears in Herz Burgin, *Geshikhte fun der Yidisher Arbayter-bavegung in Amerike, Rusland, un England* (New York, 1915), pp. 164-65.

11. Silberner, "Anti-Semitism," p. 118.

12. Cahan, *Bleter*, 3:169.

13. The resolution which, according to the official record was passed unanimously, reads: "Le Congrès ... considerant que pour les populations ouvrières de langue juive, il n'y a pas d'autre moyen d'émancipation que leur union avec les partis ouvrières ou socialistes de leurs pays respectifs;

"Tout en condamnant les excitations anti-sémitiques comme une des manoeuvres par lesquelles la classe capitaliste et la réaction gouvernementale cherchent à faire dévier le mouvement socialist et à diviser les travailleurs;

"Décide, qu'il n'y a pas lieu de traiter la question proposée par la délégation des groupes socialistes américaines de langue juive et passe à l'ordre du jour." *Congrès International Ouvrier Socialiste tenu à Bruxelles du 16 au 23 Août 1891. Rapport. Publié par Sécretariat Belge* (Brussels, 1893), p. 106.

14. Cahan, *Bleter*, 3: 164. Tscherikover says Cahan was "plainly ashamed to tell how his resolution was handled." Tscherikover, "Di ershte," p. 790.

15. *Justice*, August 22, 1891, quoted in Silberner, "Anti-Semitism," p. 120.

16. Tscherikover, "Di Ershte," p. 790.

17. Ibid.

18. The text of this response is in ibid., pp. 796–97. There was as yet no Russian Social-Democratic party.

19. Ibid., pp. 790–91.

20. Ibid., p. 791.

21. Ibid., pp. 794–95.

22. George Lichtheim, "Socialism and the Jews," *Dissent*, July–August 1968, p. 315.

23. Ibid., p. 316.

24. J. L. Talmon, *Israel Among the Nations* (New York, 1970), p. 10.

25. At the time, French banking was largely in the hands of Protestants of French, Swiss, and German origin.

26. Nathan Rotenstreich, "For and Against Emancipation: The Bruno Bauer Controversy," in *Yearbook IV* of the Leo Baeck Institute (London, 1959), pp. 7–8.

27. See English translation of "Zur Judenfrage" in H. J. Steinig, *Selected Essays by Karl Marx* (London, 1926), pp. 40–97.

28. Edmund Silberner, "Was Marx an Anti-Semite?" *Historia Judaica* 11 (April 1949): 52. The use of the most vitriolic passages of Marx's essay in recent books published in the Soviet Union, such as Trofim K. Kichko's *Judaism Without Embellishment* (1963), goes far toward incorporating anti-Jewish ideas in the official ideology.

29. Ibid.

30. Leonard Schapiro, "The Role of the Jews in the Russian Revolutionary Movement," *Slavonic and East European Review* 40, no. 84 (December 1961): 159.

31. Silberner, "Was Marx," p. 33. By contrast, Engels acknowledged the existence of a large Jewish proletariat, whose lot was an especially bitter one, and stressed the significant role of Jews in the socialist movement. Moreover, Engels emphasized the Jewish role in precapitalistic economies, finding that Jewish capital was marginal in a sophisticated capitalistic society. See Edmund Silberner, "Friedrich Engels and the Jews," *Jewish Social Studies* 11 (1949): 323–42.

32. Silberner, "Was Marx," p. 48.

33. In the very year of the violent pogroms in Russia (1881), the organ of the social-democratic movement in Germany, *Der Sozialdemokrat*, reprinted the anti-Jewish passages of "Zur Judenfrage," hardly against the will of the author. Excerpts were also reprinted in the *Berliner Volksblatt*, October 10–19, 1890. Socialist and communist writers have been reluctant to confront the issue of Marx's writings on the Jews, for they raise serious questions about his formal reputation for humanitarian and universal values. See Silberner, "Was Marx," p. 51.

Donald L. Niewyk, *Socialist, Anti-Semite, and Jew: German Social Democracy Confronts the Problem of Anti-Semitism 1918–1933* (Baton Rouge, 1971), pp. 22–23, observes that "Marxist economic dogma thus inspired an apathetic SPD attitude toward anti-Semitism in the 1890's," but that before the outbreak of World War I German Social Democrats "became increasingly impatient with the disabilities under which the Jews of Germany and Eastern Europe functioned." He finds only a "very few, isolated instances of anti-Semitism in the SPD," but admits that the "SPD attacks against Jewish capitalists . . . kept alive among the workers the stereotype of Jews as grasping capitalists who were interested only in personal gain" (p. 27).

34. Silberner, "Anti-Semitism," p. 121. See also his "German Social Democracy and the Jewish Problem Prior to World War I," *Historia Judaica* 15 (April 1953): 3–48.

35. Quoted in Silberner, "German Social Democracy," pp. 11–12, from the *Sozialdemokrat*, August 18, 1881.

36. Quoted in ibid., p. 15.

37. Mendelsohn, "The Jewish Socialist Movement," p. 132.

38. Ibid., p. 134.

39. Tscherikover, "Di Ershte," pp. 791–92.

40. Franz Kurski, *Gezamlte Shriftn* (New York, 1952), pp. 76–79.

41. Tscherikover, "Di Ershte," p. 792.

42. Ibid.

43. Quoted in Mendelsohn, "The Jewish Socialist Movement," p. 136.

44. Quoted in ibid.

45. Ibid., p. 139.

46. Ibid., p. 140.

47. Ibid., p. 144.

48. See pp. 200-01, 204, and 206 for a further elaboration of the immigration issue.

49. Silberner, "Anti-Semitism," p. 120. The Bund had given the request to Rosa Luxemberg. It is not clear whether she neglected to give the message to the steering committee of the Paris congress (1900) or whether the committee rejected it.

50. The text of the appeal is reproduced in *Social-Democrat* 7 (London, 1903): 440–41.

51. *Sixième Congrès Socialiste International tenu à Amsterdam du 14 au 20 Août* (Brussels, 1904), p. 94. The pogroms of 1903 raised serious doubts for the Bund as to whether Russian workers could be counted on to defend Jews. Many of them had joined in the slaughter, forcing the Bund not only to organize self-defense units, but also to begin a serious study of the need for a specifically *Jewish* policy.

52. Jewish Socialist Labour Confederation Poale Zion, *The Jews and the War: Memorandum to the International Socialist Bureau* (The Hague, 1916), pp. 3–4. The attempts of Poale Zion to attain the recognition of the International after 1914 (finally succeeding in 1917) are described in Mark Jarblum, *The Socialist International and Zionism*, trans. Maximilian Hurwitz (New York, 1933).

CHAPTER 8: THE EARLY LABOR PRESS AND YIDDISH POETS

1. Abraham Menes, "The Jewish Labor Movement," in *The Jewish People Past and Present* (New York, 1955), 4: 354.

2. See comments by John Commons, American labor historian, in U.S. Industrial Commission, *Reports*, vol. 15, "Immigration and Education," House Doc. No. 184, 54th Cong., 1st Sess. (Washington, D.C., 1901), pp. 325, 327.

3. Aaron Antonovsky, *The Early Jewish Labor Movement in the United States* (New York, 1961), p. 359.

4. Ibid., p. 60.

5. The use of a Hebrew alphabet for a language completely different from the

Semitic languages is grounded in the religious education of Jews—for centuries the only one availble to them. They found refuge from a hostile world in the Hebrew scriptures and Talmudic commentary. But while Hebrew was the language of prayer and study, Yiddish became the spoken language of Ashkenazic Jews, a process that began almost a thousand years ago when emigrants from northern France settled in a number of cities on the Rhine, moved eastward, and adopted the German dialects of the area. In adopting these dialects, they changed the new language to their old speech patterns and created a unique mixture of German dialects intermixed with Hebrew and Aramaic elements. Later, as Jews moved farther east, Slavic languages influenced Yiddish. The principal disseminators of old Yiddish literature were the bards and jesters; after the invention of printing, there appeared tales and legends in Yiddish and the widely popular "Women's Pentateuch," *Tseno Ureno* (Go Out and See). The stories and homilies of Isaac Meir Dyk were also very popular. However, among the immigrants to America were a considerable number, women especially, who could not read. Many had never seen a newspaper in Russia. (Winchevsky lamented a similar illiteracy among Jewish immigrants in London.)

In 1859, the Hebrew periodical *Ha-Melitz* was started in Odessa. Two years later, Mendele Mokher Sephorim and his friend Joshua Lipschutz, who subsequently published a Yiddish-Russian dictionary, influenced the editor, Alexander Tsederboim, to request permission from the government to issue a Yiddish supplement. After many appeals, permission was finally granted to publish *Kol Mvasser* (Voice of the Messenger). It had great influence, but a small circulation; some towns had only one subscriber.

6. Moses Rischin, *The Promised City: New York's Jews, 1870–1914* (Cambridge, 1962), p. 118.

7. S. Sheinfeld, "Di Geshikhte fun der Yidisher Shriftzetser-yunyon," in *Fufsik Yor Yidisher Shriftzetser-yunyon* (New York, 1938), pp. 15–16.

8. Shmuel Niger, "Yiddish Culture in the U.S.," in *Jewish Life Past and Present*, 4:284. Niger's "Onhoyb fun der Proletarish-Yiddisher Literatur" in *Zukunft*, September 1940, is a full treatment of the subject.

9. Antonovsky, *The Early Jewish Labor Movement*, p. 240. The *Nu Yorker Yidishe Folkstsaytung* was a private venture whose editors were active in the Jewish Workingmen's Association. The JWA formally acknowledged it as a workers' organ and decided to support it rather than issue its own paper, as long as it defended the interests of the working class.

10. Cahan, *Bleter*, 2:15.

11. Morris Hillquit, *Loose Leaves from a Busy Life* (New York, 1934), pp. 35–36.

12. Ibid., p. 37.

13. Ibid.

14. *Zukunft*, January 1892, pp. 1–2.

15. *Arbayter Tsaytung*, May 9, 1890.

16. *Arbayter Tsaytung*, March 7, 1890.

17. In 1889, Rosenfeld helped to organize the first association of Yiddish writers in America to improve "jargon" literature in content and form.

18. Charles A. Madison, *Yiddish Literature: Its Scope and Major Writers* (New York, 1968), pp. 151–64.

19. The first collection of Rosenfeld's poetry in book form was *Di Gloke (The*

Bell) (New York, 1888). For English translation, see Morris Rosenfeld, *Songs of the Ghetto,* tr. Leo Weiner (Boston, 1898), also published as *Songs of Labor and Other Poems,* tr. Rose P. Stokes and Helena Frank (Boston, 1914), and Max Rosenfeld and Itche Goldberg, *Rosenfeld's Poetry in English* (New York, 1964). See also Ezekiel Lifschutz, "Morris Rosenfeld's Attempts to Become an English Poet," in *American Jewish Archives* 22, no. 2 (November 1970): 121–37.

20. Hutchins Hapgood, *The Spirit of the Ghetto* (New York, 1902), p. 109.

21. Jewish Students' Bund, *Yiddish Songs of Work and Struggle* (New York, 1972), p. 1.

22. A relative of Rosenfeld who was a wealthy butcher guaranteed the cost of publishing *Di Gloke.* Two thousand copies were published, but only about a hundred were sold.

23. "Earth," tr. Joseph Singer and Raphael Singer, in Irving Howe, ed., *Treasury of Yiddish Poetry* (New York, 1969), pp. 80–81.

24. David Edelstadt, *Edelstadts Shriftn* (New York, 1923); Madison, *Yiddish Literature,* p. 139.

25. Yossef Bovshover, *Gezamlte Shriftn* (New York, 1911).

26. Eli Katz, "Bovshover, Kobrin, Libin and Pinski," *Jewish Currents,* November 1972, p. 5.

27. Joseph Opatoshu, "Fifty Years of Yiddish Literature," *YIVO Annual* (1954), 9:75.

28. Niger, "Yiddish Culture in the U.S.," p. 290.

29. Melech Epstein, *Jewish Labor in the U.S.A.: An Industrial, Political and Cultural History of the Jewish Movement, 1882–1914* (New York, 1950), p. 295.

30. *Gezamelte Verk* [of Morris Winchevsky], ed. Kalman Marmor (New York, 1927), vol. I, *Biography of Morris Winchevsky;* Melech Epstein, *Profiles of Eleven* (Detroit, 1965).

31. Winchevsky's unfinished autobiography (in English), Winchevsky Archives, YIVO, New York.

32. Epstein, *Profiles of Eleven,* p. 23.

33. Ibid.

34. *Der Poylisher Yidel,* 1, no. 1 (July 25, 1884). Quoted in Lloyd P. Gartner, *The Jewish Immigrant in England, 1870–1914* (London, 1960), p. 107.

35. Esptein, *Profiles of Eleven,* p. 30.

36. Not to be confused with the Yiddish socialist monthly issued in the United States and still being published.

37. An American edition was published by the Newark branch of the Knights of Freedom, an anarchist group, in 1890.

38. Winchevsky, *Gezamelte Verk,* 10:143–46.

39. Quoted in Antonovsky, *The Early Jewish Labor Movement,* pp. 189–90.

40. He wrote "Hert, Kinder" in June 1886, when news of the Haymarket riot reached London.

41. Epstein, *Profiles of Eleven,* p. 33.

42. Antonovsky, *The Early Jewish Labor Movement,* pp. 186–87.

43. Ibid., p. 201.

44. John Gross, "The 'Jewish Chronicles' and Others," *Commentary,* November 1963, p. 388.

45. Winchevsky was close to Eleanor Marx Eveling during his years in London. She was active in Whitechapel, helping to organize and educate Jewish workers

there. Winchevsky portrayed her as a remarkable young woman and gifted writer who translated Flaubert and Ibsen into English. She was deeply wounded by the flagrant infidelity of her husband. In striking contrast to her father, Eleanor was very consciously Jewish and loved the Jews of the ghetto. At a parade of the Socialist International in Zurich in 1893, she told Winchevsky, "We Jews have to stick together." Winchevsky published his recollections of her after her suicide in 1898.

46. *Di Fraye Velt* 36, no. 5 (July 1892).

47. Winchevsky, *Gezamelte Verk*, 10:307.

48. Winchevsky, *Gezamelte Verk*, 9:155–57.

49. The exodus from Russia following the expulsion of Jews from Moscow continued until September 1892, when the discovery of a few cases of typhus temporarily halted all immigration to the United States. From 1890 to September 1892, an estimated 100,000 to 120,000 Jews—mostly from Russia—entered the United States.

50. Antonovsky, *The Early Jewish Labor Movement*, p. 257.

CHAPTER 9: YIDDISH IN THE CULTURAL GROWTH OF JEWISH WORKERS

1. C. Bezalel Sherman, *The Jew Within American Society: A Study in Ethnic Individuality* (Detroit, 1961), p. 167.

2. Charles A. Madison, *Yiddish Literature: Its Scope and Major Writers* (New York, 1968), p. 138.

3. *Tsu der Geshikhte fun der Yidisher Presse*, ed. Jacob Shatsky (New York, 1947), p. 54.

4. Shmuel Niger, "Yiddish Culture in the U.S.," in *Jewish Life Past and Present* (New York, 1945), 4: 285.

5. Ibid., p. 289.

6. Ibid., p. 275.

7. Shmuel Niger, "Di Zukunft un di Yidishe Literatur in Amerike," *Zukunft*, May–June 1942.

8. Isaac Rabonowitz, quoted in Shlomo Noble, "The Image of the American Jew," *YIVO Annual* (1954), 9: 90.

9. *Nu Yorker Yidishe Folkstsaytung*, September 18, 1889.

10. Supplement to *Yidishe Gazetn* 11, no. 37.

11. Shlomo Noble, "Pre-Herzlian Zionism in America as Reflected in the Yiddish Press," in Isidore S. Meyer, ed., *Early History of Zionism in America* (New York, 1958), p. 41.

12. *Nu Yorker Yidishe Folkstsaytung*, June 25, 1886.

13. Maxwell Whiteman, "Zionism Comes to Philadelphia," in ibid., pp. 192, 193.

14. *Labor Zionist Handbook* (New York, 1939), p. 57.

15. Baruch Zuckerman and L. Shipzman, *Geshikhte fun der Tsionistisher Arbayter Bavegung in Tsofn Amerike* (New York, 1955), 1: 113. See also *Yidisher Kempfer* 15, no. 146 (1935), for articles on the early years of Poale Zion in America.

16. See Chapter 23, on Syrkin.

17. See Yoel Entin's introduction to Leon Kobrin's *Dramatishe Shriftn* (New York, 1952); Madison, p. 143.

18. Eli Katz, "Bovshover, Kobrin, Libin and Pinsk," *Jewish Currents*, November 1972, p. 6. Three of Kobrin's sketches have been translated and edited by Max Rosenfeld, *A Union for Shabbos* (Philadelphia, 1967).

19. Hutchins Hapgood, *The Spirit of the Ghetto* (New York, 1902), p. 202. Two of Libin's sketches have been translated into English in Rosenfeld, *A Union for Shabbos.*

20. Noble, "The Image of the American Jew," p. 103.

21. Hapgood, *The Spirit of the Ghetto,* p. 121.

22. *Arbayter Tsaytung,* April 11, 1890.

23. *Frayhayt,* October 20, 1948, quoted in Epstein, *Profiles of Eleven,* p. 148.

24. Kalman Marmor, *Yaakov Gordin* (New York, 1953); Abraham Cahan, *Bleter fun Mayn Leben* (New York, 1926–31), 3: 186–94 and 4: 344–77. In English, Melech Epstein, *Profiles of Eleven* (Detroit, 1965), pp. 135–58; Hapgood, *The Spirit of the Ghetto,* pp. 136–49.

25. Ezekiel Lifschutz, "Jacob Gordin's Proposal to Establish an Agricultural Colony," in Abraham J. Karp, ed., *The Jewish Experience in America* (New York, 1969), 4: 253–64.

26. Ronald Sanders, *The Downtown Jews: Portraits of an Immigrant Generation* (New York, 1969), pp. 304–05.

27. Epstein, *Profiles of Eleven,* p. 146.

28. Niger, "Yiddish Culture in the U.S.," p. 293.

29. Ibid., p. 294.

30. Jacob Shatzky, "Some Letters to and from Jacob Gordin," *YIVO Annual* (1954), 9:126–36.

31. Lincoln Steffens, *Autobiography* (New York, 1931), p. 318.

32. Sol Liptzin, *A History of Yiddish Literature* (New York, 1972), p. 81.

33. Niger, "Yiddish Culture in the U.S.," p. 293.

34. Sherman, *The Jew Within American Society,* p. 161.

35. Ibid., p. 165.

CHAPTER 10: STORMY YEARS, 1890-97

1. Melech Epstein, *Profiles of Eleven* (Detroit, 1965), pp. 113–34.

2. Although the Yiddish press identified De Leon as a Jew, he never acknowledged his Jewish origins.

3. Ira Kipnis, *The American Socialist Movement, 1897–1912* (New York, 1952), p. 11.

4. Morris Hillquit, *History of Socialism in the United States* (New York, 1903), pp. 286–89.

5. Quoted in Kipnis, *American Socialist Movement,* p. 14.

6. Epstein, *Profiles of Eleven,* p. 125.

7. *Fraye Arbayter Shtimme,* May 10, 1890.

8. Abraham Cahan, *Bleter fun Mayn Leben* (New York, 1926–31), 2: 26–27.

9. Melech Epstein, *Jewish Labor in the U.S.A.* (New York, 1950), p. 258.

10. Quoted in Epstein, *Profiles of Eleven,* p. 131.

11. Epstein, *Jewish Labor*, p. 258.

12. A number of the young intellectuals worked by day and studied at night. They dropped out of sight for a few years and emerged as doctors, lawyers, and teachers who were still attracted by the vitality of the radical movement and stayed within its orbit. They, too, chafed at press control by a small clique.

13. Epstein, *Jewish Labor*, p. 259.

14. Moses Rischin, *The Promised City: New York's Jews, 1870-1914* (Cambridge, 1962), p. 225.

15. *Arbayter Tsaytung*, November 4, 1892.

16. Ronald Sanders, *The Downtown Jews: Portrait of an Immigrant Generation* (New York, 1969), p. 165.

17. *Di Zukunft*, February 1892.

18. Herz Burgin, *Geshikhte fun der Yidisher Arbayter-bavegung in Amerike, Rusland, und England* (New York, 1915), pp. 637-38; *Forward*, July 8, 1897.

19. Burgin, *Geshikhte*, p. 40.

20. Cahan, *Bleter*, 3: 452.

21. Jacob C. Rich, "Sixty Years of the *Jewish Daily Forward*," *New Leader*, June 3, 1957.

22. Ibid., p. 19.

23. In an essay Cahan wrote in 1889, he has a vision of socialism and realism striding hand in hand "on the path of progress and happiness." These ideas were developed more fully as Cahan began experimenting with fictional material and began publishing in English. American writers as well as social critics began noticing him. A meeting with William Dean Howells in 1892 and conversations with American literary figures who had become fascinated with Russian Jewish culture on the East Side nourished his never fully crushed desire to be an "American writer," a need that helped precipitate his temporary departure from the *Forward*. See Cahan's essay "Realism," in *Workmen's Advocate* (organ of New York Socialist Labor party), March 15, 1889.

24. De Leon's name for the dissidents was "kangaroos"—those who jumped from one party to another.

25. Epstein, *Jewish Labor*, p. 246.

26. Chester McArthur Destler, *American Radicalism, 1865-1901* (New York, 1966), pp. 490-91.

27. Cahan, *Bleter*, 3: 490.

28. M. Osherowitch, *Di Geshikhte fun Forverts, 1897-1947*, pp. 35ff (typescript in the Jewish Division of the New York Public Library).

29. George Lichtheim, "Socialism and the Jews," *Dissent*, July-August 1968, p. 325.

30. *Abendblatt*, January 4, 1898.

CHAPTER 11: NEW FORCES, NEW DIRECTIONS, 1900-10

1. See Eduard Bernstein, *Evolutionary Socialism* (New York, 1961).

2. *Memoirs of a Russian Governor, Prince Serge Dmitriyevich Urussov*, tr. and ed. Herman Rosenthal (New York, 1908).

3. A detailed "Table of Pogroms from 1903 to 1906" appears in the *American Jewish Yearbook, 1906-1907* (Philadelphia, 1906).

4. The immigration figures reflect the urgency to leave Russia, especially pronounced after the Kishinev pogrom of 1903, and reaction to the economic crisis in the United States in the winter of 1907-8. See table, p. 67.

5. Moses Rischin, *The Promised City: New York's Jews, 1870-1914* (Cambridge, 1962), p. 162.

6. The treaty was finally ratified in 1893, largely as a result of George Kennan's momentous report on the treatment of exiles in Russia, first published serially in 1887-89 in the *Century Magazine,* and in book form *(Siberia and the Exile System)* in 1891.

7. Rischin, *The Promised City,* p. 163.

8. Abraham Liessin, *Zichroynes un Bilder* (New York, 1954), pp. 112-16. See also Lucy Dawidowicz, *The Golden Tradition* (Boston, 1967), pp. 422-25.

9. Ibid., p. 116.

10. Henry J. Tobias, *The Jewish Bund in Russia from Its Origins to 1905* (Stanford, 1972), p. 57.

11. Liessin, *Zichroynes un Bilder,* pp. 119-20.

12. Ibid., p. 120.

13. Tobias, *The Jewish Bund,* p. 57.

14. Hutchins Hapgood, *The Spirit of the Ghetto* (New York, 1902), p. 114.

15. Ibid., p. 113.

16. Ibid., p. 115.

17. Liessin never seems to have found adequate release or expression in his poetry. For several years after 1904, he stopped writing poetry altogether. In 1912, his wife's death left him with the care of a daughter crippled by paralysis. Nevertheless, in 1913 he became editor of *Zukunft* and, despite Cahan's hostility and obstructionism, crowned his life with a long tenure as editor of the leading literary monthly in Yiddish.

18. The intensified national feelings among Jewish radicals caused the formation of the National Radical Union of Poale Zion in 1903, fusing the ideals of socialism with Zionism. The development of these ideas is treated below in Part III.

19. Abraham Cahan, "Jewish Massacres and the Revolutionary Movement in Russia," *North American Review,* July 1903, pp. 49-62.

20. [Arcady Kremer], *Arkady: Zamlbukh tsum Andenk fun Arkady Kremer* (New York, 1942), pp. 230-31.

21. This break caused great consternation among the Jewish socialists in New York. See pp. 295-300 for a discussion of the reasons for this break.

22. Tobias, *The Jewish Bund,* p. 244.

23. John Mill, *Pionern un Boyer* (New York, 1946-49), 2: 179-81.

24. Ronald Sanders, *The Downtown Jew: Portrait of an Immigrant Generation* (New York, 1969), pp. 333-49, discusses Cahan's book *The White Terror and the Red* and his efforts to lay these conflicts to rest.

25. Dr. Moshe Gurevich became the Bund's permanent delegate to the United States in 1905 and founded the Friends of the Workmen's Circle. See M. Gurevich, "Der Bund in Amerike," *Zukunft,* no. 10 (1937).

26. Maximilian Hurwitz, *The Workmen's Circle: Its History, Ideals, Organization and Institutions* (New York, 1936). See also Melech Epstein, *Jewish Labor in the U.S.A.* (New York, 1950), pp. 298-305.

27. Epstein, *Jewish Labor in the U.S.A.,* p. 304.

28. B. A. Weinrebe, "Di Sotsiale Role fun di Landsmanshaften," in *Di Yidishe Landsmanshaften fun New York* (New York, 1938), p. 84.

29. Shmuel Niger, "Yiddish Culture in the U.S.," in *Jewish Life Past and Present* (New York, 1945), 4: 286.

30. Abraham Menes, "The Jewish Labor Movement," in *The Jewish People Past and Present* (New York, 1955), 4: 377.

31. Quoted in C. Bezalel Sherman, "Nationalism, Secularism, and Religion in the Jewish Labor Movement," *Judaism* 3, no. 4 (Fall 1954): 363.

32. Quoted in Rischin, *The Promised City*, p. 160.

33. *Forward*, May 22, 1901.

34. Bernard H. Bloom, "Yiddish-Speaking Socialists in America, 1892-1905," *American Jewish Archives* 12, no. 1 (April 1960): 21.

35. Ibid., p. 25.

36. *Zukunft* (1904), quoted in ibid., p. 647.

37. *Zukunft* (1904), quoted in ibid., p. 413.

38. Quoted in ibid., p. 98.

39. Quoted in ibid., p. 24.

40. Hillel Zolotarov, *Amol in Amerika* (Warsaw, 1928), p. 458.

41. *Zukunft*, October 1904, p. 34.

42. The following account is based on Zosa Szajkowski, "Paul Nathan, Lucien Wolf, Jacob H. Schiff and the Jewish Revolutionary Movements in Eastern Europe, 1903-1917," *Jewish Social Studies* 29, no. 1 (January 1967).

43. Shmuel Niger, *In Kamf far a Nayer Dertsiung* (New York, 1940), describes the shifts of some socialists and intellectuals toward a more Jewish orientation.

44. Niger, "Yiddish Culture," p. 295.

45. Quoted in Charles A. Madison, *Yiddish Literature: Its Scope and Major Writers* (New York, 1968), p. 294.

46. Chaim Zhitlovsky, *Zikhroynes fun Mayn Leben* (New York, 1935), 3 vols. Several excerpts have been translated in Lucy Dawidowicz, *The Golden Tradition* (Boston, 1967), pp. 411-21. Melech Epstein, *Profiles of Eleven* (Detroit, 1965), pp. 297-322, also contains biographical material on Zhitlovsky and excerpts from his writings.

47. Epstein, *Profiles of Eleven*, p. 393, states that in the 1930s, Zhitlovsky saw a Soviet edition of Tschedrin's works in which the editor identified the bad wolf with the tsarist regime. On re-reading the story, Zhitlovsky was still inclined to accept his own version, however.

48. Zhitlovsky also affected the Bund indirectly. In 1896-97, he formed the Group of Jewish Socialists Abroad in Berne, consisting of national-minded socialist students. By the fall of 1900, John Mill had increasing help from the Berne group for *Der Yidisher Arbayter*. Attracted to the Bund, and enlisted to write and translate articles in Yiddish, they gradually awakened to the complex problems of Jewish life. It was the very growth of the Bund's activities in Russia that made Russian students abroad conscious of the problems of their communities back home. See Tobias, *The Jewish Bund*, p. 137.

49. In 1936, overwrought by the menace of Nazism and the weakness of the West, Zhitlovsky, who had been vehemently anti-Bolshevik, began to look to the Soviet Union to stop the Nazi danger. The last phase of his life involved him in bitter controversy with old friends, and perhaps an ideological throwback to his Social Revolutionary party days.

50. Marie Syrkin, *Nachman Syrkin, Socialist Zionist* (New York, 1960), p. 158.

51. Rischin, *The Promised City*, pp. 164–65.

52. Sherman, "The Jewish Labor Movement," p. 357.

CHAPTER 12: JEWISH LABOR TRIUMPHS: FROM ZEROS TO FIGHTERS

1. See Max D. Danish, *ILGWU News-History, 1900–1950* (New York, 1950); Moses Rischin, "The Jewish Labor Movement in the U.S.," *Labor History*, vol. 4 (1963); and Louis Levine, *The Women's Garment Workers* (New York, 1924), for the history of the ILGWU in English. Abraham Rogoff, *Formative Years in the Jewish Labor Movement in the U.S.* (New York, 1945), also contains valuable material.

2. Melech Epstein, *Jewish Labor in the U.S.A.* (New York, 1950), p. 365.

3. See Rudolph Glanz, "Jewish Social Conditions As Seen by the Muckrakers," *YIVO Annual* (1954), 9: 308–31.

4. Fictional treatment of ghetto life by Russian Jewish writers who had mastered English also appeared in the muckraking magazines. For example, Cahan's *The Rise of David Levinsky* appeared in *McClure's Magazine* in 1912–13.

5. *The Autobiography of Ray Stannard Baker* [David Grayson] (New York, 1945), p. 181.

6. Moses Rischin, *The Promised City: New York's Jews 1870–1914* (Cambridge, 1962), p. 183.

7. Rose Schneiderman, "A Capmaker's Story," *Independent* 27 (April 1905).

8. Abraham Menes, "The Jewish Labor Movement," in *The Jewish People Past and Present* (New York, 1955), p. 365.

9. Epstein, *Jewish Labor*, p. 372.

10. Bernard Weinstein, *Di Yidishe Yunyons in Amerike* (New York, 1929), p. 465.

11. Epstein, *Jewish Labor*, p. 375.

12. See J. M. Budish, *A History of the Cloth Hat and Cap and Millinery Workers International Union* (New York, 1925), for the early struggles of the union.

13. Will Herberg, "The Jewish Labor Movement in the United States," *American Jewish Yearbook* (1952), 53: 17.

14. At the time, there were 41 unions in the UHT, involving about 5,000 workers.

15. Weinstein, *Di Yidishe Yunyons*, pp. 358–59.

16. Levine, *The Women's Garment Workers*, p. 154.

17. Ibid., p. 144.

18. Ibid., p. 144ff.

19. Ibid., p. 159.

20. Ibid., pp. 156–57.

21. Quoted in ibid., p. 157. See also McAllister Coleman, "All of Which I Saw," *Progressive*, May 1950.

22. *Forward*, November 25, 28, December 7, 10, 16, 21, 1909.

23. Epstein, *Jewish Labor*, p. 394.

24. At a meeting called by the New York Cloak Joint Board on August 6, 1906, the gold watch chain belonging to Max Pine, secretary of the UHT, was pledged against the $25 rental of the hall.

25. Abraham Rosenberg, *Erinerungen fun di Klokmacher un Zayere Yunyons* (New York, 1920), p. 208.

26. Levine, *The Women's Garment Workers,* pp. 161–62, 204–05, 260.

27. According to Epstein *(Jewish Labor,* pp. 405–06), the unusual name given to the settlement grew out of a disagreement between counsel on both sides. Brandeis later explained: "To make the new agreement acceptable to the rank and file, an appropriate label had to be found for it." Meyer London (counsel for the union) suggested "this collective agreement." Fearful that such a phrase might encourage rather than abate "the war spirit of the radicals in the union," Julius H. Cohen (counsel for the employers) suggested "treaty of peace," a name that London opposed. Louis Marshall, the well-known constitutional lawyer, then came forward and said, "Why not call it 'protocol'—neither group will know what that means and it will achieve the result."

London's role in the settlement brought him widespread fame and near victory that fall in the Socialist party bid for the congressional seat in the Twelfth District. See p. 206.

28. Some historians have viewed the Protocol of 1910 as a traditional Jewish way of settling disputes. For the efforts of the New York kahals to arbitrate Jewish worker-employer conflicts, see Arthur Goren, "The Jewish Labor Movement and the Kehillah," in his *Quest for Community: The Kehillah Experiment, 1908–1922* (New York, 1970).

29. Herberg, "The Jewish Labor Movement," p. 19.

30. Rischin, *The Promised City,* p. 254.

31. See Philip Foner, *The Fur and Leather Workers' Union* (Newark, 1950).

32. Benjamin Stolberg, *Tailors' Progress* (New York, 1944), pp. 41–45.

33. *Forward,* December 23, 1912.

34. Jacob C. Rich, "Sixty Years of the *Jewish Daily Forward,"* *New Leader,* June 3, 1957, p. 28.

35. *Forward,* March 1, 1913.

36. Herberg, "The Jewish Labor Movement," p. 23.

37. Rich, "Sixty Years," p. 27.

38. Ibid., p. 28.

39. Isaac Metzker, *A Bintel Brief* (Garden City, N.Y., 1971).

40. Epstein, *Jewish Labor,* p. 419.

CHAPTER 13: POLITICAL STRUGGLES AND UNSEEN QUESTIONS, 1908–17

1. Morris Hillquit, *History of Socialism in the United States* (New York, 1903), pp. 322–25.

2. Ira Kipnis, *The American Socialist Movement, 1897–1912* (New York, 1952), p. 36.

3. *The People* (Hillquit-Williams St. Faction), February 4, 1900.

4. Kipnis, *The American Socialist Movement,* p. 107.

5. Ibid., p. 214.

6. Ibid., p. 220.

7. John Spargo, "The Influence of Karl Marx on Contemporary Socialism," *American Journal of Sociology* 16 (July 1910).

8. The party also agreed not to "meddle" in internal union activities or seek endorsement by a union and abandoned the fight for industrial unionism. Victor

Berger said: "We must make the trade unionist constantly feel that the S.P. is the political complement—the other half—of the economic organization [the union]." *Socialist Party Official Bulletin,* January 1909.

9. Socialist party, *Proceedings of the National Convention,* 1912, pp. 237–48.

10. Kipnis, *The American Socialist Movement,* p. 275.

11. Abraham Menes, "The Jewish Labor Movement," in *The Jewish People Past and Present* (New York, 1955), 4: 378.

12. Melech Epstein, *Jewish Labor in the U.S.A.* (New York, 1950), p. 350.

13. The federation reached its peak membership in 1917. It was seriously split in 1921 at the time of the schism between supporters and opponents of the Communist International, as were socialist parties all over the world.

14. One issue that divided the two groups in the Arbayter Ring for seven or eight years was education. The young Bundists in the federation wanted a broad educational program, with a centralized educational department, a substantial budget, and the opening of Yiddish schools for children of members. The older members were grouped around the *Forward* and were reluctant to widen the scope of activity of the organization. Moreover, long in the leadership, centered in New York and a few other large cities, the old guard wanted the centralized organizational structure to continue. The rift in Massachusetts during this period was so great that for a time an independent A.R. was formed. By 1916, most of these differences were reconciled.

15. Marcus Lee Hansen, *The Immigrant in American History* (Cambridge, 1940), p. 95, suggests that probably more immigrant socialists were lost to the cause in the U.S. than were won from the ranks of the newcomers.

16. J. Lenz, *The Rise and Fall of the Second International* (New York, 1932), p. 68. See also Chapter 7.

17. *Socialist Party Official Bulletin,* March–April 1907.

18. See pp. 111–12 for the Bund position on immigration.

19. *New York and American Journal,* May 16, 17, 22, 1903.

20. Morris Hillquit, *Loose Leaves from a Busy Life* (New York, 1934), p. 108.

21. Kipnis, *The American Socialist Movement,* pp. 168, 171.

22. Ibid., p. 173.

23. Moses Rischin, *The Promised City: New York's Jews, 1870–1914* (Cambridge, 1962), p. 233.

24. *Forward,* September 11, October 8, 1906.

25. Rischin, *The Promised City,* p. 234.

26. Ronald Sanders, *The Downtown Jew: Portrait of an Immigrant Generation* (New York, 1969), pp. 382–83.

27. The results were: Goldfogle (Dem. and Indep. League) 7265; Adler (Rep.) 2733; Hillquit (Soc.) 3616. *New York Times,* November 8, 1906. See also Epstein, *Jewish Labor,* p. 329.

28. Quoted in Sanders, *The Downtown Jew,* pp. 378–79.

29. Milton Doroshkin, *Yiddish in America* (Cranbury, N.J., 1969), p. 118.

30. *New York Evening Call,* October 31, 1908.

31. *New York Times,* October 26, 1908.

32. Arthur Goren, "A Portrait of Ethnic Politics: The Socialists and the 1908 and 1910 Congressional Elections on the East Side," in Abraham J. Karp, ed., *The Jewish Experience in America* (New York, 1969), 4: 189.

33. Ibid., pp. 191–92.

34. *New York Evening Call,* September 12, 1908.

35. *Varhayt,* November 2, 1908; *American Hebrew,* April 3, 1908, p. 552.

36. *Tageblatt,* November 2, 1908.

37. Goren, "A Portrait of Ethnic Politics," p. 203.

38. Ibid.

39. Hillel Rogoff, *An East Side Epic* (New York, 1930), p. 18.

40. He actually supported a compromise resolution offered by Hillquit, opposing the exclusion of any immigrants because of race or nationality, but barring the immigration of strikebreakers and the "mass importation of workers . . . for the purpose of weakening the organization of American labor." See Kipnis, *The American Socialist Movement,* pp. 282-88. For London's report, see D. *Zukunft* 15 (July 1910).

41. *Forward,* October 20, 1910.

42. Goren, "A Portrait of Ethnic Politics," p. 206.

43. Ibid., p. 206.

44. Victor Berger, elected in Milwaukee in 1910, was the first Socialist congressman.

45. Zosa Szajkowski, *Jews, Wars and Communism,* vol. I, *The Attitude of American Jews to World War I, the Russian Revolution of 1917, and Communism* (New York, 1972), p. 5.

46. Ibid., pp. 180-81; and Zosa Szajkowski, "The Jews and New York City's Mayoralty Election of 1917," *Jewish Social Studies* 32 (1970): 286-306.

47. Hillquit was defeated, receiving only about 12 percent of the vote.

48. Joseph Rappaport, "Zionism as a Factor in Allied-Central Power Controversy (1914-1918)," in Isidore S. Meyer, ed., *Early History of Zionism in America,* (New York, 1958), pp. 303-04.

49. Ibid., p. 310.

50. *Yidisher Kempfer,* May 11, 1917, p. 4.

51. Rappaport, "Zionism as a Factor," p. 313.

52. Selig Adler, "The Palestine Question in the Wilson Era,"" *Jewish Social Studies* 10, no. 4 (October 1948): 305n.

53. *Proceedings of the Amalgmated Clothing Workers of America,* 1918, p. 193; *Proceedings of the International Ladies' Garment Workers Union,* 1918, p. 201.

54. Rappaport, "Zionism as a Factor," p. 315.

55. Benjamin Stalberg, *Tailor's Progress* (New York, 1944), p. 157.

56. C. Bezalel Sherman, "Nationalism, Secularism and Religion in the Jewish Labor Movement," *Judaism* 3, no. 4 (Fall 1954): 362.

57. Abraham Cahan, *Bleter fun Mayn Leben* (New York, 1926-31), vol. 5.

58. Melech Epstein, *Profiles of Eleven* (Detroit, 1965), p. 108.

59. Sherman, "Nationalism in the Jewish Labor Movement," p. 356.

60. Ibid.

61. Selig Perlman, "Jewish-American Unionism: Its Birth Pangs and Contribution to the General Labor Movement," in Abraham H. Karp, *The Jewish Experience in America* (New York, 1969), 5:208-48.

CHAPTER 14: THE JEWISH ARTISAN IN LITHUANIA-WHITE RUSSIA

1. Lieberman's writings hardly produced a ripple and he was soon forgotten, only to be rediscovered some twenty years later when he became the object of

interest and scrutiny by Bundists and socialist Zionists, who claimed him as their precursor. He was hailed as the first Jewish socialist who did not flee from his people and tried to reconcile Jewish needs and socialism.

2. Isaac M. Rubinow, *Economic Condition of the Jews in Russia* (Washington, D.C., U.S. Bureau of Labor, September 1907), 15: 496.

3. Ibid., pp. 489–90.

4. Henry J. Tobias, *The Jewish Bund in Russia from Its Origins to 1905* (Stanford, 1972), p. 8.

5. Jacob Lestchinsky, *Dos Sovietishe Idntum* (New York, 1941), p. 26.

6. Ezra Mendelsohn, *Class Struggle in the Pale: The Formative Years of the Jewish Workers' Movement in Tsarist Russia* (Cambridge, 1970), p. 7.

7. Ibid.

8. Ibid., p. 9.

9. *Historishe Shriftn*, 3: 50–51.

10. Rubinow, *Economic Condition*, p. 532.

11. Mendelsohn, *Class Struggle*, p. 10.

12. Rubinow, *Economic Condition*, p. 521.

13. Ibid., pp. 521–22.

14. Mendelsohn, *Class Struggle*, p. 22.

15. Jacob Lestchinsky, *Der Yidisher Arbayter in Rusland* (Vilna, 1906), p. 31.

16. Moshe Mishkinski, "Regional Factors in the Formation of the Jewish Labor Movement in Czarist Russia," *YIVO Annual* (1969), 14: 28. The rest of the Pale included the nine provinces in southern and southwestern Russia—the Ukraine—and the ten provinces of Poland. See map, p. 2.

17. Many localities not classified as cities were known as *miestechkos*, and in those settlements Jews had the right of domicile. The *miestechkos* served as the commercial and to some degree industrial centers of the surrounding countryside. The Russian village was usually an agricultural community, and in those villages the Jew was prohibited from settling.

18. Rubinow, *Economic Condition*, p. 495 (chart).

19. Mishkinski, "Regional Factors," p. 39.

20. *Historishe Shriftn*, 3: 1–21.

21. Rubinow, *Economic Condition*, p. 533.

22. Ibid., p. 524.

23. Mendelsohn, *Class Struggle*, p. 14.

24. Solomon M. Schwarz, *The Jews in the Soviet Union* (Syracuse, 1951), p. 19.

25. Rubinow, *Economic Condition*, p. 525.

26. Ibid.

27. Mendelsohn, *Class Struggle*, p. 11.

28. Simon Dubnow, *History of the Jews in Russia and Poland* (Philadelphia, 1918), 2: 366–67.

29. *V'period*, December 15, 1875, quoted in Mendelsohn, *Class Struggle*, p. 14.

30. Mendelsohn, *Class Struggle*, p. 14.

31. The observer was Sara Rabinowitsch, a German Jewish scholar who made a study of the early artisan guilds and *kassy* of the Jewish proletariat in Russia, as quoted in Rubinow, *Economic Condition*, p. 526.

32. Ibid., p. 528.

33. E. H. Jeshurin, ed., *Vilno* (New York, 1935), p. 83.

34. At the 1896 International, Plekhanov praised the activities of the Jewish Social Democrats: "These pariahs ... who do not even have the paltry rights the

Christian inhabitants possess, have shown so much staunchness in the struggle with their exploiters and such keenness in understanding the socio-political tasks of the contemporary workers' movement, that in some respects they may be considered the avant garde of the workers' army in Russia." Quoted in Tobias, *The Jewish Bund*, p. 61.

35. Rubinow, *Economic Condition*, p. 531.

36. Mendelsohn, *Class Struggle*, pp. 43–44.

37. Ibid., pp. 42–43.

38. Ibid., pp. 45–46.

39. Vladimir Akimov, "A Short History of the Social Democratic Movement in Russia," in his *On the Dilemmas of Russian Marxism 1895–1903*, ed. and tr. Jonathan Frankel (Cambridge, 1969), p. 212.

40. Mendelsohn, *Class Struggle*, p. 64.

41. Ibid., pp. 67–68.

42. Ibid., p. 68.

43. Abraham Menes, "Der Onhayb fun der Yidisher Arbayter-bavegung in Rusland fun Onhayb biz Sof 90er Yorn," *Historishe Shriftn*, 3:30–31.

44. Ibid., p. 30.

45. Ibid., p. 31.

46. Charles Rappaport, "The Life of a Revolutionary Emigré," *YIVO Annual* (1951), 6: 211–12.

47. Menes, "Der Onhayb," p. 32.

48. T. Kopelson, "Yidishe Arbayter-bavegung in Vilno Sof 80er un Onhayb 90er yorn," in Jeshurin, ed., *Vilno*, pp. 57–74.

49. Liuba Akselrod was later an *Iskra* collaborator and devoted philosophical disciple of Plekhanov. A number of early Bundists mention her with great affection in their memoirs. (She was not related to Pavel Akselrod.)

50. *Arkady: Zamlbuckh tsum Ondenk fun Arkady Kremer* (New York, 1942), p. 114.

51. Kopelson, "Yidishe Arbayter-bavegung," p. 61.

52. Ibid., p. 60.

53. Ibid., pp. 60, 63.

54. John Mill, "Fun di Pionern-tsayt," in Jeshurin, *Vilno*, p. 79.

55. Kopelson, "Yidishe Arbayter-bavegung," p. 64.

56. Tobias, *The Jewish Bund*, p. 14.

57. Akimov, "A Short History," p. 205. "The first Jewish Social-Democratic workers' groups," according to this report, "were founded in Vilna about the year 1887." Quoted in K. Frumkin, "Der Bund un Seine Gegner," *Zukunft*, 2 (1903): 281.

58. Richard Pipes, "Russian Marxism and Its Populist Background: The Late Nineteenth Century," *Russian Review* 19, no. 4 (October 1960): 327.

59. Tobias, *The Jewish Bund*, p. 115.

60. Plekhanov, however, in contrast with Akselrod and Vera Zasulich, accepted terrorism when it "seemed necessary in the interests of the struggle," until his break with Lenin toward the end of 1903.

61. Mill, "Fun di Pionern-tsayt," p. 84.

62. John Mill, *Pionern un Boyer* (New York, 1946–49), 1: 59.

63. Yaacov Peskin, "Di Grupe Yidishe Sotsiale-demokratn in Rusland un Arkady Kremer," *Historishe Shriftn*, 3: 544–52.

64. Ibid., p. 549. See also Koppel Pinson, "Arkady Kremer, Vladimir Medem, and the Ideology of the Jewish 'Bund,' " *Jewish Social Studies* 7, no. 3 (July 1945): 241.

65. Pinson, "Arkady Kremer," p. 242.

66. See pp. 240–43 for a discussion of *On Agitation*.

67. Mill, "Fun di Pionern-tsayt," p. 78.

68. Ibid., p. 82.

69. Kopelson, "Yidishe Arbayter-bavegung," p. 65.

70. Mill, *Pionern*, 1: 38.

71. Quoted in Ezra Mendelsohn, *Class Struggle in the Pale: The Formative Years of the Jewish Workers' Movement in Tsarist Russia* (Cambridge, 1970), p. 32.

72. Allen K. Wildman, "Russian and Jewish Social Democracy," in Alexander Rabinowitch, ed., *Revolution and Politics in Russia* (Bloomington, Ind., 1972), p. 76.

73. Quoted in ibid., p. 78.

74. Not until 1889 did the first illegal works in Yiddish start coming into Vilna. The earliest was probably Dikshtein's pamphlet, "Who Lives by What?" full of Marxist economic terminology. Tobias, *The Jewish Bund*, p. 18.

CHAPTER 15: FROM PROPAGANDA CIRCLES TO AGITATION, 1890–95

1. Moshe Mishkinsky, "Regional Factors in the Formation of the Jewish Labor Movement in Czarist Russia, *YIVO Annual* (1969), 14: 42–43.

2. Chaim Zhitlovsky, *Zikhroynes fun Mayn Leben* (New York, 1935), 2: 184ff.

3. John Mill, *Pionern un Boyer* (New York, 1946–49), 1: 69.

4. Quoted in Ezra Mendelsohn, *Class Struggle in the Pale: The Formative Years of the Jewish Workers' Movement in Tsarist Russia* (Cambridge, 1970), p. 38.

5. Ibid., p. 48.

6. Mill, *Pionern*, 1: 36.

7. Quoted in Henry J. Tobias, *The Jewish Bund in Russia from Its Origins to 1905* (Stanford, 1972), p. 24.

8. Mendelsohn, *Class Struggle*, p. 49.

9. Ibid., p. 50.

10. Ibid., p. 51.

11. Vladimir Akimov, *On the Dilemmas of Russian Marxism 1895–1903*, ed. and tr. Jonathan Frankel (Cambridge, 1969), p. 209.

12. Arkady Kremer, "Mit 35 yor tsurik," *Arkady: Zamlbukh tsum Ondenk fun Arkady Kremer* (New York, 1942), p. 397.

13. Mill, *Pionern*, 1: 95–97.

14. Quoted in Vladimer Akimov, *On the Dilemmas*, pp. 214–15.

15. Quoted in Jacob S. Hertz, "The Bund's Nationality Program and Its Critics in the Russian, Polish and Austrian Socialist Movements," *YIVO Annual* (1969), 14: 54.

16. John Mill, "Fun di Pionern-tsayt," in E. H. Jeshurin, ed., *Vilno* (New York, 1935), p. 86.

17. Mill, *Pionern*, 1: 98.

18. *Arkady: Zamlbukh,* pp. 52–53.

19. Avram Gordon, *In Friling fun Vilner Yidisher Arbayter-bavegung* (Vilna, 1926), p. 45.

20. It should be remembered that opportunities for the secular education of children of workers were very limited, especially after 1887, when Jewish quotas were greatly reduced.

21. Mill, "Fun di Pionern-tsayt," p. 87. This argument was also used by Lestchinsky in his preface to *Der Yidisher Arbayter in Rusland* (Vilna, 1906).

22. Gordon, *In Friling,* p. 35.

23. Akimov, *On the Dilemmas,* pp. 215–16.

24. Mendelsohn, *Class Struggle,* pp. 60–61.

25. Quoted in J. L. H. Keep, *The Rise of Social Democracy in Russia* (London, 1963), p. 46.

26. A Yiddish translation of *Ob Agitatsii* (On Agitation) appears in *Arkady: Zamlbukh,* pp. 293–321.

27. Ibid., pp. 309–10.

28. Ibid., p. 318.

29. Koppel Pinson, "Arkady Kremer, Vladimir Medem, and the Ideology of the Jewish 'Bund'," *Jewish Social Studies* 7, no. 3 (July 1945): 244.

30. Yaacov Peskin, "Di Gruppe Yidishe Sotsiale-demakratn in Rusland un Arkady Kremer," *Historishe Shriftn,* 3: 551.

31. Shmuel Gozhansky, "A Briv tsu di Agitatorn," *Historishe Shriftn,* 3: 626–48.

32. Leon Bernshtein, *Ershte Shprotsungen* (Buenos Aires, 1956), pp. 33–35.

33. Richard Pipes, "Russian Marxism and Its Populist Background: The Late Nineteenth Century," *Russian Review* 19, no. 4 (October 1960): 330.

34. Ibid., p. 332.

35. Ibid., p. 333.

36. Ibid.

37. Mendelsohn, *Class Struggle,* p. 53.

38. Gozhansky, "A Briv," p. 632.

39. Mill, *Pionern,* 1: 103.

40. A. Litvak, *Vos Geven: Etiudn un Zikhroynes* (Vilna, 1925), pp. 71ff.

41. Henry Tobias, *The Jewish Bund,* p. 33.

42. Eliahu Tscherikover, "Di Onhayb fun der Umlegaler Literatur in Yiddish," *Historishe Shriftn,* 3: 580–81.

43. Litvak, *Vos Geven,* pp. 69–85.

44. Several of Gozhansky's brochures are published in *Historishe Shriftn,* 3: 685–721.

45. Tobias, *The Jewish Bund,* p. 31.

46. Ibid., p. 55; Allen K. Wildman, "Russian and Jewish Social Democracy," in Alexander Rabinowitch, ed., *Revolution and Politics in Russia* (Bloomington, Ind., 1972), p. 79.

47. Excerpts from Martov's address are in *Historishe Shriftn,* 3:649–52. In 1900, it was translated from Russian into Yiddish and called "Di Naye Epoche in der Yidisher Arbayter Bavegung."

48. Mill, *Pionern,* 1:229.

49. See Martov's "Zikhroynes vegn Broshur 'Der Vendpunkt'," *Historishe Shriftn,* 3: 653–57.

50. According to his biographer, even in 1895 Martov's advocacy of Yiddish was

"tactical and utilitarian, not surprisingly, for Yiddish meant nothing to him. . . . Martov [never became] . . . one for whom the preservation and cultivation of a national Jewish individuality in language, customs, and culture are worthwhile things in themselves." (Israel Getzler, *Martov: A Political Biography of a Russian Social Democrat* [Cambridge, 1967], pp. 28–29.) Yet Getzler speculates that he "was not so detached from his own people as to play his role against the Bund without pain or misgiving" (p. 62). (Before his death, Martov spoke with the historian Marc Yarblum and expressed deep interest in the humanistic socialism of the Jewish workers in Palestine. He also sent friendly greetings to the Bund in 1917, on the twentieth anniversary of its founding, emphasizing its role in the past.)

51. Memoir by Esther Frumkina, quoted in Zvi Y. Gitelman, *Jewish Nationality and Soviet Politics* (Princeton, 1972), pp. 29–30.

52. Bernshtein, *Ershte*, pp. 23–25.

53. Mendelsohn, *Class Struggle*, p. 154.

54. Charles E. Woodhouse and Henry J. Tobias, "Primordial Ties and Political Process in Pre-Revolutionary Russia: The Case of the Jewish Bund," *Comparative Studies in Society and History* 8 no. 3 (April 1966): 398–99.

55. Ibid., p. 355.

CHAPTER 16: JEWISH WORKERS ORGANIZE, 1895-97

1. Henry J. Tobias, *The Jewish Bund in Russia from Its Origins to 1905* (Stanford, 1972), p. 41.

2. *Historishe Shriftn*, 3:591.

3. Tobias, *The Jewish Bund*, p. 41.

4. *Historishe Shriftn*, 3: 47.

5. Ezra Mendelsohn, *Class Struggle in the Pale: The Formative Years of the Jewish Workers' Movement in Tsarist Russia* (Cambridge, 1970), p. 72.

6. *Historishe Shriftn*, 3: 47.

7. Mendelsohn, *Class Struggle*, p. 54.

8. Vladimir Medem, *Fun Mayn Leben* (New York, 1923), 1:208.

9. Vladimir Akimov, *On the Dilemmas of Russian Marxism 1895-1903*, ed. and tr. Jonathan Frankel (Cambridge, 1969), p. 218.

10. Ibid., pp. 218–19. The basic principles of later Bund organization and functions of central committee, trade councils, and local committees are described in ibid., pp. 223–30.

11. Hillel Katz, *Zikhroynes fun a Bundist* (New York, 1940), pp. 39–40.

12. John Mill, *Pionern un Boyer* (New York, 1946–49), 1: 216.

13. Ibid., p. 202.

14. Tobias, *The Jewish Bund*, p. 38.

15. *Der Yidisher Arbayter*, December 1896.

16. Allen K. Wildman, "Russian and Jewish Social Democracy," in Alexander Rabinowitch, ed., *Revolution and Politics in Russia* (Bloomington, Ind., 1972), p. 84.

17. Ibid.

18. Ibid., p. 82.

19. Quoted in ibid., p. 83.

20. The other socialist party active in Polish territory—the Social Democracy of the Kingdom of Poland and Lithuania (SDKPL)—was sympathetic toward the Bund.

21. Mill, *Pionern*, 1:116–17.

22. Ibid., p. 117.

23. Ibid., p. 216.

24. Ibid.

25. Quoted in Tobias, *The Jewish Bund*, p. 50.

26. Akimov, *On the Dilemmas*, p. 215. See "Proklamatsies in Yiddish Erev dem Bund," *Historishe Shriftn*, 3: 751–52.

27. Akimov, *On the Dilemmas*, p. 216.

28. Tobias, *The Jewish Bund*, p. 47.

29. Ibid., p. 62.

30. *Arkady: Zamlbukh tsum Ondenk fun Arkady Kremer* (New York, 1942), pp. 358–61.

31. Mill, *Pionern*, 1:258–59, 267–68.

32. Quoted in Tobias, *The Jewish Bund*, p. 64.

33. See Arkady Kremer, "Di Grindung fun Bund," in *Arkady: Zamlbukh*, pp. 358–60; Mill, *Pionern*, 1: 270–71.

34. Thirteen delegates were invited, six from Vilna (Kremer, Mutnikovich, and Kosovsky, and three Vilna workers: David Katz, Israel Kaplinsky, and Hirsh Soroka); Leon Goldman, John Mill, and Marya Zhaludsky from Warsaw; Pavel Berman from Minsk; Rosa Greenblatt and Hillel Katz-Blum from Bialystok; and Yidel Abramov from Vitebsk. See *Arkady: Zamlbukh*, p. 361. Mill pointed out that of these thirteen, only five were intellectuals, in contrast with the composition of other revolutionary groups in Russia. *Pionern*, 2: 272.

35. *Arkady: Zamlbukh*, p. 164.

36. Ferdinand Lassalle's Allgemeiner Deutscher Arbeiterbund probably inspired the name proposed by Arkady.

37. Wildman, "Russian and Jewish Social Democracy," p. 85.

CHAPTER 17: THE EARLY YEARS OF THE BUND, 1897–1901

1. Henry J. Tobias, *The Jewish Bund in Russia from Its Origins to 1905* (Stanford, 1972), p. 70.

2. John Mill, *Pionern un Boyer* (New York, 1946–49), 1: 278.

3. *Arkady: Zamlbukh tsum Ondenk fun Arkady Kremer* (New York, 1942), p. 381.

4. The pamphlet was called "Di Milkhoma fun der Poylisher Partai gegn dem Yidishn Arbayter Bund," 1898.

5. *Arkady: Zamlbukh*, p. 364.

6. Mill, *Pionern*, 1: 98.

7. Ibid., p. 300.

8. *Arkady: Zamlbukh*, p. 390.

9. Tobias, *The Jewish Bund*, pp. 85–86.

10. Yaacov Peskin, "Di Grupe Yidishe Sotsiale-demokratn in Rusland un Arkady Kremer," *Historishe Shriftn*, 3: 551.

11. Eliahu Tcherikover, "Yidn Revolutsinern in Rusland..." *Historishe Shriftn,* 3: 48.

12. Tobias, *The Jewish Bund,* p. 87.

13. Ibid., pp. 88–89.

14. Ibid., p. 91.

15. Mill, *Pionern,* 2: 6, 7, 13.

16. Tobias, *The Jewish Bund,* p. 94.

17. Mill, *Pionern,* 2: 32.

18. *Der Yidisher Arbayter,* no. 7, August 1899.

19. Tobias, *The Jewish Bund,* p. 98.

20. Ezra Mendelsohn, *Class Struggle in the Pale: The Formative Years of the Jewish Workers' Movement in Tsarist Russia* (Cambridge, 1970), p. 83.

21. Described in Shmuel Gozhansky, "Der Shtot Maggid," *Historishe Shriftn,* 3: 721–30.

22. Mendelsohn, *Class Struggle,* p. 84.

23. Tobias, *The Jewish Bund,* p. 101.

24. Ber Borochov, "The Jubilee of the Jewish Labor Movement," in Abraham G. Duker, ed., *Nationalism and the Class Struggle* (New York, 1937), p. 178.

25. According to Borochov, two-thirds of all the strikes by Jewish workers involved fifty or fewer workers. Ibid., p. 89.

26. Tobias, *The Jewish Bund,* p. 100.

27. Vladimir Medem, *Fun Mayn Leben* (New York, 1923), 1: 199.

28. Leon Bernshtein, *Ershte Shprotsungen* (Buenos Aires, 1956), p. 129.

29. Tobias, *The Jewish Bund,* p. 102.

30. Mill, *Pionern,* 2:35–36.

31. Zhitlovsky and later Nachman Syrkin were especially challenging to the students.

32. Quoted in Solomon Schwarz, *The Jews in the Soviet Union* (Syracuse, 1951), p. 348.

33. Chaim Zhitlovsky, "Tsionismus oder Natsionalismus," *Der Yidisher Arbayter,* no. 6, March 1889.

34. Tobias, *The Jewish Bund,* p. 136.

35. Mill, *Pionern,* 2:72–73.

36. Ibid., p. 109.

37. Vladimir Akimov, *On the Dilemmas of Russian Marxism 1895–1903,* ed. and tr. Jonathan Frankel (Cambridge, 1969), pp. 222–25.

38. Ibid., p. 226.

39. Tobias, *The Jewish Bund,* p. 115.

40. P. Schwartz, "Revolutionary Activities of the Jewish Labor Bund in the Czarist Army," *YIVO Annual* (1965), 13: 228.

41. *Der Yidisher Arbayter,* no. 8, December 1899.

42. Schwartz, "Revolutionary Activities," p. 231.

43. Ibid.

44. *Di Arbayter Shtimme,* no. 27, June 1902.

45. "The Zubatov Idea," *The American Slavic and East European Review,* no. 3 (October 1960): 335–46.

46. Mendelsohn, *Class Struggle,* p. 144.

47. The reference is probably to the practice of hiring strikebreakers.

48. Quoted in Mendelsohn, *Class Struggle*, p. 144.

49. *Arkady: Zamlbukh*, pp. 391-92.

50. Tobias, *The Jewish Bund*, p. 139.

51. Mendelsohn, *Class Struggle*, p. 137.

52. *Arkady: Zamlbukh*, pp. 166-67.

53. Tobias, *The Jewish Bund*, p. 125.

54. Boris Frumkin, quoted in Schwarz, *Jews in the Soviet Union*, p. 298.

55. Ibid., pp. 299-300.

56. Ezra Mendelsohn, "Jewish and Christian Workers in the Russian Pale of Settlement," *Jewish Social Studies* 30, no. 4 (October 1968): 244.

57. Bernshtein, *Ershte*, pp. 85-86.

58. *Der Minsker Arbayter*, December 1900, quoted in Tobias, *The. Jewish Bund*, p. 125.

59. "Di Natsionale Frage . . ." *Der Yidisher Arbayter*, no. 8, December 1899.

60. Tobias, *The Jewish Bund*, p. 160.

61. *Di Arbayter Shtimme*, no. 10, August 1901.

62. Ibid., no. 8, December 1899.

63. Tobias, *The Jewish Bund*, p. 113. However, in 1902 the question caused serious disruption within the Bund.

64. Ibid., p. 135.

CHAPTER 18: THE STRUGGLE WITH LENIN

1. Henry J. Tobias, *The Jewish Bund in Russia from Its Origins to 1905* (Stanford, 1972), p. 170.

2. Ibid.

3. John Mill, *Pionern un Boyer* (New York, 1946-49), 1: 102-03.

4. Pavel An-Man (Rosenthal), "Belostoker Period in Leben fun Tsentral Komitet fun Bund," *Royter Pinkes*, 1:69.

5. *Der Yidisher Arbayter*, no. 12, 1901.

6. Quoted in Tobias, *The Jewish Bund*, p. 150.

7. *Di Arbayter Shtimme*, no. 29, September 1902.

8. Vladimir Medem, *Fun Mayn Leben* (New York, 1923), 1: 318.

9. *Der Yidisher Arbayter*, no. 14, October 1902.

10. According to J. L. H. Keep, *The Rise of Social Democracy in Russia* (London, 1963), p. 14, there were fourteen Bund committees that publicly supported terrorism.

11. *Di Arbayter Shtimme*, no. 27, June 1902, quoted in Koppel Pinson, "Arkady Kremer, Vladimir Medem, and the Ideology of the Jewish 'Bund'," *Jewish Social Studies* 7, no. 3 (July 1945): 234-35.

12. Tobias, *The Jewish Bund*, p. 145.

13. *Di Arbayter Shtimme*, no. 28, August 1902.

14. Tobias, *The Jewish Bund*, p. 157.

15. Vladimir Akimov, *On the Dilemmas of Russian Marxism 1895-1903*, ed. and tr. Jonathan Frankel (Cambridge, 1969), p. 228.

16. Ibid.

17. Tobias, *The Jewish Bund*, p. 159.

18. This struggle is concisely summarized in Henry J. Tobias, "The Bund and Lenin Until 1903," *Russian Review* 24, no. 4 (October 1965): 344–57.

19. Edward H. Carr, *The Bolshevik Revolution, 1917–1923* (Middlesex, England, 1966), 1: 31–32.

20. These views were vehemently argued by the RSDWP and split the party into Mensheviks and Bolsheviks in 1912.

21. *Arkady: Zamlbukh tsum Ondenk fun Arkady Kremer* (New York, 1942), pp. 370–71.

22. Quoted in Bertram Wolfe, *Three Who Made a Revolution: A Biographical History* (New York, 1964), p. 227.

23. Quoted in Allen K. Wildman, "Russian and Jewish Social Democracy," in Alexander Rabinowitch, ed., *Revolution and Politics in Russia* (Bloomington, Ind., 1972), p. 86.

24. Quoted in Tobias, *The Jewish Bund*, p. 185.

25. Ibid., p. 186.

26. Quoted in ibid., p. 197.

27. Ibid., p. 191.

28. *Israel Getzler, Martov: A Political Biography of a Russian Social Democrat* (Cambridge, 1967), pp. 56–59. "We have had to fit our propaganda and agitation to the masses . . . to give it a more Jewish character," he had said. "Our aim is to found a specifically Jewish organization which will be the leader and educator of the Jewish proletariat in the struggle for economic, civil and political liberation."

29. Ibid., pp. 60, 62.

30. Leopold H. Haimson, *The Russian Marxists and the Origins of Bolshevism* (Cambridge, Mass., 1955), p. 64.

31. Tobias, *The Jewish Bund*, p. 196.

32. See Hyman Lumer, ed., *Lenin on the Jewish Question* (New York, 1974), pp. 20–25, for Lenin's article, "Does the Jewish Proletariat Need an Independent Political Party?" in *Iskra*, February 15, 1903.

33. Leonard Schapiro, "The Role of Jews in the Russian Revolutionary Movement," *Slavonic and East European Review* 40, no. 84 (December 1961): 159.

34. Tobias, *The Jewish Bund*, p. 29.

35. *Di Arbayter Shtimme*, no. 32, March 1903.

36. Medem, *Fun Mayn Leben*, 2:6.

37. Quoted in Vladimir Medem, *Tsum Tvantsikste Yohrtsayt (1865–1935)* (New York, 1943), pp. 10–11.

38. Medem, *Fun Mayn Leben*, 2:12–13.

39. See *Unzer Tsayt*, no. 4, December 1927.

40. Medem, *Fun Mayn Leben*, 2:20.

41. See pp. 338–39, 351, and 352 for a discussion of neutralism.

42. Medem, *Fun Mayn Leben*, 1:1–170.

43. Ibid., p. 171.

44. Tobias, *The Jewish Bund*, p. 201. Lenin's attack on this resolution appeared in *Iskra*, August 15, 1903. For English translation, see Lumer, *Lenin*, pp. 31–34.

45. Medem, *Fun Mayn Leben*, 2:121. Lenin's angry condemnation of the Bund's "maximum" and "minimum" rules appeared in *Iskra*, October 1903. See Lumer, *Lenin*, pp. 35–46.

46. This was a disproportionately small number for an organization of thousands of members. The smallest Russian committee was permitted one delegate, and most sent two.

47. Medem, *Fun Mayn Leben*, 2:24.

48. Much of the material on this matter has been drawn from Tobias, *The Jewish Bund*, pp. 207-20, based largely on Russian sources.

49. Medem, *Fun Mayn Leben*, 2:24. For Lenin's attack on Liber, see Lumer, *Lenin*, pp. 27-30.

50. Quoted in Solomon Schwarz, *The Jews in the Soviet Union* (Syracuse, 1951), p. 25.

51. Ibid., p. 26.

52. David Shub, *Lenin* (New York, 1948), p. 38.

53. Quoted in Tobias, *The Jewish Bund*, p. 215.

54. Ibid., p. 217.

55. Medem, *Fun Mayn Leben*, 2: 29.

56. Ibid., p. 31.

57. Ibid., pp. 31-32.

CHAPTER 19: 1905: THE BUND AT ITS ZENITH

1. Zvi Y. Gitelman, *Jewish Nationality and Soviet Politics* (Princeton, 1972), p. 65.

2. Vladimir Akimov, *On the Dilemmas of Russian Marxism 1895-1903*, ed. and tr. Jonathan Frankel (Cambridge, 1969), p. 223.

3. See pp. 407-10 for a discussion of socialist Zionism in Russia.

4. Herzl had talks with Plehve in 1903 and came away believing in his promise to secure a charter for Palestine within fifteen years if the revolutionaries stopped their activity. Plehve's insinuation that the Jewish revolutionaries were largely responsible for the misery of the Jews in Russia was a further source of conflict between the socialists and Zionists. (During this period, the government tolerated Zionism—another reason for the Bund's hostility.)

5. Vladimir Medem, *Fur Mayn Leben* (New York, 1923), 2: 5.

6. See pp. 336-38 and 351-52 for Medem's ideas on nationality.

7. It was not until 1910 that Medem worked out his formulation of neutralism.

8. Bernard D. Weinryb, "Antisemitism in Soviet Russia," in Lionel Kochan, ed., *The Jews in Soviet Russia Since 1917* (London, 1972), p. 293.

9. Henry J. Tobias, *The Jewish Bund in Russia from Its Origins to 1905* (Stanford, 1972), p. 226.

10. Raphael Abramovich, *In Tsvay Revolutsias* (New York, 1944), 1: 189-90.

11. Tobias, *The Jewish Bund*, p. 229.

12. P. Schwartz, "Revolutionary Activities of the Jewish Labor Bund in the Czarist Army," *YIVO Annual* (1965), 13:236.

13. Ibid., pp. 236-37.

14. Solomon M. Schwarz, *The Russian Revolution of 1905*, tr. Gertrude Vakar (Chicago, 1967), pp. 31-32.

15. Ibid., pp. 53-55.

16. Ibid., p. 55.

17. Quoted in ibid., p. 57.

18. J. L. H. Keep, *The Rise of Social Democracy in Russia* (London, 1963), p. 157.

19. Bertram Wolfe, *Three Who Made a Revolution: A Biographical History* (New York, 1964), p. 283.

20. Ibid., p. 284.

21. Quoted in ibid., p. 286.

22. Afterward, Gapon's role dwindled quickly. He engaged in gun-running for a while, but soon became an isolated, hunted man. Later, he returned to Russia and became a police agent. The Social Revolutionary party declared him a traitor and sentenced him to death by hanging. The sentence was carried out in April 1906, under the direction of Pinchas Rutenberg (later a famous engineer in Palestine), who had led the famous march with Gapon and had helped him to escape. See Medem, *Fun Mayn Leben*, 2:70-76.

23. Tobias, *The Jewish Bund*, p. 281.

24. Ibid.

25. Despite the unpleasantness of this struggle, the Bund was gratified by the adoption of their resolution condemning the anti-Jewish policy of the Russian government. John Mill, *Pionern un Boyer* (New York, 1946-49), 2:164-65. At this International, the Bund was recognized as the first independent Jewish party.

26. Tobias, *The Jewish Bund*, p. 282.

27. *Di Arbayter Shtimme*, supplement to no. 39, March 1905.

28. Ibid.

29. Ibid., no. 39, January 1905.

30. Schwarz, *The Russian Revolution of 1905*, p. 205. The effects of these tensions and contradictions as they affected relations between workers and intellectuals are analyzed in Allen Wildman, *The Making of a Worker's Revolution: Russian Social Democracy, 1891-1903* (Chicago, 1967).

31. Ibid., pp. 205-06.

32. Supplement to *Iskra*, July 10, 1904, cited in Tobias, *The Jewish Bund*, p. 378.

33. Schwarz, *Revolution of 1905*, p. 211.

34. Ibid., p. 213.

35. Ibid., p. 211.

36. Ibid., pp. 89-91.

37. Ibid., pp. 94-95.

38. Quoted in Tobias, *The Jewish Bund*, pp. 295-96.

39. *Di Arbayter Shtimme*, supplement to no. 39, March 1905.

40. Quoted in Keep, *Social Democracy in Russia*, p. 169.

41. Ibid., pp. 170-71.

42. Schwarz, *Revolution of 1905*, pp. 134-37. See also A. Litvak, *Geklibene Shriftn* (New York, 1945), p. 180.

43. Schwarz, *Revolution of 1905*, p. 158n.

44. Keep, *Social Democracy in Russia*, p. 194.

45. Ibid., p. 195.

46. Lenin did not return to Russia until November 1905.

47. David Shub, *Lenin* (New York, 1948), pp. 53-54.

48. Tobias, *The Jewish Bund*, p. 239.

49. Ibid., p. 306.

50. Litvak, *Geklibene Shriftn*, pp. 178-79.

51. Tobias, *The Jewish Bund*, pp. 307-08.

52. Ibid., p. 308.

53. Abramovich, *In Tsvay*, 1: 222.

54. Melech Epstein, *Profiles of Eleven* (Detroit, 1965), pp. 328-33.

CHAPTER 20: REACTION AND INTROSPECTION, 1906-10

1. The grand duke had been the governor-general of Moscow whose army had trampled to death thousands of people who had rushed to booths filled with candy presented by the new tsar. In the rush of the crowds, the army tried to restrain the masses and crushed many Russians.

2. See "Pogromen un Selbstshuts" in *Der Bund in der Revelutsia fun 1905-06* (Warsaw, 1905), pp. 51-67. See also Simon Dubnow, *History of the Jews in Russia and Poland* (Philadelphia, 1918), 3: 113-20.

3. Estimate by Tobias, *The Jewish Bund in Russia from Its Origins to 1905* (Stanford, 1972), p. 315. Abraham Cahan, "Tsu der Geshikhte fun der Bundistisher Zelbstshuts," *Unzer Tsayt*, no. 12 (1953), has much higher figures.

4. See pp. 173-74 for role of Schiff in raising money for the Bund.

5. "Pogromen un Selbstshuts," p. 61.

6. Tobias, *The Jewish Bund*, p. 317.

7. A. Tschemerinsky, "Lodz in 1905," in *Lodzer Almanak*, Lodzer Branch 324, Workmen's Circle (New York, n.d.), pp. 59-61.

8. Ibid., p. 60.

9. Ibid.

10. Tobias, *The Jewish Bund*, p. 317.

11. Bund Central Committee, *Mir un zay (vegen der yidisher liberaler bavegung)*, March 1905.

12. Lucy Dawidowicz, *The Golden Tradition* (Boston, 1967), pp. 463-64.

13. Vladimir Medem, *Fun Mayn Leben*, (New York, 1923), 2: 90-93.

14. *Der Veker*, January 3, 14, 21, 1906.

15. Medem, *Fun Mayn Leben*, 2: 91-92.

16. Solomon M. Schwarz, *The Russian Revolution of 1905* (Chicago, 1967), p. 170.

17. Ibid.

18. Quoted in J. L. H. Keep, *The Rise of Social Democracy in Russia* (London, 1963), p. 217.

19. Schwarz, *Revolution of 1905*, p. 172.

20. *Der Bund*, no. 10, November 22, 1905.

21. Tobias, *The Jewish Bund*, p. 334.

22. Medem, *Fun Mayn Leben*, 2:94.

23. Ibid., pp. 95-96.

24. Keep, *Social Democracy in Russia*, p. 234.

25. Abramovich served briefly as the Bund representative to the St. Petersburg Soviet and was the Bund and RSDWP delegate to the Second Duma. Later in 1917 he became a leading Menshevik.

26. Schwarz, *Revolution of 1905*, p. 236.

27. Ibid., p. 238.

28. Ibid., p. 179.

29. Ibid., p. 181.

30. See ibid., pp. 189–95, for Schwarz's interesting account of an article by Lenin, written early in November 1905, which remained "unknown" until 1940 and reveals Lenin's shifting views. Schwarz believes that Lenin actually bowed to the St. Petersburg Bolsheviks; see ibid., pp. 194–95.

31. Ibid., p. 240.

32. Ibid., p. 340.

33. Sidney S. Harcave, "The Jewish Question in the First Russian Duma," *Jewish Social Studies* 6 (April 1944): 155.

34. Dubnow, *History of the Jews in Poland and Russia*, 2: 138–39.

35. Keep, *Social Democracy in Russia*, p. 266.

36. Ibid., p. 278.

37. Medem, *Fun Mayn Leben*, 2: 131.

38. Ibid.

39. Ibid., pp. 132–34.

40. Ibid., p. 135.

41. Quoted from *Nashe Slovo*, no. 4, July 1906, in Zvi Y. Gitelman, *Jewish Nationality and Soviet Politics* (Princeton, 1972), pp. 52–53.

42. Vladimir Medem, *Zikhroynes un Artiklen* (Warsaw, 1917), p. 68.

43. This essay first appeared in Russian in the illegal Bundist periodical *Vestnik Bunda (The Bund Courier)* in 1904, and was translated into Yiddish and published in *Vladimir Medem Tsum Tsvantsigste Yohrzeit* (New York, 1943).

44. *Di Naye Tsayt*, no. 7, 1909, quoted in Koppel Pinson, "Arkady Kremer, Vladimir Medem, and the Ideology of the Jewish 'Bund'," *Jewish Social Studies* 7, no. 3 (July 1945): 251.

45. *Vladimir Medem Tsum Tsvantsigste*, p. 188.

46. Pinson believes this analysis is similar to the later formula adopted by the USSR: "socialist in content and national in form," but Medem was vehemently opposed to leaving cultural problems to the mercies of a central government.

47. Medem, *Zikhroynes*, p. 73.

48. Medem, "Di Sotsial-Demokratie un di Natsionale Frage," in *Vladimir Medem Tsum Tsvantsigste*, p. 176.

49. Pinson, "Arkady Kremer," p. 253.

50. Medem, *Zikhroynes*, p. 74.

51. *Vladimir Medem Tsum Tsvantsigste*, p. 183.

52. *Fun Mayn Notiz Buch*, pp. 110–11, quoted, in Pinson, "Arkady Kremer," p. 260.

53. *Di Naye Tsayt*, no. 7, 1909, quoted in Pinson, "Arkady Kremer," pp. 253–54.

54. Medem, "Natsionalizm oder Naytralizm," in *Zikhroynes*, pp. 129–30.

55. *Vladimir Medem Tsum Tsvantsigste*, p. 217.

56. In the essay, Medem wrote: "Territorial autonomy at best frees the dominant nation of a province from oppression. It does not solve the problem of the other nationalities living there. Moreover, even the members of the dominant nation are free only as long as they remain inside the boundaries of 'their province'." *Vladimir Medem Tsum Tsvantsigste*, p. 218.

57. Under the German occupation of Poland, Medem took the lead in

organizing Jewish secular schools, planning textbooks, and laying the foundation for what later developed into the large network of Yiddish schools, known as Cysho. See ibid., pp. 160–69.

58. E. Frumkin, "Vegn natsionaler ertsihung," *Tsayt Fragn* (Vilna, 1909), 1: 24.

59. H. Erlich, "Esther Frumkin," *Der Veker* (New York), December 27, 1930.

60. *Di Shtimme fun Bund,* December 1908.

61. Charles E. Woodhouse and Henry J. Tobias, "Primordial Ties and Political Process in Pre-Revolutionary Russia: The Case of the Jewish Bund," *Comparative Studies in Society and History* 8, no. 3 (April 1966): 348.

CHAPTER 21: REASSESSMENT AND DECLINE, 1907–10

1. The so-called "unity" congress, which met in April 1906, followed the all-Bolshevik congress of 1905, whose validity the Mensheviks contested.

2. Bertram Wolfe, *Three Who Made a Revolution: A Biographical History* (New York, 1964), pp. 376–77.

3. Ibid., p. 377.

4. Vladimir Medem, *Fun Mayn Leben,* (New York, 1923), 2: 187–89. See also Melech Epstein, *Profiles of Eleven* (Detroit, 1965), p. 333.

5. Medem, *Fun Mayn Leben,* 2: 176.

6. Wolfe, *Three Who Made a Revolution,* pp. 355–56.

7. Ibid., p. 356.

8. Medem, *Fun Mayn Leben,* 2: 174.

9. Wolfe, *Three Who Made a Revolution,* p. 384.

10. Medem, *Fun Mayn Leben,* 2: 176.

11. Quoted in Louis Fischer, *The Life of Lenin* (New York, 1964), p. 57.

12. Medem, *Fun Mayn Leben,* 2: 175.

13. Wolfe, *Three Who Made a Revolution,* p. 387.

14. Leon Trotsky, *Autobiography* (New York, 1930), p. 218. The Mensheviks demanded a reckoning from Lenin, but he successfully evaded them at the congress. By the end of the year, however, these activities had created a scandal in social-democratic circles in Western Europe and were discrediting the whole movement. In 1910, party investigations revealed Lenin's guilt, but his "repentance" was short-lived. In 1911, Martov documented Lenin's complicity in the expropriations in his work *Saviors or Destroyers?*

15. Lenin very early recognized that no revolution could be made without the peasants. In the original party program of 1903, he had written the demand for the return of the *otrezki,* the pieces of common land that had been cut off from the peasant holdings in the 1861 emancipation. At the Stockholm Congress, he had proposed peasant seizure of the land or nationalization by a victorious revolutionary government. The Social Revolutionary party made its land program central, but the Mensheviks underestimated or ignored the peasant problem.

16. Edward H. Carr, *The Bolshevik Revolution, 1917–1923* (Middlesex, England, 1966), p. 65.

17. Ibid., pp. 65–66.

18. Wolfe, *Three Who Made a Revolution,* p. 363.

19. Medem, *Fun Mayn Leben,* 2: 220.

20. Ibid., p. 221.

21. Ibid., p. 222.

22. Ibid., p. 223. The newspapers were *Posledniya Izvestia (The Latest News)* and *Nashe Slovo (Our Word).*

23. In the spring of 1907, the total strength of the RSDWP was estimated at 150,000, out of an industrial population of about 3 million. The Polish SDKPIL had about the same number as the Bund. The Latvian Social Democrats had 13,000 members; the Bolsheviks, 46,000, and the Mensheviks, 38,000. See T. L. H. Keep, *The Rise of Social Democracy in Russia* (London, 1963), p. 288.

24. Charles E. Woodhouse and Henry J. Tobias, "Primordial Ties and Political Process in Pre-Revolutionary Russia," *Comparative Studies in Society and History* 8, no. 3 (April 1966): 345-46.

25. Ibid., p. 345.

26. Ibid., p. 346.

27. Ibid., p. 348.

28. J. S. Hertz and G. Aronson et al., eds., *Di Geshikhte fun Bund* (New York, 1962), 2: 557.

29. Ibid.

30. Ibid.

31. Ibid., p. 550.

32. Ibid., pp. 551-52.

33. Quoted in ibid., p. 554.

34. Woodhouse and Tobias, "Primordial Ties," p. 354.

35. Medem, *Fun Mayn Leben,* 2: 234.

36. Ibid., p. 235.

37. Koppel Pinson, "Arkady Kremer, Vladimir Medem, and the Ideology of the Jewish 'Bund'," *Jewish Social Studies* 7, no. 3 (July 1945): 258.

38. Medem, "Natsionalizm oder Naytralizm," in *Zikhroynes un Artiklen* (Warsaw, 1917), pp. 114-15.

39. Ibid., p. 116.

40. Pinson, "Arkady Kremer," p. 259.

41. Medem, *Fun Mayn Leben,* 2: 237.

42. Ibid., p. 239.

43. *Barikht fun der VIII Konferents fun Bund* (Geneva, 1910), pp. 7-8. (The seventh conference had taken place in 1906.)

44. Medem, *Fun Mayn Leben,* 2: 232.

45. Ibid., pp. 242-43.

46. Ibid., pp. 245-46.

47. Based on an account in Wolfe, *Three Who Made a Revolution,* pp. 535-57. The Bolshevik press condemned Malinowsky for "indiscipline" and desertion of "his post," but Lenin's attitude was much more tolerant. During the war, he and his wife sent food parcels and books to Malinowsky while he was in a German prison camp. There he devoted himself to propaganda among other Russian prisoners. Lenin permitted him to rehabilitate himself but later, after he came to power, Malinowsky returned to Russia and was tried and executed. Lenin did nothing to save him.

48. Medem, *Fun Mayn Leben,* 2: 229.

49. Ibid.

50. Ibid., p. 231.

51. *Lebensfragn,* April 18, 1912.

52. Medem, *Fun Mayn Leben*, 2: 247–48.

53. Quoted in Lucy Dawidowicz, *The Golden Tradition* (Boston, 1967), p. 74.

54. Medem, *Fun Mayn Leben*, 2: 248.

55. Ibid.

56. Ibid., p. 249.

57. Ibid.

58. Ibid., p. 250.

59. Bernard K. Johnpoll, *The Politics of Futility: The General Workers' Bund of Poland, 1917–1943* (Ithaca, 1967), p. 68.

CHAPTER 22: THE END OF THE BUND IN RUSSIA

1. Bertram Wolfe, *Three Who Made a Revolution: A Biographical History* (New York, 1964), p. 581. The social democratic organizations in the August Bloc were technically still in the RSDWP, a situation Lenin called "federation of the worst type."

2. Ibid.

3. Quoted in ibid., p. 577. See also Lenin's article *(Pravda,* May 8, 1913), "Separatists in Russia and Separatists in Austria," in Hyman Lumer, ed., *Lenin on the Jewish Question* (New York, 1974), pp. 65–66.

4. Robert C. Tucker, "Stalin's Revolutionary Career before 1917," in Alexander Rabinowitch, ed., *Revolution and Politics in Russia* (Bloomington, Ind., 1972), p. 168.

5. Ibid., p. 169.

6. Joseph Stalin, *Marxism and the Colonial Question* (London, n.d.), p. 8.

7. Ibid., p. 10.

8. Ibid., p. 36.

9. Tucker, "Stalin's Revolutionary Career," p. 170.

10. Trotsky believed that this essay was wholly inspired by Lenin and written and edited under his careful supervision. Isaac Deutscher, Boris Souvarine, Bertram Wolfe, and Solomon Schwarz see it as a reflection of Lenin's thinking, but Tucker and Richard Pipes *(The Formation of the Soviet Union;* Cambridge, Mass., 1954) disagree.

11. Tucker, "Stalin's Revolutionary Career," p. 171.

12. Ibid., p. 172.

13. Ibid.

14. Lumer, *Lenin on the Jewish Question*, pp. 65–72.

15. Ibid., pp. 75–82. These theses were not published until 1925.

16. Referring to Vladimir Purishkevich, a notorious advocate of extreme anti-Semitism in pre-Revolutionary Russia.

17. Lumer, *Lenin on the Jewish Question*, p. 107.

18. Ibid.

19. Ibid., p. 120.

20. Ibid., p. 105.

21. Ibid., p. 111.

22. Ibid., p. 112.

23. P. Liebman, "A Naye Oyflage fun Altn Toes," *Tsayt*, September 17, 1913.

24. Lumer, *Lenin on the Jewish Question*, pp. 106–07.

25. Quoted in Solomon M. Schwarz, *Jews in the Soviet Union* (Syracuse, 1951), p. 27.

26. Lumer, *Lenin on the Jewish Question*, p. 87.

27. A. Menes, "The Jewish Socialist Movement in Russia and Poland," in *The Jewish People Past and Present*, 2: 397.

28. Raphael Abramovich, *In tsvay revolutsias* (New York, 1944), 2:47-53.

29. J. S. Hertz and G. Aronson et al., eds., *Di Geshikhte fun Bund* (New York, 1962), 2: 95.

30. *Di Arbayter Shtimme*, August 20, 1917.

31. Zvi Y. Gitelman, *Jewish Nationality and Soviet Politics* (Princeton, 1972), pp. 88-90.

32. Quoted in Menes, "The Jewish Socialist Movement," p. 393.

33. Abraham Ascher, "Pavel Axelrod: A Conflict Between Jewish Loyalty and Revolutionary Dedication," *Russian Review* 24, no. 3 (July 1965): 262.

34. Ibid.

35. Ibid., pp. 262-63.

36. Ibid., pp. 263-64.

37. *Forward*, September 12, 1944.

CHAPTER 23: NACHMAN SYRKIN: PRECURSOR AND VISIONARY

1. For biographical details, see Marie Syrkin, *Nachman Syrkin, Socialist Zionist: A Biographical Memoir* (New York, 1961).

2. *Forward from Exile: The Autobiography of Shmarya Levin*, tr. Maurice Samuel (Philadelphia, 1967), p. 253.

3. Chaim Weizmann, *Trial and Error* (New York, 1949), p. 37.

4. Ibid., p. 38.

5. *Forward from Exile*, p. 269.

6. Ibid., pp. 273-74.

7. Ibid., p. 277.

8. Weizmann, *Trial and Error*, p. 44.

9. Syrkin, *Nachman Syrkin*, p. 40.

10. Quoted from "Toward the History of Socialist-Zionism," in M. Syrkin, *Nachman Syrkin*, p. 42.

11. Ibid.

12. Weizmann, *Trial and Error*, pp. 50-52.

13. Ibid., p. 51.

14. "The Jewish Question and a Socialist Jewish State," tr. from the German in M. Syrkin, *Nachman Syrkin*, pp. 255-93. Also published in *Studies in Labor Zionism: Nachman Syrkin*, ed. Jacob Katzman (New York, n.d.), pp. 19-35. This essay in Hebrew appears on pp. 1-59 in Syrkin's *Ktavim* (Tel Aviv, 1939).

15. Nachman Syrkin, *Essays on Socialist Zionism* (New York, 1935), p. 28.

16. "Toward the History of Socialist-Zionism," p. 64.

17. M. Syrkin, *Nachman Syrkin*, pp. 70-71.

18. Zalman Shazar, *Morning Stars* (Philadelphia, 1967), p. 91.

19. Acronym from the first Hebrew letters of a passage in Isaiah: "House of Jacob, come let us go." See Samuel Kurland, *Biluim: Pioneers of Zionist Colonization* (New York, 1943).

20. *Manifesto of the Bilu,* in Walter Laqueur, ed., *The Israel-Arab Reader* (New York, 1971), p. 4.

21. Amos Elon, *The Israelis: Founders and Sons* (New York, 1971), p. 98.

22. Peretz Smolenskin, "Am Olam," in Kol Sifrei (Warsaw, 1905–10), vol. 1.

23. Leo Pinsker, *Auto-Emancipation: An Admonition to his Brethren by a Russian Jew,* tr. D. S. Blondheim (New York, 1906), was the first English translation. The pamphlet is also included in *Road to Freedom: Writings and Addresses of Leo Pinsker* (New York, 1944).

24. No one knows exactly how much Rothschild put into Palestine. Estimates run as high as over $50 million over a forty-year period.

25. Samuel Kurland, *Cooperative Palestine* (New York, 1947), p. 10.

26. M. Syrkin, *Nachman Syrkin,* pp. 71–73.

27. Ibid., p. 73.

28. Nachman Syrkin, *A Call to Jewish Youth,* tr. from the Russian in ibid., pp. 294–305. Also in *Studies in Labor Zionism,* pp. 12–16, abridged.

29. As if foreshadowing his later acceptance of territorialism, Syrkin called "pseudoromantic" the view that colonization can only start in the "Holy Land," not in countries adjacent to Palestine.

30. See pp. 393–95 and 411 for Borochov's organizational work.

31. Ber Borochov, "Reminiscences," in Abraham G. Duker, ed., *Nationalism and the Class Struggle* (New York, 1937), p. 179.

32. Ben Halpen, "Nachman Syrkin," *Jewish Frontier* 41, no. 8 (October 1974): 15–16.

33. M. Syrkin, *Nachman Syrkin,* p. 76.

34. Ibid., p. 81.

35. Ibid., p. 82.

36. The name Poale Zion was first adopted by a club in Minsk, under the leadership of A. Litvin, who became a well-known American Jewish writer. This group denied the value of the class struggle in the Galut and anticipated the so-called Minsker Poale Zion which united with the socialist territorialists in 1907.

37. Ber Borochov, "At the Cradle of Socialist Zionism, *Di Varhayt* (New York), March 13, 1916. Quoted in Duker, *Nationalism and the Class Struggle,* p. 180.

38. Biographical sketch in ibid., pp. 11–12.

39. Ibid., pp. 27–28.

40. Ibid., p. 180. Borochov thus credits Poale Zion with the organization of the first Jewish self-defense unit, two and a half years before the Bund group organized in Gomel in September 1903. An article in *Unzer Tsayt* (J. Hertz, "Ber Borochov un zayne mfrishim") challenges Borochov, raising the point that Borochov never explains what the Poale Zion defense group *did.* Several sources are cited, indicating that there was a *plan* for a Poale Zion defense group, but nothing more at this early period. A World Zionist Commission report on pogroms in Russia 1883–1905 is also cited, but it too contains nothing on any self-defense unit in 1901.

41. Isaac Gruenbaum, *The History of Zionism,* part 2, "The Herzlian Period." (Tel Aviv, n.d.), p. 67.

42. Ibid., p. 68.

43. *Theodore Herzl: The Complete Diaries* (New York, 1960), 4: 1321.

44. J. L. Talmon, *Israel Among the Nations* (New York, 1970), pp. 118–20.

45. Quoted in ibid., p. 120.
46. Walter Laqueur, *A History of Zionism* (London, 1972), p. 116.
47. Ibid., pp. 123-24.
48. Weizmann, *Trial and Error*, p. 82.
49. Ibid., p. 83.
50. Ibid., p. 85.
51. Vladimir Medem, *Fun Mayn Leben*, (New York, 1923), 2: 33-36.

CHAPTER 24: REJECTING THE *GALUT*: FROM GORDON TO BOROCHOV

1. *David Ben-Gurion: Memoirs*, comp. Thomas R. Bransten (New York, 1970), p. 34.
2. Ibid., p. 39.
3. Ibid., pp. 42-43.
4. Ibid., p. 52.
5. The Odessa Committee emerged out of an 1887 Katowice conference of Russian Zionists who became the center of the Hovevei Zionist movement. The group was legalized in 1890 under the name The Society for the Support of Jewish Farmers and Artisans in Syria and Palestine. In that year, the committee sent an engineer, Vladimir I. Temkin, to Palestine to purchase more land for colonization, but his mission was unsuccessful.
6. Walter Laqueur, *A History of Zionism* (New York, 1972), p. 279.
7. Walter Preuss, *The Labor Movement in Israel, Past and Present* (Jerusalem, 1965), p. 22.
8. As far back as 1888, the philanthropist Baron de Hirsch had set aside a sum of 50 million francs to carry out plans for improving the condition of Russian Jewry, but the government was not interested. The expulsion of Jews from Moscow inspired Hirsch to found the Jewish Colonization Association (known as ICA) to enable Jews to migrate to Argentina and become farmers there. Meanwhile, Hibbat Zion, which had begun with ambitious dreams of a general exodus, had retreated step by step because of petty worries and pitifully small donations. Rothschild's colonies in Palestine still dominated colonization efforts. In 1899, Rothschild handed over all his Palestine interests to ICA.
9. Chaim Weizmann, *Trial and Error* (New York, 1949), p. 127.
10. Robert St. John, *Ben-Gurion* (Garden City, N. Y., 1959), p. 25.
11. Ibid.
12. Preuss, *The Labor Movement in Israel*, p. 35.
13. Quoted in *Studies in Labor Zionism*, no. 5 (New York, n.d.), p. 7. All of Gordon's writings are available in *Ktavim*, 5 vols. (Tel Aviv, 1925-29). An edited selection in English including his major writings, was published in 1938 by the League for Labor Palestine under the title *A. D. Gordon: Selected Essays*, tr. Frances Burnce.
14. From the essay "Labor," in *A. D. Gordon: Selected Essays*, p. 56.
15. From "Our Tasks Ahead" (1920) in Arthur Hertzberg, ed., *The Zionist Idea* (New York, 1959), p. 380.
16. From "Nationalism and Socialism," in *Labor Zionist Studies*, no. 5, p. 26.
17. From "Man-Nation," in ibid., p. 16.
18. Some estimate the figure may have been as high as 80 percent.

19. Bransten, *David Ben-Gurion: Memoirs,* p. 52.

20. Quoted in Samuel Kurland, *Cooperative Palestine* (New York, 1947), pp. 10-11.

21. Introduction to Borochov's *Nationalism and the Class Struggle,* ed. Abraham C. Duker (New York, 1937), p. 30.

22. Ibid., p. 32.

23. Zalman Shazar, *Morning Stars* (Philadelphia, 1967), p. 109.

24. Ibid., pp. 111-12.

25. Henry J. Tobias, *The Jewish Bund in Russia from Its Origins to 1905* (Stanford, 1972), p. 250.

26. Affiliation with Poale Zion was often kept secret as a protection against the police; some general Zionists are known to have joined Poale Zion clandestinely.

27. Itzchak Ben-Zvi, "Labor Zionism in Russia," in Jacob Frumkin, *Russian Jewry (1860-1917)* p. 212.

28. Ibid.

29. Ibid., p. 214.

30. Duker, *Nationalism and the Class Struggle,* p. 181. Borochov wrote in Yiddish, German, and Russian. However, there is no single collection of his writings in any of these languages. So far, the Hebrew collection, *Ktavim,* ed. L. Levita and D. Ben-Nachum, Hakibbutz Hameuchad, Sifriat Poalim 1955-64, is the most comprehensive. A number of his essays are available in English in a pamphlet, *Nationalism and Class Struggle,* issued by the Radical Zionist Alliance, New York, n.d.

31. *Di Varhayt,* March 13, 1916, quoted in Duker, *Nationalism and the Class Struggle,* pp. 181-82.

32. See ibid., pp. 135-66, for full text of "The National Question and the Class Struggle," on which this exposition is based.

33. Text of "Our Platform," in ibid., pp. 183-205. Ben-Zvi and Alexander Haskin also wrote the nontheoretical sections.

34. The word comes from the Greek *stichion,* which means "elements," and the Russian *stignost,* which means "spontaneity."

35. However, at the first Poale Zion regional conference in Lithuania and White Russia (June 1906), Ben-Zvi lectured to the youthful delegates on the Arab question, explaining that there was no such thing as a unified Arab nation, but varied ethnic groups, religious groups, tribes, and great families that were often hostile to each other. Their alleged spokesmen were reactionary *effendis* who enslaved the population and should not be dealt with. The Arab workers, however, would be allies of the Jewish labor Zionists as soon as they were organized and a "natural" division of labor between Arabs and Jews developed. See Shazar's *Morning Stars,* pp. 149-67, and Rahel Yanait Ben-Zvi, *Coming Home,* tr. from the Hebrew by David Harris (Tel Aviv, 1963), pp. 202-10, for vivid accounts of this conference.

36. Ben Halpern, "The Problems of Israeli Socialism," in *Israel, the Arabs and the Middle East,* ed. Irving Howe (New York, 1972), p. 48.

37. Duker, *Nationalism and the Class Struggle,* p. 138. For Lestchinsky's views, in English, see his "Economic Development of the Jewish People," in *The Jewish People, Past and Present* (New York, 1946), 1: 361-80.

38. Amos Perlmutter, "Dov Ber-Borochov: A Marxist-Zionist Ideologist," *Middle Eastern Studies* 5, no. 1 (January 1969): 40.

39. Ibid., p. 33.

40. "Dov Ber Borochov: A Biographical Sketch," in *Studies in Labor Zionism*, no. 4, *Ber Borochov* (New York, n.d.), p. 5.

41. Ibid.

CHAPTER 25: RUPPIN AND THE FIRST *KVUTZOT*

1. Walter Preuss, *The Labor Movement in Israel, Past and Present* (Jerusalem, 1965), p. 28.

2. Ibid.

3. Walter Laqueur, *A History of Zionism* (New York, 1972), p. 284.

4. Ibid., p. 282.

5. Ibid., p. 283. See Z. Even-Shoshan, *Toldot Tnuat Poalim Be'Eretz Israel* (Tel Aviv, 1968), for a history of the labor movement in Israel in Hebrew and A. Levinson, *Bereshit Hatnuah* (Tel Aviv, 1947), for the beginnings of the movement.

6. Michel Bar-Zohar, *Ben-Gurion, the Armed Prophet*, tr. Len Ortzen (Englewood Cliffs, N.J., 1968), p. 20.

7. Ibid., p. 19.

8. Manya Shochat, "In the Beginning," in *The Plough Woman: Records of the Pioneer Women of Palestine*, ed. Rachel Katzenelson-Rubashow, tr. Maurice Samuel (New York, 1932), pp. 19–26.

9. Bar-Zohar, *Ben-Gurion*, p. 22.

10. Maurice Samuel, *Harvest in the Desert* (New York, 1944), p. 122.

11. Manya Shochat was the first woman *shomer;* Rachel Yanait joined at the meeting in Meschah. See Rachel Yanait Ben-Zvi, *Coming Home*, tr. from the Hebrew by David Harris (Tel Aviv, 1963), pp. 124–25.

12. Ibid.

13. Zipporah Seid, "With the Shomrim in Galilee," in *The Plough Woman*, p. 43.

14. *Toldot Ha Haganah* (Ma'arachot, 1954), 1: 235–36.

15. Ben-Zvi, *Coming Home*, pp. 139–40.

16. Ibid., p. 142.

17. *Arthur Ruppin: Memoirs, Diaries, Letters*, tr. from the German by Karen Gershon (New York, 1971), pp. 3–59.

18. Ibid., p. 62.

19. Ibid.

20. *Die Organizationen des jüdischen Proletariats in Russland* (Karlsruhe, 1903).

21. *Ruppin: Memoirs*, p. 66.

22. Ibid., p. 74.

23. Ibid., p. 76.

24. Ibid., p. 86.

25. Ibid., p. 87.

26. "The Picture in 1907: An Address Delivered before the Jewish Colonization Society of Vienna, February 27, 1908," in Arthur Ruppin, *Three Decades of Palestine* (Jerusalem, 1936), p. 12.

27. *Ruppin: Memoirs*, p. 86.

28. Chaim Weizmann, *Trial and Error* (New York, 1949), p. 129.

29. Quoted in Esther Tauber, *Molding Society to Man* (New York, 1955), p. 21.

30. Ibid.

31. Weizmann, *Trial and Error*, p. 127.

32. *Ruppin: Memoirs*, p. 98. For the early days of settlement, in Hebrew, see Alex Bein, *Toldot Ha'hityashvut Ha'tzionit* (Tel Aviv, 1945).

33. *Ruppin: Memoirs*, p. 98.

34. Harry Viteles, *A History of the Cooperative Movement in Israel: A Source Book in 7 Volumes*, Book Two: *The Evolution of the Kibbutz Movement* (London, 1967), p. 25.

35. Ibid., pp. 25-26.

36. *Ruppin: Memoirs*, p. 102.

37. Walter Preuss, *The Labor Movement in Israel, Past and Present* (Jerusalem, 1965), p. 32.

38. "Report to the Eleventh Congress," in Ruppin, *Three Decades*, p. 42.

39. *Ruppin: Memoirs*, p. 107.

40. Ibid.

41. Ibid., p. 103.

42. Ibid.

43. Ibid.

44. *Niv Ha-Kvutza*, May 1958, in "From Petach Tikva to Um Juni," quoted in Viteles, *A History of the Cooperative Movement*, 2: 27.

45. Thomas R. Bransten, comp., *David Ben-Gurion: Memoirs* (New York, 1970), p. 54.

46. Viteles, *A History of the Cooperative Movement*, 2: 27.

47. Ibid., p. 30.

48. Shmuel Dayan, "The Early Days of Dagania," in *Hechalutz*, ed. Chaim Arlosoroff (New York, 1929), pp. 76-78.

49. Viteles, *A History of the Cooperative Movement*, 2: 38.

50. Excerpts and summary of "Sipur 50 Shnot Ha-Kvutza—Darkah Shel Degania Alef," in Viteles, *A History of the Cooperative Movement*, 2: 37.

51. Laqueur, *Zionism*, p. 291.

52. *Ruppin: Memoirs*, pp. 107-08.

53. Ibid., p. 104.

54. Laqueur, *Zionism*, p. 108.

55. After World War I, Degania developed as an independent cooperative without a guaranteed minimum wage and went over to intensive farming. A second (Degania Bet) and third (Gimmel) commune were also founded later.

56. "Buying the Emek," in Ruppin, *Three Decades*, pp. 182-84. The JNF governing board and executive director were opposed to the purchase. Ruppin credits the sale to the intervention of the Zionist Executive and the deciding vote of Weizmann (p. 186).

57. Ibid., p. 184. Even before the signing of the deeds, Hankin urged the Workers' Organization of Galilee (Choresh) to organize a *kvutzah* on the new land. Twenty-six men and four women were chosen for the "great privilege" of preparing a new Jewish position. See Deborah Dayan, "The Founding of Merchavia," in *The Plough Woman*, pp. 38-55.

58. "The Kvutzah," in Ruppin, *Three Decades*, p. 133.

59. Preuss, *The Labor Movement in Israel*, p. 33.

60. *Ruppin: Memoirs,* p. 109.

61. "A General Colonization Policy," address delivered before the Eleventh Zionist Congress in Vienna, September 1913, in Ruppin, *Three Decades,* p. 46.

62. Ibid. p. 39.

63. Ibid., p. 47.

64. *Ruppin: Memoirs,* p. 110.

65. Ibid., p. 111.

66. Ibid.

67. Ada Fishman, *Ayanoth* (Tel Aviv, 1948), p. 19.

CHAPTER 26: THE COOPERATIVE MODEL

1. Examples cited in Harry Viteles, *A History of the Cooperative Movement in Israel,* Book One: *The Evolution of the Cooperative Movement* (London, 1966), pp. 7–16.

2. Walter Preuss, *The Labor Movement in Israel, Past and Present* (Jerusalem, 1965), pp. 36–37. Kupat Holim later became a comprehensive health insurance scheme of the Histadrut and one of its largest mutual aid institutions.

3. Samuel Kurland, *Cooperative Palestine* (New York, 1947), p. 18.

4. Preuss, *The Labor Movement in Israel,* pp. 37–38.

5. Ibid., p. 38.

6. After the war, the move to establish a united socialist party was stimulated by the Third *Aliyah.* Toward this end, a new group, Achdut Ha-Avoda, was set up in 1919. But Hapoel Hatzair refused to join, and Achdut Ha-Avoda turned into a political party. This, in turn, caused Hapoel Hatzair to become more political and competitive. Berl Katznelson was the moving force behind Achdut Ha-Avoda in the 1920s. In 1930, the two groups merged to form Mapai, but for many years there was great internal strife.

7. Quoted in Kurland, *Cooperative Palestine,* p. 20.

8. Preuss, *The Labor Movement in Israel,* p. 40.

9. Ibid.

10. Ibid., pp. 40–41.

11. *Arthur Ruppin: Memoirs, Diaries, Letters,* tr. Karen Gershon (New York, 1971), p. 122.

12. Preuss, *The Labor Movement in Israel,* p. 42.

13. The rest was divided into lots and a blueprint was made which Ruppin took with him to Russia in 1913. It was published together with an explanation and a Russian translation in the journal *Razvet* (October 25, 1913). Some Russian Zionists bought plots for 1,000 roubles, not realizing that five or six years later, after they had lost everything in the Revolution, this land would be all they owned. They were destitute when they came to Palestine, and these plots became the basis of a new life. See *Ruppin: Memoirs,* pp. 123–24.

14. Arthur Ruppin, *Three Decades of Palestine* (Jerusalem, 1936), p. 62.

15. Ibid., pp. 62–63.

16. Harry Viteles, *A History of the Cooperative Movement in Israel,* Book Two: *The Evolution of the Kibbutz Movement* (London, 1967), p. 32.

17. Ibid.

18. Ibid., p. 31.

19. Preuss, *The Labor Movement in Israel*, p. 48.

20. Ibid.

21. Ibid.

22. In 1920, the left faction of Zeire Zion created the Zionist Socialist party, which later merged with the right Poale Zion, while the right faction merged with the Palestinian non-socialist party Hapoel Hatzair to form the Hitachadut. Hashomer Hatzair could not avoid organizational consolidation and developed into a Marxist movement. In 1927, it founded Kibbutz Artzi, an association of Hashomer Matzair *kibbutzim.*

23. See Roman Freulich, *The Hill of Life* (New York, 1968), and P. Lipovetzky, *Joseph Trumpeldor: Life and Works* (Jerusalem, 1953), for biographical details.

24. Freulich, *The Hill of Life*, p. 45.

25. Ibid., p. 78.

26. The Jewish Legion was officially established in London in August 1917, and some members of Trumpeldor's Mule Corps were among the first to join the new unit—the 38th Battalion. The American and Palestinian Legions were set up a little later. The London Legion took an active part in the British conquest of Palestine.

27. Freulich, *The Hill of Life*, p. 163.

28. Ibid., p. 166.

29. Quoted in Lipovetzky, *Joseph Trumpeldor*, p. 69.

30. Ibid., pp. 71-72.

31. Freulich, *The Hill of Life*, pp. 173-74.

32. Lipovetzky, *The Hill of Life*, p. 75.

33. Ibid., pp. 81-82.

CHAPTER 27: THE ARABS IN PALESTINE: THE UNRESOLVED QUESTION

1. Isaiah Friedman, *The Question of Palestine, 1914-1918: British-Jewish-Arab Relations* (New York, 1973), p. 309.

2. The elaboration of this understanding has been carefully researched and presented in ibid., ch. 18 ("The Meaning of the Declaration"), pp. 309-32, the source for my comments.

3. Neville Mandel, "Turks, Arabs and Jewish Immigration into Palestine, 1882-1914," St. Anthony's Papers, no. 17, *Middle Eastern Affairs*, no. 4 (London, 1965).

4. Malcolm Kerr, "Arab Radical Notions of Democracy," in Gendzier, ed., *A Middle East Reader* (New York, 1969), p. 72.

5. Ibid., p. 74.

6. Atallah Mansour, "The Future Is the Son of the Past," in ibid., p. 443.

7. *David Ben-Gurion: My Talks with Arab Leaders*, ed. Misha Louvish (New York, 1973), p. 3.

8. Ibid., p. 2.

9. Ibid.

10. Ahad Ha-Am, *Collected Works* (Berlin, 1895), 1: 26.

11. *Ben-Gurion: My Talks*, p. 1.

12. Chaim Weizmann, *Trial and Error* (New York, 1949), p. 41.

13. It is generally believed that there were about 700,000 Arabs in pre-1914 Palestine, but in 1907 Consul Blech estimated the number of Jews "in the whole of

Palestine ... at 100,000 out of a total population of 400,000–500,000." See *British Consulate in Jerusalem, 1838–1914*, documents edited by A. M. Hyamson (London, 1941), 2:570. More than 75 percent of the Arab population was concentrated in the Mutasarriflak of Jerusalem.

14. James Parkes, *Whose Land? A History of the Peoples of Palestine* (Middlesex, England, 1970), pp. 219–20.

15. V. D. Segre, *Israel: A Society in Transition* (London, 1971), p. 59.

16. Mandel, "Turks, Arabs and Jewish Immigration," p. 85.

17. Ibid.

18. Ibid., p. 86.

19. Walter Laqueur, *A History of Zionism* (New York, 1972), p. 212.

20. Allon Gal, *Socialist-Zionism: Theory and Issues in Contemporary Jewish Nationalism* (Cambridge, Mass., 1973), p. 117.

21. *Palestine Royal Commission Report* (London, 1937), pp. 240–41.

22. Christopher Sykes, *Cross Roads to Israel* (London, 1967), p. 100.

23. Laqueur, *Zionism*, p. 206.

24. Ibid.

25. Sykes, *Cross Roads*, p. 174.

26. *Palestine Royal Commission Report*, ch. 10.

27. Laqueur, *Zionism*, p. 212.

28. Bernard Lewis, *The Middle East and the West* (London, 1963), pp. 72–73.

29. Parkes, *Whose Land?* p. 214.

30. Ibid.

31. Mandel, "Turks, Arabs and Jewish Immigration," p. 86.

32. Ibid., p. 88.

33. Ibid., p. 89.

34. Ibid.

35. Ibid., pp. 91–92.

36. The article was called "The Arab Movement and Its Purpose," by A. Hermoni, and appeared in *Ha-Shiloah* 15 (1905): 377–90.

37. Yaacov Roi, "The Zionist Attitude to the Arabs, 1908–1914," *Middle Eastern Studies* 4, no. 3 (April 1968): 199.

38. Epstein's account was subsequently published in *Ha-Shiloah* (1907, pp. 193–206), under the title "She'ela ne'elma" (The Unseen Question).

39. Nechama Puchachevski, *Ha-shiloah* (1908), pp. 67–69.

40. Ibid.

41. Mandel, "Turks, Arabs and Jewish Immigration," p. 93.

42. Laqueur, *Zionism*, p. 215.

43. Mandel, "Turks, Arabs and Jewish Immigration," p. 93.

44. Ibid., p. 92.

45. Parkes, *Whose Land?* p. 189.

46. Roi, "The Zionist Attitude," p. 203.

47. Ibid.

48. Ibid., p. 204.

49. Central Zionist Archives (Jerusalem) W126/1, quoted in ibid., p. 223.

50. Ibid., p. 241.

51. Ibid., p. 206.

52. Central Zionist Archives, Z2/251, quoted in ibid.

53. Ruppin to V. Jacobson, September 29, 1908, quoted in ibid., p. 221.

54. Ruppin to M. Menassewitsch, April 29, 1910, quoted in ibid., p. 222.

55. Ruppin to M. Krigser in Merchavia, September 15, 1911, and the Workers' Committee in Ein Ganim, September 6, 1911, quoted in ibid., p. 222.

56. Ruppin to Zionist Central Office, July 28, 1912, quoted in ibid., pp. 223–24.

57. Amos Elon, *The Israelis: Founders and Sons* (New York, 1971), p. 128.

58. *A. D. Gordon: Selected Essays*, tr. Frances Burnce (League for Labor Palestine, 1938), p. 23.

59. Ibid., p. 24.

60. Ibid., p. 25.

61. Ibid., p. 27.

62. Roi, "The Zionist Attitude," p. 225.

63. Among them were Haim Cohen, Elias Auerbach, Aaron Aaronson, and David Yellin.

64. M. Perlman, "Chapters of Arab-Jewish Diplomacy, 1918–22," *Jewish Social Studies* 6, no. 1 (January 1944): 125.

65. *Ha-Olam* 5, no. 13 (1911), cited in ibid.

66. Mandel, "Turks, Arabs and Jewish Immigration," p. 97.

67. Roi, The Zionist Attitude," p. 226.

68. Ibid.

69. Laqueur, *Zionism*, p. 142.

70. Roi, "The Zionist Attitude," p. 210.

71. Neville Mandel, "Attempts at an Arab-Zionist Entente: 1913–1914," *Middle Eastern Studies* (April 1965): 238.

72. Ibid., pp. 244–45.

73. S. Hochberg to V. Jacobson, May 17, 1913, quoted in Mandel, "Turks, Arabs and Jewish Immigration," p. 100.

74. Mandel, "Attempts at Entente," p. 246.

75. Ibid., p. 247.

76. Ibid., pp. 247–49.

77. Ibid., p. 240.

78. C. Ernest Dawn, "The Rise of Arabism in Syria," *The Middle East Journal* 16 (1962): 148–49.

79. Mandel, "Attempts at Entente," p. 249.

80. Ibid., pp. 250, 251, 253.

81. Roi, "Zionist Attitudes," p. 215.

82. Mandel, "Attempts at Entente," pp. 253–55.

83. Albert Hourani, *Arabic Thought in the Liberal Age: 1789–1939* (Oxford, 1967), pp. 235–36.

84. Ibid., pp. 256–57.

85. Roi, "Zionist Attitudes," p. 217.

86. Mandel, "Attempts at Entente," p. 257.

87. Ibid., p. 258.

88. Ibid., p. 260.

89. Ibid.

90. Ibid.

91. Friedman, *The Question of Palestine*, pp. 222–23; and Hourani, *Arabic Thought in the Liberal Age*, ch. 9.

Index